THE MEDICAID EXPERIENCE

Edited by
Allen D. Spiegel, Ph.D.

Downstate Medical Center
State University of New York
Brooklyn, New York

Aspen Systems Corporation
Germantown, Maryland
1979

Library of Congress Cataloging in Publication Data
Main entry under title:

The Medicaid Experience.

"Contains entirely different articles, with no repetitions [from 1975 ed.]"
Includes bibliographical references and index.
1. Medicaid—United States—Addresses, essays, lectures.
2. Insurance, Health—United States—
Addresses, essays, lectures. I. Speigel, Allen D. [DNLM: 1. Insurance,
Health—United States. Medical assistance, Title 19. W275 AA1 M43]
HD 7102.U4M422   1979   368.4′2′00973   78-27669
ISBN 0-89443-088-2

Library of Congress Catalog Card Number: 78-27669
ISBN: 0-89443-088-2

Printed in the United States of America

1   2   3   4   5

CONTENTS

CONTRIBUTORS

RONALD ANDERSEN, Ph.D.
Center for Health Administration Studies
University of Chicago
Chicago, Illinois

JUDITH D. ANDERSON
Texas Medical Foundation
Austin, Texas

LAWRENCE BAILIS, Ph.D.
Senior Analyst
Urban Systems Research and Engineering, Inc.
Cambridge Massachusetts

SAM A. BANKS, Ph.D.
President
Dickinson College
Carlisle, Pennsylvania

MICHAEL BARTHEL, Ph.D.
Research and Statistics Division
Department of Human Resources
Washington, D.C.

PATRICIA BENNER
Junior Analyst
Urban Systems Research and Engineering, Inc.
Cambridge, Massachusetts

LOUISE BERENSON
Program Research Analyst
New York City Department of Health
New York, New York

PHYLLIS R. BLEIWEIS
Center for Inter-Governmental Studies
College of Law
University of Florida
Gainesville, Florida

PETER R. BREYER, Ph.D.
Co-Director
Urban Health Institute
East Orange, New Jersey

RHONA M. BRONSON
Planning Associate
Urban Health Insurance
East Orange, New Jersey

PATRICIA J. BUSH, Ph.D.
Adjunct Assistant Professor
Department of Community Medicine
and International Health
Georgetown University School of Medicine
Washington, D.C.

NEIL A. BUTLER
Former Mayor
Gainesville, Florida

PATRICIA A. BUTLER, J.D.
Health Facilities Analyst
Colorado Department of Health
Denver, Colorado

JOSEPH A. CALIFANO, Jr.
Secretary of Health, Education and Welfare
Washington, D.C.

ANTHONY P. CAPPELLI, Ph.D.
  President
  Universal Analytics, Inc.
  Playa Del Rey, California

JAMES Q. CANNON
  PACE Project Manager
  Utah Professional Review Organization
  Salt Lake City, Utah

DAVID F. CHAVKIN
  Senior Staff Attorney
  National Health Law Program
  Santa Monica, California

PHILIP K. COHEN
  Senior Health Planner
  Massachusetts Department of Public
    Health
  Boston, Massachusetts

WILBUR J. COHEN
  School of Education
  University of Michigan
  Ann Arbor, Michigan

KATHLEEN CONNELLY
  Associate Director
  Division of Long Term Care
  Massachusetts Department of Public
    Health
  Boston, Massachusetts

MAUREEN A. COTTERILL
  Research Assistant
  Alan Guttmacher Institute
  New York, New York

KAREN DAVIS, Ph.D.
  Deputy Assistant Secretary for Planning
    and Evaluation
  Department of Health, Education and
    Welfare
  Washington, D.C.

JUDITH DERNBURG
  Senior Analyst
  Urban Systems Research and Engineer-
    ing, Inc.
  Cambridge, Massachusetts

CAROL D'ONOFRIO, Dr. P.H.
  Head, Health Education Program
  University of California School of Public
    Health
  Berkeley, California

BRIGITTE DÖRING-BRADLEY
  Department of International Economic
    and Social Affairs
  United Nations
  New York, New York

DAVID ELLWOOD
  Consultant
  Urban Systems Research and Engineer-
    ing, Inc.
  Cambridge, Massachusetts

JOHN A. FLUECK, Ph.D.
  Director, Data Analysis Laboratory
  School of Business Administration
  Temple University
  Philadelphia, Pennsylvania

RICHARD FOSTER
  Research Associate
  Center for Health Administration Studies
  University of Chicago
  Chicago, Illinois

NORMAN A. FULLER, Ph.D.
  Executive Director
  National Capital Medical Foundation
  Washington, D.C.

JERRY GARBER
  Chief, Community Services Support Unit
  Division of Mental Health
  Department of Human Resources
  Atlanta, Georgia

EDWIN M. GOLD, M.D.
  School of Public Health
  University of California
  Berkeley, California

HYMAN GOLDSTEIN, Ph.D.
  Research Biostatistician
  Maternal and Child Health Program
  School of Public Health
  University of California
  Berkeley, California

CHRISTINE GUNSTON
  Supervisor, Data Control Unit
  Medicaid Fraud and Abuse
  New York State Department of Social
    Services
  New York, New York

CHARLES P. HALL, Jr., Ph.D.
Professor
Departments of Health Administration
  and of Insurance and Risk
School of Business Administration
Temple University
Philadelphia, Pennsylvania

BETTE HAMBURGER
Staff Coordinator
California Medical Association
San Francisco, California

ALFRED C. HEXTER, Ph.D.
Research Biostatistician
Maternal and Child Health Program
School of Public Health
University of California
Berkeley, California

DANIEL L. JEHL
Planning Analyst
Division of Health
Department of Health and Social
  Services
Madison, Wisconsin

MICHAEL W. JONES
Director, Division of Research and
  Socio-Economics
California Medical Association
San Francisco, California

A.R. KIRKLEY, M.D.
President
Texas Medical Foundation
Austin, Texas

ARLETTE KLEIN
Systems Department
Bradford Administrative Services, Inc.
New York, New York

CAROL A. KUNREUTHER
Research Associate
Urban Health Institute
East Orange, New Jersey

RICHARD LINCOLN
Director of Publications
Alan Guttmacher Institute
New York, New York

BARBARA L. LINDHEIM
Senior Research Associate
Alan Guttmacher Institute
New York, New York

STEPHEN F. LOEBS, Ph.D.
Associate Director
Graduate Program in Hospital and Health
  Services Administration
Ohio State University
Columbus, Ohio

DONALD MALAFRONTE
Director
Urban Health Institute
East Orange, New Jersey

IRENE MALOZEMOFF, Ph.D.
Senior Analyst
Urban Systems Research and Engineer-
  ing, Inc.
Cambridge, Massachusetts

RICHARD MARTINSON
Assistant Editor
Dental Management
New York, New York

WILLIAM F. MCKENNA
Research Associate
Department of Health Administration
School of Business Administration
Temple University
Philadelphia, Pennsylvania

EMMANUEL MESEL, M.D.
Associate Professor, School of Medicine
Information Science and Pediatrics
University of Alabama
Birmingham, Alabama

JOHN C. MILLER
Free Lance Writer
Los Angeles, California

MAURICE H. MILLER, Ph.D.
Professor of Audiology
New York University
New York, New York

HOWARD H. MOSES
Senior Associate
Urban Health Institute
East Orange, New Jersey

FRANK E. MOSS, J.D.
Former U.S. Senator

PATRICIA DOLAN MULLEN, Dr.P.H.
Associate Director
Health Education Department
Group Health Cooperative
Puget Sound
Seattle, Washington

RICHARD W. NATHAN
New York City Consultant,
Specializing in Health Care
New York, New York

GENE OKSMAN
Senior Analyst
Urban Systems Research & Engineering,
Inc.
Cambridge, Massachusetts

JAMES STUDNICKI, Sc.D.
Associate Professor
Department of Health Services
Administration
School of Hygiene and Public Health
Johns Hopkins University
Baltimore, Maryland

C. RICHARD TREADWAY, M.D.
Associate Vice-President for Medical
Affairs
Vanderbilt University
Nashville, Tennessee

TIMOTHY J. TYSON
Planning Analyst
Division of Health
Department of Health and Social
Services
Madison, Wisconsin

HELEN M. WALLACE, M.D.
Professor and Chairman
Maternal and Child Health Program
University of California School of Public
Health
Berkeley, California

WARREN OKSMAN, Ph.D.
Assistant Professor
Harvard Business School
Cambridge, Massachusetts

DAVID L. RABIN, M.D.
Acting Chairman
Department of Community Medicine and
International Health
Georgetown University School of
Medicine
Washington, D.C.

BRUCE F. REITER, M.D.
Radiologist and Novelist
New York, New York

RICHARD C. REYNOLDS, M.D.
Acting Dean
College of Medicine and Dentistry of
New Jersey—Rutgers Medical School
Piscataway, New Jersey

STEPHEN N. ROSENBERG, M.D.
Assistant Professor
Columbia University School of Public
Health
New York, New York

MARILYN RYMER
Vice-President
Urban Systems Research and Engineer-
ing, Inc.
Cambridge, Massachusetts

ROBERT M. SAYWELL, Jr., Ph.D.
Assistant Professor
Department of Public Health
Administration
School of Hygiene and Public Health
Johns Hopkins University
Baltimore, Maryland

STEPHEN C. SCHWARTZ
Executive Director
Bay Pacific Health Plan
San Mateo, California

SUZANNE STONE
Executive Associate for Policy
Committees
American Pharmaceutical Association
Washington, D.C.

HALSTEIN STRALBERG, Ph.D.
  Universal Analytics, Inc.
  Playa Del Rey, California
DIANA CHAPMAN WALSH
  Center for Industry and Health Care
  Boston University
  Boston, Massachusetts
PETER WEIL, Ph.D.
  Research Associate
  Department of Medicine
  University of Chicago
  Chicago, Illinois

WALTER WIECHETEK, M.D.
  Department of Health Services
    Administration
  School of Hygiene and Public Health
  Johns Hopkins University
  Baltimore, Maryland
DAVID D. WIRTSHAFTER, M.D.
  Associate Professor
  School of Medicine
  Information Science and Pediatrics
  University of Alabama
  Birmingham, Alabama

INTRODUCTION

On July 30th, 1965, President Lyndon B. Johnson stepped into his airplane and flew to Independence, Missouri. After the plane landed, the President went to the Harry S. Truman Memorial Library and, with ex-president Truman sitting there, signed into law the Social Security Amendments of 1965 (Public Law 89–97). This legislation established health insurance for the aged and grants to the states for medical assistance programs (Medicare and Medicaid). Ex-president Truman received the first Medicare card in the United States.

Typically, the focus of all the attention was on the Medicare program. This reemphasized the fact that the eye of the storm of the controversy over the years was on the attempt to "socialize medicine." Organized medicine had fought the battle through the terms of at least four presidents. As the June 1966 issue of *Medical World News* noted, "After nearly two decades of struggle and controversy, million dollar advertising drives, rallies, and political-action campaigns, the AMA's (American Medical Association) crusade has failed."

Very few people paid attention to Title XIX and Medicaid became the "sleeper" in the Social Security Amendments of 1965. One person who did predict a substantial impact on the private practice of medicine for the Medicaid title was economist Herman M. Somers in an interview which took place in October 1965, months before the new program took effect. Dr. Somers anticipated the large numbers of people coming into the Medicaid program and also warned about the "welfare stigma" of the program as well as the possibility of increased costs.*

However, Dr. Somers was the exception and represented the views of a small number of people who foresaw the impact of the Medicaid legislation. Yet, it did not take long for the nation to be alerted to the effect of the Medicaid provisions. The numbers of eligible persons and the costs of providing the health care services to that eligible population were evident as soon as the first reports from state and federal accountants became available. Obviously, the Medicaid program had outstripped anybody's projections in terms of costs and numbers of people who qualified for the program. This last minute addition to the more spectacular Medicare program caused

---

*H.M. Somers. "The Big Sleeper in the Medicare Law" interview by Howard R. Lewis *Medical Economics,* January 24, 1966 pp. 110–122.

reverberations throughout each state and territory as the administrators grappled with the mandate of the federal law and the precarious position of their state budget.

What the state administration did in terms of the services provided under Medicaid and in terms of the management aspects is the major focus of this book. In an earlier book,* more attention was given to the history, evolution and perspectives about Medicaid. In addition, this earlier book concentrated on analyses of the health care providers and the quality control efforts. The concluding section of that book discussed the performance, the problems and the perspectives for the future. This latest book on Medicaid puts the emphasis on the health care services provided (Section 2) and on the management of the Medicaid program (Section 3). Included in the management section are articles relating to actual administration, funding and cost containment, utilization and utilization control and surveillance/utilization review for both fraud and quality. In addition Section 1 provides a brief historical review and Section 4 discusses achievements, fraud and abuse and the future. As with the prior collection of articles, this book also stresses the lessons to be learned from the Medicaid program.

If possible, consideration should be given to regarding the two books as companion pieces. Each book contains entirely different articles with no repetitions. Subject matter in the two books are complementary and reinforce the lessons to be garnered from the Medicaid program. Now, literature continues to pile up on the Medicaid program and the selection of material for this latest collection was quite difficult. Much worthwhile material had to be deleted to keep the book within reasonable size. This wealth of data and reports should not be lost and it is possible that even more collections would be useful to people working in this health care field.

In speculating about the lessons to be learned from experiences with the Medicaid program, it is interesting to contemplate the statement by Krause* about Medicaid, "The decision to run the program through the Federal Welfare Bureau, and in each state through the welfare departments, which was a decision made at the beginning of the Medicaid program, doomed it from the start as a strategy for change." Krause commented that political opposition to the creation of genuine equal opportunity in health care for the poor, the alignment of health and welfare systems against the program and the profit motivation of the private health care system were instrumental factors in the expected demise of Medicaid. Of course, from colonial times onward common law has stated that the care of the poor, including medical care, was a fundamental function of local government. This concept established the tradition of "poor relief" as a responsibility of the smallest political unit—village, town, city, parish or county. No government should allow its citizens to die of starvation, sickness or exposure merely because they were poor. So, a tradition of local government responsibility for the administration of health care services for the poor might also be considered as part of the projected downfall of the Medicaid program. No doubt the rationales could be varied and numerous. Yet, it should be noted that despite all the huge problems and difficulties, Medicaid has survived. Maybe, that's the biggest lesson of all.

---

*Allen D. Spiegel and Simon Podair. *Medicaid: Lessons for National Health Insurance.* Germantown, Md.: Aspen Systems Corporation, 1974.

*Elliott A. Krause. *Power and Illness: The Political Sociology of Health and Medical Care.* New York: Elsevier, 1977.

SECTION ONE

A BRIEF OVERVIEW

Grants to States for Medical Assistance Programs was the official name of Title XIX of the Social Security Amendments of 1965 and part of Public Law 89–97. Medicaid was the popular name of the program.

Medicaid was added to the original legislation to meet the objections of those who felt that Medicare didn't cover everyone. Creators of the bill thought that several million unknown eligibles for Medicaid services might be discovered, but a huge hidden population sought Medicaid benefits and exceeded twenty million people in the late 1970s. In addition, the first year costs of Medicaid were estimated to be about $238 million and a recent estimate indicated that the costs will be more than $20 billion per year. Yet, the welfare provisions of P.L. 89–97 were virtually ignored by the Congress, the mass media and by most observers. Perhaps, the culmination of actually passing health care legislation for the aged overshadowed all else.

Another important factor that may have contributed to the short shrift given to Medicaid was the belief of the creators of the legislation that the bill would be short lived. It was anticipated that a national health insurance program would be in effect by 1970. Medicaid, then became a program created for reasons of convenience and expediency. As events turned out, Medicaid was a "sleeper" that burgeoned into a massive health care program.

Historically, health care in America has been a two track system; charity care for the poor and fee-for-service health care for those who could afford the payments. Medicaid became an avenue for the poor to move into the mainstream of medical care. However, the words used to describe the people on Medicare and Medicaid clearly illustrate what happened; Medicare clients were called "beneficiaries" and Medicaid clients were called "recipients." The charity and/or welfare mentality was maintained and the stigma remained, putting an indelible imprint on the Medicaid program throughout the nation.

As Medicaid was a state administered program, the "welfare stigma" overtones varied throughout the nation depending upon each state's approach to providing health care for welfare recipients. In effect, Medicaid legislation created the opportunity for more than 50 separate and unique Medicaid programs to evolve in each of the states and territories in the United States.

With the combination of the huge hidden population that became eligible for Medicaid benefits and the rising costs of health care, most state legislatures turned their attention to containing costs and reducing the numbers of people eligible for Medicaid benefits. Currently, these areas remain uppermost in the state administered Medicaid program.

On March 8, 1978, the Tenth Annual Conference of Medicaid Directors was held in New Orleans, Louisiana and the Under Secretary of Health, Education, and Welfare addressed the group. Hale Champion stated, "No matter how you choose to picture Medicaid's current state, there can be but one conclusion—we can't be proud of Medicaid as it is, and we have got to do something about it." Furthermore, the Under Secretary identified the following problems on which he thought real progress could be made in the near future:

- Health cost inflation and general economic conditions that helped undermine Medicaid's fiscal stability. This problem should be met by saving costs through elimination of nonessential services, prudent buying and contracting, by reducing error rates, and by aggressively fighting fraud and abuse.

- Constraints in the ability to make fundamental changes in benefit packages. For example, long-term care policies are biased toward institutional services. This may mean that one state does not cover a $2,000 prosthesis for a nursing home patient that will allow the patient to go home even though the state will continue to pay $400 per month to the nursing home. Rules should be changed when they don't make sense and aren't cost-effective.

- Payment policies impede access to care. In some states, only 4 out of every 10 physicians treat any number of Medicaid patients because of the severely limited payment rates. Cutting costs by lowering physician payment levels is counterproductive to the overall Medicaid program.

- Failure to explore third party liability and to collect payment from other resources that the recipient may have. This deficiency is estimated to be costing the Medicaid program as much as $1 billion a year.

- Eligibility error rates. This rate is calculated at seven percent and costs $1.2 billion per year it is estimated.

- Ill-devised penalty provisions to spur states into action. If the penalty is too small, the states will absorb the loss rather than institute the controls. If the sanction is too large, the state's Medicaid program could be crippled. Yet, sanctions to meet these problems and still have the states carry out their part of the partnership with effectiveness and good faith must be worked out.

- Medicaid is an extremely complex program to manage. Administrative resources committed by the federal government and the states have been inadequate. Resulting management weaknesses have severely impaired the ability of the federal and state governments in their efforts.

Among the considerations put forth by the Under Secretary as responses to the problems were recommendations for action on hospital cost containment, the promotion of health maintenance organizations (HMOs), the revision and/or replacement of the Early and Periodic Screening, Diagnosis and Treatment (EPSDT) provisions and the extension of services under the Rural Health Clinic Services Act of 1977. In addition, a number of management initiatives is expected to make considerable headway toward the commitment to provide health care for those on Medicaid.

This section contains only one article by Loebs that reviews the Medicaid program. In addition, a number of exhibits provide current data about the existing Medicaid program.

Starting out with the noting of the "sleeper" aspects of Medicaid, Loebs goes on to explain the intent of the legislation and to define the purpose of Medicaid. He then proceeds to review various characteristics of the programs including eligibility, medical services, administration, access and utilization, quality of care, and costs of the program.

Loebs discusses seven alternatives for cost containment and the issues raised relative to eligibility changes, reductions in medical services offered, cost sharing requirements, fraud and abuse control prior to the passage of the anti-fraud legislation, reimbursement policies, utilization review and others such as use of generic drugs and the role of primary prevention.

In commenting on state variations in Medicaid programs, Loebs quotes another source to sum up the situation, "Medicaid does not treat people in equal circumstances equally."

A fundamental question that is posed in the discussion about the future of Medicaid is, "Should Medicaid survive in its current form?" Who is to have the primary responsibility for the system—the federal government or the state government?

In summary, Loebs points out that Medicaid is a microcosm of the medical care system and that solving problems here could affect the entire American health care system. Four lessons are identified:

- Medicaid made health care accessible to the poor who wouldn't have had it otherwise.

- Many persons are still ineligible for benefits.

- Attention was focused on the quality of care and the failings of the program while emphasizing public responsibility for the program.

- State governments can dilute national goals when they play a dominant role in the administration of such a program.

In several exhibits, data on the Medicaid program presents the issues graphically.

In a nine year period, starting with 1970, the Medicaid population is projected to be leveling off at about 21 million recipients. Children under 21 have the greatest growth over the years. In addition New York and California account for 28.5 percent of the Medicaid population by themselves with the next eight states adding an additional 35 percent. By size of state program, the 20 largest states account for 81 percent of the total national Medicaid population.

Expenditures for Medicaid grew from more than $3 billion in 1969 to a projected cost of more than 20 billion in 1979. This has been a steady straight line increase. By 1976, for example, Medicaid paid for almost 50 percent of the nation's costs for nursing home care expenditures. However, the expenditures were divided disproportionately by states. New York and California accounted for 32.5 percent by themselves with the next eight states adding 33.7 percent and the 20 largest state programs spending 81.9 percent of the funds.

In comparing the numbers of eligible Medicaid recipients and the expenditures by eligibility classification, another disparity can be observed. While children under 21 comprise the largest eligibility group, the aged comprise the group accounting for the greatest volume of expenditures. In a similar vein, while inpatient hospital care was the service required most frequently by the total Medicaid group, skilled nursing care was the most frequent expenditure for the aged. Variations in the services used by the different eligible Medicaid groups indicates the potential effect of cutbacks on the various classifications.

1. Medicaid—A Survey of Indicators and Issues

STEPHEN F. LOEBS

Reprinted with permission from the quarterly journal of the American College of Hospital Administrators, *Hospital & Health Services Administration*, 22(4): 63–90, Fall 1977.

Title XIX of the Social Security Amendments of 1965, known more commonly as Medicaid, has been in effect for more than 10 years. It was a "sleeper" to the country, overshadowed by the controversies and enactment of Medicare.

In recent years, however, its visibility has changed dramatically. Medicaid has become one of the most controversial programs in the country and a major problem for hospitals. It has caused governors and state legislators to radically change their budget priorities to pay for the costs of the programs. This has effected acute reverberations for other state financed programs, such as education, which have had to cope with budget cutbacks because of the increasing and apparently uncontrollable costs of Medicaid. Investigations have exposed fraudulent practices by providers and recipients in the Medicaid program, raising bigger problems than were suspected.

Congress is considering proposals to restructure the entire Medicaid program. State governments are developing and implementing new initiatives to contain the Medicaid cost spiral. In brief, the impact and controversy generated by Medicaid was underestimated in its early years. It has emerged as one of the most complex and costly public initiatives in medical care in the last decade.

(A word of caution is necessary before proceeding. The available information on Medicaid is not as recent as we might prefer and the very nature of its administration by the several states makes generalizations practically impossible. The status of Medicaid is fluid and any firm predictions of future developments are precarious.)

DEFINITION OF MEDICAID

The intent of the Medicaid legislation has been to provide payment for medical care for certain low income individuals and families receiving public assistance and for others defined as medically needy. The underlying goal has been to improve access to medical care for the poor. The funding for Medicaid is a combination of state and federal funds with federal participation between 50–80% of the state's Medicaid program. This percentage is dependent on the per capita income of a state's population.

Medicaid is controlled and administered by the state. Within guidelines set by federal law, the states have flexibility in determining who is eligible, the types and levels of medical services for which financing is made available, and the levels of reimbursement for providers of the medical services. There is no limit set by the federal government on the total amount of money which can be spent by the states for medical services, and this open-ended funding policy has been one of the major contributors to the rapid increase in total costs and to the difficulties in controlling costs.

Federal and state financing of health care for the poor was not initiated by Medicaid. It is an expansion of programs started before the Depression and then incorporated in the Social Security Act of 1935 (2) (3).

The states were not required to develop a Medicaid program but imposing incentives were established to do so. For example, no federal funds were made available after December, 1969 for medical provider payments under categorical related programs (Aid to the Blind, Aid to the Permanently and Totally Disabled, Aid to the Aged, and Aid to Families with Dependent Children). At present, 49 states have a Medicaid program and Arizona expects to begin its program in July 1977 (4).

SELECTED INDICATORS

1. Eligibility

The Medicaid law requires the states to include in their Medicaid programs those eligible under the categorical assistance programs—Aid to Families with Dependent Children (AFDC) and Supplemental Security Income (SSI). The original categories of aged, blind, and disabled cash assistance recipients were combined under the SSI program in 1974. The states have the option of including the medically needy. These are persons in the above categories whose incomes are too high to be eligible for cash assistance but are not sufficient to pay for needed medical care. The states must define the income limits for the medically needy within certain guidelines. Twenty-nine states finance medical services for the medically needy.

An important policy decision for each state which includes the medically needy is the definition of income limits for an individual or family to be eligible. These limits vary considerably among the states. There are estimates that as many as 8,000,000 people below the poverty line are not eligible for Medicaid. North Carolina has established an income limit of $2200 for a family of four while Wisconsin's limit is $5742 (5). In addition, Davis reports that "most states in the Deep South cover only about one-tenth of the poor children, while in the Northeast nearly all poor and near-poor children receive services" (6). These state variations in defining eligibility indicate that Medicaid does not cover all the poor.

2. Medical services

The states are required to include the following medical services under Medicaid: inpatient, outpatient, laboratory and X-ray, skilled nursing, physicians, home health, and EPSDT (Early and Periodic Screening, Diagnosis, and Treatment) for children under 21 years. Beyond these, the states have the option of including a number of other services, such as drugs, eyeglasses, and dental services, for which federal matching funds are available. If a state decides to include all the optional medical services for which federal matching funds are available, its Medicaid program can be more comprehensive in coverage of medical care costs than most other financing programs, public or private.

States have the discretion of deciding on the amount (or level) of each service included in the program and they may impose other restrictions, such as cost-sharing requirements. For example, one state may decide to include 30 inpatient hospital days per Medicaid eligible person per year while another state may include 90 days. These options have led to substantial variations among the states in expenditures for medical services for eligible persons. For example, Medicaid payments per child recipient in 1970 ranged from $43 in Mississippi to $240 in Wisconsin (6).

Attempts have been made to understand the basis for these variations utilizing indicators of state characteristics and subjective estimates by program administrators, legislators, and lobbyists. This author found that a different set of factors appears to influence the optional choices for medical services than the factors which influence inclusion of the medically needy (7). These factors did not explain as much variation as Richmond detected in a case study of one state's Medicaid program. He concluded that the dominant political ideology and attitudes toward the poor held by legislators and governmental bureaucrats were the chief determinants of the responses to the optional choices in the Medicaid program (8).

3. Administration

States have had the option of selecting the agency (or department) to be responsible for administering the Medicaid program. There is variation in this selection with about 60% of the programs administered by the welfare department, about 30% administered by a combined health and welfare department, and about 10% administered by the health department.

There are controversies that a welfare department should not administer Medicaid because it is not compatible with the goals of improving the health of a population; therefore the health department is the logical administering agent. The alternative point of view concludes that the welfare department is much better prepared for administering the program because most (if not all) of the eligible recipients are already part of the welfare program. A compromise has been developed in one state by establishing a new and separate agency. There is no conclusive evidence that the Medicaid program would be better or worse if it was managed exclusively by the same department in every state.

North Carolina recently contracted with a private management firm to manage the Medicaid program. The firm agreed to assume most of the management responsibility for a fixed fee but the contract was terminated by mutual agreement due to a significant overrun on original cost estimates. The major contributors to the overrun were identified as: (1) an increase in nursing home reimbursement rates with a simultaneous expansion of long-term care facilities in the state, and (2) an underestimation of the number of persons eligible for Medicaid. Since the contract was in effect for a relatively short time, evaluation of the effectiveness of a private management firm in a public program such as Medicaid is impossible (9).

4. Access and utilization

One of the goals of the Medicaid program has been to make medical services more accessible to low income persons. The evidence indicates that progress is being made to achieve this goal. Specifically, 28% of the poor in 1964 had not seen a physician in the two previous years, but this had declined to 17% by 1974 (10). While several factors have clearly influenced this change, it is fair to conclude that Medicaid, through its financing of services, had a substantial impact on the trend. One author has concluded that Medicaid has produced two major accomplishments in its 10 years: dramatic improvement in the financial access of the poor to medical services, and a source of experience in considerations for a national health insurance program (4).

The number of persons receiving one or more medical services under Medicaid was approximately 23 million in fiscal year 1975. This represents an increase of approximately 7% from 1974. The distribution of these recipients among the eligibility categories are as follow: dependent children under 21 years made up about 34%; adults in families with dependent children 21%; persons over 65 years constitute 24%; the permanently and totally disabled persons 13%; the blind 1%; and other recipients who have been included by the states but who do not come under one of the eligibility categories account for about 7% (11).

Another perspective on the Medicaid population is the distribution of expenditures among the eligibility categories. In fiscal year 1975, payments for persons over 65 accounted for approximately 38% of total expenditures; payments for the permanently and totally disabled 23%; payments for dependent children in the AFDC program 16%; payments for adults in the AFDC program 16%; the noncategory related medically needy consumed 6% of the total expenditures; and about 1% of the payments were made to the blind (11). This pattern of expenditures for the Medicaid program reveals that more than 60% of the total dollars are spent for the aged and disabled. Davis concludes from these data that, "Medicaid has been the primary vehicle by which society has helped assist those who are no longer able physically or mentally to care for themselves . . . . it is far from being a program for welfare mothers" (12). The expenditure data also reveal about 47% of the total is spent for persons who are not receiving monthly welfare payments. Most of these become eligible for Medicaid under one of the welfare categories because they are medically needy.

The data on general characteristics of the Medicaid population do not detect if those eligible are receiving medical care when it is needed and in the same manner as those with higher income. There is some evidence to suggest that eligibility does not automatically lead to immediate utilization of services. Brook and Williams report that 20% of the eligible Medicaid population in New Mexico never used one medical service in a two-year period (1971–1973) (13). While this is only one state and it is likely that some of the non-users were basically healthy without need for medical services, it is also likely that there are persons in need of services who did not use the services due to problems in access, availability,

lack of knowledge, or lack of confidence in health providers. Much more information relating these factors to use is required before definitive conclusions are possible.

Davis has reported that the "poor do not obtain care in the same setting, from the same kind of physicians, and with the same ease and convenience as higher income persons" (12). Data reveal that persons with low incomes are more inclined to obtain physicians' services from general practitioners than specialists, in a hospital outpatient department rather than in a physician's office, and after travelling long distances and waiting substantially longer for care (13). Donabedian has presented an extraordinarily comprehensive analysis of access to medical care among Medicaid recipients and concludes that use of services may not be totally congruent with need. For certain sectors, however, such as urban communities, the total number of physician visits and hospital days used by the poor are about the same as for high income groups (14). The data are often contradictory but one of the effects of Medicaid seems to be improved access and utilization of medical services for persons previously unable or unwilling to obtain medical services.

5. Quality

The evidence on the quality of medical care provided to Medicaid beneficiaries is limited. Donabedian has summarized the most relevant studies (14). He concludes the major benefit in terms of quality is an increase in use of services. Simultaneously, efforts to watch hospital utilization under PSRO-type structures have produced reductions in hospital patient days for certain categories of Medicaid recipients (15).

There is apparently a greater tendency for overuse and fraud to occur under Medicaid than any other financing program. The basis for this is not obvious. Donabedian observes that "many of the practitioners and some of the institutions that serve the poor do so under a variety of handicaps, often in an environment in which incentives for self-control are weak and the mechanisms for self-control are absent or ineffectual'' (14).

This places Medicaid beneficiaries in a particularly vulnerable position, since they are less likely to be aware of the financial consequences and hazards of the services prescribed by private practitioners. Corrections of these problems in quality are not readily at hand. Increased attention to fraud and abuse in the Medicaid program may lead to improvements but the evidence to support such an expectation is not persuasive. If the states continue to have responsibility for quality measurement and control, then variation in quality is to be expected. For example, one study reported that only 12 states had established standards for the performance of sterilization on Medicaid beneficiaries (16).

6. Costs

Medicaid may be most well known for the rapid escalation in total costs. While the actual costs were expected to exceed projections (4), the recent annual increases have created major problems for state governments and increased Medicaid's visibility within the federal government. Expenditures made for Medicaid services in 1975 were $12.5 billion. This represents an increase of approximately 150% in five years. There was a 20.9% increase in expenditures in 1975 over 1974 which was the largest annual increase in the three preceding years (11). The expected total cost in 1976 is estimated at $14 billion (12).

The distribution of Medicaid dollars by type of service in 1975 was as follows: inpatient, acute hospital services—28%; skilled nursing home services—20%; intermediate care facility services—18%; mental hospital services—4%; physicians' services—10%; prescribed drugs—7%; outpatient hospital services—3%; clinic services—3%; and other services—8%. Inpatient services

(hospitals, skilled nursing, intermediate care facilities and mental care hospitals) accounted for more than 70% of Medicaid payments.

The largest percent of change in 1975 from 1974 expenditures is found in expenditures for intermediate care facility services which increased 36% in the one year. Inpatient hospital service expenditures increased 15%; skilled nursing, 22%; and physicians' services, 14%. The extraordinary increase in expenditures for intermediate care facility services suggest that Medicaid is rapidly becoming a major source of financing long-term care for the aged and disabled. As the age distribution of the United States population continues to shift to the older years, the expenses of Medicaid will likely accelerate under the current benefit levels and reimbursement policies.

These unanticipated high costs of Medicaid have been accompanied by a few intensive studies of the causes. Gartside identified the causes of increase in total Medicaid costs in California and their respective contributions to the increase as: (1) increases in the price of medical services—49.4%; (2) expansion of the covered population—26.3%; and (3) increases in utilization of medical services—24.3%. (17). Grimaldi identified the same causes for increase in the costs of the New Jersey Medicaid program between 1970 and 1974, but concluded that changes in utilization per eligible person was the most significant contributor to the increase rather than increases in price (18). Davis offers a refinement in the analysis of cost increases by reporting that the three factors which are almost totally responsible for the increases are: the increase in the number of Medicaid recipients covered under the AFDC program; the rise in medical care prices; and the high cost of nursing home care for an impoverished, aged, and disabled population (6).

The acute concern for the increases in Medical costs may be tempered by the comparison of Medicaid expenditures with other components of the annual state government budgets and the federal budget. Davis suggests that Medicaid's share of total expenditures has not changed markedly in several years and that its rate of change is not greater than other governmental activity (6). The latter argument is not convincing to the several state governors who have recently proposed major changes in the federal law to assist them in containing the cost increases (19). Medicaid may be a small part of a state's overall budget, but the rapid cost increases have made it highly visible. Much attention is focused on the alternatives for doing something about these costs, and this has become one of the major issues in the Medicaid program.

COST CONTAINMENT ALTERNATIVES AND ISSUES

The rapidly rising costs of Medicaid, well-publicized claims of fraud and abuse by providers, and uncertainties about the effectiveness of program management in the states have created increasing attention to the alternatives for reducing the costs or, at least, reducing the rate of increase. The analysis of alternatives and the process of implementation of changes has become very politicized and controversial. There are many issues within the general controversy of cost containment and there are many constituencies who are directly affected by program changes. Several of the alternatives for cost containment within Medicaid and related issues are described in this section.

1. Eligibility changes

States must include all cash assistance recipients under the AFDC and SSI programs. Since enactment of the SSI program, states have had the option of limiting Medicaid eligibility of SSI recipients by requiring them to meet more restrictive eligibility standards for Medicaid which were in effect on January 1, 1972, prior to the implementation of the SSI program. Fourteen states have chosen this more restrictive standard. As previously stated, 29 states have included the medically needy optional groups. Data indicate that states have not made changes in the eligibility groups of Medicaid, except for the restrictions under SSI.

Although an increasing eligible population has been one of the major contributors to increasing Medicaid costs, nothing has been done about reducing eligibility. The explanation is that most of this expansion has been the result of the mandated inclusion of certain groups (such as persons under 21 years of age for the Early and Periodic Screening, Diagnosis, and Treatment—EPSDT—program) and general economic conditions which, in turn, affect the number of people receiving cash assistance. The number of persons who are made eligible by inclusion under the optional medically needy groups is proportionately small in most states which have included these persons. To eliminate them from Medicaid would not have much impact on total costs and could be very expensive politically. While reduction in the number of eligible persons for Medicaid is a theoretical alternative to cost reduction, it is not a realistic alternative unless basic changes are made in the federal law.

2. Reductions in medical services

Each state is required to cover certain services and may include additional services if it chooses to do so. For both sets of services, the amount of coverage, such as the number of hospital days and the number of physician visits, is determined by the states. These options give the states flexibility in the extent to which the costs for medical services are covered for Medicaid eligible persons. A cost-reducing alternative for the states would be a reduction in medical services covered under Medicaid which would be expected to reduce utilization and costs. More specifically, the amount of medical services could be reduced and the optional services which the states select on their own to include could be eliminated.

These alternatives appear to be gaining favor among the states. During 1975, 11 states reduced the amount of coverage on mandatory services, and 15 states eliminated one or more of the optional services. The most common type of mandatory service reduction was the amount (or days) of inpatient hospital care, while the most common type of optional service eliminated was adult dental care. No state eliminated all of its optional services (21). Most of these changes have been related to fiscal problems in the states (22), although there may be more fundamental opposition to a medical assistance program for the low income welfare recipients which is manifested in these benefit reductions.

The states' decisions to reduce and eliminate medical services from Medicaid may not necessarily yield reductions in total costs and may lead to more serious problems. Eligible persons may shift their location for medical care to more expensive providers when reductions in one type of service occur. For example, optometrists may be excluded from Medicaid reimbursement, but a Medicaid eligible person can go to an ophthalmologist and obtain the same service, usually at higher costs. Physician office visits may be reduced but hospital outpatient clinic visits may be used, again at higher costs.

Another possible consequence of medical service reductions is increasing the unavailability of providers. When services are reduced or eliminated, providers may move away to more lucrative neighborhoods and suburbs where reimbursement is more likely. This creates a gap in availability for Medicaid beneficiaries who must contend with transportation difficulties and other similar barriers. This could, in turn, produce frustration and alienation among population groups who have come to expect more equal access to medical care.

The differences among the states in the medical services financed by the Medicaid programs can be expected to continue and it is likely reductions will occur in uneven fashion, unless the federal law is changed. Whenever states have a major role in establishing benefits, differences in those benefits will occur and states will have different degrees of response to ensuring equitable access to medical care (12).

3. Requirements for cost-sharing

The Social Security Amendments of 1972 (P.L. 92–603) provide the states with an option of imposing cost sharing requirements on Medicaid-eligible persons with certain restrictions. The intent of requiring Medicaid-eligible persons to pay part of the costs of medical services is to impose a consideration (a constraint) before use occurs to reduce unnecessary use. This is intended to yield lower total cost than would be incurred by the state if some form of cost sharing was not imposed.

A recent report indicates that cost sharing in the form of required copayments by Medicaid-eligible persons is the second most common type of cost control employed by the states other than direct reduction of services. This should be tempered by the fact that only eight states had instituted cost sharing requirements. The most common type of cost sharing is a copayment of 50¢ per prescription. Only North Carolina identified a comprehensive list of services with copayment requirements including inpatient hospital days (22). This latter amounts to a requirement that the eligible person pay $2 per inpatient day which the hospital must collect.

The impact of the copayment requirement is not well documented and conclusions on utilization and cost reductions are limited. The best evidence is derived from a California experiment between January, 1972, and June, 1973, under which the

Medi-Cal program (Medicaid in California) imposed a copayment charge of $1 on the first two doctor visits and other outpatient services and a 50¢ copayment charge on the first two drug prescriptions (23). Use of office visits among those Medi-Cal eligible persons required to copay these amounts declined relative to the use of those not required to pay. At the same time, hospitalization for the copay group increased to higher levels than the hospital use rate for those not required to pay. There were increased costs associated with higher hospital utilization rates which offset the savings derived from a decline in ambulatory care. The substitution of more expensive services with no copayment requirement for a less expensive service with a copayment requirement appears to occur (24).

Another problem associated with copayment requirements is the response and participation by providers in additional collection and paperwork procedures. The administration of copayment requirements can mean more hassle, frustration, and uncollectible charges which would in turn jeopardize providers' willingness to participate in the program. A survey of providers in the California experiment reports that private physicians, pharmacists, and nurses collected the copayments and did not believe it to be a hardship on the patients. On the other hand, hospital outpatient departments often did not collect. This tends to counterbalance the perspective of individual providers (25). The evidence suggests that selected copayment requirements do not yield significant cost savings, and they may produce higher expenditures than with no copayment requirement.

4. Fraud and abuse control

There have been lengthy analyses by the news media about provider fraud in Medicaid. The term Medicaid mills had been coined to refer to the providers who are obtaining exorbitant reimbursement amounts through fraud. The evidence on the extent of fraud in Medicaid around the country is generally sketchy, but the information about illegal prosperity in Medicaid laboratories in Illinois (26), and nursing home scandals in New York does suggest a problem exists and that cost reductions are possible.

The potential savings (or cost reductions) from closer monitoring of fraudulent practices and prosecution of providers, as well as others involved in such practices, is in dispute. One source in the Department of Health, Education and Welfare estimates that fraud accounts for 5% of total Medicaid expenditures, or $750 million (27). Davis claims that this is only a small fraction of the total costs, that abuses are inevitable in a program as large as Medicaid, and that effective cost control will only be achieved by attacking the basic causes of cost increases (6). She does, however, recommend that corrective action should be taken.

The recent changes by HEW to increase its staff capability in detecting fraud and abuse, as well as attention given to the topic by proposed changes in the federal law, indicate that expectations are increasing that Medicaid costs will be affected by a crackdown. While the impact may be rather modest on a national scale, it is more likely that the significance of provider fraud will vary from state to state.

5. Reimbursement policies

Reimbursement to providers for services used by Medicaid-eligible persons is one of the more sensitive and potentially explosive issues. Certain changes in reimbursement policies as a cost-containing alternative have made this issue more visible.

States have had flexibility to determine the reimbursement rate for services, except for hospital care. Reimbursement for hospital care must follow the Medicare reasonable cost payment system unless an alternative payment system is approved by the Secretary of HEW. Since July 1, 1976, reimbursement policies for skilled nursing facilities and intermediate care facilities must be approved by HEW, but flexibility in these arrangements does, in fact, continue.

Reductions in reimbursement amounts are assumed to be a cost-reducing alternative which is tied to factors accounting for cost increases. That is, a reversal of cost increases is assumed to occur if the states could control the increase in prices. Between January 1, 1975, and January 15, 1976, nine states made this assumption and limited or reduced provider fees (21). Mullen and Schneider provide a caution on these data because they do not reflect the reimbursement policies of those states which have kept reimbursement levels for participating providers excessively low for several years (28).

Reimbursement levels for physicians' services under Medicaid vary considerably from state to state. Some states follow the Medicare practice of paying physicians at approximately the 75th percentile of prevailing charges; others follow private insurance policies with fees at approximately the 90th percentile of prevailing charges; while others set fee schedules or rates well below the norm for other financing programs. California, for example, was recently reported to limit physician payments to 1968 levels (28). There are also reports that other states have recently reduced reimbursement levels by 30%.

There is evidence that states' efforts to contain costs by reducing physicians' fees below normal levels are producing undesirable effects; the number of physicians who will accept Medicaid patients is gradually declining because of the inadequate level of reimbursement and denial of reimbursement for services already provided (29).

There are other consequences to the limitations on provider reimbursement and subsequent nonparticipation. It impairs access to certain types of physicians, especially primary care physicians, who largely determine access to the remainder of re-

quired medical services. This reduction in access would appear to contradict the purposes of the Medicaid program. Some states may have adopted the implicit position that Medicaid beneficiaries should face increasing difficulty finding a private physician. This might then produce lower utilization of services and lower expenditures. Such a sequence is only hypothetical because it is more likely that Medicaid beneficiaries will seek medical services at a different location, such as a hospital outpatient department where services may be available and more expensive. The long-run effect would be an increase in total expenditures.

Controlling Medicaid costs by reducing physicians' fees appears to have limited impact. As long as physician participation in Medicaid is voluntary and there are other sources of income for physicians who are required to assure access to medical services financed under Medicaid, then reimbursement levels must be structured to induce participation.

Hospitals are faced with a different set of problems under Medicaid reimbursement formulae. The states are not freezing or lowering reimbursement for hospitals, but some states are establishing limits on the allowable increases. Massachusetts, for example, enacted a budget which mandated a 7% ceiling on increases in hospital and nursing home rates under Medicaid for 1977 (30). The movement to establish a ceiling, or cap, on annual increases is manifest in other arenas. The Carter administration has made such a proposal which has been well publicized. It is likely this will be a most controversial issue in the months ahead.

There are other sequela from the changing reimbursement environment. As states cut back on medical services which are usually provided outside the hospital, and as they reduce reimbursement levels for physicians, Medicaid-eligible persons can be expected to turn to the hospital as the major, and perhaps only, source of care. If reimbursement to the hospital by the state for Medicaid financed services is not equivalent to costs and if Medicaid beneficiaries are required to pay part of the costs through copayment provisions, then hospitals are forced to either deny the beneficiaries access to hospital care, attempt to collect payment from the individual users, or absorb the losses by recouping from another group of payors. This latter possibility becomes more difficult with the potential of a mandated cap on annual increases and increasing reluctance by the other payors to subsidize Medicaid patients. There is a squeeze occurring with no long-term resolution in sight.

Inpatient hospital services account for approximately 30% of Medicaid expenditures. Reductions in the prices paid for hospital services appear to most observers, certainly legislators, to be the most cost-effective effort as opposed to reductions in reimbursement to other providers. More attention to prospective reimbursement systems to be applied throughout the country and to reimbursement caps is likely. In the face of this increased pressure to hold costs, hospitals may consider boycotting the Medicaid program, as some nursing home associations have done, or instituting litigation against the states to force more reasonable reimbursement in compliance with federal law. Either alternative increases the level of conflict between hospitals and state government agencies.

6. Contracts with HMOs

The current Medicaid reimbursement policies and the traditional forms of medical care in this country favor the use of hospitals, nursing homes, and fee-for-service providers. These patterns are considered to be a major deterrent to controlling and improving the Medicaid program. Alternatives to the current reimbursement policies and patterns of organization among providers which would encourage the development of nontraditional and noninstitutional patterns of care in the medically under-

served area could offer cost savings and other improvements. One specific alternative is the Health Maintenance Organization (HMO), also known as a comprehensive prepaid health plan, with which states may develop contracts to cover Medicaid-eligible persons.

HMOs provide comprehensive medical services to an enrolled population in return for a fixed, prepaid fee. The incentives for physicians and for the sponsoring organization are different than under a fee-for-service reimbursement system, and the medical services are usually more organized and centralized. States have had the option of developing contracts with existing HMOs for Medicaid eligibles, but only 15 states have done so.

The most publicized effort to relate HMOs to the Medicaid program has occurred in California. Fifty-four prepaid health plans (PHP) had contracted with the state by the end of 1974 to provide comprehensive services to approximately 10% of the eligible population. The results have not been supportive of the expected benefits. The PHPs have tended to maximize monthly costs by enrollment abuses, denial of needed services, and low quality care (32).

The abuses and fraudulent practices of the PHPs have been the subject of state and national studies which have produced new efforts to monitor them. The intended increase in accountability and in performance has not been achieved without serious problems (33), and a Medicaid/HMO contracting program is apparently more difficult to implement than originally anticipated.

There is evidence from other studies of Medicaid/HMO arrangements that indicates more positive outcomes. A recent analysis of comparative HMO and fee-for-service rates for use and cost between matched population groups in the District of Columbia Medicaid program concluded that a significant reduction in hospital admissions and length of stay occurred among

Medicaid eligibles enrolled in the HMO. This produced an average saving of 25% during the study period for the Medicaid program (34). Such data cannot be easily generalized, but they provide additional verification of the potential efficacy of this alternative.

A comprehensive study comparing various aspects of HMO performance in ten plans across the country with the performance of the fee-for-service alternative for the Medicaid population was reported by Gaus et al. The study examined utilization differences between several types of HMOs. Group practice HMOs had significantly lower hospital utilization than those serviced by fee-for-service physicians. The foundation-type HMOs did not manifest this difference. The authors concluded that capitation payment by itself is not sufficient to produce major changes in utilization. Rather, the organized, multi-specialty group practice arrangement appears to be the most significant factor affecting utilization.

They also concluded that the Medicaid eligibles who selected the HMO were similar in all other respects to those who had selected the fee-for-service system (35). The implication from this study is that an expectation of cost savings in the Medicaid program is reasonable if a Medicaid/HMO contract arrangement is established, particularly with a group practice HMO. The initiative for these contracts and the administration of the contracts must be found in the state government agencies responsible for the Medicaid program. Reluctance on the part of these agencies to become involved with HMOs could mean a lost opportunity to improve the efficiency of the program.

7. Utilization review

The federal Medicaid legislation requires that states establish an effective system for reviewing the utilization of services provided in hospitals, skilled nursing facilities, and intermediate care facilities. This is considered an effective technique to reduce unnecessary use and subsequent costs. Despite the potential savings to the states through the implementation of a utilization review system, about half of the states had no functioning utilization review system before the local Professional Standard Review Organizations (PSROs) were organized (28). Where an effective utilization review has existed for Medicaid eligibles, savings are apparent. Massachusetts reports an estimated $15 million savings to the Medicaid program by its Certified Hospital Admissions Monitoring Program for Medicaid Eligibles in Hospitals (30).

A major study of a utilization review program for Medicaid in New Mexico was recently published by Brook and Williams (13). They conclude that a peer review system, such as developed and implemented in New Mexico between 1971 and 1973 for the Medicaid program in that state, does produce gross savings in the total amount of money which is billed for services. This is largely the result of close collaboration between the fiscal intermediary and the peer review organization. They were able to relate improvements in the quality of care to the peer review system, but their evidence indicates cost savings will not necessarily occur by pre-certification and recertification procedures. Nevertheless, the significance of this study is a demonstration that improvements in a Medicaid program can occur with concerted efforts of providers. The effectiveness of such a review process across the country is, once again, highly dependent on the environment and commitment within each of the states.

Two other areas for increasing utilization review are expected in the near future. The amount of dollars expended for skilled nursing facility and intermediate care facility services under Medicaid makes these providers highly visible and more vulnerable to closer monitoring than in recent years. One state found that about 18% to 20% of Medicaid patients in skilled nursing facilities did not need the level of medical care delivered in those facilities (30). If these patients could be moved to less intensive locations, the average savings could be about $1800 per patient, per year. The total is significant, so it is likely that there will be accelerated efforts to monitor utilization in these facilities and, perhaps, deny reimbursement for patients who should be relocated at a less intensive and less expensive location.

The second area is a second opinion program for elective surgery. There are reports that about 20% of recommendations for surgery are reversed by a second opinion. The logistics for installing a second opinion may be formidable, but these will be scrutinized as costs continue to increase.

OTHER ALTERNATIVES

The preceding survey of seven alternative strategies for cost containment is not an exhaustive list of cost containment measures. Other measures are mandated use of generic drugs, closer monitoring of Medicare reimbursement coverage for Medicaid recipients, and heavier investment in primary prevention activities. The costs of Medicaid are more visible than at any other time and the alternatives to reduce or contain these costs present the medical care system and the public at large with a major issue.

The issue has two components: (1) Can the states and federal government continue to absorb the increase in Medicaid costs without changes in the program itself or changes in other, broader policies? (2) If changes are indicated, what specific measures will have a desirable effect on the cost increase while maintaining the objectives of the program? The answer to the first question seems rather obvious. A continuous increase in Medicaid costs cannot be tolerated without a response by legislators to crack down on abusers and stem the spillover effect which is creating acute prob-

lems for other state programs who'se budgets are reduced to pay for Medicaid. Tax increases are not a popular alternative to pay for the increasing costs, so action of some other form is practically dictated.

The second question is more complex. It makes an assumption that the goal of any specific measure for improving the cost situation includes a continuation of the original objectives of Medicaid. Stated differently, can the goals of improving access to medical care for low income persons be continued while new cost containment measures are installed? Some would claim that the original goals are objectionable and cost containment measures should be designed to cut back as much as politically feasible to reduce to an absolute minimum the expenditures for welfare medicine.

Another point of view holds that the original goals of Medicaid must be retained and the scope of the program expanded. These are extreme responses but they present the difficulty in arriving at a solution in an environment in which general attitudes toward the poor and the role of the government in paying for medical care have a significant influence on the outcome.

The evidence on the various cost containment measures indicates that: (1) each has potential for reducing costs by varying amounts, (2) some are accompanied by cost shifts to other components of the Medicaid program, (3) some shift the burden for paying medical care costs to those least able to pay, (4) each usually creates controversy when implemented, and, (5) most are focused on the Medicaid program itself without consideration of more basic reasons for cost increases. This last observation was underlined in a report from Massachusetts which concluded there is a limit to the state's ability to control costs in the health field . . . . health care costs are determined to a large extent by factors over which the states have limited or no control (30). Perhaps the issues surrounding Medicaid cost containment at the state governmental level are only sideshows or preliminaries to the main event. As long as the states have primary responsibility for administering Medicaid and for establishing most of the policies which determine its scope and coverage, the states will have influence on the total costs.

STATE VARIATIONS

The issues revolving around costs and cost containment are the subject of most analyses and media attention about Medicaid. Another dimension of the Medicaid program which also creates a separate set of issues is the variation among the states in the many optional policies which they control. Several of these have already been described, and they include eligibility beyond cash assistance recipients, optional benefits, duration of both mandatory and optional benefits, and reimbursement levels. It is not well known that so much variation exists among the states and that Medicaid consists of 49 different programs. This is a direct contrast to Medicare which is similar in most respects throughout the country.

The plain truth is that the Medicaid program "does not treat people in equal circumstances equally" (6). For example, the definition of the need standard (annual income amount) to be eligible for AFDC assistance payments and subsequently for Medicaid for a family of four varies from $2208 in North Carolina to $5472 in Wisconsin. In addition, the annual income levels established by the states with medically needy programs varies from $2200 for a family of four in Tennessee and West Virginia to $5600 in certain areas of Wisconsin. There are also a variety of restrictions beyond income limits, such as allowable savings, which contribute to more complexity and unevenness.

The evidence is conclusive that there are many people with low income not covered in any way by Medicaid. Medicaid recipients total less than 20% of the poverty population in eight states (22). On a national basis, Davis estimates that between 40% and 50% of the poor population is not covered by Medicaid at any given time (6). Medicaid cannot be termed a program for all the poor. It is a program which allows each state to define terms of eligibility. It makes a difference if a low income person lives in Wisconsin or in North Carolina. This has been true, of course, for many years but the access to medical services is significantly different among the states and is likely to continue under present federal law.

Medicaid is a financing mechanism for medical care services for those eligible. States have the option of restricting the financing to a limited amount for mandated medical services or extending the coverage to an extraordinarily comprehensive group of medical services with generous levels for each service. Data presented elsewhere indicate that the variation among states is substantial. Further evidence of this variation is the average expenditure per Medicaid recipient in each of the eligibility categories. For example, for the aged eligible for Medicaid under OAA, the average Medicaid expenditures in 1973 in West Virginia was $178 per year while in New Jersey and Connecticut it was more than $2400 per year (22). There are many factors which influence this total, in addition to medical services financed, but the variation is symptomatic of the general commitment to finance needed medical services.

Fifteen states have developed Medicaid/HMO contracts which provide an option for Medicaid eligibles to obtain medical services in a more organized manner. These states have extended their Medicaid programs beyond the financing of existing patterns of care. While enrollment may not be high, there is an option made available. It is surprising that more states have not developed contracts for Medicaid eligibles where HMOs exist since the data on the effectiveness of HMOs appears so encouraging.

The state governments have a dominant role in the Medicaid program. This was incorporated in the original federal legislation which created it, but the extent of variation among the states has surprised many. The response of the states to the options they have had in administering and in developing policy for their separate Medicaid programs offers additional evidence that any major role which the states are given to implement a broadly defined federal program can result in widely divergent commitments to the program. More specifically, the states have different commitments to the goal of ensuring equal access to medical services at a high level of quality for Medicaid eligible persons. There are 49 different Medicaid programs at present and these differences will continue unless the federal law is changed.

THE FUTURE OF MEDICAID

There is a fundamental question which these lessons and the various facts illustrate. Should Medicaid survive in its current form? The basic issue is the ultimate source of primary responsibility for the system—federal government or state government (4). There is, in addition, a lengthy list of issues to be resolved before the future direction of Medicaid is known. Davis had recently listed the alternatives in concise terms (6), but the eventual choice is not at all obvious. Donabedian concludes that the accomplishments of Medicare and Medicaid "have whetted the (national) appetite for more and have cleared the way for something astoundingly larger" (14). Weikel reports that "the federal focus has shifted (in recent years) from encouraging expansion of state programs to assuring their integrity" (9). It is impossible to detect if this shift has had impact on the states, but there are definite proposals for a change in the federal presence which should be noted.

The proposals currently under debate at state and federal governmental levels form a continuum from total federal control of Medicaid, similar to Medicare, to increased accountability by the states with more stringent restrictions on payment of federal matching monies. Senator Talmadge introduced legislation in the second session of the 94th Congress, "The Medicare-Medicaid Administrative Reform Act" (S.3205) which would increase requirements on the states to improve Medicaid management. The consequence of no improvements would be a reduction in federal contributions to the costs of the program.

He listed the choices confronting the government: (1) make Medicare and Medicaid more economical and efficient, (2) reduce benefits, (3) increase taxes, and/or (4) cut payments to hospitals and doctors (36). His proposal depends on the first choice to produce positive results because he claims the others are either too distasteful or a continuation of current problems. The proposal was not taken up by the Senate, but a newer version has been prepared for debate by the 95th Congress.

Another proposal which has received attention is authored by Senators Long and Ribicoff. Their proposed legislation includes the replacement of Medicaid with a uniform national program of medical services for more than 35 million low income persons. This national program would be administered similar to Medicare and would remove the many variations among the states previously described.

The outcome of the Congressional debates on Medicaid changes cannot be accurately assessed. The commitment of the Carter administration for changes is obviously important because there are powerful forces converging on the Medicaid program. The extent to which these changes have impact on the multi-faceted nature of the Medicaid program and its related issues will not be known for an indefinite period.

SUMMARY

Medicaid was initiated in 1966 as a silent partner to the more publicized and controversial Medicare program. During the ten years of their existence, the roles have reversed. Medicaid has created intensive awareness of the multi-faceted problems of a comprehensive public financed medical care program within the framework of a state-federal partnership. Most of the problems are not restricted to Medicaid alone. They can be found in almost every nook and cranny of the medical care system, but Medicaid has made them more visible, possibly more controversial, and has certainly raised the public consciousness about the manner in which medical care is provided for a portion of the population, at least. In the midst of the criticisms, and less frequent, accolades about Medicaid, there are lessons which can be identified:

1. Medicaid has made medical care more accessible to a portion of the low income population which would probably have not received it.
2. There remain many persons in the low income or poverty category who are not eligible for the benefits of Medicaid.
3. "The greatest single contribution that Medicare and Medicaid will have made to the quality of care is to have focused attention on it, to have documented its failings, and to have asserted and institutionalized public responsibility for it." (14)
4. State governments, including elected officials and bureaucrats, can directly dilute national goals when they have such a central role as provided in the Medicaid program.

The experience with the Medicaid program in its first decade, particularly in the most recent years, will obviously influence the outcome of the debates on its future. The increasing costs, allegations of widespread fraud and abuse, inequities among the states, and problems in management are certain to dominate those debates. Medicaid is, however, an extraordinarily complex program with more dimensions and problems than the main topics for debate indicate. It is a microcosm of the entire medical care system. The resolution of problems which it presents to state governments and the federal government could very likely determine the direction for American medicine in the next decade, at the very least.

REFERENCES

1. Stevens, Robert and Rosemary, *Welfare Medicine in America: A Case of Medicaid, Free Press, 1974.*

2. Spiegel, Allen D., and Podair, Simon, *Medicaid: Lessons for National Health Insurance,* Aspen, 1975.

3. Holahan, J., *Financing Health Care for the Poor—The Medicaid Experience,* Lexington Books, D.C. Health, 1975.

4. Weikel, M. Keith and Leamond, Nancy A., "A Decade of Medicaid," *Public Health Reports,* July-August 1976, Vol. 91, no. 4.

5. Merritt, Richard E., "Medicaid: Background and Status," in *State Perspectives on Medicaid,* National Conference on State Legislatures, 1976.

6. Davis, Karen, "Achievements and Problems of Medicaid," *Public Health Reports* (July-August 1976, 91, no. 4.

7. Loebs, S.F., "*Variations Among States in Selected Optional Decisions in the Medicaid Program,*" (Ph.D. diss., University of Michigan, 1974).

8. Richmond, Frederick, "An Analysis of the Factors Influencing the Optional Policy Decisions in the Medicaid Program for the State of Ohio," (Master's thesis, The Ohio State University, 1976).

9. Comptroller General of the U.S., *North Carolina's Medicaid Insurance Agreement: Contracting Procedures Need Improvement,* Report to the Subcommittee on Health, Senate Committee on Finance, July 1976.

10. National Center for Health Statistics, 1975, DHEW Pub. No. (HRA) 76-1232, U.S. Government Printing Office, Washington, D.C. 1976.

11. National Center for Social Statistics, DHEW Pub. No. (SRS) 76-03154, *Medicaid Statistics, Fiscal Year 1975,* March 1976.

12. Davis, Karen, "Medicaid Payments and Utilization of Medical Services by the Poor," *Inquiry* 13, no. 2, (June, 1976).

13. Brook, Robert H., and Williams, Kathleen, "Evaluation of the New Mexico Peer Review System: 1971–1973," *Medical Care* (December, 1976) 14, no. 12, (Supplement).

14. Donabedian, Avedis, "Effects of Medicare and Medicaid on Access to and Quality of Health Care," *Public Health Reports* (July-August, 1976) 91, no. 4.

15. Brian, E., "Foundations for Medical Care Control of Hospital Utilization: CHAP—A PSRO Prototype," *New England Journal of Medicine* (April 26, 1973): 78–882.

16. Wallace, H.M. et al., "Study of Title XIX Coverage of Sterilization," *Journal of the American Medical Women's Association* 31 (5), (May, 1976).

17. Gartside, Foline E., "Causes of Increase in Medicaid Costs in California," *Health Services Reports* (March, 1973), 88, no. 3.

18. Grimaldi, Paul L., "An Analysis of the Causes of Increases in Medicaid Payments, New Jersey, 1970–74," *Public Health Reports* (November-December, 1975) 90, no. 6.

19. Hicks, Nancy, "Governors Will Vote on Medicaid Reform," *New York Times* (February 27, 1977).

20. Rosenblatt, Rand E., "Lurching Toward the Abyss: Medicaid Cutbacks and Health Care Inflation," *Health Law Project Library Bulletin #315,* November 1975.

21. "Summary of Medicaid Cutbacks: January 1, 1975-January 15, 1976," Medical Services Administration, Social and Rehabilitation Services, U.S. Department of Health, Education and Welfare, unpublished.

22. U.S. House of Representatives, Committee on Interstate and Foreign Commerce, Subcommittee on Health and Environment, "Data on the Medicaid Program: Eligibility, Services, Expenditures Fiscal Years 1966–76," January 1976.

23. Brian, Earl W., and Gibbons, Stephen F., "California's Medi-Cal Copayment Experiment," *Medical Care* (Supplement) (December, 1974) 12, no. 12.

24. Rosemer, M.J. et al., "Copayments for Ambulatory Care: Penny Wise and Pound Foolish," *Medical Care* (June, 1975) 13, no. 6.

25. Hopkins, Carl E. et al, "Cost Sharing and Prior Authorization Effects on Medicaid Services in California," *Medical Care* (August, 1975) 13, no. 8.

26. Downey, Gregg W., "Illegal Prosperity in Medicaid Labs," *Modern Health Care* (April, 1976).

27. *Wall Street Journal,* "U.S. Medicaid Fraud Crackdown Slated to Focus on Massachusetts, Ohio Initially," (29, March 1976).

28. Mullen, L., and Schneider, A., *Medicaid Cutbacks: A Handbook for Beneficiary Advocates,* National Clearinghouse for Legal Services, (April 1976).

29. Jones, M.W. and Hamburger, B., "A Survey of Physician Participation In and Dissatisfaction With the Medi-Cal Program," *Western Journal of Medicine,* (January, 1976).

30. Fielding, Jonathon and Wheeler, Anne P., "The State's Approach to Rising Health Costs," Presented at an Annual Meeting of American Public Health Association, October 1976.

31. National Center for Social Statistics, DHEW Pub. No. (SRS) 77-03150, "Medicaid Statistics—August, 1976," December 1976.

32. Schneider, A., and Stern, J., "Health Maintenance Organization and the Poor: Problems and Prospects," 70 *Northwestern University Law Review* 90, 126–138, (1975).

33. Mullen, L.R., and Schneider, A.G., "HMOs and the Poor: Another Look at the California Experience," *Library Bulletin* No. 323, (July, 1976) Health Law Project, University of Pennsylvania.

34. Barthel, M., "D.C. Project Analyzes Medicaid Costs in HMO Setting," *Urban Health* (December, 1976).

35. Gaus, C.; Cooper, B.S.; and Hirschman, C.G., "Contrasts in HMO and Fee-for-Service Performance," *Social Security Bulletin* (May, 1976).

36. Congressional Record, Vol. 122, No. 43, Senate, S.3205, (Medicare and Medicaid Administrative and Reimbursement Reform Act), March 25, 1976.

2. Data on the Medicaid Program: Eligibility/Services/Expenditures Fiscal Years 1966–78

INSTITUTE FOR MEDICAID MANAGEMENT
HEALTH CARE FINANCING ADMINISTRATION, HEW

Reprinted from *Data on the Medicaid Program: Eligibility/Services/Expenditures Fiscal Years* 1966–79

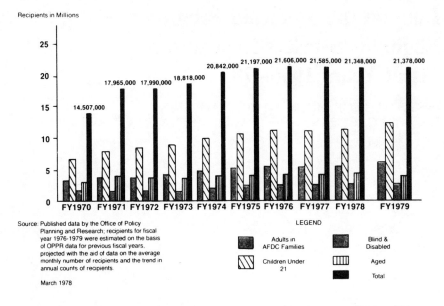

Recipients in Millions

LEGEND

Adults in AFDC Families

Children Under 21

Blind & Disabled

Aged

Total

Exhibit 1 Number of Medicaid Recipients, Fiscal Years 1970–1979

In the years since the enactment of Medicaid, the number of recipients has increased greatly. This growth in the number of Medicaid recipients is directly related to the growth in the cash assistance population during the same period due to the general linkage of Medicaid eligibility to the cash assistance programs. These increases have varied at different times by eligibility category. This Exhibit details the growth in the number of recipients by category of eligibility.

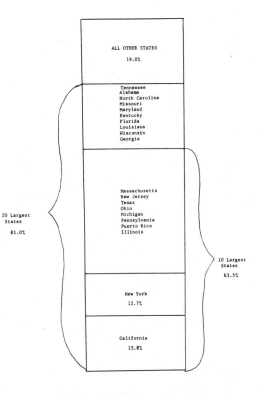

As with Medicaid expenditures, the largest states account for the greatest percentage of Medicaid recipients. California accounts for 15.8 percent followed by New York with 12.7 percent. The 10 largest states account for 63.5 percent of the nation's total recipients.

Exhibit 2 Total Medicaid Population by Size of State Programs, Fiscal Year 1975

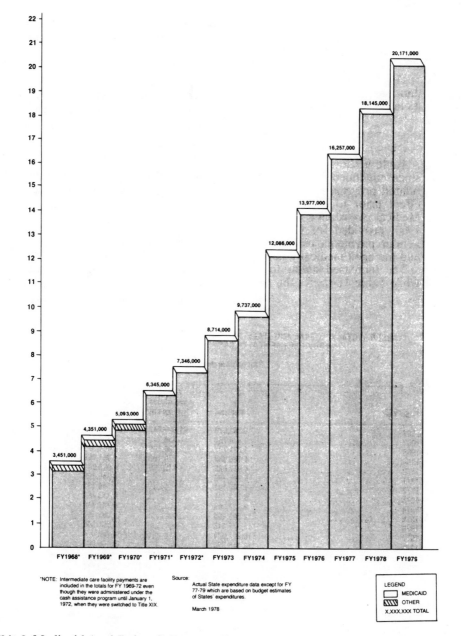

Exhibit 3 Medicaid (and Related) Program Payments to Providers of Health Care, Fiscal Years 1968–1979

This exhibit shows the dramatic growth in total Medicaid expenditures since the enactment of the program. Other in the legend refers to the vendor payment programs in effect prior to Medicaid, most notably the Kerr-Mills program, or Medical Assistance for the Aged (MAA).

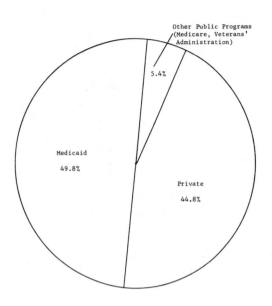

Exhibit 4 Medicaid's Share of Nursing Home Care Expenditures, Fiscal Year 1976

Medicaid has assumed an increasing proportion of personal health care expenditures in the United States since enactment of the program. Medicaid's share of personal health care expenditures rose from about 5 percent in 1967 to more than 11 percent in 1976; Medicaid's share of public expenditures for personal health care services increased from 18 percent to 30 percent in the same time period.

As this exhibit shows, Medicaid's expenditures for nursing home care comprised a major portion of the nation's expenditures for long term care services.

Exhibit 5 Total Medicaid Vendor Payments By Size of State Programs, Fiscal Year 1977

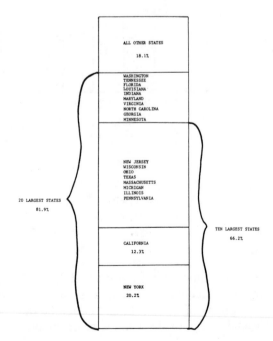

A disproportionate share of the total Medicaid expenditures are consumed by the largest states, especially New York and California; New York accounts for 20.2 percent and California for 12.3 percent. The 10 largest states account for 66.2 percent of the total vendor payments. States are listed in the order of the size of their programs in this Exhibit.

Exhibit 6 Comparison of Medicaid Recipients and Medicaid Expenditures By Basis of Eligibility, Fiscal Year 1975

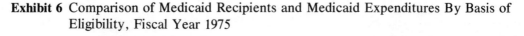

Recipients	Expenditures

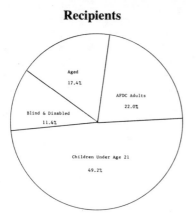 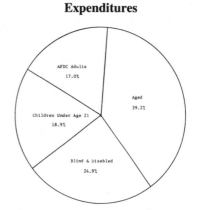

This comparison shows that the aged and the blind and disabled account for 28.8 percent of the recipients but receive services that account for 64.1 percent of the expend-

itures. On the other hand, children under 21 comprise 49.2 percent of recipients but only 18.9 percent of the expenditures.

Exhibit 7 Comparison of Medicaid Expenditures by Type of Service for Each Eligibility Category, and Graphic Comparison for All Recipients and for the Aged, Fiscal Year 1975

All Recipients	Aged

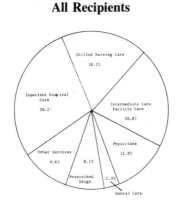 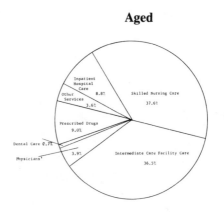

There are vast differences in expenditures for the major types of service within each of the eligibility groups. This Exhibit shows the percentages for each group and the services utilized.

Expenditures for the aged are related to the coverage of various services under Medicare. Small proportions of Medicaid

expenditures are made for inpatient hospital care and physicians' services reflecting the coverage of those services under Medicare. Larger percentages going toward nursing home care, intermediate care and prescribed drugs reflect the limitations on coverage, or lack of coverage of those services under the Medicare program.

SECTION TWO

LESSONS FROM EXPERIENCES IN PROVIDING MEDICAID SERVICES

A major purpose of the Medicaid program was to provide the poor with access to the mainstream of American medicine. Health care was to be delivered, without discrimination, to the poor as well as to those able to pay their own way. Almost immediately, the question of cost became intertwined with provision of health care services and influenced the decisions relative to the amount, scope and duration of services under Medicaid. In fact, some would say that cost has become the dominant factor in the determination of what services state Medicaid programs will provide now and in the future. Attention to the quality of health care services under Medicaid may run a distant second to cost. Public Law 93–641, The National Health Planning and Resources Development Act of 1974, specifically mandates emphasis on cost and quality in planning for health care in America. Some critics point out that the order of importance in the health planning process is also in that order of priority— cost and then quality.

However, in this section attention will be directed toward discussion of the services themselves to determine if issues other than cost have arisen and what experiences have occurred.

Once a state chose to participate in the Medicaid program, the state had to provide the following basic required services to at least everyone receiving federally supported financial assistance: inpatient hospital care; outpatient hospital and rural health clinic services; other laboratory and x-ray services; skilled nursing facility services and home health services for individuals 21 and older; early and periodic screening, diagnosis, and treatment for individuals under 21; family planning; and physician services. Service benefits could be expanded by the states and the states could also offer the services to people not eligible for financial assistance but eligible for medical assistance. This meant that a state could offer the required services to the medically needy, could add additional services for the financial assistance group or could offer the required and expanded services to both groups. Additional services for which federal financial participation was available included coverage for prescribed drugs; dental services; prosthetic devices; eyeglasses; private duty nursing; physical therapy and related services; other screening, preventive and rehabilitative services; emergency hospital services; skilled nursing facility services for patients under 21; optometrists' services; podiatrists' services; chiropractors' services; care for patients 65 or older in institutions for mental diseases; care for patients 65 or older in institutions for tuberculosis; care for patients under 21 in psychiatric hospitals; institutional services in intermediate care facilities; and clinic services. (A chart in this section identifies the Medicaid services provided by each state and territory as well as those providing only the basic required services.) Obviously, the states could come up with dozens of variations of service benefit packages depending upon a variety of data. In addition, with the approval of the Secretary of HEW, states could cover any other medical service recognized under state law.

States also had the right to impose limitations on their coverage of both mandatory and optional services. Limits could be set on the number of days of care for inpatient services and the number of outpatient visits. Prior authorization could also be required by the states for certain services such as elective surgery.

In the late 1970s, about one out of every 10 Americans received health care from a state administered Medicaid program. By population groups served, services went to children under 21 (49 percent of the services); to adults in the Aid to Families of Dependent Children (AFDC) program (22 percent); to the aged (17 percent); and to the blind and disabled (11 percent). However, by expenditures for services, the order was the aged (39 percent of expenditures); the blind and disabled (25 percent); and the other two groupings each stood at about 18 percent. Considering the types of services provided, 70 percent of the expenditures were used for institutional care; 32 percent for inpatient hospital care; 20 percent for skilled nursing care; and 18 percent for intermediate care facilities. Of the remainder, 10 percent went to physicians, seven percent for prescription drugs, three percent each for dental services and for outpatient services and eight percent for other services. Obviously, the aged, blind and disabled comprise less than 40 percent of the people being served by Medicaid programs, but more than 60 percent of the expendi-

tures are directed to them. Nationally, about 65 percent of the costs went for mandatory services.

Services for people enrolled in Medicaid programs are provided by private practitioners under a vendor payment arrangement. Payments are made directly to a provider of health care services for the care rendered to an eligible individual. Providers are required to accept the Medicaid reimbursement level as payment in full for the services rendered.

Quality of health care provided under Medicaid has varied from the usual stories of gross overutilization and outright fraud to the provision of high quality medical care. The advent of the Professional Standards Review Organizations (PSROs) has resulted in the development of standards, norms and criteria for inpatient care that must be followed if the provider is to receive reimbursement from federally financed programs such as Medicaid. These guidelines were prepared by the American Medical Association in cooperation with 38 national professional and specialty societies and resulted in a 740-page book entitled *Sample Criteria for Short-Stay Hospital Review. Screening Criteria to Assist PSROs in Quality Assurance.* Similar projects are underway to develop criteria for ambulatory care services, specifically those rendered by shared health facilities—the so-called "Medicaid Mills." In addition, the Health Systems Agencies (HSAs) created by P.L. 93–641 also are mandated to consider the quality of health care. In examining the "appropriateness" of the health care delivery system, HSAs are to review the six characteristics of the health care delivery system: acceptability; access; availability; continuity of care; cost; and quality of care.

Participation by health care providers was another consideration in the Medicaid program. Private practitioners and institutions had to decide whether to participate in the Medicaid program, then file the appropriate applications and meet whatever eligibility criteria the states established. In most instances, specialists had to be board certified or board eligible and indicate evidence of their specialization. Providers would then be certified as Medicaid providers and secure an identification number and be placed on a state registry. Frequently a small number of private practitioners provided a majority of the services to the Medicaid population with a maldistribution geographically and by specialty. Mobility of health care providers was also marked as the providers moved into and out of the Medicaid registers.

Legal issues relative to services provided under Medicaid have taken place throughout the history of the program. Lawyers representing various groups have contested the state's determinations regarding eligibility, the imposition of limitations, the reduction of services, the confidentiality of records and more recently the limitations on abortions and the deficiencies of the mandated EPSDT programs.

Regardless of all the difficulties associated with the provision of health care services to the Medicaid population, one fact does stand out—more poor people than ever received health care services. Some studies indicate that the poor approached the rest of the nation in the number of visits to a physician and in the small percentage that never visited a physician or a dentist. A large number of people received care that they probably would never have received without being in the Medicaid program. As one critic put it, "Medicaid recipients received equal amounts of health care but of unequal quality." That statement has been refuted by lower infant mortality rates and decreased health status indicators of ill health among the poor. Therefore, there can be no doubt that the health care services were needed by the poor and that an adequate mechanism to provide the health care services is vital.

With the advent of the rising costs and the larger than anticipated number of eligibles, the states began limiting the services offered under their Medicaid programs. From a legalistic viewpoint, Butler reviews the state limits on the amount, scope, and duration of services under Medicaid. By law, there was no doubt that the states had the legal right to cut back on services. Three mechanisms evolved to limit the types of services:

- *By condition*—In Pennsylvania, eyeglasses could be secured if pathology was present but not for refractive errors such as nearsightedness.
- *By eliminating items of service*—In New York, surgical services were limited to emergency services, specified procedures or on a patient-to-patient basis when the surgery could not be deferred for six months without causing possible harm or severe pain.
- *By provider of service*—In the District of Columbia, podiatry services were limited.

States also set limits on the number of days of hospital care for which they would pay. Virginia limited reimbursement to 14 days per year with an extension of seven more days with prior authorization based upon medical necessity.

Finally, Butler explains how to construct a legal case regarding the imposition of limitations by states on services provided under Medicaid.

A hornet's nest has been raised by the question of providing abortion services to Medicaid recipients. In their article, Lincoln and others talk about how the court, the Congress and the President turned back the clock on the pregnant poor. In June, 1977, the House of Representatives voted to prohibit the use of federal funds to pay for abortions. The U.S. Supreme Court followed with a ruling that the states need not pay for nontherapeutic abortions. Following this, President Carter noted that many things in life aren't fair and that wealthy people can do things that poor people can't. In his decision on the case, Supreme Court

Justice William Brennan quoted Anatole France, "The law, in its majestic equality, forbids the rich as well as the poor to sleep under bridges, to beg in the streets, and to steal bread."

Three conditions for abortions have been established by federal regulations: abortion is fundable when the "life of the mother is endangered"; when two physicians certify to the "severe and long lasting physical damage to the mother" and when rape or incest occurs.

Lincoln's article examines who is affected by the rulings and points out the Medicaid population affected. Who performs Medicaid abortions is considered next and the authors conclude that private practitioners and institutions do the great majority of the abortions.

Withdrawing public funds for abortions could increase mortality and certainly strikes most heavily on those least able to meet the problem—the very poor, the teenaged, the unwed and the rural dweller.

When sizeable income is involved, various providers of services can become embroiled in who should do what for how much for Medicaid recipients. Miller details the example of the audiologist in the Medicaid program. Political infighting by hearing aid dealers, otologists and the audiologists contributed to the situation where the audiologist was virtually eliminated from the program. Lessons to be learned from this experience are cited by the author. This type of competitive situation could take place between the podiatrist and the orthopedic physician, between the chiropractor and the family physician, between the family practitioner and the medical specialist, between the registered nurse and the home health aide and others. In each instance, professional domain is at stake and the politics requires "a strong stomach and a tough skin" as Miller concluded.

Dental care is a significant part of the Medicaid budgets of states that provide that optional service. Schwartz describes efforts to develop a model system for dental care delivery in New York City through the Health Insurance Plan of Greater New York (HIP). First, he enumerates the dental services to be provided and then the objectives of the program. Four potential mechanisms for the delivery of dental care were investigated: hospital dental clinics; contracting with other insurance companies; individual dental providers; and HIP-affiliated dentists. HIP chose to create its own system with the HIP-affiliated dentist as a major component of the system. The system that emerged charged a reasonable fee, provided quality assurance, emphasized preventive care, had accessible facilities and was a model that could be replicated easily.

Drug prescription rates are examined by Rabin, Bush and Fuller as 1,000 beneficiaries of Medicaid were voluntarily enrolled in a prepaid group practice. With respect to medicine use, the evaluation reviewed the following elements: prescription and physician visit rates; prescriptions by specific drug and therapeutic category; costs of prescription drugs per capita; and prescribing quality as compared with that for the 160,000 Medicaid beneficiaries who were in the control group. Results suggested that strategies to reduce ambulatory patients' visits to physicians are likely to reduce medicine use. Enrolling a Medicaid group in a prepaid group practice appears to be beneficial in terms of reducing prescribing and other service rates with no apparent diminution in prescribing quality or patient satisfaction with care.

Early and Periodic Screening, Diagnosis and Treatment (EPSDT) for children is a preventive aspect of the Medicaid program. States that do not provide EPSDT can be penalized and lose a percentage of their federal funds. Miller reports on a study of the effectiveness of state EPSDT activities. "To be considered a mature and fully effective national program, between 80 and 90 percent of children who are examined and found to need treatment should receive it."

This was a finding of a nine state study of treatment follow-up. An EPSDT treatment rate by state chart is included in this article. Considerable variation can be noted among the states studied. A number of steps are detailed to improve the EPSDT program throughout the country. In addition, the methodology of the study is described.

Home health care services were studied by the federal General Accounting Office in Georgia, California and Florida. After noting the legal mandate and the expenditures, the article defines the specific home health services covered under Medicaid. Then the restrictive eligibility criteria were noted along with the requirements on the allowable number of home visits per year. Discussion about the encouragement of states to establish reasonable reimbursement rates indicated that Medicaid payments were too low and thereby effectively restricted the use of home health care. This study concluded that home health care under Medicaid is subject to the whims of the states since the program is state administered. The investigators recommended that an informational program be developed to provide data to physicians and institutional providers about the home health care program. In addition, a recommendation was made that inequities among individual groups of Medicaid beneficiaries be corrected by the states.

A study of long-term care patients in the New Jersey Medicaid program concentrated on the appropriateness of the long-term care placement. The question considered was, "How many patients could live more independently, if appropriate alternate settings and services were available?" Projecting the answer secured by Malafronte and the other investigators to the total population would result in more than 1,700 persons who could be placed in appropriate settings at a lower level of care than that provided in the long-term setting. Currently, care for those 1,700 persons is more than $10 million per year. In their conclusions, the authors discuss the impact on

long-term care cost and bed need, the feasibility of independent living, the variations in Medicaid offices, the relation to mental health, the practicality of family care, congregate living arrangements, community based services, continued institutionalization, and society's role in alternate care services under Medicaid. Six recommendations are listed for the New Jersey Medicaid program to follow through on the results of this investigation and to change long-term care services.

Mental health benefits of the Tennessee Medicaid program are described by Treadway and also compared with services received in nine other southeastern states under Medicaid. Mental health services were made available to the poor through Medicaid and community mental health centers were included in the reimbursement packages. The scope of services and providers involved, according to Treadway, ". . . the decision about either which mental health disciplines are covered or which types of mental health services are covered will be made primarily around the issue of cost." Mental health benefits in Tennessee provided about $28 million per year and comprised about 14 percent of the total state Medicaid expenditures.

Nathan's article on patient preferences for ambulatory care concludes that, "Shared health facilities are evidently approved and often preferred to hospital based ambulatory care facilities by a substantial segment of the population in economically depressed areas of New York City and other major urban areas." Of course shared health facilities are sometimes referred to as "Medicaid mills." Yet, this study which involved interviews with 228 ambulatory care patients in three shared health facilities, three acute care hospital ambulatory care facilities and one community health center located in three boroughs of New York City tends to refute the general poor reputation of Medicaid mills. Accessibility appeared to be a paramount factor in the choice of a care center by the patients in conjunction with the quality of care and the waiting time. Since quality of care at shared health facilities has received so much attention, it is noteworthy to explore the definitions of quality as perceived by patients. Nathan surmises that the patient includes more than that which is strictly medical in the evaluation of quality.

Four questions are answered in the study of sterilization coverage by Medicaid. Wallace and her coauthors address these questions:

1. How many states now include sterilization under Medicaid?
2. How many individuals receive sterilization under Medicaid?
3. What are the restrictions to providing sterilization under Medicaid?
4. What are the costs in providing sterilization under Medicaid?

Results indicate that most states did include sterilization under Medicaid with most reporting restrictions such as age, residence, parental consent, consent of spouse and marital status. Procedures were performed in hospital inpatient and outpatient services as well as in physicians' offices. However, most states had not established standards for such services. A serious drawback in this investigation was the inability to secure adequate data on the number of patients sterilized and the expenditures for such services. The authors note that a change in the data collection and retrieval system is needed.

3. Medicaid Services State by State, December 1, 1977

U.S. DEPARTMENT OF HEALTH, EDUCATION, AND WELFARE
HEALTH CARE FINANCING ADMINISTRATION

Reprinted from *Data on the Medicaid Program: Eligibility/Services/Expenditures Fiscal Years 1966–79*

MEDICAID SERVICES STATE BY STATE,

DECEMBER 1, 1977 ⇓

* BASIC REQUIRED MEDICAID SERVICES Every Medicaid program must cover at least these services for at least everyone receiving federally supported financial assistance inpatient hospital care, outpatient hospital services, other laboratory and X-ray services, skilled nursing facility services and home health services for individuals 21 and older, early and periodic screening, diagnosis, and treatment for individuals under 21, family planning, and physician services Federal financial participation is also available to States electing to expand their Medicaid programs by covering additional services and/or by including people eligible for medical but not for financial assistance For the latter group States may offer the services required for financial assistance recipients or may substitute a combination of seven services.

Services provided only under the Medicare buy-in or the screening and treatment program for individuals under 21 are not shown on this chart.

Definitions and limitations on eligibility and services vary from State to State. Details are available from local welfare offices and State Medicaid agencies.

● offered for people receiving federally supported financial assistance

✛ offered also for people in public assistance[2] and SSI[3] categories who are financially eligible for medical but not for financial assistance

Additional services for which Federal financial participation is available to States under Medicaid

Column headers (left to right): Clinic services; Prescribed drugs; Dental services; Prosthetic devices; Eyeglasses; Private duty nursing; Physical therapy and related services; Other diagnostic, screening, preventive and rehabilitative services; Emergency hospital services; Skilled nursing facility services for patients under 21; Optometrists' services; Podiatrists' services; Chiropractors' services; Care for patients 65 or older in institutions for mental disease; Care for patients 65 or older in institutions for tuberculosis; Care for patients under 21 in psychiatric hospitals; Institutional care facilities (intermediate care facilities)

FMAP[4]	BASIC*	State																		
73	●	Alabama																		AL
50	●	Alaska																		AK
61		Arizona																		AZ
72	✛	Arkansas																		AR
50	✛	California																		CA
54	●	Colorado																		CO
50	✛	Connecticut																		CT
50	●	Delaware																		DE
50	✛	D.C.																		DC
57	●	Florida																		FL
66	●	Georgia																		GA
50	✛	Guam																		GU
50	✛	Hawaii																		HI
64	●	Idaho																		ID
50	✛	Illinois																		IL
58	●	Indiana																		IN
52	●	Iowa																		IA
52	✛	Kansas																		KS
70	✛	Kentucky																		KY
70	✛	Louisiana																		LA
70	✛	Maine																		ME
50	✛	Maryland																		MD
52	✛	Massachusetts																		MA
50	✛	Michigan																		MI
55	✛	Minnesota																		MN
78	●	Mississippi																		MS
61	●	Missouri																		MO
61	✛	Montana																		MT
53	✛	Nebraska																		NB
50	●	Nevada																		NV
63	✛	New Hampshire																		NH
50	●	New Jersey																		NJ
72	●	New Mexico																		NM
50	✛	New York																		NY
68	✛	North Carolina																		NC
61	●	North Dakota																		ND
55	●	Ohio																		OH
65	✛	Oklahoma																		OK
57	●	Oregon																		OR
55	✛	Pennsylvania																		PA
50	●	Puerto Rico																		PR
57	✛	Rhode Island																		RI
72	●	South Carolina																		SC
64	●	South Dakota																		SD
69	✛	Tennessee																		TN
61	●	Texas																		TX
69	✛	Utah																		UT
68	✛	Vermont																		VT
50	✛	Virgin Islands																		VI
57	✛	Virginia																		VA
52	✛	Washington																		WA
70	✛	West Virginia																		WV
59	✛	Wisconsin																		WI
53		Wyoming																		WY
●	20	●	13	19	12	14	10	5	9	4	17	18	13	13	10	13	9	11	26	
✛	33	✛	29	32	22	29	25	13	23	16	26	26	25	23	18	28	18	21	24	
	53	Total	42	51	34	43	35	18	32	20	43	44	38	36	28	41	27	32	50	

1/ Data from Regional Office reports of characteristics to State programs and State plan amendments.
2/ People qualifying as members of families with dependent children (usually families with at least one parent absent or incapacitated).
3/ People qualifying as aged, blind, or disabled under the Supplemental Security Income program.
4/ FMAP - Federal Medicaid Assistance Percentage: Rate of Federal financial participation in a State's medical vendor payment expenditures on behalf of individuals and families eligible under Title XIX of the Social Security Act. Percentages, effective from October 1, 1977, through September 30, 1979, are rounded.
5/ Including ICF services in institutions for the mentally retarded.

(Right margin note) Intermediate Care Facilities (ICF) P.L. 92-223 transferred the ICF program to Medicaid (Title XIX) as an optional service, effective 1-1-72. States may at their option include institutions for the mentally retarded, both public and private. See footnote five.

UNITED STATES DEPARTMENT OF HEALTH, EDUCATION, AND WELFARE   Health Care Financing Administration   Medicaid Bureau

Division of State Management

(HCFA)-77-801*

4. State Limits on the Amount, Scope, and Duration of Services Under Medicaid

PATRICIA A. BUTLER

Butler, *State Limitations on the Amount, Scope, and Duration of Services Under Medicaid,* CLEARINGHOUSE REVIEW (September 1977). Reprinted by permission of The National Clearinghouse for Legal Services.

INTRODUCTION

As the cost of medical care has increased, many states facing severe budget constraints have decided to cut back on their Medicaid[1] programs.[2] Cutback techniques include: reducing eligibility levels and provider reimbursement, imposing cost-sharing on Medicaid recipients, and limiting the amount or duration of various Medicaid services for which states will pay. Over the last few years, Legal Services programs have begun to challenge these limitations, based on various statutory or regulatory authorities.[3] Results have been mixed. Despite some problems in analyzing the permissible limits, it is now possible to set forth the principles upon which to base an amount, scope and duration case. In so doing, one must examine the different types of amount, duration and scope limitations states have imposed on Medicaid services, as well as the cases challenging those limits, in order to suggest approaches to protect clients from these benefit restrictions and cutbacks.

The types of Medicaid restrictions which concern Legal Services' clients limit the "amount" of services, such as the number of visits to a provider, the "scope" of services, such as types of drugs or supplies covered under a formulary, and the "duration" of services, such as the number of days of hospitalization which will be covered.

Some states have also decided not to cover certain conditions requiring treatment, even though the treatment will be provided for other conditions. Such an exclusion is probably also properly characterized as a limitation on the "scope" of care.

THE STATUTORY FRAMEWORK

Several provisions of the Medicaid law clearly recognize that states may limit the amount, scope and duration of services.[4] The preamble to the Medicaid statute, 42 U.S.C. §1396, requires states to provide "necessary" medical care to Medicaid eligibles, "as far as practicable," clearly indicating that states have some discretion over the services reimbursed. More specifically, the language in 42 U.S.C. §1396a(a)(10), which requires comparable treatment among the categorically needy recipients and medically needy recipients, uses the terms "amount, scope and duration." This language clearly implies that services must be equally available to all persons who are either categorically or medically needy. It is clear from Congress' repeal of 42 U.S.C. §1396b(e) in 1972 that whatever its intent in 1965, Congress obviously intended to provide to the states wide latitude in designing programs to meet their budgets.[5] Original

35

policy statements in the *Handbook of Public Assistance Administration, Supplement D,*[6] and HEW regulations[7] set limits on the ways in which states could limit amount, scope and duration of services, but clearly permitted some such limits. It should also be noted that the eligibility conditions analysis of *Townsend v. Swank*[8] and *Carlson v. Remillard*[9] does not advance the argument that Medicaid services must be provided comprehensively. These cases hold that the federal definitions set forth in federal public assistance programs cannot be undercut by more restrictive state definitions unless it is clear that Congress would allow such restrictive eligibility conditions. However, as has been noted, the Medicaid statute *does* permit some types of limits on amount, scope and duration of services, although it does not specify what they should be.[10]

Nevertheless, despite considerable state discretion allowed in designing Medicaid programs, the federal Medicaid statute does circumscribe state limits in various ways. First, as noted above, §§1396(a)(10)(B) and (C) require comparability within the categorically needy and the medically needy groups, and also prohibit a state from providing more services to the medically needy group than it does to the categorically needy.[11] Second, §1396a(a)(13) defines mandatory services which the states must provide to the categorically needy and to the medically needy and also requires that states pay for hospital and nursing home services on the basis of reasonable cost.[12] Third, §1396a(a)(14) imposes limits on cost-sharing that a state may impose upon beneficiaries in the form of premiums, copayments and deductibles. Finally, §1396a(a)(19) requires that the Medicaid program in each state be administered "in the best interest of recipients." This general language has been applied in a Medicaid abortion case[13] suggesting that the language is at least capable of meaningful interpretation. Furthermore, as mentioned above, HEW regulations also define

permissible limits on amount, scope and duration of services as follows:

> State plans must specify the amount and/or duration of each item of medical and remedial care and services that will be provided to the categorically needy and to the medically needy, if the plan includes this latter group. *Such items must be sufficient in amount, duration and scope to reasonably achieve their purpose.* With respect to the required services to the categorically needy . . . and the medically needy . . . the *state may not arbitrarily reduce amount, duration and scope of such services to an otherwise eligible individual solely because of the diagnosis, type of illness or condition.* Appropriate limits may be placed on services based on such criteria as medical necessity or those contained in utilization or medical review procedures. [Emphasis added.][14]

This regulation sets forth two standards, a broad one that mandatory services may not be so limited as to eliminate conditions from treatment, and a narrow one that optional services must be reasonably sufficient to achieve their purpose. HEW regulatory definitions in 45 C.F.R. §249.10(b) also arguably define the minimum services for which the states must pay.[15]

LIMITING THE TYPES OF SERVICE

By Condition

In the case of *White v. Beal,*[16] the district court provided a clear analysis of the amount, scope and duration limitations issue. The case presented a classic example of an irrational limit which also eliminated a diagnosis or condition from treatment. Although the case is perhaps too easy because of the patent irrationality of the limitation, it presents a useful framework for analyzing amount, scope and duration restrictions. Pennsylvania paid for eyeglasses under Medicaid for only those medically needy and categorically needy recipients with eye pathology or disease, but not for recipients with refractive errors, such as nearsightedness, farsightedness and astigmatism. The court applied both provisions of the amount, duration and scope regulation to invalidate the Pennsylvania limitation.

Preliminarily, the court found that eyeglasses, which are an optional federal Medicaid service under 42 U.S.C. §1396d(a)(12), were actually a mandatory service by virtue of the comparability requirements of 42 U.S.C. §1396a(10)(B)(ii), requiring that once services are provided to the medically needy, they must also be provided to the categorically needy.[17] The district court held that limiting eyeglasses to those persons with pathology eliminated a condition or diagnosis from coverage under Medicaid in violation of 45 C.F.R. §249.10(a)(5). It should be noted that the court found that the condition which was eliminated from treatment was not, as the defendant state had argued, "eye disease," because eyeglasses were "an ineffective means to deal with disease or pathology."[18] Rather, the court found that the condition which was eliminated from coverage was "visual impairment."[19] The length of time the court spent discussing what was the appropriate definition of a condition so as to trigger the application of this regulation suggests the importance of establishing a definition for a condition which is as broad as possible.

The court also found that the state's limit violated the regulatory standard as well, holding that limiting eyeglasses to eye pathology "fails to achieve the purpose of the service." It is noteworthy that the court found the *purpose* of providing eyeglasses to be as that defined in the HEW regulation section establishing maximum federal reimbursement parameters ("to aid or improve vision").[20] The most significant aspects of the district court's opinion in *White*

v. Beal are: (1) its conversion of an apparently optional Medicaid service into a mandatory one; (2) its definition of condition in applying the broad standard in §249.10(a)(5); and (3) its use of the federal matching definition to establish the purpose of eyeglasses and its finding that the limitation was unreasonable under the narrow standard in §249.10(a). One should also note plaintiffs' most effective use of experts to define the condition in question, the purpose of the service (bolstering the definitional argument) and the total irrationality of the limitation. Legal Services attorneys should imitate this use of expert testimony in handling similar cases.

White v. Beal was recently affirmed by the Third Circuit,[21] in an opinion which did not directly discuss the district court's discussion of and reliance upon the amount, duration and scope regulation. Apparently impressed by the patent irrationality of the state's eyeglass limitations, the Third Circuit found that the state had violated the Medicaid statute's requirement of "an equitable distribution of the total funds available among all in need of the service. . . ."[22] The court held that "the service must be distributed in a manner which bears a rational relationship to the underlying federal purpose of providing the service to those in greatest need of it."[23] It is not clear where the court found this requirement, but the court seems to establish a test of rational distribution of Medicaid services according to a determination of medical efficacy and necessity.[24] The court raised, but did not answer, the question of how the state could define the condition which it chose to cover, although the court implied that any designation of a condition must be reasonable.

The district court in *White v. Beal* relied upon a Third Circuit Medicaid abortion case, *Doe v. Beal*,[25] for its statutory analysis. In *Doe*, the Court of Appeals examined in considerable detail the latitude for and limits on state power to define state Medicaid programs inherent in the federal

Medicaid law. The court invalidated on two grounds Pennsylvania's refusal to pay for abortions under Medicaid which were not "medically necessary." The court held that §§1396a(a)(10)(B) and (C) require comparable treatment within the categorically needy and the medically needy groups, which a state cannot abridge without a reasonable basis. The court found that paying for prenatal care and delivery for some pregnant women who are either categorically or medically needy, but refusing to pay for abortions for other pregnant women within those categories, was not treating the women in each of those categories comparably. Essentially, the court developed a statutory equal protection argument within the federal Medicaid law. Finding no reasonable basis for the decision to limit abortion services, since neither maternal health nor cost justified this exclusion, the court struck down the limit. An independent basis for the court's decision was that under the general statutory Medicaid scheme, a state may designate conditions for which care is "necessary", such as pregnancy, but once having done so, may not limit the physician's discretion in choosing the type of care to be provided. The Supreme Court reversed *Beal v. Doe*,[26] finding that the state's decision not to pay for abortions did not infringe upon the physician's discretion to practice, but left the comparability argument intact. In footnote 11, the Court explained the comparability analysis without comment, but found a reasonable basis to justify the disparate treatment: the state's interest in promoting childbirth.

It should be noted that the Third Circuit in *Doe v. Beal* specifically held that the definitions of services for federal matching purposes found in 45 C.F.R. §249.10(b) do not define mandatory Medicaid services.[27] Nor did the court deal at all with the regulation on eliminating a condition from treatment, although the Pennsylvania abortion policy certainly seems to have violated that standard.[28]

By Eliminating Items of Service

Another case challenging limitations on amount, duration and scope of service is *Dodson v. Parham*,[29] in which the State of Georgia had limited its reimbursable drugs to those specified in a drug formulary and to those additional drugs for which a physician obtained prior approval. Since drugs are an optional service, the court analyzed these limitations according to the narrow reasonableness standard in the amount, scope and duration regulations. The court discovered the purpose of the service in the federal regulations[30] to be substances "for the cure, mitigation or prevention of disease, or for health maintenance." Despite plaintiffs' arguments, the court refused to hold that the drug formulary itself was so limited as to violate the purpose of providing drugs at all. However, the court did find that the formulary and the prior approval system taken together were "unlikely to deliver . . . the scope and quality of services necessary to achieve the prescription drug component's purpose of curing, mitigating or preventing disease, or for maintenance of health, as required by 45 C.F.R. §249.10(b)(12)(i)."[31] The court noted that the proposed formulary was "designed to be effective in the treatment in only 90–95% of the medical problems which a physician might encounter."[32] Obviously, the court was most concerned that the prior approval system did not contain emergency procedures allowing physicians to obtain approval on week nights, weekends, or holidays and that a doctor of pharmacy should not be responsible for making the decision about whether to grant approval. The court relied heavily upon *White v. Beal* and *Doe v. Beal* in its application of the amount, scope and duration regulations. It is noteworthy that, as in *White*, the *Dodson* plaintiffs effectively used expert testimony from physicians and pharmacologists in establishing the unreasonableness of the entire program, although the court did not have to rule on the unreasonableness of the formulary itself; undoubtedly, the expert testimony created an atmosphere where the court appreciated the seriousness of the limitation upon Medicaid beneficiaries and was willing to rule in their favor, albeit according to a somewhat narrower theory.

Another amount, duration and scope case which should be noted is *Medical Society of State of New York v. Toia.*[33] The State of New York had enacted an omnibus Medicaid cutback law, which limited surgical procedures to either: (1) emergency services, (2) surgery specified in regulations, or (3) surgery which would be determined on a patient-by-patient basis not to be deferrable for at least six months without jeopardizing life or causing severe pain.[34] Because the *Toia* opinion is obscure, confusing and contrary to legal precedent, Legal Services attorneys should be cautious in relying upon it.

Ignoring contrary holdings in the *Podiatry Society* case and *Doe v. Beal,* the district court interpreted as mandatory the definition of physicians' services in the statute and regulations: "those services provided, within the scope of practice of his profession as defined by state law."[35] The court incorrectly characterized the limitations on amount of service as eligibility conditions, implicitly prohibited under the *Townsend v. Swank* analysis,[36] and ignored the fact that amount, scope and duration limits are different from eligibility conditions.[37] Despite the fact that plaintiffs had never requested reimbursement for the surgical procedures in question and had therefore never been denied reimbursement for them, and despite questionable jurisdictional, standing and exhaustion analysis, the court issued a preliminary injunction against surgery limitations in the New York State plan.

It should be noted that to the extent that the surgical limitations in the state law and regulations eliminated various conditions from treatment, the limits probably violated

the broad standard of §249.10(a)(5)(i) and could have been enjoined on that basis. Nevertheless, the court's analysis in this case is far from enlightened, and the case provides questionable authority.

By Provider of Service

In the case of *District of Columbia Podiatry Society v. District of Columbia,*[38] the District of Columbia had limited podiatry services available under the Medicaid program in two ways: first, it had set a fee schedule by which it defined podiatry services for which it would pay when performed by podiatrists (some services would be paid only if performed by physicians); and second, it set different (although not necessarily higher) fees for podiatry services performed by physicians. The podiatrists challenged this discrimination as a violation of the Medicaid law which permitted states to cover "medical care . . . furnished by licensed practitioners within the scope of their practice as defined by state law,"[39] arguing that this definition in the statute and a comparable definition in the regulations[40] mandated comprehensive coverage of such optional services as podiatry once the state determined to provide them. The court examined the provisions of the Medicaid law limiting services and eligibility under the program[41] and refused to hold that the statutory or regulatory definitions of services mandate coverage of comprehensive benefits, relying on the similar language and holding of *Doe v. Beal.* The court found further support for this position in the amount, scope and duration regulation authorizing some state limits. In applying this regulation, the court noted that plaintiffs presented no evidence demonstrating that Medicaid recipients were unable to obtain needed podiatric care or that podiatrists' services were not achieving their purpose.[42]

In spite of plaintiffs' failure to prevail in this case, the result is easily reconciled with those in *White* and *Dodson* because plaintiffs did not attempt to introduce evidence to meet the regulatory standard. Furthermore, to the extent that the state's program favored one provider over another, another approach might have been more successful. Paying for podiatry services provided by a physician, but not paying for some of those same services provided by a podiatrist, violates the Medicaid freedom of choice requirement in 42 U.S.C. §1396a(a)(23).[43] As long as the real issue in the case was which provider could render certain services, rather than whether services were available as needed, the *Podiatry Society* case could be seen as not an amount, duration and scope case at all, but merely a freedom of choice of provider case.

DURATIONAL LIMITS ON INSTITUTIONAL CARE

Several cases over the past few years have challenged various state limitations on the number of days of hospital care for which a state would pay. In *Virginia Hospital Association v. Kenley*,[44] the state Medicaid agency limited reimbursable hospital care to 14 days per year, permitting an extension of seven more days with prior authorization upon a determination of medical necessity. The court summarily dismissed plaintiffs' contentions that the 21-day limit violated comparability requirements of 42 U.S.C. §§1396a(a)(10)(B) and (C), the best interest of recipients' requirements in 42 U.S.C. §1396a(a)(19), the restrictions on copayment in 42 U.S.C. §1396a(a)(14)(A)(i), and the requirement that Medicaid pay reasonable costs for hospital care in 42 U.S.C. §139a(a)(13)(D). The court held that the durational limits did not conflict with any of these provisions of the law, since they apply only to *covered* services, and do not affect the state's ability to limit amount, scope and duration of services. Although the result is unfortunate, its logic is clear: to hold otherwise would

cause various sections of the Medicaid statute to be internally inconsistent.

Plaintiffs next argued that the limitation unduly interfered with physician discretion to determine appropriate choice of treatment and therefore violated 42 U.S.C. §1395, the preamble to the Medicare Act prohibiting federal interference with the practice of medicine. The court held that the limitation was not a condition of reimbursement, since regardless of the number of days of service needed, the first 21 days would be paid for, and that the 21-day limit would have no effect on physician decision-making. Apparently plaintiffs did not present evidence on this last issue, but it certainly would have been possible to establish that as a result of the limit on reimbursable hospital days, a Medicaid patient could not be admitted to an institution because the institution feared the patient would require a longer stay than would be reimbursed and the institution would not be reimbursed for the full costs of care. Introducing such evidence might have made a difference to the court's conclusion on this point.

Finally, the court examined the amount, scope and duration regulation. The court never addressed the question of whether the 21-day limitation violated the regulation's narrow standard by eliminating certain diagnoses or conditions from coverage,[45] although it said specifically that "there are a number of medical conditions which, on the average, will require hospitalization beyond 21 days." Possibly evidence to establish this issue could have been handled better, and the argument from §249.10(a)(5) could have been made more effectively. Rather, the court examined the 21-day limitation in light of the prohibition in the amount, scope and duration regulation against services which fail to "reasonably achieve their purpose." The court looked to the purpose of providing hospitalization, not as it is required for an individual recipient's needs, but as is necessary to meet the *average needs* of the Medicaid population.

In reaching this conclusion on the purpose of the program, the court relied upon an HEW field staff information memorandum on Medicaid cutbacks issued in January 1976 which gave an example of appropriate amount, scope and duration limits as the number of days "at least adequate to cover one admission for the average days needed by those individuals covered under the program."

Even if this HEW policy correctly reflects Medicaid law, the court's reliance on it is misplaced. It refers to durational limits *per admission,* rather than per year, as was Virginia's limitation. In determining whether the limitation was reasonable in order to achieve the purpose of the service, the court examined the state's statistics on hospitalization, establishing that 92 percent of the Medicaid hospital population required fewer than 21 days of care annually. Of course, the court did not inquire about per admission days, which could vary from annual days of hospitalization if Medicaid recipients are rehospitalized more frequently than the general population. In view of this statistic, and without analyzing the regulation any further, the court held that "such a limitation is, therefore, a reasonable one." The significant difference between the *Hospital Association* case and *Dodson v. Parham*[46] is that in *Dodson* the court was willing to view the purpose of a drug treatment program as one which was necessary to cure or mitigate an individual's disease. However, in *Hospital Association* the court determined that the purpose of hospitalization related to the general Medicaid population, not to the individual patient.

A few other durational limits cases have been decided over the past several years; none is instructive because it does not analyze the regulation in detail. Furthermore, all the cases have been unsuccessful. In *Commonwealth of Pennsylvania Department of Public Welfare v. Temple University,*[47] the court held that a 60-day limit on inpatient hospital care did not violate

§249.10(a)(5) because there was no evidence in the record that 60 days is insufficient to achieve the purpose of providing hospital care. The court did not apply the second test of eliminating a condition or disease from treatment, nor did it discuss the purpose of hospital services within the meaning of the regulation.

In *Western Mercantile Agency v. Froats*[48] the court held that a 21-day annual limit on hospital care did not violate the Medicaid law. Rather than examining the amount, scope and duration regulation, the court merely followed *Dandridge v. Williams*[49] and held that the state had complete discretion in designing its Medicaid program. In *Idaho Corporation of Benedictine Sisters v. Marks,*[50] the court held a 20-day per stay limit on hospital care in a skeletal opinion, in which findings of fact indicate that the state limit is authorized by federal laws and regulations, but does not provide authority or analysis for that holding.

HOW TO CONSTRUCT AN AMOUNT, SCOPE AND DURATION CASE

It is obvious that there is little common thread among these cases and that they are difficult to reconcile. Nevertheless, a few principles can be derived to assist in developing a case to challenge amount, duration or scope limits on Medicaid services. First, if a condition is covered but the choice of treatment is limited (probably an unusual situation), the case should be governed by *Doe v. Beal*[51] as a violation of 42 U.S.C. §1396a(a)(10). Second, if a limitation on a mandatory service eliminates a condition or diagnosis from treatment, the case is governed by *White v. Beal,*[52] raising a violation of the narrow standard in §249.10(a)(5). To prevail in such a case, it is necessary to define the limited service as a mandatory one, to define the condition broadly and to get good evidence into the record on the number and frequency of conditions eliminated.

Third, if a state limits an optional service, one must demonstrate that the limitation is irrational in light of the purpose of the service. In such a case, it is important to try to define the purpose of the service broadly as the courts did in *White* and *Dodson,* and to get evidence into the record on the way in which the limit violates the purpose, especially by the effective use of experts. Furthermore, one should urge the *Dodson* approach that services must be sufficient to meet individual needs, rather than merely the average needs of the entire Medicaid population, as in the *Hospital Association* case. If a court adopts the latter approach, using statistical evidence of average needs to establish that a limit on optional services is irrational, statistics must demonstrate that a *significant* percentage of patients are not covered by the service. Apparently 92 percent is sufficient, but as yet there is no judicial guidance on what percentage would be insufficient.

It may be possible to argue that the definitions of federal matching in 45 C.F.R. §249.10(b) are mandatory.[53] This argument works well for specifically defined services such as eyeglasses, and perhaps drugs, but as the definitions are broader, such as those for hospitalization and physician services, courts are loathe to apply them mandatorily, since to do so appears to require a state to provide comprehensive services.[54] In spite of the *New York Medical Society* case, this argument is probably too weak, at least with respect to physician services.

Finally, one should keep in mind the possibility of obtaining a broad scope of certain services (such as dental care, eyeglasses and hearing aids) for children under Medicaid's program of "Early and Periodic Screening, Diagnosis and Treatment" (EPSDT),[55] even though the services might not be available to adult Medicaid recipients. As an example, plaintiffs in Maine were able to obtain orthodontia, a very expensive and usually excluded dental service, under the Maine EPSDT program, as part of the definition of necessary dental care for children in that program.[56]

CONCLUSION

It appears that as states continue to face fiscal pressures and find more creative ways of reducing services, they will probably resort to amount, scope and duration limits. Therefore, Legal Services attorneys must be alert to these issues and equally creative in their approaches to challenging such limitations in order to assure that the broadest scope of necessary medical care is available to their clients.

REFERENCES

1. 42 U.S.C. § 1396 *et seq. See* AN ADVOCATE'S GUIDE TO THE MEDICAID PROGRAM, 1976. Available from the Clearinghouse, No. 17,639 (34pp.).

2. 9 CLEARINGHOUSE REV. 392 (Oct. 1975).

3. *See* MEDICAID CUTBACKS: A HANDBOOK FOR BENEFICIARY ADVOCATES (1976). Available from the Clearinghouse, No. 18,090 (44pp.).

4. *But, see,* Medical Society of State of New York v. Toia, No. 76C1443, (E.D. N.Y., Jan. 18, 1977), CCH MEDICARE & MEDICAID GUIDE ¶28,364. It is arguable from the enactment of 42 U.S.C. §1396b(e) that Congress intended, at least in 1965, that the basic five services required by 42 U.S.C. §§1396a(a)(13) and 1396d(a) would be provided comprehensively, and that limitations were permissible only on the optional services. This is so because §1396b(e) required the states to liberalize the *scope* of Medicaid services. It is clear that by the word *scope* Congress meant the *number* of services, not the duration or amount of any given service. Handbook of Public Service Administration, Supplement D, §1100(2)(3). While the words "scope of services" might be read to mean either the breadth of each service or the number or range of services, it is clear from the use of the words "scope and extent" in 42 U.S.C. §1396a(d), and §1396b(e) that Congress intended "scope" to refer to the number of services, not the breadth (which is encompassed instead in the words "extent," "amount" and "duration"). The reference in §1396b(e) to expanding eligibility is also clear. Therefore, since the five services were mandatory, and Congress only intended by §1396b(e) that states would add additional services during the ten-

year period they were given to achieve comprehensiveness, it could be argued that Congress assumed that the basic services were to be provided in a comprehensive manner at the outset. Whatever the initial intent of Congress, however, the practical effect of this argument in prohibiting limitations of the mandatory Medicaid services was nullified when Congress repealed §1396b(e) in 1972.

5. Doe v. Beal, 523 F.2d 611, 616 (3d Cir. 1975).

6. §5140, HANDBOOK OF PUBLIC ASSISTANCE ADMINISTRATION, SUPPLEMENT D.

7. 45 C.F.R. §249.10(a)(5).

8. 404 U.S. 282 (1971).

9. 406 U.S. 598 (1972).

10. The contrary suggestions in White v. Beal, No. 76-1755 (3rd Cir., May 5, 1977) at p.5 (Clearinghouse No. 17,486G Opinion (6pp.)) and New York Medical Society v. Toia, No. 76C1443 (E.D. N.Y., Jan. 18, 1977) at p.27 (Clearinghouse No. 20,944A Opinion (41pp.)) are incorrect.

11. Doe v. Beal, 523 F.2d at 617, *rev'd on other grounds, sub nom.* Beal v. Doe, 45 U.S.L.W. 4781 (U.S. Sup. Ct., June 21, 1977).

12. *Id.*

13. Coe v. Hooker, 406 F.Supp. 1072 (D.N.H. 1976).

14. 45 C.F.R. §249.10(a)(5).

15. *See* Butler, *The Right to Abortion under Medicaid,* 7 CLEARINGHOUSE REV. 713, 719 (April 1974); N.Y. Medical Society v. Toia, No. 76C1443 (E.D. N.Y., Jan. 18, 1977) at p.27.

16. 413 F.Supp. 1141 (E.D. Pa. 1976), *aff'd* No. 76-1755 (3rd Cir. May 5, 1977).

17. In affirming the district court, the Third Circuit did not seem to understand this holding, but since it did not apply the regulation, it did not need to affirm this aspect of the district court's opinion.

18. 413 F.Supp. at 1154.

19. *Id.*

20. 45 C.F.R. §249.10(b)(iv).

21. No. 76-1755 (3rd Cir., May 5, 1977).

22. *Id.* at 5.

23. *Id.* at 7.

24. For a discussion of the dangers of using medical necessity in some contexts, *see* Butler, *The Right to Medicaid Payment for Abortion,* 28 HASTINGS L.J. 931, 953-61 (1977) [hereinafter HASTINGS]. However, the Supreme Court determined that such distinctions were statutorily and constitutionally valid. Beal v. Doe, 45 U.S.L.W. 4781 (U.S. Sup. Ct., June 21, 1977); Maher v. Roe, 45 U.S.L.W. 4787 (U.S. Sup. Ct., June 21, 1977).

25. 523 F.2d 611 (3d Cir. 1976), *rev'd on other grounds, sub nom.* Beal v. Doe, 45 U.S.L.W. 4781 (U.S. Sup. Ct., June 21, 1977).

26. 45 U.S.L.W. 4781 (U.S. Sup. Ct., June 21, 1977).

27. 523 F.2d at 620. *But see,* N.Y. Medical Society v. Toia, No. 76C1443 (E.D. N.Y., Jan. 18, 1977) at p.27.

28. The district court in White v. Beal incorrectly suggested that the Court of Appeal in Doe v. Beal applied the regulation, 413 F.Supp. at 1154, but this is incorrect.

29. No. 76-1671A (N.D. Ga., Jan. 13, 1977), CCH MEDICARE & MEDICAID GUIDE ¶28,343.

30. 45 C.F.R. §249.10(b)(12)(i).

31. Dodson v. Parham, No. 76-1671A (N.D. Ga., Jan. 13, 1977) at 16.

32. *Id.*

33. No. 76C1443 (E.D. N.Y., Jan. 18, 1977).

34. N.Y. Social Services Law §365-a(5); 10 N.Y.C.R.R. §85.1-85.2.

35. 45 C.F.R. §249.10(b)(5).

36. *See* text accompanying notes 8 and 9, *supra.*

37. *Id.*

38. 407 F.Supp. 1259 (D. D.C. 1975).

39. 42 U.S.C. §1396a(a)(6).

40. 45 C.F.R. §249.10(b)(6).

41. 407 F.Supp. at 1263.

42. 407 F.Supp. at 1265.

43. Bay Ridge Laboratories v. Dumpson, 400 F.Supp. 1140 (E.D. N.Y. 1975).

44. No. 76-0300-R (D. Va., Feb. 23, 1977); CCH MEDICARE & MEDICAID GUIDE ¶28,346.

45. Hospitalization is one of the mandatory services covered by this regulation, 42 U.S.C. §§1396a(a)(13), 1396d(a)(i).

46. No. 76-1671A (N.D. Ga., Jan. 13, 1977), CCH MEDICARE & MEDICAID GUIDE ¶28,343.

47. No. 1257 (C.D. Pa., Sept. 8, 1975).

48. 75 Or. 2225, 536 P.2d 549 (1975).

49. 397 U.S. 471 (1970).

50. No. 1-72-169 (D. Id., Aug. 29, 1973).

51. 523 F.2d 611 (3d Cir. 1975), *rev'd on other grounds, sub nom* Beal & Doe, 45 U.S.L.W. 4781 (June 21, 1977).

52. 407 F.Supp. 1141 (E.D. Pa. 1976).

53. *See* Butler, *The Right to Abortion Under Medicaid,* 7 CLEARINGHOUSE REV. 713 (April 1974).

54. *See* Doe v. Beal, 523 F.2d 611, 620 (3d Cir. 1976).

55. For a detailed description of EPSDT *see* Butler, *An Advocate's Guide to EPSDT,* 10 CLEARINGHOUSE REV. 1 (May 1976).

56. Brooks v. Smith, No. 1308 (Me. Sup. Ct., April 30, 1976); CCH MEDICARE & MEDICAID GUIDE ¶27,851.

5. The Court, the Congress and the President: Turning Back the Clock on the Pregnant Poor

RICHARD LINCOLN, BRIGITTE DÖRING-BRADLEY,
BARBARA L. LINDHEIM, and
MAUREEN A. COTTERILL

Reprinted with permission from *Family Planning Perspectives*, Vol. 9, No. 5, 1977.

"Well, as you know, there are many things in life that are not fair, that wealthy people can afford and poor people can't." President Jimmy Carter, press conference, July 12, 1977.

Safe, legal abortions are apparently to be added to the list of "luxuries" such as "faceliftings, hair transplants, expensive cars and tickets to the Kennedy Center"[1] that "wealthy people can afford and poor people can't" as the result of actions taken and policy decisions enunciated during and just preceding the summer by the President of the United States, his Secretary of Health, Education, and Welfare, the U.S. Supreme Court, the Congress and numerous state legislatures and officials.

The long hot summer began early for poor pregnant women when the House of Representatives on June 17 voted 201-155 to pass the so-called Hyde Amendment to the DHEW-Labor appropriations bill. That amendment prohibits the use of federal funds after October 1 "to pay for abortions or to promote or encourage abortions."[2] Three days later, the U.S. Supreme Court, in 6-3 decisions, ruled that states need not pay for "nontherapeutic" abortions even though they pay for childbirth, and that public hospitals need not perform such abortions, although they provide other pregnancy-related services.[3] On June 29, the Senate voted 56-39 to bar the use of federal funds for abortion except to save the life of the pregnant woman if the fetus were carried to term "or where medically necessary, or for the treatment of rape or incest."[4]

The same day, the Supreme Court vacated a ruling by New York District Court Judge John F. Dooling, Jr., that had enjoined enforcement of the previous year's version of the Hyde Amendment, passed by both houses of Congress, which banned

---

Data on the number of Medicaid-funded abortions and expenditures for Medicaid-funded abortions are from a 1977 AGI mail survey of state welfare and Medicaid agencies, followed up by telephone interviews with state officials in July 1977.

Data on the distribution of Medicaid and non-Medicaid abortions among providers, on estimates of total U.S. abortions financed by Medicaid, on average abortion costs, by type of provider, and on reduced and deferred payments are from an AGI special survey conducted during the winter of 1977 of 1,353 clinic and hospital abortion providers, of which 764 (56 percent) provided usable responses. The sample survey was partially supported by the Ford Foundation.

Data on the distribution of all abortions, by provider and by state, are from AGI's 1976 nationwide survey of health institutions and private physicians, in which 2,398 abortion providers were identified (see reference 10).

federal funding for abortions unless the pregnant woman's life was endangered;[5] on August 4, the 1976 Hyde Amendment went into effect when Judge Dooling lifted a temporary restraining order that had prevented enforcement.[6] Lest there be any misinterpretation of the extent of the ban, Attorney General Griffin B. Bell informed DHEW, on request, that it applied to all abortions "except where the victim's life is endangered," despite exceptions that had been written into the Senate-House conference report accompanying the ban.

Earlier, on July 12, President Carter had indicated at a news conference that he believed the federal government should not finance abortions "except when the woman's life is threatened or when pregnancy is the result of rape or incest." HEW Secretary Joseph Califano previously had indicated his support for congressional enactment of legislation barring the expenditure of federal funds for abortions except when performed to save a woman's life.

Encouraged by the actions of Congress, the nation's chief executive and its high court, officials from more than two dozen states announced that their states would no longer pay for abortions unless the pregnant woman's life were threatened;* and officials from numerous other states indicated that they would only fund "medically necessary," or "therapeutic," abortions— variously defined. Although most state legislatures were in recess during the summer, many legislators, courting the favor of right-to-life constituents, rushed to the media to announce that they would file bills to stop state payments for abortions. Bills

actually were filed in five states,† and one, Illinois, became the first to pass such a measure following the Supreme Court's June decisions.[7] As of this writing, however, support for continued Medicaid reimbursement has come from the governors of three of these states (Massachusetts, Michigan and New York) as well as from the governors of California, Maryland, Vermont and Washington.‡ (More than half of Medicaid-funded abortions were performed in these seven states in 1976.) Nevertheless, it is considered unlikely that many states will continue to provide Medicaid reimbursement for long after federal aid is cut off, since four-fifths of public funds for abortion have come from the federal government.

Thus, the denial of federal funds for abortions is likely, as predicted by Rep. Louis Stokes (D.-Ohio) during the congressional debate over the Hyde Amendment, to be "tantamount to . . . outlawing abortion for the poor."[8]

WHO IS AFFECTED?

The effects of the court decisions and of the executive, congressional and state actions will be felt most directly by Medicaid-recipient women of childbearing age, 85 percent of whom are AFDC mothers and their dependent children.§

---

*As of this writing, officials in the following states are reported to have stated that they will stop funding all abortions except when the woman's life is endangered: Alabama, Arkansas, Connecticut, Delaware, Florida, Georgia, Iowa, Indiana, Kentucky, Louisiana, Maine, Mississippi, Missouri, Montana, New Hampshire, New Jersey, North Carolina, North Dakota, Rhode Island, South Carolina, South Dakota, Tennessee, Texas, Utah and Vermont.

†Illinois, Massachusetts, Michigan, New York and Wisconsin.

‡It is notable that the governors of California and New York are Roman Catholic; and the governor of Massachusetts is Greek Orthodox. The Roman Catholic nun Sister Elizabeth Candon, who heads Vermont's Human Services Agency, which supervises Medicaid, also has announced that she favors continuing Medicaid-funded abortions for the poor.

§This figure is derived from two DHEW studies: National Center for Social Statistics, Social and Rehabilitation Service (NCSS), tables from unpublished study on AFDC recipient characteristics, Dec. 1976; and NCSS, *Medical Statistics, January 1977*, DHEW Pub. No. (SRS) 77-03150, NCSS Report B-1 (1/77), May 1977, Table 2, p. 8.

More than three million Medicaid-eligible women are at risk of unwanted pregnancy at any given time.

Unfortunately, no precise data are available on how many women obtain abortions that are paid for in whole or in part by federal and state funds. This is because there is no national reporting system and no compatible state reporting systems which publish data on the number of abortions that are publicly funded each year, the amount of money that is spent, the facilities where the abortions are performed, or the characteristics of the women obtaining the abortions. (Most of the necessary information should, in theory, be submitted to each state's Medicaid or Title XX [Social Services] program before fees for services rendered are reimbursed. But this information is never published and analyzed, since neither the federal government nor the state governments have required that the data be gathered, tabulated and made available. Indeed, all services under Medicaid and Title XX are poorly reported.)

However, some states have reported or estimated the number of abortions financed by Medicaid. Moreover, The Alan Guttmacher Institute (AGI) has surveyed state welfare and Medicaid agencies, as well as a large random sample of abortion providers. Based on these surveys—supplemented by other available information reported in the press—we have made rough estimates, by state, of the number of publicly funded abortions performed and the amount of money expended for these abortions in FY 1976 under Title XIX (Medicaid) and Title XX (Social Services) of the Social Security Act. These estimates in turn are used to compute approximate rates of utilization of abortion by Medicaid-eligible women in each state, and, thus, to suggest the patterns of availability of legal abortion to the poor before the summer of 1977.

As seen in Table 1, between 261,000 and 274,000 poor U.S. women obtained abortions that were paid for at least in part by

Table 1. Estimated number of abortions and total expenditures under Title XIX (Medicaid) and Title XX (Social Services) of the Social Security Act, by state, FY 1976*

State	No. of abortions	Expenditures
U.S. total	**260,800–274,400†**	**$60,907,000**
Ala.	1,300	338,800
Alaska	300	17,600
Ariz.	‡	‡
Ark.	500	61,300
Calif.	70,000§	24,411,700§
Colo.	2,800§	110,300
Conn.	2,000§	427,500§
Del.	400	44,100
D.C.	7,400§	1,419,800§
Fla.	1,600§	229,300§
Ga.	3,700§	948,600
Hawaii	1,200	212,100
Idaho	u	u
Ill.	18,300§	2,667,100§
Ind.	u	u
Iowa	1,000	297,300
Kans.	3,700§	300,000§
Ky.	900	197,400
La.	u	u
Maine	500	212,100
Md.	5,000§	1,675,000§
Mass.	5,100§	1,105,300§
Mich.	14,800§	2,432,200§
Minn.	1,300	215,700
Miss.	u	u
Mo.	2,400§	180,000§
Mont.	700§	210,000§
Nebr.	300§	11,700§
Nev.	400**	200,000**
N.H.	200§	31,300§
N.J.	10,000§	3,500,000§
N.Mex.	900**	164,700**
N.Y.	50,000§	7,875,000
N.C.	3,100**	1,109,800**
N.Dak.	u	u
Ohio	10,000§	2,000,000§
Okla.	700	59,200
Oreg.	2,000§	547,000§
Pa.	10,000§	1,913,100§
R.I.	1,000§	96,300§
S.C.	1,400**	248,900**
S.Dak.	u	u
Tenn.	1,200§	274,700§
Tex.	13,300**	3,500,000
Utah	300§	25,200§
Vt.	300§	179,800
Va.	5,200§	463,100§
Wash.	2,700**	640,000**
W.Va.	300§	91,500§
Wis.	2,500§	250,000§
Wyo.	100	12,500

*These estimates differ somewhat from those published earlier. The earlier estimates were based on actual reports from 17 states. These updated estimates include actual reports of abortions and/or expenditures from 32 states and the District of Columbia.

†The 260,800 estimate is the sum of the state totals; the 274,400 estimate is from the AGI 1977 sample survey of abortion providers.

‡No Medicaid program in FY 1976.

§Based on Title XIX state reports.

**Based on state reports of Title XIX and Title XX. Estimated expenditures and number of abortions performed under Title XX are: Nevada, 25 abortions, $12,500; New Mexico, 400 abortions, $77,800; North Carolina, 1,700 abortions, $624,855; South Carolina, 900 abortions, $162,900; Texas, 9,500 abortions, $2,491,700; Washington, 300 abortions, $39,900.

Note: u = unavailable.

one of these federal-state programs, at a total public expenditure of $61 million—or about $222-$234 per abortion.* Expenditures for about 248,000-262,000 of these abortions were made under Title XIX (Medicaid), and for the remaining 13,000 abortions under Title XX (Social Services), of the Social Security Act.

*The figure 274,400 is obtained by applying percentages of Medicaid-funded abortions performed in 1976 obtained from the AGI sample survey of abortion provider clinics and hospitals to the total number of abortions estimated for FY 1976. The figure of 260,800 abortions is based on reports or estimates obtained by AGI from state welfare and Medicaid agencies in 32 states and the District of Columbia. For the remaining states, two different estimation techniques were used. Several states unable to provide information on numbers of abortions did have data on expenditures. To estimate the number of abortions, the expenditure figure was divided by $160 in states in which most abortions occurred in clinics, and by $290 in other states. These amounts reflect the average costs of clinic abortions and a mix of clinic and hospital procedures, respectively. The resulting estimate was then refined, using the factors described below. For states in which neither numbers nor expenditures were reported, we assumed that 20 percent of all abortions performed in the state were paid for in whole or in part under Titles XIX or XX. Since approximately 25 percent of all abortions nationwide are Medicaid-financed, it therefore seemed reasonable to obtain an initial estimate by applying the more conservative 20 percent figure in these states. The estimate was then revised upward or downward depending on such factors as the known availability of abortion providers; the level of total welfare expenditures per capita; the generosity of the overall Medicaid program as evidenced by eligibility criteria; the proportion of all abortions obtained in the state by nonresidents (as reported by DHEW's Center for Disease Control); the proportion of Medicaid-eligible women among all women of reproductive age in the state; the existence of generally restrictive abortion policies or legislation; and the existence of court action enjoining state laws or policies against Medicaid funding of abortions.

Data on expenditures for abortion under Medicaid and Title XX were reported by 32 states and the District of Columbia. For the remaining states which did not report family planning and abortion expenditures separately, estimates were derived by extrapolating from the experience of states that were able to provide separate breakdowns.

Three-quarters of these abortions were reported from eight states† in which 10,000 or more procedures were paid for by public funds; more than four in 10 of the procedures were obtained in California and New York.

One state, Arizona, had no Medicaid program, and six others‡ did not report any reimbursement for abortions from public funds. Some of these indicated that a small number of abortions had been performed—mainly to save the pregnant woman's life.

Table 2 shows that utilization of legal abortion services among the poor, as measured by the rate of abortions per 1,000 Medicaid-eligible women aged 15-44, was about three times higher in FY 1976 than among the nonpoor. This is consistent with previous findings that the incidence of unwanted and mistimed pregnancies and births is much higher among poor than among nonpoor women.[9]

Abortion rates for Medicaid-eligible women would have been higher still if access to abortion services had been distributed more equitably among different areas in FY 1976. In six out of 10 of the states, abortions are concentrated in one or two large metropolitan areas, and in eight out of 10 counties, there is not a single abortion provider.[10] The need to travel, often over considerable distances, to obtain abortions has been shown to be a major barrier to utilization by individuals from lower socioeconomic groups—especially teenagers.[11] In addition, some states pay providers considerably less than the actual charge for the abortion under their Medicaid plans, or restrict payment to specified facilities, such as hospitals. Nevertheless, Medicaid abortion rates were higher than non-Medicaid rates in all but four states (Florida, Kentucky, Massachusetts and

†California, Illinois, Michigan, New Jersey, New York, Ohio, Pennsylvania and Texas.

‡Idaho, Indiana, Louisiana, Mississippi, North Dakota and South Dakota.

Table 2. Estimated rate of Medicaid-funded abortions per 1,000 Medicaid-eligible women and rate of abortions not Medicaid-funded per 1,000 women not eligible for Medicaid, by state, FY 1976

State	Medicaid rate	Non-Medicaid rate	Medicaid/non-Medicaid ratio
U.S. total	53–56	19	2.8–3.0
Ala.	20	7	3.0
Alaska	74	16	4.6
Ariz.	*	16†	u
Ark.	11	6	1.8
Calif.	100	24	4.2
Colo.	77	20	3.8
Conn.	37	17	2.2
Del.	30	17	1.8
D.C.	190	171	1.1
Fla.	16	28	0.6
Ga.	30	21	1.5
Hawaii	56	27	2.1
Idaho	u	7†	u
Ill.	60	19	3.1
Ind.	u	7†	u
Iowa	25	10	2.7
Kans.	82	24	3.4
Ky.	7	12	0.6
La.	u	9†	u
Maine	17	7	2.3
Md.	56	21	2.6
Mass.	21	28	0.7
Mich.	52	16	3.1
Minn.	22	14	1.6
Miss.	u	1†	u
Mo.	25	10	2.5
Mont.	46	5	8.3
Nebr.	16	14	1.2
Nev.	60	25	2.4
N.H.	18	12	1.4
N.J.	52	17	3.0
N.Mex.	41	17	2.4
N.Y.	85	35	2.5
N.C.	29	15	2.0
N.Dak.	u	10†	u
Ohio	46	16	2.8
Okla.	14	12	1.2
Oreg.	43	25	1.7
Pa.	39	17	2.2
R.I.	30	16	1.9
S.C.	25‡	8	3.1
S.Dak.	u	11†	u
Tenn.	15	22	0.7
Tex.	91	16	5.6
Utah	18	8	2.4
Vt.	32	21	1.5
Va.	65	15	4.2
Wash.	37	27	1.4
W.Va.	13	1	15.9
Wis.	34	11	3.2
Wyo.	28	5	5.4

*No Medicaid program in FY 1976.

†Total abortion rate.

‡Includes abortions funded under Title XX as well as under Title XIX, since in South Carolina abortion services were restricted under both titles to women who were categorically indigent.

Note: u = unavailable.

Tennessee) that reported paying anything for abortions under their Medicaid programs.

It is difficult to explain the large variations in Medicaid abortion rates among the states in terms of attitudinal differences, since there are striking differences in the rates in contiguous states, where the age and race of the Medicaid-eligible population are fairly similar. Thus, the abortion rate for Medicaid-eligible women in Virginia is 65 per 1,000, while the rate in bordering North Carolina is 29, and in West Virginia, 13. In Georgia, the Medicaid rate is 30; in Alabama, it is 20. Illinois' rate is 60, but in Missouri and Iowa it is 25. The Colorado rate is 77, but in New Mexico it is 41, and in Utah it is only 18.

Such differences among bordering states, whose populations are comparable, seem to be attributable primarily to inequitable distribution of services and/or to restrictive policies.

These estimated rates in each state make it possible to calculate approximately how many additional Medicaid-funded abortions might have been performed in 1976 under conditions of equitable distribution throughout the country; in other words, we estimated the number of Medicaid recipients who were unable to obtain legal abortions in 1976, even before the recent restrictions were implemented. To obtain this estimate, we summed the number of Medicaid abortions and of Medicaid-eligible women at risk in the three areas with the highest rates (California, Texas and the District of Columbia) to arrive at an average rate for the three states of 103 per 1,000 Medicaid-eligible women. If this rate is applied to the 48 other states, a total of over 245,000 additional abortions is obtained.

It is possible, however, that the Medicaid populations of these three areas are not varied enough—in characteristics or attitudes—to capture the range of attitudinal differences toward abortion that is thought to exist throughout the nation. The 12 states with Medicaid abortion rates at or above the national average have rates which range from 56 to 190 per 1,000*. The weighted average abortion rate is 86 in these states. If we apply this rate to the Medicaid-eligible population of the remaining 39 states, the total number of Medicaid abortions would have been 164,000 more than actually occurred.

The figure of 164,000 additional Medicaid-funded abortions that would have been obtained under conditions of high accessibility and availability is probably conservative. This is because the 12 higher-than-average abortion rate states are from all parts of the country; and it is not likely that all Medicaid-eligible women who want abortions are actually obtaining them in all these states. This analysis, while necessarily speculative, suggests that between 164,000 and 245,000 Medicaid-eligible women who needed and wanted abortions were unable to obtain them—before implementation of the Hyde Amendment—as a result of restrictive Medicaid practices and the lack of abortion services in most states.

"LET THEM EAT CAKE"

In its June 20 decisions, the Supreme Court declared that the refusal of a state to finance abortions for poor people did not interfere with their right to seek and, if they could pay for them, obtain legal abortions (a logic which dissenting Justice Blackmun likened to Marie Antoinette's injunction to France's starving peasantry: "Let them eat cake"[12]). How reasonable is it to expect poor people to be able to pay for their own abortions?

As may be seen in Table 3, the average cost of an abortion in the United States— $280—is $42 higher than the average monthly welfare payment *for an entire family* for food, clothing, shelter and all other

---

*Alaska, California, Colorado, District of Columbia, Hawaii, Illinois, Kansas, Maryland, Nevada, New York, Texas and Virginia.

Table 3. Average abortion cost, average monthly family AFDC payment and ratio of cost to payment, by state, United States, FY 1976

State	Average abortion cost*	Average AFDC monthly payment††	Cost/ payment ratio
U.S. total	**$280**	**$238**	**1.2**
Ala.	310	113	2.7
Alaska	293	297	0.8
Ariz.	207	141	1.5
Ark.	307	135	2.3
Calif.	379	297	1.3
Colo.	301	205	1.5
Conn.	409	266	1.5
Del.	460	207	2.2
D.C.	239	242	1.0
Fla.	211	139	1.5
Ga.	214	97	2.2
Hawaii	430	363	1.2
Idaho	400	256	1.6
Ill.	225	269	0.8
Ind.	244	168	1.5
Iowa	310	247	1.3
Kans.	379	229	1.7
Ky.	199	171	1.2
La.	160	119	1.3
Maine	274	193	1.4
Md.	280	175	1.6
Mass.	218	300	0.7
Mich.	232	296	0.8
Minn.	278	266	1.0
Miss.	460	48	9.6
Mo.	167	137	1.2
Mont.	383	173	2.2
Nebr.	202	210	1.0
Nev.	250	157	1.6
N.H.	321	217	1.5
N.J.	280	263	1.1
N.Mex.	289	140	2.1
N.Y.	309	363	0.9
N.C.	331	154	2.1
N.Dak.	160	256	0.6
Ohio	202	195	1.0
Okla.	169	203	0.8
Oreg.	415	260	1.6
Pa.	298	283	1.1
R.I.	448	263	1.7
S.C.	226	85	2.6
S.Dak.	160	205	0.8
Tenn.	196	104	1.9
Tex.	208	104	2.0
Utah	184	246	0.7
Vt.	181	255	0.7
Va.	253	191	1.3
Wash.	223	252	0.9
W.Va.	460	196	2.3
Wis.	241	296	0.8
Wyo.	460	196	2.3

*The average costs for a hospital abortion ($460) and clinic abortion ($160) were derived from the AGI provider sample survey. For each state, these averages were multiplied by the percentage of all abortions (from the 1976 AGI abortion survey) performed in hospitals or in clinics and physicians' offices. The results were summed to obtain the average abortion cost in the state.

†Average payment per family, from National Center for Social Statistics, DHEW, *Public Assistance Statistics, February 1977*, June 1977, Table 4A, p. 7.

necessities. In Mississippi, the average cost of an abortion is 10 times higher than the monthly family AFDC payment. In only 13 states and the District of Columbia is the cost of an abortion less than the monthly family AFDC payment. Under these circumstances, it seems clear that not very many pregnant women on welfare will be able to get together the money to pay for their own legal abortions—and if they do, it will be at the sacrifice of basic necessities of food and shelter for themselves or their families.

WHO PERFORMS MEDICAID ABORTIONS?

As may be seen in Table 4, 74 percent of abortions that are not financed by Medicaid are performed in nonhospital clinics or private physicians' offices; just four percent are performed in public hospitals and 22 percent in private hospitals. In contrast, 19 percent of all Medicaid-funded abortions are performed in public hospitals, 50 percent in private hospitals, and only 31 percent in clinics or physicians' offices.

Although only about half of all provider hospitals report that they perform *any* Medicaid-funded abortions, compared to 70 percent of clinics, seven out of 10

Medicaid-reimbursed abortions are performed in hospitals. Medicaid-financed abortions account for 60 percent of public hospital abortions and 44 percent of private hospital terminations, compared with only 13 percent of all clinic procedures.

In the recent congressional debate over the Hyde Amendment, Rep. Eldon Rudd (R.-Ariz.) argued that "those who want to pay for the abortions of others can do so by contributing privately to charity hospitals or abortion clinics without robbing [taxpayers] who prefer not to pay for them."[13] Just how likely is it that private philanthropy will be able to make up the deficit if the $61 million in Medicaid and Title XX funding is withdrawn? Data from the AGI 1977 sample survey of 1,353 abortion providers indicate that current providers are already subsidizing abortions for many poor women.

About 75 percent of nonhospital clinics, 30 percent of private hospitals and 27 percent of public hospitals provided some free or reduced-cost abortions to poor people in 1976. (In some instances—especially among clinics—reduced-fee policies reflected Medicaid reimbursement rates set at below actual abortion charges.) An estimated 14 percent of all clinic abortion patients and possibly four percent of all hospital abortion patients (a total of more than

Table 4. Estimated number and percent distribution of Medicaid-funded abortions and non-Medicaid abortions, percent of total abortions that are funded by Medicaid, and percent of abortion providers that report performing abortions funded by Medicaid, by type of provider, FY 1976

Type of provider	No. of abortions		% distribution of abortions		% total abortions Medicaid-funded	% providers that perform Medicaid abortions
	Medicaid-funded	Not Medicaid-funded	Medicaid-funded	Not Medicaid-funded		
Total	**274,400**	**800,000**	**100**	**100**	**26**	**54***
Hospitals						
Private	138,000	173,600	50	22	44	52
Public	51,700	34,200	19	4	60	46
Clinics/MD offices	84,700	592,200	31	74	13	70*

*Excluding private physicians' offices.

Note: Data on total abortions from AGI 1976 abortion survey; all other data from AGI 1977 sample provider survey.

100,000 women) obtained reduced-cost or free abortions in 1976.

In addition, about three-quarters of nonhospital clinics and public hospitals and nearly two-thirds of private hospitals offered deferred payment plans to some women in financial difficulty. Payments were deferred for an estimated 15 percent of all clinic patients and for perhaps six percent of hospital patients (for a total of about 120,000 women).

There is an unknown degree of overlap among abortions for which providers accepted reduced and deferred payments in 1976, but it is probable that providers are already subsidizing, through one or both of these channels, at least 150,000 abortions annually. If public subsidies were withdrawn, current providers would have to almost triple the number of abortions that they are now subsidizing to make up the deficit, assuming that Medicaid recipients could raise even the reduced fees.

The disparity between the potential deficit and the capacity of private philanthropy to meet it is apparent. For example, Planned Parenthood, following the Supreme Court's June 20 decisions, launched a "Justice Fund" to raise $3 million for education, litigation and some degree of subsidy for needed services. The organizers of the fund expressed the hope that perhaps as much as $4 million annually could be raised to help providers subsidize abortions for poor women; this sum compares with $61 million expended by the states and federal government last year to finance abortions under Medicaid and Title XX.

What is more, the role of private philanthropy in financing personal health services has always been very small and, according to DHEW, has been steadily declining—from 2.9 percent of total expenditures in 1960 to just 1.1 percent in 1975.[14] If private contributions to finance abortion services were five times as great as they are for all other personal health services, and if all of those contributions were spent to subsidize abortions formerly financed by Medicaid,

only five percent of the 261,000-274,000 Medicaid abortions would be covered.

TIP OF THE ICEBERG

As was noted earlier, the high concentration of abortion services in relatively few large metropolitan areas, along with restrictive Medicaid policies in some states, has limited access of poor people to abortion services even when the courts have prohibited states and the federal government from denying Medicaid reimbursement to poor women seeking abortions.

Data from the 1976 AGI abortion survey show that an estimated 654,000 women in need of abortion services were not able to obtain them in that year. More than 80 percent of public hospitals did not provide *any* abortions; 380,000 low- and marginal-income women of reproductive age live in counties in which neither the public hospital nor any other provider offers abortion services. Because of these facts, and because of the high concentration of abortion services, the study concluded that the unmet need was disproportionately concentrated among "poor, rural and very young women . . . who are least likely to have the funds, the time or the familiarity with the medical system that they need to be able to cope with the problems associated" with travel to distant cities to obtain abortions.[15] Available data confirm the validity of this conclusion, at least with respect to women of low and marginal income.

About 910,000 low- and marginal-income women and about 859,000 higher income women were estimated to be in need of abortion services in 1976.* The data suggest

---

*"Low- and marginal-income" defines women from families below 200 percent of the federal poverty standard—about $5,500 annually for a nonfarm family of four in 1976. Need estimates used here are the higher estimates made by AGI. For a description of the method of determining need, see: AGI, *Abortion 1974-1975: Need and Services in the United States, Each State and Metropolitan Area,* New York, 1976, pp. 99–102.

that a maximum of 486,000 low- and marginal-income women obtained abortions in 1976. These included 274,000 women whose abortions were financed by Medicaid; 31,000 other women who obtained abortions in public hospitals (90 percent of those public hospital abortions that were not funded by Medicaid); 150,000 women who may have received deferred or reduced payments; and 31,000 who paid themselves or received reimbursement through private insurers (the latter hypothesized to be five percent of the remaining women who obtained abortions in 1976).

Thus, even before the June 20 Supreme Court decisions, about 424,000 or nearly half of low- and marginal-income women in need of abortions still were not able to obtain them in 1976. In contrast, about 271,000 higher income women—fewer than one-third of those in need of abortions— were unable to obtain them. The Court decisions and the Hyde Amendment can only have the effect of widening this disparity by preventing the further diffusion of abortion services—especially among public hospitals—and, thus, of blocking more equitable availability of services for poor and rich alike. As Justice Marshall declared of the June 20 Supreme Court decisions, they "inevitably will have the practical effect of preventing nearly all poor women from obtaining safe and legal abortions."[16]

INCREASED MORTALITY

What will be the effect on pregnancy-related mortality if the $61 million in federal and state reimbursements for abortion is withdrawn?

Precise estimates are impossible, since it is not known how many women who would have obtained abortions under Medicaid will turn to unskilled illegal abortionists, will try to abort themselves, will get their abortions subsidized by provider agencies or somehow raise the money themselves, or

will go on to give birth to unwanted children.

A range of estimates, however, has been made by officials of DHEW's Center for Disease Control (CDC) based on Medicaid data, census enumerations, vital statistics and the CDC's own abortion surveillance reports.[17] The CDC officials estimate that:

- If all women who would have obtained a legal abortion turned to illegal channels to terminate their pregnancies, 90 additional deaths per year would result.

- If 70 percent of the women had an illegal abortion and 30 percent chose to carry their pregnancies to term, 77 additional deaths would occur—63 deaths from illegal abortion, and 14 from complications related to childbirth.

- If all women who would have obtained a legal Medicaid-funded abortion chose to carry their pregnancies to term, an additional 44 deaths would occur.

- If difficulties in obtaining funds for abortion resulted in an average delay of two weeks in obtaining a legal abortion, five additional legal abortion deaths would occur—raising the national abortion death-to-case rate by 21 percent, and increasing the death-to-case rate of women who would have had Medicaid abortions by 60 percent.

Increased mortality, of course, is only the most extreme adverse health outcome that is likely to result from withdrawal of most public aid for abortions. Major complications from illegal and legal abortion and from pregnancy and childbirth are more than one hundred times more frequent than death—especially among poor women. These health consequences are in addition to the enormous social and financial costs to the poor women involved and to their families.†

RACE

As noted by Justice Thurgood Marshall in his dissent, the effect of withdrawing Medicaid support for abortions "will fall with great disparity on women of minority races." This is because an estimated 39 percent of black women rely on Medicaid for their health care—including abortion— compared to just seven percent of white women. And the abortion-live-birth ratio is nearly two times higher among blacks than whites.[18] This differential in ratios is not surprising in view of the fact that blacks have more unwanted pregnancies than whites. We can expect, therefore, that with the sharp reduction in Medicaid-funded abortions, proportionally more black than white women will be forced to bear unwanted children.

CONCLUSION

The impact of withdrawing public funds for abortion services, in Justice Marshall's words, "falls tragically upon those least able to help or defend themselves"[19]— namely, the very poor, and among the poor, a disproportionate number who are black, teenaged, unwed or rural.

Such a cutoff of public funds will, of course, impact most immediately on the estimated 300,000 poor women annually whose abortions currently are being paid for in whole or in part under Medicaid or Title XX, or who are obtaining abortions in public hospitals under some other funding arrangement. It will affect almost as directly the 150,000 other low- and marginal-income women whose abortions are being subsidized by hospitals and clinics, and the approximately 424,000 low- and marginal-income women in need of abortion services who, last year, were unable to obtain them because of inaccessibility of providers, Medicaid restrictions and other problems.

Potentially, the withdrawal of public assistance may directly affect, at some time, any of the more than three million Medicaid-eligible women of reproductive age at risk each year of having an unwanted pregnancy, and, indirectly, the 6.3 million other low- and marginal-income women at risk.

Such an action is likely to halt or even to reverse the trend of more than a decade, in which the gap in unwanted childbearing has been substantially reduced between rich and poor, black and white, rural and urban. It may well cause teenage illegitimacy rates to rise sharply again, as they did in the late 1960s and early 1970s.

---

†The financial costs to the taxpayer of the Medicaid abortion ban are likely to be staggering. A June 4 memorandum to HEW Secretary Califano from his health financing chief, Robert A. Derzon, indicates that each unwanted birth to a poor woman costs about $1,000 a year in welfare costs and $100 in Medicaid funds. If just one-third of the women currently getting abortions financed by Medicaid were to carry their pregnancies to term, the first-year costs would be about $100.5 million. If the remainder obtained illegal abortions, many millions of additional dollars would be expended in Medicaid funds for treatment of complications. These figures probably considerably understate the financial costs the public will have to assume as a result of the ban on Medicaid-financed abortions. By updating the estimate developed by Phillips Cutright and Frederick S. Jaffe to assess the short-term costs and benefits of fertility control programs, we find that the *first-year* governmental expenditures for each birth to a Medicaid-eligible woman who would have obtained a Medicaid abortion if it were available would be $2,330. This total reflects government expenditures for medical services, public assistance and selected social welfare services minus the average Medicaid expenditure for the abortion. (See: P. Cutright and F.S. Jaffe, *Impact of Family Planning Programs on Fertility,* Praeger, New York, 1977, p. 144.) If one-third of Medicaid women desiring an abortion give birth in the absence of public funding for abortion, the first-year public costs would be about $200 million. If a higher proportion of these women are forced to go to term, this figure will increase correspondingly. In addition, the first-year costs do not reflect the increased social welfare expenditures that will be needed for at least some of these families for many years to come.

Pregnancy-related mortality and morbidity, which have steeply declined in this decade, are likely to rise again, with the poor, the black and the young the main victims.

The resulting increase in unwanted childbearing and illegal abortions among the poor will not only deepen their own physical and mental anguish, and increase the poverty in which they and their children must live, but it will also cause public expenditures for their health care and welfare support to soar.

These consequences contrast sharply with the images projected by congressmen who equate public financing of abortions for the poor with "luxuries" or "conveniences" like facelifts and hair transplants, and by the President when he dismisses the withdrawal of public funds for abortion as just one more of the "many things in life that are not fair." They also raise serious questions about the opinion of the Supreme Court majority that "an indigent woman desiring an abortion is not disadvantaged" by a state's decision to fund childbirth, but not abortion. Rather, in the words of Justice Blackmun, the denial of subsidized abortions to the poor marks "a sad day for those who regard the Constitution as a force that would serve justice to all evenhandedly and, in so doing, would better the lot of the poorest among us."[20]

REFERENCES

1. Rep. E. Rudd (R.-Ariz.), debate on the Hyde Amendment to the Labor-DHEW Appropriation Act of 1978, *Congressional Record,* June 17, 1977, p. H.6088.

2. Sec. 209, H.R. 7555, Labor-DHEW Appropriation Act of 1978, *Congressional Record,* June 17, 1977, p. H.6083.

3. *Beal v. Doe,* 97 S. Ct. 2366 (1977); *Maher v. Roe,* 97 S. Ct. 2376 (1977); and *Poelker v. Doe,* 97 S. Ct. 2391 (1977).

4. Sec. 209, H.R. 7555, Labor-DHEW Appropriation Act of 1978, *Congressional Record,* June 29, 1977, p. S.11050.

5. *Califano v. McCrae,* 97 S. Ct. 2893 (1977).

6. *McCrae v. Califano,* No. 76-C-1804 (E.D.N.Y., Aug. 4, 1977); and *New York Health and Hospitals Corp. v. Califano,* No. 76-C-1805 (E.D.N.Y., Aug. 4, 1977).

7. H.333 (1977).

8. Rep. L. Stokes (D.-Ohio), debate on the Hyde Amendment to the Labor-DHEW Appropriation Act of 1978, *Congressional Record,* June 17, 1977, p. H.6085.

9. C.F. Westoff and N.B. Ryder, *The Contraceptive Revolution,* Princeton University Press, Princeton, N.J., 1977, Table X-12, p. 297; J.E. Anderson, L. Morris and M. Gesche, "Planned and Unplanned Fertility in Upstate New York," *Family Planning Perspectives,* 9:4, 1977, Table 6; and M.L. Munson, "Wanted and Unwanted Births Reported by Mothers 15-44 Years of Age: United States, 1973," *Advance Data from Vital & Health Statistics,* National Center for Health Statistics, DHEW, No. 9, Aug. 10, 1977, Table 1.

10. E. Sullivan, C. Tietze and J.G. Dryfoos, "Legal Abortion in the United States, 1975-1976," *Family Planning Perspectives,* 9:116, 1977, Figure 3.

11. J.D. Shelton, E.A. Brann and K.F. Schulz, "Abortion Utilization: Does Travel Distance Matter?" *Family Planning Perspectives,* 8:260, 1976.

12. Justice H.A. Blackmun, 97 S. Ct. 2394 (1977).

13. Rep. E. Rudd, 1977, op. cit.

14. A.M. Skolnik and S.R. Dales, "Social Welfare Expenditures, 1950-75," *Social Security Bulletin,* Vol. 39, No. 1, 1976, Table 6, p. 15.

15. E. Sullivan et al., 1977, op. cit., p. 121.

16. Justice T. Marshall, 97 S. Ct. 2394 (1977).

17. D.B. Petitti and W. Cates, Jr., "Restricting Medicaid Funds for Abortions: Projections of Excess Mortality for Women of Childbearing Age," *American Journal of Public Health,* 67:860, 1977.

18. Justice T. Marshall, 1977, op. cit.

19. Ibid.

20. Justice H.A. Blackmun, 1977, op. cit.

6. The Politics of Hearing: Medicaid in New York City and the Audiologist

MAURICE H. MILLER

Reprinted with permission from *Asha*, Vol. 15, No. 9, September 1973.

More than five years have elapsed since audiologists in New York City first became involved in efforts to include audiological services in the program of hearing care for Medicaid-eligible adults. A directive has been issued by the local Medicaid office which leaves the decision on whether Medicaid-eligible adults should have the services of an audiologist in the hands of the physician. Those of us who have participated actively in these efforts in the past five years recognize that this directive is tantamount to the operational elimination of the audiologist as a regular participant in services for the overwhelming majority of the eligible population. The highlights of these frustrating and unsuccessful efforts to achieve recognition for the role of the audiologist need to be reported to ASHA's Members since a repetition in one form or another is likely to occur in some other part of the country.

ELIMINATION OF AUDIOLOGICAL SERVICES

In January 1968, the then executive medical director of Medicaid created a Medicaid Advisory Committee for Quality Hearing Care. The purpose of the committee was "to bring excellent health care to the medically indigent." He expressed concern about the Department of Health list of approved hearing centers and allegedly long waiting lists and wished to have the entire issue clarified. The committee first met on January 31, 1968.

Among those in attendance were otologists, audiologists, and hearing aid dealers. The audiologists were struck by the absence of otologists connected with major medical training institutions. The otologists tended to be private practitioners associated with hospitals that either had not met the Department of Health criteria for approved hearing centers or had never applied for approval. The dealers were primarily presidents and other officers of state and city dealer associations.

The general view expressed by the otologists and supported by the dealers was that the majority of hard-of-hearing adults did not need an audiologist's services. They encouraged Medicaid officials to have eligible patients referred directly from an otologist to a dealer. One otologist, for example, stated that in his private practice he sends the patient, accompanied by a relative or friend, to one of three local hearing aid dealers. He had encountered no problems with this arrangement and encouraged

Medicaid to provide a similar service for its patients. The physicians generally agreed that the referral to the dealer should be made only by an otologist and not by a general practitioner or other physician. The otologists present expressed the opinion that the existing system, using "approved" speech and hearing centers, was both expensive and unnecessary. Long waiting lists were described by the hearing aid dealers. One young otologist connected with a medical school, who was representing another physician not able to attend, reported that in his practice all patients receive audiological work-ups by competent audiological personnel prior to being referred to a dealer. He was clearly outvoted by the majority of otologists in attendance, as well as by the dealers. The dealers asked that any otologist; outpatient ear, nose, and throat clinic; or other medical facility be permitted to refer patients directly to the dealer. One dealer referred to some audiological literature suggesting that hearing aid evaluations were unreliable and a waste of professional time and stated that Medicaid should not support a procedure which in the judgment of the audiologists themselves had little value.

The audiologists argued for the inclusion of audiological evaluations and aural rehabilitation services in the care of adult hard-of-hearing patients, particularly those in the geriatric group. They acknowledged the difficulty of getting Medicaid-eligible adults into some of the approved hearing centers and suggested that such patients be referred to ASHA-certified audiologists working in a variety of settings, including free-standing institutions, rehabilitation centers, college and university speech and hearing centers, and private practice. Audiologists noted that the approved centers were created primarily to meet the need of pediatric patients and that some of the requirements, for example, an approved residency training program in pediatrics, were neither applicable nor necessary in serving adult hard-of-hearing patients.

Shortly after the meeting, the executive medical director of Medicaid announced a change in procedure for purchase of hearing aids. Under the altered procedure, which became effective on February 1, 1968, board-certified and board-eligible otolaryngologists could request hearing aids for Medicaid patients on a Medical Service Order form. The patient would then bring the completed form directly to an authorized vendor. Except for children under 21 years of age, referral to an approved hearing and speech center was no longer required.

EFFORTS TO REINSTATE AUDIOLOGICAL SERVICES AND DEALER REACTION

In an effort to restore audiological services for the adult medically indigent population, a group of audiologists formed the Committee on Hearing Care under Medicare, under the aegis of the New York State Speech and Hearing Association (NYSSHA). The committee held a number of meetings and developed a program for audiological care for Medicaid-eligible adults which included personnel standards and an enforcement mechanism. These standards were submitted through the president of NYSSHA to various city and state officials. The committee also looked at the actual waiting lists at the various approved centers and found that the situation was not as the Medicaid official and hearing aid dealers had described. While there was a waiting period at the approved hearing and speech center in one borough, the majority of facilities were able and willing to accept Medicaid-eligible adult patients for appointments within one month. Furthermore, the distance from the borough where facilities were limited into the central city where facilities were available was short enough to make referrals a practical solution had the officials wanted such a solution.

The dealer groups responded to the audiologists' efforts by mounting their own campaign to support the new Medicaid procedure. The New York Hearing Aid Dealers Guild sent registered letters to all of the board-certified and board-eligible otolaryngologists in the New York area, opening with the following statement: "Should you the otologist or otolaryngologist be relegated to the background in the vital discussion as to whether *your* patient requires a hearing aid?" The letter then went on to inform the physician that until recently the city health department required otolaryngologists to refer all hearing cases to a speech and hearing center for a decision on amplification. This practice had been stopped by recent decision of the Department of Health which enabled the otolaryngologist to make the complete diagnostic decision of what is best suited for his patient. The otolaryngologist was advised that his control of the patient was threatened by audiologists who wanted the patient referred to speech and hearing centers. He was asked to mail an enclosed card, along with his prescription blank, to Medicaid supporting the decision to eliminate audiological services.

In point of fact, the dealers erred in suggesting that the change in directive came from the City Health Department. When the director of the Health Department's Bureau for Handicapped Children was contacted for his opinion on the new proposal he stated that it would establish poor practice in so far as the vendor would also be the one who determined whether or not and what type of hearing aid was required. He considered this a potentially bad arrangement, to say the very least. He also expressed doubt about the competence of hearing aid dealers to test and evaluate individuals with hearing impairments. He suggested that some mechanism be devised which would clearly separate mercantile from professional functions. In other words, two advisory committees (the Technical Advisory Committee of the

Bureau for Handicapped Children and the Medicaid Committee) clearly differed on the advisability of the new action. The dealers were able to elicit considerable support from some members of the otological community through efforts to convince otologists that the new directive restored to them the professional management of their patients while what the audiologists wanted would result in 'the subordination of the physician's responsibility to that of another group. Doubtless the letters and prescription blanks from physicians to the Medicaid office led the medical director of Medicaid to believe there was considerable support from the professional community for the new policy.

All efforts by audiologists, and otologists contacted by the audiologists, to effect a change in the new procedure (elimination of audiologists from regular involvement in the care of hard-of-hearing patients) continued to be fruitless. In an effort to elicit additional input on this question, the altered Medicaid procedure was reviewed at a meeting of the Technical Advisory Committee on Hearing of the Department of Health. This committee endorsed the following position regarding management of adult hard-of-hearing patients: "Adults who require hearing aids should be examined by both a qualified otologist and audiologist and not necessarily at an approved hearing center. In the case of an otologist who is qualified as an audiologist the entire examination may be carried out by this individual."

MEDICAID APPOINTS HEARING AND SPEECH COMMITTEE

In July 1970, Medicaid appointed a Hearing and Speech Advisory Committee composed of audiologists from hospital programs, training institutions, and community-supported organizations. The purpose of the committee, as articulated by the new deputy executive director of

Medicaid, was to restore audiological services to Medicaid-eligible hard-of-hearing patients. He stated that there was widespread collusion between some otologists and vendors since the promulgation of the February 1968 directive. He claimed this collusion was documentable in the offices of both the city and state health departments, and he was convinced that this situation could be rectified, or at least ameliorated, by audiological involvement in the evaluation and rehabilitation of the hard-of-hearing patient. The committee welcomed the opportunity of working with him and met on a regular basis for more than two years. Two otologists were subsequently appointed to the committee. They both were connected with major medical training programs having large, well-staffed hearing and speech programs that had been approved by the Department of Health for many years.

The committee developed several drafts of a revised set of procedures that included audiological testing by an ASHA-certified audiologist, plus hearing therapy. In cases where the Medicaid patient was evaluated by other than an approved hearing and speech center (approved by the Department of Health), prior approval from the medical director of the Bureau of Health Care Services (Medicaid) was necessary. The suggestion was that the advisory committee would review such applications on a form it had developed and would submit its recommendations to the Medicaid director.

RECOMMENDATIONS BY AUDIOLOGISTS REJECTED

Months elapsed and the committee received no word from Medicaid about the disposition of the new set of directives. It did learn that the officers of Medicaid who had created the advisory committee were no longer with the program and that a new executive medical director had been appointed. The new director had been holding a series of meetings with hearing aid dealers and had asked them to develop a set of procedures and standards which they would find acceptable. Needless to say, their recommendations did not include audiological evaluation (by audiologists) of adult hard-of-hearing patients. During the time the new Medicaid official was meeting with the dealer group, Medicaid launched an investigation regarding over-recommendation of hearing aids by some dealers to Medicaid residents in nursing homes. Medicaid created a peer review committee of several hearing aid dealers to evaluate the charges and make appropriate recommendations. The peer review committee concluded from the deliberations that at least two dealers recommended hearing aids to large numbers of nursing home residents who were either unable to use them or so deteriorated physically and psychologically that the benefits from amplification could not be demonstrated. The peer review committee decided that these dealers must make restoration to Medicaid of $16,000 in the case of one dealer and $10,000 in the other for hearing aids issued to residents who could not benefit from them. During the course of these investigations, a separate set of hearing aid procedures applicable to the nursing home population was developed by the dealers.

The Medicaid Advisory Committee on Hearing and Speech was not consulted during the period when Medicaid's medical director was meeting with the hearing aid dealers. However, two audiologists on the committee assumed responsibility for attempting to determine what was happening to the committee's recommendations and suggested procedures. These audiologists were subsequently contacted by another audiologist who claimed that she was serving as Medicaid's intermediary between the audiologists and the dealers.

The "audiological mediator" stated that the main point of disagreement between the two groups was whether sound field testing with hearing aids was an essential part of the evaluation of the adult hard-of-hearing patient, and she asked the two audiologists on the committee to state an opinion. The two audiologists with whom she consulted informed her that this was not the critical question and that the dealers focused on this point because most of them, in contrast to audiologists, were not tooled up to perform such evaluation. Those two audiologists continued to insist upon a meeting with the Medicaid official, which was finally held.

The Medicaid official stated first that he was unable to obtain an audiological consultant to review the prior authorization forms. However, at least two audiologists on the committee had not been asked by his office to serve, and both would have been willing to perform this service gratis.

The official then summarized the dealer objections to the revised set of procedures, focusing again on the question of sound field testing and adding the additional argument that there were not enough audiologists to serve the population. The audiologists stated that (1) he was going over areas which had been exhaustively explored in meetings held with his predecessors, and (2) sound field testing was not the important issue. Rather, the question of the professional's role in the management of the hard-of-hearing patient was the critical consideration.

The two audiologists continued to stress the contribution of the audiologist to the management of the adult hard-of-hearing patient. They stated that audiologists working with the geriatric population tended to recommend fewer hearing aids than dealers, thus affording a significant saving to the funding agency. In addition, audiologists usually accompany a hearing aid recommendation with the necessary aural rehabilitation services, bringing the patient a more successful adjustment to and performance with amplification.

The official listened to this discussion but apparently had been persuaded by the dealers of their ability to manage almost all geriatric patients without the participation of an audiologist. He agreed with the dealers that audiological involvement in these recommendations resulted in the subordination of the dealer to a professional group and this was unfair to the established dealers in the community.

The two audiologists asked the official whether, if he had an aged hard-of-hearing relative or friend requiring a hearing aid, he would secure the services of an audiologist. He stated that he did not know but appreciated the question and promised to contact a number of otologists of his acquaintance regarding how they manage these problems. We asked him to communicate with knowledgeable otologists with experience and interest in the problems associated with sensorineural hearing impairment. The audiologists also agreed to submit publications from the Veterans Administration and the Department of Health, Education, and Welfare regarding how to go about purchasing a hearing aid.

No word was received until August 1972, when the audiologists were advised that the Medicaid official had reached his decision. He felt that he could not adjudicate the controversies, and he had decided to leave the decision with the otolaryngologists. If they wish to call upon the services of an audiologist in the management of patients, they could do so; otherwise, they could refer directly to a vendor as in the past. Appreciation was expressed for the time and effort spent by the advisory committee in developing the set of standards that had not been accepted.

LESSONS TO BE LEARNED: RECOMMENDATIONS TO AUDIOLOGISTS

It is difficult to draw any conclusions from the long and unhappy tale recited above. However, certain warning notes might be directed at members finding themselves in comparable situations.

1. The hearing aid dealer group is generally well organized, well funded, strongly motivated, and speaks with one voice to official government agencies. The dealers recognize that their livelihood is involved in these issues and they will organize well-financed public relations efforts to bring their side of the story to the professional and the public. Audiologists are not as well organized or funded. Furthermore, the entire question of hearing aid recommendations and services affects a minority of members of the speech and hearing profession, and many of the majority are unwilling to fund the efforts of their audiological colleagues.

2. Great disservice can be done by members of the audiological group who do not coordinate their efforts with other audiologists. For example, the audiologist who was contacted by Medicaid to serve as an intermediary should not have agreed to serve in this capacity unless her efforts were coordinated with the entire Medicaid Advisory Committee. Furthermore, she fell into the trap of focusing on the question of whether sound field hearing aid evaluations were a necessary part of the process of selecting and recommending a hearing aid. The dealers tend, at least in this part of the country, to control the actions and public statements of members of their group much more effectively than we, presenting themselves to the government agency as a cohesive, well-functioning group.

3. The ties between hearing aid dealers and some otologists are quite close, going back over many years. Audiological involvement is viewed by some members of these groups as a threat to the long-established functioning patterns of patient care, which many feel serve the public well. Dealers are capable of summoning otological support at all stages of the negotiations and, in turn, support the predominant role of the physician in the management of these patients. Within this context, the arguments of audiologists often appear to be self-serving and discipline-oriented rather than patient-oriented.

4. Medicaid services are oriented to supporting and reproducing the level and type of patient handling characteristic of the majority of field practitioners. Strong audiological services tend to be, at least in this part of the country, associated with large medical training institutions and not with proprietary or small voluntary hospitals. Therefore, the argument is raised whether Medicaid should support a type of service which the private patient of the field practitioner often does not get. In other words, audiologists are seen as arguing for the highly specialized, expensive service characteristic of the medical school and large voluntary teaching hospital and not that of the practitioner in private practice. Medicaid sees itself not in the role of trend setter or upgrader of medical care but, rather, of making available to the Medicaid-eligible patient the average level of service provided in the community. The failure of the audiologist to be licensed becomes a major obstacle to his recognition as a provider of services and in the establishment of a fee schedule. Other things being equal, the audiologist who fights these battles in a state which licenses audiologists and speech pathologists will have a greater chance of success.

5. When speaking to government representatives about audiological services, it is advisable to specify "performed by a qualified audiologist." Dealers consider themselves qualified to perform "audiological evaluations."

The following is a definition of a "qualified audiologist":

(1) Holds a valid Certificate of Clinical Competence in Audiology from the American Speech and Hearing Association; or,

(2) Meets equivalent academic, practicum, and work experience standards and successfully completes the National Examination in Audiology necessary for such certification; or,

(3) Where applicable, holds a valid license in the state.

6. Each group has its own militant, highly vocal extremists who tend, through overstating the case, to incur the wrath and hostility of the opposing group. If possible, the representatives chosen as spokesmen should be from the "mainstream" of the prevailing audiological point of view. They should be clinical practitioners involved at the time in rendering service to patients, rather than professors at universities having limited or no current exposure to clinical problems.

7. In statements to the press and in private and public meetings, it is well to avoid giving examples of how members of the other group "messed up" a particular patient or exploited him financially. When we refer to the dealer who extracted more than $800 from the blind, aged patient whose only problem was wax in the ears, we should remember that the other group can cite equally cogent examples of mishan-dling by members of our profession. Such arguments are counterproductive and serve only to incite hostility, aggravating the situation and encouraging an attitude of non-cooperation.

8. Finally, audiologists entering into this arena of negotiation should have a strong stomach and a tough skin. They are bound to encounter repeated frustration and difficulty at every point. The amorphous status of our profession in the eyes of the professional and lay community will become evident to them at every stage. The clearer public image of the dealer and the ease with which his role can be defined place the audiologist at a disadvantage. Finally, the cooperation and recognition an audiologist enjoys with professional colleagues at his own institution may not be present as he negotiates with other practitioners in the field. What is obvious to the audiologist may be difficult to establish when confronting the unsympathetic ears of other groups.

7. A Model System for Dental Care Delivery

STEPHEN C. SCHWARTZ and LUCILLE FALLON

Reprinted with permission. APHA paper, October 31, 1977.

INTRODUCTION

In the Fall of 1975, the Health Insurance Plan of Greater New York (HIP), a prepaid health plan having contractual relationships with 26 medical groups in New York City was approached by the City of New York regarding the possibility of providing an expanded program of health care benefits to a portion of the City's A.D.C. (Aid to Dependent Children) Medicaid population. The anticipated enrollment was to be approximately 100,000 persons, roughly 70 percent (under 21 years), and 30 percent adults. Care was to be provided in the five boroughs of New York. Among the services to be provided was a dental component:

Dental care under Medicaid requires the following:

1. oral prophylaxis, including education on plaque control and oral disease
2. x-rays, appropriate to the age of the enrollee
3. an annual oral exam based on clinical exam and x-rays together with a second prophylaxis, when necessary
4. sodium fluoride applied topically for children who have not lived continuously in a fluoridated area
5. treatment as authorized
6. dental care as delineated in the federal Early and Periodic Screening Diagnosis and Treatment (EPSDT) program:
   a. soft tissue inspections
   b. oral hygiene—cleanliness of oral cavity and adequacy of tooth brushing technique
   c. inspection of the teeth; noting abnormalities of morphology and eruption patterns, obvious gross or early decay, malignant and discoloration

OBJECTIVES

Because HIP does not provide dental care as one of its benefits, a subcontractual arrangement had to be developed to provide the care. Our objectives in planning the system of dental care delivery were as follows:

1. cost containment through the development of a payment agreement on a capitated basis
2. quality assurance
3. emphasis on preventive care
4. utilization of providers located within easy access for enrollees because of the comprehensive family (one-stop) approach HIP attempts to deliver to its enrollment in addition to the requirement under Medicaid mandating

transportation reimbursement for recipients

5. development of a useful model which could be applied to a variety of populations.

METHODS

Investigation of Potential Providers

Our basic approach was to seek to utilize existing facilities and providers in order to avoid the cost and man-hours involved in duplicating a system which was already in place. We looked at several methods of providing the care:

Hospital Dental Clinics

We identified 51 hospital dental clinics in the five boroughs—Manhattan, Bronx, Brooklyn, Queens and Richmond. After investigation, however, this option was considered not feasible because of the high costs associated with hospitals and because of the difficulty involved in effectively controlling the number of referrals. In addition, because of the volume of patients involved, treatment in the clinics is primarily episodic.

Contracting with Other Insurance Companies

We explored the possibility of contracting with another insurance company which presently has a relationship with dental providers. However, such an arrangement would have required payment not only for services but of an administrative fee as well making this plan unacceptable.

Independent Dental Providers

In the New York City area there are many large dental providers which employ dentists and have centralized offices located throughout the Metropolitan area. While this option initially seemed to be the most attractive due to its composition and its readily adaptable conformity to the HIP

capitation and delivery system, it was decided that the total adoption of this approach would most likely hinder marketing by adding an additional treatment site which the patient must utilize while also increasing transportation expenses.

HIP-Affiliated Dentists

After surveying HIP medical group facilities, it was found that a majority of groups had, located on their premises, dentists who could conceivably be used to provide the major portion of the required care. These dentists were in actuality tenants within HIP medical group centers. A closer examination of this situation revealed that 67 percent of the present HIP-Medicaid ADC population utilized medical groups that either presently have or in the past have had a tenant affiliation with a practicing dentist.

After much consideration and deliberation with the affiliated medical groups, HIP chose to create its own dental delivery system. The major component of this system is the HIP-affiliated dentist who will provide the required dental care in locations centered at our affiliated medical groups.

THE SYSTEM

Costs

A capitation rate of $40.46 for adults and $19.24 for children ($25.50 composite) was negotiated with the dental providers, closely paralleling the amount designated in HIP's premium submission to the City for estimated dental care costs. HIP is receiving premiums for $44.43 for adults, and $21.12 for children ($28.00 composite) from New York City. The difference of $2.50 or 8 percent (composite) represents the required amount for the HIP administration of this program. For specialty care (orthodontic, endodontic, oral surgery, etc.), a special services fund was established by retaining a small portion of the capitation. HIP administers and monitors this special services fund.

Quality Assurance

A peer review and quality assurance system was already in place in the existing Medicaid program which will be utilized in the HIP Program. This system employs as one component pre and post-operative radiographs to insure the integrity of the dental treatment provided. In addition, HIP has made arrangements to employ their own dentists to monitor the overall quality assurance program. It is these dentists' responsibility to review charts, pre and post-operative radiographs, conduct routine inspection of dental facilities and to recall random patients to conduct dental examinations of services previously provided. In addition, the contract will mandate that all credentials of participating dental providers be submitted to both HIP and city and state departments of social services for approval. Any dentist who had been previously disqualified from participation in the general Medicaid program will not be eligible to participate in the HIP-Medicaid program.

Preventive Care

The most effective form of assuring preventive dental care as well as limiting over-utilization is the capitation payment system itself. Participating dentists, whether salaried or not, have little incentive to over utilize services and, therefore, aggressive preventive measures, particularly with children, can be employed.

Both HIP and the participating dentists agreed that a strong emphasis is to be placed on the formulation of a program for preventive dentistry. It was felt that such a program is necessary in order to educate and motivate patients toward better oral health. Dental assistants and dental hygienists will, at the direction of the dental practitioner, provide instruction in such areas as plaque control, toothbrushing and flossing techniques, timely application of fluorides, home-care instruction, and will disseminate literature to promote this concept.

Accessibility of Facilities

As stated previously, one of HIP's major objectives in developing a dental delivery system was to utilize providers located within easy access for enrollees. HIP is responsible for reimbursing Medicaid enrollees for transportation expenses. Therefore, the availability of multiple facilities in each borough would be desirable to decrease transportation costs. At the same time, however, HIP views dental care as a single component within a total health care delivery system. HIP firmly believes that full service medical centers offer the optimum type of care available to its enrollment. Therefore, it was felt that the utilization of HIP-affiliated dentists having their offices located at the group health centers represented the most efficient method of providing care while at the same time maintaining HIP's tradition of one-stop health care. In addition to easy accessibility, having dental services available at the group centers provides a continuity of total health care: the patients' records travel with him while physicians, dentists and allied health personnel are able to interact, discuss and evaluate the total health needs of the enrollee. Moreover, the use of multiple dental providers in the five boroughs allows for cost containment because of savings in patient transportation reimbursements.

A Replicable Model

It is our belief that the system developed by HIP is both flexible and easily adaptable to either multicentered prepaid health plans such as our own or to single site plans. The delivery system is a simple one which stresses the delivery of preventive dental care. At the same time, dentistry is also viewed as one of many components involved in the overall health care of the individual. Therefore, all attempts have been made to incorporate it into a larger, more all-inclusive delivery system.

8. Drug Prescription Rates Before and After Enrollment of a Medicaid Population in an HMO

DAVID L. RABIN, PATRICIA J. BUSH, and NORMAN A. FULLER

Reprinted from *Public Health Reports*, Vol. 93, No. 1, January-February 1978

As health care costs continue to mount and as more of these costs are borne by the public sector, there are increasing pressures to contain costs and to assure that dollars are well spent in terms of quality and equity. Prepayment through enrollment in health maintenance organizations (HMOs) has been found to reduce costs most notably through reduced hospitalization (1-5). The effect on quality of care is less certain. With respect to equity, however, there is evidence that enrollment of low-income families in HMOs will raise their levels of use of physician visits and hospital days at least to those of other enrollees (6,7).

Because prescription drugs are neither the major component nor an increasing proportion of health care costs, they have not received as much attention as have other components. However, national rates of medicine use are steadily increasing (8) with the consequences of increasing not only costs but the risks of drug interactions and adverse reactions.

Because medicines are prescribed at more than 50 percent of the visits of ambulatory patients, according to the National Ambulatory Medical Care Survey (9), the effects of HMO enrollment on number of visits to physicians may also be reflected in the use of prescribed medicines. Moreover, HMO physicians may prescribe differently than others. For example, certain therapeutic categories of drugs such as antiobiotics (10) and tranquilizers (11,12) that are considered to be prescribed excessively for the population may be used more conservatively by HMO physicians. Thus HMO enrollment may decrease rates of prescribed medicine use and the associated costs by increasing the quality of prescribing.

In 1971, the District of Columbia enrolled 1,000 Medicaid beneficiaries in a prepaid group practice, Group Health Association, Inc. (GHA) of Washington, D.C. GHA, one of the oldest prepaid plans in the United States, is cooperatively owned by its 80,000 subscriber population. The terms of the contract for this project provided for a broad range of health services that were evaluated over a 3-year period (1971–74), pre- and post-enrollment. In this project, medicine use for the enrollees was evaluated and compared with that for the entire

The project was supported by grant No. 97–P–00034 and contract No. SRS–74–14 from the Social and Rehabilitation Service and by grant No. 1–R21 HS 01722–01 from the National Center for Health Services Research, Department of Health, Education, and Welfare.

universe of the 160,000 Medicaid beneficiaries in the District of Columbia. Specifically investigated were (a) rates of drug prescriptions and physician visits, (b) prescriptions by specific drugs and by therapeutic category, (c) per capita costs of prescription drugs, and (d) quality of drug prescribing.

METHODS

In early 1971, approximately 4,000 letters were sent to heads of Medicaid households living in the service area of a GHA outpatient clinic. The letter announced this program of the D.C. Medicaid Agency and invited recipients to enroll. In addition to the continued availability of the full range of title XIX benefits, two special benefits—waiver of eligibility redetermination for the 3 years of the project and free dental care—were offered as inducements to volunteer for the project.

The D.C. Medicaid population consists of those on public assistance (PA) and those who are medically indigent and classified as nonpublic assistance (NPA). Enrollment in GHA required exchange of the Medicaid card, which beneficiaries used to purchase medical services from any health care provider participating in Medicaid, for the GHA card, which entitled participants to obtain services only from the four clinics run by GHA. Those who volunteered for the project were permitted to revert to regular Medicaid status if they so desired at any time during the study. The voluntary termination rate was less than 3 percent for the entire 22-month study period. These terminations, and the involuntary terminations caused by death, change of residence, or incarceration reduced the GHA study group from 1,000 to 934 persons.

Data on newborns' use of health services were incomplete because of the administrative lag in issuing Medicaid cards, and Medicaid data on use of health services by persons over 65 years were unavailable.

Therefore, children under 1 year old and persons over 65 years old were excluded, reducing the Medicaid control group to 142,268 and the study group to 834. The study group consisted of 781 persons in the Aid to Families with Dependent Children Program (AFDC) of whom 257 were NPA, and 53 persons in the Aid to the Permanently and Totally Disabled Program (APTD) of whom 4 were NPA.

The project was designed to compare the study group's use of health services before and after enrollment in GHA and with the use of health services by a control group, the D.C. Medicaid population for the ages corresponding to the study group. In such an experiment, randomization into study and control groups would guard against selection bias. However, in this instance the GHA study group volunteered from a randomly selected population.

A comparison of the GHA and the control populations by age, sex, public aid program category, and eligibility for public assistance revealed that the 834-person study group had an age-sex distribution similar to the control group, consisting mostly of women and children with virtually no men between 22 and 64 years. In both groups, 61 percent were females. There was no significant difference by program category but, by eligibility, the study group had fewer medically indigent enrollees (31 percent were NPA) as compared to 41 percent in the control group. Since per capita expenditure of an NPA recipient was more than twice that of a PA recipient in 1972, the study group, consisting of fewer medically indigent persons, was expected to have somewhat lower rates of health services use than the Medicaid control population.

Changes in rates of use of health services by a Medicaid population enrolled in a prepaid health plan must be assessed over time. When any group changes health care providers, new conditions may be diagnosed which lead to transient increases in the use of services.

Accordingly, the study group's use of health services and medicines was observed at 6 intervals at 12, 18, and 22 months, 3 before and 3 after enrollment in GHA on July 1, 1971; data were annualized for each period. The Medicaid control group was observed during fiscal year 1972. Use data were not calculated for the control group for fiscal year 1971 because the District of Columbia Master Eligibility File maintains reliable data only for the most recent 2 years. Therefore, it was not possible to calculate the annualized population at risk. However, use data per recipient (not per annualized person at risk) for the control group showed an increase in their rates of use of physician visits and prescription drugs from fiscal years 1970 to 1972.

Data on use of health services were obtained in the following ways. For the Medicaid control group and the pre-GHA Medicaid study group, all claims were transferred to magnetic tape on a daily basis in the sequence they were received. A computer checked them for eligibility and computed the amount to be paid. Physicians' claims identified the patient, the provider physician by specialty or institution, the service performed, and the date of the service. Pharmacy claims identified the patient, the pharmacy, and the name and quantity of the drug. Because the claims file was maintained by date of payment rather than date of service, some services rendered in fiscal year 1971 were counted in fiscal year 1972 and so on. The D.C. Master Eligibility File determined the denominator (annualized population at risk) for the rates of use for the control group for fiscal year 1972.

For the study group, each service rendered was reported on a punched card which provided the information for the three periods after enrollment. Cost data were obtained from GHA annual membership reports and from data provided the D.C. Government prior to renewal of each year's contract.

The D.C. Medicaid formulary listed 2,772 drug items. These were collapsed to 1,541 drug names by combining those with the same brand name but of different strength or form. Removal of nonlegend (over-the-counter) drugs from the formulary left 1,197 brand or generic name prescription drugs that were entered into the study. These were categorized into 90 therapeutic categories as derived from "AMA Drug Evaluation" (13).

RESULTS

Comparisons of the study and control groups are reported in five areas: (a) rates of use of prescription drugs by age and eligibility status, (b) physician visit rates, (c) costs of drugs, (d) rates of use of prescription drugs by therapeutic category and by specific drug, and (e) prescribing quality.

As shown in the chart, both the average number of prescribed drugs and physician visits were reduced for the AFDC recipients in the GHA study group in the 12 months after, as compared to the 12 months before, enrollment. Further, the study group's rates of use of these services were less after enrollment as compared to the rates of the Medicaid control group. Because it was known that the rate of use of services per user and costs increased in the control group from fiscal years 1970 to 1972, one can infer from the chart that those who volunteered for the study group were higher than average users of services since their fiscal year 1971 prestudy use rates were much higher than the fiscal year 1972 use rates of the controls.

Table 1 shows that, 22 months after enrollment in GHA, the average annualized prescription use rate was 18 percent less (2.4 prescriptions per enrollee per year) than before enrollment (2.9 prescriptions per enrollee per year). The t-value differences between before and after periods were -5.88 at 12 months, -6.33 at 18

Average number of prescriptions obtained and physician visits by AFDC recipients aged 1–64 years 12 months before and after enrollment in GHA and by Medicaid control group

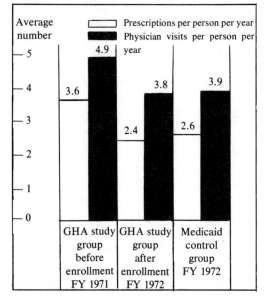

months, and −3.09 at 24 months. (Values less than −1.96 are required for significance at the .05 level.) Rates were less at 12 months after than before enrollment among all age groups except for the 7 persons aged 55–64 years, and the difference persisted over the 22 months of observation. The most marked reductions were in the two age groups 20–34 years; their rates were nearly halved. Note that while the average rate of use for the 781 AFDC recipients increased from 2.9 at 22 months to 3.6 at 12 months before enrollment, they were stabilized after enrollment (2.4 at 12 and also at 22 months). By 12 months after enrollment, rates of use of GHA enrollees were 9 percent less than the Medicaid controls—2.4 prescriptions per GHA enrollee compared to 2.6 in the control group.

For the 53 disabled persons (APTD), the pattern of use was similar, with increasing rates in the observed pre-enrollment periods and relatively stable post-enrollment rates. However, the t-values of differences in the rates of use in the comparable pre- and post-enrollment time periods were not significant at the .05 level. In all periods, disabled persons in the study group had higher rates of prescription use than disabled persons in the control group.

Comparing the average number of prescriptions dispensed to the study group and to the controls in fiscal year 1972 by eligibility category (NPA and PA) reveals that, as expected, the medically indigent had higher rates of use in both groups (and also among both males and females) than those on public assistance. The average NPA rate of use was lower for the study group (3.9) than for the controls (4.9), particularly for females (4.7 and 6.2 respectively). The average use rates for PAs were identical (2.8) and varied little by sex between the study and control groups.

Because prescriptions derive from physician visits, lower rates for ambulatory physician visits in the study group after enrollment than in the control group may account for the difference in the rates of prescribed medicines. Table 2 shows the average annualized rates of physician visits for the study group 22 months before and after entering into GHA and for the controls for fiscal year 1972. All encounters of ambulatory patients with GHA physicians were counted as physician visits. For persons aged 1–64 years, annual rates for physician encounters were steadily and significantly reduced ($P<.05$ using a two-tail t-test) at 12, 18, and 22 months after enrollment in GHA. Rates were reduced 15 percent (4.2 to 3.5 visits) between the 22-month period before enrollment compared to the 22 months afterward. Five of the nine age groups showed a decrease; the most marked decreases were in age groups 20–44 years. Visit rates for the disabled showed little change over the study period.

A comparison of the study group and the control population for the same period, fiscal year 1972, shows that the Medicaid control group had somewhat higher (3.9) rates of encounters than did the study group (3.8) at 12 months after enrollment (table 2). However, there are some notable dis-

Table 1. Annualized rates of prescription use per enrollee for the study group at 12, 18, and 22 months before and after enrollment and FY 1972 rates for the Medicaid control group, by age group

Age group (years)	Number of persons	Study group before enrollment			Study group after enrollment			Control group	
		22 months	18 months	12 months	12 months	18 months	22 months	FY 1972	Number of population [1] at risk
1–4	123	1.7	2.0	2.2	1.6	1.2	1.1	2.2	23,716
5–9	157	1.1	1.0	1.1	0.8	0.7	0.8	0.9	27,987
10–14	160	0.9	1.0	1.0	0.9	0.9	1.0	0.7	24,471
15–19	135	1.8	2.1	2.3	2.2	2.2	2.2	2.0	20.411
20–24	46	5.8	7.3	7.8	3.7	3.7	4.1	5.7	11,110
25–34	65	7.9	9.6	9.9	4.8	4.4	4.7	6.0	11,741
35–44	57	7.6	8.8	9.0	6.2	5.9	6.1	5.7	6,802
45–54	31	8.9	10.8	11.3	8.1	7.4	9.1	7.6	3,335
55–64	7	4.4	5.1	0.9	6.6	5.5	7.0	9.0	1,240
Subtotal 1–64 years	781	2.9	3.4	3.6	2.4	2.2	2.4	2.6	130,813
Disabled	53	10.1	12.3	12.7	12.6	11.2	12.5	7.0	11,455

[1] Number of person years.

parities by age and disabled groups. In the control population, visit rates were higher for persons 20–34 years and lower for persons 35–64 years and for the disabled than in the study group.

Prescription use rates (table 1) dropped 18 percent compared to the 15 percent drop in physician visit rates (table 2) for the 22 months before and after joining GHA. A Pearson product-moment correlation (r^2) between prescribed medicine use rates and physician visit rates using the 12-month study periods, by age groups, was 0.92. This is a high and significant correlation, a perfect correlation being ±1. Thus, the decrease in physician visit rates appears to account for most of the decrease in prescribed medicine use for the enrollees over the study period. The most marked decreases in both prescribed medicine use and physician visit rates were in the same age groups, 20–34 years, which were 95 percent female.

Furthermore, the average number of prescriptions per physician visit decreased from 0.74 at 12 months before enrollment to 0.63 at 12 months after enrollment. The Medicaid controls averaged 0.68 prescriptions per visit during fiscal year 1972.

The decrease in prescription rates was reflected in considerable cost savings for drugs. Total cost for benefits per annualized person at risk per year for comparable benefits in the GHA study group in fiscal year 1972 was $282, of which 5.5 percent was attributable to drugs as compared to $373, of which 7.0 percent was attributable to drugs in the Medicaid control group. The 18 percent difference in the average number of prescriptions per person meant a 41 percent drug cost saving for those enrolled in GHA as compared to the control group. Drug costs per person in fiscal year 1972 for the GHA study group were $15.51, compared to $26.11 for the controls. Part of this difference may be accounted for by a greater propensity for GHA physicians to prescribe nonlegend drugs which are usually cheaper than legend drugs. Of all drugs

prescribed, 20.2 percent were nonlegend medications in the GHA study group compared to 17.2 percent in the Medicaid controls.

Factors in addition to the prescribing rates may have had an effect in lowering costs. These include differences in the tendency to prescribe cheaper brand-name drugs, differences in the average quantity of drugs per prescription, differences in prescribing patterns, and differences in the proportion of drugs that were generically prescribed. (In general a drug prescribed generically is cheaper than a drug prescribed by brand name.) No information was available on the quantities of drugs prescribed per prescription, but comparisons were made by therapeutic category, individual drugs, and the proportion of generic drugs prescribed.

In table 3 the GHA study group and the D.C. Medicaid controls are compared by therapeutic category of prescription drugs. The data are combined for all ages and both sexes and for public assistance (PA) and nonpublic assistance (NPA). The top 30 categories accounted for more than 90 percent of medicines for both the study and the control groups. Eight of the top 10 categories in table 3 are the same, but expectorants and antidiabetic agents were prescribed more frequently for the GHA study group and adrenal-corticosteroids and broncho-dilators were prescribed more frequently for the control population. The top three categories are identical: diuretics, mild analgesics, and antianxiety agents. The top 10 categories account for more than half of drugs prescribed for both the GHA and the control populations.

While the rank ordering of drugs for patients by frequency of categories was very similar for the two groups, the rates were different. Rates of drugs dispensed per 1,000 persons by therapeutic category were consistently higher for the controls; for example, the rate of diuretics was 287 among the control population and 257 among the GHA study group per 1,000 per-

Table 2. Annualized rates of physician encounters [1] per enrollee for the study group at 12, 18, and 22 months before and after enrollment and FY 1972 rates for the Medicaid control group, by age group

Age group (years)	Number of persons	Study group before enrollment			Study group after enrollment			Control group	
		22 months	18 months	12 months	12 months	18 months	22 months	FY 1972	Number of population [2] at risk
1–4	123	2.4	2.7	2.7	3.3	2.8	2.8	3.0	23,716
5–9	157	1.7	1.8	1.6	1.8	1.7	1.6	1.9	27,987
10–14	160	2.2	2.4	2.4	1.8	1.9	1.8	1.7	24,471
15–19	135	2.8	3.4	3.6	3.8	3.6	3.5	3.7	20,411
20–24	46	9.3	11.2	12.0	4.6	4.3	4.5	8.1	11,110
25–34	65	10.2	12.2	12.0	6.4	5.9	5.7	8.3	11,741
35–44	57	10.1	10.7	11.1	8.5	8.6	8.6	7.2	6,802
45–54	31	8.1	10.1	10.3	10.5	10.1	9.6	7.6	3,335
55–64	7	6.0	6.4	6.7	7.7	7.5	7.2	6.5	1,240
Subtotal 1–64 years	781	4.2	5.0	4.9	3.8	3.6	3.5	3.9	130,813
Disabled	53	10.2	11.8	11.3	11.1	10.3	10.1	6.3	11,455

[1] Includes ambulatory patient encounters for mental and physical conditions at home, office, outpatient department, and emergency room.   [2] Number of person years.

sons. Differences persist for the less commonly prescribed drugs among the 10 categories; for example, penicillins were dispensed at the rate of 232 per 1,000 persons for the controls and 152 per 1,000 persons for the study group.

In comparing specific drugs, one would expect much more variation since there are 1,197 specific drugs as compared to 90 categories. GHA physicians may favor a narrower spectrum of brand or generic named drugs in contrast to the more numerous and dispersed physicians giving care to the Medicaid controls. Of the top 10 specific drugs, 6 were the same in both groups. As predicted, a narrower prescribing spectrum was found for GHA physicians, but the difference was not great; 125 drugs accounted for more than 90 percent of drugs prescribed compared to 147 drugs for the control population.

To compare national rates with the rates of use of categories of prescribed drugs for both the study and control groups, some drug categories were collapsed to be consistent with available national data. Rates of use of antibiotics and hormones were lower in the GHA study group while the controls' rates were almost identical with national rates. The study and control groups used cardiovascular (including antihypertensive) and diuretic medicines at similar rates. These rates were higher than national use rates but were consistent with the greater rates of hypertension among the population of the District of Columbia compared with national rates for this condition. Rates for ataraxics, analgesics, and antispasmodics were similar among the three groups. Sedative-hypnotics and vitamins were prescribed at similar rates for study and control groups, but both were lower than national rates.

Despite considerable differences in the age, sex, and race distribution of the D.C. Medicaid population and the U.S. population, the comparison of prescribing suggests that the GHA and control group prescribers differed little from each other and from national prescribers.

It is difficult to assess prescribing quality in the absence of diagnostic information. The reduction in prescribing rates after enrollment in GHA indicates that prepaid group health plans may reduce drug use among their members. Since it is generally felt that prescribing rates are high and costs and risks of medicine use are considerable, lowered rates of use can be considered desirable. Two more direct indicators of quality of prescribing are the proportion of generic drugs prescribed, reflecting cost consciousness, and the proportion of "irrational" drugs prescribed among the study and control groups.

With few exceptions, there is little evidence that brand name drugs are more efficacious than their generic equivalents, although generically prescribed drugs are usually less expensive. If the rates that generic drugs were prescribed are used as a measure of cost consciousness, the study and control groups differed little. Ten percent of the study group's prescriptions were generic compared with 8 percent of the control group's when the 50 most frequently prescribed drugs for each group were examined.

According to "AMA Drug Evaluations" (13) certain drugs are "irrational" in that they are inappropriate mixtures or they are not recommended for the purposes for which they are prescribed. Of the 50 most frequently prescribed drugs, 11 (22 percent) fell into this category for the GHA study group as compared to 9 (18 percent) for the control population.

Thus, although there was a decrease in rates and costs in the GHA study as compared to the control group, there is no indication that the study group received better quality of prescribing by the yardsticks of generic and irrational drug prescribing rates.

A decrease in rates of use, with resultant savings from enrolling a Medicaid population in a prepaid group plan, is not in itself

Table 3. Cumulative percentage and number of prescription drugs per 1,000 persons per year dispensed to study and control groups in FY 1972, by therapeutic category

Rank	Study group			D.C. Medicaid control group		
	Therapeutic category [1]	Cumulative percent	Number per 1,000 persons per year	Therapeutic category [2]	Cumulative percent	Number per 1,000 persons per year
1	Diuretics	8.3	257	Diuretics	8.3	287
2	Mild analgesics	15.9	236	Mild analgesics	15.6	251
3	Antianxiety agents ...	23.5	235	Antianxiety agents ...	22.8	249
4	Antihypertensives	28.7	162	Penicillins	29.5	232
5	Estrogens, progesterones, and oral contraceptives	33.8	159	Antihistamines	35.7	215
6	Expectorants and inhalants ..	38.8	153	Estrogens, progesterones, and oral contraceptives	41.5	199
7	Penicillins	43.7	152	Antihypertensives	45.8	148
8	Antihistamines	48.0	132	Tetracyclines	49.8	138
9	Tetracyclines	51.8	118	Adrenal corticosteroids	53.6	129
10	Antidiabetics	55.6	117	Broncho-dilators	57.2	122

[1] 30 categories account for 90 percent of study group's prescriptions.
[2] 31 categories account for 90 percent of control group's prescriptions.

Note: 8 of 10 categories are the same for the study and the control groups.

justification for doing so if patients are not satisfied with the services. Therefore, the reasons persons terminated from the plan during the study period were investigated. The annual termination rate was 7 percent, but only 2.5 percent (62 persons in 22 families) dropped out because of dissatisfaction with convenience, accessibility, or some aspect of the delivery of services. The few voluntary terminations for dissatisfaction indicated a general acceptance and satisfaction with GHA services (14).

DISCUSSION

Results in this study indicate that enrollment of a Medicaid population in a prepaid health plan may decrease rates of use of prescribed drugs and costs without an apparent diminution in quality and with high enrollee satisfaction. Rates of medicine use dropped significantly and stabilized for the enrolled study group compared with their former use and with the nonenrolled Medicaid controls. However, the GHA study group was expected to have lower rates of use of services because of the smaller proportion of medically indigent persons (NPAs) as compared to the Medicaid controls. The decrease in rates of medicine use by the study group was limited to the NPAs and was greatest for women aged 20–34.

The decrease in the average number of prescriptions per visit, associated with the decrease in the average number of physician visits, was greatest among women 20–34 years. A drop in the number of pregnancies may have been responsible. Hospital admissions of obstetric patients decreased from 47 during the 12 pre-enrollment months to 27 for the 12 post-enrollment months.

Although the overall volume of prescriptions decreased for the study group, the pattern of therapeutic categories of prescribed drugs differed little from that of the controls. There was more variation, however, in the individual drugs prescribed. The study group received a somewhat narrower spectrum of drugs, as would be expected from a group of physicians sharing a similar work environment, and an in-house pharmacy. The pattern of prescribing for both study and control groups by drug categories was also quite similar to national patterns despite considerable differences in age-sex distributions of the populations. Thus, decreases in costs for the study group after enrollment are largely attributable to volume, rather than drug category, and to an apparently greater cost consciousness by GHA prescribers.

The similarity in prescribing patterns but the difference in volume is borne out by the similar proportions of drugs generically and irrationally prescribed. Without diagnostic information, prescribing quality cannot be precisely assessed. However, more generic prescribing of drugs and less of irrational mixtures would indicate better prescribing quality. GHA physicians did not significantly differ from the control group's prescribers in these measures of quality. However, in the absence of evidence for an increase in prescribing quality, it remains desirable to decrease rates of use and costs.

Results suggest that strategies that reduce ambulatory physician visit rates are likely to reduce medicine use as well. These strategies are likely to be more successful in prepaid group practice HMOs than in medical foundations; prepaid prescription plans alone may increase prescribed medicine use (15). Prepaid group practice HMOs, more than other forms of practice, have incentives to keep their enrolled populations both well and satisfied while controlling costs. This study supports the hypothesis that enrolling a Medicaid group in such a plan reduces prescribing costs. Not only are savings observed from the decrease in costs of prescribed medicine but there are uncounted savings in decreasing risks of drug interactions and adverse drug reactions. Although this study does not show better prescribing quality through enrollment in a prepaid group plan, the lower rate of prescribing per patient per visit was beneficial if outcomes were not compromised. There are no direct measurements of outcome, but inferences derived from measures of disenrollment suggest that satisfaction with services was favorable.

Experiments such as the institution of drug utilization review and the implementation of drug therapy protocols are currently underway in several prepaid group plans. These efforts are more readily undertaken in prepaid group practices than among other health care providers because common data systems provide an opportunity to review and assess the quality and costs of care. If widely instituted, such programs may increase prescribing quality and decrease costs. Meanwhile, this study suggests that the decrease in medicine use rates and in other services with no decrease in patient satisfaction may justify enrolling welfare groups in prepaid group plans.

REFERENCES

1. Densen, P.M., Shapiro, S., Jones, E.W., and Baldinger, I.: Prepaid medical care and hospital utilization. Hospitals 36: 63–68 (1962).

2. Donabedian, A.: An evaluation of pre-paid group practice. Inquiry 6: 3–27 (1969).

3. Shapiro, S.: Role of hospitals in the changing health insurance plan of greater New York. Bull New York Acad Med 74: 374–381 (1971).

4. Social Security Administration: Medicare experience with prepaid group enrollees. Office of Research and Statistics, Washington, D.C., 1971.

5. Roemer, M.I., and Shonick, W.: HMO performance: The recent evidence. Milbank Mem Fund Q 51: 271–319, summer 1973.

6. Greenlick, M.R., et al.: Comparing the use of medical services by medically indigent and a general membership population in a prepaid group practice program. Med Care 10: 187–200 (1972).

7. Sparer, G., and Anderson, A.: Utilization and cost experience of low income families in four prepaid group-practice plans. New Engl J Med 289: 67–72, July 12, 1973.

8. Rabin, D.L., and Bush, P.J.: The use of medicines: historical trends and international comparisons. Int J Health Serv 4: 61–87 (1974).

9. National Center for Health Statistics: National ambulatory medical care survey: 1973 summary, United States, May 1973–April 1974. Vital and Health Statistics Series 13, No. 21. U.S. Government Printing Office, Washington, D.C., 1975.

10. Simmons, H.E., and Stolley, P.D.: This is medical progress? Trends and consequences of antibiotic use in the United States. JAMA 227: 1023–1028, Mar. 4, 1974.

11. Mellinger, G.D., Balter, M.B., and Manheiner, D.I.: Patterns of psychotherapeutic drug use among adults in San Francisco. Arch Gen Psychiatry 25: 385–394 (1971).

12. Stolley, P.D., et al.: Drug prescribing and use in an American community. Ann Intern Med 76: 537–540 (1972).

13. AMA Council on Drugs: AMA drug evaluations. Publishing Science Group, Inc., Littletown, Mass., 1973.

14. Fuller, N.A., Patera, M.W., and Koziol, K.: Medicaid utilization of services in a prepaid group practice health plan. Med Care 15: 705–737 (1977).

15. Greenlick, M.R., and Darsky, B.J.: A comparison of general drug utilization in a metropolitan community with utilization under a drug prepayment plan. Am J Public Health 58: 2121–2136 (1968).

9. Study Finds EPSDT Program Growing in Effectiveness

JOHN C. MILLER

Reprinted from Health Care Financing Administration *Forum*, Vol. 1, No. 2, November-December 1977.

The program for assessing the health of children of low-income families and treating the problems found has had less than its share of good news since getting off to a slow start in 1969. Only in the last two years did activity markedly increase and nearly as many children were examined as in the previous five years.

But examination for health problems was one thing and their treatment quite another. State Medicaid agencies were unable to determine whether or not the problems found in examination were treated.

The lack of data on treatment was highlighted by a 1975 study, *Shortchanging Children*. This study, commissioned by the House Subcommittee on Oversight and Investigations, showed that less than one-sixth of the 12 million eligible children were being examined, and only 60.4 percent of the children needing treatment received it. It then concluded that the remaining children not examined were "at risk."

However, subsequent analyses by the Medicaid Bureau have shown that only about half of the children eligible for the program could be expected to be examined, considering the degree of program acceptance and the intervals states set between examinations. In addition, half of the children who were examined were found to be perfectly healthy, and the remaining half averaged about 1.5 problems per child. However, the relatively low treatment rate of 60 percent remained unchallenged until a recently-issued study* commissioned by the Medicaid Bureau revealed more encouraging figures.

It shows that 78 percent of the children who were examined in eight states and Puerto Rico received initial treatment for at least one problem, with 72 percent receiving treatment for all their problems. The report concludes: "To be considered a mature and fully effective national program, between 80 and 90 percent of children who are examined and found to need treatment should receive it. Medicaid's Early and Periodic Screening, Diagnosis and Treatment program is now rapidly approaching this range."

The study, performed by an organization with long experience with EPSDT, the Health Services Research Institute of The University of Texas, suggested why previous reports indicated that a significantly lower percentage of children were being treated.

---

*Reviews of Shows for Treatment EPSDT—a Nine-State Study.

One reason: the new study gathered data at the local level by actually tracking children from examination to treatment. The routine reports received by the Medicaid Bureau came from state Medicaid offices, and some data on treatment may have been lost in the reporting process. Indeed, the study often found a greater number of children were treated than reports from state Medicaid offices indicated. The House Subcommittee on Oversight and Investigations also gathered its information at the state level.

Another reason for variation was that the new study covered a more recent period than previous reports. As it matured, the program reached a higher level of effectiveness.

CHILDREN NOT TREATED

Of the children with problems who were not treated, slightly more than one-third either refused treatment, were no longer eligible because of a change in their family income, no longer appeared to have a problem or failed two or more times to keep appointments for treatment. Another six percent were on the waiting list to receive treatment when the study was made.

But what of the rest of the children who were not treated? Many times, the information necessary to determine if these children received treatment was lacking, even though there were five separate records that should have showed whether or not a child was treated. In these cases, either the name of the professional to whom they were referred was not listed or the address or telephone number of the childrens' parents was missing.

Typically, records showed: "No record of child," "No record of Medicaid number," or "Files incomplete."

A major segment (27 percent) of children who were not treated missed appointments or refused treatment. Since it is "often times necessary to convince a parent or guardian that a seemingly well child needs to go to the doctor, the probability of achieving a 100 percent participation in the program . . . . is exceedingly remote, if not outside the realm of possibility," the study points out.

Of the four categories of problems identified, significantly fewer children were treated for dental problems. The study found this was due to low rates of reimbursement for dentists. Indeed, it points out that the lack of dentists accepting referrals was a frequent concern of local EPSDT program workers.

Another reason for a low dental-treatment rate was probably that parents did not recognize the value of preventive medicine. Of the children who refused treatment, nearly half refused dental treatment.

In an effort to improve the rate of treatment, a requirement for a better information system was written into penalty regulations and reporting requirements published in September. The requirement would become effective January 1979.

CASE MONITORING A FACTOR

Another factor that appeared to affect the states' rate of performance was case monitoring—the system for notification of eligibility and following a child from examination through treatment until eligibility ceases. The rate of treatment was significantly higher in those states which recognized case monitoring as a specific function of the EPSDT program and assigned that task to a single state agency.

But where the responsibility for case monitoring was assigned to the provider of treatment or to an agency not responsible for the entire program, or where case monitoring was not clearly identified as a separate and highly desirable task within the program, the state's performance tended to be low. This was the case with each of four states that had the lowest treatment performances.

Money spent for case monitoring varied considerably among states. Generally, the more allocated to this function, the better the overall performance. Expenditures ranged from just pennies per child examined to an estimated $10 to $15 per child.

The Medicaid Bureau is developing a model system for tracking children from the time they are first informed of their eligibility for the program, through examination, and until the problem is resolved.

STATE PERFORMANCE VARIES

The 78 percent treatment factor was an average performance for the eight states—California, Georgia, Iowa, Michigan, Ohio, Pennsylvania, Tennessee and Texas—and Puerto Rico. However, the range of performance was extremely wide—from 87 percent in Pennsylvania to 55 percent in Tennessee. Interestingly, Pennsylvania had the lowest number of undocumentable cases and Tennessee had the most.

These ratings do not, however, indicate the effectiveness of each state's program, because the costs of the programs were not considered. A number of factors, aside from sufficient resources to do the job, were cited as possibly influencing a state's performance. These include:

- Whether the EPSDT program was operated by a state agency or contracted to a private organization.
- Socio-economic variations among the states.
- Environmental conditions, including factors such as the amount of fluorides in drinking water.
- Cultural norms.

Generally, a state EPSDT program was organized as follows: (1) the state department of public welfare was responsible for the overall program and located children who needed examinations; (2) the state health department performed the examinations; (3) referrals for treatment were made to private clinics; (4) case monitoring was performed by the agency responsible for locating the children for examination.

It should be noted, however, that this structure varied considerably from state to state and in some cases within the same state.

EPSDT Treatment Rate by State

	Number of Children With Problems	Children Treated at Least Once		Adjusted* Number of Children With Problems	Adjusted* Percent Treated
		Number	Percent		
Texas	368	263	71.5%	342	76.9%
Pennsylvania	579	466	80.5	528	88.3
Georgia	313	234	74.8	311	75.3
Tennessee	407	247	60.7	384	64.3
Michigan	439	351	80	421	83.4
Puerto Rico	280	179	63.9	271	66.1
Iowa	287	216	75.3	287	75.3
California	371	267	71.9	331	80.7
Ohio	378	299	79.1	365	81.9
Total	3,422	2,522	73.7%	3,240	77.8%

*After deletion of children who refused treatment and those who no longer had a problem.

Note: These data, in themselves, do not indicate the degree of effectiveness of state programs since the costs of the programs are not included in this study.

IMPROVING THE SYSTEM

The study focused on poor documentation, which made it difficult or impossible for some states to determine whether health problems found in the screening were actually treated. The new proposed reporting requirements and the Medicaid Bureau's model program for tracking children through the system represent efforts to address this deficiency.

However, the variety of other shortcomings found suggests that each state program must be evaluated within the frame of its own organizational structure, eligibility requirements, and frequency and extent of examination of children. To improve the EPSDT program throughout the country, a number of steps are being taken. These include:

Program Improvement Plan

The EPSDT program of each state is examined to pinpoint problems that are keeping the states from filling program objectives. A plan is then developed to help each state upgrade its program.

Technical Assistance

The Office of Child Health offers technical assistance to help a state implement its Program Improvement Plan. When the central or regional office is unable to help solve a problem, an independent contractor is often available to provide technical assistance.

Case Monitoring

A model information system designed to reenforce case management is now being completed and will be available to states in early 1978.

Interagency Agreements

Because of the many child care programs operated by various agencies, it is important to insure that unnecessary overlapping does not occur. Interagency agreements are developed in such areas for identifying the population to be served, the objectives of the program and the methods that will be used to accomplish the objectives.

Provider Participation

OCH encourages the states to publicize the EPSDT program to providers and to set their reimbursements for providers high enough to attract a sufficient number of them. To ease the paperwork burden for physicians, the AMA is working with the agency to develop a standard billing form that can be used by physicians for all health care programs.

METHODOLOGY OF THE STUDY

The study focused on a random sample of 3,240 children who were examined between January 1 and April 30, 1976, and found to have problems. Four-hundred children were scheduled to be chosen from each of eight states and Puerto Rico, each of which had a high number of children examined during the preceding quarter. But the random quality of the study suffered when three states declined to participate and other states were substituted.

The eight states and Puerto Rico had about 44 percent of all children who were eligible for EPSDT and coincidentally, they examined 44 percent of all children in the program during the third quarter of 1976.

Each state was asked to submit a list of five urban sites and five rural counties, each with a minimum of 400 children. Three urban and two rural sites in each state were randomly selected. Each child was assigned a number, and a sample of 80 children was drawn from each site.

Because an extremely high incidence of dental problems was found, it was decided that, if necessary, the number of dental cases checked at each site could be limited. This would insure that there was a sufficient number of other problems to make the study statistically valid. The limitation was imposed in only one state. Cases of deficient immunization were deleted for the same reason.

Other factors limiting the random quality of the study were:

- A site had to have examined at least 400 children during the period designated or it was not considered. This requirement insured there would be adequate numbers of children with referrable problems.
- The decision to use three urban sites and two rural ones in each state to assure the proper urban-rural representation was arbitrary.

- The degree to which the examination uncovered problems and identified them varied.
- Of the sites considered, there was extensive variation in the maximum number of children examined.

The data was collected by questionnaires sent to the local EPSDT staffs. Whether or not a child was treated was determined by checking clinic, welfare and Medicaid payment records, or through a visit or telephone call to the provider or the patient's parent.

A member of the survey team visited each site to resolve questions and insure that survey questionnaires were as complete as possible. While at the site, team members also verified a random sample of 20 percent of the forms, finding an error rate of between three and five percent.

10. Home Health—The Need for a Rational Policy to Better Provide for the Elderly

GENERAL ACCOUNTING OFFICE

MEDICAID HOME HEALTH CARE

Home health care became a required service for the categorically needy under Medicaid on July 1, 1970. Home health agencies which are qualified to participate in Medicare are also qualified to participate in Medicaid.

The 1967 Amendments to the Social Security Act required coverage of home health services as a step toward requiring states to provide a comprehensive program of services to Medicaid beneficiaries. Although home health services were optional under the Medicaid program until July 1, 1970, states now are required to provide home health services, which have been defined as part-time and intermittent services by a certified home health agency. Home health services provided under Medicaid have varied considerably from state to state. With the publication of Medicaid regulations on August 25, 1976, all states were required to provide nursing services, home health aide services, and medical supplies and equipment.

Any person eligible for skilled nursing home services, and if home health services were prescribed by a physician, is eligible to receive home health care.

The Medicaid home health care benefits differ from Medicare benefits because they do not require skilled nursing care or physical or speech therapy for a person. Also, they do not provide for medical social services. In contrast to Medicare part A, to be eligible for Medicaid home health care benefits a person does not need prior hospitalization nor is the number of visits limited by federal law or regulation, although states may impose a limitation.

For fiscal years 1975, 1976, and 1977 total state expenditures were, or were estimated to be, about $73 million, $126 million, and $154 million, respectively, for home-health care benefits under their Medicaid programs. The federal share was about $40 million, $71 million, and $87 million, respectively. In contrast, total federal and state Medicaid expenditures for institutionalized care in skilled nursing and intermediate care facilities were $4.2 billion, $4.7 billion, and $5.8 billion, respectively.

CLARIFY AND DEFINE SPECIFIC HOME HEALTH SERVICES COVERED UNDER MEDICAID

In 1974 we reported (Home Health Care Benefits under Medicare and Medicaid, July 9, 1974) that services covered under state Medicaid programs varied greatly and that some states had adopted Medicare eligibility criteria which were more restrictive than Medicaid intended. We recommended that the Social Rehabilitation Services department clarify the specific services eligible for federal financial participation.

Each of the states we visited had different requirements for the number of visits, and all three states still used more restrictive eligibility criteria than established under the federal Medicaid law. Recent HEW actions clarified home health services and eligibility requirements.

Limited Visits

Each of the three states we reviewed had different requirements concerning the number of allowable home health visits. Georgia limited home health care to 100 visits a calendar year. California did not establish a limit on total visits, but therapy visits were limited to two per month. Florida imposed no limit on the number of visits for Medicaid recipients, but applied the Medicare 100 visits limit for buy-in* patients. This limitation was not shown in Florida's Medicaid plan.

Florida's policy conflicts with federal Medicaid regulations which require equal services for all eligible Medicaid beneficiaries. When Medicare buy-ins exhaust the 100 visits, the beneficiaries must either

- obtain home health care at no cost to them,
- obtain funds to pay for some or all of the home health care,
- enter a nursing home, or
- do without the needed health care services.

The Visiting Nurse Association in Dade County, Florida, provided free services to several Medicare buy-ins who had exceeded the 100 visits. Had these patients

*Buy-ins are people for whom Medicaid funds are used to pay premiums for Medicare Supplementary Medical Insurance Coverage (part B).

been regular Medicaid beneficiaries, the state probably would have paid for all services provided.

Restrictive Eligibility Criteria

The three states used different eligibility criteria for home health care. California law and its Medicaid plan provided that these services would be covered only when a physician prescribed them in a written plan which indicated the need for skilled nursing care. Before Georgia changed its program to reflect the August 25, 1976, federal regulations, the state not only required that recipients need skilled care, but that they be homebound—similar to Medicare criteria. Florida imposed Medicare restrictions—skilled care and homebound—on its Medicare buy-ins only.

Recent HEW Initiatives

HEW's August 1976 home health regulations should clarify some of the confusion about the types of home health services covered by Medicaid. These regulations require the following services be made available:

- Nursing services on a part-time or intermittent basis by a home health agency or by a registered nurse licensed in the state when a home health agency does not exist in the area.
- Home health aide services provided by a home health agency.
- Medical supplies, equipment, and appliances suitable for use in the home.

All these services must be made available for all Medicaid eligibles. Until the new regulations were issued, states were allowed to provide less than all of the services. In addition, states can now provide physical therapy, occupational or speech pathology, and audiology services provided by a home health agency or by a state approved facility licensed to provide medical rehabilitation services as home health care. Previously, these covered services were not included as home health care.

State officials in Florida and Georgia believe that the new regulations adequately define Medicaid home health care services.

In addition to the new regulations, on February 16, 1977, HEW issued guidelines on home health care which answered some frequently asked questions about the program. The guidelines state that states may not limit home health services to individuals who require a skilled level of care as defined by Medicare.

An official in the California Department of Health said in July 1977 that he had not seen the Social Rehabilitation Services' February guidelines. He said he believed that Medicaid eligibles still had to require skilled services to qualify for home health care. He said California's program would probably have to be changed in order to comply.

ENCOURAGE STATES TO ESTABLISH REASONABLE REIMBURSEMENT RATES

Our 1974 report showed that in some states the reimbursement rates for Medicaid home health care services were not adequate. We recommended that the Secretary of HEW direct Social Rehabilitation Services to encourage states to establish payment rates at a level that would stimulate greater use of home health care. On June 20, 1975, HEW reported to the Congress that a survey had indicated wide-spread changeover of states' reimbursement systems to liberalize payments.

States still use a variety of reimbursement systems to pay home health care providers. According to a 1976 HEW report, most states use the Medicare method of reimbursing Medicaid home health care providers—paying the lowest charge. However, many states continue to use a system of fixed fees, negotiated rates, or schedule of maximum allowances.

States' reimbursement systems do not always encourage more home health agencies to participate in the program. The systems used in the three states we visited restricted the use of home health care.

Many home health care providers in Florida and Georgia said Medicaid reimbursement rates were very low, and several said they did not participate in the states' Medicaid programs because of the low rates. Florida had established a "fee" for visit reimbursement rate, whereas Georgia reimbursed its Medicaid providers on the basis of negotiated percentage—from 90 to 100 percent—of the interim rates established by Medicare.

Florida's Medicaid reimbursement rates, which had not increased since 1974, were based on a fee for visit with a maximum rate of $13.50 for a skilled nursing visit and $7.50 for a home health aide visit. Both were considerably less than the average Medicare payments for the same services. For five providers we visited in Florida, Medicare reimbursements ranged from $9.09 to $16.52 for a home health aide visit and from $13.90 to $39.93 for visits by other than aides.

Officials in both states acknowledged that Medicaid payment rates were too low. They generally agreed that the payment rates restricted the use of home health care and that until the rates were increased the use of the program as an alternative to inappropriate institutionalization would never be maximized. A Florida Medicaid official told us that Medicaid should reimburse all reasonable costs of providing home health care. He said, however, that this could be done only if the state legislature appropriated more funds for home health care.

Florida officials also said that the state legislature had historically been reluctant to appropriate funds for Medicaid home health. In fiscal year 1977, the legislature increased the appropriation for home health by more than $469,000—an increase of about 250 percent over the fiscal year 1976 appropriation for $189,000. However, because of the limited use of home health—believed to be caused primarily by the low-reimbursement rates—the total expenditures for state projects will increase by only about $76,000. The state officials recognize that the rates are unreasonably low and as a result only those providers which have other sources of funds, like the visiting nurse association, could afford to serve Medicaid patients. State officials acknowledged that the low rates restricted the use of home health care and limited the effectiveness of the program. They said that they hoped the state would increase payment rates in the near future.

The reimbursement system in California also restricts use of home health care. The state reimburses on a fee-for-service basis, with limits on the maximum allowable rates. In December 1976 the California Association for Home Health Services requested the state to study home health provider rates. As a result of the study, home health care rates were increased on August 1, 1977. For example, the rate for skilled nursing visits was increased from $19.60 to $24.60 and home health aide visits were increased from $11.50 to $11.70. California's study of Medicare reimbursement rates showed a range from $6.36 to $29.96 for home health aide visits and $14.38 to $73.71 for visits by other than aides.

Officials of California's Department of Health acknowledged that rates have traditionally lagged behind the costs incurred by providers. However, they said this problem is similar for skilled nursing facilities, acute hospitals, and other providers of medical services.

Until recently HEW had done little to encourage California, Florida, or Georgia to make their reimbursement rates more reasonable. An HEW San Francisco region official said the state was responsible for establishing Medicaid payment schedules. Officials of the California Department of

Health noted that HEW has not provided the state with feedback as to the appropriateness of its payment schedules.

The HEW Associate Regional Commissioner in Atlanta said that HEW indirectly encouraged the states to pay at least reasonable costs for home health services during technical consultations with the state and while processing the state plan. He said in some instances the low rates discouraged the use of home health care and more use might be made if rates were higher. However, state Medicaid officials in both Florida and Georgia told us that HEW had done little to encourage the states to increase reimbursement rates to stimulate use of home health care. State officials acknowledged that the reimbursement rates were too low and that higher rates would increase the use of the program.

An HEW headquarters official said HEW can do little to encourage states to use reasonable payment rates because federal law does not require states to use any specific reimbursement formula for payment rates. She said more states were using the Medicare formula since our 1974 report, but the rates still vary considerably from state to state.

In June 1977, HEW sent a letter to 13 states that reportedly used a fixed fee, negotiated rate, or schedule of maximum allowances in 1974. The letter stated that these methods of reimbursement do not encourage home health agencies to provide services to Medicaid patients. It was also pointed out that "* * * home health services are mandatory and that every effort must be made to provide the services to all eligible individuals." Two states responded and stated that their revised reimbursement structures should encourage home health care.

CONCLUSIONS

HEW analyses of intermediaries screens and processed claims showed that Medicare's guidelines for home health services were not followed in many instances, and the screens and parameters of intermediaries often differed. However, the problems between intermediaries and providers on whether and to what extent home health services are covered have largely been resolved. Providers say they now know, through experience, what Medicare will cover. Denials of claims are minimal.

HEW has (1) taken action to increase awareness and support of home health care by the health field, (2) issued a National Directory of Home Health Agencies, and (3) reviewed and revised various Medicare publications.

Also, HEW plans to involve intermediaries and carriers promoting home health care as part of their professional relations activities. This appears to be a reasonable promotional initiative.

HEW has tried to impress upon states that home health care under Medicaid should be used as an alternative to institutionalization when it is less expensive and meets the patients needs. Home health care has been publicized through HEW's procedures for issuing revised regulations and holding public hearings in 1976 on home health care.

Since Medicaid is essentially a state program, it is each state's prerogative to use home health care as it wishes. Services varied among the states we visited. The states used more restrictive eligibility criteria than established under the federal Medicaid law. Under its buy-in program, Florida has provided unequal benefits to Medicare buy-ins which was contrary to HEW regulations and the state's approved Medicaid plan. Recent HEW initiatives should help to clarify some of the confusion on the services covered.

Reimbursement systems for home health care vary among the states. Most states use a system similar to Medicare, which pays the lowest cost or charge. Many use a fixed-fee or schedule of maximum allowance system. Some states' systems do not encourage increased use of home health care.

The reimbursement systems used in California, Florida, and Georgia all restricted the use of home health care because rates were low. HEW had taken little action to encourage states to establish higher reimbursement rates. HEW has no authority to require states to adopt higher rates.

RECOMMENDATIONS TO THE SECRETARY OF HEW

We recommend that the Secretary of HEW direct the Administrator of the Health Care Financing Administration to:

- Have the carriers and intermediaries, in conjunction with their proposed promotional efforts, provide data to physicians and institutional providers on the home health agencies in their service areas. Such data should include the services each agency provides and the geographical area in which it will provide care.
- Identify state programs which do not provide equal treatment to individual groups of Medicaid recipients and take steps to correct such inequities. Particular attention should be given to restrictions resulting through states buy-in programs, such as that identified in Florida.

11. Appropriateness of Long-Term Care Placement:
A Study of Long-Term Care Patients in the New Jersey Medicaid Program

DONALD MALAFRONTE, HOWARD H. MOSES,
RHONA M. BRONSON, CAROL A. KUNREUTHER and
PETER R. BREYER

DESCRIPTION OF THE STUDY

Introduction and Purpose

Medicaid is the joint federal and state program of medical care for welfare recipients and other needy persons authorized by the Social Security Amendments of 1965 and subsequently adopted by all states, some as early as 1966, one as late as 1975. New Jersey's program began January 1, 1970. It is administered by the Division of Medical Assistance and Health Services, Department of Human Services, formerly the Department of Institutions and Agencies. The Medicaid program is headquartered in Trenton and has 16 local offices covering the state's 21 counties.

Medicaid is a broad program and some of its elements have been the subject of public questioning prompted, in large part, by the program's unanticipated cost. Elements required by law include physicians' care, outpatient and inpatient care at hospitals, lab and x-ray services, long-term care services and screening and treatment of eligible individuals under age 21.

This study is concerned with only one aspect of Medicaid: its institutionalized, long-term care patients and the question of how many could live more independently, if appropriate alternate settings and services were available. Financial eligibility and reimbursement policies which might affect placement were not included in the study.

Categories of Long-Term Care

In cooperation with the New Jersey Medicaid program, the Urban Health Institute studied a sample of cases from the category of long-term care classified in New Jersey as IV(B), an intermediate level of care that provides minimal nursing services and residential services to those for whom life in the community is judged impractical but who are not sick enough to require skilled or a higher level of intermediate nursing services. New Jersey regulations describe such patients as ambulant or semi-ambulant with physical and/or mental dysfunctions requiring minimal assistance with personal care needs on a daily basis. Level IV(B) is the lowest level of long-term care covered by Medicaid. It was selected for examination in this study because by definition IV(B) patients are closest to the need for alternate care and most likely to provide accurate indicators of the types of alternate settings and services required in New Jersey.

Other levels of long-term care in New Jersey are Level III, which involves skilled nursing care for persons with acute or sub-acute medical or mental dysfunctions requiring continuous skilled nursing care, and Level IV(A), the upper level companion to IV(B). Upper level IV(A) patients are judged to require *substantial* assistance with personal care needs on a daily basis rather than the *minimal* assistance required in IV(B).

Most IV(B) patients are elderly and most are in nursing homes. A minority are in special hospitals or other types of long-term care institutions. The classifications used for analysis in this study are those of the state Department of Health, which licenses such facilities. Medicaid does not distinguish among classifications of facilities offering long-term care.

Cost of Care

The IV(B) category is relatively new—it was established in New Jersey in 1974—but it is significant in number of persons served and in cost. During an average month during the last fiscal year, there were 4,920 IV(B) patients in long-term care facilities in the state at a total cost to Medicaid of $32,114,231, shared equally by the state and federal governments. The IV(B) expenditures accounted for over 20 percent of overall Medicaid expenditures of $154,789,041 for long-term care in New Jersey in 1976.

Study Methodology

In conducting the study, eight local Medicaid offices were randomly selected from among the 16 in New Jersey. Local office medical evaluation teams, consisting of a physician, nurse and social worker, completed a questionnaire concerning their perceptions of every case reviewed for re-certification during a three-month period. The social worker was utilized by Medicaid as a team member for the duration of the study. Presently, a social worker participates only in initial assessments, cases of prospective denials of benefits and in cases involving special problems. The teams are responsible for certifying the level of long-term care required, if any, and periodically re-evaluating need and quality of care rendered to the patient.

The eight offices were Bergen, Burlington, Camden, Essex, Hudson, Hunterdon—which includes Hunterdon, Warren and Somerset Counties—Mercer and Middlesex. The sample offices included 96 licensed facilities serving IV(B) patients: 70 nursing homes; 15 incorporated homes for the aged, virtually identical to nursing homes; four licensed as intermediate care facilities; and seven general and special hospitals. The classifications are those of the state Department of Health, which licenses such facilities. All are approved by Medicaid to offer an intermediate level of care.

Preliminary questionnaires were developed and pretested during a three-week trial period, March 4–25, 1976, in the Mercer office. Urban Health Institute staff were present at each conference during the pre-test period to observe team reactions to the survey instrument and to note difficulties in either question interpretation or question completion. As a result of the pretesting, a number of changes in the questionnaire were made.

Medical evaluation teams began utilizing the final study questionnaire in the eight sample offices on May 10, 1976. Urban Health Institute staff were present at all conferences held during the first two weeks at each office to observe the teams at work. A third week was spent with those teams that were judged to require additional observation.

The study continued for a three-month period, ending August 6, 1976. The three-month period was selected to permit the sampling of approximately 50 percent of all IV(B) residents in the eight offices. Since each IV(B) resident is reviewed every six months, approximately half of the total residents are reviewed in any three-month period. Cases reviewed numbered 1,250, a sample of 25 percent of all cases in the IV(B) category.

The sample size produced a statistical probability of 97 percent for its findings to be true for all IV(B) cases.

Questionnaires were gathered by the local administrators in each local office. They labeled each questionnaire with an identification number to protect confidentiality of records and forwarded the questionnaires bearing only the number to the Urban Health Institute for processing.

The questionnaires were computer coded and processed through computer services provided by the Celanese Corporation. A preliminary report on findings was presented to Medicaid in December 1976.

FINDINGS

1. The medical evaluation teams judged that 35 percent of those currently institutionalized at the IV(B) intermediate care level could be discharged if appropriate alternate settings and services were available. There is considerable variation in recommendation for discharge among the offices, from a low of 16.9 percent in Hudson to a high of 79.8 percent in Burlington.
2. Level IV(B) patients were judged by the medical evaluation teams to suffer an average of 2.1 medical problems each, but there is considerable variation among offices. The Hudson team listed almost twice as many primary diagnoses per patient as did Bergen and Burlington.
3. Cerebral arteriosclerosis, frequently related to senility and similar dysfunctions, is more prevalent among those recommended for continued institutional care, than among those recommended for discharge. Those suffering musculoskeletal disorders, including arthritis and fractures, were more likely to be recommended for alternate care. There was some variation among offices in the findings related to cerebral arteriosclerosis, particularly in Hudson, where most such cases were judged to require continued institutionalization, and Burlington, where most were judged suitable for lower levels of care.
4. Most IV(B) patients are in nursing homes. Residents of hospitals receive recommendations for alternate care less frequently, while patients in nursing homes receive that recommendation most frequently, again with some office variation.
5. Most IV(B) patients have been institutionalized for less than three years.
6. The majority of IV(B) patients were institutionalized in the county in which they lived prior to institutionalization.
7. Most IV(B) patients are female and most are well over age 65. Among patients below the age of 75, men tend to receive recommendations for alternate care slightly more frequently than women.
8. The medical evaluation teams held that 72 percent of those cases recommended for alternate care—or 25 percent of all IV(B) patients—could be cared for in alternative, congregate living arrangements.
9. Most IV(B) patients recommended for release need one or more of four categories of nursing and other supportive services.

CONCLUSIONS

Impact on Long-Term Care Cost and Bed Need

The percentage of IV(B) patients who could be discharged if appropriate alternate settings and services were available is significant in terms of the number of patients involved and the cost of their care. The percentage is also significant in terms of the number of beds which could be made available to others presently awaiting appropriate placement and in reducing the need for costly construction or conversion to produce additional long-term care beds.

Projected for the entire IV(B) population, the study findings indicate that more than 1,700 persons could be placed in more appropriate lower levels of care. The annual cost of this care for these persons in their present institutional setting amounts to more than $10 million.

The 1,700 beds which would become available through more appropriate placement constitute nearly 10 percent of all long-term care beds in New Jersey and are sufficient in number to accommodate most of the 1,500–2,000 persons estimated by Medicaid to be awaiting placement in New Jersey. The cost of adding 1,700 beds through new construction would be approximately $28 million, using a conservative construction estimate of $17,000 per bed, based on a 1976 survey of nursing home construction in the New York-New Jersey area.

The high percentage of IV(B) patients who can be moved to a lower level of care, combined with the underutilization of many acute care hospitals in the state that could be utilized to offer services to patients in need of higher skilled care, suggest that coordinated planning could produce sufficient long-term care beds to meet New Jersey's present needs without additional construction.

These conclusions are based on findings regarding the physical and mental condition of patients and do not take into account financial eligibility and reimbursement policies which tend to favor institutionalization and therefore stand in the way of simple, direct transfer of patients to more appropriate, alternate care.

Feasibility of Independent Living

Independent living is not considered a viable alternative for IV(B) patients. Only 14 of the 437 persons recommended for discharge were judged capable of fully independent living. This represents about three percent of those recommended for alternate care and just one percent of all those studied.

The only alternatives judged practical involved lower levels of care which tended to blur the difference between institutional and noninstitutional care, since it is difficult to be precise about the difference between institutionalization in a nursing home and placement in a sheltered or other congregate living arrangement.

Reasons for Office Variations

Local office variations in recommendations for alternate care are attributable in part to the mix of patient illness and type of institution in each office, but the variations also appear closely related to office caseloads and the subjective personal judgments of individual medical evaluation teams. This conclusion is supported most strongly by the virtually opposite findings in Burlington, where strong patterns supporting release were found, and Hudson, where equally strong patterns for continued institutionalization exist.

In a number of offices, the prevalence of cerebral arteriosclerosis with attendant senility or mental confusion tended to affect the rate of recommendations for release. Over 70 percent of persons suffering from such dysfunctions were judged to require continued institutionalization.

However, variations in district recommendations occurred even in terms of this illness. In Burlington, two out of three such cases were judged suitable for release. In Hudson, almost nine out of ten were held to require continued institutionalization.

The persistence of variations throughout the office and case findings suggest that in a nonmedical category such as IV(B), where institutionalization rests as much on the need for residential care as it does on nursing care, the personal and subjective opinions and beliefs of individual team members as to the practicality of alternate care are crucial.

In addition, a correlation appears to exist between the number of cases in an office and recommendations for release. The larger the number of cases in an office, the lower the rate for release. This correlation persisted even though in theory staffing patterns at the offices permit teams the same amount of time per case.

Long-Term Care and Mental Health

The number of persons in New Jersey psychiatric hospitals suffering from organic brain syndrome—a condition typically related to cerebral arteriosclerosis, senility and related dysfunctions—decreased from 1,763 to 809 between the years 1964–74. This reduced such cases from 42 percent to 21 percent of all cases in the psychiatric hospitals. It is probable that some of these cases found their way into long-term care facilities.

The prevalence of cerebral arteriosclerosis and its attendant senility and similar dysfunctions among those recommended for continued institutionalization suggests long-term care facilities may serve an appropriate role in serving such cases. Institutionalization in a nursing home for persons suffering from mild mental confusion, senility and similar problems appears preferable to the previous practice of placing such persons in large, state-operated psychiatric hospitals. In fact, placement in long-term care facilities, which have an average of less than 100 beds, could be considered a form of deinstitutionalization for patients in psychiatric hospitals, which often have 1,000 or more beds.

The Practicality of Family Care

Recommendations for family care are impractical, by Medicaid's own definition of responsible family. Medicaid regulations hold only spouses and parents of minors responsible. Only 12 of the 437 recommended for alternative care had spouses. The regulations, promulgated by the federal government, take precedence over the New Jersey Poor Laws which define responsible family as the parent, child or spouse of a poor, old, blind or lame person.

Residence and Cross-County Placements

The study provided no data corroborating the belief that substantial numbers of IV(B) patients covered by New Jersey Medicaid were prior residents of other states. Almost 97 percent of the persons studied were prior residents of New Jersey.

Furthermore, the Medicaid offices seem to be largely self-contained with almost three-quarters of all IV(B) patients being institutionalized in the counties in which they previously lived.

In regard to the cross-county placement which does exist, there is a widespread belief that it is desirable to institutionalize the aged in close geographic proximity to the community in which they previously lived. Presumably this is intended to facilitate continued interaction with family and friends and to attenuate the impact of adopting an institutional lifestyle. However, others believe once long-term institutionalization occurs, interaction with the community-at-large tends to diminish or disappear and that the primary task of the resident of an institution is to create new and effective intrainstitutional relationships, regardless of the location of the institution. In the presence of the former belief, cross-county placements may be undesirable, whereas in the presence of the latter belief, cross-county placement is not a significant issue.

Congregate Living

The setting most recommended for those who could be released suggests a need for either a lower level of institutional care or a higher level of community care, neither of which was judged to be available.

The preferred setting recommended by the medical evaluation teams is some form of congregate living arrangement.

While the description of the most frequently recommended setting appears similar to that used by the state Department of Health to define a sheltered boarding home, the area remains, as it has for some years in long-term care, a broad gray zone, a zone ranging from something more than room, board and some personal services at the lower level to something less than 24-hour per day nursing care and other professional services at the nursing home level.

The primary intention in creating Level IV(B) was to establish a more appropriate level of care for those already institutionalized at an inappropriately high level. It was not intended primarily to provide an institutional level of care for those still in the community who seemed to require institutional disposition, but were not sufficiently ill to qualify for admission to a medical level of care. However, if it were to become public policy to establish or enrich the setting recommended by the medical evaluation teams, developments in the alternate care field of congregate living might produce a new population, presently at home and receiving no services, who might be placed in those settings.

Community-Based Services

The services which could be required to facilitate more appropriate placement of IV(B) patients are of the type which could be provided at the community level.

In order to facilitate appropriate placement among all IV(B) patients, the study finding projects that it would be necessary to provide community-based licensed nursing services for about 530 people. Home health aide/homemaker services would be required by about 240 people. This does not include provision for nursing services and home health aide/homemaker services for those 180 persons recommended for congregate living arrangements with professional services since, by definition, those services would be routinely available in the setting itself. These estimates are of the volume of services which would be required by persons no longer institutionalized in settings providing the services.

In addition, a variety of therapeutic services would be required by about 425 people while communication/transportation and similar support services would be required by 576 people. In addition, day care services would be required for approximately 620 people.

Alternate Care Data

An accurate inventory of available alternate settings and services is essential to determine the practicality of releasing IV(B) patients recommended for alternate care.

Continued Institutionalization

At least 65 percent of IV(B) patients must continue to remain in intermediate care facilities and improvement in the quality of their lives is dependent on the ability of institutions to respond effectively to their human needs.

Even if the support of alternate care is adopted as a major policy, many patients must remain institutionalized and this will continue to be so, during any period of change and after it. A parallel movement for humanistic care within institutions is a logical, linked step. The focus of this movement will most likely be on the psycho-social aspects of institutionalization, rather than on medical and custodial services.

Medicaid, Society and Alternate Care

Decisions regarding alternate care and deinstitutionalization have issues at their core larger than medical decisions and Medicaid policy; instead they center on beliefs (independent living is more desirable and possibly even healthier); fears (we are getting older and we don't want to end up that way); desires to help (let's do something for the needy and the aged); and human impulse to grow (let's change things). In addition to these broad societal concerns is public pressure upon the government to stabilize health care costs. This has often been translated with regard to long-term care as pressure to get people out of nursing homes purely as a means to save money. In fact, although the human factors associated with deinstitutionalization are rarely disputed, cost factors are unclear. Involved at the least are significant money and other cost transfers. Many money costs presently borne by Medicaid could be transferred to other programs, presumably also publicly financed, to support the increased need for alternate care services. For example, the cost of care to Medicaid for the 35 percent of patients recommended for alternate care was more than $11 million in 1976. However, Medicaid's role could instead be recast, leaving it to utilize its funds to become as pertinent a force in alternate care and deinstitutionalization as it is today in supporting long-term institutional care.

RECOMMENDATIONS

1. The New Jersey Medicaid program should adopt the development of alternate care resources as a major long-term care policy.

2. The availability of alternate long-term care resources in New Jersey should be inventoried, classified and kept current. Definition of terms used to describe alternate care resources is also required.

3. The present system of matching people in need with appropriate resources should be re-examined, with consideration given to centralizing responsibility for administration, clarifying the role of county welfare and other agencies, and establishing medical evaluation teams and other Medicaid staff as active agents in insuring placement in alternate care.

4. Reimbursement practices which encourage deinstitutionalization and support of alternate care resources should be tested, including waivers of restrictions on reimbursement for home care and other community-based services.

5. Training of local office medical evaluation teams should be reviewed and redesigned to encourage more consistent assessments among teams.

6. Present pressure for new long-term care beds should be met through coordinated, interagency planning which takes into consideration (1) the high percentage of long-term care patients who can benefit from alternate care and (2) the current oversupply of acute care beds in general hospitals. Another element in such planning should be coordination with the present deinstitutionalization activities of the Division of Mental Health and Hospitals. Involved in such interagency coordination should be the Medicaid program; Department of Health; Division of Mental Health and Hospitals; and the five Health Systems Agencies (HSAs) in New Jersey.

12. Mental Health Benefits of the Tennessee Medicaid Program

C. RICHARD TREADWAY

Reprinted with permission from *Journal of the Tennessee Medical Association*, Vol. 69, No. 10, October 1976.

INTRODUCTION

Until 1972 no benefits had been provided for mental health services given to Tennessee Medicaid patients. The exclusion of services had represented a decision of the State Legislature and State Medicaid Policy Committee and had not been necessitated by Federal law or regulation. Federal law and regulation had permitted states to include limited mental health services if they so chose.

Even the limited mental health benefits possible had been excluded in Tennessee for two primary reasons. One was the control of cost. Tennessee had attempted to get into the Medicaid program slowly and had limited its basic Medicaid program in such a way as to limit cost. This fiscally conservative approach had been suggested by the rapid escalation of cost in other states which had early adopted a comprehensive form of coverage.

A second factor in the denial of mental health benefits was the belief that the state had already discharged its responsibility to the medically indigent psychiatric patient by the provision of state funds for both state hospitals and state supported community mental health centers. The extension of Medicaid benefits to mental health centers

and private psychiatrists was therefore seen as a duplication.

COMMUNITY MENTAL HEALTH CENTERS

Of some interest is the fact that inclusion of community mental health centers in Medicaid reimbursements preceded that of psychiatrists. The decision to include mental health centers was made in 1972 and was implemented in 1973. This decision permitted reimbursement to mental health centers of any physician services provided to Medicaid eligible persons. Eligibility for Medicaid was essentially synonymous with welfare status.

In community mental health centers, services supervised by licensed physicians but provided by psychologists, social workers, or nurses are also reimbursed. This reimbursement of allied health professionals occurs only in the mental health centers.

In order to control costs of the Medicaid reimbursement of physician services in mental health centers, it was decided initially to offer reimbursement only for outpatient visits and not to extend coverage to inpatient care or day hospitalization.

Another cost control was the decision of the Department of Mental Health not to exceed thirty-five dollars reimbursement per visit regardless of cost. The thirty comprehensive community mental health centers are currently being reimbursed at a rate of $100,000 per month or a total of 1.2 million dollars a year.

Although the Medicaid program at mental health centers has generally gone well, there were some initial abuses which required correction. These abuses at times involved the absence of physician supervision for services that must be physician supervised or provided in order to be eligible for reimbursement. Another problem was the initial occasional submission of inappropriate charges such as recreation therapy or social services. These problems have now largely been corrected.

PSYCHIATRIC SERVICES BY PRIVATE PHYSICIANS

In 1975 the Tennessee Medicaid program was broadened for the first time to include payment for psychiatric services. Coverage under Medicaid had been provided for most medical services in Tennessee, but dental and psychiatric services had been specifically excluded. Psychiatric services by licensed physicians are now reimbursed whether or not they are psychiatrists and whether they are provided on an outpatient or inpatient basis.

The decision to include psychiatric services came as a result of the encouragement of private psychiatrists, the Tennessee District Branch of the American Psychiatric Association, and the Department of Mental Health. The Department of Public Health was willing to consider the matter if the inclusion could be shown to be fiscally sound and designed in such a way as to eliminate unnecessary duplications.

Although it was extremely difficult to project a total cost for the inclusion of psychiatric services, administrators of the state

Medicaid program did postulate initial estimates for psychiatric benefits based upon discussions with the Department of Mental Health and private psychiatrists. They believed this decision would increase the cost of the total Medicaid program by no more than 10 percent. This estimate appears to have been correct, since the actual reimbursement of psychiatric services in 1975–76 amounted only to an estimated $200,000.

As for the matter of duplication of effort, it was not thought important whether medically indigent persons were served by mental health centers or by private psychiatrists as long as they were served by a competent professional provider. Duplication of effort was not thought to be a genuine issue.

Forty-three of the 50 states now provide psychiatric benefits under Medicaid.

MENTAL HEALTH INSTITUTIONS

Coverage for Mental Health and Mental Retardation Institutions began in the 1971–72 fiscal year. Reimbursement is provided to qualified extended care (ECF) and intermediate care (ICF) facilities for patients who have been certified as eligible under the Medicaid program. Reimbursement grew to 13.5 million in support of the three Mental Retardation institutions in 1974–75 and 10.9 million for support of the state psychiatric hospitals. Total Medicaid support for Mental Health and Mental Retardation Institutions in 1974–75 was thus 24.4 million dollars. It is projected to be 26.8 million dollars for 1975–76.

EXTENT OF TENNESSEE'S MEDICAID REIMBURSEMENT FOR MENTAL HEALTH SERVICES

Funds expended for mental health services have increased dramatically over the initial three years of coverage. In 1971 there were no Medicaid dollars expended on mental health. In fiscal year 1975–76 more than 28 million dollars will be expended. (Table 1 and Fig. 1)

Figure 1 Percentage of Medicaid Expenditures

1975–76 (Projected)

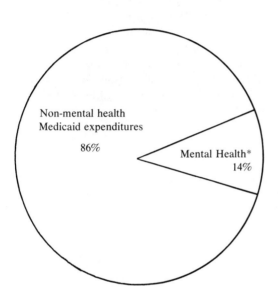

*Of total projected state Medicaid expenditures of $200,000,000, $28,200,000 are for mental health services.

Table 1

Total Medicaid Reimbursement for Mental Health Services	1975–76 (Projected)
Psychiatric Services by Private Physicians	$200,000 (estimated)
Community Mental Health Centers	1,200,000
State Mental Health and Mental Retardation Institutions	26,800,000
Total	28,200,000

NON-MEDICAL MENTAL HEALTH SERVICES

An interesting point recently raised in regard to the coverage of mental health services by Medicaid is whether only those services provided by or supervised by physicians will continue to be covered under Medicaid or whether Medicaid will also reimburse non-physician supervised services provided by clinical psychologists, social workers, nurses, clinical pastoral counselors, alcoholism counselors, drug abuse counselors, and other mental health professionals involved in the direct provision of care. This issue will of course be determined by a multitude of factors. Some of these are professional, having to do with competence and capacity for independent judgments. Another is political, having to do with whether or not psychologists are able to pass a state law requiring Medicaid to reimburse clinical psychologists. Another important factor is cost. The broader the mental health coverage under Medicaid, the more costly the Medicaid program will become.

A somewhat different approach would be to reimburse only for the medical components of mental health services. In this approach a psychiatrist might be reimbursed for medical diagnostic interviews, inpatient hospital care, psychiatric visits in which medication is prescribed, but not for group psychotherapy, family counseling, or individual psychotherapy. These latter activities might be construed as non-medical mental health services which could be provided by a psychiatrist, a clinical psychologist, or any one of a number of other mental health professionals.

In our judgment the decision about either *which mental health disciplines* are covered or *which types of mental health services* are covered will be made primarily around the issue of cost, which has been a predominant concern of the state Medicaid program during the past year, and will likely remain so during the next few years. The earlier projected deficit of $18 million in the 1975–76 fiscal year makes it highly unlikely that any major expansion of Medicaid coverage will occur in the near future. Additional funds had to be appropriated above the original appropriation just in order for the program to continue operation beyond the spring of this year when funds had been projected to run out. The Federal congress has also recently expressed concern about the steady escalation in Medicaid and Medicare programs nationally. Congressional action now being considered may result in a decrease of federal Medicaid and Medicare expenditures in the future. At any rate attitudes in both state and federal legislative bodies would appear to be inimical toward any expansion of the program.

MEDICAID REIMBURSEMENT OF MENTAL HEALTH SERVICES IN OTHER SOUTHEASTERN STATES

Alabama reimburses physicians for recipients seen in mental health clinics. Reimbursement is also provided for short-term inpatient care in general hospitals, both for physicians and hospitals. Outpatient care by private psychiatrists is not reimbursed. The program also covers mental patients placed in nursing homes.

Florida Medicaid provides vendor payments to state mental hospitals for Medicaid patients of 65 years and older. It will reimburse a board eligible or certified psychiatrist provider (MD or DO) the allowable charges for covered psychotherapy

Table 2 Mental Health Medicaid Benefits Received in Southeastern States

	Physician Services	State Institution Inpatient Care	General or Private Hospital Inpatient Care	Psychologists	Limits
Alabama	yes	yes	yes	no	Outpatient physician services eligible only if provided in Mental Health Center
Florida	yes	yes	no	no	Currently have a maximum reimbursement of $156 Patient per six months for psychiatric services
Georgia	yes	yes	yes	yes	Limit of 10–12 days of inpatient care per year
Kentucky	yes	yes	yes	no	Also reimburses psychiatrists, psychologists, psychiatric nurses, or master's social workers in Community Mental Health Centers
Mississippi	yes	no	no	no	Annual limit of $250 for services of the psychiatrist
North Carolina	yes	yes	yes	no	Physician services limited to 2 visits per year except at Mental Health Centers
South Carolina	no	no	no	no	No specified mental health benefits under State Medicaid program
Tennessee	yes	yes	yes	yes	20 day limit on inpatient—no outpatient limit. Psychologists may participate only if patients are referred by physicians
Virginia	yes	yes	yes	no	Limit of 50 one-hour psychotherapy sessions per lifetime. Inpatient limit of 14–21 days per year
West Virginia	yes	yes	yes	no	Limit of 10–60 days of inpatient care per year

services rendered a Medicaid recipient. At the present time, a cap of *$156.00* per patient for the 6 month period ending June 30, 1976 has been established for psychiatric services due to a projected Medicaid deficit for this fiscal year.

Georgia provides a relatively full range of mental health benefits under Medicaid. Psychologists are also included.

In *Kentucky,* mental health and psychiatric benefits are covered primarily under two program areas, the physician services segment and the community mental health center segment.

Physicians who are not board certified or board eligible in psychiatry may be reimbursed for no more than four (4) psychiatric procedures/examinations per patient per calendar year, while board certified or board eligible physicians in psychiatric practice may bill for their services without limitation, provided, that the services are necessary and otherwise included in program coverage.

Community mental health centers may be reimbursed for services rendered by a psychiatrist, psychologist, psychiatric nurse or master social worker. In accordance with Federal regulations, inpatient services rendered in psychiatric facilities are available to recipients under age 21 and over age 65. Psychiatric admissions to a general hospital may be covered during the treatment of an acute phase of such a condition, subject to program staff review for appropriateness of treatment and length of stay.

The *Mississippi* Medicaid program does not have specific separately provided services for psychiatric or mental health coverage, but rather covers it just as any other illness or accident with a $250.00 annual limit for the services of the psychiatrist. There is a provision in the Mississippi law providing for coverage for individuals over 65 in an approved psychiatric hospital, though the state does not have a facility that is qualified under this provision of the law.

North Carolina Medicaid patients are permitted two outpatient visits per year to private psychiatrists. Third and subsequent outpatient visits require prior approval except when at mental health centers. Acute inpatient care is reimbursed only at general hospitals, private hospitals, and mental health centers. State hospitals receive ICF funds.

In *South Carolina,* there are no specified mental health benefits under the state Medicaid program.

The *Virginia* Medical Assistance Program provides for the equivalent of 50 one-hour psychotherapy sessions per recipient for life. A Psychiatric Appeals Board meets monthly and considers extensions of this maximum upon request of the treating psychiatrist. All sessions are considered within this limitation wherever conducted, whether in a private office, general hospital, or mental health clinic. Short-term hospitalization for psychiatric reasons is restricted by a general limitation of 14 days hospitalization per admission, with a possible extension to a total of 21 days. Virginia also provides psychiatric care in the state mental institutions for those aged 65 and over.

West Virginia covers the first 10 days of inpatient care for the categorically needy and medically indigent for acute psychiatric disorders. The next fifty days may be preauthorized by the State office for maximum hospitalization per year of 60 days for all patient care including psychiatry. West Virginia also pays for outpatient visits, with no distinction between community mental health centers and private practitioners.

CONCLUSION

Mental health coverage under the Tennessee Medicaid program was nonexistent prior to 1972. Its inclusion since that time has grown to the point of providing $28 million annually for the provision of mental health services to those eligible for Medicaid benefits. Mental health benefits now constitute 14 percent of the total State expenditures under the Medicaid program.

The inclusion of mental health benefits has been associated with substantial improvements in the quality of care provided in State mental health institutions and community mental health centers. None of the eight mental health institutions was accredited prior to 1972 while five of the eight are now accredited by the Joint Commission on Accreditation of Hospitals. The new support provided by Medicaid to mental health institutions has played an important role in the achievement of accreditation status for the majority of the institutions.

The inclusion of mental health benefits has undoubtedly also had the effect of avoiding unnecessary hospitalizations by providing psychiatric patients with the financial means for purchasing outpatient care either from community mental health centers or from private physicians. The inclusion also helps to mark the end of an era in which mental health services were considered outside the mainstream of health care delivery.

Acknowledgments

The author wishes to express appreciation to the Department of Public Health, and especially its Division of Medicaid Services, for information which has been provided for this paper. Acknowledgment is also made of additional assistance provided by the Department of Mental Health and Mental Retardation of the State of Tennessee.

REFERENCES

1. "Action Against Mental Disability." The Report of the President's Task Force on the Mentally Handicapped, pages 47 through 48, September, 1970.

13. Patient Perceptions and Preferences for Alternative Forms of Ambulatory Care

RICHARD W. NATHAN

INTRODUCTION

The National Health Planning and Resources Development Act (Public Law 93–641) identifies, in Section 1502, several national health priorities. The first priority is:

The provision of primary care services for medically underserved populations, especially those which are located . . . in economically depressed areas

Medical group practices providing Medicaid reimbursable ambulatory care on a fee-for-service basis treat a substantial number of patients in economically depressed urban areas across the country. Municipal and voluntary hospitals and a relatively small number of community health centers are the only major providers of ambulatory care in these areas. Private physicians in solo practice, in these areas, are scarce.

In New York City, Medicaid group practices, known as shared health facilities (SHF)*, are not required to be registered by any public authority. The number of such facilities and the size of their operations are, therefore, not known. Estimates of the number of shared health facilities operating in New York City range from 350 to 600. Estimates of annual patient visits to such facilities range from 3.6 million to 6.2 million annually.

There are fifteen municipal hospitals and 62 voluntary hospitals in New York City which provide either or both emergency room and outpatient department (OPD) ambulatory care. In 1974, municipal and voluntary hospitals in New York City accounted for a total 11.4 million ambulatory care patient visits.

A small number of community health centers (CHC) have been established in the last decade in New York City, mostly with strong federal financial assistance. Statistics are not readily available on the total

---

*As defined by the New York City Department of Health, a shared health facility is:

. . . three or more providers delivering health care, either independently or in association with each other, within a single structure and (a) two or more of whom share common waiting areas, examining rooms, treatment rooms, equipment, supporting staff or any shared space, (b) one or more of whom receives payment on a fee for service basis from the [Medicaid] Program, and (c) the providers receive from the Program a total aggregate monthly remuneration in excess of five thousand dollars for any one month during the preceding twelve months, in return for ambulatory care services rendered within the facility.

number of these facilities or the magnitude of their operations.

The quality of care provided by some SHFs (and by some hospitals), in the view of many public health officials and others, is questionable. Nonetheless, they are evidently approved and often preferred to hospital based ambulatory care facilities by a substantial segment of the population in economically depressed areas of New York City and other major urban areas. The comprehensive care and neighborhood control of CHCs assure their favor with others living in these areas.

PURPOSE OF THIS STUDY

The purpose of this study was through primary research to determine the basis and intensity of patient preferences for these alternative forms of ambulatory health care.

METHODOLOGY

Task 1—*Orientation*

The first task in this study involved review of selected literature and interviews with local health officials, representatives of provider organizations and others to gain a greater understanding of the nature of the facilities which are the subject of this study and the patient universe which they serve.

Task 2—*Defining the Universe/Identifying a Sample*

The second task involved identifying a sample, for interviewing purposes, reasonably representative of those who select and utilize these alternative forms of ambulatory care in economically depressed areas of New York City. Three widely separated neighborhoods were selected for study: (1) the South Bronx, (2) Williamsburg/Brooklyn, and (3) the Lower East Side of Manhattan. It was decided to interview an approximately equal number

of patients who were actually waiting for ambulatory care for themselves or those whom they accompanied e.g., spouse or children, in one SHF and one hospital in each of the three neighborhoods.

Three SHFs slightly larger than average (to assure an adequate number of interviewees) and three hospitals (two municipal and one voluntary hospital) were selected in each neighborhood taking into account proximity within the selected neighborhood of each to one another, availability of public transportation to each and the demographic unity of the respective community each pair of facilities served. Additionally, one well established community health center was selected on the Lower East Side.

Two hundred and twenty eight patient interviews were completed in these seven facilities and utilized in this study. The number of patients in each of the selected facilities is shown in Table 1.

Of 228 respondents, 60 percent were Hispanic, 77 percent were female. Respondents were evenly spread in three adult age groups. Seventy-seven percent had

Table 1 Interviews by Location and Type of Facility

Location/Type of Facility		Respondents	
South Bronx			
Shared Health Facility		31	
Municipal Hospital		28	
	Total	59	59
Williamsburg/Brooklyn			
Shared Health Facility		35	
Municipal Hospital		33	
	Total	68	68
Lower East Side/Manhattan			
Shared Health Facility		31	
Voluntary Hospital		35	
Community Health Center		35	
	Total	101	101
Total			228

Note: Seventeen patient interviews were terminated before completion and/or otherwise disqualified.

third party coverage (mostly Medicaid) for ambulatory care costs.

Hispanic female patients predominated in SHF and CHC interviews. Black female patients predominated in municipal hospital interviews. White and Hispanic female, somewhat older, patients predominated in the voluntary hospital interviews.

The lowest percentage of respondents having third party coverage (62%), excluding the CHC, was in the municipal hospitals. Third party coverage of patients by type of facility where interviewed is shown below:

Type of Facility	No. Respondents	No. Covered	% Covered
Shared Health Facility	97	92	94.8
Voluntary Hospital	35	32	91.4
Municipal Hospital	61	38	62.2
Community Health Center	35	14	40.0
Total	228	176	77.1

Only the municipal hospital and CHC will provide nonemergency ambulatory care to persons on demand without charge. Lack of third party coverage obviously limits patients' choice of other sources of care.

Patients of Hispanic extraction are somewhat more represented in the sample drawn than reported as a proportion of total patient load by the facilities in which interviews were conducted. In other known respects, the sample appears to be reasonably representative of the patients served in the facilities visited.

Task 3—*Develop Interview Guide*

Patients were to be interviewed in open reception areas while waiting to see a doctor. It was believed necessary, therefore, to limit interviews to ten minutes. Basic common information had to be obtained from all respondents; additional data could be obtained from selected sub-samples. One interview guide was developed and used for all interviews in the South Bronx and Brooklyn (see Exhibit A). Another guide was developed and utilized on the Lower East Side. The second guide (see Exhibit B), in addition to some differences with the first guide respecting the nature of data to be obtained, sought to determine the criteria and process by which patients select from among alternative forms of health care in an open-ended, rather than directed manner.

Task 4—*Interview Patients*

Patients were interviewed during daytime hours. All patients interviewed at each facility were interviewed on the same day. Interviews were conducted during seven weekdays in the last two weeks of February and the first week of March, 1976. Interviews were conducted by a personable and attractive young woman equally fluent in English and Spanish. Interviews were conducted in the language chosen by the respondent.

Task 5—*Inspect Facilities*

Each facility was inspected and its manager or director was interviewed by the author. Four sites were clean, orderly and attractive. Three sites were crowded.

Task 6—*Tabulate and Analyze Interview Data*

Data obtained from 228 patient interviews was interpreted and tabulated at the conclusion of all interviews. Analysis of these tabulations is contained in the findings section of this report.

Task 7—*Prepare the Report*

The final task was to prepare this report which provides background information on the subject, the purpose of the study, the methodology employed, and findings, conclusions, and tabulations.

Exhibit A Patient Preferences for Alternative Forms of Ambulatory Care

1. How many times since Thanksgiving have you come to this clinic to see a doctor?

2. How many times since Thanksgiving have you gone somewhere else to see a doctor?

3. Where else have you gone to see a doctor since Thanksgiving?

4. What other clinics or emergency rooms do you know of near here?

5. Why do you go most often to _____ ?

6. How do you feel about going to some of those other places that you have been to in the past or that you know about?

7. Which of the following are most important to you when it comes to going to a clinic, a hospital, or a doctor's office?

   A. It's close to home.

   B. It has convenient office hours.

   C. You don't have to wait long to see a doctor.

   D. It offers more services.

   E. The people there are nice to you.

   F. The doctors there are good.

   G. You don't need an appointment.

   H. The offices are attractive.

8. How are you going to pay for this visit?

9. Patient's age _____   Sex _____   Race/ethnicity _____

FINDINGS

Basis For Selection of Alternative Forms of Care

Criteria used by respondents in selecting from among alternative forms of care, in order of frequency reported, are shown in Table 2. Clearly, accessibility or proximity of a chosen facility to a respondent's home was the criterion cited by most respondents in choosing where to obtain ambulatory care. The quality of care respondents have received in the past and the length of time they have waited in the past to see a doctor were also reported to be major determinants. Respondents on the Lower East Side, none of whom were given suggested criteria from which to choose for selecting from among alternative sources of care, also ranked accessibility and "good doctors" as important. Many however, emphasized familiarity with a particular facility and the desire to continue treatment where they began. Finally, a substantial number of these respondents said they choose a facility on

Exhibit B Patient Preferences for Alternative Forms of Ambulatory Care

1. *How many times* since last summer have you come to this clinic to see a doctor?

2. What do you *like most* about this clinic?

3. *Where else* have you gone since last summer to see a doctor?

4. Where do you *go most often* to see a doctor?

5. *Why* do you go there *most often?*

6. What do you *dislike most* about the other clinics and hospitals that you have visited?

7. *How do you decide* where to go to see a doctor?

8. Does your *entire family* usually go to the *same place* to see a doctor?

9. *How* are you going to *pay* for this visit?

10. Patient's age _____ Sex _____ Race/ethnicity _____

the basis of recommendations by relatives and friends.

Reasons for Selecting Particular Forms of Care

Every respondent was asked and reported the particular ambulatory care facility he used most and the reasons for the apparent preference.

Of 228 respondents, 77 or 34 percent indicated they utilized a SHF most often. "Good doctor," a satisfactory outcome in previous treatment received at a particular SHF and its closeness to the respondent's home were the pre-eminent reasons given for utilization of a SHF by respondents interviewed in a SHF. "The doctors are good here" and "I feel better here and it's closer to home" were comments expressed by two respondents typical of those expressed by many who utilize a SHF. "They take good care of the kids. They're not repugnant with you. They're very patient," said another which suggests that at least for some the quality of medical care provided

Table 2 Basis for Selection of Alternative Forms of Ambulatory Care Identified by Patients

Criteria Cited*	South Bronx/ Brooklyn	Lower East Side
Block 1		
Accessibility	40	30
Good Doctors	37	14
Short Waiting Time	27	3
Staff Courtesy	11	7
Comprehensive Services	17	
Convenient Office Hours	10	2
No Appointment Needed	12	
Attractive Facility	2	4
Block 2		
Recommended		2
No Answer		13
Familiarity/Continuity of Care		13
Available at Low or No Cost		9
To Obtain Emergency Care		8
Good Treatment Outcome		7
Personal Interest/ Attentiveness		7

*Patients interviewed in the South Bronx and Brooklyn, constituting 55% of the sample, were asked to indicate importance of suggested criteria shown in Block 1. Patients interviewed in Manhattan were asked to suggest their own criteria. Those which they suggested encompass some of those in Block 1 and all of those in Block 2 as shown.

may, in some instances, encompass rapport with patients, personal interest and attentiveness, and staff courtesy—other reasons also frequently cited for utilizing a SHF.

Significantly, patients interviewed at SHFs also expressed several reasons for *not* using a hospital. Chief among them were: "bad doctors," poor outcome and long waiting time, "The city hospitals are too big, too abrupt. They exhibit contempt for people" typified many negative comments directed at hospitals by respondents. Nonetheless, SHF patients do continue, also, to use hospitals and they most often gave as reasons for utilizing a hospital: (1) the need to obtain emergency care when SHFs were not open or not considered ca-

pable of responding to the nature of an emergency and (2) the need or preference for a particular doctor or service. "If I'm very sick, I go to the hospital," said one respondent. "If it's urgent, I go to the hospital," said another and SHFs encourage patients in these circumstances to go.

Of 228 respondents, 99 or 43 percent indicated their principal source of ambulatory care was a municipal or voluntary hospital. Reasons most frequently cited for using a hospital by respondents interviewed in hospitals were: familiarity with a particular institution and the desirability of continuing treatment which they began there, the hospital's accessibility and closeness to their home and "good doctors." Unlike those who were interviewed in SHFs and who seldom had negative comments to make about SHFs, nearly 18 percent of patients interviewed in hospitals complained of the long waiting time to see a doctor.

Accessibility and the personal interest and attentiveness of staff ranked highest with regard to selecting a community health center as a source of care by the 37 or 16 percent of respondents who indicated that a community health center was their principal source of care. CHC respondents complained of long waiting times in hospitals.

Utilization of Particular Forms of Care

Respondents interviewed in two SHFs and in the two municipal hospitals reported an average of nearly six visits to a doctor somewhere in the past three months. More than half saw physicians in different types of facilities.

Frequency of physician visits was substantially higher for respondents interviewed in SHFs than in municipal hospitals. Of the 67 respondents who were interviewed in a SHF which they identified as their principal source of care, 79 percent reported seeing a doctor at that facility, in addition to physicians they may have seen elsewhere, at least once each month. Only 51 percent of patients interviewed in municipal hospitals which they identified as their principal source of care reported that frequency of utilization. Sixty-nine percent of those respondents who reported a voluntary hospital as their principal source of care reported utilization of that type of facility more than once per month.

Several reasons may be hypothesized for the apparent greater frequency of utilization of those who were interviewed in and prefer SHFs. They range from the relatively higher percentage of persons interviewed in SHFs with third party coverage, to the accessibility and relatively shorter waiting time for care afforded by these facilities, to the possibly larger numbers of nonemergent chronic conditions treated by SHFs than municipal hospitals, to the possibility, in some instances, of SHFs more frequently encouraging patients to make repeat visits. However, patients interviewed in SHFs were more aware of alternative sources of care than those interviewed in municipal hospitals. Patients whose principal source of care is a SHF or voluntary hospital more frequently use alternative sources of care in addition to their principal source of care than those who principally utilize municipal hospitals. It is reasonable to conjecture that patient initiative—at least the initiative of those patients with third party coverage—is more likely the causative factor with respect to frequency of utilization than the comforts, convenience and importuning of particular types of facilities. Patients whose principal form of care is a SHF are even prepared to travel longer to obtain care. This underscores the possibility that patients, themselves, rather than the facilities which they utilize have more to do with the frequency with which they seek medical care.

CONCLUSIONS

The appearance*, atmosphere, personal attentiveness of staff and rapport between doctor and patient both reported by re-

spondents and observed by the author are substantially different between hospitals on the one hand and shared health facilities and community health centers on the other. The relative closeness of preferred SHFs to respondents' homes and the relative waiting time to see a doctor are additional noted significant differences between these types of facilities. Moreover, some respondents reported a difference in the quality of care delivered by these different types of facilities. It is reasonable to surmise however, both from respondents' total response and the generally recognized calibre of the medical staff at the hospitals visited that perceived qualitative differences between types of facilities encompass aspects of the respondents' relationship to the medical staff of each facility beyond those strictly medical.

Hospital based ambulatory care facilities, compared with most SHFs, invariably are bigger, more crowded, and more noisy than SHFs and for reasons not sought in this study, they appear less willing or less able than SHFs to ameliorate negative characteristics in their delivery of care as perceived by patients. They are less inclined to schedule medical services in a manner designed to reduce patient waiting time.** They are less apt to have on their staff physicians fluent in Spanish—the only language of a substantial number of ambulatory care patients. In addition, because hospitals treat a greater number and range of critical medical conditions than SHFs or CHCs, they are less likely to be responsive to the often relatively less critical chronic

---

*Respondents seldom commented on the purely physical appearance of any facility visited although there were substantial differences between them. "Appearance" in this context relates to crowdedness, noise, and size of facilities observed.

**Less than 20 percent of respondents sought or apparently were given specific appointments to see a doctor at SHFs, hospitals, or the CHC although many visit a facility on a day or at a specific time when they know a particular physician or service will be available.

condition of many patients who perhaps more often visit SHFs.

Third party coverage, in nearly all instances Medicaid, has enabled millions to exercise choice of provider in seeking medical care. While the nature of the sample interviewed in this study does not permit a defensible inference with respect to relative preference of those given freedom of choice, clearly SHFs, CHCs, and hospitals each have their adherents. The factors previously noted partly account for this distribution. Sociocultural and emotional factors, beyond the scope of this study, may also be responsible. Future study with respect to patient preferences for alternative sources of ambulatory care could usefully be directed to (1) in-depth examination of the full extent and reasons for the large number of individuals who apparently utilize multiple sources of care and (2) expanded examination of the reasons a truly representative sample of the economically depressed urban population has for preferring various alternative sources of care. Such an examination ought to develop and use two subsamples in order to eliminate the bias introduced by the availability to some, but not others, of third party coverage.

14. Study of Title 19 (Medicaid) Coverage of Sterilization

HELEN M. WALLACE, HYMAN GOLDSTEIN,
EDWIN M. GOLD, and ALFRED C. HEXTER

Reprinted with permission from *Journal of the American Medical Women's Association*, Vol. 31, No. 5, May 1976.

Individuals and families eligible for care under the Medicaid program are generally a high risk group of our population. In addition to their need for basic economic support, they frequently have health, housing, social, and vocational support needs. Those who are included in the maternal and child health age group have higher birth and fertility rates, more unwanted pregnancies, more out-of-wedlock pregnancies, higher infant and perinatal mortality, and greater incidence of infants with low birth weight—all conditions requiring a concentration of improved comprehensive preconceptional, maternal health, infant children and youth, interconceptional (and day care) services. Among those services needed is the spectrum of family planning, including contraception, abortion, and sterilization.

A previous study by the authors investigated the coverage of abortion under the Medicaid program.[1] The present study provides data to answer the following questions:

1. How many states now include sterilization under Medicaid?
2. How many individuals receive sterilization under Medicaid?
3. What are the restrictions to providing sterilization under Medicaid?
4. What are the costs in providing sterilization under Medicaid?

METHOD OF STUDY

During the winter of 1973 and spring of 1974, a study form was developed and mailed to the State Commissioners of Health and Welfare of all states in the United States, with three follow-up mailings.

Response to the Study

Table 1 shows the response to the four mailings. Of the total 56 states and territories, 3 (5.4%) have no Medicaid program. Of the remaining 53 states and territories, 43 returned the study form (81.1%). Of the remaining 10 states, 8 did not return the study form; 2 reported that Medicaid does not cover sterilization. Of the 51 states with Medicaid programs that cover sterilization, 43 or 84.3% completed the study form (Table 1).

RESULTS

State Administration of Medicaid Program

Of the 45 states providing information on their Medicaid program, in 26 (57.8%)

115

Table 1 Number and Percent of States Responding to Study by Type of Response and Medicaid Program

Type of Response	No.	Percent
Total	56*	100.0
With Medicaid program	53	94.6
Completed study form	43	76.8
Did not complete study form	8	14.3
Medicaid program does not cover sterilization	2	3.6
No Medicaid program	3	5.4

*Includes 50 states, District of Columbia, the Commonwealth of Puerto Rico, 3 territories, and 1 trust territory.

Table 2 Number and Percent of States with Medicaid Programs by Administrative Location of Program Responsibility

Administrative Location	No.	Percent
Total states providing information	45	100.0
Welfare Department	26	57.8
Health Department	5	11.1
Combined Health and Welfare Department	13	28.9
Separate Commission	1	2.2

Medicaid is administered by the State Welfare Department; in 5 (11.1%) by the State Health Department; in 13 (28.9%) by a combined Health and Welfare Department; and in 1 (1.8%) by a separate Commission (Table 2).

Coverage of State Medicaid Program

Of the 45 states reporting on their Medicaid program, 42 (93.3%) reported coverage of those on public assistance; 37 (82.2%) reported coverage of those on Aid to Families with Dependent Children; 24 states (53.3%) reported coverage of medically indigent; and 23 states (51.1%) reported coverage of other groups (Table 3).

Coverage of Sterilization by Medicaid

Of the 45 respondent states which completed the study form, 43 (95.6%) reported coverage of sterilization by Medicaid. Of the 2 states where the Medicaid program does not cover sterilization, one reported

that inclusion of sterilization is in the planning stage; the other gave as the reason for non-coverage the current legal controversy about sterilization of minors and the mentally incompetent.

Data were requested from the states regarding the number of patients sterilized under Title 19 and the expenditures for such services. Only 8 states reported data on number of patients sterilized, 15 states on average cost, and 4 states on expenditures. The number of respondent states for these specific questions is considered too small to discuss the reported findings. The remainder of this report summarizes the data provided by the 43 states with sterilization coverage under Medicaid.

Eligibility Restrictions for Sterilization under Medicaid

Most respondent states (36) report financial eligibility restrictions. Over half of the

Table 3 Number of States with Medicaid Coverage for Specified Welfare Categories

Welfare Category	Response			Percent		
	Total with Medicaid	Yes	No	Total	Yes	No
Those on public assistance	45	42	3	100.0	93.3	6.7
Aid to families with dependent children (AFDC)	45	37	8	100.0	82.2	17.8
Medically indigent	45	24	21	100.0	53.3	46.7
Other	45	23	22	100.0	51.1	48.9

Table 4 Number of States Reporting Eligibility Restrictions for Sterilizations Under Medicaid

	Response				Percent			
Type of Restriction	Total	Yes	No	Question not answered	Total	Yes	No	Question not answered
Only married are eligible								
Males	43	2	37	4	100.0	4.7	86.0	9.3
Females	43	0	40	3	100.0	0.0	93.0	7.0
Minimum age	43	25	17	1	100.0	58.1	39.6	2.3
Parental consent for minors	43	25	.7	11	100.0	58.1	16.3	25.6
Financial eligibility	43	36	6	1	100.0	83.7	14.0	2.3
Residence	43	23	20	0	100.0	53.5	46.5	0.0
Consent of spouse if married	43	14	26	3	100.0	32.5	60.5	7.0
Minimum parity	43	1	40	2	100.0	2.3	93.0	4.7

states (25) report an age restriction, and the same number report a requirement of parental consent for minors. About half of the states (23) have a residence requirement. One third of the states (14) require the consent of the spouse. Two states require that males applying for sterilization under Medicaid be married; this is not required for females. One state has a requirement concerning minimum parity (Table 4).

With regard to age restriction, 12 states reported that sterilization under Medicaid is not covered for those under 21 years; 6 additional states reported that it is not covered for those under 18 years; and 4 other states reported that it· is not covered for "minors." Three states indicated that there was a minimum age but did not specify what it was.

In regard to parental consent for a minor, 12 states require parental consent for those under 18 years; and an additional 7 states require it for those under 21 years (Table 5).

Indications for Sterilization under Medicaid

In 7 states (16.3%) a patient request was sufficient indication for doing a sterilization, in 6 states (14.0%) a medical reason was sufficient. However, in 27 states (62.8%) either a patient request or a medical reason was sufficient (Table 6).

Services Paid for by Medicaid and Offered to Patients Applying for Sterilization

Most respondent states provide funds for the testing and treatment of venereal dis-

Table 5 Number of States Requiring Parental Consent for Minors by Age Requiring Consent

Age in Years	No. of States	Percent
Total	25	100.0
Under 16	1	4.0
Under 18	12	48.0
Under 19	1	4.0
Under 21	6	24.0
"Minor"	2	8.0
Age not stated	3	12.0

Table 6 Number and Percent of States Reporting Reasons for Doing Sterilization under Medicaid by Reason Reported

Reason for Sterilization	No.	Percent
Total	43	100.0
Patient request only	7	16.3
Medical reason only	6	14.0
Either patient request or medical reason	27	62.8
Socioeconomic factors, including multiparity	1	2.3
Reason not stated	2	4.7

Table 7 Number of States Offering Additional Services Under Medicaid to Sterilization Patients by Type of Service

Type of Service	Response				Percent			
	Total*	Yes	No	Not answered	Total	Yes	No	Not answered
VD testing	43	42	0	1	100.0	97.7	0.0	2.3
VD treatment	43	41	1	1	100.0	95.4	2.3	2.3
Papanicolau smear	43	42	0	1	100.0	97.7	0.0	2.3
Breast examination	43	41	1	1	100.0	95.4	2.3	2.3
Pregnancy testing	43	39	3	1	100.0	90.7	7.0	2.3
Sperm examination	43	32	10	1	100.0	74.4	23.3	2.3
Sperm count	43	33	9	1	100.0	76.7	20.9	2.3
Counseling	43	36	6	1	100.0	83.7	14.0	2.3
Follow-up	43	35	7	1	100.0	81.4	16.3	2.3
Psychiatric	43	37	5	1	100.0	86.1	11.6	2.3
Genetic diagnostic studies	43	32	10	1	100.0	74.4	23.3	2.3
Genetic counseling	43	29	13	1	100.0	67.4	30.2	2.3

*Including 13 states that indicated that whatever the physician ordered would be provided.

eases, for Papanicolaou smears, for breast examinations, for pregnancy testing, and for psychiatric services. Services less likely to be paid for are genetic diagnostic studies, genetic counseling, sperm examination, and sperm counts (Table 7).

Sterilization Procedures Paid for by Medicaid

Most respondent states provide funds for all forms of sterilization—tubal ligation, hysterectomy, and vasectomy (Table 8).

Table 8 Number of States Providing Sterilization Services Under Medicaid by Type of Procedure Offered

Type of Procedure	Response				Percent			
	Total	Yes	No	Not answered	Total	Yes	No	Not answered
Tubal ligation	43	42	0	1	100.0	97.7	0.0	2.3
Vaginal	43	40	2	1	100.0	93.0	4.7	2.3
Abdominal-surgical	43	41	1	1	100.0	95.4	2.3	2.3
Laparoscopy	43	41	1	1	100.0	95.4	2.3	2.3
Hysterectomy	43	39	3	1	100.0	90.7	7.0	2.3
Vasectomy	43	41*	1	1	100.0	95.4	2.3	2.3
Other								
X-ray where indicated	43	1	41	1	100.0	2.3	95.4	2.3
Bilateral oophorectomy	43	1	41	1	100.0	2.3	95.4	2.3
Vas ligation	43	1	41	1	100.0	2.3	95.4	2.3
"Any medically accepted surgical procedure"	43	1	41	1	100.0	2.3	95.4	2.3

*Includes one state which indicated that vasectomy may be performed only as required to treat an existing medical condition.

Places Where Sterilization Can Be Done under Medicaid

For males, sterilization can be done in a doctor's office or in a hospital inpatient or outpatient service in most states. For females, most states reported that sterilization can be done in a hospital inpatient service (42 states); 30 states reported that it can be done in a hospital outpatient service and 23 in a doctor's office (Table 9).

Requirement for Consultation Prior to Doing Sterilization under Medicaid

Twelve states (27.9%) require a consultation prior to doing sterilization under Medicaid, and 29 states (67.4%) do not (Table 10). The question was asked about the type of consultant required. One state reported requiring an obstetrician or urologist; 1 state reported requiring medical and psychiatric consultants; 1 state reported requiring a social worker; 5 states reported requiring physicians. The number of consultants required is 1 to 2. The other 4 states that required consultation prior to sterilization did not specify the type of consultant required.

Medical Specialty Permitted to Perform Sterilization under Medicaid

Most states permit sterilizations to be done by any physician (37 states). In addition, this includes obstetricians (27 states), general surgeons (27 states), and urologists (25 states). Twenty-four states permit an osteopath to do sterilizations (Table 11).

Use of Consultants by Medicaid

Twenty-seven states (62.8%) reported that consultants are used by the Medicaid program; 13 states (30.2%) reported that consultants are not used (Table 12). The types of consultants used are most frequently physicians in association with dentists, pharmacists, nurses, and social workers (Table 13).

Table 9 Number of States Providing Sterilization under Medicaid by Place Where Sterilization May Be Performed and Sex of Patient

Place of Operation	Sex	
	Male	Female
Total	43	43
Hospital inpatient service	38*	42*
Hospital outpatient service	39*	30*
Doctor's office	41	23
Ambulatory surgical center	1	1
Family planning clinics	2	1
Other clinics	1	1

*Includes one state which indicated that hospital must be "certified."

Table 10 Number and Percent of States Requiring Consultation Prior to Performing Sterilization under Medicaid

Consultation Required	No.	Percent
Total	43	100.0
Yes	12	27.9
No	29	67.4
Not answered	2	4.7

Table 11 Number and Percent of States Providing Sterilization Services under Medicaid by Medical Specialty Permitted to Perform Sterilization

Medical Specialty	No.	Percent
Total	43	100.0
"Any physician"	37	86.0
General surgeon	27	62.8
Obstetrician	27	62.8
Urologist	25	58.1
Osteopath	24	55.8

Table 12 Number and Percent of States Reporting Consultant Use for Sterilizations under Medicaid Program

Consultation Used	No.	Percent
Total	43	100.0
Yes	27	62.8
No	13	30.2
Not answered	3	7.0

Table 13 Number of States Using Consultants for Sterilizations under Medicaid Program by Type of Consultants Used

Type of Consultant	No.	Percent
Total using consultants	27	100.0
Physician	7	25.9
Physician, dentist	2	7.4
Physician, dentist, pharmacist	2	7.4
Medical foundation	2	7.4
"All types" of health professionals	2	7.4
Miscellaneous*	7	25.9
Not answered	5	18.5

*One each of the following were reported: advisory committee, physician, podiatrist; physician and nurse; physician and social worker; physician, nurse, social worker, physical therapist; physician, social worker, pharmacist; physician, pharmacist; physician, dentist, pharmacist, optometrist, chiropractor, podiatrist, psychologist.

Requirement of Authorization Prior to Doing Sterilization

Thirteen states (30.2%) require an authorization prior to doing a sterilization; 28 states (65.1%) do not have such a requirement. When a prior authorization is required, it is usually required in writing (Table 14).

Requirement of Review by Review Committee Prior to Authorization of Sterilization

Ten states (23.3%) require a review by a review committee prior to any sterilization

Table 14 Number and Percent of States Requiring Authorization Prior to Performing Sterilizations under Medicaid by Type of Authorization Required

Type of Authorization	No.	Percent
Total	43	100.0
Prior authorization required	13*	30.2
In writing	7*	16.3
By telephone	0*	0.0
Either written or by telephone	2	4.7
Type not specified	4	9.3
Not required	28	65.1
Not answered	2	4.7

*Includes one state where prior authorization is required for hysterectomies only.

Table 15 Number and Percent of States Requiring Committee Review Prior to Sterilization under Medicaid

Review Requirement	No.	Percent
Total	43	100.0
Review required	10	23.3
In all cases	5	11.6
Only when hysterectomy is done	1	2.3
Only when mentally retarded or other incompetents are involved	3	7.0
Only on petition by any other two people for sterilization	1	2.3
Not required	31	72.1
Not answered	2	4.7

under Medicaid; 31 states (72.1%) have no such requirement (Table 15). Seven states reported on who does such a review; it is usually done by a committee composed of a group of physicians. Criteria used by the review committee include medical necessity, special protection of the mentally incompetent, and the criteria included in federal guidelines.

Medical Complications

Only two states reported any medical complications known to have occurred in patients sterilized under Medicaid. They consisted of bleeding and severe symptoms requiring subsequent hysterectomy.

Problems Encountered

Problems encountered in sterilization under Medicaid were reported by a number of states. They consist of delays (5 states); these include delays due to legal aspects in the case of mental incompetency and minors, delays in appointments for workup and counseling, or delays associated with required procedures. Another type of problem reported by 3 states is that related to physicians' fees, i.e., fees requested are too large. One state reported abuse of the program, i.e., frequent hysterectomy following tubal ligation may indicate the possibility of abuse of the program. An additional problem reported by one state is the lack of availability of federal funds for sterilization of minors or the legally incompetent.

Rejection of Patients for Sterilization

No patients were reported as having been rejected for sterilization under Medicaid in 1973.

Establishment of Standards

Twelve states (27.9%) reported the establishment of standards for the performance of sterilization under Medicaid; 26 states (60.5%) reported that no standards have been established. The 12 states indicated that standards were established by the state agency responsible for Medicaid, or by the federal guidelines.

DISCUSSION

The situation with regard to certain aspects of sterilization under Medicaid is un-resolved, and this directly affects the number of individuals currently receiving this service under Medicaid. It is pertinent to point out that this study was conducted during a national controversy about the performance of sterilization on minors and the mentally incompetent. In September 1973, proposed federal regulations were published in the Federal Register, setting forth the policies regarding the use of federal funds for sterilization procedures. On February 6, 1974, these regulations were published in the Federal Register.[1] Shortly thereafter, the effective date was delayed to permit resolution by the U.S. District Court. On March 15, 1974, the U.S. District Court in Washington, D.C., declared in effect that no federal reimbursement will be made for sterilization unless (1) the patient is legally of age in the state, (2) the patient is competent to give informed consent, and (3) the consent form shows prominently at the top that a refusal or withdrawal of consent does not jeopardize other benefits.[1-4]

On April 18, 1974, the Secretary of the U.S. Department of HEW continued a moratorium on sterilization of individuals under the age of 21 years and individuals legally incapable of consenting to sterilization. In addition, new regulations for Medicaid were set forth for sterilization of legally competent individuals over the age of 21. HEW instituted a new requirement of a 72-hr waiting period between the giving of informed consent and the performance of any non-therapeutic sterilization using federal funds. The regulations set forth elements that the Department considers necessary to informed consent: (1) a fair explanation of the procedures to be followed; (2) a description of the attendant discomforts and risks; (3) a description of the benefits to be expected; (4) an explanation concerning appropriate alternative methods of family planning and the effect and impact of the proposed sterilization, including the fact that it must be considered to be an irreversible procedure; (5) an offer to answer any inquiries concerning the procedures; and (6) an instruction that the individual is free to withhold or withdraw his or her consent to the procedure at any time prior to the sterilization without prejudicing his or her future care and without loss of other project or program benefits to which the patient might otherwise be entitled. Involved are all HEW programs under the Society Security Act, including Medicaid.[4]

Most states in 1973 permitted sterilization under Medicaid. However, as is evident from Table 4, there are restrictions in many states. These restrictions relate to financial eligibility, the requirement of parental consent for minors, age, residence, and the requirement of consent of the spouse. These restrictions undoubtedly account for the small reported number of sterilizations under Medicaid.

The question of other relevant services paid for by Medicaid (Table 7) is an important one in considering the need for comprehensive health care. While it is gratifying that most states reported that such services as venereal disease testing and treatment, Papanicolaou smears, and breast examinations are covered, fewer states reported the inclusion of such services as genetic diagnostic studies and counseling, and sperm examination and counts. Comprehensive health programs need to be more inclusive. Persons considered for sterilization often have other problems requiring attention. Each person should receive such other services as VD testing, Papanicolaou smear, breast examination, pregnancy testing, counseling and follow-up, and, where indicated, genetic studies and counseling, psychiatric services, and medical consultation.

Only 12 states (27.9%) reported the establishment of standards for the performance of sterilization under Medicaid. It would appear advisable that more states proceed to the step of standard setting. This would seem especially needed because the procedures are being done in hospital outpatient services and in doctors' offices (Table 9) and also because of the fact that consultation is required in only 12 states (Table 10).

It is important to realize that only a small number of states was able to provide data for 1973 on the extent of sterilization under Medicaid. For example, 8 states provided data on number of patients, 15 states on average cost, and 4 states on expenditures. Since the study herein reported antedates the legal and procedural changes in the status of federally supported sterilization, mentioned above, their impact is not reflected in these data. Nevertheless, insofar as the legal and procedural changes reflect increasing conservatism in the effort to avoid abuses of "informed consent," the expected reduction in prevalence of sterilization in the public sector contrasts with the growing acceptance (and prevalence) of sterilization in the public at large.

No data are available from the National Reporting System for Family Planning Services regarding sterilizations performed under Medicaid.[5] This is a serious handicap in attempting to determine the prevalence of this procedure, the age and marital status, parity, and other characteristics of those undergoing sterilization, and the costs involved. In order that inequities in availability of as important a preventive health measure as sterilization may become readily apparent as new mechanisms for health services delivery evolve, ready access to relevant statistics is needed.

Medicaid now represents one of the largest public medical care programs in this country. The difficulty in obtaining such data, as illustrated by the present study,.argues strongly for a change in its data collection and retrieval system in order to provide this important information.

Acknowledgment

The authors wish to express their appreciation to Dr. Donald H. Minkler for his assistance in preparation of the manuscript.

REFERENCES

1. Federal Register: Sterilization restrictions. 39:26:III: 4730–4733 6 Feb. 1974.

2. U.S. Department of Health, Education and Welfare: Restrictions applicable to sterilization procedures in federally assisted family planning projects. Deferral of effective date of regulations. 12 Feb. 1974.

3. Federal Register: Restrictions applicable to sterilization procedures in federally assisted family planning projects. 39:76: 13872–73, 13887–88, 18 Apr. 1974.

4. American College of Obstetricians and Gynecologists: *ACOG Newsletter,* p. 3, June 1964.

5. Tyler, C.W., Jr.: Reported in the *Family Planning Digest, 3:* p. 10, 4 July 1974.

SECTION THREE

LESSONS FROM ADMINISTRATIVE AND OPERATIONAL ASPECTS OF MEDICAID PROGRAM MANAGEMENT

Federal Medicaid legislation allowed the states wide latitude in the options that they could choose in their opting for participation in the program. However, while Public Law 89–97 encouraged experimentation, the law was also restrictive at the same time in many of its requirements. States could make choices relative to the following areas:

- Serving welfare recipients alone or people with low incomes but not on welfare.
- Providing any one of dozens of possible benefit packages.
- Administering the Medicaid program through any one of several state agencies.
- Sharing the costs with the federal government on a percentage unique for each state.
- Licensing, auditing and reviewing the performance of providers in any of a number of ways.

Consideration of the restrictive aspects of the Medicaid legislation raises the question of the interface between regulations and administration of a program. Management personnel are provided with regulations which interpret the law and set down

guidelines for operational procedures. Regulatory dilemmas that may cause disruption within the administration of the program include the following:

- Complex regulations permit greater discretionary behavior than simple regulations. Can complex regulations be monitored is the issue that needs consideration.
- Severe sanctions often create a sanction-free environment. Administrators know that severe sanctions are less likely to be carried out.
- Frequent updating of regulations destroys the intent of the regulations. Administrators tend to ignore constantly changing regulations.
- Intervening in the behavior of all program participants wastes resources and may create aberrant or undesirable behavior.

To add to the mixture of experimentation with restrictions, long standing jurisdictional rivalries and power struggles between state departments of welfare, health, education and other agencies also corrupted the development of a smooth running administrative scheme for the state's Medicaid programs. Who was going to run the Medicaid program in each state? Currently, the breakdown by states is as follows: in 27 states welfare departments run the program; in 17 states the program is administered in conjunction by health and welfare departments; in 8 states the health department administers the Medicaid program; and in Mississippi a free standing agency administers the program. Overall, welfare departments have the major role in administering Medicaid programs in the states. This occurred despite the well documented evidence of problems in welfare administration of similar type activities.

Data management became a serious roadblock in the administration of many Medicaid programs. State administrators were unprepared for the volume of information that had to be processed in terms of technology as well as in terms of people. Computerization took time and in the interim, the problems mounted up and resulted in massive tie-ups of red tape.

Financial aspects of the Medicaid program tended to dominate the management operations as well as the services offered. Prior to paying attention to the establishment of a smooth running administrative Medicaid program, top level management were ordered to concentrate on cost containment by their state legislatures. Therefore, cost considerations usually preceded any operational administrative edicts.

Health care providers were reimbursed in two ways: fee schedules were established for services or providers were paid based on their "usual, customary and reasonable charges." Some states reimbursed providers using records from prior years to show how much the provider charged and then paying a percentage of that usual fee, say 75 percent. Of course, the percentage could be lowered and the fee schedule could always be reduced and some states did that to cut costs.

A number of policy choices were open to states as they looked for ways to control the seemingly endless spiral of rising costs for providing health care under the Medicaid program. Policy choices included the following:

- Establish fees paid to providers closer to the real costs. This could cut down the "demand" for services.
- Where fees paid are low, increase the payment. Perhaps more health care providers would then participate in the Medicaid program.
- Develop an effective utilization review program. Unnecessary services could be reduced and save funds.
- Set fixed budgets for all Medicaid financed services provided by physicians, hospitals, nurses, etc. Expenditures must remain within budget limitations.
- Develop and make greater use of capitation reimbursement—similar to a fixed budget in that all services are covered by the capitation payment.

Obviously, these choices do not have to be made on a one only basis. Combinations or all could be used simultaneously.

Cost-sharing as a containment mechanism is allowed under Section 1902(2) (14) of the Social Security Act. Three requirements are stated in the law for the states to follow in the imposition of cost-sharing as follows:

- Cost-sharing fees may be imposed only on the optional services for cash assistance recipients.
- Cost-sharing may be imposed on both the optional and the mandatory services for the medically needy group.
- Cost-sharing fees imposed by the states must be nominal.

Meeting the three requirements, the states usually considered three types of cost-sharing for the Medicaid recipients:

- Copayments—The patient pays a fixed charge per unit of service such as one dollar for a prescription or two dollars for an evening office visit.

- Coinsurance—The patient pays a percentage of the bill such as 10 percent of the fee.
- Deductible—The patient pays up to a set sum and then the Medicaid program pays the remainder. Each patient has to pay the first $25 with no more than $100 for a family and then Medicaid pays the rest of the bill.

Those opposing the imposition of cost-sharing by the states have raised questions relative to the mandated requirements. What is an optional service? How can drugs be considered optional when they are required as part of the treatment regimen. What is the point of being examined for eye problems and then not being allowed to buy the eyeglasses? What is a "nominal" fee? Does the imposition of cost-sharing fees cause the patient to delay seeing a physician until the condition is more serious? If that happens, doesn't the Medicaid program defeat itself because the state then has to spend much more for the more serious problem?

Evidently, cost containment can raise as many problems as it attempts to solve. Nevertheless, a number of recommendations have emerged from a consensus review of state activities.* In order of their potential savings, the following cost containment actions are advised:

- Federal government should impose a limit on total hospital revenues.
- Federal government should increase its financial share for long-term care services through Supplementary Security Income payments.
- States should be required to institute and operate a surveillance/utilization

review (S/UR) system with the federal government funding the total cost.
- Early and Periodic Screening, Diagnosis and Treatment (EPSDT) should be targeted at specific diseases within specific groups of children.
- States should be allowed to experiment with limiting benefits by diagnoses.
- States should be required to issue Medicaid clients photo identification cards.
- States should be allowed to institute nominal copayments for physician ambulatory care.
- Freedom of choice of provider provision should be deleted.
- All nursing homes certified by either Medicare or Medicaid must participate in both programs.

Another administrative concern is the utilization of services provided under the Medicaid program. Components that impinge upon utilization consider whether patients and providers accept the services; whether there is easy access to the services; whether the services and resources are available; whether continuity of care is provided so that someone acts as the coordinator of services; whether there is any cost factor that deters utilization; and whether the services are of high enough quality to attract utilization. Utilization can also be affected by the following elements:

- Desires and attitudes of the professional providers regarding the type of patients they wish to treat.
- Willingness of patients to provide the time and effort to obtain the services.
- Procedures established by the state that affect the quantity and the distribution of services.
- Alternatives available to both recipients and providers.

---

*John Holahan, William Scanlon and Bruce Spitz. *Restructuring Federal Medicaid Controls and Incentives*. Washington, D.C.: The Urban Institute, June 1977. pp. 64–86.

Both of these groupings of factors affecting the utilization of health care services have much in common. Yet, both point out that utilization is not merely a matter of opening the doors and saying, "Here we are." State Medicaid programs removed a major barrier to utilization by the poor of health services by providing the funding and the free choice of participating providers. However, the Medicaid program also had to consider utilization controls to counter possible abuse of the system.

Utilization controls are usually classified by the timing of the delivery of services; before, during or after services are rendered, as follows:

- Predelivery controls—This can be accomplished with prior review and/or prior authorization. Before services are rendered to the Medicaid patient, the health care provider must receive an authorization from the state to proceed. This could be for specific services such as elective surgery or for hospitalization or for a broader range of services where there might be abuses.
- Concurrent review—This control takes place at the same time that the patient is receiving the services. During hospitalization, a concurrent review could be undertaken to determine the required services, the length of the hospital stay and the health care personnel required.
- Posttreatment review—This is probably the most common utilization review technique and involves the reviewing of the patient's chart to determine if the proper treatment was given, if the hospital stay was appropriate and if the medication was suitable. Reviews of this nature are undertaken by institutional utilization review committees, by Professional Standards Review Organizations and by computerized surveillance utilization review systems.

Utilization reviews seek to discover when medically unnecessary services are rendered, when medically inappropriate services are rendered, when fraud and abuse takes place, when misutilization occurs and when socially inappropriate services are rendered where the costs exceed the benefits. Usually, the utilization reviews are guided by norms, standards and criteria established by the concerned professional groups. Surgeons would outline the criteria for performing various operations including the required lab tests, the diagnostic characteristics, the rationale for discharge and also the components that are considered inappropriate for that specific condition. In actual operation, a nurse coordinator could then use the established criteria to check against the patient's record and flag any deviations for investigation. In a similar fashion, computer programs have been prepared to identify deviations for utilization control programs.

Surveillance/Utilization Review (S/UR) programs have the following major characteristics and abilities:

- Production of a prescreened set of profiles based on comparing individual program participants (either providers of recipients) against the average pattern in the state.
- Limiting the profiles produced to those of providers and recipients whose behavior is statistically aberrant or in whom the reviewer has a special interest.
- Making postpayment utilization review a useful and manageable process.
- Providing the user with options in the approach to utilization review.

Acronyms relating to S/UR are AMOEBA, HEWCAS and MEDRX. AMOEBA (Automated Medicaid Overutilization and Erroneous Billing Auditor) is a less complex system that operates on the level of individual procedure codes and is both an editing and surveillance system. HEWCAS (H.E.W. Computer Audit System) is a computer application that is designed to allow an auditor entry to a computer data file in a state. Computer programs are written by HEWCAS to allow for information retrieval—for the compiling of the data. MEDRX (Medicaid Exception Reporting System) was designed to bring providers with questionable practices under closer scrutiny by the responsible Medicaid officials. Various screens are used that are classified by categories of providers and practitioners, indicator screens of practice characteristics and pattern screens of services. These are listed below:

1. *Provider Categories*—physicians with predominantly office practices; physicians whose practice includes a large number of procedures, or surgical type services; physicians whose practice is primarily office practice, but also provide numerous procedural or surgical services; dentists; dental surgeons or orthodontists; podiatrists, optometrists, other nonphysician practitioners; laboratories; pharmacies.
2. *Indicator Screens*—total amount of charges; total number of encounters; total number of service incidents; average amount charged per encounter; average amount charged per incident; average number of incidents per encounter; ratio of expensive service incidents to total number of service incidents; ratio of service incidents identified with fraudulent or abusive practices to total number of service incidents.
3. *Pattern Screens*—indication of yo-yoing; indication of ping-ponging; indication of gang visits; indication of unreasonability; indication of exceptional charges; indication of overutilization; indication of misutilization; indication of disutilization.

A perusal of the various screens indicates the scope of the MEDRX program in controlling utilization.

Utilization is directly related to the quality of health care. This would be particularly pertinent when norms, standards and criteria are used as part of the review. Since the guidelines were developed by peer professional groups, the assumption can be made that the quality of health care is also being defined. Using the commonly accepted categories of structure, process and outcome, the quality of health care rendered under the Medicaid program could be examined. However, the same difficulties that exist for the evaluation of the quality of health care in the total system also apply to the Medicaid system. Structure can be checked comparatively easily by noting the facilities, the personnel and the equipment in use. Process can be checked against the guidelines developed by peer groups for the treatment of specific illnesses and conditions. Outcomes can be examined using mortality and morbidity statistics. However, the relation between process and outcome needs much better documentation and valid measurement techniques. Most of the quality evaluations emphasize the process of health care. As the old proverb goes, "The operation was a success but the patient died." Evaluation of the quality of care rendered under the Medicaid programs will supply the same problematic data as previously until the improved measurement techniques are available.

All these aspects of the Medicaid program—management, funding, utilization and quality—offer numerous lessons for private practice, governmental programs and for future health care activities.

In his article about the Medicaid Management Information System (MMIS), Chavkin begins the article thusly, "Poor administration has plagued the Medicaid program since its inception." MMIS was developed to improve Medicaid administration. The following six interdependent computer subsystems comprise the MMIS schema: recipient subsystem; provider subsystem; claims processing subsystem; reference file subsystem; surveillance and utilization review (S/UR) subsystem; and management and administrative reporting subsystem. Each of these subsystems is explained in detail and charted. Chavkin cites the positive and negative aspects of the MMIS system with reference to eligibility, fraud, provider payments, and the quality of health care. Since all states and jurisdictions will be required to implement MMIS type systems, one may be coming to your state in the near future.

Mesel and Wirtschafter continue the discussion of the use of computers as they report on an on-line billing system for physicians' services. This approach was implemented and tested in 100 offices throughout Alabama over a 2 and 1/2 year period. Providers used a standard Touch Tone (R) telephone and received instructions and confirmation from the central facility via voice answer-back. Time spent billing and labor were reduced substantially. Errors were also reduced as data was edited at the source of transmission. An example illustrates the user-machine dialogue.

Some states decided to administer all or part of their Medicaid programs by contracting with private firms for insurance coverage for Medicaid eligibles. For a predetermined per capita premium, the contractor is responsible for paying all valid claims. Thusly, states fix their expenditures and private contractors run the risk of losses if the claims exceed the premium payments. The General Accounting Office reported on such programs in Arkansas, California, Florida, Louisiana, Maine, North Carolina, Pennsylvania and Texas. Seven different firms and the services they offered to the states are explained individually. In addition, the GAO report details the legal and regulatory basis for these Medicaid agreements, specifies HEW regulations governing the agreements and briefly reviews the Medicaid program and its administration. Recommendations centered about HEW efforts to assist the states, legislation to stimulate competitive

bidding on agreements and improvements needed in contract monitoring and approval.

Rymer and her associates studied Medicaid eligibility intensively and developed five administrative reform packages. Each set of reforms was labeled and the major areas addressed are noted as follows:

- *Administrative Reform Package*— Recommendations are made about staff development and technical assistance, program coordination, SSA and Medicaid relations, federal monitoring, data collection and computer systems, quality control, the interpretation and dissemination of policies, public information and clients' rights, federal regulations and unclear policies.
- *Minor and Technical Reforms*—These reforms talk about coverage of groups, income levels, disregards, special needs, retroactive coverage, extended Medicaid coverage, residency, spend-down and grandfather clause coverage.
- *Major Cross-Program Standardization*—Suggestions are made here relative to interprogram coordination, disregards, income levels, resource criteria, deeming and relatives' responsibility, categorical definition, alternatives to institutionalization, and compliance and performance standards.
- *Minor State Flexibility Reforms*— Recommendations refer to the medically needy eligibility, income disregards, financial criteria affecting the institutionalized, SSI recipients eligibility, adult medically needy coverage, specific eligibility policies and data systems and quality control.
- *Major State Flexibility Reforms*— Here, the authors discuss cash assistance coverage, Medicaid only coverage, Medicaid only administration and the federal role in the program.

Obviously, even this brief outline indicates the scope of the comprehensive approach to the vital issue of eligibility in this report.

In July 1976, the Massachusetts State Legislature, despite strenuous opposition by the state medical society, mandated a second opinion program for all Medicaid patients scheduled to undergo any of the following eight elective operations: tonsillectomies; hysterectomies; cholecystectomies; varicose vein excisions; hemorrhoidectomies; rhinoplasties; disk surgery-spinal fusions; and menisectomies. After a year of operation, 12 percent of the cases reviewed by consultants in the Boston area resulted in canceled operations. Medicaid administrators predict a saving of about $1 million over and above the annual cost of the program. Official operational descriptions of the second surgical opinion programs and a flow chart spell out the Massachusetts mandate. Western Massachusetts, where the surgical rates are two to three times higher than the state average, operates a little differently so that procedure is given separately. At some future date, there will probably be a comparison of the mandated and voluntary second surgical opinion programs.

Garber uses a light touch to describe the maze that a provider must travel in order to receive payment from Medicaid. He calls it—The Medicaid Game. Participants in the game include the players, kibitzers, referees, cheerleaders, adversaries and allies. As the game proceeds, the players learn the rules. When the author is hired to secure payment for community mental health center services to Medicaid recipients, he enters the game as a player and relates his own experiences. After ten months of playing the Medicaid game, Garber won his first game and collected payment.

Contributions of price and use to health care expenditure increases during the 1953–1970 period were examined by Andersen, Foster and Weil. This time period includes the pre- and post-Medicaid era. Expenditures for hospital inpatient and outpatient care, for in and outpatient care by private physicians, for dental care and for prescribed and nonprescribed drugs and medicines were compared over the time periods. The authors concluded that the institution of the Medicaid program accelerated some trends that were already taking place such as relatively high rates of increase in the use of health services for the low income population and the aged. Overall, price increases contributed substantially more to expenditures than did use increases. Hospital price increases contributed the most to total expenditure increases. In addition to the young and the aged, there were use increases by the 55–64 year old group. In addition, during the 1963–1970 period, "free services" added a substantial increase in use while apparently making no contribution during the 1953–1963 period.

A report of the Program Review and Investigations Committee of the Connecticut General Assembly presents a legislative program to contain Medicaid costs in that state. Four types of cost control are identified and then recommendations are given for each type as follows:

- *Eligibility Control*—In 1975, 20 percent of the Medicaid population were either overpaid or actually ineligible. Legislative recommendations include home visits when fraud is suspected; annual redeterminations for the medically needy group; adoption of a caseload system; development of training programs for Medicaid employees; and the matching of Medicaid rosters with the Department of Labor, Motor Vehicles and others to discover Medicaid ineligibles.
- *Price Controls*—Connecticut has five rate setting bodies to cause confusion. Suggestions include the issuance of a handbook describing the rate determination process for Medicaid; experimentation to see if incentives can be made more attractive; utilization of a

bid system for pharmaceutical services to nursing homes; conduct a review of the "relative value scale" of payment to physicians; review ambulance cost operations; and contract out for equipment such as wheelchairs.

- *Utilization Review Controls* — Recommendations include the auditing of ambulance claims; use of a second surgical opinion program; and the use of more medical review teams to conduct prior authorization audits.
- *Expenditure Controls* — It was suggested that additional staff be hired to fill vacancies and speed up the review and processing procedures; third party payers should be checked to see if they cover some Medicaid services; investigate vendor fraud more intensively; use generic drugs; and conduct overpayment audits.

In addition the Legislative Committee suggested that alternatives to institutionalization such as home health care, foster care and adult day care be investigated.

Budgeting for medical assistance programs is a complex process and Tyson and Jehl describe a technique used in Wisconsin. Budget projections are related to policy changes, utilization increases, reimbursement changes and caseload growth. A 270 equation econometric model forecasts personal income, unemployment rates, employment in specific industries, financial activity of banks and loan companies and state government revenue. For this study the data base entered into a stepwise regression analysis, included the consumer price index, the unemployment rate, personal income, disposable income, population, personal tax liability and employment in medical services. Then, the authors report on predictive budget models based on medical assistance as a function of time and as a function of prior medical assistance data. Expenditure models and beneficiaries models are compared. The authors conclude that traditional trend analysis techniques may be better for short-term projections with the predictive and econometric models better for long-term projections.

If a family meets the categorical requirements for public assistance, but has income in excess of the medically needy eligibility level, it can still qualify for Medicaid by "spending down" the income in excess of the eligibility level. Urban Systems Research and Engineering, Inc. evaluated Medicaid spend-down in seven locations in three states. Specific objectives were to analyze the implementation and administration of the spend-down, to determine various characteristics of successful and unsuccessful spend-down applicants and to estimate the extent of the enrollment of the eligible spend-down population in the Medicaid programs. Answers to these objectives constitute the majority of this article. In addition, there is a discussion of what objective spend-down really fulfills. Three options are raised in the form of the following questions:

- Is spend-down an equalizer?
- Is spend-down an emergency health insurance program?
- Is spend-down an ongoing health insurance program?

Eight recommendations are made to fill in the serious gaps and inconsistencies regarding the spend-down provisions.

Barthel compared the utilization of services rendered to Medicaid patients enrolled in an HMO (Health Maintenance Organization) setting against people on Medicaid who used a fee-for-service setting. Hospital admissions, physician encounters, pharmacy services and X-ray, laboratory and other provider services were compared and analyzed. The conclusion of the study stated, ". . . the HMO system, when offered as an alternative to fee-for-service delivery of health care, can represent a significant overall reduction in the rates of utilization and costs of services. For the three year period examined here, the average saving in cost is about 25 percent."

On December 13, 1977, President Carter signed into law (Public Law 95–210) the Medicare and Medicaid Reimbursement for Rural Health Clinics Act. A summary of the major provisions of the bill is presented in a memo from the federal Health Care Financing Administration. Of major importance is the fact that the services of a physician's assistant or nurse practitioner can be reimbursed by Medicaid for 100 percent of the cost. In addition, the bill allows for demonstration projects to take place in urban medically underserved areas with similar reimbursement policies. The range of covered services is equal to those that can be provided under Medicaid by a physician.

Under the Freedom of Information Act, Martinson requested the listing of dentists receiving more than $100,000 a year from the Medicaid program. In 1975, the list showed that 312 dental practices received $100,000 or more and 14 of these earned more than $400,000 in Medicaid payments. A detailed two page questionnaire was sent to each of the 312 dentists that asked about their gross and net income, offices, staff, type of practice and practice location. Well over half of the dentists responded with 10 percent returned as undeliverable. Key findings indicated that most of the dentists grossed between $100,000 and $150,000 in 1976 from Medicaid. For the most part, they practiced in the center city. About 60 percent were in group practices with 20 percent each in solo practice and in partnerships. The inference was made that the total dollar amount listed by the federal government was divided up into an average of three slices. Thusly, the figures released were misleading. A Detroit practitioner commented, ". . . not only does the public think I'm a crook, many of my fellow practitioners think so as well." In rounding out the article, Martinson cites the advantages and disadvantages of working with Medicaid patients and includes a composite profile of a "Medicaid dentist."

Cappelli and Stralberg focus on the impact of utilization controls on Medicaid. Inpatient institutional services such as acute hospital care, skilled nursing facility (SNF) care and services from an intermediate care facility were studied in California, Michigan and Virginia as these services constituted the largest share of Medicaid expenditures. Four assumptions about the impact of utilization controls were identified to be evaluated:

- UC is cost effective in that it reduces overall institutional Medicaid expenditures.
- UC leads to changes in use patterns producing more efficient utilization of health care resources.
- UC means that fewer unnecessary or inappropriate services are rendered.
- UC leads to improved quality of care for Medicaid patients.

Generally, the conclusions of the study upheld the four assumptions.

Data on more than 8,000 Medicaid recipients in Atlanta, Little Rock, Oklahoma City and Trenton were collected relative to the utilization of health care services. People were asked about their use of hospitals, physicians, dentists, eye doctors and prescription services. Comparisons by categorical eligibility status (Old Age Assistance, Aid to the Disabled, Aid to Families with Dependent Children) of out of pocket expenses and unmet needs are also included. Hall, Flueck and McKenna concluded, "The results of the study leave little doubt that the presence of Medicaid coverage does, other things being equal, clearly remove a significant barrier to the availability of health care services. In addition, the comprehensiveness of the Medicaid package appears to have a substantial effect on the utilization of each individual service."

While Hall and his colleagues found that Medicaid coverage clearly removes a barrier to health care, Reynolds and his coworkers commented that more is needed than the mere removal of the financial barrier. Their study of 259 Medicaid recipients in North Florida showed that most knew about coverage for hospital care, physician services and prescription drugs. The majority of the recipients did not know other services were available to them. In addition the poor perceived their health status as bad seven times more often than a comparable sample of the nonmedicaid population. The authors recommend improvements to facilitate access to health care and a public information effort to make Medicaid recipients aware of the services and resources available to them. Furthermore, they suggest that more be done to motivate private providers to accept Medicaid patients.

In line with the interest in providers, Studnicki, Saywell and Wiechetek investigated the disproportionate share of care rendered to Medicaid patients by graduates of foreign medical schools (FMGs). While FMGs constitute 22 percent of all physicians in Maryland, they comprise 36 percent of the Medicaid vendors. From a specialty viewpoint, 32 percent of all FMGs in Maryland are board certified but only 22 percent of the FMG Medicaid vendors are board certified; concentrated in general surgery, internal medicine and general practice. In addition, FMGs tend to concentrate in areas with a large Medicaid population. Findings suggest that a special relationship exists between the FMGs and Medicaid medicine. A question to be considered is, "Does this special relationship perpetuate the two class system of health care—rich care and poor care?"

A general practitioner in California commented on the Medicaid (called Medi-Cal there) program regarding participation and personal satisfaction in the article by Jones and Hamburger:

I practice in a high Medi-Cal area, and I refuse three or four new Medi-Cal patients per week. I quit taking new patients when the total came to 25 per-

cent of my practice. Since my expenses are about 50 percent of my receipts, I felt very uneasy about having half of my personal income dependent on Medi-Cal, to be reduced or deferred as they see fit.
I would accept more Medi-Cal patients if I could feel that the program was dedicated to fair treatment of both patients and doctors.

Almost 700 physicians in California responded to a questionnaire about their degree of participation in the Medi-Cal program, their plans for future participation, their acceptance of new Medi-Cal patients, referrals and consultations and about their personal involvement. More than 250 physicians responded to another survey seeking to discover dissatisfactions with the Medi-Cal program. About half of the responding physicians expected to be treating a similar number of Medi-Cal patients in the future with about 25 percent expecting to be treating a smaller proportion. Critical problems causing dissatisfaction cited by almost half of all respondents dealt with the inadequate level of reimbursement, the denial of reimbursement for services provided and the bureaucratic interference with patient care. In addition, the authors analyze the physicians' reactions to the treatment authorization request (TAR) system.

B.P. Reiter, M.D. describes his life and hard times in a Medicaid mill. He answers the question, "If Medicaid clinics are so lousy, why work in them?" His answer is, "Because I needed a job." Participation of providers can be that basic in the motivational aspects. From a management viewpoint, Reiter details the ins and outs of daily health care delivery including the red tape, the borderline and over the border techniques employed by the operator of the Medicaid clinic, the battle of the guidelines and the balancing of the books. Reiter's summation also does not jibe with the image of the rich Medicaid provider:

During the 10 weeks or so that I worked at the Medicaid clinics, I wrote out checks for medical society dues, malpractice insurance, fees, assessments, and, of course, rent to The Entrepreneur's corporation. The checks came to $7,030. To date, I've received payments of $7,323 from Medicaid. I've earned $293.

Quality control in a fee-for-service Medicaid system is described in specific detail by Rosenberg and his coauthors. In addition to the detailed data about the computer system used, the article provides illustrations of individual provider profiles, statistical provider profiles, quality of care exception reports and a sample printout of flagging criteria. A focus on patterns of practice, the use of multiple assessment techniques and a concentration on unequivocally substandard care overcome limitations related to current evaluation technology. In concluding, the authors explore the implications for national health insurance and for Professional Standards Review Organizations.

Periodic medical review (PMR) as a technique to assess the quality and appropriateness of care in skilled nursing facilities is discussed by Connelly, Cohen and Walsh. Strengths and weaknesses of the PMR are identified. Advantages include an emphasis on the individual patient, attention to the patient's functional status and the relatively low cost of PMR. On the debit side, the assessments may lack objectivity and the narrow perspective of appropriate placement rather than total care may limit the optimal outcome.

Both quality and utilization are addressed in Cannon's narrative on the Physician Ambulatory Care Evaluation (PACE) program. PACE uses claims data and an auto-mated system to build patient case histories and screens them for compliance with clinical guidelines. Examples are given of the clinical criteria currently in use in Utah and cover required service or therapy, contraindicated therapy, utilization limits and untoward symptoms during therapy. A schematic diagram shows the regular PACE processing cycle. Outputs of the PACE system include patient treatment profiles, requests for review and summary reports of various types. Cannon also describes staff screening activities, professional reviews and cites other uses of the PACE system. Results, costs and conclusions all point to PACE being a system that could impart a good deal of knowledge to the issue of ambulatory care evaluation.

Kirkley and Anderson report that 172 Texas hospitals elected to have the Texas Medical Foundation (TMF) conduct their Medicaid utilization reviews. This constitutes 62 percent of all Medicaid review performed in Texas. Review criteria were developed based on medical care patterns of practicing physicians in the state. The review process involves the interaction of three groups of people within the hospital: the utilization review committee, physician advisors and medical care analysts. Day-to-day reviews are conducted by the medical care analysts, many of whom are registered nurses or medical record administrators. A unique feature of the Texas review program is their emphasis on an evaluation of discharge planning. Cost effectiveness of the Texas admissions and review program has also been demonstrated. However, as the authors note, ". . . the greatest benefit is to the patient—*more* people receive *better* care with the funds now available, and physicians once again are able to assume a proper role in patient care."

15. An Introduction to the Medicaid Management Information System (MMIS), or Your Friend, The Computer

DAVID F. CHAVKIN

Chavkin, *An Introduction to the MSIS, or Your Friend, The Computer*, 12 CLEARINGHOUSE REV. (June 1978). Reprinted by permission of the National Clearinghouse for Legal Services.

INTRODUCTION

Poor administration has plagued the Medicaid program since its inception. Medicaid beneficiaries are routinely denied benefits which are theoretically available under the state plan. Providers refuse to participate in Medicaid citing red tape in billing and delays in payment. Eligibility processing significantly delays receipt of services.[1]

The Medicare and Medicaid Anti-Fraud and Abuse Amendments of 1977 established standards for the processing of claims and for administrative accountability.[2] In order to meet these standards, states must establish sophisticated computerized information systems. The prototype of these information systems is the Medicaid Management Information System (MMIS).[3]

Like any computer system, MMIS is complicated and riddled with technical jargon. It is not difficult, however, to develop a working knowledge of the system that will be more than adequate for negotiations and litigation. This article provides an introduction to MMIS.

WHY SHOULD MMIS BE IMPORTANT TO LEGAL SERVICES?

Implementation of an MMIS system may affect Legal Services clients both positively and negatively. Positive aspects include the following: (1) eligibility processing time for recipients may be shortened; (2) eligibility can be more easily verified for beneficiaries who have lost their Medicaid cards; (3) more providers may be willing to participate in the Medicaid program because claims may be paid more promptly; (4) more accurate and complete information on utilization and cost of services will be available to health advocates seeking to contest proposed cutbacks in eligibility or scope of services in the program; (5) providers who are guilty of fraud and abuse may be more easily identified; and (6) providers who provide unnecessary or substandard services may be more easily identified.

Negative aspects include the following: (1) fraud and abuse investigations of recipients may be greatly enhanced with the result that innocent recipients may be subjected to increased verifications of eligibility; (2) recipients who are believed to be abusing the program may be more easily identified and subjected to provider lock-in

137

or mandatory counseling; (3) although providers may be paid more quickly, they also may be subjected to even greater red tape in the billing process, thereby resulting in decreased participation in the program; and (4) fear of unjustified fraud and abuse investigations may lead innocent providers to withdraw from participation in the program.

These are only some of the ways in which MMIS can affect Legal Services clients. In addition, discovery in pending litigation may depend on information contained in the MMIS system and proposals by Legal Services for expansion of Medicaid eligibility may depend on accurate cost estimates which are available through the MMIS system.

WHAT ROLE CAN LEGAL SERVICES PLAY WITH REGARD TO MMIS?

Implementing MMIS involves more than just purchasing some computer time and pressing some buttons. MMIS systems vary greatly from state to state. States may identify different concerns as priorities or may identify different data as desirable for future operations. In addition, states must decide whether to contract with outside consulting firms or with groups like Blue Cross/Blue Shield for the processing of claims or whether to perform the operation in-house. All of these decisions will affect the scope and availability of information under the system and all will have some effect on Legal Services clients.

WHAT IS MMIS?

MMIS, the Medicaid Management Information System, is a system of six interdependent computer subsystems that perform specific functions.[4] Although these six subsystems may be designated differently in different states, the following descriptions have been used by HEW: (1) Recipient Subsystem; (2) Provider Subsystem; (3) Claims Processing Subsystem; (4) Reference File Subsystem; (5) Surveillance and Utilization Review (S/UR) Subsystem; and (6) Management and Administrative Reporting (MARS) Subsystem.

The Claims Processing Subsystem is the heart of the MMIS system. Information is fed into it from the Recipient Subsystem, which checks recipient eligibility, the Provider Subsystem, which checks provider eligibility, and the Reference File Subsystem, which checks the reasonableness of provider charges. Questionable claims are selected out by the Claims Processing Subsystem to be resolved by administrative personnel. When resolved, they are fed back in for further processing. Prior authorizations are also fed into the Claims Processing Subsystem.

Information coming out of the Claims Processing Subsystem consists primarily of authorization and payment of claims. It also includes (1) information about possible fraud and abuse, which in turn goes into the Surveillance and Utilization Review Subsystem; (2) explanations of benefits and remittance statements which go directly to recipients or providers; and (3) budget information, which goes into the Management and Administrative Reporting Subsystem.

The Recipient Subsystem

The Recipient Subsystem maintains current records on all recipients eligible for Medicaid and provides the mechanism for frequent and timely updates to all recipient eligibility records. It provides the mechanism for identifying potential third party liability and Medicare Part B Buy-In processing. Lastly, it allows access to recipient eligibility records for claims processing, surveillance and utilization review activities, and management reporting.

When a recipient is found eligible for Medicaid, his name and identifying information are added to the computerized eligibility file. This information is updated as appropriate; file maintenance will ordinarily be conducted by an operator in a centralized communications center with information provided by workers throughout the state.

In addition to file maintenance, inquiry/response is conducted through the Recipient Subsystem. Authorized state personnel and medical service providers may inquire as to the current payment status of a recipient. While departmental personnel have access to complete case information, payment data, recipient eligibility, and current and historical Medicaid data, providers are limited to that information necessary for providing medical service and subsequent claim processing. Information available to providers can be used where a recipient has lost his card and the provider wishes to verify eligibility prior to rendering service. Inquiries are usually made by a telephone call to the central communications center or by using terminals located in the local offices or in the billing offices of major providers.

Confidentiality is usually protected through two measures. First, persons entering or requesting data must be able to respond to an operator request for a given security code. Second, update terminals are located in a central, physically secure area with access permitted only to authorized personnel. Local terminals can only be used for inquiry purposes.

Use of the Recipient Subsystem can shorten the time for issuance of Medicaid cards. In those states with operational MMIS systems, Medicaid cards are issued within five days from the final eligibility determination. In addition, delays in budgeting can be greatly reduced. The Recipient Subsystem is also used in some states for the processing of AFDC, Food Stamps, and General Assistance eligibility.

Use of the Recipient Subsystem can also have advantages for providers. Payment of claims may be accomplished in days rather than months. Daily updating of files can reduce the number of claims rejected for re-

cipient ineligibility, and inquiries about Medicaid eligibility can be handled promptly. Each of these benefits may increase provider participation in the program and thereby improve recipient access to health services.

The Provider Subsystem

The Provider Subsystem enrolls providers for participation in the Medicaid program after the filing of an agreement to comply with Title XIX requirements. It ensures that only qualified providers are reimbursed under the program and creates and maintains a computer file on all eligible providers to support claims processing, surveillance and utilization review activities, and management reporting.

After an application/agreement is completed by the provider, the information is verified. The respective boards are contacted to determine if the provider is licensed and eligible for the specialties listed. Once the information is verified, the provider is assigned an identification number, the Provider Subsystem is updated to authorize the provider's participation, and the provider is notified of billing procedures and program requirements.

The Claims Processing Subsystem

The Claims Processing Subsystem verifies the eligibility of both the recipient and the provider and the validity of the claim information submitted. It ensures that correct payment is made to providers on a timely basis. It creates a computer file of adjudicated claims to support surveillance and utilization review activities and management reporting. Lastly, it assembles and maintains a record of claims pending because of errors.

Claims are submitted on standard invoice forms which vary with the type of provider. These forms should be uniform with the private insurers operating in the state to simplify billing procedures. These claims are then reviewed by an optical character scanner which scans the forms for errors. Forms with coding errors are then manually re-entered.

Claims invoices then pass through a series of "edits." Claims submitted by providers who are not certified for participation in the program are rejected after comparison to the Provider Subsystem. Claims submitted for recipients who were not eligible at the time that services were rendered are also rejected after comparison to the Recipient Subsystem.

Claims are then subjected to a series of further edits. These edits might include sex/diagnosis (to ensure that the provider is not billing for an abortion for a male patient), procedure/diagnosis (to ensure that the procedure is consistent with the diagnosis), and length of stay (to ensure that a patient has not been hospitalized for too long a period without prior authorization).

Claims that are not approved for payment are then "pended." These pended claims are either returned to the provider with an explanation of the errors in the invoice or they are referred to a Claims Resolution Unit. Resolution might take the form of a review of additional documentary data submitted by the provider in support of his request for a fee in excess of the normal levels. All such pended claims appear on information reports submitted to the provider so that it is possible to keep track of all claims submitted.

Those claims that are approved for payment are then sent to an approved claims file and a warrant is written for the provider and a remittance statement is issued. In those states with approved MMIS systems, as many as 85 percent of all claims are paid within 15 days of submission. This is well within the requirement of the Medicare and Medicaid Anti-Fraud and Abuse Amendments of 1977 that 90 percent of all claims be paid within 30 days of submission.[5]

The Reference File Subsystem

The Reference File Subsystem provides the Medicaid practitioner with the usual and customary charge data and incorporates Medicare usual and customary charges in the Medicaid system. It provides a record for the updating of prices and charges for drugs and services. Invoices may then be compared to this record to determine the amount of charges that will be reimbursed under the program. This subsystem is essentially a compendium of prices and charges that can be used by the Claims Processing Subsystem to determine the amounts that will be paid for services, including prescription drugs.

The Surveillance and Utilization Review Subsystem

The Surveillance and Utilization Review (S/UR) Subsystem maintains data on activities and characteristics of individual Medicaid providers and recipients from paid claims. It classifies providers and recipients into peer groups according to demographic, medical and utilization characteristics and develops a statistical profile of each peer group classification to be used as a base line for evaluation. It develops a statistical profile, compatible with peer group profile, of each individual provider or recipient, compares individual providers or recipients to appropriate group profile and reports individuals who deviate significantly from their group norm or from predetermined standards.

Utilization review has historically led to across-the-board controls. In the past, if a state Title XIX agency believed that overutilization of prescription drugs by *some* recipients was a problem (whether or not there was data to support it), it established controls for *all* recipients. The MMIS S/UR Subsystem would allow the state to identify those recipients who actually are using services in excess of some defined levels.

Controls may then be tailored to individual recipients' utilization patterns.

In addition, the S/UR Subsystem can actually be used to improve a recipient's health. Drug interactions pose a significant danger. Ordinarily, drug interactions are monitored by the prescribing physician and by the dispensing pharmacist. If the recipient obtains prescriptions from several doctors and fills these prescriptions at several pharmacies, there is no opportunity to monitor such interactions. The S/UR Subsystem may be programmed to identify all those recipients who obtain prescriptions at more than two pharmacies in a particular month. Recipient profiles may then be reviewed to identify problem situations that should be referred for counseling or other services.

Utilization and surveillance review of providers is also assembled on providers in the community. A provider who deviates significantly from the profile can then be identified for further investigation. Services that might be reviewed are the number of office injections made by a physician, the number of hysterectomies performed on a physician's patients, over-prescribing of certain drugs, or other indices of potential abuse. In-depth peer review of such a provider's activities might then be undertaken.

The Management and Administrative Reporting Subsystem

The Management and Administrative Reporting Subsystem (MARS) provides the state Title XIX agency with financial data for proper fiscal planning and control. It also provides the agency with information to assist in the development of improved medical assistance policy and regulations. MARS monitors the progress of claims processing operations, including the status of provider payments. It analyzes provider performance in terms of the extent and adequacy of participation, analyzes recipient participation in terms of the nature and extent of services received, and provides the necessary data to support federal reporting requirements.

It has traditionally been difficult to obtain precise data from state Medicaid agencies on administrative aspects of the program. Many states, for example, know how many physicians have enrolled in the Medicaid program for participation. Few states, however, have any real idea as to the actual number of physicians participating or the extent of their participation. The MARS Subsystem can provide exact figures in order to determine the level of participation. This may be essential for demonstrating to a legislature or court that fee levels are so low that recipients have little access to necessary services.

Similarly, budget requests and program decisions are often based on data that is extremely unreliable. The availability of precise and extensive data can be used to propose alternatives to the state legislature, administrative agency or court. As a result, the program can be run more efficiently, delivering the maximum level of services possible for the monies available.

CONCLUSION

By April 1978, 15 states had implemented certified MMIS systems. All 53 states and jurisdictions with Medicaid programs will be required to implement such systems in the near future. MMIS will therefore be coming to your state soon, if it is not there already.

REFERENCES

1. Current issues in Medicaid administration are discussed at programs presented by the Institute for Medicaid Management (IMM) of the Health Care Financing Administration (HCFA). These programs are open to Legal Services workers. For more information, contact Institute for Medicaid Management, Room 4628—Mary Switzer Bldg., 330 C St., SW, Washington, D.C. 20201.

2. Pub. L. No. 95–142, §2(b)(1)(c)

3. Concern over rising Medicaid costs and inflation in the health care field led to the establishment of a task force on Medicaid in 1969. The task force examined deficiencies in the Medicaid program and submitted final recommendations to the Secretary of Health, Education and Welfare in 1970. One of the deficiencies noted was a lack of administrative controls and statistical data necessary to administer the program efficiently.

In response to this report, the Medicaid Services Administration (MSA) established a Division of Management, Information and Payment Systems. This division developed the prototype of the MMIS system. The expressed objective of MMIS was to improve the capability of the Title XIX State Agencies to administer the Medicaid program within the states. A system was therefore developed to process claims effectively and to provide management with the necessary information for planning and control.

4. Much of the information on the operation of an MMIS system was obtained from a review of the Michigan MMIS program and is published with the permission of the Michigan Department of Social Services. The Michigan MMIS system was one of the earliest certified by HEW, on January 1, 1976. The Michigan Department of Social Services, Bureau of Medical Assistance, conducts seminars periodically on their MMIS system. The seminar takes two days and provides a working knowledge of the capabilities of MMIS. For further information, contact Gary McGaffey, Michigan Dept. of Social Services, Bureau of Medical Assistance, 412 Commerce Center Bldg., 300 S. Capitol Ave., Lansing, Mich. 48926, (517) 373–8168.

5. 42 U.S.C. §1396a(a)(37).

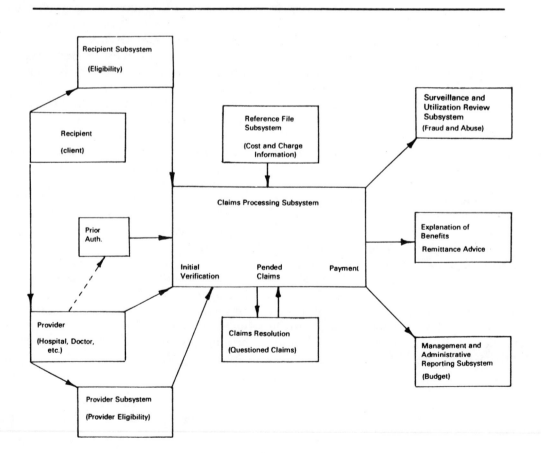

16. On-Line Medicaid Billing System for Physicians' Services

EMMANUEL MESEL and DAVID D. WIRTSCHAFTER

Reprinted with permission from *Computers and Biomedical Research*, Vol. 8, pp. 479–491, 1975. © Academic Press.

PERSPECTIVE

The cost of submitting an insurance claim for professional services is a disproportionate fraction of the amount paid for providing the service.[1] For general practitioners, who provide the largest number of individual services, this share may be more than one fourth of the payment for most common services. Submitting a claim involves furnishing approximately 15 items on a standard form, usually in the following sequence: (1) determination of eligibility or contract number for services under a sponsored program (Medicaid, Medicare), or private insurance; (2) recording of demographic information, usually a transcription from business records; (3) abstracting and transcribing of services and diagnoses from the clinical record; (4) obtaining the patient's and the physician's signature; (5) making a copy of the claim for office records; and (6) mailing the claim to the intermediary or carrier. Most of these steps represent the recording of information twice, once for business and once for clinical purposes. If some of the steps could be eliminated, the cost of submitting claims would be substantially reduced.

Similarly for the insurance carrier or Medicare or Medicaid intermediary, the cost of preparing and recording data from source documents is a large part of total processing cost. For most claim processors, it takes three steps to convert source documents into computer usable form: (1) checking the claim to be sure it contains all necessary data; (2) encoding of procedures and diagnoses; and (3) translation of the data into machine readable form (cards, tapes, disks). Processing costs would be substantially reduced if these labor-intensive steps could be eliminated.

To put the problem in more concrete terms, it is estimated that the cost to physicians to prepare insurance claims varies from $1.25 to $2.50 (1), each claim composed of an average of two service items. Carrier performance data published by the Bureau of Health Insurance (2) shows that our local Medicare intermediary spent an average of $2.35 to process a claim in 1973. Thus the combined cost of billing and claims processing could average $3.60 to $4.85 per claim. This estimate would be even higher in Washington, DC, and Chicago, IL, where claims processing costs alone exceed $4. Comparison of claims

This work supported by Contract HSM 110-71-252, Health Care Technology Division, National Center for Health Services Research and Development.

preparation and processing costs with the average per claim payment for ambulatory medical services of $10 (personal communication: Equitable-Alabama Medicaid office) demonstrates the need for reducing paperwork, especially multiple transcriptions of the same data elements in provider offices and carrier systems.

Under sponsorship of the National Center for Health Services Research and Development, and with the cooperation of the Medical Services Administration of the State of Alabama, Blue Cross-Blue Shield of Alabama, and the Equitable Life Assurance Society, the Clinical Information Systems group of the University of Alabama in Birmingham (UAB) contracted to design a system using point-of-service terminals tied on-line to a central computer in a project to reduce the costs of submitting claims from the physician's office as well as the costs of data preparation in the carrier's system.

Why an On-Line System?

The Bureau of Health Insurance has found that 15% of all Part B Medicare claims become rejects within a carrier's system because the patient's identification number for benefits is invalid (3). A major source of annoyance and expense to both providers and carriers is the return of such claims for correction not only of identification numbers but of other data elements as well. By editing the inputs at their source and providing branching capability to handle complex transactions (e.g. the medication and volume injected for an "injection procedure," "time" for anesthesiology procedures, etc.), much of the frustration and cost of the manual processing can be eliminated. Direct interaction also permits entry of multiple procedures in one claim transaction, entry of multiple diagnoses for a single procedure, and switching between slow and painstaking instructional and fast, efficient modes of data entry. Imprinting with embossed plastic cards like a credit card used to prepare gasoline charge slips,

and also used for pharmacy claims in the Alabama Medicaid Program, was considered impractical because of limited input capabilities.

Choice of Data Entry System for the Physician's Office

Since physicians are universally involved in billing third parties, it was apparent that the cost of the terminal chosen for the physician's office would be the major determinant of the cost of the total hardware package needed to operate the billing system. For a group of 1000 physicians (there are 2500 potential users in Alabama) the least expensive video or printing terminal would cost five to seven times as much as a voice answer-back system using a standard telephone set equipped with a numerical keyboard and card reader (Touch Tone (R) pad and Carddialer (R)). The incremental cost for hardware to an office already equipped with a telephone is less than $8 a month including a pro-rata share of the voice answer-back device. For a group as small as 100 users, the cost to each user would be less than $25 per month.

System Specifications

To provide satisfactory service to users the following general functional specifications were considered essential:

1. The system should operate continuously from 9 am to 7 pm, Monday through Friday.
2. The user should be able to enter 99% of all claims without resorting to manual preparation of a document.
3. The user should be able to determine patient eligibility before completing a claim.
4. All data elements entered must be edited.
5. Instructional and fast modes of operation must be provided.

6. A claim control number must be assigned to each claim entered and fed back via voice answer-back to the user for easy reference if later communication with the carrier becomes necessary.
7. Accuracy of transmission and encoding of information should equal the present manual system at the very least.
8. The system must be capable of expansion to accept data not currently on claims but which will probably be required for PSRO purposes, e.g. results of laboratory tests, the blood pressure measurement for hypertensive patients, etc.

Design, Development and Operation

The following sections describe the design, development, and operation of an on-line system for professional services billing to the carrier in a statewide Medicaid program in Alabama. Software development began in July of 1971. The voice answer-back equipment and telephone interface were installed in late November and service to users began on December 13, 1971. The system has been in continuous operation providing 40 hr per week scheduled service since that date.

A total of 165,845 complete claims representing 319,246 "lines" or individual services had been entered by the termination of the contract on April 30, 1974. During September 1973, the last month of free service, the volume entered exceeded 50% of the statewide load. At that time there were 110 offices participating in the project billing for services provided by 343 physicians accounting for 17% of all providers of service in the Alabama Medicaid program.

From October, 1973, through April, 1974, computer services were provided at the rate of 25¢ per billed medical service. During the 7 months of fee-for-service operation, 65,872 claims were entered compared with 76,361 during the previous 7 months of free service.

METHODS

1. The Basic System

Access to the system was provided via the "dial up" telephone network using modems (Bell 403D3) to decode the multifrequency tones and to interface the user terminals to the voice answer-back device, which was directly connected to the central processor. The funding agency made the initial decision to append the on-line hardware to the UAB central computer facility's main-frame computer (rather than to support an independent preprocessor), so the choice of rentable voice answer-back equipment was limited to IBM's Audio Response Unit 7770 and associated 8721 vocabulary drum. A tentative vocabulary was selected from IBM's library of recorded words to support the claims application expeditiously. Words not available were generated by spelling the word (or contraction) letter-by-letter. A revised vocabulary later replaced this clumsy procedure. The various files that support the on-line system as well as the file of incoming claims transactions are stored on an IBM 3330 disk drive. A dedicated core partition on the 370/158 handles programs for line-control of incoming claims and the interactive user dialogue. To enhance exportability a determined effort was made to write programs in a 32K core partition so that these same programs could be run on smaller stand-alone systems.

2. Recruiting Participating Physicians

To determine which providers generate the highest volume of paperwork (dollar volume of claims is not indicative because of the high unit value of surgical procedures), we sorted the paid claims data for 1971, and ranked physicians according to the total number of "lines" submitted. (A "line" on a claim refers to a single service to the patient). Recruiting for participation in the project was directed primarily toward the 300 providers who accounted for two-thirds of all services to beneficiaries of the Medicaid program. Most of these physicians were in general practice.

3. On-Line System Software

Line control. This program was written with the constraint that it be flexible enough to work in a highly interactive environment. Unlike most commercial applications of voice answer-back, it involved a complicated flow of data and messages. A simplified version of the user-machine dialogue is shown in Table 1.

Mapping of claim form onto transaction file. To make the on-line system compatible with the manual system employed by the insurance carrier (Blue Cross–Blue Shield of Alabama), the Medicaid claim form M-19-65 was mapped onto the transaction file carried on disk with a few minor changes which were agreeable to the carrier.

Instructional/quick modes of data entry. Two voice answer-back procedures were implemented to accommodate novices and experienced users. The instructional mode guides the novice who is learning to use the terminal. A series of messages prompts the user through step-by-step entry of each required data element. Each entry is edited and accepted only when in the proper range for that element. Error messages are generated when faulty data are detected. As the user becomes proficient, the prompting messages become annoying and unnecessary. At this point the user can select the quick entry mode for data entry. In this mode, the user enters a stream of input in-

TABLE 1

SIMPLIFIED USER–MACHINE DIALOGUE FOR INSTRUCTIONAL INPUT

Voice message	User input	Edits performed
"Medicaid claim system, slow input, enter doctor number"	4337	Checks for valid number in provider file
"Enter patient number"	337-1-123456-789	Calculate check digit Check patient eligibility in recipient file
"Enter date"	040174	Check for valid date or range of dates
"Enter point of service"	1	Check for valid point of service code
"Enter number of visits"	1	$1 \leqslant \text{Number} \leqslant 99$
"Enter procedure code"	90040	Check for valid procedure code Program branches and asks for additional input for the following procedures: 90030 Injection (drug code, volume) 40XXXXX Anesthesia (time) 12000 Suture laceration (length)
"Enter diagnosis code"	5020	Check for valid diagnosis code
"Enter next diagnosis, or sign (#) to proceed"	#	Check for valid diagnosis code or "#"
"Enter charges"	750	Check for valid range of charges
"Charges seven point five zero"	1	Check for a valid code
"Claim seven four six"	(User records claim control number)	

terrupted after each data element by an audio tone from the computer to indicate a valid element has been received. Only two voice messages are generated: one after "charges" are entered to permit the user to recheck the entry, the other gives the user the claim control number for that claim. Both modes of data entry are completely compatible, and a user may switch back and forth from one to the other during a single transaction.

Eligibility check. The system can respond to inquiries from doctors' offices, county health clinics, administrators in Medical Services Administration, and the insurer by supplying current eligibility information on any of the 300,000 recipients in the Medicaid program so that providers of costly services can determine if a given patient is eligible for benefits.

Prepunched card verification. To verify the accuracy of the prepunched cards used for much of the data entry, cards can be read by the terminal and interpreted by voice answer-back.

Injectable medications—a specific problem. Approximately two-thirds of all claims processed by the intermediary contain a charge for an injection. Therefore, one of the potential stumbling blocks in automating claims processing was the handling of charges for injectable medications in doctors' offices. In traditional systems, processing injections requires a manual "look-up" and setting of an allowable charge for the procedure. Irrespective of the drug injected, the code 90030 (injection) is assigned to all such transactions. To facilitate automation, we prepared a list of all injectable drugs found in the computerized Drug Product Information File (DPIF) of the American Society of Hospital Pharmacists (ASHP), and the unique five digit number, the DPIF Brand Product Package Number (BDPPK#), was chosen as the code number to identify the drug injected. In our system, each time the procedure code number 90030 is encountered in a transaction, the user is asked to enter the drug

code (BDPPK#) and the volume given. Since we also have the average wholesale price for each drug in our file, it would be a simple matter to *calculate* the allowable charge, compare it with the submitted charge, and determine which is lower. This degree of automation is lacking in current carrier processing systems.

Procedure modifiers. Procedure modifier codes, two digit prefixes to the AMA-CPT procedure codes discussed below, were adopted to cause program branching when claims for anesthesia, assistance at surgery, multiple surgical procedures, etc., were being entered. This allows the fiscal agent to determine allowable charges since special procedure codes do not exist for all possible anesthesia procedures, e.g. anesthesia for tonsillectomy. (There are more than 2500 surgical procedure codes alone!) We are indebted to the 1969 California Relative Value Study for the concept of modifiers to reduce the number of procedure codes required.

4. Off-Line System Software

Off-line programs have been written to convert the transaction file on disk into hard copy claims and tape files for submission to the insurer.

The data elements entered by the user are listed in Table 1. Other items needed to produce a hardcopy claim were retrieved from off-line files. To avoid manual translation errors, we printed both the AMA-CPT and the local carrier's procedure codes. The claim control number, which was "voiced" to the user at the time of input, was also shown on the document. By arrangement with the Medicaid program director, no signature was required to submit these claims for payment.

Eligibility file. A disk resident file of all current recipient numbers is created monthly from the eligibility tape file supplied by Medical Services Administration. It occupies 15 cylinders on an IBM 3330 disk pack.

Cross-referencing procedure codes. To make the system generally applicable in claims processing, and to maintain impartiality toward all carriers, the American Medical Association's Current Procedural Terminology (CPT) code was selected. Though the text descriptions of the codes are sometimes lengthy and circuitous, they represent a great deal of thought by the medical profession and the list is complete. We have also acquired from OCHAMPUS (Office of Civilian Health and Medical Programs for the Uniformed Services) a cross reference between CPT and 1964 CRVS, and CPT and the 1970 National Association of Blue Shield Plans (NABSP) procedure codes to expedite cross referencing between AMA's CPT and Equitable's and Blue Cross' codes, derivatives of 1964 CRVS.

Diagnosis file. The complete set of 4 digit codes and their descriptions abbreviated to 90 characters (for purposes of hardcopy formatting) were keypunched from the eighth revision of ICDA, International Classification of Diseases, Adapted.

Provider file. Physicians are identified by a 5 digit code supplied by Blue Cross–Blue Shield of Alabama, the Medicare intermediary for this state. Monthly updates of this file keep our file current.

5. Aid to physicians' offices

Prepunched cards. Analysis of paid claims records for 1971 furnished by Equitable showed that the 10 commonest procedures accounted for more than ¾ of all services and the 50 most frequent diagnoses for more than 2/3 of all conditions submitted by all physicians participating in the program regardless of specialty. The paid claims file was further sorted by specialty of practice: for each specialty, procedures performed and patient diagnosis were ranked by frequency of occurrence and prepunched decks of the 50 most common procedures and diagnoses for the type of practice were distributed to each participant.

The paid claims file was also scanned for recipients seen by any of the physicians participating in this project and cards were prepared for each patient except where the number seemed excessive; in these cases, cards were prepared only for patients with five or more visits. The prepared patient cards were distributed to the appropriate physicians.

User instruction. Each user in the office of a participating doctor was trained by one of our instructors until competent to enter claims without assistance. Six hours of instruction, divided into three 2-hr sessions, was usually required.

RESULTS

Physician Participation

Our minimum performance goal was to enlist the participation of enough physicians to account for 50% of the statewide Medicaid billing load, using a maximum of 150 terminals. By September, 1973, we had agreements to participate with 110 offices, but 10 did not yet have the phone equipment because of problems with small independent phone companies in rural areas of the state. Of the remainder, 70 were submitting claims weekly and another 27 at least once monthly. Three did not use the system although adequately trained. Despite the small number of offices using the system regularly or intermittently, users entered 28,455 procedures in 14,368 complete claims during September 1973. This monthly rate exceeded the formal contract goal and was more than 50% of the statewide load processed by the carrier.

System Performance

Time to enter claims. The histogram in Fig. 1 shows the distribution of the time required to input claims. The small number

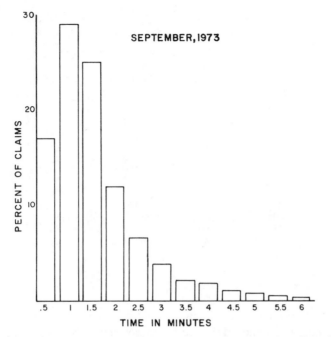

Fig. 1. Distribution of time to transmit complete claims. The average number of services per claim is 1.9. Data for September 1 to September 28, 1973, the last 4 wk of free service and the highest volume period during the project.

of claims entered in less than 30 seconds represent claims submitted by six County Health Departments involving Pediatric Screening program visits. The average time to enter a claim, which usually contains two procedures, is less than 1½ min. The average time per procedure is consistently less than 1 min. Since some users are still being trained, a few outlying claims take more than 7 min to enter. A maximum of 13 procedures may be entered as one claim, but fewer than 1% of claims have so many procedures.

Telephone Loading

The number of input channels required to handle a given billing load can be estimated from current experience. Table 2 shows the loading of the various telephone lines as a function of time of day for the last week of September 1973. It should be noted that although we made no attempt at scheduling input, users achieved a reasonable distribu-

tion of claims entry during the day and during the week. Because most high volume users are outside the local dial-up area of the central facility, we have installed three WATS lines in addition to two local lines. These five lines easily handle 50% of the statewide load—our project goal. (Our original projections were that 13 lines would handle 100% of the load—based on a 1-min. average time per "line," a 50% duty cycle for a phone line, and 40 hr/wk operation.)

Acceptance by Intermediary

The initial cautious attitude of both carriers involved in this project has gradually moved toward more enthusiastic acceptance of the potential for cost reduction in claims processing, not only for Medicaid claims, but for their private Blue Shield contracts with subscribers as well. The carriers also realize that there is no basic conflict between our system and their own efforts to implement "direct entry" of claims,

TABLE 2

SYSTEM LOADING AS A FUNCTION OF DAY OF WEEK AND TIME OF DAY[a]

Hour		Number of Claims			
	Monday	Tuesday	Wednesday	Thursday	Friday
8–9	0	38	25	0	8
9–10	7	67	205	112	145
10–11	123	104	146	159	123
11–12	173	77	153	193	105
21–1	31	70	157	129	65
1–2	76	93	165	112	67
2–3	55	136	150	142	102
3–4	133	123	193	120	79
4–5	50	86	114	113	136
5–6	23	66	57	84	1
6–7	0	64	0	48	10
Total	671	924	1365	1212	841

[a] Data for last week of September 1973.

an improvement that eliminates the preparation of coding forms from standard source documents. Throughout the project the carriers processed hard copy produced by our system just like manually prepared claims submitted by other physicians' offices. Although confident that the encoding of information by office personnel was accurate and that cross-referencing of CPT to local codes was also accurate, neither carrier processed claims directly from magnetic tape. Blue Cross tested the feasibility of processing Pediatric Screening claims and found no technical barriers to a successful outcome, but has been unwilling to attempt this on a general basis because of conflicting internal priorities.

Cost Analysis

The high volume achieved permits a realistic estimate to be made of the cost for providing on-line computer services for medical billing. Variable costs for computer processing need little extrapolation. The projected annual budget for a system which handles a minimum of 400,000 service entries per year assuming all reporting offices have been trained is approximately $100,000 including overhead based on a

cost per unit of service billed of 25¢. Most offices report halving in personnel time required for billing and improved collections resulting from accurate and complete claims.

DISCUSSION

The use of voice answer-back systems is not innovative in itself. These systems have been used extensively by the banking industry for simple account balance inquiry systems, by industry for inventory control, and tracing jobs within a plant. Experimental work in the biomedical field was reported by Allen and Otten (4) who demonstrated the applicability of such systems to medications ordering, laboratory test ordering, and inquiry systems on an experimental basis. The novelty in the application is in the complex data flow with extensive user–machine interaction and in the flexible branching program structure which can be expanded to obtain additional information for PSRO. This contrasts sharply with the imprinter billing system under consideration by SSA (3) which does not even capture diagnosis in machine readable form and is limited to "one procedure" claims.

We gained a number of revealing insights in the process of training doctors' office personnel to use the on-line system. Frustrated by previous experience with the bureaucracy, the physician's role in claims processing is often passive/aggressive. A physician, who is either too busy to care or unaware of the significance of how the procedure or diagnosis he specifies on a claim form is translated into a code by the intermediary, may use nonstandard terminology to describe services rendered, not realizing the effect this may have on reimbursement. When payments for services are not checked against the claim submitted, a feeling of hostility may develop when the physician finds that payment for the same service varies and he may refuse to see other sponsored patients.

Errors generated in the process of translating procedure descriptions to procedure codes were estimated by comparing a list prepared manually by the office clerk working for each physician with a comparable list derived from paid claims data supplied by the intermediary. Except for two of the most common services ("routine office visit" and "initial office visit") these two lists did not coincide for general practitioners and surgeons. In contrast, the agreement for radiology and clinical pathology laboratories was excellent. The discrepancies noted indicate that coding of procedure by the intermediary may be too subjective or too arbitrary, or, more likely, that the physician did not state clearly and explicitly what services he provided. It is clear that laboratory and X-ray examination descriptions are concise, and that there is adequate standardization of terminology for these procedures among all physicians. Surgical procedure names, on the other hand, are notably nonuniform. There is enormous variance between the AMA-CPT, the NABSP, and the 1964 and 1969 CRVS procedure code manuals; and enormous variation among individual physician's descriptions of these procedures.

Installing a telephone terminal to the on-line system and attempting to use the system has brought these problems into clear focus for the average physician for the first time. Use of the system requires a certain discipline not always typical of a doctor's business office. A clerk who understands the encoding of procedures and diagnoses must often ask the physician many questions to resolve an ambiguous description. (Some personnel state they had never previously dared question the physician about what he had written on a claim form.)

When an office goes "on-line," there is a period of about 1 wk during which the user makes obvious mistakes, revealed by direct manual comparison of our hardcopy with office records. After this initial period, errors in encoding procedure and diagnosis with the on-line system are less than 1%. The difference between new and old systems is undoubtedly a reflection of the various "edits" that are built into the on-line system, and a new awareness of what the whole process of claims processing involves on the part of doctors' office staff.

A positive conclusion on cost-effectiveness cannot be made at the present time. This crucial issue can be resolved only by objective cost accounting studies of the on-line billing system, physicians' business office, and carrier operations. It has been very difficult to obtain cost data from carriers either because most customary carrier accounting methods aggregate costs into centers that are not directly comparable to the functions performed by our on-line billing system, or because carrier operations are highly competitive business enterprises, these data are closely guarded business secrets. Anecdotal evidence from several of our high-volume group practices indicates that the labor cost has been reduced to one third the previous cost using manual methods. If this proves to be true for small offices as well, a significant cost reduction to physicians' office operations as well as of carrier's should be possible.

CONCLUSIONS

The following conclusions may safely be drawn from our experience in operating the system:

1. The numeric keyboard/card dialer telephone used in conjunction with audio feedback via computer is completely adequate for gathering and editing data to produce a physician's claim for service in the Medicaid program.
2. Fifty prepunched cards for procedures and diagnoses, when carefully selected for the individual office, reduce manual entries of these data elements to fewer than 5% of the total number entered.
3. User acceptance of this mode of data entry is conditioned to a large degree by the type of practice (group vs solo practitioner) and the amount of basic office organization predating the installation of the terminal. With persistence, however, reluctant users can be retrained to take advantage of this system. This may be accompanied by improved performance in other aspects of office management.

Acknowledgments

The authors wish to acknowledge the assistance and cooperation of the following individuals and groups without whose help this project could not have succeeded: all our physician participants and their office staffs; Dr. Paul I. Robinson, Director of MSA (Medicaid); Dr. Thomas H. Alphin, previous Director of MSA; Mr. Joseph Vance, Senior Vice-President of Blue Cross–Blue Shield of Alabama, Mr. John Anderson, District Director of Equitable–Alabama Medicaid; Dr. Robert Holzworth of OCHAMPUS; Dr. William Barclay of AMA; Dr. Josiah Macy, Jr., Director of the Division of Biophysical Sciences of UAB; Mr. Jack Davis, Manager of Operations for UAB Central Computer Facility; and to Ms. Sybil Klein, Ms. Betty Doyle, and Ms. Sandra Brown, former and present project managers without whose patience, encouragement, devoted service, and loyalty this effort would not have gotten beyond the initial feasibility study.

REFERENCES

1. Krinsky, Joel and Hampton, Phillip Community Profile Data Center, Technical Paper Series No. 2, Contract HSM-110-70-43, Community Health Service, HSMHA, DHEW.
2. Statistical Report on Administration Costs for Medicare contractors, July 1973 through December 1973, Bureau of Health Insurance, Social Security Administration.
3. Report on Simplified Physician Billing Project. Division of Systems, Social Security Administration, April 1973.
4. Allen, Scott I. and Otten, Michael. The telephone as a computer input–output terminal for medical information. *JAMA* 208, 673–679 (1969).

17. Medicaid Insurance Contracts—Problems in Procuring, Administering, and Monitoring

GENERAL ACCOUNTING OFFICE

SCOPE OF REVIEW

We directed our review toward (1) ascertaining the extent of HEW's involvement in developing and awarding contracts for Medicaid insuring agreements, (2) evaluating HEW's capability to monitor insuring agreements, (3) evaluating states' policies and procedures for obtaining and monitoring insuring agreements, and for reviewing contractors' financial performance under insuring agreements.

Our review was conducted at HEW headquarters in Washington, D.C., and at the HEW regional offices in Atlanta, Georgia; Boston, Massachusetts; Dallas, Texas; Philadelphia, Pennsylvania; and San Francisco, California. Also, work was performed at state agencies in Arkansas, California, Florida, Louisiana, Maine, North Carolina, Pennsylvania, and Texas. The state agencies are responsible for administering and monitoring state Medicaid activities and developing and awarding state contracts. In addition, work was performed at the facilities of the contractors and subcontractors involved in administering state Medicaid programs under insurance-type contracts, except for Group Hospital Service, Inc.

We reviewed federal and state legislation, regulations, guidelines, policies, and procedures pertaining to Medicaid activities and to the use of private industry and insurance-type contracts for administering Medicaid programs. Our work also included reviews and analyses of reports, records, and other data pertaining to state contract procurement and monitoring activities and to HEW's involvement in these activities. At the contractors' and subcontractors' facilities, we reviewed financial records, various reports required by the contracts, data used by contractors to develop contract proposals, and proposals for rate adjustments under existing contracts.

We also visited or telephoned several firms that either received a request for proposals or expressed interest in being awarded a Medicaid insurance-type contract. This was done to obtain their views concerning the use of insuring agreements to administer state Medicaid programs, and the effectiveness of state practices and procedures relative to awarding Medicaid insurance-type contracts.

A list of contracts included in our review is shown in Exhibit 1.

INTRODUCTION

Medicaid is a federal/state program for financing the health care of public assist-

153

Exhibit 1 Medicaid Insurance-Type Contracts Included in Our Review

State	Name of contractor/ subcontractor	Medical services covered by the contract	Actual contract period[a]
Arkansas	PAID/HAS	drugs	9/1/73– 6/30/76
California	PAID/HAS	drugs	12/1/72– 9/30/75
	[b]CDS/none	dental	1/1/74–12/31/77
Florida	PAID/HAS	drugs	7/1/74– 6/30/76
Louisiana	[cd]LNL/PCS	drugs	10/1/75– 6/30/76
Maine	PAID/HAS	drugs	8/1/74– 6/30/75
North Carolina	PAID/HAS	drugs	12/1/72– 6/30/76
	HAS/none	multiservice	5/1/75– 6/30/76
Pennsylvania	PAID/HAS	drugs	2/1/75– 6/30/76
Texas	[e]GHSI/none	multiservice	9/1/67–12/31/76

[a]Includes contract renegotiations and extensions effected without competition through June 30, 1976.
[b]California Dental Service.
[c]Lincoln National Life.
[d]Pharmaceutical Card Systems.
[e]Group Hospital Services.

ance recipients and other low-income individuals and families. States have the primary responsibility for creating and operating their Medicaid programs. At the federal level, Medicaid was administered until March 1977 by the Social and Rehabilitation Service (SRS) of the Department of Health, Education, and Welfare (HEW). On March 8, 1977, the Secretary of HEW announced a reorganization which abolished SRS and transferred federal Medicaid administration to the newly established Health Care Financing Administration (HCFA). Our fieldwork for this report took place before March 1977, therefore, this report refers to SRS as the federal administrative agency for Medicaid.

Normally, states have either administered their Medicaid programs directly or contracted with firms to administer the Medicaid claims payment process, paying such firms on a cost reimbursement or fixed-price-per-claim-processed basis. Firms with these claims processing agreements are called fiscal agents. However, some states have decided to administer all or part of their Medicaid programs by contracting with private firms for insurance

coverage for Medicaid eligibles. Under insuring agreements, the contractor is responsible for paying all valid claims for covered services received by eligible persons in exchange for a predetermined per capita premium. The contractor is at risk because, if the costs of paying claims exceed premium payments, the contractor could suffer a loss.

Texas has had a Medicaid insuring agreement covering several types of medical services (primarily inpatient hospital and physician services) since 1967. Since 1972 Arkansas, California, Louisiana, Florida, Maine, North Carolina, and Pennsylvania have used insuring agreements for administering their Medicaid drug programs. California also entered into an insuring agreement in 1974 for dental services under its Medicaid program; and, in April 1975, North Carolina entered into an insuring agreement that covered all aspects of its Medicaid program, except for determining program policy and recipient eligibility, inspecting and certifying medical providers, and processing and paying drug claims (which were already administered under a separate insuring agreement). All these contracts were included in our study.

By letter dated May 22, 1975, the Chairman, Subcommittee on Health, Senate Committee on Finance, requested that we review North Carolina's multiservice insurance contract as the first stage of a broader review of HEW's and various states' policies and procedures for awarding insurance-type contracts.

The Chairman expressed concern about:

- the extent of HEW's involvement in the North Carolina contract award and
- HEW's capability to monitor such contracts and to assess contractors' performance.

The results of our North Carolina review are contained in our report of July 1, 1976, to the Chairman, Subcommittee on Health, Senate Committee on Finance.* The report pointed out that:

- competition for the contract was limited because of a number of conditions surrounding the procurement;
- the contractor's proposed price received limited evaluation;
- the state directed its negotiations at obtaining advantages which, in fact, were already in the contractor's proposal;
- most benefits claimed for the contract would either not materialize or were not related to the contract's insurance feature;
- HEW had limited involvement in preselection activities but more involvement in contract negotiations; and
- the contractor was having financial difficulties under the contract and notified the state that it was contemplating termination.

---

*"North Carolina's Medicaid Insurance Agreement: Contracting Procedures Need Improvement" (HRD-76-139).

In August 1976 the contract's insurance aspect was terminated effective July 1, 1976. The state agreed to pay the contractor an additional $16 million and the state hired the contractor to act as the state's fiscal agent.

The results of our broader review of HEW and state policies and procedures for awarding insurance-type contracts are discussed in this report.

The Medicaid Program and Its Administration

Title XIX of the Social Security Act (42 U.S.C. 1396) authorizes federal financial participation in state medical assistance (Medicaid) programs which conform to the provisions of the act. The federal government pays 50 to 78 percent (depending on the state's per capita income) of the costs for providing Medicaid medical services.

Medicaid recipients include persons or families receiving or entitled to receive cash assistance payments under the Supplemental Security Income or Aid to Families with Dependent Children programs. These recipients are referred to as the categorically needy. In addition, states may pay for medical care to medically needy persons and their families (individuals whose income exceeds the state's standard under the appropriate cash assistance plan, but is insufficient to meet their medical costs). As of January 1977, 49 States, the District of Columbia, Guam, Puerto Rico, and the Virgin Islands had operational Medicaid programs, and 32 of these jurisdictions had elected to pay for care to the medically needy.

The Social Security Act requires that a state desiring federal sharing in the costs of its Medicaid program submit to the Secretary of HEW a plan for medical assistance which meets the conditions specified in the act, and that the Secretary approve any state plan which meets those conditions. The approved state plan is the basis on which the federal government shares in the costs of a state's Medicaid program.

Until March 1977 the Secretary of HEW had delegated the responsibility for federal Medicaid administration to the Administrator of the Social and Rehabilitation Service. Authority to approve state Medicaid plans had been delegated to the SRS regional commissioners, who administered the program's field activities through HEW's 10 regional offices. The commissioners were to determine whether state programs comply with Federal requirements and approve state plans.

For a state to get federal approval for its Medicaid plan, the state must provide inpatient and outpatient hospital care, physician services, X-ray and laboratory services, skilled nursing facility services, home health services, family planning services, and early and periodic screening, diagnosis, and treatment services for eligible recipients under 21 years of age. States can, at their option, cover virtually any other medical or remedial care under the Medicaid plans.

Legal and Regulatory Basis for Medicaid Insurance Agreements

The Social Security Act specifies, in section 1902(a)(4)(A) (which deals with the requirements for state Medicaid plans), that the plan must provide for ". . . such methods of administration . . . as are found by the Secretary to be necessary for the proper and efficient operation of the plan." The act also states, in section 1903(a)(1)(B) (which deals with federal sharing of Medicaid costs), that funds are available for sharing the costs of ". . . insurance premiums for medical or any other type of remedial care or the cost thereof." Based on these two provisions, the Secretary has determined that insurance agreements are an acceptable method for administering all or part of a state Medicaid program.

To determine the congressional intent in allowing federal participation in the costs of Medicaid insurance agreements, we researched the provision's legislative history. We found that the sharing provision was a carryover from the Kerr-Mills Act (Public Law 86–778, Sept. 13, 1960), which preceded Medicaid and provided medical assistance to the aged. The provision in the Kerr-Mills Act was, in turn, a carryover from the medical assistance provisions contained in the preceding cash assistance programs for the aged, blind, disabled, and dependent children. The sharing provision was added to the Social Security Act by the 1956 Amendments (Public Law 85–239, Aug. 30, 1957), but the congressional legislative committee reports relating to those amendments did not say why the provision was included. We found, however, that H.R. 81–1300 on the Social Security Amendments of 1950, (Public Law 81–734, Aug. 28, 1950), which first provided medical assistance to the aged stated:

Some [state] assistance agencies consider it preferable to pay the medical practitioner or institution that supplies the medical care directly. Some state agencies have wanted to insure their clients' needs for medical care with organizations for group care such as Blue Cross.

Thus, it appears that the provision providing for federal participation in Medicaid insurance agreements was included because some states desired this method for administration as long ago as 1949.

HEW Regulations Governing Medicaid Insurance Agreements

HEW Medicaid regulations (45 C.F.R. 249.82) provide for federal financial participation in costs paid by a state to health insurance organizations, fiscal agents, or private nonmedical institutions under contracts for administration of a state's program.

When the contracts included in our review were initially proposed, negotiated, and awarded, regulations did not require HEW's prior insurance contract approval. The regulations were amended effective August 9, 1975, to require prior approval of all contracts costing more than $100,000.

States are also required to follow the procurement standards listed in 45 C.F.R. 74.150 through 74.159 when they procure Medicaid insuring agreements. These procurement standards prohibit conflict of interest in procurement actions, require free and open competition, establish procedural requirements and criteria for the types of procurements that can be negotiated, require the inclusion of certain clauses in contracts, and require states to have adequate contract administration systems. States are not required to follow the Federal Procurement Regulations, but instead can use their own procurement policies as long as they meet the standards contained in 45 C.F.R. 74.150, *et seq.*

Contractors and Subcontractors Involved in Medicaid Insuring Contracts

Between 1967 and 1976, seven different companies entered into insurance-type contracts with one or more states to administer some benefits of the state Medicaid programs. We reviewed state contracts with six of these companies.* A discussion of the contract arrangements with the states, and the organizational relationships and business involvements of these six contractors and their major subcontractors follows.

Group Hospital Service, Inc. (Blue Cross of Texas)

Blue Cross of Texas, a not-for-profit health insurance corporation, through its fiscal agent organization, Group Hospital Service, Inc., has had an insurance-type contract** with Texas since 1962 for several types of medical services provided under the state's medical assistance programs. In 1967 when Texas consolidated its previous medical assistance programs into a Medicaid program, it unsuccessfully attempted to solicit bids from additional firms—Group Hospital Service thus retained the program with the original contracts. The state resolicited the contract in 1976 and received three proposals.

Paid Prescriptions, Inc.

Paid Prescriptions, Inc. (PAID), is a California not-for-profit corporation which either currently has, or until recently had, insurance-type contracts with Arkansas, California, Florida, Maine, North Carolina, and Pennsylvania to administer these states' Medicaid drug programs on a prepaid capitation basis. In addition to its Medicaid drug contracts, PAID has numerous drug contracts with insurance firms and private organizations.

PAID had an agreement with Health Application Systems, Inc. (HAS), under which PAID was obligated to subcontract with HAS for computer and marketing services for all PAID's contracts. HAS had exercised control over PAID since 1969 through a series of such agreements.

Developments in February and March 1977 affected the relationship between PAID and HAS. These changes are discussed in the next section.

---

*Prudential Insurance Company had Medicaid insurance agreements with two states in the late 1960s. Since these contracts were not in force at the time of our review, they were not included.

**Actually there were three essentially identical agreements covering different categories of eligible recipients. In this report we will consider the three contracts as one.

Health Applications Systems, Inc. (HAS)

HAS was a for-profit corporation which offered systems consulting, design, and implementation, and computer processing services in the health care area. HAS was a wholly owned subsidiary of the Bergen-Brunswig Corporation, a manufacturer of health products and a leading distributor of pharmaceutical products.

In addition to its relationship with PAID, HAS contracted directly with North Carolina to undertake all aspects of the state's Medicaid program except for determining program policy and recipient eligibility, inspecting and certifying providers, and processing and paying drug claims. The agreement, which covered all benefits except drugs, was executed on April 28, 1975, and called for HAS to function as a fiscal agent during May and June 1975 and as an insurer from July 1, 1975, through June 30, 1977. However, HAS exercised its option under the contract to cancel on 120-days notice and the state and HAS agreed to terminate the agreement effective June 30, 1976, 1 year before the scheduled expiration date.

On February 26, 1977, PAID, HAS, and Bergen-Brunswig entered into an agreement which would grant PAID many of HAS' assets and most of HAS's contractual requirements. Bergen-Brunswig had decided to divest itself of data processing activities performed by HAS because of financial difficulties HAS was having. HAS's Medicaid insuring agreement with North Carolina had been terminated, effective June 30, 1976, but HAS continued to administer the program as a fiscal agent. HAS lost this fiscal agent arrangement in January 1977.

The Department of Defense notified HAS in August 1976 that it would not exercise the Department's option to extend HAS's fiscal agent contract for the Department's health insurance program for dependents of active duty and retired military personnel.

HAS then asked for and was granted early termination of the contract.

Also, in March 1977, PAID was considering converting itself (including the acquired portion of HAS) into a for-profit corporation called Professional Health Services, Inc., which had been incorporated in Delaware on February 16, 1977.

The relationship between PAID and HAS discussed in this report relates to the relationship which existed between the two entities prior to February 1977.

Lincoln National Life Insurance Company

Lincoln National Life, a for-profit corporation, entered into a 9-month contract, renewable for an additional year and effective October 1, 1975, with Louisiana to administer that state's Medicaid drug program. Lincoln, with corporate offices in Indiana, is the nation's tenth largest life insurance company.

Under the contract's terms Lincoln assumed risk under the contract and subcontracted for a percentage of contract premiums with Pharmaceutical Card Systems, Inc., to perform all the program's administrative functions. Lincoln and Pharmaceutical Card have been involved as insurers and administrators on other drug programs, but no corporate relationship exists between the two companies.

Pharmaceutical Card Systems, Inc.

Pharmaceutical Card is a for-profit company which develops prescription drug claim administration systems and processes drug claims. It is a wholly owned subsidiary of Foremost-McKesson Incorporated, which is the parent company of McKesson and Robbins Drug Company, the world's largest drug wholesaler.

Pharmaceutical Card's Louisiana operation was incorporated as a wholly owned subsidiary solely to administer the Louisiana drug program. The Louisiana drug contract is Pharmaceutical Card's first experience with a Medicaid drug program; however, it administers prescription drug plans covering individuals in employee groups of all kinds throughout the United States and has bid on several Medicaid drug contracts.

Electronic Data Systems Federal Corporation (EDSF)

EDSF is a wholly owned subsidiary of Electronic Data Systems (EDS) Corporation. Formed in 1962, EDS designs, programs, installs, operates, and maintains management information systems under long-term fixed-price contracts with corporate customers and government agencies. EDSF, incorporated in 1969 under the Texas Business Corporate Act, provides claims processing services mostly as a fiscal agent or as subcontractor for a fiscal agent for various government health care programs, including Medicaid in several states. Effective August 1, 1976, North Carolina awarded EDSF a prepaid insurance-type contract for that state's Medicaid drug program, the first prepaid Medicaid contract received by EDSF. EDSF also bid on the 1976 solicitation for Texas' Medicaid insurance agreement and was awarded that contract, effective January 1, 1977.

California Dental Service, Inc.

California Dental Service, Inc., is a not-for-profit health services organization administering prepaid dental programs in California. It was formed by the California Dental Association and incorporated in 1955, designated as the California Dental Association Service. The California Dental Service entered into its first dental service contract in 1957. Effective January 1, 1974, the California Dental Service was awarded a 4-year prepaid dental service contract for California's Medicaid recipients.

Conclusions

Some states, trying to have better control over Medicaid costs, used insurance contracts for administering their Medicaid programs.

However, the insurance contracts have not solved states' Medicaid funding and budgeting problems.

Many private firms have declined to participate in Medicaid programs under insurance contracts due to the lack of accurate, reliable program cost and utilization data, and the inability to predict recipient eligibility. This makes the venture too risky.

Several firms that did enter into insurance contracts experienced severe financial difficulties. They charged that inaccurate, unreliable, and incomplete Medicaid program data caused them to underbid. These firms then terminated their agreements, refused to extend them, or pressured the state to renegotiate the contract in the contractor's favor so that they could avoid losses and reduce their underwriting risk.

The Department of Health, Education, and Welfare (HEW) reviewed and approved contracts for federal financial participation; however, weaknesses in the review resulted in its approving

- one contract that contained a loss recoupment provision in violation of existing federal regulations,
- one contract that included estimated costs of $3.7 million ineligible for federal sharing, and
- Federal sharing at incorrect rates on costs of about $181,000 under two approved contracts.

HEW also failed to make certain that a state complied with conditions placed on approval of a contract.

In the procurement actions, states generally did not follow federal Medicaid standards when obtaining their insurance contracts.

Open and free competitive practices were not followed, contractors' proposals were not adequately evaluated, and contract negotiation records were not maintained. In addition, they did not evaluate various alternatives, such as state administration, fiscal agent arrangements, or insurance contracts.

There had been little federal contract monitoring and no contractor financial assessments because HEW regional officials responsible for administering Medicaid programs believed that these functions were state responsibilities. HEW got involved only if the states requested it.

Most states, however, had not assigned sufficient staff to adequately perform these functions. They were relying on unverified financial and program data provided by contractors for use in assessing contractor performance, renegotiating contracts, and determining the state and federal governments' share of contract savings.

This information contained inaccurate and unreliable data. In some instances it did not fully disclose overall contract results because some contract revenues and costs were excluded.

GAO reviewed the financial performance of one nonprofit contractor who had six Medicaid insuring agreements. Its affiliated, for-profit subcontractor realized an average profit of 32 percent of costs. Five of the six contracts included provisions whereby the state would share in contractor profits. However, since almost all profits accrued to the affiliated subcontractor, the states could not share them.

Recommendations to HEW

HEW should:

- improve its assistance to states procuring Medicaid insurance contracts,
- improve its contract approval and monitoring functions, and
- revise its Medicaid contracting regulations.

Recommendations to the U.S. Senate Subcommittee on Health

GAO identified a number of state laws which restricted competition for Medicaid insurance contracts or gave a competitive advantage to some potential contractors. The Subcommittee should:

- develop legislation to amend the law to prevent federal sharing in the cost of Medicaid contracts when state laws have restricted competition or provided competitors with a competitive advantage.

HEW, State, Contractor, and Subcontractor Comments

HEW agreed with GAO's findings. It said that the report should be useful to HEW and the states in improving Medicaid contracts and contracting procedures. It concurred in all of GAO's recommendations and said it was taking actions to implement them.

Some states and contractors disagree with some of the information in this report. However, the data GAO gathered supports the information.

18. Comprehensive Review of Medicaid Eligibility

MARILYN RYMER, GENE OKSMAN,
LAWRENCE BAILIS, JUDITH DERNBURG,
PATRICIA BENNER and DAVID ELLWOOD

Prepared by Urban Systems Research & Engineering, Inc. for the Health Care Financing Administration

Between 1968 and 1976, Medicaid expenditures rose from \$3.5 billion to \$14 billion. During the same time, the number of Medicaid recipients rose from 11.5 million to about 24 million. If there had been no increase in recipients, Medicaid costs in 1976 would have stood at only \$6.6 billion even allowing for all the growth in medical prices and utilization. Eligibility policy, then, should be of critical concern. Yet many people who claim to be knowledgeable about Medicaid are surprisingly ignorant about two of its most important aspects—*who* is eligible and *how* that eligibility is determined.

Medicaid is one of the most significant public transfer programs available to poor people. With rising medical costs, eligibility for Medicaid is often more valuable than cash assistance. Yet getting on Medicaid can be a nightmare of red tape and regulations. Public understanding of Medicaid eligibility requirements is hampered because the requirements vary so by state and by type of applicant. The rules are even more complex than those used in cash assistance. And the complaints do not end with program applicants and recipients. State and local staff also complain that Medicaid eligibility determination is an administrative "chamber of horrors."

What is it about Medicaid policy that arouses confusion and frustration from recipients and staff alike? What in the policy is unfair? And what procedures are largely unworkable?

This study, sponsored in 1976 by the Department of Health, Education and Welfare (DHEW), was directed to answer such questions and to recommend a series of alternative reforms to remedy the policy and administrative problems plaguing Medicaid eligibility. The reforms stop short of what most people call National Health Insurance; instead, the focus is on minor to major changes which can be made to Medicaid (see Exhibit 1).

THE ADMINISTRATIVE REFORM PACKAGE

Much could be done to improve the administration of Medicaid eligibility immediately. The major thrust of this package is to correct those aspects of Medicaid program administration that are acutely in need of reform but do not necessitate significant legislative or regulatory change. The reforms in this package would not affect the policies or administration of the cash assistance programs, nor would they result in

Exhibit 1 Continuum of Reform Packages

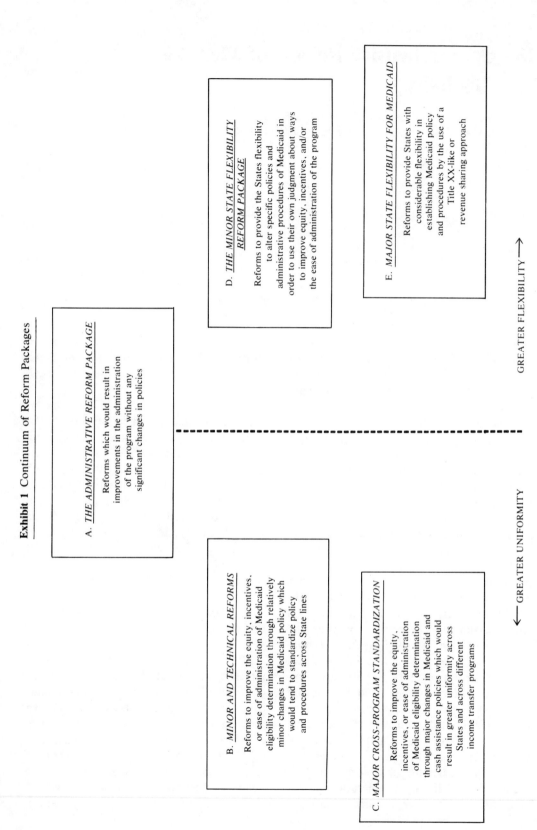

A. *THE ADMINISTRATIVE REFORM PACKAGE*

Reforms which would result in improvements in the administration of the program without any significant changes in policies

B. *MINOR AND TECHNICAL REFORMS*

Reforms to improve the equity, incentives, or ease of administration of Medicaid eligibility determination through relatively minor changes in Medicaid policy which would tend to standardize policy and procedures across State lines

C. *MAJOR CROSS-PROGRAM STANDARDIZATION*

Reforms to improve the equity, incentives, or ease of administration of Medicaid eligibility determination through major changes in Medicaid and cash assistance policies which would result in greater uniformity across States and across different income transfer programs

D. *THE MINOR STATE FLEXIBILITY REFORM PACKAGE*

Reforms to provide the States flexibility to alter specific policies and administrative procedures of Medicaid in order to use their own judgment about ways to improve equity, incentives, and/or the ease of administration of the program

E. *MAJOR STATE FLEXIBILITY FOR MEDICAID*

Reforms to provide States with considerable flexibility in establishing Medicaid policy and procedures by the use of a Title XX-like or revenue sharing approach

GREATER FLEXIBILITY →

← GREATER UNIFORMITY

significant increases in program costs. These reforms do not depend upon decisions about what direction future reform should take. As such, this reform package is the least difficult to implement of the five packages. It is essentially value-free, and *it is also the only reform package that should be implemented regardless of whether or not any other reforms are enacted.*

This package focuses on an assortment of administrative problem areas in Medicaid eligibility ranging from understaffing at all levels of operation to poorly written federal regulations to lack of coordination between Medicaid and Supplemental Security Income. The often-neglected area of data collection and data processing for eligibility information is addressed, as is the problem of public understanding of Medicaid eligibility provisions. Again, it should be stressed that only changes that require little if no legislative or regulatory actions are included in this package.

Since administrative expenses are particularly hard to estimate, especially at the federal level, no dollar cost estimates are given for any of the reforms in the Administrative Reform Package. For those reforms which Urban Systems Research and Engineering, Inc. (USR&E) felt some cost discussion could help crystallize relevant tradeoffs, the discussion is included. For the others, no comments are included.

Staff Development and Technical Assistance

The staffing capability for Medicaid eligibility at the federal, state, and local levels should be improved.

- increase the rate of Federal Financial Participation (FFP) for the states to seventy-five percent for the salaries of staff involved in Medicaid eligibility
- develop "recommended" standards of staff/caseload ratios to states for local eligibility determination staff
- increase the HEW Central and Regional office staff so that a sufficient

number of well-trained full-time Medicaid eligibility specialists are available to provide prompt and accurate guidance to the states
  - provide sufficient staff to develop policy interpretive materials promptly
  - provide sufficient staff to respond to specific questions or requests for technical assistance from the states
  - provide at least one Medicaid eligibility specialist per region
- develop additional mechanisms through the Medicaid Management Institute to support improvements in the management of eligibility determination in the Medicaid program:
  - provide federal funds for federal-to-state and state-to-state technical assistance
  - develop procedures for identifying and disseminating exemplary practices, e.g., written materials, forms
  - assist states in the development of corrective action plans based on quality control results
  - assist states in areas of special need, i.e., State Data Exchange (SDX) and Beneficiary Data Exchange (BENDEX) training

Program Coordination

Coordination between the Medicaid program and other income transfer programs should be improved.

- mandate the development of "cross-program impact statements" for all proposed changes in major income transfer programs so that policy inconsistencies, excessive benefit reduction rates, and unplanned-for repercussions can be fully explored before final decisions are made
- establish ongoing eligibility policy coordination units within HEW with

major responsibility for coordinating Medicaid with other major income transfer programs

SSA/Medicaid Relations

Changes need to be made to improve the operations of SSA and the interface between SSA and Medicaid.

- improve the referral procedures between SSA and welfare/Medicaid offices at the local level
  - a standard referral form should be developed
  - better training on Medicaid should be provided to SSA claims representatives
  - the outstationing of Medicaid eligibility staff in SSA offices should be encouraged
- SSA should assume responsibility for eligibility determination of nursing home cases and cases needing retroactive coverage
- SSA should make its Quality Assurance program more useful
  - states should be regularly informed of quality assurance results
  - SSA should assist states in making an assessment of the cost of SSI errors to Medicaid
  - SSA should establish more stringent quality assurance procedures and/or clearer guidelines to ensure the consistent application of disability criteria across states
- SSA should revise its termination and denial letters so that SSI applicants and recipients are not misled about their potential Medicaid eligibility
- SSA should expedite its appeals process for SSI so that Medicaid claims can be settled in a reasonable time period
- SSA should use the same time limits as states (i.e., sixty days) in determining eligibility for disabled SSI applicants; in the interim, states should receive

full FFP for all Medicaid presumptive disability cases
- SSA should develop record-sharing policies with state disability determination units in order to avoid unnecessary duplication of the disability determination process
- SSA should undertake a complete review and modification of the State Data Exchange (SDX) system to improve its content, timeliness, accuracy, and usefulness to states
  - much SDX data currently transmitted to states is useless and thus should be deleted
  - the carrier name and policy number for private insurance coverage should be on the SDX instead of the current Yes/No indicator
  - the Medicare claim number and the Medicare buy-in status for each SSI recipient should be on the SDX
  - clearer codes should be developed for suspended SSI cases so that states can easily and accurately determine Medicaid eligibility status
  - the actual date of disability onset, up to three months prior to application, should be on the SDX
  - the actual date of death for a deceased person should be included on the SDX to aid in retroactive coverage determinations
  - eligibility start and stop dates should be clear for each case, as well as the current eligibility status of the case
  - SSA should stop transmitting case records that are known to have errors on the SDX
- SSA should provide states with extensive training in the SDX and BENDEX systems
- SSA should test the installation of an on-line system linking the SDX to a

state Medicaid system, since the tape-to-tape approach continues to cause delays

Dissemination of Policies and Policy Interpretations

Federal Medicaid policy should be transmitted to the states in a more timely, consolidated, and organized manner.

- restrict dissemination of changes in federal Medicaid policy to a single information channel
- provide states at least forty-five days lead time before new policy materials must be implemented
- provide states with interpretive materials concerning new federal policies at the same time the new policies are issued
- provide states with alternative interpretations of federal policies when more than one alternative is acceptable
- establish formal mechanism for states to comment upon all policy interpretive materials

Federal Monitoring

HEW should devise a more effective system for monitoring state compliance with federal policy.

- revise the State Plan Pre-print
- establish a periodic Central Office review of all state Medicaid eligibility plans
- base monitoring activities upon state Medicaid manuals and not upon the State Plan Pre-print
- revise approach to citing State compliance issues so that federal policy is better enforced
- rethink the current role of HEW Regional Office staff who *must* serve both as compliance monitor and as provider of assistance at the same time

Data Collection and Computer Systems

Improvements should be made in the process whereby states collect and process data concerning Medicaid eligibility.

- mandate to states a minimum data set regarding eligibility information
  - Federal reporting requirements should be expanded to insure that data already collected by many states is available for program planning purposes
- provide increased FFP for any state effort to automate the Medicaid eligibility determination process (not just linked to MMIS)
- improve the MMIS for eligibility purposes
  - loosen the MMIS guidelines so states can develop and implement components only
  - upgrade the MMIS recipient eligibility module so that it is equal in sophistication to the claims payment component (e.g., a prototype eligibility system)
  - encourage development of data systems linkage between a more developed eligibility module and the claims payments module
- improve HEW efforts at collection, analysis, and dissemination of Medicaid eligibility data on a periodic basis
- assist states in improving their linkages with data systems of other programs important to Medicaid eligibility
  - SDX
  - BENDEX
  - Medicare Buy-In

Quality Control

Procedures should be improved to increase the utility of Medicaid Eligibility Quality Control (MEQC) data.

- revise MEQC sampling procedures
  - the MEQC sample should be drawn from Medicaid cases rather than claims
  - the MEQC sample should include rejected applicants as well as recipients
  - MEQC should look at all paid claims for a given time period rather than a single claim
  - the MEQC sample size should be increased to a level which allows greater statistical precision
- insure that MEQC reviewers have complete and up-to-date knowledge of state and federal Medicaid eligibility criteria
- increase the federal MEQC subsample and compare eligibility decisions with Federal Medicaid policy as well as with state policy
- increase technical assistance to states for improving their eligibility determination system
  - assist states in the analysis of MEQC data and the development of corrective action plans
  - assist states in the use of error-prone case profiles
  - assist states in analyzing the cost effectiveness of their verification procedures
- expand MEQC to broaden its utility
  - develop a cross-program eligibility QC system which draws a single sample and reviews AFDC, Medicaid, SSI and Food Stamps cases at the same time
  - explore broadening MEQC to include Utilization Review of the cases already included in the sample

Public Information and Client Rights

HEW should take steps to insure that Medicaid recipients and potential recipients are adequately informed about the program and their rights and responsibilities as recipients and/or applicants.

- develop standards to insure that states provide the public with clear, easy-to-read, comprehensive information about Medicaid eligibility, e.g., a standard that all materials be comprehensible to an individual with an eighth grade education. Such information would include:
  - material for public service announcements on radio and television
  - material on rights and responsibilities of applicants and recipients to be distributed in welfare offices and Social Security offices
  - application forms and notices to applicants concerning eligibility decisions, the reasons why they were made, and the procedures whereby appeals can be filed
  - general information which compares AFDC, SSI, Food Stamps, Medicaid, and Medicare
- monitor state operations to insure that all state Medicaid materials meet these standards, i.e., that public understanding is adequately promoted
- enforce deadlines for fair hearings
- enforce deadlines for decisions on new applications and redeterminations (including SSI)
- require states and the Medicaid Bureau to set up ombudsman offices to insure that recipient concerns get adequate attention

Federal Regulations

The Federal regulations for Medicaid should be rewritten and reformatted to increase their clarity and utility. The SSI regulations (20 CFR 416) should serve as a prototype.

- develop a usable index for the regulations

- include a definition-of-terms section
- eliminate extensive cross-referencing
- use short, self-contained discussions of specific topics in the regulations

Unclear Policies

Federal regulations and other policy materials should be clarified in a number of specific eligibility policy areas. These areas include:

- *spend-down:* the definition of in-hand and available income, accounting periods, use of non-eligible family members' medical expenses in meeting spend-down, relationship of third-party insurance, definition of incurment, and countable medical expenses
- *State residency requirements* for the institutionalized placed out-of-state, foster children, and institutionalized children whose guardians move out-of-state, and migrants
- *State-administered optional supplements:* definition of "reasonable classification" for purposes of Medicaid eligibility
- *personal needs allowance* (PNA) of the institutionalized: monitoring the PNA; when and how the PNA can be reduced or increased
- setting the *medically needy level*
- *retroactive coverage provision:* definition of "in hand," extent to which separate determinations are required for specific retroactive periods
- continuity of eligibility for *Medicaid-only grandfathered cases*
- applicability of *Medicaid maximum on gross income for categorically needy* (i.e., "Medicaid cap")
- how *relatives' responsibility* provisions relate to SSI and SSI-related cases
- allowable *income disregards* and income exclusions by category
- extent to which states can impose *additional conditions of eligibility*, e.g.,

Medicare buy-in and current medical need
- *termination procedures:* extent to which fair hearings are required and required procedures
- *treatment of non-citizens*
- *extent to which states must engage in independent verification of all SSI eligibility criteria*

MINOR AND TECHNICAL MEDICAID REFORMS

If it were decided that only minor change to the current Medicaid law and regulations on eligibility were feasible at this time, the following reform package would apply. Generally, this package consists of a series of relatively minor amendments to Title XIX law and regulations. None of these changes would affect the cash assistance programs, nor would they alter the current federal-state Medicaid relationship. Instead, the general purpose of these reforms would be to increase the efficiency of administration and equity of the program to the greatest extent possible without necessitating major legislative or regulatory change in Medicaid or the cash programs. The specific goals of this package in terms of equity and administration are:

- to eliminate certain inequitable eligibility criteria;
- to amend particularly troublesome and difficult-to-administer Medicaid eligibility provisions; and
- to increase uniformity among states in their Medicaid coverage.

Coverage Groups

Medicaid eligibility for cash assistance recipients should be standardized with only limited exceptions.

- require states to use cash assistance criteria for categorically needy

Medicaid eligibility (but allow separate applications for SSI recipients) with only two permissible exceptions:
— allow states to impose transfer of assets prohibitions
— allow states to impose relatives' responsibility for the institutionalized, provided that adequate standards of living are maintained for the non-institutionalized relatives

Income Levels

Current statutory maximums on Medicaid income levels should be removed.

- eliminate current maximum limitation on medically needy levels, i.e., 133% of the highest AFDC amount paid
- eliminate current 300% "Medicaid cap" on gross income for categorically needy aged, blind, and disabled persons

Disregards

Medicaid-only disregards should be simplified, consolidated, and standardized.

- substitute a mandatory rise in Medicaid income levels with each rise in Title II benefits instead of the current Title II cost-of-living disregard
- require states to use the AFDC earned income disregards for AFDC-related cases in their medically needy programs and for other Medicaid non-cash groups
- require states to protect income for maintenance of the home for the short-term institutionalized who do not have any dependents

Special Needs

States which cover special needs in their cash programs should be required to pro-

vide them in their medically needy programs.

- require states to include special needs in determining eligibility for medical assistance if they are included in the cash programs

Retroactive Coverage

The eligibility determination process for retroactive coverage should be modified to simplify administration.

Extended Medicaid Coverage

Provisions for extended Medicaid coverage should be consolidated and simplified.

- establish one three-month extended coverage provision for both AFDC and SSI recipients who become ineligible because of losing their categorical relatedness or because of increased earnings
- modify the requirement that a complete redetermination be done for extended coverage cases and require only that the reason for ineligibility be reviewed
- eliminate the requirement that workers monitor the continued eligibility of extended coverage cases; rather, the responsibility for reporting a change in circumstances should rest with the recipient

Residency

Conflicts in state residency policies should be resolved.

- require states to consider an individual a state resident for Medicaid purposes until (s)he has established residence in another state
- develop a legally binding definition of "intent to reside" for Medicaid purposes (using arbitrary criteria)

- insure that migrants are not denied Medicaid because of questions of state residence

Spend-Down

Unworkable provisions of the spend-down program should be eliminated.

- eliminate the requirement that states prioritize application of spend-down expenses to excess income
- require states to establish clear guidelines on allowable medical expenses for meeting the spend-down liability, for example, transportation and over-the-counter drugs

Grandfather Coverage

Medicaid grandfather provisions should be phased out.

MAJOR CROSS-PROGRAM STANDARDIZATION

This reform package consists of very major reforms to both the cash assistance and Medicaid programs which would help to achieve considerable uniformity in Medicaid coverage across programs and across states. These reforms would require substantial changes in Titles IV-A, XVI, and XIX of the Social Security Act. Specifically, these reforms involve:

- simplification and standardization nationwide of eligibility criteria and procedures for Title XIX,
- consolidation and standardization nationwide of eligibility criteria and procedures across all major transfer programs, and
- expansion and uniformity of Medicaid coverage groups nationwide.

This reform package should be considered in conjunction with the Minor and Technical Medicaid Reforms package. Together they represent the range of changes needed to standardize and simplify the Medicaid program nationwide.

Estimating the costs for this major reform package was difficult because simple extrapolation of current program data was rarely feasible for most of the reforms. The numbers provided are based on numerous assumptions necessitated by the severe lack of current program data. The numbers should be seen as rough guideposts, not accurate predictions.

Here, more than with the other reform packages, the participation rate question is vital. Most of the estimates were derived assuming little change in current participation rates. But, if dramatic improvements are made in interprogram coordination, and if a potential recipient can apply for several programs with the same application, participation is certain to increase. Publicity is another potential influence on participation. A major legislative thrust such as mandatory coverage of low-income persons under eighteen is certain to increase public awareness of the program.

Interprogram Coordination

The eligibility determination process should be standardized and consolidated across the major transfer programs.

- establish uniform definitions for eligibility criteria to be used by all major transfer programs
- require a single multipurpose application form for cash and health care benefits in each state, abolishing the separate AFDC, SSI, Food Stamps, and Medicaid eligibility determinations, but still allowing for some differences in exact eligibility criteria among the programs
- Social Security offices should determine all program eligibility for adult applicants; State welfare agencies

should continue to handle eligibility determination for families and children
  — fiscal liability for the programs would remain the same, but control procedures would have to be worked out

Disregards

Disregards for all cash and medical assistance programs should be standardized.

- provide a $20 disregard of any income for the SSI, AFDC, and medically needy programs; eliminate all other unearned income disregards
- standardize the earned income disregards for the SSI, AFDC, and medically needy programs
  — abolish the $30 and one-third earned income disregard for AFDC and use instead a standard disregard for earned income for the AFDC, SSI, and medically needy programs, with a *fixed maximum;* it should include all work expenses except child care
  — all program applicants as well as recipients should receive the earned income disregard

Income Levels

Income levels for the cash and medical assistance programs should be simplified and standardized.

- require states to use a uniform methodology in establishing the AFDC needs standard
- mandate that the medically needy level for a state, at a minimum, should be the adult payment level or the AFDC needs standard (whichever is higher)

Resource Criteria

Resource definitions and limitations should be simplified and standardized

across the cash and medical assistance programs.

- establish a uniform resource definition and a uniform minimum resource level for the AFDC, SSI, and medically needy programs
- mandate a one-year transfer of assets prohibition for the AFDC, SSI, and medically needy programs

Deeming and Relatives' Responsibility

Deeming and relatives' responsibility policies should be established which are equitable and uniform across the cash and medical assistance programs.

- establish a deeming of income policy to apply nationwide to AFDC, SSI, and Medicaid; do not use the SSI approach
- include in whatever criteria are developed provision for spouses and parents of child recipients to share in the cost of care when recipients are institutionalized

Categorical Definition

The categorical definitions should be amended to better identify the target population for cash and medical assistance.

- revise the definition of disability for cash assistance and Medicaid
  — use a six-month time frame for length of disability
  — eliminate the use of an arbitrary income level for determining substantial gainful activity; other more flexible criteria should be developed
  — establish that sedentary work should only be grounds for denial when it is actually available in the locality in which the applicant lives
  — allow the combination of multiple disabilities of a less severe nature

to be sufficient to qualify persons as disabled
— eliminate the use of arbitrary IQ levels in determining disability
• require the submission of psychosocial histories as well as medical information for use in the review process for disability determination
• expand the definition of the eligible unit for cash and medical assistance to include "essential persons"
• revise the MA-21 program so that it becomes medical assistance to low-income children under age 18 (MA-18)

Coverage Group Expansion

States should be required to phase in Medicaid coverage of all groups currently allowable under SSI, AFDC, and Medicaid regulations.

• mandate coverage of all the medically needy
• mandate coverage of all SSI and State Supplement (SSP) recipients
• mandate coverage of AFDC-UF
• mandate coverage of all children in poor families, including the unborn (MA-18 program)

Alternatives to Institutionalization

Provision should be made among the major transfer programs to meet recipient special needs which would prevent unnecessary institutionalization.

• establish criteria for including certain special needs in the eligibility determination process of AFDC, SSI, and Medicaid
— the list of special needs should include, at a minimum, homemakers and domiciliary care

Spend-Down

State Medicaid programs should collect the spend-down liability, thus assuming total administrative responsibility for the spend-down program.

• require states to establish reasonable payment schedules for recipients to pay off spend-down liabilities
• prohibit states from denying medical coverage because of non-payment of the spend-down liability; however, states should make every attempt to enforce collection of the liability

Compliance and Performance Standards

Performance standards should be established for Medicaid eligibility with incentives for policy compliance as well as sanctions.

THE MINOR STATE FLEXIBILITY REFORM PACKAGE

The previous two reform packages contained modifications of the Medicaid program which would tend to standardize the program nationwide, and, as such, reduce State flexibility in implementing the program.

While many state Medicaid officials are for national standards, few can agree on what the standards should be. The only standards that would be satisfactory to the majority of states are ones that are liberal enough so that no state would have to cut back its program. However, imposing liberal standards nationwide would be extremely costly, and none of the states is willing, or able, to pay for it. Once cost constraints are introduced into the decision making, states tend to disagree widely on what Medicaid policy should be. One thing they all are in agreement on, however, is that the states are in a much better position than the federal government to make and implement sound policies.

States believe that many of the problems of the Medicaid program are due to the fact that the policymakers (i.e., HEW and the Congress) are *not* the ones who have to implement the policies. The result is a proliferation of policies that are administratively unworkable. Many state Medicaid officials feel that if they were given the flexibility to administer the Medicaid program as they wish, they would contribute significantly to the development of exemplary models or innovative approaches which could be adopted by other states as well. They also believe that they are closer than Congress and HEW to their constituents and are, therefore, in a better position to develop policies that are responsive to recipient needs.

These arguments form the basis for this reform package and the one which follows. The reforms in this package leave the basic structure of the federal-state Medicaid program in place and permit departures from specific eligibility policies and/or procedures. Reforms in the package presented last represent a major change in the overall philosophy of the Medicaid program and would involve adoption of a Title XX-like approach to the provision of medical assistance to the needy.

The reforms in this package generally consist of those modifications in Medicaid eligibility policy and procedures which:

- would provide states additional flexibility in planning and implementing Medicaid programs,
- do not involve changes in cash assistance programs, and
- do not involve major changes in the nature of the current federal-state relationship in public and medical assistance.

Many of the reforms in this package would require changes in some parts of Title XIX

of the Social Security Act as well as in the current federal regulations.

Certain of these reforms would give the states the flexibility to expand the program more gradually than they have done in the past. Others would give states the flexibility to cut back on the program in areas which they feel are of low priority. It is hard to predict how states would respond to this new flexibility, and thus, it is impossible to predict the cost impact of this package. But the cost implications should not be short-changed. These reforms, unlike most of the others, are almost certain to provide some fiscal relief. Given the chance, most states would cut back. If costs must be cut, allowing states to decide where programs must be slashed would serve to increase local control over who gets benefits.

Medically Needy Eligibility

States should be given greater flexibility in setting eligibility requirements for the medically needy.

- permit states to provide medically needy coverage for only selected categories
- eliminate the maximum on medically needy levels (133% of the highest amount paid for AFDC), and retain current regulations on minimum levels
- permit states to set gross income maximums on medically needy levels
- permit states to recognize special needs in determining eligibility for the medically needy program
- permit states to establish additional conditions of eligibility should they so choose, e.g.,
  — enrollment in Medicare Part B
  — current medical need
  — transfer of assets prohibition

Spend-Down

States should be allowed more flexibility in administering specific elements of spend-down.

- allow states to require that the spend-down liability be paid before granting Medicaid eligibility
- permit states to set up spend-down collection accounts
- provide states full discretion as to which expenses can be counted toward spend-down beyond Medicaid-covered services

Income Disregards

States should be given more flexibility in determining what kinds of earned and unearned income should be disregarded in determining financial eligibility for Medicaid.

- permit states to decide for themselves whether or not to continue using current unearned income disregards for Medicaid such as:
  - August 1972 Social Security cost-of-living increase
  - further Social Security cost-of-living increases
  - educational stipends
  - stipends for VISTA-like programs
  - cash bonus value of Food Stamps
  - per capita payments to Indian tribes
  - benefits under Title VII of the Older Americans Act
- permit states to alter the current treatment of work-related expenses and earned income for AFDC medically needy cases
  - permit the states to use a flat disregard for work-related expenses (without any provision to permit higher disregards if actual expenses can be demonstrated to be higher)
  - permit the states to apply a modified "thirty and a third" rule which imposes time and/or money limits

Other Financial Criteria Affecting the Institutionalized

States should be given more flexibility to set financial standards for Medicaid coverage which affect the institutionalized.

- eliminate the "Medicaid cap" for adult categorically needy recipients (i.e., the 300% of SSI limit on gross income) and, in its place, require only that gross income be less than total medical (at Medicaid cost-related reimbursement rates) and maintenance costs (including maintenance of the home)
- eliminate the requirements that the personal needs allowance must be at least $25.00 and allow states to vary the allowance according to actual personal needs

Medicaid Eligibility for SSI Recipients

Changes should be instituted in the options available to states for coverage of SSI recipients in order to provide greater flexibility.

- repeal 209(b) and allow states at their option to establish for Medicaid *any* criteria more restrictive (than SSI) for the aged, blind, and disabled
  - permit states using more restrictive criteria to rely on selected data from the SDX in eligibility determination without additional verification
  - continue allowing states to use SSI criteria but require a separate application for Medicaid; also allow those states to rely on the SDX without additional verification
  - no spend-down provisions would be mandatory, no disregard of SSI income would be required; neither would states be limited to their January 1972 eligibility criteria

— continue to make the 1634 agreement option available to states

Adult Medically Needy Coverage

All states should be permitted to provide medically needy coverage to certain aged, blind, and disabled persons not currently eligible because of SSI categorical criteria.

- permit states to provide coverage for "essential persons"
- permit states to use a more liberal disability definition for Medicaid coverage

Specific Medicaid Eligibility Policies

States should be able to modify other specific Medicaid eligibility provisions when, in their judgment, these revisions would improve the program in their jurisdiction.

- permit states to set their own eligibility requirements and monitoring procedures for extended coverage
- permit states to set their own eligibility requirements for retroactive coverage
- permit states to provide federally-matched Medicaid for whatever groups of low-income children they wish, e.g., all children under a certain age

Data Systems and Quality Control

HEW should provide states with increased flexibility to collect and analyze program data and to conduct quality control activities they feel to be appropriate.

- permit states to develop and implement MMIS or any parts of it in an incremental fashion
- permit states with consistently low MEQC rates to reduce the size of their sample and/or to sample less frequently within federally set limits

and/or to use error prone profiles for their MEQC sample
- increase the administrative matching rate to states with good MEQC results

MAJOR STATE FLEXIBILITY FOR MEDICAID

This package of reforms provides major flexibility to states in establishing Medicaid eligibility requirements and thus represents a radical departure from the current thrust of Medicaid policy. Instead of requiring states to model their programs according to criteria established by the federal government, states would be free to provide Medicaid eligibility beyond the cash assistance population however they wished. States would be required to automatically cover all cash assistance recipients under Medicaid and would have unlimited federal matching funds for this effort. With the medically needy and all other noncash assistance groups, however, there would be a fixed amount of federal funds available to each state (derived from a formula involving the number of poor people in a state and the state's current non-categorically needy Medicaid expenditures) for Medicaid matching purposes. This approach is somewhat similar to that employed in the current Title XX Social Service program. It would not be a "block grant" approach because matching would still be involved.

The primary assumptions upon which a package such as this is based include the following:

- A state is in a better position to judge which of its people most need medical coverage than is the federal government.
- States would be more likely to extend medical coverage beyond the recipients of cash programs if they had complete control over which groups of people would receive this coverage.
- States are in the best position to develop specific policies for administer-

ing the Medicaid program because they operate the program.

This reform package provides a means by which Medicaid expenditures could be better controlled. Given the current cost constraints facing states and the federal government, the issue of cost control is indeed an important one.

The issue of whether or not states should be able to vary the benefit package for the Medicaid-only population has not been addressed in this reform package, because benefit coverage is clearly beyond the scope of this project. However, this issue would need to be addressed. The extent of benefits provided is obviously equally important to eligibility criteria in controlling costs.

Serious thought would have to be given to how the ceiling on available federal funds would be revised each year. The rate of increase in medical costs has been tremendous in recent years. Thus, some means would need to be devised to insure that this approach would not require states to cut back their overall level of effort for Medicaid to the noncash assistance population.

With such a broad set of reforms, no specific cost estimates can be given. But the simple appeal of this sort of approach is that it puts stronger financial pressure on states. It also allows more extensive state experimentation with methods of cost control on both the eligibility and the payments sides. In a health system where no one has succeeded in controlling costs, such experimentation might be very valuable.

Cash Assistance Coverage

All states should be required to automatically extend Medicaid eligibility to all cash assistance recipients.

- include mandatory coverage for all persons who would be eligible for cash if they were not institutionalized

- continue to make available to states unlimited federal matching funds for coverage of these groups

Medicaid Only Coverage

States should have maximum flexibility for establishing eligibility criteria to extend Medicaid only to low-income persons.

- eliminate federally-mandated categorical requirements for Medicaid-only coverage
- eliminate federally-mandated income levels for Medicaid-only coverage
- eliminate federally-mandated disregards for Medicaid-only coverage
- eliminate federally-mandated spenddown for Medicaid-only coverage
- establish a ceiling on federal funds available for Medicaid matching to each state for coverage of Medicaid-only recipients

Medicaid Only Administration

States should develop their own administrative procedures for implementing the Medicaid-only program within broad federal guidelines.

- require states to submit to the federal government a state plan for the Medicaid-only program which would specify all eligibility criteria
- require states to make available to the public and the Federal government a manual which clearly specifies all administrative procedures for eligibility determination
- establish certain minimal federal requirements regarding fair hearings, nondiscrimination, time frames for eligibility determination, public information, recipient rights, and the like

Federal Role

The federal role should largely be to monitor state operations.

- develop criteria for State plan approval
- monitor state operations to insure that plans are being fully implemented and equitably administered

SUMMARY OF FINDINGS

- Medicaid eligibility policy does not encourage recipients to work, does not promote family stability, and encourages unnecessary institutionalization.
- Medicaid eligibility policy is unfair and inequitable.
    - Many poor people who need medical assistance cannot become eligible for Medicaid.
    - Medicaid rules often cause two applicants with identical income and assets to be treated differently; one will be eligible for all Medicaid benefits and the other will be totally ineligible.
    - There are extreme interstate differences in coverage groups and financial eligibility levels.
- Medicaid eligibility policy is so complex and administratively unworkable that many States modify, or simply ignore, numerous Federal policies.
- Responsibility for determining Medicaid eligibility for the aged, blind, and disabled is split between the Social Security Administration and the states. This fragmentation leads to:
    - inconsistent and inappropriate policies,
    - frequent long delays in certifying Medicaid eligibility,
    - wasteful duplication of effort, and
    - undue confusion to recipients.
  It is one of the major causes of the problems in Medicaid eligibility today.
- Other causes of the problems in the Medicaid eligibility system are:

    - Medicaid is required to follow basic eligibility policies established for the cash assistance programs.
    - "Workability" or administrative feasibility has been of minor concern in the establishment of eligibility policy. State and local input to federal policy development has been minimal.
    - Legislation directed at other programs and human needs is enacted without considering effects on Medicaid eligibility.
    - Policies change too often.
    - Federal financial support for state administrative improvements is inadequate and too restrictive. Sanctions are ineffective.
    - Too few federal resources are allocated for policy interpretation and dissemination, monitoring, and technical assistance to states.
- Several immediate administrative changes can alleviate some of the current operational problems, but other problems would remain.
- More substantial reform requires several decisions and judgments:
    - Should Medicaid-only eligibility continue to be closely linked to cash assistance?
    - Should eligibility criteria be more uniform across states, or should States have more flexibility in structuring their programs?
    - Is major legislative change feasible?
- Whatever reform direction is chosen, a clear understanding of the nature and causes of today's Medicaid eligibility problems is crucial as policymakers consider welfare reform and national health insurance.

19. Mandated Second Opinions for Elective Surgery in Massachusetts

MASSACHUSETTS DEPARTMENT OF PUBLIC
WELFARE

In March of 1978, the Massachusetts welfare department started to require second opinions for all Medicaid patients scheduled to undergo any of the following eight elective procedures: tonsillectomies and adenoidectomies; hysterectomies; cholecystectomies; varicose vein excisions; hemorrhoidectomies; rhinoplasties; disk surgery-spinal fusions; and meniscectomies. At that time, no other Medicaid program mandated a second opinion and neither did Medicare.

Despite strong opposition from the state medical society, the second opinion program was authorized by the state legislature in July 1976. After a year long trial in the Greater Boston area, welfare officials estimated that the statewide program would save about $1 million above the anticipated $450,000 annual cost of operating the program. During the trial year more than 12 percent of the second opinions resulted in canceled operations, mainly tonsillectomies and hysterectomies.

Even though the physicians opposed the program, they agreed to participate in the administration through the state's five PSROs (Professional Standards Review Organizations).

Following are the operational descriptions of the second surgical opinion program as supplied by the Massachusetts Department of Public Welfare. In addition, a flow chart graphically shows the sequence of events. An additional description is supplied for Western Massachusetts since there is a slight variation. PSROs will waive consultations if the doctor's supporting documentation meets preset criteria for the operation in question. In the operational descriptions and the flow chart, the word "Foundation" refers to the PSROs since that word is included in the official name of the organization.

OPERATIONAL DESCRIPTION OF THE SECOND SURGICAL OPINION PROGRAM

1. The proposing surgeon (he/she who has examined the patient and intends to perform the surgery) or his designee, or the patient contacts the Foundation either by telephone or in writing and gives the following information: Patient's name, age, sex, address, telephone number, diagnosis, and Medicaid number, and along with this data, we need to know the hospital in which the procedure is to be performed and which specific procedure the surgeon intends to perform subject to the consultation. After obtaining the proposing surgeon's name, specialty, address, and telephone number, the Foundation requests that all pertinent medical documentation and procedure or pathology results be forwarded to us so that we can furnish this material to the consulting physician. This is done to prevent having any unnecessary duplication of laboratory tests or procedures done to the patient.

2. Once all the necessary initial intake information has been gathered, the Foundation contacts a consulting physician, who is board certified or board eligible and is usually within ten miles of the patient's home or within ten miles of the place of practice of the proposing surgeon, to set up an appointment for the patient. The Foundation then forwards to the consulting physician the patient's medical record or appropriate portions thereof and a Pre-Surgical Screening Consultation Form to be completed and returned to the Foundation.

3. After a Foundation employee speaks with the patient on the telephone, the Foundation notifies him in writing as to when, where, and with whom his consultation has been arranged. One of the reasons for this is that a large percentage of these patients either do not have telephones, or they are unlisted, or unpublished. If for any reason the patient cannot keep his/her appointment, he is instructed to call us immediately.

4. At the time of the appointment, the initial consulting physician will conduct a physical examination of the patient, and order any additional diagnostic tests that may be required to make the decision as to the medical necessity of the proposed elective surgery. He will notify the Foundation of such tests in his report to the Foundation, along with the consultant's opinion and recommendations which are made on the Consultation Form. These must be returned to the Foundation within three working days of the patient's examination. If we have not received the Consultation Form within one week after the patient's appointment, we contact the consulting

physician and request that he/she forward this information immediately.

5. If the initial consulting physician concurs that the surgery is medically necessary, the proposed surgery is reimbursable. At this point, a letter is sent to the proposing surgeon, the patient, and the admitting office of the hospital in which the surgery is to be performed, stating that the patient has been approved and to go ahead and schedule that surgery. If the initial consult *does not* concur with the medical necessity of the proposed surgery, a letter is sent to the proposing surgeon and the patient stating this and explaining the two options the patient has. 1.) *Not* to have the surgery, or 2.) Contact the Foundation and request a *second* consultation. The proposed surgery is *not* reimbursable at this stage.

6. If the patient accepts this decision, he/she will not have surgery. If the patient chooses to refuse this decision, he/she will call the Foundation, and they will go through the whole process again of setting up an appointment with a second consulting physician, furnishing him/her with the same medical documentation, and notifying the patient in writing of his/her appointment. The second consultant will not be told that the patient's condition has been assessed by an initial consulting physician unless the patient chooses to do so. The second consulting physician will render an opinion to the Foundation in the same manner as the first.

7. If the second consulting physician concurs with the proposing surgeon, a letter will be sent to the patient, proposing surgeon, and admitting office. This letter states that the patient has undergone a *second* consultation, and the consulting physician concurs with the medical necessity of the proposed elective surgery, therefore, they may now schedule the patient for the surgery.

8. If the second consultant *does not* concur with the proposing surgeon, a letter will be sent to the patient and proposing surgeon stating that it is the judgment of two

Second Surgical Consultation Program Flow Chart

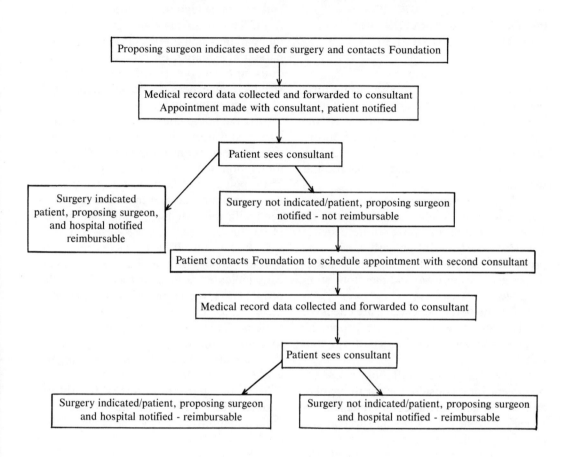

qualified specialists in the field, that the proposed elective surgery is not medically necessary. The patient may still choose to undergo the surgical procedure and providers of services rendered in this case will be reimbursed, but the proposing surgeon will be contacted and informed that two of his/her peers disagreed with his/her recommendation for surgery.

9. There is a separate category of patients which is called "Special Consideration Cases." This is for patients who are not classified as "emergency" admissions, but their medical management cannot wait

the four weeks it may take to complete the program. An example of this type of case would be a patient who has a definite diagnosis of carcinoma-in-situ documented by a cone biopsy. An approval is given for these cases by the Foundation without the patient seeing a consulting physician with the understanding that the proposing surgeon forward to the Foundation copies of any procedures or previous pathology results, his/her operative report, pathology report, and discharge summary so that this documentation can be reviewed retrospectively for medical necessity.

OPERATIONAL DESCRIPTION OF SECOND SURGICAL OPINION PROGRAM AS OPERATING IN WESTERN MASSACHUSETTS

1. When a surgeon proposes to perform one of the eight second opinion procedures he/she completes the top portion of the "indications for surgery check-off form" and if applicable checks the indication which describes the patient's condition at that time.

2. The proposing surgeon then submits this form to the foundation where it is reviewed. If one or more indication is checked the foundation will notify the proposing surgeon, patient and hospital that the surgery is approved and therefore reimbursable.

3. If none of the indications are checked, the foundation will notify the proposing surgeon and patient of the need for a consultation.

4. The foundation will obtain an appointment for a consultation for the patient and will collect all necessary medical information from the proposing surgeon and forward it to the consultant.

5. At the time of the appointment, the initial consulting physician will conduct a physical examination of the patient, and order any additional tests as may be necessary in order to determine the medical necessity of the proposed surgery. He/she will notify the foundation of his/her opinion and recommendations on the consultation form. This form must be returned to the foundation within three working days of the patient's examination. If the foundation does not receive this form within the specified time period, the foundation will contact the consultant.

6. If the initial consulting physician concurs that surgery is medically necessary, the proposed surgery is reimbursable. The foundation will notify the proposing surgeon, patient and hospital that the patient has been approved and that they may proceed with the scheduling and performance of the surgery.

7. If the consulting physician does not concur that the proposed surgery is medically indicated, a letter is forwarded to the proposing surgeon and patient informing them that at this time the patient has two options: (1) not to have the surgery, or (2) to contact the foundation and request a second consultation. The proposed surgery is *not* reimbursable at this stage.

8. If the patient chooses to obtain another consultation, he/she will contact the foundation and they will arrange for this final consultation.

9. Regardless of the outcome of this final consultation the choice to have surgery is the patient's. If the patient chooses to undergo surgery even when there may have been two negative opinions, providers of services will be reimbursed for the surgery.

20. The Medicaid Game: A Personal Experience in Playing and Winning

JERRY GARBER

Reprinted with permission from *Hospital & Community Psychiatry*, Vol. 28, No. 3, March 1977.

The Medicaid game, monitored nationally by the Department of Health, Education, and Welfare, is played individually and differently by each state that elects to participate. The governor of a participating state must designate a single state agency (SSA) to run the game. The SSA may be a social services agency, a health agency, or an agency set up specifically to run the game.

The playing field is called the maze; it is a confusing network of interlocking passages. There are obstructions called "No" walls that spring up of their own volition in otherwise unobstructed passages. "No" is the most common word used in the game. It is printed on the walls that unsuspecting players walk into; it is used by members of the SSA instead of "good morning"; and it is used by referees instead of a whistle.

The game is subject to various interpretations and may change at any turn within the maze. This condition is known as the black-box phenomenon—one learns the rules by playing the game.

PARTICIPANTS IN THE GAME

Players. Players are selected from various organizations that wish to be paid for services by Medicaid. Any number of players can enter the game at any time. Players can all be on the same team, can switch allegiance during the game, or can play alone. Players must have stamina.

Adversaries. Adversaries usually represent power blocks such as the state's medical association, psychiatric association, dental association, nursing home association, or any other politically strong force. Adversaries can enter and leave the game at will.

Kibitzers. Kibitzers may be from any organization inside or outside the state. A kibitzer's status is measured by how much useless advice he is able to give to how many players.

Referees. Referees are supplied by the HEW regional social and rehabilitative services office (SRS). Referees' interpretations of the rules are subject to political persuasion, personal feelings, and guidance from the regional director of SRS. Rules vary from region to region and from state to state within each region, depending on the referee. HEW has made things more interesting for the players by separating the referees of SRS from the regional financing and health economics office, whose members are allowed to assist the players, talk to the cheering section, and trip the ref-

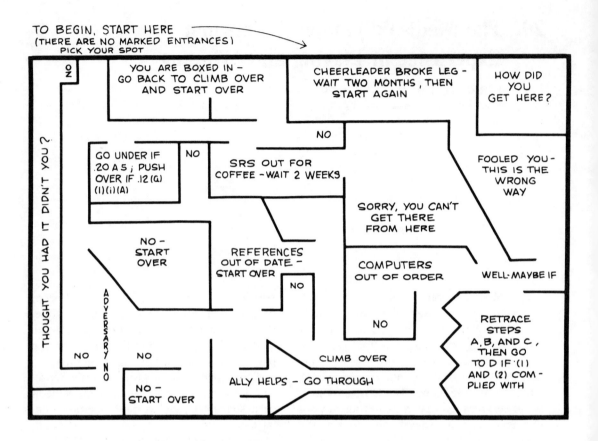

TO BEGIN, START HERE
(THERE ARE NO MARKED ENTRANCES)
PICK YOUR SPOT

erees. Referees are also separate from the regional health services office (HSO).

Cheerleaders. Individuals in the HSO are allowed to cheer from the sidelines. They are not allowed to talk to the referees.

Allies. Allies give support, encouragement, and assistance to players—usually surreptitiously.

Providers. This is an endearing term applied to any player who has successfully completed the game.

A GAME IN GEORGIA

Until 1972 Georgia's Medicaid program was housed in the Department of Public Health, which was governed by one of the adversaries—the state board of health. The board was heavily dominated by the medical profession. A state agency's partici-

pation in the Medicaid game was frowned on; the philosophy was that only private providers should partake of the federal largesse.

In 1972 the Department of Human Resources (DHR) was formed by combining all the state agencies that dealt with human problems. Medicaid was moved within the DHR to the benefits payments division (welfare) and subsequently to a separate Medicaid management improvement project (MMIP).

The national trend of inflation and recession deepened, and Georgia was not immune to its effects. In August 1974 the governing board of DHR passed a resolution encouraging all agencies within DHR to seek out and make the most of all available sources of federal funding and other third-party resources. There was no new state money to pump into DHR programs.

The division of mental health approached the SSA for assistance in establishing a reimbursement mechanism for clinic services, which states may opt to provide under Medicaid. The SSA did not deny the division's right to play the game, but it erected a formidable "No" wall. The SSA told the division that whatever it did, it would have to do alone. The SSA already had enough problems with nursing homes, doctors, and dentists; it had no time to help new players.

The division of mental health felt strongly enough about the need to find new money for 34 community mental health centers that it signed me on as a new player to bring the clinic-service option into reality. I had no background in Medicaid and knew none of the rules of the game. I did not even know which of the "No" walls had already been penetrated.

I began by making a thorough study of three contiguous states that had been using the clinic-service option for a number of years. All three had successfully navigated the maze and were now providers. To win their games, all three had produced a statewide average cost per covered visit. The figure was based on all of the allowable outpatient mental health costs of the state divided by the number of covered visits. The referees had accepted this interpretation of the rules and had granted provider status to the three players.

Therefore, we gathered cost information from as many sources as we could think of and, with great difficulty, got figures on patient contact from our community mental health centers. We combined all those data into a package similar to those used by the three neighboring states. We presented the package to the SSA, assuming the SRS referees' approval would be rubber stamp.

We also requested permission to proceed with the next phases of the game, which would include modifying the state Medicaid plan, working out administrative details, and designing forms. No such luck. When the liaison from the SSA presented the package to the referee at SRS, it was re-

jected out of hand. The SSA told us to forget the clinic-service option since we had run into a "No" wall (SRS) that we could not get around.

I was unhappy with this decision and decided to get an official ruling from the referee on a personal basis. I felt sure that although we had run into a "No" wall, there was a way around it. If we could not play the same way as our neighboring states, exactly how and under what conditions could we play?

The referee was very helpful. (Although he was not the referee for our neighboring states, he felt sure that they would have to change their methods.) He said that if we wanted to get into the game, we would have to cost out every service offered in every program in each of the 34 mental health catchment areas. We were overwhelmed. None of our community mental health centers had cost-accounting procedures established, and we had no way to cost out services. Still unhappy, and now frustrated, I went to the regional health service office for coaching. Although the office was unable to intervene on our behalf, it did set up another meeting for me with SRS and promised to come to the game to cheer me on. I made it around another corner of the maze.

At the meeting SRS agreed—as an interim measure—to let us calculate an average cost per covered visit for each of the 34 catchment areas. Costs for an entire fiscal year were to be determined by using the federal guidelines on allowable costs. The referee glibly quoted passages from several sets of federal regulations as if I knew exactly what they were and where to find them. These were mere hurdles. I was on my way.

The second passage. The DHR had contracted with a leading consulting firm to help mental institutions refigure costs for inpatient care in existing programs. An amendment to include community mental health centers in the contract soon had us back in the game. We devised a rate-calculation schedule acceptable to the SRS referee, to the SSA, and to our community mental health centers.

We hit the road, and in three months had been to each of the centers and had determined a rate for each based on the previous fiscal year's audited financial reports and the number of contacts for the same period of time. With the completed cost studies in hand, I approached the SSA again, only to find a new "No" wall blocking the entrance. In Georgia the state-to-federal ratio for the Medicaid dollar is 33.90 to 66.10 percent. The SSA was in serious financial trouble, and although the DHR backed the division's game plan, the 33.90 percent state money to support the clinic option was not in the SSA budget.

The third passage. Based on the cost schedules for each center, I calculated the reimbursements we would receive in the coming fiscal year if we gained provider status. The division was impressed by these projections. It therefore persuaded the DHR budget office to ask the legislature to reallocate state money from line-item appropriations for mental health grants-in-aid to the SSA budget. The legislature approved.

I drew a deep breath and rounded another corner of the maze, only to find another "No" wall. Even if there was now enough money to support the clinic-service option of the centers, there was no money in the SSA budget to pay the state's share should any private clinic enter the game.

The fourth passage. I went back to the referees at SRS. Again they were helpful and supportive. They said if the state plan for Title 19 was amended to pick up the clinic-service option, we could elect to bring the option in "with limitations": we would have to write standards for participation stipulating that a broad range of services be provided to a target population. (The requirement for a broad range of services would eliminate specialized clinics from participating.) In addition, we would have to guarantee individualized written treatment plans with stated goals and re-

views for all clients and reimbursement rates that would be based on calculated costs and not on "reasonable and customary charges" as are rates for some of the private providers.

When the standards were written, the amendment to the state plan was approved by the regional director of SRS. The "No" wall disappeared, and I entered a new hallway.

The fifth passage. For some time I had been trying to get my cohorts in mental health to agree on which services provided by community programs were reimbursable. I got lists ranging from nine to 197 services. After several unsuccessful attempts at compromise, I discussed my difficulties with an ally in the SSA and asked if there was any way I could make an end run on my cohorts. We came up with a very simple plan. The SSA computer would be set up to accept exactly 16 specific psychiatric procedures for private providers. I told my cohorts that the problem had been solved by the SSA—if we could live with the 16 existing procedures. We could.

Now there was light ahead, but stumbling blocks were strewn about. Provider numbers had to be assigned by the SSA. Forms agreed on by the centers and the SSA had to be preprinted and distributed to the centers, along with instructions for completing the forms. And standards had to be introduced to the centers. We thought it would be smooth sailing after these administrative details were worked out, but we were wrong. We had problems with the computer.

The sixth passage. The SSA computer programs were written in 1966 and had not been updated. As new Medicaid programs were added to the state plan, they were simply "back-ended" or "front-ended" to the computer. The language the computer understood was obsolete; programmers who remembered the language were hard to find. In addition, the computer itself was run down. I was informed that a feasibility study would have to be undertaken to see if a new program could be written for the computer. The study would cost $10,000.

An additional problem lay in the department of administrative services (DOAS), which runs the state's computer services. The department was so far behind in priority work that it could not begin any new programming for six to eight months. Fortunately, over the seven months that I had been playing the game, I did gain a few allies in the SSA hallways. One such ally, who had helped me jump administrative hurdles in earlier passages, came to my rescue.

Earlier in the game I had instructed the centers to send all of the claims through me so that I would know how much of "our" money (33.90 percent) the SSA was spending. I had one month's worth of claims sitting in my desk drawer—waiting until someone found the $10,000 to conduct the feasibility study. My ally photocopied 50 of the claims and quietly placed them in line for processing and payment. The dummy batch sailed through the entire computer process, with all of its edits, and was withdrawn by my ally just before the checks would have been written. Therein ended the need for the $10,000 study.

I had discussed time frames with my ally at various stages of the game. The SSA and DOAS were about six months behind in processing claims. The processing involved, in part, coding, editing, and keypunching to tape. I said that my community mental health centers could do their own coding; my ally suggested that I contract with an outside agency to do the keypunching. In that way we could put our tape in line for editing and payment and circumvent the software processing.

I then discovered another rule of the game: all state-level agencies must use DOAS computer services. I learned quickly, however, that local programs were under no such obligation. In about two days I persuaded the local programs to make verbal agreements with a local comprehensive health center's federally funded computer center to do the taping process. We now have a turnaround time of ten days.

The seventh passage. By this time the centers had submitted service claims for two months and were screaming for their money. (I had warned them that it might be six months before they saw a dime.) In an attempt to expedite payment, I handcarried the claims first to the computer and then to the SSA, where I hovered about like an expectant father. At last the first checks were printed and were in my hands.

It had taken me ten months to navigate the maze. Although I knew that a great deal more effort would be required to implement an effective cost-accounting system and improved monitoring methods, I experienced an indescribable high. I had won my first game.

21. Rates and Correlates of Expenditure Increases for Personal Health Services: Pre- and Post-Medicare and Medicaid

RONALD ANDERSEN, RICHARD FOSTER, and
PETER WEIL

Reprinted with permission of the Blue Cross Association, from *Inquiry*. Vol. XIII, No. 2 (June 1976). pp. 136–144. Copyright © 1976 by the Blue Cross Association. All rights reserved.

A question of continuing interest from a policy perspective is the extent to which health expenditure increases represent increased delivery of services or rising prices. A number of studies have allocated observed expenditure increases to these and other factors using data from institutional sources.[1]

This study examines the contributions of price and use to health expenditure increases over the 1953–1970 time period using data from a series of household interview surveys. In addition to confirming some of the general findings of studies based on other data sources, data from household interviews permit separate analyses to be done for different population groups. This study examines the contributions of price and use to expenditure increases by different age, sex, income, race, and residence groups and by source of payment. In addition, some categories of expenditure have been included that have not previously been studied in this way.

We shall first describe the data and examine rates of increase in per capita expenditures for different types of health serv-

The study is funded through Contract #HSM-110-70-392, with the Bureau of Health Services Research, Health Resources Administration, DHEW.

ice. A discussion of the issues involved in allocating these increases to price and use factors will then be followed by a price-use breakdown of increases by health service category. Within each service category increases in free and nonfree care will be examined. Finally, price-use breakdowns are presented for different demographic groups.

Throughout the paper, increases will be analyzed separately for the 1953–1963 period and the 1963–1970 period. The first period from 1953–1963 can be characterized as one in which a primary shift in financing patterns was from consumer out-of-pocket payments for medical care to payments by voluntary health insurance. The coverage was mainly for hospital and inpatient physician services. The groups that benefited most from the growth in voluntary health insurance were the working population and their dependents.[2] The second period from 1963–1970 witnessed the passage of the Medicare and Medicaid legislation. Both programs went into effect in mid-1966, although, of course, the time of implementation and range of benefits for Medicaid varied from state to state. In this latter period, the proportion of the personal health care dollar accounted for by voluntary insurance remained relatively constant. The main trend here was a decrease in the percentage covered directly by the consumer and an increase in the percentage paid for by government. Also, given the target populations of Medicare and Medicaid, it seems fair to say that in a relative sense the change in financing mechanisms was greatest for the elderly and the medically indigent during this period.[3]

Specifically, we will address four questions concerning these two time periods:

1. What was the relative increase in total expenditures and expenditures for various types of health services?
2. What was the relative contribution of price and use to expenditure increases in each time period?
3. What part did different types of service and payers play in the overall expenditure increases noted in each period?
4. What was the increase in price and use for various population groups defined by age, sex, income, race and residence?

DATA AND FINDINGS

The estimates in this paper are based on data provided by parallel social surveys of representative samples of the nation's families conducted in 1953, 1958, 1964, and 1971 by the Center for Health Administration Studies (CHAS) and the National Opinion Research Center (NORC) of the University of Chicago. In the most recent survey, 3,765 families and 11,619 individuals were interviewed in their homes in early 1971. The weighted completion rate was 82 percent. The interviews averaged about one and one-half hours. One or more members of each family provided information regarding use of health services, the cost of these services, and how the cost was met for the calendar year 1970. In each study, information was collected on the population's use of health services, how much these health services cost, and how they were paid for.

The comparable nature of these studies allows documentation and analysis of trends in utilization, expenditure, and methods of payment.

In addition to data provided by sample families, information was collected in the latest study from doctors, clinics, hospitals, insuring organizations and employers about the families' medical care and health insurance for the survey year. This additional information serves to verify the family information, as well as to provide additional details on services, expenditures, and conditions treated and not known by the family. The following analysis is based on the verified expenditures for hospital services, but is limited to family reports of expenditures for the other services. This procedure maximizes the comparability of the data of the current study with the earlier studies since only the expenditures for hospital services were previously verified.

The total expenditures reported include what we refer to as both a "non-free" and a "free" component. The non-free component includes expenditures for which the consumer is himself responsible, either directly or through some third party to which he pays premiums or has premiums paid on his behalf. It includes payments by voluntary insurance and those made out-of-pocket, as well as Medicare. Medicare is considered non-free because it is defined as a social insurance rather than a group subsidy program; there are no income restrictions on eligibility for its use; and because in large part it replaces voluntary health insurances carried by people 65 and over in the earlier studies.

The free component includes services provided to the family at no direct cost or at substantially reduced rates and without benefits being provided by any type of health insurance plan. Components are expenditures for medical care by public aid departments on behalf of their recipients, as well as expenditures for those people not on welfare but with incomes sufficiently low to qualify them for payment for some or all of their medical bills. Also included here is the estimated monetary value of care provided by locally tax-supported hospitals and institutions, including city and county hospitals, state mental and tuberculosis hospitals, and Board of Health clinics.

Expenditures for the free services were not estimated in the studies done prior to 1971. However, due to their increasing importance they were included in the most recent study. For this analysis, the free component of total per capita expenditures for the earlier studies was estimated using aggregate data published by the Social Security Administration (SSA).[4] Since SSA estimates are based on the total population, while the CHAS studies include only the noninstitutionalized population, these aggregate estimates were adjusted to exclude expenditures for the institutionalized population.[5]

Findings

Table 1 shows that the rate of increase in medical care expenditures was twice as high in the period from 1963–1970 as it was in the earlier period (9.9 percent versus 4.9 percent per year). The component for which expenditures increased most rapidly in both periods, with higher acceleration in the second period, was the hospital component. Expenditures for drugs and medicines behaved most erratically, showing the highest rate of increase in the first period and the lowest rate in the second period.

ALLOCATION TO PRICE AND USE

Any effort to discuss price and use increases in the health field is inevitably complicated by quality considerations. In this section, we attempt to clarify what we mean by price and use and discuss the ways that quality affects these, both conceptually and through the price indices we shall employ later.

Conceptually, a *price increase* means that more money is spent to purchase the same service. All other expenditure increases are properly considered *use increases*.[6] If a "completely new" product or service is purchased, the entire expenditure represents a use increase. If a "higher quality" product is purchased at greater expense than the lower quality product purchased previously, the difference between the cost of the new product and the cost of

Table 1 Mean expenditures per person for the noninstitutionalized population of the United States by type of service, 1953, 1963 and 1970

Service	Expenditure 1953[f]	Expenditure 1963	Expenditure 1970	Average annual percent increase[g] 1953–1963	Average annual percent increase[g] 1963–1970
Hospital[a]	$16	$ 34	$ 96	7.2%	14.8%
Physician[b]	26	36	62	3.1	7.8
Dental[c]	10	15	28	3.9	8.9
Drugs[d]	10	24	32	8.3	4.1
Other[e]	8	10	20	2.1	9.9
Total	71	119	238	4.9	9.9

[a]Includes inpatient and outpatient services provided by hospitals, nursing homes and extended care facilities.
[b]Includes inpatient and outpatient services provided by physicians and osteopaths other than those provided by salaried staff physicians of hospitals which are included in the hospital component.
[c]Includes charges by a dentist for his services and those of his auxiliary personnel and for dental appliances.
[d]Includes prescribed drugs and nonprescribed medicines.
[e]Includes charges by non-M.D. practitioners, such as optometrists, and charges for laboratory tests and medical appliances, such as glasses.
[f]Corresponds roughly to *fiscal* year 1953, while 1963 and 1970 are calendar years.
[g]Computed by the natural logarithm technique outlined in: Barclay, G. *Techniques of Population Analysis* (New York: Wiley, 1953) pp. 28–33.

the old one represents purchase of additional services. It is for this reason that Klarman, *et al.*, refer to our use category as "all other."[7] While a further division of our use increase category into "increased use of the same services" categories would be desirable, it would require a more detailed specification of the services purchased than the specification for which we have data.

While the concept of price employed here is the conventional one in economics, and is the one that guides the Department of Labor in the construction of its Consumer Price Index (CPI), another concept lies at the base of some of the price indices familiar in the health field. Hospital expense per patient day, for example, is better suited to answering the question, "how rapidly is the amount that a patient should expect to pay for a day in the hospital increasing?" than is the hospital component of the CPI. However, hospital expense per patient day includes tests and other ancillary services that have been increasing in cost over time. Consequently, we feel the CPI, which is based only on room and board charges, is conceptually better suited to measure price as used in this paper.

In practice, an index that captures only "pure price" increases is often difficult to construct. The hospital component of the CPI, for example, is unable to make any adjustment for the increases in intensity of services that presumably have accompanied higher nurse staffing levels and employment of growing numbers of RNs relative to LPNs, although these are included in room and board charges. The effects of such changes in the nature of the product will therefore be attributed to price increases. It is for such reasons that we are unwilling to assert generally that the effects of technology and changing quality are included in the use term, although that is clearly the intent of the method. The success with which pure price increases are measured varies by type of expenditure; these differences will be discussed as results are presented.

COMPONENTS OF EXPENDITURE INCREASES

Following the conceptual discussion of the previous section, we compute average annual percentage increases in price, attributing the remainder of expenditure increases to use. Price increases are computed using various components of the CPI,[8] although alternative price measures are discussed as appropriate.

Table 2 indicates that price increases account for more of the increase in per capita expenditures than do use increases, both over the 1953–1963 period and over the 1963–1970 period. Although prices increased much more rapidly during the 1963–1970 period than previously, use also increased more rapidly, with the relative contributions of price and use not greatly changed. If adjustments are made for changes in the general purchasing power of the dollar—by subtracting the rate of increase of the CPI for all items (1.4 percent for the 1953–1963 period and 3.4 percent

Table 2 Average annual percent increase per person in price and use by type of health service, 1953–1963 and 1963–1970

| | Annual percent increase | | | |
| | 1953–1963 | | 1963–1970 | |
Service	Price[a]	Use[b]	Price[a]	Use[b]
Hospital	6.1%	1.0%	10.5%	3.9%
Physician	3.0	0.1	5.4	2.3
Dental	2.3	1.6	4.5	4.2
Drugs	0.8	7.4	0.4	3.7
Other[c]	1.4	0.7	3.4	6.3
Total[d]	3.3	1.5	6.1	3.6

[a]Price increases are estimated on the basis of the medical care component of the Department of Labor's Consumer Price Index.
[b]The residual increase in expenditure not accounted for by price increase was defined as increase due to use.
[c]Uses the CPI component for optometrists' fees and glasses.
[d]Computed using as weights the expenditure by service in the initial time period.

for the 1963–1970 period) from the rates of price increase in Table 2—the rate of increase in medical prices in real terms is seen to have increased from 1.9 percent per year in the 1953–1963 period to 2.7 percent per year in the 1963–1970 period.

During both periods, the component showing by far the highest rate of price increase is hospital care. Since the hospital price index is based on daily service charges and the quality of room, board, and nursing services is presumed to have increased over time, there is some concern that the figures in Table 2 may overstate hospital price increases (and, correspondingly, to understate use increases by excluding "use of higher quality services" from use increases).

One means of assessing this possibility is to compare the results in Table 2 with results obtained using different price indices. Hospital expense per inpatient day and per adjusted patient day both have the characteristic that expenditure increases resulting from greater use of ancillary services per day in the hospital will be allocated to the price effect. Since increased use of ancillary services is known to have occurred, we would expect the per diem expense indices to show greater price increases than an index based on changes in the price of a uniform product. In fact, expense per inpatient day and expense per adjusted patient day give results virtually identical to those in Table 2.[9] We conclude that much of the effect of increasing quality of hospital care has been attributed to price in Table 2.[10]

Still another method of determining price and use increases is to determine use increases from direct measures of use and attribute the remainder of per capita expenditure increases to price. As long as the price index measures the price of the same "unit of service" measured by the use index, this should give the same results as the method used in constructing Table 2. Price and use increases were computed using short-term hospital days per capita as the use measure. The results are virtually identical to those in

Table 2 for the 1953–1963 period (a 6.2 percent rate of price increase and a 0.9 percent rate of use increase), but gave a much smaller rate of use increase (1.5 percent) over the 1963–1970 period. This discrepancy is probably in part attributable to the inclusion of care in long-term hospitals, nursing homes, and extended care facilities in the expenditure data but not in the patient days data. We thus conclude that much of the hospital use increase reported in Table 2 actually represents increased use of these institutions.[11]

Physician Services

Price increases also exceeded use increases for physician services. Although some increases in quality of physician services may be attributed to price in Table 2, the physician fee component of the CPI probably comes much closer to pricing a uniform product than does the hospital component.[12] There is no physician index comparable to hospital expense per patient day, however. The only direct measure of physician use available from survey data is the number of office visits, and even this is only available since 1963. Physician office visits per capita actually declined at the rate of 1.4 percent per year over the 1963–1970 period, in contrast to the 2.3 percent rate of use increase indicated in Table 2. If a crude direct measure of physician use is constructed by adding to the number of office visits the number of hospital patient days (our expenditure data include payments to physicians for services provided to inpatients, as long as the physician is paid separately from the hospital), the result is still a slight reduction (−0.8 percent per year) in physician use over the 1963–1970 period.

We conclude that virtually all of the 2.3 percent per year use increase reported in Table 2 represents changes in the nature of services rendered per physician contact. Such changes would include more surgery, greater tendency to be seen by a specialist, and provision of more separately billed services per physician contact.[13] While Table 2 indicates virtually no change in physician use over the 1953–1963 period, this may understate the rate of increase in use by as much as 1 percent per year due to the increased rate at which the customary fees priced by the CPI were actually collected over this time period.[14] However, the rate of increase in physician use over this period would still be less than the rate of increase from 1963–1970.

Dental Care

Dental care also showed a greater rate of use increase from 1963–1970 than during the earlier period. Although survey data on dental visits is available only for 1970, data from other sources[15] indicate that dental visits per capita declined at the rate of 1 percent per year from 1963–1970. All of the increase in dental use, then, represents changes in the nature of a dental contact. Such changes can include greater number of restorations per visit, greater incidence of orthodontal work, and greater incidence of cleaning by hygienists.

Drugs

Drugs were the only component of health expenditures to show a slower rate of use increase over the 1963–1970 period than earlier. Drugs also showed by far the lowest rate of price increase of any of the expenditure components. Both the expenditure data and the CPI component used in Table 2 include both prescription and nonprescription drugs. The CPI drug component has been the object of substantial criticism because of the limited number of prescription items priced, and also because the items that are priced do not include "new" drugs even though new drugs account for a substantial share of the market. Firestone, however, constructed a much more broadly based index with the items priced changed frequently and found that, except over short time periods, it gave virtually the

same results as the prescription component of the CPI.[16] Firestone also showed that indices such as average price per prescription have overestimated price increases due to increases over time in the average dosage per prescription. We conclude that virtually all of the increase in drug expenditures is attributable to use when use is defined more broadly than the number of prescriptions.

RELATIVE IMPACT OF TYPE OF SERVICE AND PAYER

Table 3 indicates the contribution of each service to the total expenditure increase per person and also to the expenditure increase attributable to increased use.

Increases in hospital expenditure accounted for 37 percent of the total per capita expenditure increase in 1953–1963, and over one-half of the total increase in the later period. In contrast, they accounted for a much smaller proportion of the increase in expenditures attributable to use in each period. Still, hospitals accounted for one-third of the total use increase between 1963 and 1970. Physician services accounted for almost one-fifth of the expenditure increase in each period, but were a factor in the use increase only in the second period. Table 3 suggests that dental services contributed between 10 and 15 percent to both total expenditure and use increase in both periods. Drugs appeared to be a much bigger factor in both expenditures and use increase in the earlier period than in the latter one.

Table 3 also allows us to assess the relative impact of the free and non-free sources. An assumption is made that price increases are the same in the free and non-free sector. Table 3 shows that increasing expenditures by the free sources accounted for only 5 percent of the expenditure increase in the early period, and apparently did not contribute at all to use increase. In the latter period, however, the free sources accounted for 16 percent of the increase in

Table 3 Percent of the increase in expenditure per individual accounted for by type of service and source of payment in current and constant dollars, 1953–1963 and 1963–1970

Service	Source of payment[a]	Percent increase			
		1953–1963		1963–1970	
		Total ex-penditures[b]	Use[c]	Total ex-penditures[b]	Use[c]
Hospital		37%	13%	52%	32%
	(Non-free)	(33)	(14)	(43)	(26)
	(Free)	(4)	(−1)	(9)	(6)
Physician		19	−1	22	18
	(Non-free)	(20)	(3)	(18)	(10)
	(Free)	(−1)	(−5)	(4)	(8)
Dental		11	13	11	15
	(Non-free)	(11)	(12)	(10)	(11)
	(Free)	(*)	(1)	(1)	(3)
Drugs		27	72	7	21
	(Non-free)	(26)	(69)	(6)	(17)
	(Free)	(1)	(2)	(1)	(4)
Other		5	4	8	15
	(Non-free)	(5)	(4)	(7)	(13)
	(Free)	(*)	(*)	(1)	(2)
All services		100	100	100	100
	(Non-free)	(95)	(102)	(84)	(76)
	(Free)	(5)	(−2)	(16)	(24)

*Less than ½ of 1 percent. Numbers may not total due to rounding.
[a]*Non-free* are generally considered to be expenditures for care that the consumer pays for himself, either directly or through some third party, or has premiums paid on his behalf. Medicare is included here. *Free* are expenditures provided to the family at no direct cost or at substantially reduced rates without benefits being provided by any type of health insurance plan. Medicaid and welfare payments are included here.
[b]Proportional expenditure increase with no consideration of price changes.
[c]Expenditures in the latter period are deflated (by appropriate components of the Consumer Price Index) to price levels in the earlier period before percentage increases are computed.

expenditures and almost one-quarter of the total use increase. Contributions to the increase in expenditures and use by the free component was primarily for hospital and physician services. In general, Table 3 permits the conclusion that the free component in expenditure increases trebled in the period 1963–1970, and that actual use of health care services that were paid for on behalf of the needy accounted for one-fourth of the overall use increase.

PRICE AND USE INCREASES BY POPULATION CHARACTERISTICS

Table 4 provides an opportunity to examine the impact of price and use increases for various subgroups of the population. Since separate price indices are not available by population group, this requires the assumption that the rate of price increase for each service is the same for all population groups. Differences in rates of

Table 4 Average annual percent increase per person in price and use for all personal health services by selected characteristics of the population, 1953–1963 and 1963–1970

| | Annual percent increase | | | | |
| | 1953–1963 | | 1963–1970 | | Mean 1970 |
Characteristic	Price[a]	Use	Price[a]	Use	expenditure[c]
Age					
0– 5	3.3%	1.5%	5.5%	5.2%	$106
6–17	3.1	0.5	5.3	1.0	96
18–34	3.4	1.4	6.6	2.1	246
35–54	3.3	2.7	6.2	−0.4	244
55–64	3.2	1.7	6.0	5.0	379
65+	3.3	2.1	5.9	5.1	429
Sex					
Male	3.2	2.3	5.9	4.7	213
Female	3.3	1.2	6.2	2.6	260
Income[b]					
Low	3.2	3.1	6.4	6.2	280
Middle	3.2	1.1	6.2	3.3	216
High	3.2	0.6	5.8	2.8	239
Race					
White	*	*	6.0	3.3	245
Non-white	*	*	6.6	3.5	166
Residence					
Urban	3.3	1.2	6.0	3.9	259
Rural nonfarm	3.3	0.9	6.2	3.0	202
Rural farm	3.3	1.0	6.1	4.7	184
Total	3.3	1.5	6.1	3.6	238

*Information not available for 1953.
[a]Price increases are adjusted according to the mix of services purchased by each group.
[b]Low, middle and high designation of family income included the following income ranges in each time period:

Year	Low	Middle	High
1953	$0–2,999	$3,000– 4,999	$ 5,000 and over
1963	0–3,999	4,000– 6,999	7,000 and over
1970	0–5,999	6,000–10,999	11,000 and over

[c]Source: Andersen, Ronald, *et al. Two Decades of Health Services: Social Survey Trends in Use and Expenditure* (Cambridge, Mass.: Ballinger Publishing Co., forthcoming).

price increase in Table 4 therefore reflect differences in the distribution of medical expenditures among services with varying rates of price increases. While it is often argued that prices paid by different population groups vary (especially between white and non-white and between urban and rural), reasons for expecting different *rates of increase* are unclear.[17] Table 4 suggests that price increases as here defined are relatively constant over the various population groups examined. In both periods, the ratio

of price increase tends to be somewhat higher for groups that tend to be high users of hospital services (the service with the highest price increases)—for example, women at childbearing ages, 18–34. Also, price increases for non-whites in the latter period are slightly over the norm.

Use increases showed considerably more variance particularly in the period from 1963–1970. In the pre-Medicare/Medicaid period, those with the greatest use increases were the middle-aged population, males, and the low-income population. The smallest use increases were found among children, ages 6–17. In the latter period, with the advent of Medicare and Medicaid, the rate of increase in use of the low-income population accelerated, and the male rate of increase continued to exceed that of females. Also, as might be expected, the rate of increase was greater for those 65 and over than for the population as a whole. However, similar high rates of use increase were seen for the 0–5 and 55–64 age groups. One group, those aged 35–54, apparently had a decrease in annual rate of use.

Rates of use increase appeared similar for the white and non-white population. Even though the non-white population is disproportionately low-income, their rate of use increase was considerably lower than for the low-income population as a whole.

SUMMARY AND CONCLUSIONS

This investigation of the increases in expenditures for medical care of the noninstitutionalized population of the United States in two recent periods suggests the following:

- Price increases contributed substantially more to overall expenditure increases in both periods than did use increases.
- Hospital price increases contributed most to overall price increases in both

periods. Drug use in the first period and hospital use in the second period contributed most to overall use increases.
- The so-called "free services" made a substantial contribution to increases in use between 1963 and 1970, while apparently making no contribution in the earlier period.
- In the pre-Medicare/Medicaid period, use increases were greatest among the working-age and male population. However, increases in use also seemed to be relatively high among the low-income group.
- In the more recent period, use increases shifted not only to the elderly and the very young, but also to the group 55–64. The relatively high rate of use increase for males and the low-income group continued.

These findings, then, suggest that institution of the Medicare and Medicaid programs was accompanied by acceleration of some trends that were already taking place, i.e., relatively high rates of increase in the use of health services for the low-income population and the aged. Some groups not considered to be target populations for the programs, such as those 35–54, showed a reduction in their use rates; others, those 55–64, increased their use. Finally, the non-white population showed no greater rate of increase in use of health services than the white population, even though the former would presumably be considered a target group.

REFERENCES AND NOTES

1. See, for example: Klarman, H.E., *et al.* "Accounting for the Rise in Selected Medical Care Expenditures, 1929–1969," *American Journal of Public Health* 60:1023–1039 (June 1970), which also gives references to other studies.

2. Andersen, R. and Anderson, O. *A Decade of Health Services* (Chicago: University of Chicago Press, 1967).

3. Andersen, R., *et al. Expenditures for Personal Health Services* (DHEW Publication #HRA 74-3105, October 1973).

4. "National Health Expenditures, Calendar Years 1929–71," *Research and Statistics Note,* No. 3 (Social Security Administration, DHEW Publication #SSA 73-11701, March 6, 1973.)

5. The following procedure was used to obtain estimates for free care in fiscal 1953: Using Tables 8 and 9 of the Social Security estimates (see note 4), an estimate for 1953 fiscal year was arrived at by adding to the free estimate for 1950 one-half of the difference between the 1950 and 1955 free estimate. The CHAS value was determined for the noninstitutionalized population by the following ratio:

$$\frac{1970 \text{ free CHAS} \times \text{SSA free 1953}}{\text{SSA free 1970}} = \text{CHAS free estimate 1953.}$$

The identical procedure was employed in obtaining CHAS estimates for free care in 1963 using SSA free estimates for 1960 and 1965, with the exception that the difference was multiplied by .6 since we are interested in calendar 1963.

6. When price and use are both increasing, some of the increase in expenditure results from the interaction of the two. That is, higher prices are paid on the additional services, as well as on services purchased originally. Use of annual average percentage increases drastically reduces this interaction effect, however. A fuller discussion of this point is given in the appendix to: Klarman, H.E., *et al.* "Sources of Increase in Selected Medical Care Expenditures, 1929–1969," Social Security Administration, Office of Research and Statistics, Staff Paper No. 4 (1970).

7. See notes 1 and 6.

8. U.S. Department of Labor. *Handbook of Labor Statistics, 1973.*

9. Using expense per inpatient day as the price index gives price increases of 6.5 percent in the 1953–1963 period and 10.5 percent in the 1963–1970 period. Using expense per adjusted patient day gives a rate of price increase of 10.6 percent over the 1963–1970 period (adjusted patient days have not been published for years prior to 1963).

10. Unfortunately, we still have no measure of the amount by which "pure price" increases are overstated.

11. It seems reasonable to expect that utilization of these institutions increased more rapidly during the 1963–1970 period than during the earlier period due to extended care facility coverage under Medicare and the general aging of the population. Use of long-term hospitals and nursing homes is still not as great a factor as the reader might initially suspect, even for 1970, since our data cover only the noninstitutionalized population.

12. Although the nature of a family physician's office visit (an important element of the CPI physician fee component) may have changed somewhat over time, changes in the nature of medical practice are believed to be more related to use of procedures for which physicians price separately. It is not at all clear that the nature of the surgeon's input to such procedures as tonsillectomies and herniorrhaphies (other important components of CPI) has changed appreciably over time.

13. If physicians do not provide additional services, but merely begin to price separately for items that used to be included in the price of an office visit, the result will be an overstatement of use increases and corresponding understatement of price increases. The magnitude of such a fractionation effect is unknown, however.

14. Klarman, *et al., op. cit.*

15. See: National Center for Health Statistics. *Volume of Dental Visits, United States, July 1963–June 1964* (Washington, D.C.: Public Health Service Publication #1000, Series 10, No. 23, 1965); and National Center for Health Statistics. *Current Estimates from the Health Interview Survey, United States, 1970* (Washington, D.C.: Public Health Service Publication #1000, Series 10, No. 72, 1972).

16. Firestone, J.M. *Trends in Prescription Drug Prices* (Washington, D.C.: American Enterprise Institute for Public Policy Research, 1970).

17. The major concern with possible differences in rates of increase appears to be with respect to the urban-rural differential. Direct evidence on this point is available from the CPI only since 1967. Annual rates of increase in the CPI for all items between 1967 and 1973 ranged from 5.1 percent for cities with populations of 3.5 million or more to 4.5 percent in cities with populations of 2,500 to 50,000. Evidence that is less direct with respect to the urban-rural distinction but more direct with respect to the items considered in this study can be obtained by examining rates of increase in hospital expense per patient day in the 10 most rural versus the 10 most urban states. Annual rates of increase were 5.9 percent in the rural states versus 6.6 percent in the urban states over the 1952–1963 period, and 10.1 percent versus 10.8 percent over the 1963–1970 period. Both sets of evidence are consistent with the belief that prices in urban areas have risen only slightly more rapidly than in rural areas.

22. Containing Medicaid Costs in Connecticut

LEGISLATIVE PROGRAM REVIEW AND
INVESTIGATIONS COMMITTEE OF THE
CONNECTICUT GENERAL ASSEMBLY

The purpose of this report is to provide an indepth analysis of the state's Medicaid program, to identify problems and to recommend solutions designed to improve performance and reduce the rate of growth in program costs. Medicaid expenditures in Connecticut have been increasing at an average annual rate of more than 15 percent since FY 1971, and are expected to exceed $200 million in FY 1977.

The scope of the study included four main types of cost controls—eligibility controls, price controls, utilization controls, and expenditure controls.

Data were gathered from numerous sources, including documents and reports, more than one hundred interviews, a survey of eligibility workers, field visits and a public hearing. Approximately 28 person months were consumed by the Committee's multidisciplinary staff in collecting and analyzing the data presented in this report. Some four dozen recommendations are made on ways to improve Department of Social Services (DSS) operations and to contain Medicaid program costs. Some of these recommendations require relatively small increases in appropriations for administration in order to save large sums of misspent funds due to inadequate controls. Further, many of the recommendations will have spillover benefits of reducing other welfare program costs through improved administrative controls.

INTRODUCTION TO MEDICAID

Title XIX of the Social Security Amendments of 1965, provides for grants to states for medical assistance (Medicaid). In Connecticut, the Department of Social Services (DSS) administers the Medicaid program together with other state welfare programs.

Two groups of persons may be covered under Medicaid: the "Categorically Needy," such as AFDC recipients, and the "Medically Needy," who receive no cash assistance. States are required by federal law to provide medical assistance to persons receiving cash assistance under any of the federal categorical programs (Categorically Needy). States may elect, as Connecticut has, to provide medical assistance to an intermediate group (Medically Needy) whose income and assets exclude them from cash assistance, but who are unable to afford necessary medical care.

Federal law provides a comprehensive list of services that a state Medicaid plan may include. Of these, certain services must be provided, and others are optional.

Connecticut provides the full range of optional medical services.

While the number of Medicaid recipients has only doubled from about 90,000 in 1967 to about 180,000 in 1976, Medicaid expenditures were *six* times higher in 1976 ($188 million) than in 1967 ($32 million).

A major cause of Medicaid cost increases in Connecticut is the imbalance in levels of care provided by the nursing home industry. Connecticut spends nearly half of its Medicaid budget on expensive skilled nursing care, while other states average only 20 percent. Conversely, other states average about 16 percent of Medicaid budgets for lower cost intermediate care, while Connecticut spends only 4 percent.

ELIGIBILITY CONTROLS

DSS makes efforts to ensure that only those eligible for program aid receive it. The most recent Quality Control Report (July-December, 1975) shows that 20 percent of AFDC cases are either overpaid or ineligible. Misspent funds (cash and medical assistance) due to errors in the AFDC program alone are estimated at *$15.5 million* annually. This does not include medical payments for ineligible Medically Needy recipients.

While an increasing proportion of errors in the AFDC caseload are attributed to clients rather than the agency, LPR&IC analysis suggests that some of these may result from agency inaccessibility. Improvements, especially in telephone service, are recommended.

As part of its latest corrective action plan, DSS proposes to study expansion of a pilot project (High Risk Unit) which has been successful in reducing errors in earned income cases. *It is recommended that DSS expand the High Risk Unit statewide if justified by a cost-benefit study. It is also recommended that the Department make better use of Quality Control Reports in the district offices by scheduling more frequent meetings with district directors on Quality Control findings and corrective action plans.*

Verification of recipient resources are attempted only when income or assets are reported by the client. In addition, the system for verifying the presence of children and absence of fathers in AFDC homes is weak and does not include home visits. *It is recommended that home visits be made on a sample of cases or when fraud is suspected.*

A redetermination of eligibility is required on all AFDC cases every six months and on all Medically Needy cases annually. While timely AFDC redeterminations are being done, Medically Needy redeterminations are not being accomplished as required. Because a pilot project in the Hartford district office shows that substantial savings could be made by reexamining the eligibility of Medically Needy cases, *it is recommended that Medically Needy redeterminations be performed annually as required by federal law and that the General Assembly fund the additional staff necessary to perform this important cost-saving function.*

DSS administrative structure for managing caseloads is separated into three main units: eligibility services, income maintenance, and social services. *Because workers in eligibility services and income maintenance perform similar tasks, it is recommended that the two units be combined.*

The system for managing caseloads is a "bank" approach in which cases are serviced by workers randomly or alphabetically. This system has major weaknesses since it is difficult to assign responsibility for particular actions or errors to particular workers. Therefore, *it is recommended that the Department study the feasibility of moving to a "caseload" system in which specific cases are assigned to each worker for long-range service.*

Adopting a caseload system may require other changes. For example, it was found that some workers lack basic skills needed to perform their jobs. *It is recommended that the specifications for the entry level position of "welfare aide" be revised to require passing a job-related competency test.*

The workload and financial responsibility (excluding adult and CAMAD cases) of eligibility workers in DSS is incommensurate with qualifications and salary. On average, each worker handles cases totalling over $1 million annually in cash assistance and medical aid and which account for over $100,000 per year in errors.

It is recommended that the Department study more thoroughly the process time for case actions so that reasonable workloads can be developed for workers. In addition, because work output is monitored poorly in some work units, *it is recommended that the Department develop performance standards by which workers can be evaluated.*

It was found that management practices and application of policy varies, sometimes considerably, from one district office to the next. To improve program administration, *it is recommended that DSS interpret policy clearly at the central office and apply policy uniformly in the districts. Furthermore, staff/workload ratios should be equalized and uniform management guidelines should be implemented statewide.*

A survey of eligibility workers was conducted to determine worker attitudes toward their training, working conditions, and morale. Workers reported that training was inadequate, and that they were dissatisfied with working conditions, salary, and opportunities for career development offered by DSS. *It is recommended that an effective and meaningful training program for workers be implemented, and that training of supervisors be improved. It is also recommended that working conditions be upgraded in the district offices.* It is suggested that the state personnel system be reviewed to determine if changes are needed to make the system more responsive to state manpower needs. A suggestion is also made that the Departments of Personnel and Finance and Control, the State Personnel Policy Board, and the Legislature cooperate with DSS efforts to implement a flexible career ladder for employees.

AFDC Quality Control Reports suggest that willful misrepresentation by clients may cost the state as much as $9.2 million in AFDC cash assistance and $1.5 million in Medicaid services. Further, the number of "client errors" is increasing at an alarming rate.

Fraud referrals from DSS to the Department of Finance and Control may be reviewed as many as six times and take three months or more to process. In spite of this, 50–75% of the fraud referrals contain inadequate information, according to Finance and Control investigators. *It is recommended that the fraud referral procedure be simplified and that Connecticut statutes be amended to require DSS to refer to Finance and Control only those cases in which recipient overpayment exceeds $500. It is also recommended that resource unit supervisors in the district offices serve as fraud referral specialists and act as liaison to the Central Collections Unit in the Department of Finance and Control. In addition, it is recommended that DSS publicize its public fraud referral program.*

Most data on recipients is not checked by DSS unless specific information is supplied by clients. Because an increasing number of recipients fail to report information or report inaccurate information, *it is recommended that DSS evaluate the feasibility of cross matching eligibility files with records at the Departments of Labor and Motor Vehicles, Court Registries and school districts.*

To recover child support payments from absent parents, LPR&IC supports full compliance with the federal Title IV-D program. *It is recommended that a separate line-item be contained in the budget to facilitate oversight of this program.*

PRICE CONTROLS

In Connecticut there are five rate-setting bodies, each having jurisdiction over particular types of vendors.

Hospitals—The Commission on Hospitals and Health Care (CHHC) sets private rates for hospitals and long-term care facilities. Based on CHHC rates and other factors, the Committee on State Payments to Hospitals establishes Medicaid reimbursement rates for these services. In the case of inpatient hospital services, interim rates are set in advance, payment is made at the interim rates, and year-end adjustment is made to reflect utilization and actual costs. The retrospective adjustment for cost increases substantially undermines the potential effectiveness of the "prospective" rates.

Outpatient clinics and emergency room rates are based on data 21 months out of date. A time lag adjustment is made, but it appears inadequate. In addition, statutory caps on rates are too low and should be removed to allow CHHC more flexibility. Multi-purpose, community-based outpatient clinics are an important resource, and their growth should be fostered in needed areas.

Nursing homes—Long-term care accounted for 53% of Connecticut Medicaid expenditures in FY 1976. Numerous abuses nationwide have prompted HEW to require a strict cost-related reimbursement system.

While a new system was being developed, an interim reimbursement system was put into effect. The system was based on 1974 costs plus a 5% adjustment for inflation. Many nursing homes in Connecticut have reported significant financial losses as a result of the interim rates. Therefore, *LPR&IC recommends that the Committee on State Payments accept and expedite rate appeals from homes able to fully document such losses.*

Connecticut's proposed cost-related reimbursement system was not implemented on July 1, 1976 as planned, due to numerous objections from the industry including the failure of the Committee on State Payments to comply with the Uniform Administrative Procedures Act. Although LPR&IC endorses the proposed system, adequate information has not been provided to explain how the reported data will be used to establish rates. *It is therefore recommended that the Committee on State Payments issue a handbook specifically describing the rate determination process.*

Each facility's audited costs will be separated into controlled cost centers, uncontrolled cost centers and asset valuation. Because there is widespread concern that the asset valuation method of the proposed system will severely jeopardize the future of the nursing home industry in Connecticut, *it is recommended that the Committee on State Payments contract for an independent examination of the Fair Rental Value System of asset valuation for its long-range impact on the nursing home industry.*

To induce efficiency, financial incentives will be offered to homes meeting certain criteria. However, *it is recommended that the incentives be reviewed to determine if they should be made more attractive.*

Drugs—Connecticut presently employs a cost plus professional fee method for reimbursing pharmacies. Although this appears appropriate for walk-in customers, an estimated $900,000 could be saved if pharmaceutical services were provided to nursing homes on a low bid contract system. *It is recommended that the Department of Social Services examine reinstitution of the bid system for providing pharmaceutical services to nursing homes.*

Doctors—Reimbursement for physician services is based on a "Relative Value Scale," which assigns units of value to each medical procedure according to time and complexity. A single unit is reimbursed at the rate of $4.50 for basic medical services and $5.00 for surgery and radiology. These rates have not been updated since 1973.

Ambulances—Recent increases in ambulance rates were based on unaudited costs presented at a public hearing. *It is recommended that the Department of Health provide the Office of Emergency Medical Service the use of a financial analyst for the ambulance rate determination process.*

Equipment—Until recently the state stocked durable medical equipment (wheelchairs, crutches, braces) to be dispensed upon DSS authorization. This procedure resulted in many problems, and the state will soon contract out for this service.

UTILIZATION REVIEW

Utilization review (UR) is a system used to determine the appropriateness of medical care provided and to identify and prevent overutilization of medical services.

Most nonemergency medical services provided in Connecticut require prior authorization from the DSS Medical Review Team (MRT). This team is composed of several part-time specialists and a Medical Director. The workload is such that an average of six minutes can be spent on each prior authorization request. Because policy communication with providers is essential, because an effective prior authorization system is a deterrent to overutilization, and because MRT positions are 75% federally reimbursed, *it is recommended that DSS expand its Medical Review Team to include one or more additional full-time consultants and a full-time Medical Director.*

The Department has considered decentralizing its MRT staff to the various district offices. *The Committee recommends that the MRT operation remain in the Central Office.*

DSS has no formal regulations that effectively control the use of nonemergency ambulance service. *It is recommended that a procedure be established for the daily reporting and sample auditing of ambulance claims.* In addition, welfare recipients should be made aware of alternative types of medical transportation available to them.

Connecticut spends nearly $3 million annually on elective surgery, one-third of which the Department estimates as being unnecessary. DSS intended to implement a second medical opinion requirement for six surgical procedures by January 1, 1976. Because of administrative delays and failure to adopt formal regulations, the plan has not yet taken effect. As much as $1 million may already have been lost in calendar 1976.

In FY 1975, drug utilization per Medicaid recipient rose at the alarming rate of 18%. DSS pharmaceutical reviewers should periodically review a sample of pharmacy billings to determine whether departmental policy is being followed with regard to drug quantity, refills and narcotic and alcoholic drugs. Further, DSS should reduce its restriction on the number of refills allowed for birth control prescriptions.

Federal regulations require that pharmaceutical services provided at a skilled nursing facility be under the supervision of a qualified pharmaceutical consultant. Many such consultants provide these services without fee, *but* usually when they also provide upwards of 70% of the drugs used in the home. Uncontrolled, these financial arrangements have the potential of creating a direct conflict of interest. *It is recommended that the State Pharmacy Commission and State Department of Health promulgate regulations which will effectively control the professional services provided by nursing home pharmaceutical consultants.* All pharmaceutical consultants should be paid on a fee basis.

As a means of safeguarding against unnecessary surgery and other excessive treatments, the federal government has mandated states to establish local "Professional Standards Review Organizations" (PSRO's). Connecticut has four PSRO's which have begun limited operations. PSRO's will perform hospital length of stay (LOS) reviews by patient age and diagnosis for each Medicaid beneficiary.

EXPENDITURE CONTROLS

The Medical Payments Section, which is responsible for manual review and preparation for computer processing of all Medicaid claims, was found to be understaffed. *LRP&IC recommends that existing vacancies be filled and that Medical Payments Section positions be reviewed for possible reclassification* to attract and retain staff qualified to perform the important and complex manual review operations.

A separate "Suspended Payments Unit" also is recommended to relieve the Medical Payments Section of some of its current workload, to increase accuracy in the payment system, and to improve provider relations.

The Department's lack of adequate staffing and effectiveness data on which to base cost-benefit analyses, as well as the lack of written instructions and formal training of personnel are noted. *The LPR&IC recommends that a systematic study of claims processing be undertaken, and that appropriate detailed staff instructions be developed, along with the development of pre-service and in-service training program.*

The Medicaid program *must* be the payor of last resort. Yet, the Department's system for holding other "third parties" (private insurers, Medicare) liable is weak. *The LPR&IC recommends that a separate "claims recovery" unit be established to follow-up insurance and accident liability.* With proper organization and training, this unit could recover significant amounts of erroneous Medicaid payments. *Additionally, it is recommended that the Department explore the use of a private contractor, as the Departments of Health and Mental Health have, to recover Medicaid payments where the Medicare program had primary liability.*

The Post-Payment Audit Group is also understaffed, limiting their capability to effectively make use of the available post audit reports. *The LPR&IC recommends that the staff of this section be augmented to increase the detection and recoupment of overpayments.* An automated claims recovery system is also suggested which would allow the Department to withhold payments to vendors until overpayment balances are recouped.

To control rising drug costs, and fully realize projected savings of the drug substitution law (P.A. 76–166) *the LPR&IC recommends that DSS implement a policy which will reimburse pharmacists only for the lowest cost generic equivalent.*

DSS conducts a very limited review of drug bills using a pharmaceutical reviewer and a computer edit routine which suspends only those line-items which exceed $16. It has been demonstrated in other states that some private contractors have pharmaceutical cost auditing and utilization control systems which would cost significantly less to operate and would generate additional savings through cost and utilization controls. *The LPR&IC recommends that formal bids be solicited for such a system.*

Vendor fraud is a topic of growing national concern. *HEW has recently established a Medicaid Fraud and Abuse Unit and LPR&IC recommends that DSS seek this unit's assistance in establishing a vendor fraud and abuse unit for Connecticut.* The Department has not promulgated regulations regarding vendor fraud as required by P.A. 76–242. Since very few (approximately one per year) vendor fraud cases are prosecuted, regulations should be issued to facilitate the prosecution of vendor fraud cases.

MEDICAID MANAGEMENT INFORMATION SYSTEM

HEW has developed a computerized system (MMIS) to help states contain Medicaid costs by reducing processing errors and facilitating control of misuse and abuse of the program.

HEW grants financial assistance for 90% of development costs to states which develop an approved MMIS. When the system becomes fully operational, HEW increases the federal reimbursement for its operation from 50% to 75%.

Although the Department's MMIS development staff have been able to identify the problems of the existing system and to propose an appropriate solution, they have had problems implementing it.

Unless management of the MMIS project is improved, the project will not meet its scheduled two-year completion date. *Therefore, LPR&IC recommends that DSS recruit a full-time director to assume responsibility for the MMIS project.* To aid project managers in controlling, monitoring, and reporting on the progress of the MMIS project, *LPR&IC recommends that the Department of Finance and Control's State Data Processing Division make available to the Department of Social Services a project management system.*

To help plan for the transition from the old system to the new, *LPR&IC recommends that the Department of Social Services include, as part of the organizational analysis required for MMIS development, a Personnel Resource Impact Statement.* It should identify all changes in agency staffing required for the new system, including staff increases or decreases.

Unless Connecticut takes an aggressive approach in following up its surveillance and utilization reports to recoup overpayments and to refer fraud cases, it will not realize the full potential savings from MMIS. The computer can only generate information which must be interpreted and followed up with investigatory work and, in some cases, court action. It is essential that DSS plan ahead for different staffing needs after MMIS is implemented if maximum benefits are to be experienced.

INSTITUTIONAL PROVIDERS OF LONG-TERM CARE

The high percentage of Connecticut's Medicaid funds spent on skilled nursing facility care warranted in-depth discussion of the reasons why so many elderly Medicaid patients are placed in skilled nursing homes and what can be done to reduce nursing home costs.

While the new cost-related reimbursement system will go far to improve nursing home accountability and assure that Medicaid only pays legitimate costs, other changes are needed to correct the current imbalance in levels of care provided and to assure that patients are appropriately placed. As many as 20–50% of Medicaid patients in long-term care facilities may be inappropriately placed in skilled nursing homes at an excess cost of at least $6 million for FY 1977. New federal regulations require appropriate placement of Medicaid patients and noncompliance could mean substantial loss of federal funds to the state. *The Committee recommends that the Department of Social Services establish a policy that skilled nursing facilities caring for reclassified (ICF) Medicaid patients either accept ICF reimbursement or the patient will be transferred to a facility that will accept the ICF reimbursement.*

Providers of long-term care involve problems of limited information about Medicaid convalescent populations. *It is recommended that DSS analyze general convalescent characteristics and trends to aid in planning and budgeting.*

Determining appropriateness of Medicaid long-term care is the function of two federally-required utilization review groups—Utilization Review Committees (URC's) and DSS Patient Review Teams (PRT's). PRT effectiveness in controlling overutilization of skilled nursing homes has been hindered by staff shortages and insufficient training. *The Committee recommends that DSS seek funds for additional PRT staff and improved training to improve effectiveness in this important cost control area.*

Appropriate and timely discharge planning and patient placement is recognized as still another means of controlling overutilization and reducing long-term care costs. Suggested improvements in long-term care planning include *a recommendation to increase the number and training of district office adult service workers who are responsible for arranging care and services for elderly clients.*

Needed revision of the state's outdated Public Health Code to facilitate development of a broader continuum of long-term care, multilevel facilities able to adjust care to patient needs, and compliance with federal regulations is outlined. *The Committee recommends amendment of the Code to establish two levels of intermediate care. In addition, a recommendation is made for statutory annual review of the Code to insure its continued relevance.*

Quality of care is related to the revision of standards and costs. While LPR&IC is not in a position to issue a definition of quality care, the Governor's Blue Ribbon Committee is studying the relation of quality to standards. *It is recommended that the findings of this important Committee be fully considered during Code revision.*

Many older persons require care (other than skilled nursing) which is not covered by Medicare. As a result, the Medicaid program has had to assume increasing responsibility for long-term care of the elderly. Since revisions in Medicare and Medicaid legislation are now being considered by Congress, *it is recommended that DSS prepare and submit to the Connecticut Congressional Delegation, a document outlining current deficiencies and recommending specific changes.*

ALTERNATIVES TO INSTITUTIONALIZATION

Alternatives to institutionalization in the continuum of long-term care for the elderly are needed. Many services exist such as home health care programs, adult day care, elderly foster homes, the Triage program and a proposed home care demonstration project.

It is suggested that home health care, a Medicaid reimbursable service, is not being utilized to its full potential despite the possible cost-savings. Utilization of home care, like other alternatives, is hampered by confusion over Medicaid reimbursement, an institutional bias, and the difficulties in coordinating an appropriate alternative care plan.

While savings cannot be accurately estimated, the State Department on Aging (DOA) is conducting studies to determine the cost-effectiveness of alternative care.

23. On the Development of Medical Assistance Projection Models

TIMOTHY J. TYSON and DANIEL JEHL

Printed with permission of authors.

Wisconsin, like other states, is undergoing mounting pressures to moderate increases in the expenditures for the Medical Assistance Program. From 1967 to 1975 total Medical Assistance expenditures increased in Wisconsin at an average annual rate of 15 percent. Over the same time period, the number of Medical Assistance recipients increased at an average annual rate of 10 percent. Medical Assistance now consumes $561,000,000 total expenditures. As a result of these rapidly escalating expenditures, it is not surprising that there is a growing need for improved methods for developing accurate budgets. The problem is one of national importance—"HEW has shown considerable concern over the accuracy of state budgetary projections which are used to request federal funds as input to the federal budget process." Similar thinking has been expressed by state officials in Wisconsin. This paper describes our effort at developing statistical models which can be used in estimating Medical Assistance expenditures and caseload. Before getting into a description of these models, a review is in order as to how projections are currently being made.

BACKGROUND

The Wisconsin Medical Assistance is projected at least every two years for state budget purposes. Projections are made by the Division of Health, State Budget Office and the State Legislature. Forecasters employ past trend analysis techniques to project future expenditures. At the most general level, past expenditures are subjected to trend analysis using yearly expenditure figures. Either straight line or nonlinear analysis can be used. At a more specific level, trend analysis can use either all services on a service by service basis with a sum total being produced; or the most costly service categories can be individually projected and the remaining services aggregated as a miscellaneous category with the same technique employed.

This approach is workable also with monthly data. The preferable approach is to use monthly data, the major services treated individually, and a smoothing of cyclical variation through an appropriate time series technique. A regression model can be employed projecting expenditures as a function of time or as a function of past expenditures with or without inclusion of an inflation factor for medical care cost increases not projected through the regression per se. Regression is an appropriate technique and can deal with cyclical variation. Most regression techniques are used as checks upon the simpler historic trend analyses techniques. The fact is that however reliable regression techniques may be, sophisticated techniques are not understood nor trusted by legislators, budget directors, and others who ultimately render the final decisions on the Medical Assistance budget projections.

In Wisconsin, for the 1975–1977 biennial budget, forecasters used a method of straight-line past trends analysis for major service categories (nursing home, hospital, physician); a straight-line analysis was also used for a catch-all category reflecting all other services; and the totals were summed to produce a grand base total. In addition, several policy changes were enacted with each costed out and added to the base total. For example, eligibility was expanded, and a projection of caseload growth due to the policy change was estimated. An average annual Medicaid payment per additional caseload was multiplied times the additional projected caseload to produce a cost projection due to the policy change.

For the 1975–1977 biennium, the base total was projected by using the previous year's estimates as a base and adding to this base 4 components: (1) policy changes each costed out individually as explained above; (2) projected cost of annual utilization increases (1 percent times the base total); (3) projected cost of annual increase due to reimbursement policy changes and medical care cost increases (6 percent of base); and (4) projected costs of projected caseload growth, with estimated caseload type increases (e.g. SSI, AFDC, etc.) multiplied times the estimated cost for each. The sums of each were totaled to produce a grand total, and regression models were used to "test" the reasonableness of the result. The regression techniques produced outer limits

for the results based upon the conventional approach since discussion of the more sophisticated regression models could have served to alienate policy makers and possibly jeopardize the "selling" of the projections. The techniques and models used are described below.

ECONOMETRIC MODEL

Some economic models are designed with the primary objective to produce accurate predictions. Others are intended to provide an explanation of the underlying structural relationship contained in the data. Of course, in practice many models have characteristics of both types. The overriding philosophy in building the forecasting models described here is to minimize the predictive error or, in other words, to produce as accurate a forecast as possible. Two general model development approaches are described. The first approach makes use of a large scale econometric model, and the second approach strictly relies on past information generated by the Medical Assistance Program.

The Departments of Revenue and Administration have been working jointly with Data Resources, Inc. a consulting firm located in Lexington, Massachusetts to design an econometric model of the Wisconsin economy. The effort which started in July, 1975, is producing 10 quarter forecasts of key economic variables.

State models developed by DRI are income models. Economic activity in the domestic sector of the state's economy is based on measures of total state income— net disposable and an index of purchases. Wage and salary disbursements are made by combining forecasts of employment with forecasts of the appropriate non-manufacturing wage rates. Economic activity in the export sector is related to national economic conditions and the relative cost of producing in Wisconsin. Employment is the measure of economic activity in this sector. For agriculture, Wisconsin's production of milk, beef, hogs, and crops is estimated directly and combined with national price forecasts to arrive at an agricultural income.

In addition to the increased understanding of the structure of Wisconsin's economy, the 270 equation model is aimed at improving fiscal analysis and planning and revenue estimates. Estimating the effect on Wisconsin's economy of changing national economic conditions is also possible. Specifically, the model forecasts personal income, the unemployment rate, employment in a host of manufacturing and non-manufacturing industries, financial activity of banks and savings and loans, state government revenue and expenditures as well as a number of other Wisconsin specific indicators and aggregates. The equations in the model can be thought of in reduced form since the model is based on empirically available data and not on economic constructs. The intent of our effort was to make use of the DRI data base for purposes of projecting MA expenditures and beneficiaries. If a model can be developed which relates Medical Assistance data to DRI data we will be able to forecast Medical Assistance given forecasts of the DRI data.

The data base for this study was formed by summing monthly observations into quarterly observations for the period July 1967–December 1975. The data were obtained from the fiscal intermediary for Wisconsin. These data were then merged with the DRI data base and the following variables selected and entered into a stepwise regression analysis program:

1. Consumer Price Index
2. Unemployment rate
3. Personal Income
4. Disposable Income (1967 dollars)
5. Population
6. Personal Tax Liability

7. Employment in Medical Services (SIC 80)

In addition, dummy variables were created to capture the effect of the freeze on Medical Assistance rates which went into effect December 1974 and to account for seasonable variations of the data. In all instances, two separate logarithmic equations were estimated, one for total beneficiaries and one for total expenditures. After the initial stepwise regressions, the models were re-estimated retaining variables significant at the .05 level. The equations were:

(1) $\ln BEN = 12.72 + .74 \ln CPI +$
          (123.07)   (2.97)

      $.17 FREEZE + .36 \ln TAX - .034 Q_1$
       (5.27)   (3.40)   (−2.04)

                $R^2 = .97$
                $D.W. = 1.75$

(2) $\ln DOL = 18.10 + 4.90 \ln CPI -$
          (13.36)   (13.36)

      $1.86 \ln EMPLOY - .057 Q_1 - .097 Q_2$
       (5.83)   (2.08)   (3.58)

                $R^2 = .97$
                $D.W. = 1.75$

where:
BEN   = number of Medical Assistance Beneficiaries or Recipients
CPI   = Consumer Price Index
FREEZE   = dummy variable representing the freeze on rates
TAX   = personal tax liability
DOL   = Medical Assistance Expenditures
EMPLOY   = employment in medical services
Q_1 = dummy variable–quarter 1
Q_2 = dummy variable–quarter 2

PREDICTIVE MODELS

The second major model development approach consisted of techniques thought to be strictly predictive in nature. Two sets of models were developed, one based upon time as a predictor of Medical Assistance and the other based upon previous values of Medical Assistance as a predictor of current Medical Assistance. Again, monthly data as reported by the fiscal intermediary were used. Regression equations were calculated for two time periods—1967–75 and 1972–75; the rationale being that the program has changed significantly enough in scope of services that the early information may no longer be relevant as a predictor of current Medical Assistance. Additionally, the period 1972–75 was chosen to allow sufficient degrees of freedom required for statistical analysis.

MEDICAL ASSISTANCE AS A FUNCTION OF TIME

The simplest relationship which can be expressed is that medical assistance expenditures or caseload is a linear function of time, i.e.,

$$MA = a + B_1 \text{ TIME}$$

This is nothing more than the common straight line projection method. However, by allowing TIME to take on higher order terms, nonlinearity in the data can be taken into consideration. Thus, equations were also specified to include TIME to the squared and cubed power. All equations contained monthly dummy variables to account for seasonal fluctuations.

MEDICAL ASSISTANCE AS A FUNCTION OF PREVIOUS MEDICAL ASSISTANCE DATA

A generalized autoregressive model is of the form,

$$MA_t = a + B_1 MA_{t-1} + B_2 MA_{t-2} + B_3 MA_{t-3} + \ldots .$$ where the level of M.A. expenditures or beneficiaries is a function of the values in previous time periods (months). Since this model utilizes past experience of the program rather than time as the predictor, it would be expected to be more sensitive to cyclical fluctuations.

PREDICTING THE CHANGE IN MEDICAL ASSISTANCE

All the previous discussion on model development referred to the level of medical assistance expenditures and caseload. Especially for short term forecasts, a better prediction may result by concentrating on the change from one period to the next as opposed to the level. Change is a somewhat more sensitive measure. As a result, models were developed to project the monthly change in medical assistance. The general form of the equation is:

$$\Delta MA_t = a + B_1 \Delta MA_{t-1} + B_2 \Delta MA_{t-2} + B_3 \Delta MA_{t-3} + \ldots .$$

MODEL COMPARISON

Since monthly data were utilized for the period through December, 1975, to develop the models, and since data were available, at the time, through July, 1976, means were available for checking the predictive ability of the various models.

Table I compares the actual and predicted values for each of the models previously discussed. An average monthly error rate is given as well as the error for the sum of the seven month figures.

Regarding Beneficiaries,
- the time model based upon 1967–75 data performed the best in terms of the average error rate.

Table I
Expenditures Models

	Time Models		Lag Models		Lagged Change Models	
	1967–75	1972–75	1967–75	1972–75	1967–75	1972–75
Average Monthly Error	25.5	12.0	11.0	10.4	7.5	8.0
7-month Error	24.6	11.8	6.1	5.2	1.9	.9

Beneficiaries Models

	Time Models		Lag Models		Lagged Change Models	
	1967–75	1972–75	1967–75	1972–75	1967–75	1972–75
Average Monthly Error	6.3	8.4	7.9	6.9	13.3	8.2
7-month Error	5.7	7.8	4.8	3.4	4.5	2.4

- the lagged change model (1972–75) did the best for the sum of the seven month period.

Regarding Expenditures,
- the lagged change model had the smallest error of any of the models.

By summing, monthly projections into quarters, a comparison can be made between the state econometric model and the "predictive models". Selecting the single "best" model of the monthly models (lagged change 1972–75) and comparing to the econometric model yields:

Beneficiaries

	Actual	Econometric Model	Lagged Change Model
Jan.–June	1,184,604	1,125,259 5.0%	1,171,327 1.1%

Expenditures

	Actual	Econometric Model	Lagged Change Model
Jan.–June	206,087,208	220,937,000 7.2%	221,386,216 2.6%

Interestingly, the lagged change model performs considerably better for the six month period than the econometric model. Six months is a relatively short time period, and as the length of the forecast period increases the more difficult it will be to obtain reliable estimates from a model which does not include factors exogenous to the Medical Assistance Program. Since the econometric model encompasses various exogenous factors it may be expected to provide more accurate long run projections.

Conclusions we reached:

- It is difficult for a simple model to adequately predict claims data. More elaborate growth models are being developed.
- There is considerable month to month variation in the data which is important to model for accurate short-term projections. Even with seasonal dummy variables, it was difficult to project even for very short time periods. The lowest average monthly error in prediction was 6.3 percent for beneficiaries and 7.5 percent for expenditures. This error was greatly reduced when projecting for somewhat longer time periods. Comparable error rates

for a seven month period were 2.4 percent for beneficiaries and .9 percent for expenditures. We do not as yet have any validation for projections covering longer time periods (2 years).
- Variables omitted from this initial effort such as real equivalent number of work days in the month may be a strong predictor.
- Traditional trend analysis techniques may be more reliable than sophisticated models for short-term projections. The models may be better forecasting methods for long-term projections.

Future efforts:

Several activities remain to be done:

1. Projections need to be disaggregated into Medical Assistance services and programs.
2. Omitted variables need to be tested.
3. A causal model needs to be developed to better predict long run behavior.
4. There is a need to educate policy makers on the utility of regression models for forecasting to foster acceptability of non-traditional techniques.

24. Evaluation of Medicaid Spend-Down

MARILYN RYMER, WARREN OKSMAN,
LAWRENCE BAILIS, DAVID ELLWOOD AND
IRENE MALOZEMOFF

Reprinted with permission.

"Spend-down" is a part of the medically needy program directed at extending medical assistance coverage beyond those who are normally included. It is based on the provision of the Medicaid law which stipulates that "in computing a family's income there shall be excluded any cost (whether in the form of insurance premiums or otherwise) incurred by such family for medical care or for any other type of remedial care recognized under state law."* Thus, if a family meets the categorical requirements for public assistance, but has income in excess of the medically needy eligibility level, it can still qualify for medical assistance by "spending down" the income in excess of that eligibility level.

DHEW sponsored the present study under Contract #SRS-74-58 to analyze in depth the problems and issues surrounding spend-down. The specific objectives of the study have been:

- To analyze the implementation and administration of the spend-down program among several States;

- To determine various characteristics (sociodemographic, economic, behavioral and health care utilization) of successful and unsuccessful spend-down applicants compared to other Medicaid populations; and

- To estimate the spend-down participation rate, i.e., the extent to which the potentially eligible spend-down population is actually enrolled in Medicaid.

In meeting the first study objective, administrative structures for the implementation of spend-down in five states were assessed and compared. Spend-down policy and procedures at both the state and local levels in Maryland, Massachusetts, Michigan, North Carolina, and Utah were reviewed to determine the clarity, consistency, efficiency and general regulatory compliance of states in running the spend-down program.

To meet the second study objective, which involved a description and comparison of the spend-down population, Urban Systems Research and Engineering sampled 1,277 Medicaid case records in Massachusetts, North Carolina, and Maryland, and then conducted a personal survey with

---

*42 U.S. Code 1396 b(f) (2).

953 Medicaid applicants and recipients in these three states. The sites selected were:

- Lynn, Massachusetts
- Boston, Massachusetts
- Springfield, Massachusetts
- Forsyth County, North Carolina (Winston-Salem)
- Guilford County, North Carolina (Greensboro)
- Baltimore City, Maryland
- Montgomery County, Maryland

Extracting information from agency records and administering a structured questionnaire to survey respondents at the seven sites, Urban Systems Research and Engineering studied successful and unsuccessful spend-down applicants, as well as a control group of medically needy recipients (who did not spend-down) in order to establish sociodemographic profiles, health care utilization patterns (and changes in these patterns as a result of medical assistance), the economic impact of spend-down, and the behavioral aspects of spend-down. It should be noted that the survey group did not include long-term care recipients.

Also related to the second study objective, Urban Systems Research and Engineering obtained Medicaid claims payment data during 1974 for the survey population from two of the states — Massachusetts and North Carolina. Eligibility and claims data from the state automatic data processing (ADP) files were also obtained for a sample of categorically needy recipients from these two states to provide for further comparison with the spend-down population.

Finally, the third study objective, which involved the estimation of the spend-down participation rate for one state, was accomplished by the development of a computer-based model which simulated the Medicaid eligibility process. Using information from the National Health Use and Expenditure Survey of 1970 and specified Medicaid eligibility procedures, USR&E approxi-

mated for Massachusetts the Medicaid eligibility process and attempted to calculate the potentially eligible spend-down population as compared to those actually enrolled. Estimates were also calculated for other eligible population groups for Medicaid in the state.

The study findings can be best stated by answering the following three questions:

- Whom is spend-down helping?
- How efficiently is spend-down being implemented?
- What objectives does spend-down fulfill?

WHOM DOES SPEND-DOWN HELP?

Although there is some variation between states, a profile of the successful spend-downer can be developed. Exhibit 1 presents the major conclusions regarding characteristics of the spend-down population.

Before further describing the spend-down population, it seems prudent to place them in some perspective with regard to the overall Medicaid program. Across the survey sites, spend-downers were not found to be a significant part of the non-institutionalized Medicaid population. In Massachusetts they constituted less than 2 percent, as an average, of those eligible for medical assistance, and in North Carolina they were approximately 6 percent of the Medicaid population not living in long-term care. The categorically needy by far (63 to 87 percent) make up the majority of those eligible in both of the states, with the balance being medically needy recipients.

Looking only at the medically needy populations, spend-downers are also relatively insignificant in two of the study states. By site, they represent 0.6 and 4 percent of the medically needy caseload in Maryland, and 4, 6, and 12 percent in Massachusetts. These figures contrast sharply with each of the two North Carolina sites in which spend-downers represent close to one-quarter of the medically needy caseload.

However, it would be a mistake to write the spend-down program off as being insignificant. The computer simulation of Medicaid eligibility for Massachusetts indicated that during 1974 the state's Medicaid program was only enrolling about 5 percent of the potentially eligible spend-down population. If this estimate is at all accurate, then spend-downers should be considered to be a vastly under-represented group in state Medicaid programs.

The Spend-Down Experience

The majority of successful spend-down cases already have incurred, at the point of application, all the health expenses which they need to fulfill their spend-down liability. Also, most cases are able to use all the health expenses which they have toward meeting their spend-down (i.e., there is not a problem with nonallowable expenses).

It is impossible to predict the likely size of a spend-down liability. However, it can be expected that most successful spend-down cases will not have spend-downs over $275. Furthermore, many spend-downs are less than $100. Generally, aged cases have the smallest spend-down liabilities. The spend-down liability represents for most spend-downers a major portion of their annual income, usually from 7% to 15%.

According to spend-downers themselves, the majority of spend-down liabilities are eventually fully paid. There is no definite pattern as to how the spend-down is paid off—some cases indicate they pay all at once while others report they work out a payment schedule with providers. However, the extended payment approach is the method most frequently used. It should be noted that all the providers interviewed for the Administrative Analysis phase of the study reported that most spend-downers do not pay off their liabilities. Unfortunately, no conclusive data could be obtained in this regard.

As had been anticipated, case records indicate that hospitals are assigned the major dollar proportion of spend-down liabilities. As a matter of fact, it can usually be expected that well over half of any case's spend-down liability will go to a hospital.

Exhibit 1 Profile of Medicaid Spend-Downer
(Excluding those in long-term care)

- Poor, income slightly above protected income level
- Main income source OASDI
- May be related to any category of assistance
- May or may not be likely to be previously eligible for Medicaid, or first-time spend-downer, depending upon state
- Had recent change in health status; had higher ambulatory care utilization in past year than general population; previous year's annual health expenses were over $1,000.
- Has had health insurance coverage of some type
- Found out about spend-down itself through the welfare office
- Has already incurred expenses needed to meet the spend-down liability at point of application
- Spend-down liability is less than $275 and from 7% to 15% of annual income
- Most of spend-down liability is assigned to hospital
- Understands the spend-down procedures
- Shows higher health care utilization patterns on Medicaid than national average in ambulatory and hospital care
- May or may not show greater Medicaid benefit utilization than other recipients, depending upon state

Medicaid Utilization Patterns

Once on Medicaid, spend-downers have a slightly higher encounter rate with ambulatory care than the general population. Disabled spend-down cases show higher encounter rates and costs per visit than AFDC cases. There is no distinct pattern to the encounter rate for ambulatory care for aged cases. Also, the impact of Medicare makes it impossible to draw conclusions about the average cost for this category.

Conclusions cannot be reached about the differences in Medicaid ambulatory care utilization among spend-downers, the medically needy and the categorically needy except by state. In Massachusetts no consistent pattern emerged across sites with regard to the encounter rates for each group. At two sites, the medically needy showed the higher rates, while at the third site spend-downers did. All three groups are slightly above the national average, but not that different from each other.

On the other hand, in North Carolina spend-down cases show considerably higher ambulatory care encounter rates than the medically needy or categorically needy. They are only slightly above the national average, while the medically needy and categorically needy are below it.

Spend-downers, once they are eligible for Medicaid, show a higher hospital utilization rate than the national average. The disabled spend-downers spend many more days in the hospital per month eligible than any other category. Aged figures are lower, but are no doubt affected by Medicaid coverage.

Medicaid cash recipients make less use of hospital care than the medically needy and spend-downers. However, the effect is more pronounced in North Carolina than Massachusetts.

The same categorical patterns for hospital usage are seen for the medically needy and categorically needy as shown for spend-downers, i.e., blind, disabled and aged cases far surpass AFDC cases in hospital usage. Not only are they more likely to be hospitalized, but they tend to stay longer for each visit.

Medicaid drug utilization data was only available for Massachusetts, but it would indicate than only between 30 to 50 percent of spend-downers are likely to have drug bills while on Medicaid. As an average Medicaid drug expenditures for spend-downers ran $2 to $6 a month. The aged and disabled spend-downers have the highest average drug expenditures among the categories. The categorically needy in Massachusetts are more likely to have drug expenditures than are the medically needy or spend-downers.

The average annual health care cost to Medicaid for a spend-down case varies considerably. By site, it is $261, $834, and $4324 in Massachusetts, and $809 and $2356 in North Carolina.

Spend-downers do not necessarily incur greater expenses in Massachusetts than the medically needy or the categorically needy. However, a pronounced pattern is seen in North Carolina, primarily due to the unusually low expenditure there on health care for the categorically needy. Although spend-downers in North Carolina are only 6 percent of the Medicaid caseload at each site, they account for 11 to 21 percent of the annual Medicaid expenditures.

The most striking result of the Medicaid utilization findings is the contrasting patterns seen between Massachusetts and North Carolina. In North Carolina, Medicaid is serving a fairly stable and consistent recipient population. Spend-downers there show a markedly greater utilization of Medicaid health care benefits than the other eligibility groups. Massachusetts, on the other hand, shows considerable variation among sites in its Medicaid caseload composition; furthermore, the utilization patterns do not show spend-downers to necessarily require any greater health care services than other Medicaid recipients. These differences between the states make it impossible to generalize much about spend-downer benefit utilization within the Medicaid system, except by state.

HOW EFFICIENTLY IS SPEND-DOWN ADMINISTERED?

The common refrain of the spend-down Administrative Analysis is that there is a wide variability in the implementation of spend-down not only among but within states. The variations observed among the states can be attributed to some extent to the latitude deliberately allowed within the regulations. However, in other instances, the variation represents either a misunderstanding or ignorance of federal intent, or a decision that the federal regulations are unworkable. Variations observed within the study states can be explained in turn by the vagueness of the policies and regulations states themselves have developed for administering spend-down. Due to the lack of superimposed structure and precise definitions, decisions about how to implement spend-down are often made at the local level. How spend-down is administered in each state, then, is largely the result of a piecemeal accretion of rules and procedures—significantly lacking in a broader framework which unifies them to a common objective.

As a result, spend-down applicants are differentially treated among and at times within states. Additionally, spend-down causes certain inefficiencies in the overall administration of state Medicaid programs. The essence of spend-down administrative problems can be boiled down into three points:

- Spend-down is a complicated program and would be difficult to administer under any circumstances.
- The paucity and vagueness of federal and state guidelines and regulations substantially exacerbate the inherent administrative problems.

- Although spend-down is legislatively part of the Medicaid program, administratively it does not integrate easily into that program.

Clearly, some states have implemented spend-down better than others, but generally spend-down is not administered as efficiently or effectively as it could be.

Administrative Difficulties with Spend-Down

At the most rudimentary level, there are two basic administrative functions that must be performed to implement the Medicaid program. The first is eligibility determination which identifies the beneficiaries of the program. The second is invoice payment: paying for the health bills of the beneficiaries. All other administrative functions are essentially controls on the accurate implementation of these two.

Spend-down complicates both procedures. It presents problems for invoice payment because controls must be built in to assure that bills paid are not part of the spend-down liability, or for services received before spend-down eligibility commenced. Spend-down complicates eligibility determination because the spend-down case is generally more time consuming and more difficult to process than other Medicaid applications.

Spend-Down and Invoice Payment

The major function of the Medicaid process which spend-down significantly impacts is invoice payment. Spend-down introduces new requirements into a system designed to handle the relatively simple procedures involved with paying bills for the categorically and medically needy.

Spend-down causes problems in claims processing because by the very structure of the program, spend-down recipients are involved along with Medicaid in paying for their health care expenses. Consequently, administrative procedures have to be developed which insure that proper billing occurs and payments are not duplicated.

Claims processing for spend-downers is further complicated because federal regulations stipulate (1) a prioritization for spend-down liabilities; (2) that spend-down liabilities only have to be incurred; and (3) that third-party insurance cannot be used to mitigate the spend-down liability. *Significantly, each of these federal requirements was being violated by study states either by oversight, poor management or in the interests of efficiently integrating spend-down into the Medicaid program.*

Looking first at the issue of prioritizing the expenses used for the spend-down liability, the federal regulations seem reasonable and straightforward in principle: apply health insurance premiums first, non-Medicaid covered medical expenses next, and Medicaid-covered expenses last. However, in actuality, this issue of assignment constitutes a major problem in implementing spend-down. Prioritizing such as that specified in the regulations falls down because spend-down applicants of course want to become eligible for Medicaid as soon as possible, and states cannot determine eligibility until the spend-down liability has been satisfied. Furthermore, states are more interested in efficient claims processing than in the effort which would be required to prioritize the spend-down liability.

A strict implementation of prioritization would require for many cases waiting until *after* the six-month accounting period was over to fully insure that, for example, non-Medicaid covered items were used first as part of the spend-down liability.

In any event, all study states have largely disregarded the federal regulations regarding prioritization in lieu of more pragmatic assignment policies. Three methods of assignment have been devised which deal with this problem with variable success—chronological assignment of the liability, assignment of the liability to specific providers, and requiring that the spend-down

liability be paid instead of incurred. Each of these alternatives appears to have been developed primarily in the interests of efficient management and the need to control against erroneous expenditures, not in any effort to sabotage the spend-down program.

However, the chronological approach to spend-down liability assignment breaks down when bills are submitted late by practitioners. Then, the spend-down date has to be redetermined, and the liability reassigned. Another problem with using the chronological accumulation of spend-down expenses and the assignment of an exact date of eligibility occurs when multiple charges in excess of the spend-down liability occur on a given day (such as in a hospital). If a claim were submitted to Medicaid for the entire day's charges, it would probably be honored since states using the exact date approach would have no way of knowing that a spend-down liability was involved.

A second method for controlling against erroneous expenditures is assigning the spend-down to a specific provider and noting it on the Medicaid eligibility file so that the charges are not later paid by Medicaid. This approach most often occurs with hospitals. However, this method has problems because it seems unfairly discriminatory against larger providers. Also, providers report that spend-down liabilities are rarely collected* and thus result in bad debts for providers and eventual increased charges for everyone.

Two of the study states have found that neither of these two methods is efficient in controlling against Medicaid overpayments and, therefore, have added a third method—restrictions on whether the spend-down expenses are to be paid or incurred. Even though these states in their

---

*In contradiction to this, a majority of the spend-downers interviewed in the personal survey reported that they had fully paid their spend-down liabilities.

Medicaid plans endorse the incurment principle, they require that expenses used for meeting the spend-down that could be covered by Medicaid must be paid, so that the invoice will not be sent in to Medicaid for reimbursement.

Perhaps spend-down's major complication centers on this issue of incurment. The problem begins with the regulations. Since they are so nonspecific, they can be interpreted to contradict a major premise of the entire spend-down principle. Neither the law nor the regulations specify whether incurred expenses must eventually be paid. If they do not, then the spend-down amount technically does not have to be paid. This violates the principle on which spend-down is founded: that in order to become eligible, the recipient must share in the cost of medical expenses.

States have not found the incurment principle to be administratively feasible, especially for applicants with chronic health care needs who may be utilizing the services of several health care providers. As a result, the spend-down liability is required to be paid. Although effective, this does not represent an acceptable solution for controlling against erroneous expenditures because it is out of compliance with Federal regulations. Furthermore, it can prevent many applicants from successfully spending-down simply because they do not have available six months' worth of cash.

A final issue with regard to spend-down and invoice payment involves third-party insurance. Although third-party coverage is not unique to spend-down recipients, spend-down enforces recognition of this Medicaid-related problem of third-party liability because as a population, most spend-downers have some form of third-party insurance. The problems involved are (1) identification of third-party liabilities; (2) division of bills between the third-party payment, the spend-down amount and the Medicaid contribution; and (3) collection of amounts overpaid or advanced by Medicaid

which rightfully should have been paid by the third party. Little direction exists for guiding workers in how to review an applicant's insurance coverage. There is confusion as to whether or not insurance can mitigate the spend-down liability. Finally, pursuit of reimbursement from third-party coverage is left largely to providers.

It is clear from the preceding discussion that spend-down imposes extra burdens on the management of Medicaid operations. Inefficiencies arise in the extra tasks required for spend-down that are inserted into the general invoice processing system. Thus, unnecessary control measures are instituted on the entire system just for the sake of the minority of spend-downers in the system. In each of these instances, where spend-down necessitates an added control, the outcome is a less efficient procedure for the whole; furthermore, the approaches introduced continue to be problematic.

Spend-Down and Eligibility Determination. Spend-down applications mean extra work for the case worker. The spend-down amount must be calculated, and the process of spending down must be explained to the applicant. This latter task is said by workers to be the most time-consuming aspect of handling a spend-down case since there are so many contingencies and technicalities involved such as incurment versus payment, what expenses are allowable, the relationship of third-party insurance, etc.

A major problem in spend-down eligibility determination involves the determination of allowable expenses for meeting the spend-down. Determining the legitimacy of the medical expenses used in spending down is an area left almost entirely to caseworker discretion. It is not surprising, therefore, that most local offices visited defined the medical expenses allowed for meeting the spend-down differently. Only one state has produced an exact list of allowable expenses which should be counted in the spend-down. As a result, what expenses are allowable for spending-down can vary considerably. This clearly influences who spend-downers are.

Although spend-down is acknowledged by all states to be a difficult area of Medicaid eligibility, few adequate explanatory materials exist for workers, providers or applicants. Consequently, a second major problem involving spend-down and eligibility determination is that although spend-down is a more complicated and less familiar approach to Medicaid eligibility, inadequate guidance is available to those who are involved with it. As a result, confusion and frustration occur more frequently than with other Medicaid cases.

Because spend-down cases are more difficult and time-consuming, it is not surprising that informal screening procedures have been set up which discourage spend-down applications, particularly those without acute or immediately obvious health needs. Only North Carolina encourages potential spend-downers to go through the eligibility process "just in case" health care expenses over a six-month period are adequate to satisfy the spend-down liability.

A final indication of the way spend-downers are differentially treated in the Medicaid eligibility determination process can be seen in the termination procedures for spend-downers in several of the study states. Most states have special controls whereby spend-downers are automatically terminated at the end of a six-month eligibility period. Reapplication is not expected, as with other medically needy recipients, because it is felt spend-down is primarily there to serve emergency health needs. Again, North Carolina is the exception to this trend as shown in the stability of its spend-down population. Utah also encourages spend-downers to reapply.

The Utah Approach. While all of the administrative problems summarized here were present to some extent in each of four study states, one state (Utah) managed to avoid most of these difficulties through its unique approach to spend-down.* Utah essentially operates its spend-down as an insurance program. Recipients become enrolled on the basis of anticipated health needs and the state collects a monthly premium equal to the monthly excess income. In return for paying this premium, the recipient receives a Medicaid card and enjoys the attendant benefits. The problems related to assignment of spend-down liabilities, proper accounting of third-party reimbursements, verification of dates on provider invoices, and incurment as opposed to actual payment largely disappear. The state is saddled with the task of collecting the spend-down from the recipient, but in Utah this has not proven to be a problem. Most importantly, in Utah recipients do not have a problem of access; providers are not confused; and recipients and workers do not have to go through the process of liability accumulation and assignment.

This is not to say that the Utah system is without problems. First of all, payment, not incurment, is eventually required. Utah's approach makes it more difficult to use nonMedicaid covered health expenses in meeting the spend-down liability. Additionally, care has to be taken with such a system to insure that federal matching monies are not confused with whatever expenditures the state's program may make to cover those expenses which are the spend-down liabilities.

Nevertheless, Utah's system is an example of how the essential administrative functions specific to spend-down can be removed from the mainstream Medicaid process. The remaining functions that are left in the overall Medicaid administrative process are those that are common to all Medicaid recipients, i.e., where spend-downers are *not* a special group. Thus, the problem of integrating the entire spend-down process into the Medicaid framework is remedied.

---

*Utah's approach has been ruled out of compliance with federal regulations.

The Impact of Spend-Down Administration Problems on Applicants and Recipients

The variations in state and local administration of spend-down are not without their repercussions for the potential spend-down population. Specifically, the way states have approached the implementation of spend-down affects applicants in the following ways:

- Many potential spend-down applicants are not aware of the program's existence.
- Inadequate explanation and guidance are available to those who do apply so that participation is further discouraged.
- State approaches to protecting against erroneous expenditures favor the potential spend-downer with acute health care needs and the potential spend-downer who has the ability to pay rather than only incur the spend-down liability.
- Even for those spend-downers who become eligible, States' procedures are not designed to make them an ongoing part of the Medicaid population.

The Spend-Down Participation Rate. The Recipient Survey findings indicate that spend-downers are only a small part of the current Medicaid population in most states. Furthermore, there is strong indication that state Medicaid program are far from enrolling all of those potentially eligible for spend-down.

The results of the eligibility simulation for Massachusetts indicated that the state's Medicaid program was reaching only about 5 percent of the potentially eligible noninstitutionalized spend-down population. Furthermore, some 2.7 percent of the state's general population would be eligible for Medicaid through spend-down if they were aware of it. Of these the sizeable majority in Massachusetts were estimated to be MA-21 cases, which is an optional state eligibility group. Nevertheless, the adult and AFDC categories were also substantially underenrolled. If these estimates are at all accurate, there are many persons with health care needs and expenses who are apparently eligible but are not benefiting from spend-down provisions. It seems safe to assume that most of them would choose to pursue Medicaid eligibility if they were aware of it.

Survey findings substantiated that the public is not familiar with the spend-down provisions of Medicaid. Most successful *and* unsuccessful applicants indicated that they did not know about spend-down *per se* until they applied for medical assistance.

Most state Medicaid programs do very little in the way of publicizing eligibility provisions. Few written materials are available. However, most of the study states did not feel this to be a problem. Since they tend to see spend-down as an emergency health care program, they seem to assume that people in real need will somehow get to welfare departments for assistance. As a result, obviously, many persons never even apply.

A common assumption seems to be that providers will refer those to Medicaid spend-down who really need the coverage. However, the survey results indicate that providers are not the main referral source. Furthermore, many potential spend-downers out of cost consideration may severely restrict the health care which they obtain, thereby reducing the likelihood that they would be referred to the spend-down program. Also, many providers are not interested in having Medicaid patients so that they would not be apt to refer potential spend-downers. Finally, it is not clear that providers (especially physicians and druggists) are familiar with the program themselves.

Spend-Down Intake Procedures. Even for those potential spend-downers who make it to their local welfare departments to apply for Medicaid, actually becoming eligible can be difficult and confusing. Applicant "screening" often takes place in state Medicaid intake procedures. The potential spend-downer with a large spend-down or not immediately obvious health care needs can be discouraged by workers from even completing an application. The difficulties and complications involved in processing the spend-down case and explaining the procedure to the applicant cause many intake workers to screen out potential spend-downers. Almost all local offices visited were understaffed, so that it is not surprising that the more time-consuming spend-down application is discouraged.

Potential spend-downers are also affected at the point of intake by the extent to which an adequate explanation is given to them of the necessary steps involved in spending down. Explanatory materials, if they exist at all, are often confusing. Equally important, workers vary in the extent to which they take the time to explain to the applicants the mechanics of spending down.

Of relevance to this discussion, a substantial number of unsuccessful spend-downers included in the Recipient Survey reported that they did not attempt to spend-down because they did not adequately understand the spend-down procedures.

The Incurment Problem. The principle of incurment as set forth in the enabling legislation for spend-down would seem to work for the benefit of the spend-down applicant. In reality, allowing the spend-downer to incur the spend-down liability has not turned out to be as helpful as it would appear. Three conclusions can be made about incurment with regard to its impact on the spend-down applicant population:

- It is often difficult for spend-down applicants to get providers to extend them credit; therefore, they do not have access to health services and are unable to incur.

- Incurment is easier for spend-downers with acute health care needs than for those in need of chronic care.
- Some states, even though endorsing the principle of incurment in their Medicaid plans, do not allow spend-down applicants to incur health expenses for Medicaid-covered services.

Staying in the Medicaid System. States vary considerably in how they see spend-downers within the Medicaid system. North Carolina, as shown in the survey results, treats spend-downers as they do other Medicaid recipients. They are encouraged to reapply every six months. Spend-down cases there even receive a priority for redetermination since workers know the timeliness of the reapplication is more critical to spend-downers than the other medically needy or the categorically needy Medicaid recipients. As a result, the North Carolina spend-down population has many spend-down "repeaters."

Massachusetts and Maryland automatically terminate spend-downers at the end of their eligibility period, and do not encourage reapplication. Although recipients can, of course, reapply, the burden for this is on them. Spend-downers are regarded by most local offices to be one-time-only or emergency cases and are not considered to be an ongoing part of the Medicaid population.

WHAT OBJECTIVES DOES SPEND-DOWN FULFILL?

So far we have described the spend-down process, explained its administration by state Medicaid programs, and reviewed its impact on the recipient population. However, these features of spend-down shed only limited light on the issue which is of critical concern in a study such as this—the purpose of the spend-down program.

Spend-down can reasonably be viewed as anything from a "disregard" to a form of "national health insurance." Since objectives for the spend-down provision were not prescribed by the law or by Congress, states are left to interpret individually the purposes spend-down must serve. In effect, states can make spend-down into whatever kind of program they want, as long as none of the broad restraints set out by the regulations are violated. In none of the state plans and regulations of the five study states are objectives of spend-down clearly articulated either. Therefore, assessing how well spend-down meets its goals is impossible. Instead, to achieve an assessment of the results of spend-down, current practices and performance can only be evaluated with respect to the achievement of hypothetical objectives of spend-down. The findings of the present research can be analyzed in terms of the extent to which states fulfill these three hypothetical objectives:

- *Spend-down is an equalizer.* (Spend-down graduates the line between those automatically qualified for medical assistance and those who have sufficient resources to meet their usual expenses but whose financial security is threatened by large medical costs.)
- *Spend-down is an emergency insurance program.* (Spend-down functions as catastrophic insurance with the spend-down as an income-related deductible for categorically-related persons.)
- *Spend-down is an ongoing primary care type of health insurance.* (Spend-down functions as most private health insurance with an income-related deductible for categorically-related persons.)

Is Spend-Down an Equalizer?

One theory of what spend-down is trying to do is to remove the sharp division between who can potentially receive Medicaid benefits and who cannot. This was the objective most frequently articulated by top-level staff in the Title XIX agencies in the five study states. Spend-down allows the line between the "haves and have-nots" to be graduated. Ideally, the individual with several dollars of "excess income" is not penalized and pushed into financial ruin while an individual with several dollars less income never runs this risk. The excess income is merely spend-down and the individual obtains Medicaid coverage.

However, both administrative findings and survey results show that spend-down does not, in actuality, function as an equalizer in the financing of health care. First, the procedures required for a spend-downer to become eligible are often a barrier. Accumulating medical expenses is a confusing, often poorly explained process that spend-down applicants must often accomplish on their own initiative. For ambulatory (nonacute) spend-downers, the problem of access often obstructs meeting the spend-down liability, i.e., providers often will not allow incurment of medical expenses from spend-down individuals because of their poor "credit rating" and lack of assured reimbursement. Since many local offices require payment of the expenses used for the spend-down (although this violates federal regulations), another obstruction to meeting the spend-down is amassing not only the expenses but also the "extra" cash to pay off six months' worth of excess income. The spend-downer with acute needs, on the other hand, obtains immediate care because hospitals usually will allow incurment. According to providers, acute care spend-downers rarely pay their liability, which makes the difference between acute and ambulatory spend-downers even more inequitable.

Thus, spend-down is not an equalizer between "haves and have-nots." Unless an emergency need is present, spending-down even a small excess income is a difficult procedure. The individual with excess income in the ambulatory setting is clearly penalized, and often never attains eligibility for Medicaid. These conclusions are borne out by the data results comparing the successful versus the unsuccessful spend-downers. The unsuccessful applicants had more income and thus larger liabilities. Furthermore, the unsuccessful spend-downers had fewer past (already incurred) health bills, while among the successful spend-downers, prior incurment of a portion of the spend-down was a frequent occurrence. It seems, therefore, that for a spend-downer to become eligible requires a small excess income and large medical needs. The probability of successfully spending-down decreases as the size of the spend-down amount increases, even when the medical need stays the same.

The implications of these observations are that spend-down is only an "equalizer" for borderline cases, i.e., individuals who are virtually medically needy anyway. Furthermore, these individuals usually must have acute medical needs for them to successfully achieve Medicaid eligibility. With these caveats, it is difficult to conclude that spend-down in reality functions as an equalizer.

Utah represents the only exception to this conclusion. Utah's system of handling spend-down by assignment of the total excess income amount to the state circumvents the problem of access discussed above. Furthermore, as long as the applicant's declared, projected medical needs are larger than the excess income, there is no deterrent to becoming a "successful spend-downer." The size of the spend-down does not forestall attainment of eligibility; nor does the lack of current large medical expenses.

Is Spend-Down an Emergency Health Insurance Program?

Perhaps the most conclusive finding of the Administrative Analysis and Recipient Survey was that spend-down helps people with emergency needs. The most expeditious and administratively "easy" way of spending-down is with a past or impending hospitalization. The spend-down amount is incurred as a portion of the hospital bill and Medicaid picks up the remainder. In this situation if the hospitalization costs are greater than the excess income, spend-down does, in fact, provide emergency health insurance coverage. However, it provides much more as well. Medicaid will pick up all other health charges for that spend-down individual for the balance of the accounting period. Given the liberal Medicaid benefit package in most states, Medicaid is providing very broad coverage for usually relatively little money. (At six of the seven survey sites, average spend-down amounts were less than $300.) Therefore, Medicaid provides more expansive medical coverage than an emergency health insurance plan.

In summary, spend-down does function to an extent as emergency health insurance. However, taking as given the emergency insurance nature of spend-down, its insertion into the mainstream of the Medicaid program denies efficient and consistent fulfillment of its role. First, the deductible (here the spend-down liability) is seldom paid in hospitals. And second, once the emergency is covered, there are often three months or more of additional coverage for all types of health expenses. Thus, if spend-down is intended to be solely an emergency insurance program, it overreaches its aim, and therefore has significant cost implications in terms of the non-essential health bills Medicaid may pay.

Is Spend-Down an Ongoing Health Insurance Program?

Spend-down, as usually administered, does not provide access to an expansive health maintenance type of insurance plan (with the major exception of Utah and, to some extent, North Carolina). Its inability to extend care to ambulatory clients with primary care (chronic and occasional medical) needs was repeatedly found. Administrative mechanisms are not devised to bring ambulatory or "in own home" spend-downers into the Medicaid system. A variety of deterrents and disincentives exist. Not the least important of these is the issue of access to community health providers unless the medical need is emergent.

That is to say, spending-down is a necessary prerequisite to becoming enrolled in Medicaid, and until an applicant has spent-down, access to care is limited by the cash available to him or the credit providers are willing to extend. As mentioned earlier, Utah provides an exception to this statement by enrolling recipients on the basis of anticipated needs, whether acute or primary, and subsequently requiring monthly payments to the state. As a result enrollment precedes the completion of the spend-down, rather than follows it.

Another deterrent to spend-down working as a type of ongoing health insurance is that the spend-down liability represents such a significant portion of available income for spend-down cases (usually 7–15 percent). As such, the spend-down liability is relatively greater than the cost incurred by the general population for health insurance premiums, deductibles and out-of-pocket health expenses.

In conclusion, then, of all objectives hypothesized for spend-down, functioning as an emergency health insurance program seems to describe most accurately what actually happens with spend-down today. Recipient data clearly supported this conclusion since spend-downers characteristically had large past and ongoing medical expenses. Furthermore, most spend-down liabilities were assigned to hospitals. And finally, the largest proportion of medical charges paid by Medicaid on behalf of spend-down goes to hospitals.

RECOMMENDATIONS

Obviously, spend-down is a critical provision in Medicaid eligibility, since it effec-tively extends Medicaid benefits to a group in need of health care coverage. Without question, it is a significant dimension to Medicaid eligibility and policy.

However, indications are that spend-down, as currently implemented, is not coming close to enrolling the potentially eligible population. It is also obvious that the administration of spend-down is difficult. Spend-down complicates Medicaid operations; consequently, states are forced into violating some of the spend-down regulations in order to achieve management control. As a result, spend-down implementation varies considerably, and the program operates in several different ways among States.

Accordingly, there are some serious gaps and inconsistencies that need to be addressed regarding the spend-down provisions. Recommendations regarding these gaps and inconsistencies include:

- *A clear statement of the federal intent for the spend-down program is the critical first step towards improving spend-down administration.* The federal government and states should be clear on the objectives for the spend-down program so that more specific policies and procedures for its efficient operation can be established.
- *In addition to clarification of federal intent, existing regulations on spend-down with regard to prioritization of the spend-down liability, the incurment principle, the relationship of third-party insurance to the spend-down liability, the accounting period and "in hand" concept need to be refined and modified to insure that they are implementable.* As it currently stands, there are a number of spend-down related regulations which are not complied with by states because they are administratively infeasible or because state officials do not understand them clearly.

- *The administrative efficiency of spend-down could be substantially improved through the creation of procedures expressly designed to handle spend-downers as opposed to other Medicaid recipients.* The use of a distinct administrative structure for spend-down such as that used in Utah would appear to result in substantial improvement toward the integration of spend-down into the overall Medicaid program. Many of the contingency procedures and special checks required for spend-downers in other states are eliminated by Utah's approach; however, Utah's system has not been tested in any large state and continues to have some problems which would require further attention. Use of the Utah approach would require revision of the Medicaid regulations.

- *Spend-down as a means of Medicaid eligibility needs to be restructured so that it is equally available to applicants with both acute and primary (chronic) health care needs.* To remedy the current discrimination, access to medical providers and thus the ability to incur medical expenses should be made equivalent. Utah's administrative approach could be used. Assistance could be given to potential spend-downers by better informing the provider community of spend-down requirements and providing applicants with provisional Medicaid eligibility identification. The use of variable accounting periods which would reduce the size of the spend-down liability is a third alternative.

- *Incentives need to be developed for spend-downers with regard to increasing their incomes and/or maintaining private insurance coverage.* The mar-ginal tax rate for any increased income to spend-downers is 100 percent, and there is no benefit to having third party coverage. The solutions to these problems are difficult, but are worthy of further research.

- *Steps should be taken to improve public knowledge and information of the spend-down provision.* Two types of public information are needed—easy-to-read written materials for potential spend-downers, service agencies, welfare departments and all types of health care providers; and more in-depth information and analysis for policy-makers in the health care and social welfare fields.

- *The medically needy protected income levels should never be lower than the highest payment standard for a given case size used by a state.* The regulations should be changed so that negative bands cannot exist for any category. This currently is allowed through the Section 209(b) of P.L. 92–603 provisions and by the 133⅓% of AFDC payment level limitations for the protected income level.

- *The spend-down provision as a means of Medicaid eligibility should be extended to states which do not have a medically needy program.* The regulations should be amended so that states can set a protected income level for each category of cash assistance at the current payment standard. A uniform level across categories would not be required. A second type of medically needy program consisting of only spend-downers would result; only one income level per category would be relevant to Medicaid eligibility. All Medicaid recipients would be either categorically needy or spend-downers.

25. D.C. Project Analyzes Medicaid Costs In HMO Setting

MICHAEL BARTHEL

Reprinted with permission from *Urban Health* (December 1976). pp. 28. 31. 41.

There continues to be a lively interest in alternatives to the traditional fee-for-service delivery of health care. This has been especially true in urban areas where for some time the alternative most often attempted is the Health Maintenance Organization (HMO) system of delivery of health services.[1]

Since the enactment of P.L. 93-222 (the HMO Act of 1973) this interest has resulted in establishment of a number of HMO's in "medically underserved" populations, including rural and urban areas. Since 1971, the Department of Human Resources of the District of Columbia, in administering the District's Title XIX (Medicaid) program, has offered HMO membership on a voluntary basis to persons eligible for Medicaid.

There are approximately 180,000 Title XIX-covered persons in the District, the great majority of whom receive their health care on a Fee-For-Service (FFS) basis. At the present time 3,000, of those covered, receive their health care service from HMO's. Two HMO's now enroll District residents covered by Medicaid, and a third HMO, plans to open enrollment in the near future.

The D.C. Department of Human Resources (DHR) pays HMO providers or clinics a prepaid fixed monthly fee called the capitation rate. The amount of the fee is set by negotiation of a contract between DHR and each clinic individually and is the same for each Medicaid member at that HMO. The member relinquishes the usual Medicaid card and is issued instead a membership card which is honored only at the HMO in which he is enrolled. The member is free to disenroll at any time and return to the FFS Medicaid system. Medicaid eligibility is recertified on a regular basis for HMO members just as it is for other Medicaid-eligible persons.

To assess the merits of the HMO alternative to FFS health care delivery, enrollment in one of the HMOs was structured according to a research design set up to study comparative results in the two forms of delivery over a three-year period. For this study, DHR entered into a contract in 1971 with Group Health Association (GHA) for GHA to deliver the entire range of health care services to approximately 1,000 Medicaid recipients on a prepaid capitation rate basis. GHA is a long-established HMO with a large enrollment in metropolitan Washington, D.C. This plan for the delivery of comprehensive health services in such a way that the merits of the system might be evaluated was called the DHR-GHA/HMO Demonstration Project.

To control as much as possible all variables which might affect the delivery of health services except for the single variable of the mode of delivery, HMO enrollment of Medicaid eligibles was drawn from a list of volunteers on a random basis, subject to the preservation of demographic characteristics that closely matched those of the District's Medicaid enrollment rolls. Thus, the HMO Medicaid membership featured race, age, sex, and family-size characteristics comparable to some of those of the far greater number of Medicaid eligibles who were receiving health care on a fee-for-service basis.

In addition, a waiver of the necessity of periodic recertification of Medicaid eligibility was obtained (through Section 1115 of Title XIX of the Social Security Act) for the HMO members for the three-year evaluation period. This waiver permitted as thorough an examination as possible of the HMO group's usage and costs of health services, including the collection of extensive utilization and cost data through the three years of the Demonstration Project, without loss of membership through ineligibility. The HMO membership changed, however, through birth, death, voluntary disenrollment, and replacement of members lost from the list of Medicaid volunteers for HMO membership. In this way, the HMO Demonstration Project had a membership of about 1,000 that preserved demographic characteristics comparable to those of the FFS Medicaid system throughout the entire three-year life of the probject.

The HMO members were interviewed on a regular basis, through a questionnaire survey, in regard to numerous consumer aspects of their health care experience. Similarly, a number of selected FFS Medicaid members were surveyed for comparison purposes. Another interview of HMO members was conducted upon their disenrollment, if they chose to withdraw before three years.

In general, consumers were found to be pleased with their experience in the HMO system as compared with their experience with the Medicaid FFS system. The best-liked and least-liked features of the HMO system, and comparative demographic characteristics of its satisfied, dissatisfied, and drop-out consumers, have been reported in greater detail elsewhere.[2, 3]

The remainder of this article presents a closer look at the comparative rates of utilization of health services, comparative cost rates for populations-at-risk, and comparative unit costs of services between the standard FFS Medicaid system and one HMO Medicaid system preserving similar population characteristics.

UTILIZATION AND COST OF SERVICES

The comparison is made between the experience of the two populations in their uses of four kinds of health service transactions over a period of three fiscal years, covering July 1, 1971 through June 30, 1974, the period of the HMO Demonstration Project. These four transactions are: (1) hospital admissions; (2) physician encounters—office visits and hospital visits including inpatient, out-patient, and emergency room encounters, by physicians of all kinds except any specialties within number 4, below; (3) pharmacy transactions (mostly prescription drugs); (4) X-rays, laboratory services, and other providers' services, the latter including services by optometrists, opticians, podiatrists, and visiting nurses.

Table I compares FFS and HMO experience for fiscal years 1972, 1973, and 1974 for each of the above kinds of transactions. The comparison is made specifically on each of three numerical values, (a) *number of uses per person:* the total number of transactions divided by the number of persons-at-risk (mid-year FFS population or monthly average HMO population); (b) *cost per person:* total dollar cost of the type of transaction divided by the number of persons-at-risk; and (c) *unit cost:* dollar

Table I Comparative HMO and Fee-For-Services Rates for Uses, Cost, and Unit Cost, For Comparable Services, During Three Years

Type of Service	Fiscal year	(a) Uses per Person		(b) Cost per Person		(c) Cost Per Use	
		FFS	HMO	FFS	HMO	FFS	HMO
1. Hospital	1972	0.32	0.09	225.98	100.94	713.46	1073.13
Admissions	1973	0.28	0.05	224.03	75.30	786.87	1457.27
	1974	0.27	0.09	229.23	107.72	839.51	1141.35
2. Physician	1972	5.09	4.99	85.78	118.09	16.84	23.68
Encounters	1973	5.99	4.26	105.25	118.51	17.56	27.84
	1974	6.35	3.98	110.40	129.93	17.39	32.66
3. Pharmacy	1972	6.13	3.73	24.07	15.55	3.93	5.06
services	1973	6.54	3.36	26.19	16.93	4.00	6.03
	1974	6.80	4.13	28.12	19.88	4.13	4.81
4. X-Ray, Lab,	1972	0.70	8.22	9.01	47.97	12.87	5.84
& Other	1973	0.76	4.05	10.48	29.37	13.79	7.25
providers	1974	0.79	4.27	10.31	38.27	13.05	8.96

cost divided by the number of transactions of the type.

The numbers of persons-at-risk for all three years are presented in Table II for both delivery systems.

The costs of the services listed above do not, in sum, represent the total cost of all three years of health care paid through either the FFS or HMO systems. The kinds of services taken for inclusion in Table I are the same ones for the entire three years and for both systems.

In addition to these services, the District of Columbia Medicaid program included services that could not be used in the comparison because: (1) a few services paid by FFS payments were not given in the HMO system, and vice-versa; (2) additional services were offered year-to-year in both systems; and (3) in a few instances there was too great a disparity of methods of tabulation to permit a valid comparison.

As an example, the HMO offered from its beginning an entire range of dental services to its Medicaid members, and the Medicaid FFS system has not included these. (These dental benefits were a strong contributor to consumer satisfaction with the HMO

clinic). Table III shows comparative total Medicaid costs per person-at-risk for all three years of the HMO Demonstration Project for the FFS and HMO systems as well. The pairs of columns headed by (a) and (b) of Table III represent: (a) comparable services (the sum of all services presented in Table I); (b) all services paid by Medicaid for the two modes of delivery.

It is seen that comparable services as combined from Table I represent the major part of the total health care costs in either system.

The data of Table I lends itself well to some statistical inference. The arrangement of the set of three numerical rates (a), (b), (c) may be taken as a two-way ("fiscal years" and "transaction types") layout of a

Table II Number of Persons-at-Risk

Fiscal year	Persons in FFS System	Persons in HMO
1972	132,529	893
1973	160,520	987
1974	169,274	943

Table III Comparative Total Costs

Fiscal year	(a) Comparable Services combined from Table 1		(b) All Services paid by Medicaid	
	FFS	HMO	FFS	HMO
1972	$344.84	$282.55	$345.61	$341.45
1973	365.95	240.11	393.00	299.36
1974	378.06	295.80	416.96	372.21

factorial experimental design. The relative rankings of these rates are then used in calculation of the suitable rank-test statistic (mult variate extension of Friedman's Q for analysis of variance based on rank sums).[4] The statistical hypothesis to be tested is that of similarity in the HMO and FFS numerical rates. The result is $X^2 = 19.6$, with $p = .02$.

The inference to be drawn from this is that the overall usage rates, cost rates, and unit costs, taken as an aggregate, are significantly lower for the HMO group than for the FFS group.

Due to the great contribution of hospital usage to the overall cost of health care,[5] a further table is included for the purpose of comparing the three-year hospitalization experience of the two modes of delivery of Medicaid services.

Table IV suggests that within an HMO system, hospital admissions tend to be far less frequent and to carry a shorter length of stay in number of days per admission than is found using the FFS system. This result is in line with the usual conjectures about the possible advantages that an HMO might be expected to offer: this system of delivery encourages "preventive care," reinforcing efforts to prevent hospitalization except when truly necessary.

APPLICATION OF FINDINGS

It may be concluded that the HMO system, when offered as an alternative to fee-for-service delivery of health care, can represent a significant overall reduction in the rates of utilization and cost of services. For the three-year period examined here the average saving in cost is about 25 percent.

There are, of course, some possible ways in which the above conclusion could be qualified or limited. It seems fair to mention two areas of such a possibility in this study. (a) *Voluntary HMO membership.* Even with the exercise of control over the demographic compositions of HMO and FFS groups, there could still remain some uncontrolled factors that affect the use of health services. Most obvious is the possible influence of the selection of the HMO group from a list of volunteers. It is a matter

Table IV Comparative Hospital Days

Fiscal year	(a) Number of Days per Person		(b) Average Cost per Hospital Day		(c) Average Number of Days per Admission	
	FFS	HMO	FFS	HMO	FFS	HMO
1972	4.08	0.83	55.39	122.14	12.88	8.79
1973	4.62	0.54	48.45	140.23	16.24	10.39
1974	4.01	1.07	57.10	100.77	14.70	11.33

of guesswork as to what is the nature of this influence, or if it really exists. (2) *Medicaid eligibility.* Some characteristics of the universe of Medicaid eligibles, e.g., the preponderance of single-female-parent households and relatively few males in the 15-44 age group may seem to limit application of any findings only to one city's Medicaid population. However, the great number of Medicaid eligibles in the District of Columbia (currently 180,000, or about one-fourth of the District's population) appears large enough for inclusion of sufficient numbers within every demographic subgroup to permit a fairly safe application of the inferences more broadly.

In sum, the findings of this study of comparative HMO rates of cost and utilization verify the desirability of the continued growth of prepaid group practice as a worthwhile delivery system for health care services.

REFERENCES

1. (Special Feature): "HMO: Its working in Detroit." *Urban Health.* Vol. 4, No. 2, April 1975, p. 30ff.

2. D.C. Department of Human Resources, Office of Planning and State Agency Affairs: *Final Report on HMO Evaluation.* Report Submitted to U.S. Department of Health, Education, and Welfare under Research grant No. 97-P-00034/3-01, April 1974.

3. Michael Barthel and Barbara Humphries: "Dropouts from a Medicaid HMO plan." *DHR Journal* (In press).

4. M.L. Puri and P.K. Sen: *Nonparametric Methods in Multivariate Analysis.* New York: John Wiley and Sons, Inc., 1971. p. 266ff.

5. *U.S. News and World Report.* Vol. 78, No. 2 June 16, 1975, p. 53.

26. Medicare and Medicaid Reimbursement for Rural Health Clinics, Public Law 95–210

ADMINISTRATOR'S REPORT, HEALTH CARE FINANCING ADMINISTRATION NUMBER 3, DECEMBER 14, 1977.

Number 3   *December 14, 1977*

On December 13, 1977, President Carter signed into law (Public Law 95–210) a bill which provides for Medicare and Medicaid reimbursement to rural health clinics.

Many isolated rural communities have not been able to attract or retain a physician and have come to rely on clinics which do not follow the traditional model of physician delivery of medical services. These clinics are, in many instances, staffed only by specially trained nurse practitioners and physician assistants who are trained to provide medical care traditionally performed by physicians. Although there is physician supervision, it is generally indirect rather than "over-the-shoulder".

Unlike clinics where there is a physician present full-time, these rural health clinics had not been eligible prior to this legislation for any Medicare reimbursement. Services provided by nonphysicians to Medicare beneficiaries have either been paid for out-of-pocket by the beneficiary, picked up under a grant, or written off by the clinic as bad debts. This law is the result of some concern on the part of the Administration and the Congress that without Medicare reimbursement these clinics would not be able to become self-sufficient.

Following is a summary of the major provisions of P.L. 95–210.

Robert A. Derzon
Administrator
Health Care Financing Administration

COVERAGE OF CLINICS IN RURAL AREAS

Medicare and Medicaid coverage will be provided for services furnished in clinics which are located in areas designated by the Bureau of the Census as rural, and by the Secretary as medically underserved, where the supply of physicians is not sufficient to meet the needs of the local residents. Such clinics may be either physician-directed or those which do not have a full-time physician. Once a clinic establishes its eligibility with respect to being located in a rural, medically underserved area, the clinic may retain its special status under this law even if the area changes.

COVERED SERVICES

Services provided by a physician assistant or nurse practitioner working in a rural clinic will be covered under Medicare and Medicaid if: (1) they are otherwise covered when provided by a physician; and (2) the physician assistant or nurse practitioner is legally authorized under State law to perform the services. Services and supplies which are presently covered when provided as incident to a physician's service will also be covered. In addition, if there is a shortage of home health agencies in the area, covered services will include part-time nursing care furnished by a nurse to a homebound patient.

COST-RELATED REIMBURSEMENT FOR RURAL HEALTH CLINIC SERVICES

Medicare payment to the clinic will be equal to 80 percent of the costs which are reasonable for the efficient delivery of services to Medicare beneficiaries. Clinics will be required to accept the amount determined by the Secretary as the full charge for the services and may bill the beneficiary only for the amount of the Medicare deduct-ible and coinsurance. Medicaid plans are required to reimburse the clinics for covered services at a rate equal to 100 percent of the reasonable cost as determined for Medicare purposes.

REQUIREMENTS OF RURAL HEALTH CLINIC

Clinics will be required to make arrangements with a physician for periodic review of all services covered under Medicare and Medicaid which are provided by the physician assistant, nurse practitioner, or nurse. The physician must be available to prepare necessary medical orders, for referral of patients when necessary, and for assistance in medical emergencies, but not be required to be physically present when the services are provided.

The clinics are required to make arrangements with one or more Medicare and Medicaid certified hospitals for referral and admission of patients who need services not available at the clinic. Clinics will also be required to maintain medical records on all patients; develop written policies governing the provision of covered services with the advice of professional personnel, including one or more physicians and one or more physician assistants or nurse practitioners; directly provide routine clinical laboratory services as prescribed by the Secretary; have available drugs and biologicals that are needed in medical emergencies; have appropriate procedures for storing, administering, and dispensing drugs and biologicals; and meet other standards the Secretary determines are necessary for the health and safety of patients.

PARAPROFESSIONAL PERSONNEL COVERED BY THE LAW

A physician assistant, nurse practitioner, or nurse midwife may perform such services as he/she is legally authorized to perform under State law and must meet such training, education, and experience requirements (or any combination thereof) as the Secretary prescribes in regulations. For purposes of providing nursing services to homebound beneficiaries, the term nurse includes a registered or licensed practical nurse under applicable State law.

DEMONSTRATION PROJECTS

The law contains authority for several demonstration projects. In order to evaluate changes which might be made in the Medicare program to provide more efficient and cost-effective reimbursement, the law requires the Secretary to conduct demonstrations in urban medically underserved areas with respect to physician-directed clinics which employ physician assistants or nurse practitioners. The Secretary is required to report his findings and recommendations for legislative changes to Congress with respect to this project by January 1, 1981. The Secretary is required to conduct a study and report within one year to the Congress concerning the feasibility and desirability of substituting a copayment for each clinic visit for the deductible and coinsurance required in present Medicare law. The Secretary is also required to study the advantages and disadvantages of extending Medicare coverage to mental health, alcoholism and drug abuse centers and to report his findings to the Congress within 6 months.

EFFECTIVE DATES

The law will apply to services provided to Medicare beneficiaries on or after March 1, 1978. The law will apply to services provided to Medicaid beneficiaries on or after July 1, 1978, with additional time permitted where enabling State legislation is necessary to allow implementation.

27. Puncturing the Myths about Those Medicaid Moneymongers

RICHARD MARTINSON

Reprinted from the August 1977 issue of *Dental Management*. This article is copyrighted, 1977, by Harcourt Brace Jovanovich. All rights reserved.

There is perhaps no more maligned professional group in America today than those who provide medical and dental care to the nation's indigent—and earn big money by doing so. For a time last year, hardly a day went by that some physician or dentist wasn't accused of making exorbitant amounts at the expense of our government and our poor. Six-figure incomes regularly got banner headline treatment in our largest and most prestigious newspapers. Charges of fraud were leveled at Medicaid practitioners with alarming regularity.

Adding fuel to fire, the Department of Health, Education, and Welfare announced that, in 1975, 312 dental practices in the United States received $100,000 or more in Medicaid payments. Of these, some 14 practices earned more than $400,000 in Title XIX receipts. And people began asking the obvious question:

Is this the gold fleecing, the something-for-nothing dream that all people search for—and the press and politicians claim that these dentists have found?

Under the Freedom of Information Act, anyone can ask for and receive the complete roster of dentists and physicians receiving more that $100,000 a year under the Medicaid program. *This magazine did exactly that!* And then we took the unprec-

edented step of sending a detailed two-page questionnaire to every one of the 312 listed dental practices, asking explicit questions about their gross and net income, offices, staff, type of practice, and practice location.

The reaction to our survey was overwhelming, with well over half responding (another 10 per cent were returned as undeliverable). Despite our assurances that all replies would be held in confidence, many volunteered to sign their questionnaire returns.

Clearly, this is a subject that Medicaid dentists want to be heard about. And, indeed, the responses were noteworthy for more than just the fact that they came from the highest-paid Medicaid dentists in the U.S. They were noteworthy for what they said and for what the dentists who participated in the Medicaid program feel about that program.

The DM survey sought to identify the Medicaid dentists in three ways: by their gross income, the type of area in which they practice, and the type of practice they have. The key findings:

- Most of the surveyed dentists grossed between $100,000 (the government's cutoff point for gross income publication) and $150,000 from Medicaid in 1976 (though the Department of Health, Education and Welfare released names for 1975, the responding dentists supplied figures for 1976). Some 20 per cent of the respondents grossed more than $150,000—and about 6 percent grossed over $200,000.

- For the most part, the Medicaid dentists practice in the center city—because, as one surveyed practitioner puts it, "That's where the poor people are."
- The predominant type of practice for the Medicaid dentist is the group practice. Some 60 percent of the surveyed dentists reported that this is the type of practice they have. The remaining 40 per cent are divided equally between solo practices and partnerships.

Thus, in about 80 per cent of the cases, the amount of money a Medicaid dental office grosses is hardly the amount the individual dentist grosses. To find out just how many slices come out of each Medicaid pie, the DM survey asked the group and partnership practitioners just how many dentists they were associated with. The average: three—with several dentists working with as many as a half-dozen other practitioners.

The logical inference is in this case the correct one: The higher the Medicaid billings, the more dentists working in the office.

To a certain extent, this also held true for dental assistants and hygienists, though as a general rule the Medicaid dentists all employed a relatively large number of assistants. Specifically, the DM survey found that the typical Medicaid dentist employs three assistants; and one full or part-time hygienist. But there are almost as many exceptions here as there are typical dentists. A Covina, Calif., dentist who works with four other dentists, employs eight assistants. A San Francisco practitioner who works in a group with five other dentists (one full timer, four part-timers) employs 11 full-time assistants and 15 part-timers. A Paterson, N.J., dentist working in partnership with two other dentists employs eight assistants and one hygienist. So whether by design or circumstances, Medicaid dentists have large staffs—and large payrolls.

In many instances, they also have more than one office. In fact, 30 percent of the surveyed dentists work out of more than one office. Moreover, virtually every dentist surveyed by DENTAL MANAGEMENT has more than one treatment room—often far more. Five is the average number.

What emerges, then, is a profile of a Medicaid dentist that is far different from the one painted by the consumer press: We see a man who grosses a large sum of money, but pays out a good deal of it in employee salaries, office rent and overhead.

But these statistics of the Medicaid dentist's practice don't tell the full story about the type of practice he has, how much money he brings home, and whether or not he feels that being a Medicaid dentist really pays.

Medicaid dental offices see many patients in the course of a day—often as many as 100. However, as many as three and four dentists share this patient load. For the individual dentist, the patient load is between 20 and 30 patients a day. This figure is not much different from the patient load handled by the typical fee-for-service dentist.

The difference, say critics of the Medicaid program, is in the amount of money these dentists earn. Just how much do they net after expenses. According to the DENTAL MANAGEMENT survey, the typical Medicaid dentist took home between $30,000 and $50,000 from Medicaid last year—and, in most cases, that figure represented the bulk of his total income. There were as well a handful of dentists whose total net income after expenses exceeded $100,000—though here, just a small percentage of that income usually came from Medicaid.

Generally, the figures would seem to indicate that a dentist who devotes a substantial portion of his practice to welfare patients can make a good living from Medicaid—if he can cope with the problems. The Medicaid dentists, as a group, find much wrong with Medicaid—and very little right.

To look at what's right first, dentists did find some advantages with Medicaid. Foremost among them: the opportunity to perform a valuable service for people who might otherwise not receive it. Says a St. Petersburg, Fla., dentist: "If it weren't for us, these people could never secure dental care." Adds a San Francisco practitioner: "Medicaid makes it possible for economically disadvantaged persons to receive dental care. These persons might not otherwise be able to afford such care." And this, from a large Medicaid provider in Hawaii: "The state is sincerely concerned that the recipients receive proper dental care. They are willing to discuss treatment with us, process forms promptly, and pay promptly."

Other dentists talk about the advantages of guaranteed payment, the ability to treat entire families simultaneously, the elimination of the need to discuss money with patients. A Philadelphia dentist lauds the fact that he deals with a similar patient load each day, while a man from Palos Heights, Ill., cites the advantages of not having to convince patients that they need dental care or having to spend time detailing treatment, and the opportunity for the dentist to earn additional money.

So much for the advantages. The surveyed dentists were far more vehement in citing the disadvantages of working with Medicaid. Broadly speaking, their objections fall into five categories and the dentists cited them all with almost equal frequency:

1. There is an inordinately high rate of failure to keep appointments—and very little sense of responsibility concerning these appointments.
2. The economic restrictions of the program dictate inferior care in many instances.
3. Politicians, the general public—and even some dentists—view Medicaid dentists with more than a bit of distaste.
4. Payments are almost always late, and almost never adequate.
5. The paperwork burden is all-consuming—and approval is often needed for other than routine procedures.

Says one Minneapolis dentist: "Over one-third of the patients don't keep their appointments. On some days we will schedule over 50 patients—and see just 20. Since they aren't paying, they don't care. Moreover, if you question them about it, they simply change dentists."

Adds a Boston practitioner: "The system does not penalize patients for breaking appointments; rather, it ignores the problem."

Finally, this from a Los Angeles dentist: "The failure to keep appointments is part of a larger problem: These people simply don't give a damn. Maybe if they had to pay, they'd care more."

There is equal animosity over state control of Medicaid—and program restrictions. "We are at the mercy of the state," says a doctor from Baltimore. "Last year in Maryland, without warning, they cut out all dental care on patients over 21 except for emergency work." Notes a practitioner from Flushing, N.Y.: "If you want to do something other than routine dentistry, you must wait for approval . . . and wait . . . and wait . . ." A Jamaica, N.Y. dentist adds that "the Medicaid program simply doesn't cover necessary procedures."

The stigma of being a Medicaid dentist is very real to the people who work with the program—and very much resented. "The politicians and the media assume that you are dishonest," says a Chicago practitioner. "It's as cut-and-dried as that."

The image of the Medicaid dentist is awful," says a New York City practitioner. "People think you're either incompetent or crooked." An Atlanta dentist resents the fact that he's been cast as a villain—and feels that dentistry in general must share the blame. "Sure I billed $100,000 through Medicaid in 1975. But I'm involved in Medicaid only because I feel it's my moral obligation to help. If every dentist shared my views, you wouldn't find my name on the list of $100,000 dentists—because more dentists would be participating in Medicaid. And speaking of the Medicaid list, it took three of us to bill that much dentistry, but because the practice is incorporated the money came to me. In 1976 we only produced $60,000 in billings among the three of us."

"People feel I'm a cheat and a fraud, a man who makes his money at the expense of poor people," comments a Cleveland dentist. And a Detroit practitioner adds that "not only does the public think I'm a crook, many of my fellow practitioners think so as well. Because of this stigma and other problems, those dentists who really wanted to serve are turned off and are no longer accepting Medicaid patients. The hassle simply isn't worth it."

Perhaps the biggest complaint that Medicaid dentists have about Medicaid is the slow rate of payment. "It is absolutely ridiculous to have to wait four, five and six months to get paid." grouses a San Francisco dentist. "What do we tell our creditors—that the government doesn't always pay on time? I don't know what the solution is—except for me to get out of the Medicaid business."

A Chicago practitioner remarks that "the biggest drawback to Medicaid comprises two parts: a low fee schedule, and extreme difficulty in receiving the proper reimbursement for work performed." A Boston dentist feels that the biggest drawback is the "lack of coordination between different levels of the welfare structure which necessitates extra help to fill out forms and contact social workers for clarification of decisions of the welfare departments."

For a Hollywood-based dentist, the biggest problems are "fees that are 20 per cent less than usual, a 3-month wait for payment, the usual bureaucratic hassles."

A Baltimore dentist laments the fact that fees haven't been raised since 1970. And this, from an Ohio dentist: "The program prevents the practitioner from doing the best work possible because of indiscriminate pricing according to computer profiles, not according to patient needs. At least one service has not had a fee in 13 years."

For one Atlanta practitioner, the late payment problem has gone to the ridiculous. "Would you believe 12 to 18 months—and sometimes longer?" he asks.

Finally, there's the paperwork—and many of the comments about late payments also hold true for the red tape involved. An Irvington, N.J. dentist has noticed an increase in the paperwork of late, along with a corresponding increase in the administrative chores and headaches. And a Hartford dentist remarks that the "paperwork involved in the preparation, correction and submission of invoices is intolerable."

There are other complaints as well—complaints about having to work in high crime areas, complaints about drugs, complaints about the lack of gratitude Medicaid patients have for the dentists who treat them.

As a result, many of the "moneymongering Medicaid dentists," those grossing more than $100,000 from the program, are disillusioned with Medicaid, more would like to get out than stay in, and more feel Medicaid is an obligation rather than an easy way to make money in the dental profession.

Which brings us full circle. Do dentists strike it rich in Medicaid—at the expense of the patient and the taxpayer?

Hardly. Undoubtedly some shoddy dentistry exists in Medicaid dentistry—as it does in every area of the health profession. But most Medicaid dentists view themselves as honest, hard working—and, in their opinion, underpaid for the services they perform. They are also more than a bit chagrined that the government has published a list of incomes which is, in itself, clearly a distortion of reality.

As a Chicago dentist put it in responding to the DM survey: "It is obviously unfair to publish 'gross' income figures—ie., the amount of money paid to a dentist—since that implies that his figure is net taxable income. The press and the government never point out that the dentist must pay from this money all his expenses, including lab bills, salaries, rent, utilities, insurance, and supplies."

There are many Medicaid dentists who share that view—and a growing number who are getting tired of having to defend it. Consider just one of them. . . .

PROFILE OF A 'MEDICAID DENTIST'

There's no such thing as a "typical" Medicaid dentist, any more than there's any other kind of typical dentist. Yet, Dr. Kenneth Webster is as representative as any responding to the Dental Management survey.

The Long Beach, Calif., dentist feels that much of the fault in Medicaid should be laid at the doorstep of the recipients, and steps should be taken to prevent them from taking advantage of the system.

More specifically, Dr. Webster feels that "this reform should begin with a schedule of mandatory co-payments structured around individual needs. All recipients should pay some amount into the program to share the enormous burden of the taxpayers. I find a large majority of those treated at my clinic are seeking public welfare merely because it is as lucrative as many menial jobs."

The clinic Dr. Webster refers to treated nearly 5,000 patients last year under California's Medi-Cal program. In return, the clinic received approximately $144,000 in fees. The average fee per patient: $288.

To provide this service, Dr. Webster employs three other dentists, five chairside assistants, four clerical assistants, two hygienists, two laboratory personnel, and a nurse-anesthetist. They operate out of 10 treatment rooms located in a center in a large urban neighborhood. On an average day, Dr. Webster and his colleagues treat 60 patients, of which 25 per cent are covered by Medi-Cal.

According to Dr. Webster, the single biggest drawback to Medi-Cal is the lack of appreciation most people have for that which they get free. "Certainly it is hard for me to imagine someone not showing up for several hundred dollars worth of 'free' dental work, but it apparently holds little value since it is basically unearned."

Dr. Webster is asking some tough questions about the Medicaid program and his role within that program. He appears ready to wait for some answers—and to deal with the system as best he can until those answers are forthcoming.

28. Impact of Utilization Controls (UC) on Medicaid

ANTHONY P. CAPPELLI and HALSTEIN STRALBERG
Reprinted with permission.

SRS Comments to the Reader

This study should be helpful to individuals and organizations attempting to determine ways and means of controlling the costs of health care services. The study outlines specific mechanisms which were found to be effective in reducing costs in the three state Medicaid programs studied. Most importantly, the study indicates that there are administrative mechanisms that can be established which effectively reduce costs.

A word of caution, however, is required. For ease of reference, the authors of this report have used the term utilization control (UC) to identify any management mechanism utilized by states to control utilization of services and the quality of care found in institutional health care settings. Some of the management mechanisms studied by the contractor were implemented as a result of section 1903(g). Others are mechanisms which the states have independently chosen to establish and which others may wish to utilize. It should be clearly understood that the authors have not used the term utilization control to refer collectively to all those mechanisms specifically outlined in section 1903(g) of the Social Security Act. *For example, the study does not include an analysis of any UR committee, obviously one of the major components of section 1903(g).*

Health care costs have risen dramatically on a yearly basis over the last decade. Such increases have focused the attention of Congress, the administration, health professionals, and the general public on improving cost control and accountability in health services financing and delivery. Simultaneously, there is a growing concern that increases in health care costs have not been accompanied by equal growth in access to or quality of health care.

Recent legislation (e.g., PL 92-603 and 1903(g)[1]) has strengthened the federal requirements for control of utilization by defining minimum Utilization Control (UC) standards to be met by state Medicaid programs as a condition for full federal financial participation. In response to these requirements, states have adopted a variety of UC methods/programs which focus on improving the management of the Medicaid program by emphasizing accountability while maintaining the provision of necessary care. Many of the states have had effective UC programs in place prior to the recent federal legislation.

Earlier studies undertaken by HEW, state agencies, and private organizations have provided incomplete and partly contradictory conclusions as to the effectiveness of the various UC programs implemented. The lack of firm evidence regarding the effectiveness of UC has caused doubts about the program's usefulness, particularly in view of the increases in total Medicaid expenditures in spite of intensified UC efforts by most states.

The objective of this study undertaken by Universal Analytics, Inc., (UAI), was to analyze, in depth, the effectiveness of UC procedures in selected states, and to develop a general analytical methodology which could be applied to measure the effectiveness of UC in other states. The study focused on *inpatient institutional services* only, i.e., acute hospitals, skilled nursing facilities (SNFs) and intermediate care facilities (ICFs), which constitute the largest share of Medicaid expenditures.

To further define study objectives, UAI's initial step was to isolate the assumptions or hypotheses implicit in the federal UC legislation. Four such assumptions were identified: (1) UC is cost effective, i.e., reduces overall institutional Medicaid expenditures, (2) UC results in changes in utilization patterns of Medicaid services leading to more efficient use of health care resources, (3) fewer unnecessary or inappropriate services are rendered, and (4) UC leads to improved quality of care for Medicaid patients. The verification or disprovement of of these hypotheses was a primary objective of the study. An additional objective was to evaluate the relative effectiveness of different UC procedures.

The term Utilization Control (UC), for purposes of this study, refers to the procedures employed by health care professionals for the review and certification of the necessity, appropriateness, and quality of institutional care provided Medicaid patients. During Phase I of this study,[2] a classification scheme was developed to identify specific review/certification procedures. The subsequent study focused on the following state-administered general review procedures: (1) Preadmission Review, aimed at avoiding unnecessary admission; (2) Periodic Concurrent Review, to determine the medical necessity of continued stay; and (3) On-Site Medical Review (MR) and Independent Professional Review (IPR), aimed at assuring the quality and appropriateness of long-term care.

As discussed later in the state reports, the analysis of hospital UR committees and retrospective review procedures were excluded from the present study because data required was not available. Recent federal legislation requiring concurrent review (within three days) of hospital admissions has caused significant changes in operations of many UR committees and makes the study of retrospective review less relevant.

Three states were selected for the in-depth study of UC impact: (1) Michigan, (2) Virginia, and (3) California. This selection was based on the criteria that these specific states (1) employed differing UC methods, (2) agreed to cooperate in the study, and more important, (3) maintained the historical data records required in the analysis. Data collected in each state included: (1) computerized records of all paid claims for Medicaid institutional services, covering a period of time before and after implementation of the UC procedure under study; (2) samples of manual records of review activity, used to trace specific service denials and transfers between care levels; (3) Medicaid eligibility statistics; and (4) detailed institutional cost data.

The detailed results obtained in each state will be presented later in this report. However, the following *major conclusions* which emerged from the analysis can be reported:

- All of the state review methods studied appear to be *cost effective* (i.e., cost avoidances exceeded administrative costs).
- UC has been associated with significant *changes in institutional utilization* patterns (generally in the direction of less expensive modes of care).

- Declining denial rates seem to indicate that UC is an on-going *deterrent* to unnecessary utilization.

The magnitude of the net cost savings estimates for the years studied varied from 2.5 percent in Virginia to over 11 percent in Michigan and 14 percent in California of the total institution-related Medicaid expenditures. The changes in utilization patterns were in the direction of fewer admissions, reduced lengths of stay, and a shift from higher to lower levels of care.

The preadmission review programs studied were found to be the most cost effective; that is, they were associated with the highest savings at lower administrative costs than other review methods. In Michigan, the initial rate of SNF admission denials was 25 percent, dropping later to around 15 percent. California's preadmission review program was associated with a hospital admission rate drop of 13 percent and contributed also to reducing length of stay through prior determination of the number of days appropriate for each patient. Concurrent Reviews were found linked with additional savings that could not be realized through preadmission review. Comparing the hospital concurrent review program in Virginia (applied to stays over 15 days) and California (using length of stay guidelines based on ailment diagnosis), the California system was clearly more effective, although it also resulted in higher administrative costs.

The on-site MR/IPR programs studied in California and Michigan resulted in detection of additional cases of inappropriate or unnecessary care that could not be observed from the forms analysis conducted during preadmission or concurrent review. The net effect was a shift towards lower care levels, from SNFs to ICFs and from ICFs to homes for the aged or supervised residential care programs.

An important objective of MR/IPR is to ensure proper quality of care for SNF and ICF patients. In fact, the MR/IPR require-ments were in large part an outgrowth of a number of reports on scandalous conditions in some nursing homes [3]. The reduced utilization rates (particularly in expensive care) associated with UC are not inconsistent with the quality-of-care requirements. Samples of medical review records revealed patient transfers both to higher and lower care levels, indicating that patients were simply being assigned to the level of care appropriate to their medical needs. By accompanying California MR personnel on on-site patient reviews, UAI obtained first-hand evidence of the positive impact these review teams have on improving the quality of care.

The findings on cost effectiveness must be tempered by a consideration of the timing of the study data and the methodological techniques employed. The following qualifications should be considered:

1. The 1972 period was a time when ICFs were being covered under Medicaid for the first time and the nursing home industry was reacting to the stringent HEW standards for SNFs. Although MR was found to be the mechanism for shifting patients to lower levels of long term care, it must be recognized that the industry was ripe for that type of shift and only after 1972 was this financially feasible. Consequently, the effects noted are consistent with a stiffened state attitude regarding appropriateness of level of care being provided to patients.

2. The project was not commissioned to investigate the disposition of patients denied institutional admission, so the costs of their alternate care are not included. Consequently, the inclusion of this consideration would have reduced the extent of cost effectiveness found for UC.

3. The methodology used addressed the increased unit cost of hospital care for Medicaid patients that results from occupancy losses due to denials of

admissions and extended stay. If it had also included the increased costs to the public at large because of occupancy loss, the computed cost effectiveness would have been much lower.

4. For many of the admission/extension denials resulting from UC, a portion of the cost (for some older patients, 90 percent) would have been paid by the Medicare program. Thus, if cost savings to the Medicare program had been included, total savings estimates would have been higher.

5. In estimating total SNF patient days avoided, an assumption based on the expected continued stay for an average SNF patient was used in determining SNF patient days avoided per denial or transfer.

6. Since the study considered only a necessarily methodologically-biased sample of three states, extreme caution should be exercised in extending these conclusions to other states.

In addition to the above conclusions, the study led to important insights regarding the effect of external factors on UC effectiveness. This insight, although not part of the original study objectives, may have some bearing in shaping future UC policy decisions. Some of the factors found to be of importance regarding UC effectiveness included: (1) population density (UC impact was greater in urban areas), (2) type of institution (e.g. impact of UC was greater in proprietary than in community institutions), (3) on-site review team composition (e.g., MR teams with a physician present exhibited higher transfer rates than nurse-only teams), (4) previous care level (e.g., SNF admission denials were less for patients previously hospitalized), and (5) availability of alternative levels of care. It is clear that the effectiveness of a UC program is affected by the environment in which it operates. As will be discussed later, UAI believes important conclusions

could be obtained from further studies of these factors that influence UC effectiveness.

Some of the above conclusions, particularly those regarding UC cost effectiveness, may appear surprising in view of the results reported in an earlier study [4]. Considering this, special importance was attached to the validation of all major results. The primary validation approach was based on the comparison of results obtained from two independent analytical models applied to different sources of raw data. The two models basically involved: (1) trend analysis of utilization statistics before and after UC implementation, and (2) sampling of manual review records to determine the UC effects traceable to specific denials or care level transfers.

In the development of these models [5], we attempted to avoid the pitfalls encountered in earlier studies. The basic analytical approach used was to establish trends in Medicaid utilization by operating on data for the period prior to or "before" implementation of the review method studied. These trends were projected to periods "after" UC implementation and compared with "after UC" utilization data to estimate the impact of UC. All trends were adjusted for changes in factors affecting utilization, including the size and composition of the eligible population, patient age distribution, and diagnostic case mix. Focusing directly on trends in utilization, rather than costs as was done in Reference 4, avoided the many factors that influence Medicaid costs such as inflation, price controls, reimbursement policy changes, variations in co-insurance coverage, etc. These economic distortions make it difficult, if not impossible, to isolate the effects of UC by a direct study of cost trends. The measured utilization impact, of course, can be later translated into UC cost savings estimates.

The trend analysis approach was selected for a variety of reasons. The month-to-month availability of detailed utilization data from paid claims tapes allowed for the detection of reversals in utilization trends at the time specific UC methods were implemented. An earlier comparative study of analytical techniques [6] indicated that a trend analysis approach is most reliable for predicting changes in medical utilization.

To attain accurate results, it was found crucial to use detailed computerized data, which allowed a separate analysis for each Medicaid aid category, as well as for different geographic areas within each state. This detailed study approach allowed adjustment for different growth patterns in each area and aid category as well as isolation of data anomalies. Conclusions reached through this approach were not apparent from aggregate data summaries maintained by the states. Appropriate statistical tests were incorporated to ensure the validity of results obtained (i.e., apparent trend reversals were not simply due to random data variations) and to establish confidence intervals for specific impact estimates. In the study of utilization trends before and after UC, adjustments were also made for factors affecting these trends. For example, to appropriately assess the length of stay impact, it was necessary to make adjustments for changes in patient age distribution and diagnostic case mix (using available CPHA [7] hospital length of stay statistics). The importance of this adjustment was illustrated in Virginia where the average length of stay was reduced by 1.05 days over the study period. This reduction, however, was in part due to the reduced average age among Medicaid hospital patients. The adjusted estimate indicated that the reduction associated with UC was only 0.64 days per admission. To validate the trend analysis results, UAI also estimated UC impact based on samples of manual review records to determine the UC effects traceable to specific denials or care level transfers. This method is based on totally different raw data, and compatibility of results between the two methods is therefore a strong indication of the validity of the conclusions reached.

An interesting conclusion emerged from comparison of the results of the two models. In the period immediately following the implementation of a new UC review procedure, the two methods yield approximately the same result, i.e., the total impact determined from trend analysis is traceable to specific review decisions. Over time (six months or less), however, the traceable impact declines significantly. The observed trend of declining denial rates strongly suggests that UC has an on-going deterrent effect as providers become familiar with review criteria over time. A corollary of the above observation is that when a UC procedure has been in effect for a long time, its full benefit may no longer be apparent. Because there are relatively few denials and patient transfers, the review procedure may come to be seen as a case of unnecessary bureaucracy, while its main benefit has been in the deterrent effects, which can be ascertained only by going back to the time when the review process was first implemented.

The above discussion has focused on the study of UC impact on Medicaid utilization. To translate the measured impact on utilization into current estimates of cost savings, two important considerations were required: (1) the effect of reduced hospital occupancy rates, and (2) UC administrative costs. As a result of reduced utilization, UC has had the effect of reducing hospital occupancy. An in-depth study of sampled hospital cost reports indicated that over 60 percent of hospital costs are fixed (i.e., basically independent of the occupancy rate). These fixed costs are distributed over fewer patients when occupancy rates are reduced. It follows that 60 percent of the potential UC cost savings may be negated due to higher hospital per diem rates. The actual savings to the Medicaid program may still be significantly higher than 40 percent, since the fixed costs are distributed over all patients, not only Medicaid. As an example, it was estimated that in Virginia 89 percent of the total gross cost avoidances were actually realized as savings by the Medicaid program. These cost savings estimates would, of course, be lower (i.e., 40 percent) if the increased costs to the public at large due to occupancy losses are included.

The administrative costs of UC were obtained from the state agencies in order to estimate net UC cost savings. In each case, administrative costs were significantly less than costs avoided. In other words, the UC programs were cost effective. It should be recognized, however, that this conclusion may not apply to other non-institutional Medicaid services such as outpatient clinics, physician visits, drug prescriptions, etc. The study of UC impact on these services was outside the scope of the present study.

A brief summary of the study performed in each state and major conclusions reached, is provided below.

MICHIGAN

The study in this state concentrated on long-term care facilities (SNFs and ICFs) since insufficient data was available to consider hospitals. The review methods studied included: (1) Preadmission Review (PA) for admission to Skilled Nursing Facilities (SNFs), and (2) Semi-annual On-Site Medical Review (MR) in Skilled and Intermediate Care Facilities (ICFs).

Both Preadmission Review (PA and Medical Review (MR) became effective in Michigan during 1972. During that year, dramatic changes occurred in the utilization patterns for SNFs and ICFs. However, it should be recalled that coverage for ICF care was mandated for the first time. To study these changes, over 1,800,000 computerized payment records for the years 1969 through 1973 were analyzed to determine trends in admissions, discharges, patient days, and cost with and without UC. At the same time, 6,500 manually sampled records of review recommendations were

analyzed to determine traceable UC effects.

With due consideration to the qualifications discussed earlier, the Michigan study clearly established the utilization impact and cost effectiveness of the PA/MR program. These conclusions were arrived at both by trend analysis of the computerized utilization data and analysis of the sampled review records. Additionally, the study provided considerable insight concerning the factors that influence UC effectiveness.

Some of the specific conclusions reached were:

1. *Number of Patient Days* in SNFs dramatically declined in 1972 after the introduction of PA/MR. Prior to 1972, the number of patient days reimbursed at SNF rates had been steadily increasing since 1969. An estimated 4,288,000 SNF patient days were saved in 1973 (i.e., a 46 percent decline). This estimate was confirmed both by trend analysis and manual record sampling. The number of patient days reimbursed at ICF rates increased at the same time by 2,653,000. The difference (1,613,000 patient days) were transferred from SNF to care levels lower than ICF.

2. *Cost avoidances were conservatively estimated at $20,586,000 (11.4 percent of total SNF/ICF per diem costs) in 1973,* based on the above patient-day impact and the prevailing rate differential between care levels. The estimate includes an adjustment of $530,000 to account for UC administrative costs.

3. *Admission/Discharge Rates.* Admission rates for SNF reimbursed care declined and discharge rates increased significantly after implementation of PA/MR. The admission denial rate was 25 percent in the first six months of the preadmission review program, later stabilizing at around 15 percent. The increase in SNF discharge rates

can be illustrated by the expected continued stay for SNF patients. Prior to 1972, the average SNF patient could be expected to remain 496 days before discharge. In 1973, the expected continued stay was down to 300 days (a 40 percent reduction).

4. *The directly traceable effects of PA and MR decrease over time as providers adapt to new review criteria.* In the first six months of 1972, 47.2 percent of patients classified by their attending physician as SNF patients were transferred to ICF or lower care levels or re-assessed as getting ICF level care. In 1975, a sample survey conducted by the state showed only 18.7 percent transfers. Since the utilization patterns established in 1972 continued into 1975, one may conclude that the reduced transfer rate is due to deterrent effects.

5. *Physician-composed MR teams* resulted in 11 percent higher transfer rate to lower case levels than nurse-only MR teams.

6. Both PA and MR had greater impact in densely populated areas, and the impact on private nursing homes was significantly larger than for county medical facilities and hospital long-term care units.

VIRGINIA

The UC impact study in this state was concentrated on Acute Hospitals. The state's Utilization Control in hospitals focuses on Long Stay Review (LSR) of all hospital stays exceeding 15 days. In addition, the state performs retroactive post-payment review of providers, based on exception reports generated by the post claims processing. The study was based primarily on 160,000 computerized payment records for fiscal years '72 through '74, covering a total of 112,000 Acute Hospital stays. In addition, 3,000 LSR records were sampled to determine the traceable effects of LSR.

Results were obtained by comparing utilization patterns in FY '72 and '74. In 1972, the LSR review limits were also reduced from 30 to 15 days. Also during this period, coverage for ICF stays was included in the Virginia Medicaid plan, and the state took over responsibility for the retroactive reviews from the fiscal intermediary (Blue Cross). The results cited in this study reflect the accumulative effect of each of these changes.

Based on original indications, it was expected that computerized payment records would be available from 1969. It was discovered, however, that only records from July 1971 were usable. In addition, LSR records were maintained only from September 1973. The limited data available had an adverse impact on the preciseness of the conclusions. Nevertheless, two major conclusions emerged from the Virginia study.

- The *cost effectiveness* of the state's Long Stay Review (LSR) program was demonstrated, both by analysis of the computerized paid claims records and through the sampled LSR records.
- A *significant reduction* in hospital utilization was found over the study period.

Some of the specific findings in the Virginia study were:

1. Net Cost Avoidances of $7,128,000 annually (16 percent) were estimated due to reduced hospital utilization. Approximately $312,000 of these savings could be directly traced to effects of Long Stay Review (LSR) procedures.

2. *Average Length of Stay* was reduced by .64 days after proper adjustment for diagnostic case mix, patient age, and aid category mix.

3. *Number of Hospital Admisssions* were reduced by 11.2 percent, coin-

ciding with increased availability of ICF beds during this period.

4. *Intensive Care Utilization* dropped dramatically (27.4 percent) during this period. No significant change in ancillary services was observed.

CALIFORNIA

The UC impact study in California included acute hospitals, hospitals for extended care, nursing homes (SNFs), and intermediate care facilities (ICFs). The review methods studied were: (1) preadmission review, required for all admissions except emergency hospital admissions; (2) periodic concurrent reviews of the need for extended stay in hospitals, SNF's, and ICF's; and (3) on-site medical review (MR), performed annually in SNF's, and ICF's. These review procedures are all administered by state-employed medical consultants and nurses; in this respect California differs from other states (i.e., Virginia) that emphasize cooperation with institution-based utilization review (UR) committees.

The California study appears to demonstrate the cost effectiveness of each of the above review methods. Furthermore, the state's preadmission review program was shown to be the most cost effective, leading to higher savings with lower administrative costs than the concurrent and on-site medical reviews. These other review methods, however, were shown to lead to additional savings that could not be realized from preadmission reviews alone. The above conclusions were derived based on a study of 25 computer tapes (containing over 6 million payment records) as well as extensive manual records obtained from the state agency.

The preadmission and concurrent review requirements became effective in April 1970. A dramatic impact on hospital utilization by Medicaid (Medi-Cal) patients could be observed in the following months, resulting in lowered admission rates, shorter average length of stay and significant overall cost savings. To illustrate the magnitude of the impact, a typical Medi-Cal hospital patient in January 1970 stayed 1.8 days, or 27 percent, longer than other patients (i.e., non-Medi-Cal) with similar age and ailment diagnosis. By the end of 1971, the length of stay was the same as for other patients.

The Medical Review (MR) program in California started in July 1970. The effect of this program, as well as the preadmission and concurrent reviews in SNF's and ICF's, could not be observed at the time of their implementation due to incomplete data from that period. However, analysis of manual records of review activity, available since January 1972, appears to indicate the cost effectiveness of UC in California SNFs and ICFs.

Some of the specific findings in the California study were:

1. After implementation of preadmission review in April 1970, hospital admission/discharge rates for the remainder of the year were 13.1 percent lower than expected based on the trends prevailing before UC. Length of stay dropped by 12.9 percent, and continued to decline in 1971.

2. Coinciding with the drop in admissions and length of stay, per diem rates showed an incremental increase (on top of the prevailing inflation rates), of 5 percent; reflecting lower occupancy rates and increased use of ancillary services per admission.

3. The hospital UC impact that could be traced to specific admission/extension denials was only a fraction of the total impact. This suggests, as in the other states, the importance of the deterrent effects of UC.

4. The number of SNF patient days avoided in fiscal year '73 was conservatively estimated at 3.33 million. Of

these patient days, approximately 2.08 million were transferred to ICFs, and the remainder mostly to board and care homes.

Comparing with the Michigan results, we see that the estimated savings in SNF patient days and costs are of the same order of magnitude, even though California's SNF/ICF population is almost 3 times larger than Michigan's. However, in view of the impact of deterrent effects observed earlier, it is likely that the traceable effects in 1970,

when UC in SNF's first started, were significantly higher than indicated above.

A direct comparison of the hospital UC impact with the impact observed in Virginia is difficult, due to the great difference between the two states' approaches. California's comprehensive review system has led to savings that are of an order of magnitude higher than those observed in Virginia, however, the difference should be seen in the light of the fact that California's hospital length of stays tend to be shorter also for non-Medicaid (Medi-Cal) patients.

REFERENCES

1. "Compilation of the Social Security Laws," as amended through January 1, 1973, Volume 1, U.S. House of Representatives, U.S. Government Printing Office, Washington, D.C., 1973.

2. "UC Impact Study, Phase I - Analytic Framework for Utilization Controls (Tasks I.1 and I.2)," Universal Analytics, Inc., for DHEW Contract #SRS–74–45, November 15, 1974.

3. Claire Townsend, et al., *Old Age, the Last Segregation,* Ralph Nader's Study Group Report on Nursing Homes, Grossman Publishers, New York, 1971.

4. "A Benefit-Cost Analysis of Utilization Review Techniques," prepared for DHEW Medical Services Administration (Contract #SRS–72–26) by Minnesota Systems Research, Inc.

5. "UC Impact Study, Summary Report of Task 5 - UC Impact Model Design," Universal Analytics, Inc., for DHEW Contract #SRS–74–45, July 17, 1975.

6. Paul J. Feldstein, and Jerimiah J. German, "Predicting Hospital Utilization: An Evaluation of Three Approaches," *Inquiry*, II, June 1975, pp. 13–36.

7. *Length of Stay in PAS Hospitals, United States, Regional,* commission on Professional and Hospital Activities, Ann Arbor, Michigan, issued annually.

29. Medicaid and Cash Welfare Recipients: An Empirical Study

CHARLES P. HALL, JR., JOHN A. FLUECK and
WILLIAM F. McKENNA

Reprinted, with permission of the Blue Cross Association, from *Inquiry*, Vol. XIV, No. 1 (March 1977), pp. 43-50. Copyright © 1977 by the Blue Cross Association. All Rights reserved.

Title XIX of the Social Security Act, popularly known as Medicaid, became effective January 1, 1966. Its primary objective was to encourage the establishment of unified state medical assistance programs with a common content of care for everyone receiving Federally aided monetary payments under any of the categorical public assistance programs. From the beginning, participating states were required to provide at least a basic set of mandatory benefits, with state options for additional services. The long-term goal was to encourage states to work toward liberalizing eligibility standards and expanding the content of care with a view to ultimately providing comprehensive services for substantially all individuals who met the state's financial eligibility standards.

However, as of December, 1973, there was considerable variability among states. The diversity among various state Medicaid programs resulted from several factors, including the ability of the respective states to provide the needed matching dollars as well as different perceptions of need by their legislatures as they took advantage of the availability of Federal funds.[1]

This paper is based on some of the findings of a broader study of Medicaid. The specific objectives of the study were:

1. Primary objectives—to determine: the proportion of Medicaid eligibles actually receiving health care services; what specific services were being used; where the services were received (i.e., from what type of provider); and how and by whom services were paid for.

2. Secondary objectives—to determine: the "utilization effects" (i.e., whether optional services were obtained through the substitution of one of the covered services) and to make comparisons between jurisdictions providing different coverages of optional services regarding the proportions of eligibles receiving various other health care services; and the proportion of eligibles who had perceived a need for health care services but who did not receive them, and to ascertain the reason(s) why they did not receive them.

3. Tertiary objective—to determine, to the extent possible, the perceived health status of the eligibles.

The focus in this paper will be on the findings with regard to two of the most utilized basic services, inpatient hospitalization and physicians' services, and three of the more heavily used optional services, dental

251

care, eye care and prescription drugs. The other mandatory services were outpatient hospital, laboratory and X-ray, skilled nursing home, early and periodic screening for children and youth, home health services for those entitled to nursing home services, and transportation. Permitted optional services included virtually all health services.[2] There has been little in-depth research into the impact on the poor of the failure of some states to provide optional services. The significance of the omission of optional services under medical assistance programs on the accessibility and use of medical services has, at the same time, been a matter of concern. This concern has been both with the effect of the omissions on the receipt of medical services not covered by the state program and the effect of the omissions on the complete range of medical services for which Medicaid eligibles have a perceived need. Knowledge gained from measurements of such effects should be of significant value in the resolution of policy questions affecting future Federal and state legislation respecting the scope and content of provisions for making needed medical services accessible to the American people—whether through the Medicaid program for the poor or a national health insurance program for all.

At the time of this study, the minimum mandated Federal requirement was that all cash welfare recipients under categorical public assistance programs had to be eligible. This included Old Age Assistance (OAA), Aid to the Blind (AB), Aid to the Permanently and Totally Disabled (APTD), and Aid to Families with Dependent Children (AFDC). On January 1, 1974, this was modified by the implementation of the Supplementary Security Income (SSI) program, but this came after the collection of data under the present study. In addition to the categorically needy, a state could opt to serve the "medically needy," that is, those found by the application of state standards to have income and resources exceeding those necessary for financial maintenance assistance but insufficient to meet the costs of medical care. This latter category of Medicaid eligibles was not investigated in the present study.

It is important to note that the target population of this study was Medicaid eligibles. Other studies have investigated Medicaid recipients[3] utilizing paid claims tapes. This approach deals only with persons who have entered and been served by the system, and it relies on data whose quality has been questioned. Only by dealing with eligibles (here defined as cash welfare recipients) is it possible to address questions about the extent to which the target population is being served. In addition, this also permits other kinds of judgments; e.g., how well-informed are the poor about programs for which they are eligible?

Methodology

Data on Medicaid eligibles were collected by a personal interview survey that produced completed questionnaires for more than 3,000 cash welfare cases, encompassing more than 8,000 recipients (i.e., all AFDC cases included more than one recipient) in the metropolitan areas of Atlanta, Ga., Little Rock, Ark., Oklahoma City, Okla., and Trenton, N.J. The interviews were conducted by Marketing Information Services, Inc., of Atlanta, under the direction of the authors. These four sites were purposively chosen in order to provide a spectrum of optional service coverage with local agency cooperation.

Specifically, the New Jersey Medicaid program provided comprehensive benefits including all of the optionals here under consideration; Georgia, with a somewhat more limited benefit structure, provided full coverage for prescription drugs, but included no program benefits for dental services or vision care except through a screening and treatment program for children to age nine. Arkansas Medicaid included full dental benefits, partial vision care (only for children to age 21) and no prescription drug benefits. Finally, Oklahoma lacked any coverage for dental care, vision care and prescription drugs except through the screening program for eligibles to age 21. An evaluation of the availability of health care services and facilities in each of the four locations, as well as a study of general utilization patterns, was made before the survey was initiated.[4]

Initial research suggested that institutionalized individuals probably had different health care needs and a different delivery system than individuals not in an institution. For this reason, the survey deleted the welfare recipients who were currently institutionalized (mainly nursing and convalescent home patients). Recipients under the Aid to the Blind program were also eliminated because they were small in number and were typically serviced by other specialized programs. Thus, the survey population of interest consisted of cash welfare recipients not in institutions in the Aid to the Permanently and Totally Disabled (APTD—hereafter abbreviated AD), Old Age Assistance (OAA), and Aid to Families with Dependent Children (AFDC) programs in each of the four local areas.

Stratified random sampling with proportional allocation was used in the survey.[5] The sampling unit was the Medicaid eligible. Data were collected during June, July and August, 1973, utilizing household interviews with recall periods varying from a minimum of six months (for prescriptions)

to a maximum of 18 months (for inpatient hospitalization and physican visits). While there are limitations to this interview technique, it has been used successfully by the National Center for Health Statistics and others for many years.[6] A number of the questions in this study were taken directly from the National Center's Health Interview Survey.[7] Sample sizes and response rates are reported in Table 1. The analyses were conducted partly from an exploratory viewpoint[8] utilizing tabular displays and comparisons of proportions (via the student ''t,'' Pearson's goodness of fit test, and multiple comparisons[9]). Above all, subject matter interpretation was stressed in all results.

General Findings

Table 1 displays some interesting indications on the utilization of the five selected health services by site and welfare category. As can be seen, there were wide variations both among eligibles in different aid categories in the same city and between eligibles in the same aid category in different cities. In general, intracity differences were somewhat predictable among aid categories, and many of the intercity variations also appeared to be consistent with the previously mentioned Medicaid covering patterns.

More specifically, since the disabled are, almost by definition, not in good health, it

Table 1 Percentage of Eligibles Utilizing Medical Service, By Site and Welfare Program

Service	Trenton			Atlanta			Little Rock			Oklahoma City		
	OAA	AD	AFDC	OAA	AD	AFDC	OAA	AD	AFDC	OAA	AD	AFDC
Hospital, 1972–73	34	45	25	26	42	20	29	29	16	34	43	24
Physician, 1973	68	81	56	73	81	56	59	65	44	64	68	55
Dentist, 1972–73	18	36	43	10	34	50	15	28	37	14	23	31
Eye doctor, 1972–73	48	45	32	41	36	21	33	28	27	29	24	17
Prescription, 1973	51	61	41	47	54	32	44	37	27	42	50	39
Sample size*	86	132	2433	174	111	1831	316	102	1519	298	164	904
Response rate	.70	.92	.86	.76	.89	.79	.89	.87	.85	.82	.79	.69

*The indicated sample sizes shown in this table also apply to Tables 2–4, and 8.

was not surprising that they had the highest levels of utilization for both hospitalization and physician visits in all four sites. They also had the highest utilization of prescriptions in three of the locations (Table 1).

Comparing the OAA and AFDC groups, the general age-relatedness of disease was quite apparent. The OAA had more hospitalization, physician visits, eye problems and prescriptions than the child-dominated AFDC group. On the other hand, the OAA displayed much lower use of dental care, a fact that was consistent with the fairly high frequency of dentures among the elderly and the orthodontia and cavity repair among the young. Note that the relatively ·high utilization of physicians (greater than 50 percent in 11 of the 12 cells of Table 1 during an approximately six- to eight-month recall period) tends to refute the suggestion that primary health services are not available to the poor. However, these data say nothing about the quality of services received.

Turning to inter-city comparisons, Trenton, with the most comprehensive Medicaid benefits, had the highest percentage of utilization in 13 of 15 categories (the five services listed in Table 1 for each of the three programs—OAA, AD and AFDC), and both of the exceptions were compatible with known site information. Specifically, the two exceptions were attributable to Grady Hospital in Atlanta, which was known to be an easily accessible facility that provided a tremendous volume of free care. Many of the elderly who saw a physician there had probably been doing so since before the establishment of Medicare and Medicaid. Similarly, the Grady dental clinic as well as several other dental programs—including the Emory University dental school clinic—tended to increase the utilization of dentists in Atlanta. Hence, these results suggest that the total Medicaid benefit structure (basic and optional services) is an important factor in the utilization of all services.

One might suspect that the dominance of Trenton over the other three sites was attributable primarily to unspecified North-South differences rather than Medicaid coverage patterns. However, in comparing only the three Southern cities, Atlanta dominates in nine of 15 categories, and this is consistent with Medicaid coverage patterns. Atlanta's coverage of Medicaid optionals is more extensive than in either Little Rock or Oklahoma City.

One of the initial objectives of the study was to determine whether a Medicaid program that failed to provide a fairly generous package of optional services, i.e., "comprehensive coverage," might have the effect of leading to more heavy use of the mandatory—and generally more expensive—facilities/services. For instance, inability to get prescriptions could permit a mild problem to worsen to a point requiring an office visit or even hospitalization. Alternatively, it was felt that some providers, frustrated by the inability of their patients to get prescriptions filled, might try to "beat the system" by prescribing additional office visits during which medication might be administered by injection. Since the office visit is a mandatory benefit, this would be covered by Medicaid.

The data in Table 1 provided little, if any, support for this suggestion. A more plausible interpretation of these results might be the analogue to the old saying about "a hospital bed built is a hospital bed used." That is, the more medical services that are available without charge, the more these services will be used. It may simply be that greater availability in Trenton leads to greater awareness, which leads to still greater utilization. Compare, for example, the utilization of prescriptions in Atlanta and Trenton and the utilization of dental care in Little Rock and Trenton. In both instances (despite the fact that the Medicaid coverage was virtually the same for these options), all the Trenton welfare categories had the relatively higher utilization. Furthermore, there was no evidence available to suggest that New Jersey Medicaid was any more aggressive in "marketing" its program than the other states.

Table 1 also indicates that Little Rock has the lowest utilization in five of six cells dealing with the basic services (hospitalization and physican). This may be largely explained by the serious shortage and maldistribution of physicians and facilities in that city, which was uncovered by the study, and may have been further aggravated by a poor public transportation system.

Oklahoma City was reported as having the most restricted Medicaid program (i.e., fewest optional services) and the utilization fits the Medicaid coverage pattern. In six of nine welfare categories for the three optional services, it had the lowest utilization values for all four sites. The relatively high utilization of hospital and physician services in Oklahoma City is surprising and may be partly attributed to ethnic differences among eligibles.

Table 2 sheds some light on another basic question addressed in the study — how were the services paid for? While there are some surprising intra-site differences by aid category, the most dramatic results can be noticed among the three optional services. For all three, Trenton had by far the lowest proportion of eligibles paying out-of-pocket costs (significant at less than .01 level). As the only city providing optional vision care services, Trenton was sharply lower in the proportion of eligibles who paid on both

adult welfare categories, although Atlanta was lower for the AFDC. But all cities provided coverage for children through the screening program, and Atlanta had, in addition, several voluntary eye programs, including the Grady Hospital and Benjamin Massell eye clinics. It was interesting to note, however, that for prescriptions in Atlanta and for dental care in Little Rock, although they showed a lower frequency of out-of-pocket costs than the cities without Medicaid coverage, they were themselves well above the corresponding values for Trenton despite similar benefit provisions.

Table 3 presents the proportion of eligibles who reported unmet needs for various services. Predictably, Trenton, with the most comprehensive Medicaid benefits and the highest levels of use of services, reported the smallest proportion of unmet needs in 11 of 12 categories. In keeping with the Medicaid coverage pattern, Oklahoma City had the highest proportion of unmet needs in eight of 12 categories.

The eligibles were given an opportunity to rate their health status during the interview. Table 4 reports on those who said their health was "poor." On an inter-city basis, Trenton was the "winner" in all aid categories. Predictably, in each site, the highest proportion of "poor" responses came from the group which, by definition, was not in good health, the AD. The exceptionally high figure in Atlanta can be traced to the fact that it had, by quite a margin the largest proportion of chronically disabled

Table 2 Percentage of Eligibles Incurring Out-of-Pocket Expenses For Medical Service, By Site and Welfare Program

Service	Trenton			Atlanta			Little Rock			Oklahoma City		
	OAA	AD	AFDC	OAA	AD	AFDC	OAA	AD	AFDC	OAA	AD	AFDC
Hospital, 1972–73	14	3	7	22	11	10	20	10	17	12	11	16
Physician, 1973	19	5	5	13	6	8	34	24	16	11	14	13
Dentist, 1972–73	13	4	3	77	24	26	54	36	17	68	55	34
Eye doctor, 1972–73	12	6	8	39	17	2	66	55	22	38	39	33
Prescription, 1973	4	3	5	48	33	33	96	84	84	91	91	94

persons.[10] It was to be expected, of course, that more OAA than AFDC would report their health as "poor."

Specific Findings: AFDC

AFDC is the largest subpopulation in the survey (Table 1). It contains both adult and children eligibles and because of its size, it is generally the most expensive component of the Medicaid program. In accordance with the general view, sharp and predictable differences in utilization patterns were present for every service studied when AFDC eligibles were classified by age (i.e., adult versus child — 20 years old or younger).[11]

Tables 5-8 present results on a basis of site-race classification. It can be seen in Tables 5 and 6 that more whites than blacks used designated health services in 11 of 12 use categories, the only exception being hospitalization in Trenton, where white and black proportions were equal. As shown in

Table 3 Percentage of Eligibles Reporting an Unmet Medical Need, By Site and Welfare Program

	Trenton			Atlanta			Little Rock			Oklahoma City		
Need	OAA	AD	AFDC	OAA	AD	AFDC	OAA	AD	AFDC	OAA	AD	AFDC
Physician, 1973	9	12	3	29	34	6	21	20	5	22	31	6
Dentist, 1972–73	13	24	8	24	31	22	22	33	16	25	41	23
Eye doctor, 1972–73	19	14	3	41	41	12	38	32	10	41	41	13
Prescription, 1973	5	10	11	10	12	9	10	26	24	11	23	16

Table 4 Percentage of Eligibles Reporting Their Health Status As "Poor," By Site and Welfare Program

	Trenton			Atlanta			Little Rock			Oklahoma City		
Service	OAA	AD	AFDC	OAA	AD	AFDC	OAA	AD	AFDC	OAA	AD	AFDC
"Poor"	15	41	5	36	62	6	37	46	6	30	45	7

Table 5 Percentage of AFDC Eligibles Utilizing Hospitalization and Dental Services, Reporting Out-of-Pocket Dental Expenses and Unmet Dental Needs, By Site and Race*

	Race	Trenton	Atlanta	Little Rock	Oklahoma City
Hospitalized, 1972–73	White	26	26	22	31
	Black	26	20	16	22
Saw dentist, 1972–73	White	57	56	51	39
	Black	40	50	35	26
With out-of-pocket expense for last dental visit	White	7	36	29	49
	Black	2	28	16	26
With unmet dental need	White	7	28	24	27
	Black	8	21	15	21
Citing lack of money as reason for unmet need	White	0	80	76	89
	Black	10	50	61	36

*The percentages shown in Tables 5–7 are based on the number of users of the specified services. These are subsets of the sample sizes presented in Table 1. (See: Hall, Charles P., Jr., *et al. Final Report—Medicaid Basic and Optional Services: Impact on the Poor,* Temple University, Philadelphia, October 1974).

Table 6 Percentage of AFDC Eligibles Utilizing Eyeglass Services, Reporting Out-of-Pocket Eyeglass Expense and Unmet Needs, By Site and Race

	Race	Trenton	Atlanta	Little Rock	Oklahoma City
Obtained glasses after 1/1/72	White	24	11	10	10
	Black	23	7	7	6
With out-of-pocket expense	White	16	73	55	50
for glasses	Black	17	70	55	69
With unmet need for glasses	White	4	16	8	13
	Black	6	14	11	13
Citing lack of money as reason	White	20	62	86	79
for unmet need for glasses	Black	13	53	77	66

Table 7 Percentage of AFDC Eligibles Utilizing Prescription Services, Reporting Out-of-Pocket Expenses For New Prescriptions, By Site and Race

	Race	Trenton	Atlanta	Little Rock	Oklahoma City
Eligibles with new prescriptions	White	94	78	82	74
after 1/1/73, chronic*	Black	78	67	63	70
Eligibles filled all new	White	96	89	89	92
prescriptions, chronic	Black	97	95	93	90
Eligibles with new prescriptions	White	77	65	81	66
after 1/1/73, nonchronic	Black	73	54	60	58
Eligibles filled all new	White	97	97	96	91
prescriptions, nonchronic	Black	97	94	91	90
All eligibles with new prescriptions	White	6	52	87	97
and out-of-pocket expense	Black	4	32	85	97

*For purposes of the survey, chronic was described as a "lingering condition requiring periodic medical attention." The project's medical consultant prepared a list of conditions typically viewed as chronic; the interviewers used the list as a guide in classifying answers. It included such problems, for example, as diabetes, high blood pressure/hypertension, and emphysema.

Table 8 Percentage of AFDC Eligibles Reporting Their Health Status and Health Services As "Poor," By Site and Race

	Race	Trenton	Atlanta	Little Rock	Oklahoma City
Eligibles rating health as "poor"	White	7	9	15	9
	Black	5	6	4	6
Eligibles rating available health	White	0	6	4	10
services as "poor"	Black	2	3	7	7

Table 7, proportionally more whites than blacks were issued prescriptions in every grouping, both for chronic and nonchronic conditions. Interestingly, in three of these eight groupings, more blacks than whites actually filled their prescriptions, despite the fact that out-of-pocket expenses were incurred by more whites in every location except Oklahoma City.

Again referring to Tables 5 and 6, more whites than blacks—by significant margins (P value less than .01)—incurred out-of-pocket expenses in all four sites for dental care, while for glasses more blacks had such costs everywhere except in Atlanta. In the latter case, however, the difference between the racial proportions was greater than 3 percent only in Oklahoma City. Unmet needs for dental care were cited more frequently by whites than blacks everywhere except in Trenton; for glasses, no clear pattern emerged with respect to unmet need. More whites than blacks reported lack of money as the reason for an unmet need to get glasses in all four cities—again by significant margins (P value less than .01). The margins were even greater, however, in the case of dental care—except for Trenton, where no whites offered this reason.

·While these few examples provide merely a hint of a pattern, when viewed over all listed classifications for the five services, the general pattern of proportionally more whites than blacks reporting both utilization of services and out-of-pocket payments is strongly upheld. Surprisingly, the two racial groups were exactly evenly divided in the number of times that they recorded the highest proportion of eligibles with unmet needs.

Table 8 shows how health status ratings compare by race. Note that although more whites than blacks rate their health as poor in all locations, the margin is smallest in Trenton where benefits are most comprehensive and utilization is highest. At the same time, note that in ranking the quality of health services, there are some significant switches that suggest that many Medicaid eligibles may be sophisticated enough to realize that personal health status is affected by many factors other than health care per se.

Concluding Remarks

The results of the study leave little doubt that the presence of Medicaid coverage does, other things being equal, clearly remove a significant financial barrier to the availability of health care services. In addition, the comprehensiveness of the Medicaid package appears to have a substantial effect on the utilization of each individual service. However, it is equally clear, as in the case of Little Rock, that serious shortages and/or maldistributions of providers and facilities can more than offset the benefits of programmatic coverage.

There is some indication that where there are comprehensive benefits and eligibles who are well-informed as to their benefit entitlement (as in Trenton), interracial differences in utilization, out-of-pocket payments and perceptions of need tend to disappear. In the other three locations, which appear to lack these dual conditions, interracial differences were substantial. On balance, the findings appear to support a tentative conclusion that whites generally seek more health care services than blacks, but they tend to obtain many of them outside of the Medicaid system, and therefore, they more often incur out-of-pocket expenses.[12]

Given the substantial sample sizes used in the survey and the high overall response rates that were obtained, these findings carry considerable weight. Additionally, they are supported by the fact that they pass the "plausibility test."

One very specific conclusion is suggested on a policy matter of some concern. A highly controversial—and potentially costly—benefit, whether incorporated under Medicaid or, perhaps, a National Health Insurance program, is full coverage of prescription medicines. Our findings are quite clear on the point that of the three major optionals (vision care, dental care and prescriptions), prescriptions were most desired as an additional benefit over all locations where they were not covered by Medicaid. The survey results showed relatively high utilization of prescription drugs in all programs in each of the four locations (Table 1); the number of eligibles incurring out-of-pocket expenses for their prescriptions varied widely by site, however, clearly reflecting differences in the program benefits available—e.g., 3 percent in Trenton to 96 percent in Little Rock (Table 2).

Yet, when reporting their perceptions of unmet needs under the four major service categories (Table 3), respondents in seven of the 12 columns ranked prescription drugs as lowest. In only two of the 12 columns were unmet prescription drug needs ranked highest. Furthermore, it was found that of those Medicaid eligibles who actually received new prescriptions during the period covered by the survey, an average of more than nine out of 10 in each of the locations were successful in having the prescriptions filled, despite a range of from 4 percent (Trenton) to 97 percent (Oklahoma City) having to use their own money to do so (Table 7).

This evidence strongly suggests that relatively few Medicaid eligibles in the sites studied were deprived of the benefits of prescribed medication, regardless of program coverage. Since a major policy concern of most health benefits programs is to reduce or eliminate unequal access to care, it could thus be suggested that for any future program which must for economic or other reasons stop short of full coverage for all benefits, prescription drug coverage could be excluded with only minimal impact on the health status of the covered population.

REFERENCES

1. See: Stevens, Rosemary and Stevens, Robert. "Medicaid: Anatomy of a Dilemma," *Law and Contemporary Problems* 35:348–425 (Spring 1970) for a detailed early discussion of some of the changes in services required and dates of implementation that have characterized the Medicaid program.

2. See: Hall, Charles P., Jr., *et al. Final Report— Medicaid Basic and Optional Services: Impact on the Poor,* Temple University, Philadelphia, October 1974.

3. School of Public Health and Administrative Medicine, Columbia University. *Effect of Medicaid on Health Care of Low-Income Persons,* Contracts WA-406, SRS-ORAT-68-01 and SRS-69-50, DHEW.

4. Hall, *et al., op. cit.,* pages 21–22, 48–49, 70–71 and 93–94.

5. Cochran, William G., *Sampling Techniques,* 2nd edition (New York: John Wiley and Sons, 1963).

6. See, for example: National Center for Health Statistics. *Health Survey Procedure: Concepts, Ques-* *tionnaire Development and Definitions in the Health Interview Survey,* Series 1, No. 2 (Washington, D.C.: DHEW, May 1964); and National Center for Health Statistics. *Interview Data on Chronic Conditions Compared with Information Derived from Medical Records,* Series 2, No. 23 (Washington, D.C.: DHEW, May 1967).

7. See: Hall, *et al., op. cit.,* chapter 2 and appendices D and E for more details on methodology.

8. Mosteller, F. and Tukey, J.W. "Data Analysis Including Statistics," in: Lindzey, G. and Aronson, E. (eds.) *Revised Handbook of Social Psychology* (Reading, Mass.: Addison-Wesley, 1968) chapter 22.

9. Brownlee, K.A. *Statistical Theory and Methodology in Science and Engineering,* 2nd edition (New York: John Wiley and Sons, 1965).

10. Hall, *et al., op. cit.*

11. *Ibid.*

12. For a discussion of other possible causal factors that need further investigation, see: Hall, *et al., op. cit.*

30. Health Service Used By North Florida Medicaid Recipients

RICHARD C. REYNOLDS, PHYLLIS R. BLEIWEIS,
SAM A. BANKS, and NEIL A. BUTLER

Reprinted with permission from the *Journal of the Florida Medical Association*, Vol. 65, No. 1
(January 1978).

In 1965 the enactment of Title XIX of the Social Security Amendments established the Medicaid program. Its purpose was to make health care more accessible to the poor citizens of the United States. Federal grants were made to states who also committed some of their funds toward this goal. The federal government established guidelines for state eligibility as prerequisites for receiving Medicaid money. Each state plan had to include as a minimum: inpatient hospital services, outpatient hospital services, laboratory and x-ray services, nursing home services, and physicians' services. Other provisions remained optional until 1969 when screening and diagnostic follow-up were added for the Medicaid eligibles under age 21. Home health services were added in 1970 and in 1972 family planning became an obligatory service provided by all state Medicaid programs.

Eligible citizens for a state Medicaid program include the categorically indigent, that is, the aged, blind, poor families with dependent children, and the permanently and totally disabled. Medically indigent citizens, as defined by the individual states, were also eligible for benefits.

Each state evolved its own version of Medicaid. Some were generous in the definitions of eligibles and provision of health services; others conservative. Since the program was initially intended to yield to the health vendors their usual and customary fees for services, the states were concerned about the costs of the program. Significantly less attention has been directed, however, at utilization characteristics of beneficiaries of this health care program. How often and what kind of services do the eligible citizens obtain through Medicaid? What do they know about its benefits? How does the utilization of health care services by the Medicaid constituents compare to utilization by other population groups? For most programs these questions go unasked.

The responses to these questions will vary according to the individual, state plan, and availability and accessibility of health care providers.

The state of Florida initiated its Medicaid program in 1970 at an annual cost of approximately \$100,000,000. Today the program spends \$250,000,000 a year to serve over 400,000 citizens, all of whom are

The authors gratefully acknowledge the help of Sara Kenaston and Marilyn Uelsmann of the Florida Division of Family Services who provided information on Florida Medicaid and Dr. Ronald Marks of the University of Florida Division of Biostatistics who assisted in analysis of the data.

categorically indigent. There have been no attempts to provide services for the medically indigent. Whenever there has been danger of overspending the budget, services have been curtailed or reimbursement of vendors has been reduced. During one brief, critical time physician fees were established at 15% of the 75th percentile of their "usual and customary" charges. However, this was never implemented.

METHODS

The purpose of this study was to explore the impact of Medicaid on the health care behavior of a sample of Medicaid beneficiaries in a north Florida county and to examine their knowledge of the Medicaid program.

Two hundred and fifty-nine recipients of Medicaid benefits (or a spouse or guardian of a recipient) in Alachua County were interviewed between October 1973 and October 1974. This amounted to 5% of all recipients enrolled in the county. The Division of Family Services of the Florida Department of Health and Rehabilitative Services provided randomly selected lists approximately every three months (four lists) from the files of Region III (North Central Florida) Medicaid eligibles. Approximately half the respondents were eligible as members of the Aid for Dependent Children program, and the remainder were from the categories of the aged, blind, or permanently or totally disabled. Rural and municipal families were interviewed in proportion to the population of the county. Alachua County is 30% rural.

All participants were notified of the character and confidentiality of the proposed interview by letter and telephone prior to receiving an appointment. Interviews were conducted in the respondents' homes. Fewer than 2% of those contacted refused to be interviewed.

The five interviewers included a research associate and a research assistant in the Department of Community Health and Family Medicine and three graduate sociology students from the University of Florida. They were instructed to interview an adult in the family who was either a Medicaid recipient or responsible for a Medicaid recipient. An estimation was made by the investigators (on the advice of administrators in the Division of Family Services) that among all the people included in the households involved in the study, at least 80% were Medicaid recipients. That is, of the 999 people in the 259 families interviewed, approximately 800 were Medicaid beneficiaries. Unfortunately not all household members knew if they were eligible for Medicaid. All interviews were discarded where reliability of the respondent was strongly questioned.

A questionnaire of 125 items was prepared. Many of the questions had been used in earlier surveys of other constituencies, two of which were citizens of Alachua County and migrant farmworkers of the St. Johns River Basin in northeast Florida. Responses to the interview were coded, computed and analyzed. Statistical analysis included frequency histograms and chi square comparisons.

To pretest the questionnaire, 38 Medicaid names were selected from the patient roster of the Northeast Volunteer Community Health Clinic in Gainesville. Thirty-two agreed to participate in the interview. Subsequently only a few changes were made in the questionnaire. None of these interviews was included in the final report.

RESULTS

The Medicaid population of Alachua County (Table 1) is predominantly black (79.5%), female (87.6%), unmarried (86.9%) and has little formal education. Over 70 percent have not completed high school. Sixty percent are unemployed. Among the 259 individuals interviewed, 46 or 18.4% were 70 years of age or older.

Table 1 Demographic Characteristics of 259 Households with Medicaid Recipients*N = 259

	Number	Percent	Mean		Number	Percent
Adults in Household			1.9	Marital Status		
1 person	122	47.1		Single	57	22.0
2 persons	77	29.7		Widowed	63	24.3
3 or more	59	22.8		Separated	71	27.4
Not answered	1	.3		Divorced	29	11.2
		99.9		Common Law	5	1.9
				Married	34	13.1
Children in Household			2.4			99.9
None	43	16.6				
1 - 3	141	54.4				
More than 3	56	21.6	Employed		
Not answered	4	1.5	Yes	101	38.9
Not applicable	15	5.7	No	156	60.2
		99.8		Not answered	2	.7
						99.8
Race						
Black	206	79.5				
White	53	20.5	Spouse Employed		
		100.0		Yes	13	5.0
				No	37	14.2
Sex				Not applicable	190	73.3
Male	31	11.9	Not answered	13	5.0
Female	227	87.6	Don't know	6	2.3
Not answered	1	.3			99.8
		99.8				
Age				Education		
19 and under	11	4.2	Less than 8 years	82	31.6
20 -29	59	22.7	Some high school	93	35.9
30 - 39	56	21.6	H.S. or trade graduate	53	20.4
40 - 49	34	13.1	Some college	13	5.0
50 - 59	33	12.7	College graduate	3	1.1
60 - 69	15	5.7	Not answered	9	3.4
70 and above	38	14.6	Don't know	6	2.3
Don't know	4	1.5			99.7
Not answered	9	3.4			
		99.5			

*Sums of these percentages may differ from 100% due to rounding error.

The number of children living in households which were studied ranged from zero to nine. Although the average number of children per household was 2.4, among these households with children 54 had two, 52 had three, 26 had four, 10 had five, 11 had six, and one each had eight and nine children. Sixteen percent of the households with two or more occupants had no children. One hundred and twenty-two, or 47.1%, of those interviewed resided in single member households.

Perceived Health Care Status

All respondents were asked seven questions which subjectively characterized their functioning health status. These questions and the responses are presented in Table 2. The range of responses is narrow. Twenty-

Table 2 Perception of Health Status

Health Status Indicator	Medicaid Population N = 259	Alachua County Population N = 1645
	Percent	Distribution
Feels present health status is poor	27.8	4.3
Feels health status is worse or much worse than a year ago	22.8	11.9
Feels health status is worse or much worse than five years ago	39.0	23.5
Has often had to go easy on work because of ill health	27.4	8.0
Has been unable to work in the past year because of ill health	37.5	data not available
Has had to miss more than three weeks of work or usual activity because of ill health during the past year	24.3	data not available
Seldom or never feels healthy enough to carry out the things they would like to do	28.2	5.5

four to 39% of the population indicated that their health status was poor, was worsening or was interfering with their work or usual activity.

Thirty-nine percent of the population gave negative responses to all seven questions, indicating that the perception of their health status was good. Among the remainder, 25% gave positive answers to four or more questions.

In addition, the responses to five of these questions by a sample of the entire population of Alachua County are included in Table 2. The increased sense of bad health by the poor population of this county is marked.

Utilization of Health Care Facilities and Providers

The Medicaid beneficiaries were asked to indicate what type of health care provider they consulted. The results are recorded in Table 3. The responses of the Medicaid population are compared to two other groups. The heads of households of migrant farmworkers were interviewed in 1973 in a study of health care needs of migrant workers in three north Florida counties. Alachua County residents (70% of whom live in Gainesville) were studied in 1970.[1] Nearly 73% of the Medicaid patients state that they had seen a physician during the past year. This figure no doubt represents some duplication since the survey instrument did not specify only physicians seen in their offices. The 73% probably included physicians seen at clinics and hospitals as well. This figure is comparable to the 80% of Alachua County residents who had seen a physician in one year, and similar to the 72% recorded in the National Health Survey.[3]

In Alachua County, because of the presence of the academic health center, which includes a teaching hospital and Veteran's Administration Hospital, there is one doctor for every 250 residents. The citizens of the county do not have access, however, to many of the doctors. Of the physicians in private practice it is estimated by county Medicaid administrators that fewer than 40% participate in the Medicaid program. Alachua County sponsors an adult and pediatric clinic for its medically indigent constituents which was used by 47% of the study population. The central office of the North Central Florida Community Mental Health Center is in Gainesville. This was identified by 6% as a source of health care. A similar percentage of respondents also sought care from a provider such as a faith healer or spiritualist. Probably most of the

Table 3 Use of Health Care Facilities and Providers By Population Groups During One Year

Agency	Alachua County Medicaid Recipients 1974 N = 259	St. Johns River Basin Farmworker Heads of House (1973) N = 291[b]	Sample of Alachua County Residents (1970) N = 1645[1]
	Percent Distribution		
Medical Doctors[a]	72.9	47.4	80.3
Public Health Nurse	33.6	28.2	3.7
Health Clinic	47.1	39.8	12.6
Hospital Inpatient	19.7	10.3	30.0
Community Mental Health Center	5.8	.003	0.8
Faith Healer or Spiritualist	5.8	.003	1.6
Psychiatrist or Psychologist	6.5	.003	5.1
Social Worker	67.5	4.1	5.9

[a]National Health Survey national average is 72.6% (1972).[2]
[b]The Health and Health Care Needs of Migrant Agricultural Farmworkers in Three Rural North Florida Counties, HSMHA Contract No. PHS-NSA-105-74-42.

6.5% who stated they saw a psychiatrist or psychologist did so at the Community Mental Health Center.

Traditionally the public health nurses have served the poor population. One third of the surveyed Medicaid group recalled a visit from the public health nurse during the previous year. Two thirds of the Medicaid recipients had consulted with a social worker. This is accounted for in part by the Division of Family Services' employment of social workers to administer the Medicaid program.

Dental Visits

In Table 4 there is assembled the percent of various groups who indicated they had visited a dentist at least once during the previous year. Altogether 22% of the Medicaid sample had seen a dentist. This was less than one half of the percentage of Alachua County residents who had seen a dentist in one year[1] and comparable to the sample of the national population adjusted for low income.[4] The migrant farmworkers, by nature of their rural location and trans-

iency, have less access to a dentist and visit one significantly less than the majority of the Medicaid population. The 2.3% of the total Florida Medicaid population represented only those under age 20 who saw a dentist.

Physician Visits

An effort was made to determine the number of times each year a Medicaid eligible person visited a physician and to com-

Table 4 Visits to the Dentist During Previous Year

Population Samples	Percent Distribution
Alachua County Medicaid Recipients	22.4
Eligible Florida Medicaid Recipients (1973–74)[a,b]	2.3
Alachua County Residents (1970)[1]	51.6
St. John Sample (1973)[c]	13.3
National Sample (1974)[3]	49.3
National Sample by Income (1969)[4] Under $2,000	26.6

pare this with other groups. These data are presented in Table 5. Little difference exists (1.89 vs. 1.25 visits per person per year) between the Alachua County Medicaid recipients and those from Florida at large in estimated annual physician visits. The remaining data depict little variation among the total number of annual physician visits despite the variation in patient constituency. There is a decrease in physician visits by migrant farmworkers

and household members, but the range of annual numbers of physician visits by the other population samples is 3.8 to 4.9.[5]

Knowledge of Medicaid

The use of Medicaid by eligible persons is related to their knowledge of this program. Each person was asked questions to ascertain his familiarity with the Florida Medicaid Program. Among those interviewed, 98.5% had heard of Medicaid, and 86.9% had used, at some time, health services provided by this program. Although all interviewed were presently receiving Medicaid benefits, 68.8% did not know who could receive benefits from Medicaid. Fourteen percent thought everyone was eligible, 29.3% were correct concerning eligibility, and 25.5% thought anyone medically indigent could receive benefits. Medical indigency is not a qualification for eligibility in Florida.

In Table 6 there is presented the responses of the study population to specific questions concerning their knowledge of the Medicaid program. Those health services used most often were recognized as a Medicaid benefit by most of the respond-

Table 5 Physician Visits Per Person Per Year For Selected Population Samples

Population Samples	Number of Visits Per Person Per Year
Alachua County Medicaid Recipients	1.89[a]
Florida Medicaid Recipients (1973–74)	1.25[b]
Alachua County Residents (1970)	4.7
St. Johns River Basin (Florida) Farmworker Heads of House (1973)[c]	3.5
St. Johns River Basin (Florida) Farmworker Household Members (1973)	2.8
National Health Survey Sample (1971)[5]	4.9
National Sample: Nonwhite	4.4
National Sample: Under $3,000 Income Per Year	6.2
National Sample: South	4.8
National Sample: Outside SMSA's —Farm	3.8
National Sample: 5 - 8 Years of Education	4.6

[a]This figure is obtained by dividing the number of visits per family by the mean number in each family.
[b]Given the estimated figure of 400,000 persons on Medicaid at any one time during FY 1973–74.
[c]The Health and Health Care Needs of Migrant Agricultural Farmworkers in Three Rural North Florida Counties, HSMHA Contract No. PHS-NSA-105-74-42.

Table 6 Recipients' Knowledge of Services Provided by Medicaid

Service	Percent of Recipients Who Think Medicaid Does/Does Not Provide Service
Service Not Provided	
Non-prescription Drugs	66.8
Services Provided	
Prescription Drugs	4.3
Hospital Care	19.3
Physician's Service	26.3
Laboratory and x-ray	58.7
Nursing Home Care	74.1
Home Health Care	78.4
Family Planning	70.7
Transportation	79.5
Screening	56.0

ents. This includes hospital care, physician services and prescription drugs.

While 73.7% of the respondents know that Medicaid provides for physician services, only 55.2% believe they can use Medicaid benefits in a private doctor's office.

Seventy percent did know where to seek information about eligibility for the Medicaid program. This was correctly identified as the Division of Family Services, or by the older nomenclature, the State Welfare Office.

Discussion

Medicaid was introduced to lessen the economic impediments between the poor citizens and the health care provider. Ideally the success of any health care program would indicate that the beneficiaries are healthier and more productive in some measurable fashion as a result of the program. Such clearcut outcomes, however, are difficult to measure. As a result the investigator often studies processes of health care delivery that reflect change in behavior or attitude of the program recipient toward health care.

The characteristics of the Medicaid population of Alachua County reveal no surprises. The eligibility requirements established by the state of Florida define a poor. black, female, unmarried, unemployed and undereducated population. The perception of present health status as poor or worsening is several-fold greater than that for other citizens of Alachua County. The Medicaid population receives a good portion of their health services from public health nurses and hospital clinics established to serve the indigent.

Although most of the people served by Medicaid had some knowledge of the program, over two thirds had incorrect information. Over 50% also believed they could not use Medicaid benefits in a private doctor's office.

A study of Baltimore Medicaid recipients in 1968-69 revealed that they were the highest users of health services in that community. They saw physicians more often, were admitted more frequently to hospitals and stayed longer than other residents of Baltimore.[6] In 1967-68, the Kaiser program in Portland, Oregon, extended its prepaid group health care plan to 1,200 families that met Office of Economic Opportunity eligibility criteria. This impoverished group of citizens were compared to other members under age 65 of the Kaiser Health Plan. The OEO membership had 11.5% greater number of doctor visits per 1,000 members and 14% more hospital days.[7]

The utilization of health services involves the definition of need by the user, his ability to come in contact with the provider of health care, his access to the provider once he is there, and the attitude and capability of the provider toward the individual seeking his services. The provider can represent either a single physician, group of doctors, multispecialty clinic, hospital emergency room, mental health center or any other person or unit engaged in dispensing health services.

Alachua County, site of a college of medicine, teaching hospital, Veteran's Administration Hospital and two community hospitals, has by any standard a surfeit of health providers. Nevertheless, the recipients of Medicaid are receiving fewer health services than other local residents. This probably represents an amalgam of factors including a different definition of health needs by poor citizens, inability to engage health practitioners, and hesitation on the part of some providers to serve the Medicaid beneficiaries.

The conclusion is simple. A health care program directed primarily at removing the economic barriers between the poor and health providers is by itself not successful. Until Title XIX is revised or replaced, however, improvements should be made to facilitate easier access to the health care system wherever possible.

Improvements can be made in two directions. Medicaid beneficiaries need to be made more aware of the benefits of the program and the resources available to them. At present they receive little information of an educational nature specifically about the Medicaid program. There is a brochure outlining eligibility and benefits but according to the respondents in this study few people are aware of it. It is only when medical care is necessary that inquiries are made about specific benefits. This means the Medicaid eligibles in this county rarely, if ever, understand the whole program.

Secondly, improvements can be made in the direction of the provider. The problem of Medicaid program acceptance by private practice physicians was not included in this study. It should be investigated further and the results of these investigations used to create means for increased participation by health providers.

REFERENCES

1. Schwab, J.J.; Warheit, G.J., and Fennel, E.B.: Epidemiologic Assessment of Needs and Utilization of Services, Evaluation 2:65–67, 1975.

2. U.S. Department of Health, Education, and Welfare, Public Health Service: Current Estimates from the Health Interview Survey, United States: 1972. HRA Publication 74-1512. Washington, D.C., U.S. Government Printing Office, 1973.

3. U.S. Department of Health, Education, and Welfare, Public Health Service: Current Estimates from the Health Interview Survey, United States: 1974 HRA Publication 76-1527. Washington, D.C., U.S. Government Printing Office, 1975.

4. U.S. Department of Health, Education, and Welfare, Public Health Service: Dental Visits: Volume and Interval Since Last Visit, United States: 1969. HRA Publication 72-1066. Washington, D.C., U.S. Government Printing Office, 1972.

5. U.S. Department of Health, Education, and Welfare, Public Health Service: Physician Visits: Volume and Interval Since Last Visit, United States: 1971 HRA Publication 75-1524. Washington, D.C., U.S. Government Printing Office, 1975.

6. Rabin, D.L.; Bice, T.W., and Starfield, B.: Use of Health Services by Baltimore Medicaid Recipients, Med Care 7:561–570, 1974.

7. Greenlick, M.R.: Medical Services to Poverty Groups. In Somers, A.R. (ed.) The Kaiser-Permanente Medical Care Program. New York, NY, The Commonwealth Fund, 1971, pp. 138–148.

31. Foreign Medical Graduates and Maryland Medicaid

JAMES STUDNICKI, ROBERT M. SAYWELL, JR.,
and WALTER WIECHETEK

Reprinted, by permission, from the *New England Journal of Medicine*, (Vol. 294, pp. 1153-1157, 1976).

In spite of some recent questioning of the actual magnitude of the migration of foreign medical graduates (FMG's) to the United States,[1] approximately one out of five licensed physicians and one out of three hospital residents in this country are trained abroad.[2] Two basic questions concerning FMG's that have major public-policy implications are whether they provide medical care that is generally equivalent in quality to that rendered by United States medical graduates (USMG's) and whether they are providing services to populations that are discernibly different socioeconomically from populations served by USMG's.

Quality assessment depends on the reliability and validity of the various methods used to evaluate physician performance.[3] What we see in the context of the FMG is the use of certain "proxy" indicators of quality or substitutes for more direct measures. Variables such as board-certification status, licensure status, performance on various state licensing examinations,[4] performance on the Education Council of Foreign Medical Graduates (ECFMG) examination,[5] performance on various specialty board examinations,[6] and certain types of intuitive judgments related to cultural shock[7] and language ability have been used to generate some suggestive trends.

The question of differences in populations served by FMG's has been fueled by their disproportionate representation among hospital house staffs and public institutions,[8] suggesting that the services rendered by the FMG are channeled to society's unfortunates. Absent from the literature, however, are studies that link certain patient characteristics to FMG providers of care. Of special interest in this context is the role of the fully licensed FMG in private practice and the nature of his patient population as compared to that of his USMG peer.

One such socioeconomically defined patient population is a state's medical-assistance recipients. The objective of our study was to determine whether there are identifiable differences in FMG representation among Medicaid physician participants (vendors) as compared to the total population of all licensed physicians within the State. Total Maryland physicians and Medicaid vendors were subdivided into

Supported in part through a contract (HRA 106-74-164) with the Bureau of Health Manpower, Division of Medicine, International Programs Staff, National Institutes of Health, U.S. Department of Health, Education, and Welfare, but does not necessarily represent the views of those agencies.

FMG and USMG subpopulations and compared for licensure status, selected specialty distribution, board-certification status, and patterns of geographical distribution within the State.

STUDY POPULATION, DATA SOURCES, CONSTRAINTS

The study population consisted of 1842 physicians who had received from the highest amount to just under $1,000 in payments from the Maryland Medical Assistance program in fiscal year 1974. These physician "vendors" are licensed practitioners who must, in addition, be formally certified by the program before they are eligible to receive Medicaid funds. Physician groups and institutional sources of physician services were not included in the study. Payments for all physician services accounted for 9.3 per cent of the total payments of the Maryland Medicaid program in fiscal 1974. Of the nearly 16 million dollars paid for physician services during the period, the physician study population accounted for approximately 10.4 million dollars, or 65 per cent of the total dollars paid for physician services.

All the information included in this study was computed or taken directly from three sources: *Maryland Medical Assistance Program, Statistical and Fiscal Information, Fiscal Year 1974,* Maryland Department of Health and Mental Hygiene, December, 1974; Maryland Medical Assistance Program, Physician Vendor Summary 11A, 1974 Fiscal Year, Listing of Participating Physicians, Ordered by Total Payments (unpublished); and American Medical Association, "Physician Biographical Record," 1973.

The total Maryland statistics are compiled as of December 31, 1973. Medicaid vendor data are for the period July, 1973, through June, 1974. In addition certain individual physicians appearing on the vendor list were not included in the AMA bio-graphical summary. Physicians for whom a complete data set was not available were excluded from the study. These 16 physicians demonstrated no consistent profile of characteristics that could be identified by the research team. Also, it was not possible to identify physicians who were primarily engaged in research, administration or education as opposed to patient care in the total Maryland statistics. This drawback could influence the numbers for metropolitan areas, but especially for Montgomery and Prince Georges counties, which include large numbers of physician employees of governmental health agencies. Although we know that generally USMG's have a higher proportional representation in these positions, the exact proportions are not known, and this discrepancy may be a source of some error.[9] The AMA biographical survey asks physicians to identify a primary and secondary "specialty" that describes their practice. All data reviewed here reflect only the primary specialty choice. In addition, this self-selected identification is decided by the individual physician without the use of explicit criteria such as the completion of special training or the relative proportions of certain types of patients seen. Finally, as has so often been mentioned, the aggregation of physicians into two groups on the basis of country of medical education is not without statistical and interpretational problems.

LICENSURE

As of December 31, 1973, 7077 physicians were licensed to practice in the state of Maryland. Of these, 78 per cent (5514) were USMG's and 22 per cent (1563) were FMG's. Of the Maryland Medicaid vendors, 64 per cent (1183) were USMG's and 36 per cent (659) were FMG's. A comparison of a five-year period of licensing figures is more revealing. The FMG proportion of all newly licensed physicians (by reciprocity and examination) in the state of Maryland has increased from 20 per cent in 1969 to 40 per cent in 1973, with the largest increase between 1972 and 1973 (14 per cent). If we compare these figures to a breakdown of all fiscal 1974 Medicaid vendors according to year of licensure, we can note some suggestive trends. First of all, FMG's appear to participate in the Medicaid program at a consistently higher rate than USMG's for a given licensure year. Secondly, the dominance of the Medicaid vendor population by FMG's in recent years is dramatic: of the 1974 program participants, 122 of the 130 Medicaid vendors licensed to practice in 1972 and 1973 were FMG's (Table 1). Since the Medicaid vendor data are a summary for fiscal year 1974 and not a composite review of annually determined licensure figures, it is possible that a part of such a dramatic difference may be attributed to differences in the interval between medical licensure and Medicaid participation—that is, FMG's may simply participate in the Medicaid program much sooner after licensure than their USMG peers for any licensure year. Although complete and comparable 1975 data are not available at this writing, indications are that the trends identified in this five-year period are continuing.

SPECIALTY

The three specialties of general surgery, internal medicine, and general practice account for 50 per cent of all the FMG Medicaid vendors but only 30 per cent of all the FMG physicians statewide. If we calculate FMG's as a percentage of total physicians within certain specialties, we can see more clearly the disproportionate representation of FMG's among Medicaid vendors clustering into these specialties. For example, FMG's account for 29 per cent of the general surgeons in Maryland, but 57 per cent of the general surgeons who are Medicaid vendors. Likewide, FMG's account for 21 per cent of the internists in Maryland, but 52 per cent of the internist Medicaid vendors. FMG general practitioners are also disproportionately represented among the Medicaid vendors, but the difference (Medicaid vendors minus Maryland total) is small—only 6 per cent. For other specialties, FMG's tend to be variably under-represented among Medicaid vendors. Although it is difficult to generalize a trend from this information, it appears that FMG's are most underrepresented among Medicaid vendors in the

Table 1 Total Maryland Physicians Licensed by Years, Fiscal 1974 Medicaid Vendors by Year of Licensure, and Index of Medicaid Participation as of June, 1974.*

Yr.	Maryland Physicians Licensed			Fiscal 1974 Medicaid Vendors/Yr of Licensure			Index of Medicaid Participation (MVL/MPI)† as of June, 1974	
	Totals	FMG	%FMG	Totals	FMG	%FMG	FMG	USMG
1969	748	148	20	50	34	68	0.230	0.027
1970	861	217	25	71	35	49	0.161	0.056
1971	1010	270	27	103	53	51	0.196	0.068
1972	1131	299	26	60	53	88	0.177	0.008
1973	1330	529	40	70	69	99	0.130	0.001

*Calculated from American Medical Association, "Physician Biographical Record," 1973, & Maryland Medical Assistance Program, Physician Vendor Summary 11A, 1974 Fiscal Year, List of Participating Physicians, Ordered by Total Payments (unpublished).

†Medicare vendors licensed/Maryland physicians licensed.

specialties that have either small absolute numbers of Medicaid vendors (e.g., dermatology and psychiatry) or an overwhelming domination of the specialty within the state by USMG's (e.g., ophthalmology) (Table 2). These differences in specialty distribution are closely related to the differences in board-certification status.

BOARD CERTIFICATION

Thirty-two per cent of all the FMG's in Maryland are board certified physicians. Among the Medicaid vendors, only 22 per cent of the FMG's are board certified. For USMG's, 48 per cent are board certified statewide, whereas 52 per cent of the USMG Medicaid vendors are board certified. These findings reflect both a clustering of FMG Medicaid vendors into the specialties that have relatively low board-certification percentages and the domination of certain specialties by USMG's. Interestingly enough, in the specialties in which the percentage of FMG's and USMG's who are board certified is about equal for the total Maryland physician

population (e.g., pediatrics, ophthalmology and dermatology), the Medicaid vendors are almost exclusively USMG's (Table 3). We may generally conclude that the FMG general surgeon and internist, usually not board certified, is much more likely to participate in the Medicaid program than his USMG peer. On the other hand, the board-certified FMG ophthalmologist, dermatologist, pediatrician or psychiatrist is less likely to participate in the Medicaid program than his USMG peer. These identified differences in board certification do not necessarily indicate differences in the length of formal postgraduate medical training received. It is possible that the inability to take or pass the board examinations is related to factors other than the length of training.

GEOGRAPHICAL DISTRIBUTION

Is the pattern of geographical dispersion of FMG Medicaid vendors within the State different from that of FMG's as a whole?

The 24 Maryland subdivisions (23 counties and Baltimore City) were arrayed in

Table 2 Foreign Medical Graduates as a Percentage of Selected Specialties—Total Maryland Physicians and Medicaid Vendors Only, According to Percentage Differences.*

Specialty	Total Maryland Physicians			Medicaid Vendors			% Differences
	USMG	FMG	% FMG	USMG	FMG	% FMG	
General Surgery	359	146	29	108	144	57	+ 38
Internal Medicine	836	220	21	113	125	52	+ 31
General Practice	582	115	16	206	59	22	+ 06
Obstetrics & gynecology	355	161	31	110	46	29	− 2
Pediatrics	383	122	24	68	19	22	− 2
Anesthesiology	119	143	54	39	43	52	− 2
Family practice	110	14	11	33	3	8	− 3
Ophthalmology	219	20	8	151	3	2	− 6
Dermatology	81	8	9	31	1	3	− 6
Psychiatry	551	157	22	21	3	12	− 10
Radiology	182	25	12	46	1	02	− 10

*Calculated from American Medical Association, "Physician Biographical Record," 1973, & Maryland Medical Assistance Program, Physician Vendor Summary 11A, 1974 Fiscal Year, List of Participating Physicians, Ordered by Total Payments (unpublished).

Table 3 For Selected Specialties, Board-Certification Status, Foreign and American Medical Graduate Percentages—Total Maryland Physicians and Medicaid Vendors Only.*

Specialty	Total Maryland Physicians					Medicaid Vendors		
	FMG	% Certified	USMG	% Certified	USMG	% Certified	FMG	% Certified
General surgery	359	55	146	24	108	59	144	13
Internal medicine	836	41	220	17	113	30	125	1
General practice	582	09	115	3	206	4	59	19
Obstetrics & gynecology	335	70	161	33	110	69	46	43
Pediatrics	383	58	122	58	68	40	19	16
Anesthesiology	119	62	143	31	39	69	43	0
Family practice	110	62	14	28	33	70	3	33
Ophthalmology	219	58	20	55	151	79	3	0
Dermatology	81	62	8	62	31	100	1	100
Psychiatry	551	41	157	25	21	4	3	0
Radiology	182	70	25	72	46	52	1	0
All specialties	5514	48	1563	32	1183	52	659	22

*Calculated from American Medical Association, "Physician Biographical Record," 1973, & Maryland Medical Assistance Program, Physician Vendor Summary 11A, 1974 Fiscal Year, List of Participating Physicians, Ordered by Total Payments (unpublished).

order by use of a simple population-to-physician ratio. Also, for each subdivision, the percentages of FMG total Maryland physicians and Medicaid vendors were listed. Finally, the percentage difference was listed for each subdivision, and quartile average percentages were computed for each group of six subdivisions (Table 4).

The six counties with the highest population-to-physician ratios have very small numbers of Medicaid patients and Medicaid vendors. Although the use of percentages can be misleading, we can conclude that, with a few exceptions, FMG's are disproportionately represented among Medicaid vendors throughout the entire range of population-to-physician ratios. More importantly, the disproportional representation of FMG's among Medicaid vendors is highest, on the average, in the subdivisions with the lowest population-to-physician ratios—that is, in the subdivisions that are relatively "physician rich."

We can construct a "fifth quartile" from the six subdivisions that account for nearly 74 per cent of the total Medicaid payments to physicians and 81 per cent of the total number of in-state physician accounts: Bal-timore City, and Baltimore, Prince George's, Montgomery, Anne Arundel and Washington counties. If we compute quartile average percentages for these subdivisions—percentage of FMG total Maryland physicians = 23.2, percentage of FMG Medicaid vendors = 39.2, percentage difference = 16.0—we may conclude that the disproportional representation of FMG's among Medicaid vendors is even higher within the subdivisions that account for the highest percentages of total Medicaid payments.

DISCUSSION

The numerical differences that we have identified are open to varied interpretation. However, the findings do support the hypothesis that a special relation exists between the FMG and "poverty medicine" and that this relation extends beyond institutional sources of care to the sole licensed practitioner. The clustering of FMG Medicaid vendors into certain specialties indicates that there may be differences in the services provided to

Table 4 Maryland Counties and Baltimore City, Population per Physician, Percentage of Foreign Medical Graduates, Total Maryland Physicians and Medicaid Vendors Only, Quartile Average Percentages.*

County	Population/ Physician	% FMG's/ Total Maryland Physicians	Quartile Average (%)	% FMG's/ Medicaid Vendors	Quartile Average (%)	% Differ- ence	Quartile Average (%)
Caroline†	3312	17		20		+ 3	
Queen Anne†	2709	14		0		− 14	
Calvert†	2215	30		67		+ 37	
Charles†	2090	44		68		+ 24	
Somerset†	2079	0		0		—	
Garrett†	1983	9	19.0	0	25.8	− 9	6.8
Worcester†	1540	12		0		− 12	
Prince George's	1521	36		62		+ 26	
St. Mary's†	1512	27		11		− 16	
Baltimore County	1383	34		38		+ 4	
Cecil	1164	40		58		+ 18	
Anne Arundel	1144	27	29.3	34	33.8	+ 7	4.5
Frederick†	1124	13		16		+ 3	
Harford	1067	33		26		− 7	
Carroll	1040	42		62		+ 20	
Washington	912	13		33		+ 20	
Kent	861	10		8		− 2	
Allegheny	839	31	23.7	47	32.0	+ 16	8.3
Dorchester	624	40		43		+ 3	
Wicomico	517	22		36		+ 14	
Howard	417	23		33		+ 10	
Talbot†	338	8		20		+ 12	
Montgomery	325	7		29		+ 22	
Baltimore City	299	22	20.3	39	33.3	+ 17	13.0

*Calculated from American Medical Association, "Physician Biographical Record," 1973, & Maryland Medical Assistance Program, Physician Vendor Summary 11A, 1974 Fiscal Year, List of Participating Physicians, Ordered by Total Payments (unpublished).

†County contains < 15 FMG's. The 10 counties so indicated, in fact, contain a total of only 44 FMG's. Percentages from such small numbers can prove misleading (e.g., Calvert County's 67% of FMG Medicaid Vendors is only 2 physicians!).

Medicaid patients by FMG Medicaid vendors as compared to USMG Medicaid vendors. For example, given the preponderance of FMG general surgeons, one might suspect that FMG's provide a relatively greater proportion of Medicaid inpatient hospital services than they do services in an ambulatory setting. The board-certification differences may be a reflection of a branch in the career pathway of the FMG in which certification status marks a professional independence with respect to public sources of financing for care. The relatively low level of participation of the board-certified FMG in the Medicaid program may also represent a desire on his part to avoid association with allegedly second-class medicine and, thus, to reinforce his equality. Finally, it also appears that the Medicaid program, for whatever reasons, exerts enough of an attraction for the FMG vendor that he is likely to locate in the areas of the State that contain the greatest numbers of medical-assistance recipients, despite the fact that these areas also tend to be "physician rich." Certainly, given this finding, the existence of some division of labor in these areas between FMG's and

USMG's on the basis of socioeconomic differences in the patient population must be considered. Obviously, each of these questions requires a more detailed scrutiny.

It is recognized that each state is a unique composite of medical manpower mix, licensure requirements, physician-vendor eligibility, patient medical-assistance eligibility, population characteristics and other special influences. At this point, it is not known how representative the Maryland situation may be of other states.

We are indebted to Annette W. Press for general research and to Kathleen Moore for assistance.

REFERENCES

1. Stevens R., Goodman LW, Mick SS, et al: Physician migration reexamined. Science 190:439–442, 1975

2. Williams KN, Lockett BA: Migration of foreign physicians to the United States: the perspective of health manpower planning. Int J. Health Serv 4:213–243, 1974

3. Brook RH: Quality of Care Assessment: A comparison of five methods of peer review (DHEW Publication No. HRA-74-3100). Washington, DC, Government Printing Office, 1973

4. Luy MLM: FMGs—do they create a double standard in U.S. medical care. Mod Med 42 (23):18–24, 1974

5. Weiss RJ, Kleinman JC, Brandt UC, et al: The effect of importing physicians—return to a pre-Flexnerian standard. N Engl J Med 290:1453–1458, 1974

6. Pass/fail rates from the boards. Resident Staff Physician: 149–152, November, 1974

7. Stevens RA, Goodman LW, Mick SS: What happens to foreign-trained doctors who come to the United States? Inquiry (Chicago) 11:112–124, 1974

8. Derbyshire RC: Warm bodies in white coats. JAMA 232:1034–1035, 1975

9. Mick SS: The foreign medical graduate. Sci Am 232 (2):14–21, 1975

32. A Survey of Physician Participation in and Dissatisfaction with the Medi-Cal Program

A Socioeconomic Report of the Bureau of Research and Planning, California Medical Association

MICHAEL W. JONES and BETTE HAMBURGER

Reprinted with permission from *Western Journal of Medicine* Vol. 124, No. 1., pp. 75-83 (January 1976).

In late 1974, the California Medical Association's Bureau of Research and Planning sent questionnaires about participation in Medi-Cal (California's Medicaid program) to a random sample of 1,200 members in private medical practice. Questions covered degree of current participation in the program; plans for future participation; patterns of acceptance of new Medi-Cal patients, referrals and consultations, and similar questions about personal involvement in the program. Responses were received from almost 70 percent of physicians sampled.

Subsequently, respondents who have curtailed participation in Medi-Cal or plan to do so were sent a follow-up questionnaire to elicit information about their perception of various problem areas within the program. From these data, evaluations can be made concerning the types of reform that might be most fruitful in eliciting the broadscale physician participation on which the program is conceptually based. Well over three-quarters of the 336 physicians in this subsample group provided data.

These findings represent highlights of a detailed report, single copies of which are available on request from the CMA's Division of Research and Socioeconomics.

PART I—THE BROAD-SCALE SAMPLE

Most Physicians Participate in Medi-Cal Program

As seen in Table 1, approximately one patient in ten (9.7 percent) being treated by the average physician is covered under the Medi-Cal program. However, the table clearly shows that a substantial number of physicians (14.9 percent) practice in a situation where over a quarter of all their patients are under Medi-Cal, while a relatively small proportion (6.3 percent) treat no Medi-Cal patients whatever. More than a fourth of all respondents (25.6 percent) conduct practices in which fewer than 5 percent of their patients are on Medi-Cal.

Understandably, participation differs according to medical specialty. Pediatricians tend to have a relatively higher proportion of Medi-Cal patients than do most other physicians, while internists, obstetrician/gynecologists and orthopedists have below-average proportions. Many pediatricians, general practitioners and psychiatrists have a patient load of which more than a fourth is made up of Medi-Cal patients. At the other end of the spectrum, above average proportions of obstetrician/gynecologists and psychiatrists treat no

Table 1 Proportion of Total Patients Covered Under Medi-Cal, by Medical Specialty, January 1975

| Specialty | Total Respondents | | Proportion of Patients Under Medi-Cal | | | | | | | | | | | Medi-Cal Patients Taken by Avg. Practitioner |
| | | | None | | Under 5% | | 5-10% | | 11-15% | | 16-25% | | Over 25% | | |
	Number	Percent	Number	Percent	Number	Percent	Number	Percent	Number	Percent	Number	Percent	Number	Percent	Percent
General/Family Practice	160	100	5	3.1	38	23.8	35	21.9	22	13.8	21	13.1	39	24.4	10.9
Internal Medicine[1]	126	100	6	4.8	47	37.3	32	25.4	23	18.3	9	7.1	9	7.1	6.7
Pediatrics[1]	41	100	0	..	5	12.2	9	22.0	10	24.4	5	12.2	12	29.3	13.7
Other Medical[2]	31	100	2	6.5	8	25.8	7	22.6	7	22.6	4	12.9	3	9.7	9.3
General Surgery[3]	57	100	2	3.5	16	28.0	12	21.0	16	28.0	7	12.3	4	7.0	9.8
Other Surgery[4]	32	100	2	6.3	9	28.1	4	12.5	6	18.8	9	28.1	2	6.3	11.3
Obstetrics/Gynecology	59	100	7	11.9	23	39.0	7	11.9	8	13.6	8	13.6	6	10.2	5.0
Ophthalmology	37	100	1	2.7	8	21.6	9	24.3	8	21.6	8	21.6	3	8.1	10.8
Orthopedic Surgery	35	100	3	8.6	12	34.3	7	20.0	4	11.4	8	22.9	1	2.9	7.0
Otolaryngology	19	100	0	..	6	31.6	3	15.8	4	21.1	4	21.1	2	10.5	11.4
Psychiatry[1]	58	100	8	13.8	9	15.5	12	20.7	6	10.3	10	17.2	13	22.4	10.5
All Other	35	100	9	25.7	7	20.0	7	20.0	3	8.6	7	20.0	2	5.7	6.2
Total (excluding Anesthesiology, Radiology and Pathology)[5]	690	100	45	6.5	188	27.2	144	20.9	117	17.0	100	14.6	96	13.9	9.3

[1]Including subspecialties
[2]Includes allergy, dermatology, neurology, physical medicine.
[3]Includes abdominal surgery, colon and rectal surgery, pediatric surgery.
[4]Includes cardiovascular surgery, neurological surgery, plastic surgery, thoracic surgery, urology.
[5]Excludes two respondents who did not answer this specific question.

Medi-Cal patients whatever. One psychiatrist, who formerly treated Medi-Cal patients, commented that he would participate "only if Medi-Cal patients would be permitted as many visits as were necessary to help them."

Generally, however, the table suggests that Medi-Cal patients are reasonably well distributed among physicians, since in the aggregate very few physicians have no Medi-Cal patients and relatively few have practices dominated by Medi-Cal patients.

Few Respondents Want More Medi-Cal Patients

Table 2 provides information about patterns of acceptance of new Medi-Cal patients, according to medical specialty. Data from anesthesiologists, radiologists and pathologists have been excluded, since they are generally unable to make an independent decision about whom they treat. Also excluded are data from respondents who have never treated Medi-Cal patients.

Table 2 Acceptance of New Medi-Cal Patients, by Medical Specialty and Level of Current Involvement in the Program

Specialty/Level of Current Participation	Total Respondents		Acceptance of New Medi-Cal Patients							
			Probably Would		Might		Probably Not		Definitely Not	
	Number	Percent	Number	Percent	Number	Percent	Number	Percent	Number	Percent
General/Family Practice	155	100	52	33.5	32	20.6	37	23.9	34	21.9
Internal Medicine[1]	121	100	30	24.8	23	19.0	51	42.1	17	14.1
Pediatrics[1]	41	100	23	56.1	11	26.8	5	12.2	2	4.9
Other Medical[2]	31	100	18	58.1	3	9.7	8	25.8	2	6.5
General Surgery[3]	57	100	32	56.1	11	19.3	10	17.5	4	7.0
Other Surgery[4]	32	100	18	56.3	7	21.9	6	18.8	1	3.1
Obstetrics/Gynecology	57	100	24	42.1	13	22.8	16	28.1	4	7.0
Ophthalmology	37	100	28	75.7	3	8.1	4	10.8	2	5.4
Orthopedic Surgery	33	100	10	30.3	6	18.2	11	33.3	6	18.2
Otolaryngology	19	100	13	68.4	6	31.6	0	..	0	..
Psychiatry[1]	54	100	24	44.4	13	24.1	10	18.5	7	13.0
All Other	26	100	14	53.8	4	15.4	5	19.2	3	11.5
Total (excluding Anesthesiology, Radiology and Pathology)[5]	663	100	286	43.1	132	19.9	163	24.6	82	12.4
Formerly treated, none now	24	100	1	4.2	1	4.2	9	37.5	13	54.2
Under 5 Percent	189	100	43	22.8	34	18.0	77	44.9	35	18.5
5 to 10 percent	156	100	66	42.3	35	22.4	35	22.4	20	12.8
11 to 15 percent	127	100	62	48.8	33	26.0	22	17.3	10	7.9
16 to 25 percent	109	100	69	63.3	20	18.3	15	13.8	5	4.6
Over 25 percent	109	100	87	79.8	11	10.1	7	6.4	4	3.7
Total[6]	714	100	328	45.9	134	18.8	165	23.1	87	12.2

[1-4]See footnotes to Table 1.

[5]Excludes 23 respondents who have *never* treated Medi-Cal patients, and 8 who did not respond to this specific question.

[6]Excludes physicians who have *never* treated any Medi-Cal patients.

Among other respondents, 43.1 percent probably would accept a new Medi-Cal patient, 19.9 percent might accept one, 24.6 percent probably would not accept one and 12.4 percent definitely would not accept a new Medi-Cal patient. Thus, it is clear that only a minority of California's private practitioners would willingly provide care to a new Medi-Cal patient seeking their services if the circumstances were such that they could make such a choice.

Data about physician willingness to accept new Medi-Cal patients according to their current level of participation are also shown in Table 2. Excluded from this portion of the table are respondents who indicated that they have never treated patients under the program; included, however, are anesthesiologists, radiologists and pathologists.

The data show a close association between degree of current Medi-Cal involvement and willingness to continue treating patients under the program. Among physicians whose case load is currently over a quarter Medi-Cal patients, almost four out of five respondents (79.8 percent) indicated that they probably would accept a new Medi-Cal patient who requested care, while just over 10 percent indicated that they either probably or definitely would not accept a new Medi-Cal patient seeking services at this time.

At the low end of the spectrum of current Medi-Cal participation, more than six out of ten respondents (63.4 percent) indicated that they probably would not or definitely would not accept a new Medi-Cal patient, while fewer than a fourth (22.8 percent) said that they probably would accept one. This close association suggests that the base of Medi-Cal participation by California physicians is gradually narrowing and that, absent program changes, the future will find fewer physicians treating more patients under the program.

Many Plan to Curtail Medi-Cal Involvement

Table 3 provides information about the future plans of physicians who are currently treating Medi-Cal patients. Most physicians indicated that they will continue treating Medi-Cal patients, as well as family members. However, a substantial proportion (17.0 percent) intend gradually to lower the number of Medi-Cal patients under their care, while some others (6.4 percent) plan to curtail caring for Medi-Cal patients as rapidly as feasible.

Internists and orthopedists showed particular reluctance to offer services to "family members" not currently under their care. "Other" surgeons, such as neurosurgeons and urologists, obstetrician/gynecologists, orthopedists and psychiatrists seem especially anxious to lower the proportion of Medi-Cal patients under their care. This proposed course of action was noted by very few pediatricians, ophthalmologists or otolaryngologists.

Information about future plans regarding Medi-Cal participation according to level of current involvement by physician respondents is also contained in Table 3. Most physicians with significant current involvement expect to remain involved, while those with a low level of participation plan to limit their participation even more or, in fact, curtail it entirely. The data again show that the base of physicians available to provide care under the program is narrowing and that relatively more care will be provided in the future by those physicians who already have significant involvement in the program.

Further Evidence of Narrowing Base

As seen in Table 4, most respondents (52.3 percent) indicated that they expect the proportion of Medi-Cal patients under their care in three years to be similar to the cur-

Table 3 Physicians' Continued Treatment of Current Medi-Cal Patients During the Coming Year by Medical Specialty and Level of Current Involvement in the Program

Specialty/Level of Current Participation	Total Respondents		Treatment of Current Medi-Cal Patients							
			Continue, Plus Family Members		Continue Patients Only		Gradually Lower Number of Patients		Curtail Number of Patients Soon	
	Number	Percent	Number	Percent	Number	Percent	Number	Percent	Number	Percent
General/Family Practice ..	154	100	98	63.6	27	17.5	22	14.3	7	4.5
Internal Medicine[1]	119	100	46	38.7	41	34.5	21	17.6	11	9.2
Pediatrics[1]	41	100	32	78.0	6	14.6	2	4.9	1	2.4
Other Medical[2]	29	100	16	55.2	8	27.6	4	13.8	1	3.4
General Surgery[3]	55	100	32	58.2	10	18.2	9	16.4	4	7.3
Other Surgery[4]	30	100	17	56.7	3	10.0	7	23.3	3	10.0
Obstetrics/Gynecology ...	52	100	25	48.1	12	23.1	11	21.1	4	7.7
Ophthalmology	36	100	29	80.6	3	8.3	3	8.3	1	2.8
Orthopedic Surgery	31	100	10	32.3	10	32.3	9	29.0	2	6.5
Otolaryngology	19	100	18	94.7	0	..	1	5.3	0	..
Psychiatry[1]	49	100	26	53.1	7	14.3	13	26.5	3	6.1
All Other	26	100	11	42.3	4	15.4	7	26.9	4	15.4
Total (excluding Anesthesiology, Radiology and Pathology)[5]	641	100	360	56.2	131	20.4	109	17.0	41	6.4
Under 5 percent	190	100	76	40.0	61	32.1	27	14.2	26	13.7
5 to 10 percent	156	100	92	59.0	27	17.3	30	19.2	7	4.5
11 to 15 percent	126	100	74	58.7	26	20.6	21	16.7	5	4.0
16 to 25 percent	109	100	67	61.5	12	11.0	25	22.9	5	4.6
Over 25 percent	110	100	86	78.2	9	8.2	13	11.8	2	1.8
Total[6]	691	100	395	57.2	135	19.5	116	16.8	45	6.5

[1–4]See footnotes to Table 1.

[5]Excludes 23 respondents who have never treated Medi-Cal patients, 24 who have no current Medi-Cal patients, and 7 who did not respond to this specific question.

[6]Excludes physicians with no Medi-Cal patients currently under their care.

rent proportion. Among others, 27.5 percent plan to be treating a smaller proportion. Since it is unlikely that many respondents expect the program itself to contract, one can assume that this group of respondents propose to achieve a diminished proportion by reason of their own voluntary actions with respect to participation in the program.

While only 7.3 percent of physicians whose current case load is under 5 percent Medi-Cal expect to increase this proportion, almost two in five (37.7 percent) plan to reduce it. Conversely, among those physicians whose current complement of patients is over a fourth Medi-Cal, well over a third (36.0 percent) expect to be treating an even larger proportion in the future, while only one in five (20.7 percent) expect the proportion to diminish.

Although the association between these two variables is extremely close, it should also be noted that a small but nonetheless significant proportion of physicians who are heavily involved in the program apparently wish to curtail their degree of involvement. The data also suggest that an almost negligible proportion of physicians not currently

Table 4 Medi-Cal Patient Load Expected in Three Years, by Current Level of Program Participation

| Proportion of Patients Under Medi-Cal | Total Respondents | | Proportion of Medi-Cal Patients in Three Years | | | | | | | |
| | | | Larger | | Same | | Smaller | | No Answer | |
	Number	Percent	Number	Percent	Number	Percent	Number	Percent	Number	Percent
Under 5 percent	191	100	14	7.3	99	51.8	72	37.7	6	3.1
5 to 10 percent	158	100	18	11.4	97	61.4	42	26.6	1	0.6
11 to 15 percent	129	100	24	18.6	66	51.2	36	27.9	3	2.3
16 to 25 percent	109	100	33	30.3	57	52.3	19	17.4	0	—
Over 25 percent	111	100	40	36.0	46	41.4	23	20.7	2	1.8
Total[1]	698	100	129	18.5	365	52.3	195	27.5	12	1.7
No Medi-Cal Patients Currently Under Care ...	47	100	3	6.4	44	93.6	0	0.0	0	0.0

[1]Excludes physicians with no Medi-Cal patients currently under their care.

treating any Medi-Cal patients expect to begin participating in the program in the future.

Although not shown in Table 4, among physicians who expect to be treating relatively more Medi-Cal patients, an overwhelming majority indicated that this is based on their own feeling of responsibility. Many also anticipate that more Medi-Cal patients will be seeking a new physician in the future. Relatively few physicians considered the program "reasonably easy to work with," while an almost negligible proportion indicated a preference for Medi-Cal patients to other types of patients. Almost half of these respondents expected that they would be treating a larger proportion of Medi-Cal patients because other physicians in their geographic area are limiting their Medi-Cal practice.

PART II—THE FOLLOW-UP

Who Provided the Data

Information contained in the follow-up survey is based on responses from a sample of 336 California Medical Association members who, in answer to Part I of the "Medi-Cal Participation Survey," indicated that they either treat no patients under the Medi-Cal program or had cut back on their participation or planned to do so in the future. This represents 45 percent of the total group of physicians who responded to the earlier questionnaire.

Usable responses were received from 258 of the 336 physicians sampled, or 76.8 percent. This high rate of response assures that the data represent with reasonable accuracy the opinions of physicians sufficiently alienated by Medi-Cal to have taken action with respect to their own personal participation in the program.

Medi-Cal Problem Areas Identified

Table 5 indicates how respondents rated various potential problem areas within the Medi-Cal program. Over half of all respondents (51.2 percent) consider inadequate level of reimbursement a critical problem to them with reference to participation in the Medi-Cal program. Almost as important are the problems of denial and reimbursement for services already provided and bureaucratic interference in patient care. Totals of 46.3 and 45.9 percent, respectively, called these problems "critical." Interestingly, a total of 26.8 percent of respondents considered bureaucratic inter-

Table 5 Respondent Ratings of Various Potential Problem Areas in the Medi-Cal Program

Problem Area	Total Responding[1]		Seriousness of Problem							
			Critical		Major		Minor		Not a Problem	
	Number	Percent	Number	Percent	Number	Percent	Number	Percent	Number	Percent
Inability to determine amount MD will be paid ..	243	100	57	23.5	109	44.9	62	25.5	15	6.2
Excessive paperwork	294	100	92	36.9	101	40.6	52	20.9	4	1.6
Delays in payment	243	100	73	30.0	83	34.2	66	27.2	21	8.6
Difficulty in securing prior authorization	230	100	43	18.7	83	36.1	70	30.4	34	14.8
Inadequate level of reimbursement	244	100	125	51.2	90	36.9	26	10.7	3	1.2
Denial of reimbursement for services provided	231	100	107	46.3	81	35.1	27	11.7	16	6.9
Bureaucratic interference with patient care	242	100	111	45.9	66	27.3	40	16.5	25	10.3

[1] Excludes physicians who indicated "don't know" or who did not respond to specific portions of the question.

ference only a minor problem or not a problem at all in the program.

Excessive paperwork was rated as a critical problem by well over a third of all respondents (36.9 percent) and a major problem by another two fifths (40.6 percent). Combining these two categories, in fact, results in an evaluation that this problem is more important than that of bureaucratic interference in patient care.

Slightly lower in severity are the delays experienced by physicians in receiving payment for services and their inability to determine the amount they will be paid for services. Approximately two thirds of all respondents consider each of these problems either critical or major. With reference to delays, a gastroenterologist in Orange County commented:

We have a deadline of 2 months to get our claims in, yet we have claims that have not been paid by Medi-Cal for over a year. When inquiries are sent, we receive a letter—"Claims are being processed. No further inquiries needed."

An obstetrician/gynecologist in the same community, concerned with the problem of being able to determine how reimbursements are based, said:

Doctors receive different fees for obstetrical care even though all have charged the same. There is a $41 difference depending on the doctor billing. We have contacted the representative and submitted documentation as requested but never receive answers to our inquiry.

Lowest ranking among the seven suggested problem areas is that of difficulties experienced by physicians in securing prior authorization to provide care. Well over half of all respondents consider this problem critical in nature, however, while just over 14.8 percent indicated it is not a problem for them. In obvious frustration, a Los Angeles general practitioner remarked:

To sit on the phone for 45 minutes to get authorization is an unbelievable waste of time!

Who Rates Which Situations "Critical"

Some of the more crucial problems showed an association with specific variables such as medical specialty or geographic area in which physicians practice. Although detailed data concerning these relationships cannot be included in this report, the following highlights are extracted from the full report of findings.

The problem of inadequate level of reimbursement under Medi-Cal is considerably more critical for surgeons of all types and somewhat more so for psychiatrists than for other types of physicians. A Los Angeles orthopedic surgeon, for example, provided the following example:

I adjusted my accounts down over $900 on my usual and customary fees in January 1975; these were all Medi-Cal patients.

A San Francisco neurosurgeon commented:

A professional responsibility is increasing relative to my patients, the financial return is getting less and less for my efforts at patient care. I receive approximately 60 cents return for every $1 billed for Medi-Cal patients, with no incréase in my fees in 5 years.

Although the factor of difficulty in securing prior authorization ranked lowest in overall terms, it is nonetheless relevant and data concerning its association with medical specialty and with geographic area are of importance in evaluating the functioning of the program.

Physicians in the fields of neurosurgery, plastic surgery, thoracic surgery, urology, internal medicine (including its subspecialties), "other" medical specialties (dermatology, allergy, pediatrics) and psychiatry consider this more of a problem that do other physicians. A psychiatrist from Santa Clara County said, for example:

My practice is largely concerned with long term psychotherapy. Authorization is given for short times and I must watch expiration dates and submit new requests or lose payment. This situation plus the uncertainty of obtaining continuing authorizations more than any other reason causes me to limit my participation.

The problem of denial of reimbursement for services already provided appears to be particularly acute among certain surgical specialties, such as general surgery, ophthalmology, otolaryngology and orthopedic surgery. Almost all internists called it either critical or major. An Orange County otolaryngologist commented, for example:

We have recently written over $400 of services which were authorized but have never been paid even after all of the initial paperwork and the follow-up work.

Almost half of general and family practitioners (49.2 percent) consider this problem critical. One general practitioner from San Diego, who no longer accepts Medi-Cal patients, stated:

During my last year of real participation, two-thirds of bills were denied after service rendered, even though prior authorization was obtained. Entire program has been handled by state officials in an arbitrary and unreasonable and incompetent manner.

The problem of excessive paperwork appears to be considered more critical by surgeons than by physicians in medical specialties. A substantial majority of ophthalmologists, otolaryngologists, orthopedic surgeons and general surgeons consider this problem either critical or major. On the other hand, relatively fewer internists, physicians in "other" medical specialties (pediatrics, dermatology, allergy) and in "other" surgical specialties (neurosurgery, plastic surgery, thoracic surgery, urology) consider the problem critical.

Other Insights into Problem Areas

The full report of findings also provides information about problem areas physicians consider most serious within the program, according to medical specialty, geographic area and current degree of involvement in Medi-Cal. The following are some highlights:

• Ophthalmologists, otolaryngologists, orthopedic surgeons, psychiatrists, physicians heavily involved in Medi-Cal and physicians who are willing to accept new Medi-Cal patients are particularly concerned about excessive paperwork requirements. One psychiatrist put it this way:

When considering that I do not get my usual fee, and that I do not get paid for the time spent in the enormous amount of paperwork required, I conclude that I provide an awful lot of free service. I am willing to do this for patients with whom I have developed a physician-patient relationship before they went on Medi-Cal, but not otherwise.

• Low levels of physician reimbursement are considered especially critical by general surgeons, obstetrician/gynecologists, orthopedic surgeons, practitioners in Orange County, San Diego County, and the west Bay Area, and physicians who plan to accept no new Medi-Cal patients. As a Los Angeles internist said:

I would be glad to do the paperwork, carry the accounts receivable (often 9 to 12 months) if my secretary's time were reimbursed and my usual and customary fee were paid. But $6 for an office visit and $7 for a 2 a.m. emergency room visit is ridiculous if the patient takes more than 3 to 5 minutes of my time.

• Retroactive denial of reimbursement is particularly critical to physicians in "other" medical specialties (pediatrics,

dermatology, etc.), to physicians in the Bay Area and in Orange County, and to physicians who plan to continue accepting new Medi-Cal patients. A general surgeon from San Bernardino County noted the following:

Our major problem is in emergency surgery cases with retroactive authorization. The hospital is usually paid. The surgeon is rarely paid. We have no choice other than treat people and I feel we should have a least some pay.

• Bureaucratic interference in patient care constitutes a special problem for general and family practitioners, ophthalmologists, otolaryngologists, "other" surgeons (neurosurgery, plastic surgery, thoracic surgery, urology), physicians in Los Angeles County, physicians who do not treat Medi-Cal patients and those who indicated that they only "might" accept a new Medi-Cal patient for care. One Los Angeles psychiatrist made this observation.:

I can understand the need to restrict certain care, but it is too painful for me to have to deny a patient after we have started the program.

TAR's Cause Several Concerns

Table 6 provides information about respondent opinion concerning the effect of the treatment authorization request (TAR) system. Respondents were asked to agree or disagree with each of five possible effects of the system in terms of its pertinence to their own particular experience with the Medi-Cal program.

Among those who were sufficiently familiar with the system to respond, the area of concern with which most agreed (85.5 percent) was that the system results in "inconsistencies due to apparently ill-defined criteria." A psychiatrist from San Diego said: "Since the Medi-Cal rules fluctuate,

Table 6 Respondent Agreement or Disagreement with Various Statements Concerning Effects of the Treatment Authorization Request (TAR) System

Statement	Total Responding[1]		Response			
			Agree		Disagree	
	Number	Percent	Number	Percent	Number	Percent
Treatment is often delayed	186	100	144	77.4	42	22.6
System interferes with case management	186	100	153	82.3	33	17.7
Follow-up care reduced or denied	177	100	128	72.3	49	27.7
Inconsistencies due to ill-defined criteria	165	100	141	85.5	24	14.5
Needed treatment is often denied	166	100	90	54.2	76	45.8

[1]Excludes physicians without a TAR requirement in their area and those who indicated "don't know" or who did not respond to specific portions of question.

the procedures are unclear and require excessive amounts of time to unravel."

Significant proportions of physicians also felt that the system interferes with case management (82.3 percent), that treatment is often delayed (77.4 percent) and that appropriate follow-up care is often reduced or denied (72.3 percent). Regarding the problem of follow-up care, one orthopedic surgeon from Orange County said:

A major problem in orthopedics is obtaining adequate post injury or post operative physical therapy—enough of a problem that the patient is better off being referred to a county facility for any surgical procedure which requires post-op. therapy.

Only a slight majority (54.2 percent) agreed with the proposal that "needed treatment is often denied." However, there is little consistency in the thinking of respondents with respect to this issue. Although not shown in the tabular data, certain associations between this problem and medical specialty, as well as geographic area, appear to exist.

The problem of treatment denial is particularly prevalent among internists, psychiatrists and physicians in "other" medical specialties such as dermatology and pediatrics, as well as among general and family practitioners. A Los Angeles cardiologist commented, for example:

The biggest problem I face is the statutory limitation of the kinds and amounts of service I can render. Most of my patients are chronically ill with multiple system disease. On a full day I see maybe 8 to 10 people. This is so out of phase with what Medi-Cal will allow, that I will not work with a Medi-Cal recipient unless I have some personal commitment to that person or their family.

With respect to geographic area, almost four out of five respondents in Los Angeles County acknowledged a problem of treatment denial. Conversely, the situation appears much less prevalent in areas such as San Diego, Santa Clara, Riverside and San Bernardino Counties, as well as in counties where there were too few respondents to permit individual identification. In most cases, these counties are smaller metropolitan areas or rural areas.

Several respondents commented that they try to avoid the necessity of securing a TAR, often merely absorbing the cost of providing the service. As one Los Angeles internist put it:

We do not ask for TAR unless absolutely necessary. We cannot turn a seriously ill patient away so we see them whether we receive payment for the treatment or not. We feel this is an unfair situation.

Many Experience Retrospective Denial

Table 7 relates to the problem of retrospective denial and how frequently it results in nonpayment for services already provided, according to medical specialty. Among all respondents, slightly over a fourth (25.8 percent) indicated that they often experience retroactive denial, while almost half (49.8 percent) indicated that they experience it occasionally. The remaining respondents stated that the problem seldom (16.7 percent) or never (7.7 percent) occurs.

Over a third of respondents in general and family practice (34.5 percent) and in internal medicine (34.0 percent) indicated that the problem often occurs, while relatively few orthopedic surgeons (13.3 percent) or psychiatrists (10.0 percent) have experienced this situation. An example of the frustrations physicians experience in securing payment for services already provided are the following comments of a Los Angeles internist:

The most galling factor is as follows: a bill is submitted by this office for Medi-Cal services. Many months go by . . . no answer. A follow-up tracer letter is written asking for payment. Again many months go by. Finally 2 payments are made for 2 months, and 2 payments for 2 visits during earlier months are not. Attempts to receive explanation by long distance telephone, correspondence (from Los Angeles to San Francisco) is like putting your body into a barrel of taffy. The harder you try, the more involved you get. The stupid answers one gets from the retarded personnel employed by Medi-Cal is enough to raise my renin-angiotensin levels to astronomical heights. Finally, in desperation and total

Table 7 Frequency with Which Respondents Experience Retrospective Denial Resulting in Nonpayment for Services Rendered to Medi-Cal Patients, According to Medical Specialty

Medical Specialty	Total Responding[1]		Frequency of Occurrence							
			Frequently		Occasionally		Seldom		Never	
	Number	Percent	Number	Percent	Number	Percent	Number	Percent	Number	Percent
General/Family Practice ..	55	100	19	34.5	24	43.6	8	14.5	4	7.3
Internal Medicine[2]	47	100	16	34.0	25	53.3	3	6.4	3	6.4
Other Medicine[3]	17	100	3	17.6	7	41.2	5	29.4	2	11.8
General Surgery[4]	13	100	4	30.8	5	38.5	3	23.1	1	7.7
Obstetrics/Gynecology	12	100	3	25.0	6	50.0	3	25.0	0	..
Ophthalmology/ Otolaryngology	9	100	2	22.2	7	77.8	0	..	0	..
Orthopedic Surgery	15	100	2	13.3	6	40.0	5	33.3	2	13.3
Other Surgery[5]	12	100	3	25.0	6	50.0	1	8.3	2	16.7
Psychiatry	20	100	2	10.0	11	55.0	5	25.0	2	10.0
All Other	9	100	0	..	7	77.8	2	22.2	0	..
Total	209	100	54	25.8	104	49.8	35	16.7	16	7.7

[1]Excludes physicians without a TAR requirement in their area and those who indicated "don't know" or who did not respond to specific portions of question.

[2]Includes subspecialties.

[3]Includes allergy, dermatology, neurology, physical medicine.

[4]Includes abdominal surgery, colon and rectal surgery, pediatric surgery.

[5]Includes cardiovascular surgery, neurological surgery, plastic surgery, thoracic surgery, urology.

frustration, I hang up, turn to my secretary and state: "Write the damn unpaid bill off and don't take any more Medi-Cal patients." . . . and that's where it stands today. It is amazing how efficiently that Medicare bills are paid and how promptly I receive answers to any inquiries I might make.

Medical Advisors Elicit Mixed Reactions

Table 8 provides information about respondent opinion of medical advisors within the Medi-Cal system according to geographic area. Among all respondents, most felt that medical advisors were at best inconsistent in handling requests for authorization. As one general practitioner commented: "Personal idiosyncrasies of the medical consultant are impossible to overrule." A substantial minority (22.8 percent) felt that advisors appear more concerned with the money than with patient care, while a considerably smaller but nevertheless significant group (9.6 percent) indicated that advisors are often arbitrary in dealing with requests for authorization. At the other end of the spectrum, almost three respondents in ten (29.4 percent) felt that

medical advisors are generally understanding and willing to authorize recommended treatment, while another large group (14.2 percent) were of the opinion that medical advisors are fair but stringent in providing treatment authorization. A family practitioner from San Diego expressed the feeling that advisors are "hamstrung by state regulations."

Respondents in Los Angeles County were particularly critical of medical advisors, while those in Alameda, Contra Costa, Orange and San Diego counties appeared to be somewhat less critical. Almost two respondents in five from Orange County (38.9 percent) indicated that advisors are inconsistent in handling requests for authorization. In San Diego and in the Riverside-San Bernardino area, however, half of all respondents indicated that advisors are "generally understanding."

Although not shown in the tabular data, findings show that there is only a limited degree of association between physician opinions about medical advisors and medical specialty. However, physicians in strictly medical specialties (internal medicine, pediatrics, dermatology and so forth) tend to be somewhat more critical of

Table 8 Respondent Opinion Concerning Medical Advisors Within the Medi-Cal System, According to Selected Areas and for the State

Geographic Area	Total Responding[1]		Opinion[2]									
			Understanding		Fair		Inconsistent		Arbitrary		Dollar Oriented	
	Number	Percent	Number	Percent	Number	Percent	Number	Percent	Number	Percent	Number	Percent
Alameda/ Contra Costa	20	100	6	30.0	4	20.0	4	20.0	3	15.0	3	15.0
Los Angeles	66	100	11	16.7	11	16.7	16	24.2	9	13.6	19	28.8
Orange	18	100	3	16.7	4	22.2	7	38.9	2	11.1	2	11.1
San Diego	12	100	6	50.0	2	16.7	2	16.7	0	..	2	16.7
Santa Clara	16	100	6	37.5	1	6.2	4	25.0	2	12.5	3	18.8
Riverside/ San Bernardino ...	10	100	5	50.0	0	..	2	20.0	0	..	3	30.0
Other Areas	55	100	21	38.2	6	10.9	12	21.8	3	5.5	13	23.6
Total State	197	100	58	29.4	28	14.2	47	23.9	19	9.6	45	22.8

[1]Excludes physicians who did not respond to specific question.
[2]See text for full content of statements.

medical advisors or of the system, than do physicians in most other specialties. An internist in Santa Clara County said:

> It is seldom that we are able to communicate with the medical advisor personally. Most requests are relayed to him (and his questions to me) through a clerk who has little medical knowledge.

A General Practitioner Sums It Up

Summing up various concerns with the Medi-Cal program experienced by physicians, especially those with considerable involvement in the program, one general practitioner from Alameda County made the following comments:

> I practice in a high Medi-Cal area, and I refuse three or four new Medi-Cal patients per week. I quit taking new patients when the total came to 25 percent of my practice. Since my expenses are about 50 percent of my receipts, I felt very uneasy about having half of my personal income dependent on Medi-Cal, to be reduced or deferred as they see fit.
>
> I would accept more Medi-Cal patients if I could feel that the program was dedicated to fair treatment of both patient and doctors.

33. My Life and Hard Times in a Medicaid Mill

B. P. REITER

What's a New York City Medicaid mill like? As awful as you can imagine—and just as awful as my own first impressions, which I described in an article last year about my job interview at one of them.*

From the response to that article, a lot of you didn't believe me. Sure, there might be problems, a number of you wrote to this magazine, but that guy Reiter must have exaggerated. Well, I didn't, and perhaps the following account of my experience while actually working for about 10 weeks at a couple of Medicaid clinics will convince you of that.

Let's start with an obvious question: If Medicaid clinics are so lousy, why did I decide to work in them? Because I needed a job. By six months after I finished my radiology residency, neither of the medical employment agencies I'd visited had called me back. I couldn't afford to start my own practice, either. Resignedly, I filled out forms to qualify as a "Medicaid provider" so that I could go to work somewhere. And I started answering ads for doctors to work at Medicaid clinics.

Then one morning I got a call from the operator of one of the clinics I'd contacted.

He could be called, very accurately, The Entrepreneur. He was about my age, only *he* knew how to make money.

He wanted me to come to work for him. I explained that New York City hadn't issued me a Medicaid number yet, but, incredibly, he offered to let me work for free. Until I got my number I wouldn't even have to pay him the standard, immediate rent—$500 a week—that these clinic operators demanded for office space and use of equipment. I should have guessed from his offer that something was wrong, but I said O.K.

First, though, I had to buy malpractice insurance. That meant I had to join the state medical society before I could apply for a policy. The society membership totaled $405, and the insurance bill was $998 for a little less than a half year's coverage. I was in the red $1,403.

"ANYTHING YOU WANT— YOU'RE THE DOCTOR"

The Entrepreneur had two clinics on the East Side of Manhattan. I introduced myself to the X-ray technician at one of The Entrepreneur's clinics. The technician was a very pleasant fellow, and he took terrible films.

*"How Seamy Can Medicine Get? Let Me Tell You." MEDICAL ECONOMICS, Oct. 27, 1975.

"No, no," I said, "these are inadequate studies." I showed him what he was doing wrong, explained what views he should take, and asked him if he knew what I was talking about.

"Sure," he said. "Anything you want—you're the doctor." Then he went right on taking awful films.

He said the equipment was no good. I said it was certainly minimal, but functional. "I'm not asking for cerebral angiograms," I told him, "just adequate plain films." He promised to do better—and continued taking terrible X-rays.

I went to The Entrepreneur. "Listen," I said, "the technician is not taking the proper number of views on these cases. I can't interpret films unless I get the right views." The Entrepreneur was not a doctor. He was a businessman, and not very interested in my problems with the X-rays. He made soothing noises.

"If I don't get adequate studies," I said, "I'm not going to sign the invoices."

That did the trick. The Entrepreneur promised to talk to the technician, and I signed the invoices. Next day, the technician quit.

I couldn't understand why there was a problem. The Entrepreneur was bound to have enough money to hire a good technician. The equipment didn't look very expensive; it definitely wasn't the quarter-million-dollar setup that one X-ray company had wanted to sell me to start my own practice.

"How much did this room cost?" I asked The Entrepreneur.

"About $8,000," he replied. I guess he must have had a lot of other expenses.

He hired a new technician, who tried harder. Some of the time I even got the views I wanted.

The two Medicaid centers began to take up a lot of my time. I love looking at films, but I'm also compulsive; I look at everything about six times to be sure I'm not missing anything. I was also typing up the reports, and that took even longer because I can't type. And I was signing a blank invoice for each case. "Don't worry," The Entrepreneur told me. "My people will take care of filling out the invoices. All you have to do is sign them."

"JUST MAKE OUT A CHECK"

My Medicaid number came! The Entrepreneur licked his chops. He and his assistant—the girl who'd been filling out my signed invoices—presented me with a bill.

"You owe me $2,000 in rent," The Entrepreneur said, looking delighted.

"I do? Have I been here that long already?"

"You signed all the invoices."

"Yeah, but they were blank when I signed them."

The Entrepreneur shrugged, "Just make out a check to the corporation," he said.

After hastily borrowing the money from my family, I gave a check to his assistant. "Who owns this corporation?" I asked her.

"He does—I think. With a bunch of other people."

The Entrepreneur, I found out, ran both of the Medicaid clinics, but each was owned by a separate corporation. Who owned the corporations was never detailed to me. I once suggested that I had some money to invest in the business, hoping to get a glimpse of the ownership arrangements, but nothing came of it. I think The Entrepreneur knew I didn't have any money of my own.

I'm pretty conscientious, and I was very good at the professional part of this venture. The business side was something else again. I was still reading films, typing reports, and signing blank invoices, but now I was also paying rent. And, of course, I couldn't keep track of half of what I'd signed.

While I waited for Medicaid to get around to paying me for my work at the clinics, I borrowed more money from my family.

GUIDELINES
AND MORE GUIDELINES

Medicaid does not like to pay doctors if it can avoid doing so. What it likes to do is send out guidelines. The guidelines are complex, detailed, and exacting. They revolve mainly around the filling out of forms. All the forms must be filled out precisely right or Medicaid won't pay you.

The forms keep changing, and so do the guidelines. Sometimes Medicaid tells you about the new guidelines, and sometimes not. And sometimes you end up better off if you *don't* receive the new rules because Medicaid may abruptly go back to the old ones.

For instance, there was the merry-go-round with Form W-303G. The following missive, dated June 1, 1975, was sent out by the Human Resources Administration, the agency that runs New York City's Medicaid program:

*Dear Health Care
Professional:*

As you may know, the City of New York has begun to implement a new Medicaid computer system [that] will be a major improvement on the old Medicaid payment process. Computerization, however, has necessitated the adoption of new forms and procedures.

One [change] concerns the billing procedures for laboratory services. Effective June 1, 1975, when you bill for performing your own laboratory services, you will use the new revised Form W-303G. . . .

It is imperative that you. . . become familiar with the above procedure. . .

That seems pretty definite, right? O.K., throw out all of the old W-303Gs. Four days later, on June 5:

. . .due to the failure of the printing company to deliver new 303G forms on

schedule as per contract specifications, we are unable to control the June 1, 1975, implementation date for having new W-303Gs in the hands of providers.

As a result of this problem, please continue to bill on the old W-303G form until you receive new invoices with the revision date of 5/2/75. . . . When you receive the new invoices, use them immediately. If you have already received new 303Gs (revised 3/20/74), continue to use these new forms. . . .

Which new forms? I've already got rid of the old ones. What are they talking about?

But there was more. Medicaid had created bigger patient identification numbers to go along with the new forms they didn't have. So:

If the situation should arise whereby you administer treatment to a patient who has an 11-digit identification number, write all 11 digits in the space allotted for the 8-digit identification number . . . .legibility is important. . . .

This was followed by the guideline dated Aug. 4, 1975, and addressed to "Medicaid Providers" (Medicaid cannot bring itself to call a physician "Doctor"). It read in part:

c. Form W-303G must be signed legibly by the primary-care physician personally. He must also list his Medicaid certification number and service address. . . .

d. Form W-303G is forwarded to the radiologist. This form will then be utilized by the radiologist as his invoice for Medicaid payment. The Medicaid program will accept only Form W-303G (or its successor) from radiologists submitting payment requests."

Assuming you could get your hands on the new—or newest—W-303G form, you discovered there were two places it could be signed. On the left was a box for "Physician's Signature"; on the right, a box for

"Provider's Signature." Obviously the radiologist and the primary-care physician are both doctors. Who was supposed to sign where?

It wasn't easy to find out. Something called "Doctors' Control" at the city's Medicaid headquarters told radiologists to sign on the *right*. But factoring companies—the outfits that lend doctors money so they can pay clinic owners rent until Medicaid finally makes *its* payments—would accept invoices from radiologists only if they were signed on the *left* side. An attempt to get a ruling produced the news that the Medicaid administrator who'd written this set of guidelines was on vacation. No one else seemed to know where the forms should be signed.

It appeared that the Medicaid computer was being given a fair chance not to pay anybody for anything. But then it turned out that Medicaid, New York City, had neglected to clear the new guidelines with the Department of Health, New York State. The guidelines were postponed.

"YOU'RE GOING TO HAVE TO LEAVE"

Disgusted with the whole system, I was ready to give up. I took a brief vacation and thought about what to do. The most reasonable thing, probably, was to quit. I had no money left, and I'd already accumulated plenty of material to write about the Medicaid mess, as I was determined to do.

Yet I felt a little guilty about leaving the centers with no radiologist. When I called The Entrepreneur's assistant, she laughed at me. "What are you worried about? One of the clinics just burned down. Besides, I think he wants to get rid of you."

I went to the remaining clinic to talk to The Entrepreneur. He'd mentioned something earlier about replacing me, but I had ignored that. Who else would be willing to pay this guy for the privilege of working here?

The Entrepreneur motioned me into one of the tiny examining cubicles and shut the door. Whenever he shut a door, that meant he was going to discuss money.

"I'm sorry," he said, "but some people have just made me a terrific offer, and it means there have to be changes made. You're going to have to leave. Don't worry, though. I'm taking over another place uptown. In a while you can work there."

He walked me out, and on the way he spied a mother bringing her kids in to see the clinic pediatrician. He abandoned me, neatly cornered the woman, and pointed convincingly toward the examining rooms.

"You too, Mama," he said. "When's the last time *you* went to the doctor?"

"$35 A POP"

After I left, I heard, The Entrepreneur tried some new tricks. One morning he instructed all the girls working for him to roam through the apartment houses in the neighborhood and get people to come to his clinic. The X-ray technician refused to do it and got fired.

The Entrepreneur even tried to talk *me* into going back to work. When he offered to sell me some old X-ray equipment and I refused, he said, "O.K., if you were happier the other way, you can go back to paying me rent."

"No, thank you."

"This place has wonderful potential," he said of the clinic. "I want to put in a mammography unit. That's $35 a pop."

Not with me, you won't, I thought to myself. "No, thank you," I repeated.

BATTLING THE CODE

About three months after I'd begun submitting invoices, I heard from Medicaid. They had a surprise for me. A certain proportion of my claims were being "reduced." That means they don't pay you any money for them. There were some explanations included as to why my claims were reduced, but unfortunately the explanations consisted only of code numbers: "77 . . . 71 . . . 70."

Medicaid didn't bother to say what the numbers meant. I called to find out. The bureaucracy at Medicaid loves to send out guidelines, but it doesn't particularly want to answer questions. Whichever number you call, whomever you talk to, and whatever you want to find out—you've got the wrong number. The number they give you to call instead is also wrong. The next number you're given is usually correct—but the individual you're supposed to talk to likely as not has gone off on vacation.

The type of question you're asking is important as well. If it's a fill-in-the-blank kind of question, you may get a deceptively facile answer. The problem is, the answer is wrong as often as it's right. If you ask for the latest edition of some revised form, Medicaid says sure, we'll send it right away. They told me they'd send the payment-reduction code right away. They never did, of course.

Code or no code, I'd already paid The Entrepreneur his rent, naively counting on the fees I was supposed to receive from Medicaid. I wrote and asked him for my money back. The Entrepreneur called and said I was upset for no reason, that these were only procedural difficulties. All I had to do was resubmit the invoices, which his people would prepare, and Medicaid would pay me. Of course, if I *didn't* get paid, he added, he would gladly give back my rent money.

"Wait a minute," I said. "Is this going to take another three or four months, too? I have loans to repay."

Well, he wasn't sure about that. It might take a while, yeah.

BALANCING THE BOOKS

More statements from Medicaid. More reductions. No word from The Entrepreneur. Finally, I sent him a nasty letter threatening to get a lawyer.

He called again. "What are you so excited about?"

"My money is what I'm excited about—the money I borrowed to pay you rent!"

No problem, he said. He would send me new invoices to sign, as soon as I sent him copies of the old ones. Hadn't he asked me for the copies before? Oh, he was sorry about that. He must have forgotten.

I'm still waiting for my money. During the 10 weeks or so that I worked at the Medicaid clinics, I wrote out checks for medical society dues, malpractice insurance, fees, assessments, and, of course, rent to The Entrepreneur's corporation. The checks came to $7,030. To date, I've received payments of $7,323 from Medicaid.

I've earned $293.

34. An Eclectic Approach to Quality Control In Fee-For-Service Health Care: The New York City Medicaid Experience

STEPHEN N. ROSENBERG, CHRISTINE GUNSTON, LOUISE BERENSON, and ARLETTE KLEIN

Reprinted with permission from the *American Journal of Public Health*, Vol. 66, No. 1, pp. 21–20 (January 1976).

As the vague outlines of a national system of health care delivery, or at least a unified system for the financing of such care, begin to appear on the horizon of political possibility, the evaluation of health care quality has become a leading topic of research articles and conversation in health care circles.

There has been considerable academic research concerned with refining definitions of optimal health care quality, and developing precise techniques for its measurement. Operational evaluation systems in third-party financing programs such as Medicaid, Medicare, and Blue Cross/Blue Shield have concentrated on peer review of medical records and on electronic data gathering at a program management level. Unfortunately, much less attention has been given by either researchers or third parties to the *use* of quality-of-care information once it has been gathered and evaluated.[1] Thus, the typical evaluation program is not designed in a pragmatic fashion to serve as a data base for intervention in the wide spectrum of health care services with which PSROs and national health insurance will have to deal—a spectrum in which patterns of care vary from outstanding, through adequate and mediocre, to unnecessary and dangerous.[2,5]

If competent health care is to be made available to most Americans, and if it is to be provided at less-than-prohibitive costs, the programs which succeed or supplement current financing systems must implement workable control measures based on realistic evaluation of quality and medical necessity. Some have predicted a worsening of quality under national health insurance, as a response to a sizeable increase in demand for ambulatory care which can only be met through dilution of quality.[6] It is vital that national health insurance avoid a repetition of the experience common to several state Medicaid programs; an ambitious start, followed by runaway costs resulting in periodic across-the-board cut-backs in fees and eligibility unrelated to health care priorities.[7,8] In acting to prevent these potential crises, the highest priority should be given to the elimination of expenses which are due to fraudulent billing, the provision of unnecessary services, and the provision of services which are of clearly unacceptable quality.

This paper will attempt to demonstrate that currently available techniques can be effective in assessing the quality and appropriateness of health care services, and acting to improve them. Efforts to advance the state of the art should continue, but implementation need not be delayed until the ultimate in sophisticated evaluation methodology is perfected.

BACKGROUND

For seven years, the Bureau of Health Care Services of the New York City Department of Health has carried out integrated surveillance, evaluation and corrective activities aimed at preventing, detecting, and eliminating instances of poor quality health care and related fiscal abuse in the City's Medicaid Program.[9,10] In 1973 and 1974 this program underwent a major reorganization. A computer system—the "Medicaid Vendor System" (MVS)—was introduced to expand the Department's profiling and case-finding capabilities and to enhance its capacity to refute or confirm suspected deficiencies and take corrective action. The system also provides basic data for use in program management and policy-making.

While most computerized evaluation units are designed to stand alone, as the sole major source of data on quality within a health care program, MVS was designed as the central component of an eclectic system. MVS is relatively unsophisticated in terms of data collection and manipulation, but highly effective in terms of the specific questions it answers, as part of a coordinated system of multiple, complementary evaluation techniques, and quality control activities.

Until recently, the New York City Health Department's Medicaid surveillance activities consisted of a manual clerical and professional audit of samples of Medicaid fee-for-service billing invoices,*[11] on-site peer surveys of offices, places of business, and institutions,[12] and the reexamination of samples of patients.[13] Whenever one of these monitoring activities, or a complaint received by the Department, disclosed a possible quality or fiscal problem, an intensive evaluation was initiated. Confirmed

problems resulted in appropriate educational and enforcement activities. At the same time, the administrators of the program relied on these sampling procedures to form impressions of typical patterns of practice in the system.[14]

In 1973 the New York City Medicaid Program received in excess of 15 million invoices from non-institutional, fee-for-service providers of care. Approximately one and one-half million were clerically screened for indications of fiscal or quality discrepancies, of which 480,000 (3.2 per cent of the total) were profiled and reviewed in detail by clerical and professional staff members. Although many sampling techniques were tried over the past few years, no method was found which would eliminate three basic problems. First, estimates of average or "normal" Medicaid practices were impressionistic at best. Second, isolated discrepancies (e.g., the occasional provision of a medication, such as a Vitamin B_{12} injection, without medical indication) would sometimes be detected and deleted from payment (after a telephone call to the provider), and at other times would slip by and be reimbursed. This "hit or miss" approach was not only incomplete as a control mechanism, but, more importantly, tended to create an impression of arbitrariness and inconsistency in the minds of professional providers. Third, the manual screening and review of a small sample of invoices was a method poorly suited to the detection of *patterns* of poor quality care. Detection and correction of deficient patterns, affecting large numbers of pa-

---

*Fee-for-service providers include professionals (physicians; podiatrists; dentists; optometrists; opticians; physical, occupational, and speech therapists; and chiropractors), and health-related businesses (pharmacies; optical retail establishments, visiting nurse and home health agencies; clinical, X-ray, EKG, and EEG laboratories; and vendors of appliances, shoes, and transportation services).

tients, was felt to be of far greater importance than detection of isolated discrepancies.

Several of the sampling schemes which were tested involved the professional audit of all invoices received from each of a sample group of providers over a one or two month period. One of the most common suspicious patterns found in such an audit was that a particular professional billed for an extremely high number of patient visits per day. A high enough number would indicate possible inability to spend enough time with each patient to provide adequate care, and/or fraudulent billing for fictitious visits. The documentation of such a case in the manual system required an average of 15 man-hours of clerical time, to profile between one and two thousand invoices by date of service. Not only was such profiling time-consuming, it was also incomplete, since the invoices received by Medicaid over a one or two month period might reflect only a fraction of the services rendered in the preceding few months, with additional invoices being submitted later.

In 1973, the Department of Health, in conjunction with the data processing division of the City's Health Services Administration, set out to develop a system of automated Medicaid invoice review.* The basic requirements for the new system were that it be inexpensive to develop, that it be able to profile virtually all invoices from all fee-for-service providers, and that it produce data which could be directly utilized in quality and fiscal evaluation and correction. The latter task required a system which would answer questions raised by on-site peer surveys and patient reexamination, and which would itself raise questions to be answered by these other review modalities.

The new system was phased in during 1974, and has been used to profile all services rendered since the beginning of 1973.

DESCRIPTION OF THE COMPUTER SYSTEM

In developing the Medicaid Vendor System, the New York City Department of Health aimed for an inexpensive interim system for rapid practical implementation, to be eventually superceded by a more sophisticated system.

To achieve these goals, the input chosen for MVS consists of data currently existing on city computer tapes: the name of each fee-for-service health care provider, Medicaid participation (billing) number (based on license number in the case of a licensed professional), billing address, "provider type" (e.g., physician or orthopedic shoe dealer), specialties if any, the service code assigned by Medicaid to each covered service or object billed (e.g., appendectomy, pediatrician's initial office visit, monaural hearing aid, chest X-ray etc.), the amount paid, the date of service, and the beneficiary's year of birth.**

Three types of report are produced by the system, based on services rendered during calendar quarters. These reports are compiled three months after the close of the quarter in question. Analysis of billing during the past few years indicates that over 80 per cent of all bills for services rendered during a quarter have been received, and are on tape, three months after the close of the quarter. The reports are as follows:

Individual Profiles of each fee-for-service provider (Figure 1). Each profile is labeled with the provider's name, Medicaid number, profession, and specialties. If he is a high volume provider or has violated a quality of care flagging parameter this is

---

*Although it had been recognized for some years that manual processing of Medicaid forms was inadequate, administrative constraints made it impossible to inaugurate electronic data processing at an earlier date.

**The current data base does not reliably identify individual beneficiaries, since client numbers are assigned to entire families or "cases".

Figure 1 Individual Provider Profile

NYC Department of Health	Run Date 07/15/74 Page 561
	Medicaid Vendor System Individual Profiles

Provider Category—Physician. Services provided from 01/01/74 thru 03/31/74 and paid thru 06/30/74

Name	Address	Participation#
Smith, John	2245 Park Avenue Bronx, NY 10453	100308989

Specialties
None (General Practice)

This provider appeared on quarterly search reports as follows:
This quarter yes preceding Q. No 2nd preceding Q. No 3rd preceding Q. No

Service	THIS QUARTER FIGURES					FROM PRECEDING QUARTERS PREVIOUSLY UNREPORTED	
	Services	%	Dollars	%	Avg Fee	Services	Dollars
0L115 GP—Complete Blood Count	51	6.7	193.80	5.5	3.80	3	11.20
0L577 GP—Chemical Urinalysis	83	10.8	83.00	2.3	1.00	3	2.80
0L578 GP—Microscopic Urinalysis	76	9.9	76.00	2.1	1.00	2	1.80
09000 GP—First Visit, Office	125	16.3	900.00	25.3	7.20	15	113.44
09001 GP—Subs Visit, Office	362	47.3	2005.48	56.5	5.54	37	215.80
09048 GP—Injection	46	6.0	46.00	1.9	1.00	47	46.80
09101+ GP—EKG	22	2.9	247.50	7.0	11.25	4	43.20
Total	765	99.9	$3551.78	100.6	$ 4.64	111	$435.04

Total Dollars from Reports for	10-73 thru 12-73 $2,279.04	10-73 thru 03-74 $6,265.86	04-73 thru 03-74 $20,538.82

noted. The body of the profile consists of a listing of all services for which the provider has billed during the quarter in question. Each service code is followed by a descriptive "service label", the number of such services billed for, the per cent of that provider's total services this number represents, the amount paid for these services, the per cent of all his payments this amount represents, and the average payment per service.† Certain categories of services which would result in unmanageably long listings (e.g., individual surgical procedures and pharmaceutical items) have been grouped into "service categories" (e.g., all tetracyclines). These are denoted by a + following the service code. Component services of special interest (e.g., abuse drugs) are reported separately. The bottom of the report shows the total number of services, average overall cost per service, and total payments made for the quarter in question, the previous quarter, the last six months, and the last year. Listed to the right of the body of the report are services and payments provided in previous quarters but not billed until the current reporting period.

Statistical Profiles (Figure 2). A statistical profile is produced quarterly for each provider type, and for each physician specialty and subspecialty. Annual summaries

---

†The data on average cost is most meaningful for items with variable cost, such as drugs (which vary by brand and by size of prescription). Most services, such as a gynecologist's initial office visit, have prices which are fixed by the Medicaid fee schedule. "Average price" actually paid by Medicaid is slightly less than this fee, as a small percentage of patients is required to co-pay 20% of each bill, and others have combined Medicaid/Medicare coverage.

Figure 2 Statistical Provider Profile

NYC Department of Health

Medicaid Vendor System Statistical Profiles
For Services from 01/01/74 thru 03/31/74 and paid thru 06/30/74

Run Date 07/15/74
Page 297

Provider Category—Optometrist
Specialty—Entire Category

| | | | THIS QUARTER | | | | | UNREPORTED IN PREVIOUS QUARTERS | |
Service	Services	%	Dollars	%	Av Fee	# Prov	%	Services	Dollars
E001 Complete Exam	51,905	26.9	413,488.00	30.8	7.97	394	96.6	7,561	60,204.30
E002 Subnrml Vision Exm	15	.0	142.08	.0	9.47	5	1.2	4	27.20
E003 Dispens 1st Pair	49,242	25.5	196,067.98	14.6	3.98	373	91.4	5,920	23,598.08
E004+ Adjustments & Reprs	8,928	4.6	22,781.50	1.7	2.55	294	72.1	845	2,233.06
E006 Orthoptic Evaltn	199	.1	1,185.12	.1	5.96	29	7.1	14	84.80
E007 Orthoptic Traing	549	.3	1,926.40	.1	3.51	8	2.0	88	400.00
E008 Visual Field Exam	123	.1	778.56	.1	6.33	17	4.2	14	88.00
E009+ Special Aides	35	.0	3,339.00	.2	95.40	20	4.9	17	1,999.90
E010 Materials	58,336	30.2	644,212.24	48.0	11.04	378	92.6	7,036	79,422.10
E011 Home Visit	64	.0	350.68	.0	5.48	34	8.3	5	32.60
E016 Tonometry	17,282	8.9	27,726.72	2.1	1.60	356	87.3	2,712	4,338.76
E018 Dispens 2nd Pair	5,748	3.0	22,896.44	1.7	3.98	292	71.6	660	2,617.06
9999 Service Code Error	841	.4	6,141.08	.5	7.30	86	21.1	55	639.70
TOTAL	193,267	100.0	$1,341,035.80	99.9	$6.94	408		24,931	$175,685.56

of these quarterly reports are also produced.

Each statistical profile identifies the profession (and specialty) being described, and lists service codes, labels, payments, etc. exactly as on the individual profiles. In addition, there is an indication of the number of providers billing for each code one or more times, and the per cent of all billing providers which this represents. The bottom line indicates this total number of providers.

In addition, "high provider" profiles are produced which depict the aggregate pattern of the providers receiving the largest Medicaid payments within each specialty and provider type. The "high provider" group was initially defined as the top 10 per cent of providers in each specialty or profession in terms of income. This can be modified as experience with the reports suggests more informative cutoff levels. It was hypothesized that the "high provider"

groups, representing practitioners or businesses with patient loads which are predominantly Medicaid, would differ significantly from the majority of participating providers who see few Medicaid patients. Some of the expected differences would be entirely reasonable. Others may reflect undesirable patterns due to the structure of the Medicaid program or other factors.

Exception Reports (Figure 3). An exception report, or "quality of care search report", is a listing of providers who exceed a limit relating to the distribution of service codes on their individual profiles. While the individual and statistical profiles produced by MVS are similar to those involved in several other profiling systems, MVS exception reports differ greatly from those produced elsewhere, revealing the action-oriented origin of the system as a whole.

Figure 3 is a composite of examples of the three basic types of exception report produced. Each report identifies the pro-

Figure 3 Quality of Care Exception Reports

NYC Department of Health   Run Date 07/15/74
Medicaid Vendor System Exception Reports
Services Provided from 01/01/74 thru 03/31/74 and paid thru 06/30/74

Provider Category—Pharmacy
Specialty—Entire Category

Flagging Criterion #503: 20 or more prescriptions with 4, 7 or 8 appearing as tens-digit of unit
number

1. 510073869   Jones Pharmacy   1100 Eastern Parkway   Brooklyn   NY   11216
   Tens-Digit   4-7-8 billed   103 times this quarter representing $386 in payments

2. 510082646   New York Pharmacy   9263 Broadway   New York   10026
Tens-Digit   4-7-8 Billed   82 times this quarter representing $264 in payments

---

Provider Category—Physician
Specialty—GP, Family Practice, Allergy, Pediatrics, Pediatric Allergy

Flagging Criterion #601: More than 50 visits per day on more than 20/of the days on which any
visits were billed

1. 100602132   John Kidd   62 East 14th Street   New York   NY   10012
   Visits exceed 50 per day on 90% of days this quarter. Visits represent $6,384 in payments

---

Provider Category—Podiatry
Specialty—Entire Category

Flagging Criterion #402: Number of X-ray sets equal to or exceeds 24% of all office visits.

1. 310264931   Ralph Foote   961 West 110 Street   New York   NY   11061
   X-ray sets equal 53% of all office visits this quarter. X-rays represent $1962 in payments

vider type (and specialties) concerned, and describes the limit beyond which a provider will be flagged for intensive review or investigation. When the system was designed, the initial limits were adopted from previous manual invoice auditing procedures. All variables (the specialties included and all numerical parameters) may be changed, and entire new criteria added as experience with the system indicates more appropriate flagging tolerances and new problems to be monitored. The identifying information for each listed provider is followed by a description of his violation in terms of the size of the alleged abuse and payments made for the abused service.

The first example in Figure 3 is a flagging criterion based on an absolute number of suspect services during the quarter: 20 or more prescriptions for 40 to 49, 70 to 79, or 80 to 89 doses of medication. Legitimate prescriptions for 80 pills are so rare that even a few such prescriptions raise the possibility that "30's" are being modified ("kited") to "80's" by the billing pharmacy.

The second section of Figure 3 exemplifies a time constraint criterion—the number of patient visits per day. It is assumed that, for most professions and specialties, there is a number of patient visits per day beyond which the quality of care probably becomes unacceptable—the average visit is just too brief. It is important to emphasize that these limits are merely flagging criteria for further review. A given professional may be able to totally justify an "excess" of visits by demonstrating that his office equipment and ancillary personnel permit extraordinary efficiency.

The third section concerns an interrelationship between two service code frequencies; the number of X-rays per podiatric patient visit. Again, and this is true for all the exception report criteria, an "excess" may be justified. The criteria used, however, were chosen because our seven years of manual auditing experience indicated that *most* exceptions cannot be justified, and re-

flect a pattern of care of unacceptable quality, and/or fraudulent billing.

Statistical summaries of exception report findings are also produced. These are used in assessing trends and setting action priorities, and are described below.

FUNCTION OF COMPUTER REPORTS IN THE EVALUATION PROGRAM

Each of the MVS reports plays a vital role in the Bureau's overall quality control program.

Statistical Profiles give us, for the first time, an objective and quantitative picture of norms for provider groups in their Medicaid practices. The detailed content of the statistical profiles, i.e., "what Medicaid paid for in 1974," is the subject of a separate paper in preparation. Insofar as the norms displayed by the profiles are reasonable, they provide baselines against which the practices of individual providers may be measured. They enable us to refine our exception report criteria in a more realistic manner.

When certain patterns of relationships among services on the statistical profiles suggest previously unexpected varieties of abuse or poor quality, new exception reports or manual techniques are instituted to identify possible abusers. On occasion, the aggregate pattern of practice of an entire provider type or specialty (or, more frequently, its "high provider" component) departs significantly from professional acceptability. This usually calls for a change in the local Medicaid program, e.g., an increase or decrease in a fee to provide an incentive or disincentive, a program of provider education, a new billing regulation, or a revision of the professional qualifications necessary for participation in the program. When, for instance, it was found that many transportation companies were providing more services than their vehicles could actually handle, it was required that each bill be accompanied by a receipt from the treating facility acknowledging arrival of the patient. In addition, of course, improperly claimed funds were repaid to the program, and referrals were made for possible prosecution.

Individual Profiles are primarily used to quickly support or rebut suspicions of poor quality or fiscal abuse which arise from other input sources. A provider's individual profile may satisfactorily explain his appearance on an exception report. For example, a podiatrist is identified as taking X-rays equal to 82 per cent of patient visits. His individual profile shows that his practice is confined almost entirely to surgery. The X-rays are thus appropriate preoperative diagnostic procedures, and not unnecessary adjuncts to the treatment of corns and fungal infestations.

The individual MVS profiles are particularly productive in conjunction with three other sources of quality-of-care data: patient reexamination, on-site office surveys, and complaints and referrals. Each of these provides data unavailable from claims review, and complementary to MVS.

Since 1969, the Bureau has conducted reexamination of randomly selected Medicaid patients. These currently include patients who have received eye glasses from optometrists and opticians, foot moulds and podiatric surgery, dental care—especially prostheses—and hearing aids. These patients and their services and devices can be objectively reexamined by peers of the providing professionals. The Department employs dentists and an audiologist for some of these examinations, and contracts with colleges of podiatry, optometry, and ophthalmic dispensing for the remainder. In 1973, 12,925 patients responded to our invitations to be reexamined. In the main, the care that had been billed for was found to have been fully provided, necessary, and of acceptable quality. When isolated cases of unacceptable quality are discovered, the provider is requested to make all necessary corrections free of charge. When isolated instances are revealed in which is appears that not all

billed services were provided, the provider is requested to explain and/or refund the fee involved. When, however, a *pattern* of poor quality or improper billing is suggested, an investigation ensues. The individual MVS profiles greatly simplify many of these investigations. If, for example, five out of ten of an optometrist's reexamined patients seem to have received unnecessary eye glasses, his profile is consulted to determine the percentage of examinations that result in the dispensing of glasses. If this greatly exceeds the norm for all optometrists, the suspicion of generalized overprescribing is supported.

On-site surveys of 509 offices, businesses, and institutions were carried out in 1973. Items evaluated include general cleanliness and safety, professional equipment, and, of course, patient records. A relatively minor problem such as incorrect disposal of hypodermic needles would be dealt with through discussion, and a request for correction prior to an unscheduled revisit. Major problems require investigation. Again the profiles can be valuable. If a physician's X-ray machine, while safe, is unsuitable for certain radiographic procedures commonly used in his specialty, his profile will tell us whether or not he bills for such procedures.

One hundred eighty-two complaints and referrals were received in 1973—from patients, professionals, anonymous sources, other agencies, and other units in the City Health Department such as the Radiation Control Bureau. In addition, referrals arise from the sections of our own Bureau concerned with prior approvals (for limited services), and from our Professional Registry. In the past, such complaints and referrals necessitated voluminous manual work for rebuttal or confirmation. The MVS individual profiles perform this function handily. A common complaint (from a patient or an anonymous source) is that a certain professional discourages necessary follow-up visits, and concentrates on more lucrative initial work-ups. If his profile indicates that the percentage of his visits which appear as first visits is at or below the norm for his profession, the complaint is probably not worth pursuing.

Exception Reports are the third category of MVS output. While the individual profiles find their primary importance in the follow-up of problems revealed by other sources, the exception reports or quality of care flagging reports are themselves becoming the single most important source of cases to be evaluated in depth or investigated. Table 1 is a listing of some of the exception reports generated by our review of services for the second quarter of 1974. The exception criteria being used to screen current data are based on these, with sev-

eral changes and numerous additions. The number of providers screened and flagged for each criterion is listed.

In only four instances were more than ten per cent of the practitioners in a provider group identified as exceeding a single flagging level: podiatric X-rays, and initial/subsequent visit ratios for three types of primary physicians (suggesting inadequate follow-up care). These flagging levels require further validation. If they are indeed confirmed as legitimate indicators of poor quality, administrative measures to change professional practice patterns within the program will be necessary.

The large number of providers identified, even when they represent only two or three

Table 1 Sample Violations of Quality of Care Flagging Criteria, April - June, 1974

Profession: Specialties	Criteria for Flagging for Detailed Review	Number of Providers In This Profession (and Specialties) Providing One or More Services This Quarter	Number of Providers Flagged and Percent of All Providers	
Optometrist	#101: More than 10 examinations of patients less than 4 years old per quarter	402	31	7.7%
	#102: More than 20 examinations per day on more than 20% of the days on which any examinations were done	402	8	2.0%
Ophthalmic Dispenser	#201: Glasses dispensed to patients less than 5 years old more than 10 times per quarter	91	3	3.3%
Chiropractor	#301: More than 50 visits per day on more than 20% of the days on which any visits occurred	231	7	3.0%
	#302: Number of x-rays equal to or exceeds 35% of all office visits			
Podiatrist	#401: More than 50 visits per day on more than 20% of the days on which any visits occurred	635	13	2.0%
	#402: Number of x-ray sets equal to or exceeds 25% of all office visits	635	11	18.1%
Pharmacy	#501: Drug abuse items and narcotics, more than 3% of all prescriptions	1,564	118	7.5%
	#502: Drug abuse items and narcotics, more than 100 prescriptions per quarter	1,564	20	1.3%

Table 1 continued

Physician: *GP, Family Practice, Allergy, Pediatrics, Pediatric Allergy*	#601: More than 50 visits per day on more than 20% of the days on which any visits occurred	3,123	68	2.2%
Physician: *All Specialties Except GP, Family Practice, Allergy, Pediatrics, Pediatric Allergy, Anesthesiology, Pathology, Radiology*	#602: More than 30 visits per day on more than 20% of the days on which any visits occurred	5,014	234	4.7%
Physician: *Psychiatry*	#603: More than 10 hours of psychotherapy per day on more than 20% of the days on which any psychotherapy is done	1,251	56	4.5%
Physician: *Entire Category*	#604: Number of first GP office visits equal to or exceeds 65% of all GP office visits*	7,772	1,598	20.6%
Physician: *Internal Medicine*	#605: Number of first internist office visits equal to or exceeds 65% of all internist office visits	1,295	332	25.6%
Physician: *Pediatrics*	#606: Number of first pediatrician visits (any location) equal to or exceeds 65% of all pediatrician visits (any location)	579	313	54.1%
Physician: *Entire Category*	#607: Number of injections equal to or exceeds 20% of all visits	7,772	349	4.5%
Physician: *All Specialties Except Cardiology*	#608: Number of EKGs on patients less than 40 years old equal to or exceeds 5% of all visits	7,616	184	2.4%

*All specialists bill as general practitioners when providing services out of their specialties.

per cent of a profession, necessitates a system of priorities for allocating departmental resources in follow-up evaluations and investigations. For this reason, *Exception Report Summaries* are also produced.

Exception Summary I lists all violators of a given criterion in descending order of violation magnitude (e.g., number of suspect prescriptions, per cent of days with over 50 visits). The dollar value of the allegedly abused service follows each entry.

Exception Summary II is a graphic display of the violations within each specialty and provider category. Flagged providers are listed vertically in order of their Medicaid identification numbers. Across the top of each graph is a horizontal listing of all criteria codes (#101 to #608). For each flagged provider, an asterisk appears in the column beneath each criterion violated. This presents a clear visual display for each provider and for the aggregate group, showing which criteria and combinations of criteria were exceeded and in what volume.

The exception summaries assist in setting and acting on priorities for investigation. A provider who exceeds five criteria would probably be investigated before another who exceeds only one. The amount of each violation, in terms of its magnitude and/or the dollar value of services involved, can be considered. Violations believed to have the most impact on quality of care receive the highest priority. A violation of one such criterion by even a small amount will merit review before a large but purely fiscal abuse with little impact on patients.

Utilizing these quality of care priorities, providers identified in exception reports are evaluated by their peers on our staff. The first step is a review of a provider's individual profile (with his profession's statistical profile as a reference), any other exception reports on which he is mentioned, and any previous evaluations on file for him. These procedures may satisfactorily explain the apparent discrepancy as part of a legitimate pattern, terminating the review. They may, alternatively, confirm the continuation or resumption of a previously documented pattern which is not acceptable, indicating the need for an immediate enforcement procedure (see below).

In many cases, however, the initial review is inconclusive, and we seek confirmation or explanation of a suspected abuse through the "focused" use of one or more of our manual data-gathering techniques; a visit to the provider's office to look at specific items (especially in patient records), reexamination of a selected sample of patients, and/or intensive manual review of invoices with special attention to items excluded from computerized review (primarily diagnosis). If use of these techniques is inappropriate or inconclusive, we may turn to special investigative techniques. Health Department investigators may visit the provider's office as "patients". Patients may be interviewed at our offices, in their homes, or by mail questionnaire. Such interviews are always conducted as "surveys", with no direct interrogation concerning the suspect provider, to avoid harming his reputation should our allegations prove unfounded. The most dramatic special investigative technique has been the collection of physical evidence. For example, pharmacies will occasionally be suspected of "shorting" (billing correctly but dispensing only part of the prescribed medication) or "kiting" (dispensing correctly but altering the prescription to bill for an inflated quantity). People often retain empty pharmacy vials and bottles. If shorting or kiting occurs, we can often show that the containers dispensed could not have physically held the quantities billed for.

At the end of an investigation which confirms suspicions of abuse, the provider in question is almost always invited to our offices for an informal discussion, during which we attempt to resolve the matter in a mutually acceptable, voluntary manner. In 1973, there were 212 such discussions. If a mutually agreeable settlement is impossible, a formal hearing may be requested by either party (there were only two in 1973) or referral may be made for civil suit or criminal prosecution. In instances where the Bureau and the practitioner reach an impasse over a matter of professional judgement, an opinion may be sought from an appropriate professional society.

As a result of the above activities in 1973, $1,293,202 in claims for services were disallowed, restitutions of $640,150 were paid to the City, 63 warnings or special conditions for participation were issued, 41 providers were suspended from the program, 12 providers were referred to law enforcement agencies, and two providers were sentenced to prison terms. Although it is difficult to measure the deterrent and corrective effects of this system on providers not directly exposed to corrective actions, we would like to believe that it's greatest contribution has been higher quality health care services than would have been rendered in its absence.

DISCUSSION

The evaluation activities of the New York City Health Department Medicaid Program are based on the Department's dual obligations, to the recipients of Medicaid health care services and to the taxpayers who finance the program, to assure that services are medically necessary and of adequate quality.

Early evaluation efforts in the program led to three related conclusions: (1) It was quickly apparent that significant numbers of health care practitioners and businesses were guilty of fiscal abuses and/or were providing significantly deficient care; (2) It also became clear that an evaluation effort which hoped to answer questions about quality, and to document the answers as a basis for corrective action would have to utilize a variety of surveillance techniques, each best suited to revealing or confirming certain types of problems; and (3) One technique which emerged as particularly useful was a focus on the pattern of practice of a professional or business, as opposed to summary statistics such as total income, or details on specific cases. Each of these lessons has importance for Professional Standards Review Organizations and for national health insurance planners.

A number of studies in various settings have revealed the existence of significant numbers of substandard health care practitioners. This is consistent with the Medicaid findings outlined in Table 1. If an evaluation program sets as its first task the identification and correction of these obvious deficiencies, it can easily proceed with current methods of assessment. A comment in the introduction to the *Medical and Dental Procedure Manual* used in Morehead's evaluation of federally-funded health centers is equally applicable to the evaluation of fee-for-service health care:

> "The peer review approach used in these studies is simplistic in the extreme compared to more recent ventures into tracer studies, outcome measures, health status and patient satisfaction assessments. However, for better or worse, the state of medical practice in the vast majority of ambulatory care settings is such that, in the opinion of the senior author, complex instruments with detailed study designs are not necessary to identify major areas of strength or, more important weakness in the provision of health services."[15]

The second lesson learned in the early assessment of New York City Medicaid services is that no single technique of evaluation can answer all the types of questions which are posed. Most third-party quality-of-care evaluation programs rely on audits of medical charts (as in Medicare utilization review activities) or computerized analyses of billing forms (in numerous Medicaid, Medicare, and private "Surveillance and Utilization Review" systems).[16] Very few of these systems are supported by other case-finding methods, such as patient reexamination and office audits, or by investigative techniques. They are not designed in large part to confirm or refute findings from other sources, or to generate cases for evaluation with other techniques. Rather than debate the relative merits of evaluating the structure, process, or outcome of health care, the New York City program looks at all three, in a mutually supportive manner. The MVS reports which generate most in-depth evaluations are basically analyses of process variables, such as time per patient in a podiatric practice. The questions raised are often best answered by obtaining structural data (e.g., paraprofessional staffing levels) or outcome information (e.g., the quality and medical necessity of foot appliances provided by the podiatrist.) The interplay of structure, process, and outcome subsystems gives definitive answers. It also provides validation of the parameters used in each component or indicates necessary changes.

The third principle which emerged from early Medicaid evaluation efforts was the value of focusing on patterns of practice. Many of the computerized Surveillance and Utilization Review (SUR) systems in existence elsewhere are more sophisticated than MVS in terms of the completeness of the data entered, and the ability to manipulate it. The most significant data elements missing in MVS and present in many other systems are patient identification and diagnosis (verbatim or coded). The potential capabilities of such systems are impressive, but their utility in affecting health care is often limited by the nature of the reports they are called upon to generate. In most cases, reports are either too generalized or too detailed to be readily used as a basis for corrective actions.

At one extreme are SUR systems which are limited to managerial reports on "what the program is purchasing", similar to the MVS statistical profiles, with or without printouts analogous to our exception reports. These latter "flagging reports" in most systems are limited to rather generalized, conceptual criteria: e.g., all providers earning over X dollars (total, or per patient), all providers rendering more than Y services (total, or per patient), or all providers rendering one or more services with an unusually high frequency. This last criterion is used in several alternate ways in various SUR systems. Each provider is compared with the average for his profession or specialty for each type of service he provides. He is flagged if he deviates from this average (in an upward direction only, in most systems) by more than a certain per cent or number of standard deviations. These norms are usually expressed in terms of annual rates for services, e.g., cardiograms per 100 patients, or per 100 services of all types.[17]

The deviant patterns identified by these generalized parameters may frequently be explained by sub-specialization, patient mix, or the presence of ancillary staff. Although high earnings and high volumes of one or more services are useful parameters in detecting most forms of overutilization, they are not sensitive to poor quality patterns other than overutilization, such as those flagged by some of the exception reports in Figure 3 and Table 1 (high volume on specific days, potential kiting, etc.). Reports in other SUR programs would proba-

bly flag many of the same providers (as high earners, etc.) but would not pinpoint the reasons *why* these high earnings are not entirely acceptable, thus leading to appropriate corrections. Thus, computerized SUR, at this generalized level, forfeits the primary advantage of evaluating the process or content of health care—its potential for indicating corrective actions.

In contrast to the generalized reports discussed above, some computer SUR systems produce extremely detailed chronological listings of services rendered by individual providers and/or received by individual patients. A very sophisticated program utilized in a few SUR units is the "Model Treatment Profile", which outlines appropriate medical services and their appropriate frequencies by diagnosis.[18] A bill with acute bronchitis as the only diagnosis will be flagged for review if an inappropriate service (such as lumbar puncture) or an appropriate service rendered too often (e.g., a fourth office visit in the same month) is claimed.

These detailed systems of computerized review and detailed manual chart review procedures may be highly useful to groups of competent physicians who are interested in self-assessment and self-improvement. When this type of evaluation is applied, however, by a third-party program to health professionals and health-related businesses whose competence covers a wide range, within a program which contains rather ambiguous fiscal inducements (e.g., fee-for-service incentives favoring high volumes), the results are not impressive. It has been the experience of the New York City Medicaid Program that discussions with practitioners based on their treatment of small numbers of patients, or on deviations from standards of a Model Treatment Profile nature, tend to result in non-productive arguments about professional discretion and governmental interference in individual cases.[19] Allegedly poor practice—short of malpractice—is much more difficult to substantiate in individual cases than in aggregate statistics.*

The Medicaid Vendor System asks selected questions about patterns of practice. This approach is more specific than tabulations of overall income, numbers of procedures per patient, etc., but less detailed (and less expensive) than patient/provider histories or Model Treatment Profiles. Six years of manual invoice review, patient reexamination, and office audit have shown that pattern-level data is most useful and reliable,† and have highlighted those specific questions about patterns which are most productive. It may be difficult to determine the appropriateness of a single radiograph, given the complexity of secondary diagnoses and atypical symptoms. It is less difficult to assess the propriety of a pattern in which ninety per cent of general pediatric office visits are accompanied by radiographs. This latter pattern might be revealed by those systems which flag providers who deviate from their profession's mean within the program. But this assumes that the norms themselves are proper, an assumption brought into ques-

tion by some of our findings and those in other programs.[22] Medicare reviews in New York City, for example, flag those physicians who use proctoscopy in legitimate ways, since mose of their peers in the program underutilize this procedure. The deviation-from-the-norm approach is a very useful scanning tool for possible abuses. As an on-going case-finding system, however, it can produce very large volumes of unnecessary data on random deviations unassociated with any abuse.

CONCLUSIONS

PSROs or national health insurance quality control units would be able to deal with the highest priority problems they are bound to encounter by utilizing an unsophisticated pragmatic approach such as the one we have described. A major obstacle to the implementation of a system for detecting and correcting significantly poor practice may be a reluctance to admit that this level of care exists. Once these high priority problems are recognized and brought under control, it will be appropriate to use the latest evaluation research to build a "second generation" system devoted to the correction of more subtle quality deficits.

Fortunately, programs which already produce detailed profiles and gross managerial statistics can, in most cases, simply and rapidly adapt their systems to produce intermediate data on patterns of care. If they do, they will find that they have greatly increased their ability to upgrade the quality of services received by their client populations. It is somewhat more difficult to institute the kinds of supplementary evaluation techniques described in this paper, but these are necessary if judgments of quality and medical necessity are to be documented and used in taking corrective actions.

This paper has stressed the use of evaluation in the correction of individual provider deficiencies. Of even greater long-range

---

*We fully appreciate the importance of several other uses to which patient-related data can be put. These include the compilation of patient utilization statistics for program planning, the identification of underutilizers (e.g., children who have not been adequately immunized) and screening for certain significant types of patient-initiated overutilization such as the use of multiple providers to obtain controlled drugs.

†Studies of detailed profiles based on fee-for-service billing forms have demonstrated that the widespread inaccuracies and gaps common in this data base seriously compromise such profiles.[20] While awaiting an adequate data base for detailed profiling, it is important to note that gross statistical profiles and intermediate-level, "pattern" profiles are much less sensitive to inaccuracies in current data, when such inaccuracies are randomly distributed. Also, screening and preliminary evaluation based on pattern level information is not dependent on the identification of individual patients and their diagnoses—the two most expensive and least reliable data elements in computerized SUR.[21] These items can be addressed in smaller scale confirmatory procedures such as medical records review.

import is the use of evaluation feedback to restructure the system itself in terms of incentives for high quality, cost-effective care. The latitude for such a restructuring within a local Medicaid program has been small.[23] Planners of national health insurance proposals will have the opportunity to incorporate Medicaid and Medicare evaluation findings in their systems of incentives, their regulations, fee structures, and benefit packages.

REFERENCES

1. Bellin, L.E. PSRO—Quality Control? Or Gimmickry? Med. Care 12:1012–1018, 1974.

2. Peterson, O.L., Andrews, L.P., Spain, R.S., and Greenberg, B.G. An analytic study of North Carolina general practice, 1953–54, J. Med. Educ. 31: Part 2, 1956.

3. McClure, W.J. Four Points on Quality Assurance. Quality Assurance of Medical Care—Monograph U.S. Department of Health, Education, and Welfare (HSMHA) 329–346, 1973.

4. Morehead, M.A., Donaldson, R.S., and Seravelli, M.R. Comparisons Between OEO Neighborhood Health Centers and Other Health Care Providers of Ratings of the Quality of Health Care. Am. J. Public Health 61:1294–1306, 1971.

5. Anderson, H. Statistical Surveillance of a Title XIX Program. Am. J. Public Health 59:275–289, 1969.

6. Newhouse, J.P., Phelps, C.E., and Schwartz, W.B. Policy Operations and the Impact of National Health Insurance. New Eng. J. Med. 290:1345–1359, 1974.

7. Rosenberg, S.N., Kavaler, F., and Rabby, A.D. Materia Medicaid New York City: A Compendium of Selected Data on Trends in Medicaid, 1966–1971. New York City Health Department, 1972.

8. Butler, P.A. State Controls Over Utilization and Medical Services Under the California Medi-Cal Program. Medicaid: Lessons for National Health Insurance. Rockville, Md., Aspen, 1975.

9. Rosenberg, S.N. and Posner, J.R. Medicaid Surveillance and Utilization Review. Medicaid: Lessons for National Health Insurance. Rockville, Md., Aspen, 1975.

10. Bellin, L.E. and Kavaler, F. Policing Publicly Funded Health Care for Poor Quality, Overutilization, and Fraud—The New York City Medicaid Experience. Am. J. Public Health. 60:811–820, 1970.

11. Kavaler, F., Bellin, L.E., Green, A., Gorelik, E.A., and Alexander, R.S. A Publicly Funded Pharmacy Program under Medicaid in New York City. Med. Care 12:361–371, 1969.

12. Kavaler, F., Folsom, W.C., Rosenthal, J., Bellin, L.E., and Herbst, E. A Review of On-Site Visits in Optometry, Under the New York City Medicaid Program. American Journal of Optometry and Archives of American Academy of Optometry 47:728–735, 1970.

13. Fisher, M.A. Quality Controls. New York State Dental Journal 37:21–27, 1971.

14. Rosenberg, S.N., Berenson, L.B., Kavaler, F., Gorelik, E.A., and Levine, B. Prescribing Patterns in the New York City Medicaid Program. Med. Care 12:138–151, 1974.

15. Evaluation Unit. Department of Community Health, Albert Einstein College of Medicine. Medical and Dental Audit Procedure Manual. New York 1974.

16. U.S. Department of Health, Education and Welfare, Community Health Service. Peer/Utilization Review Activities Inventory. Rockville, Md., 1972.

17. Electronic Data Systems Federal Corporation. Professional Utilization Review. Dallas. 1971.

18. Harrington, D.C. The San Joaquin Foundation Peer Review System. Med. Care 11:185–189, Supplement. 1973.

19. Bellin, L.E., and Kavaler, F. Medicaid Practitioner Abuses and Excuses Vs. Counterstrategy of the New York City Health Department. Am. J. Public Health 61:2201–2210, 1971.

20. Berkanovic. E. An Appraisal of Medicaid Records as a Data Source. Med. Care 12:590–595, 1974.

21. Doyle, D.N. Accuracy of Selected Items of Blue Cross Claims Information. Inquiry 3:16–27, 1966.

22. Rucker, T.D. The Role of Computers in Drug Utilization Review. American J. of Hospital Pharmacy 29:128–134, 1972.

23. Bellin, L.E. Foreshortened Frank Memoirs of a Former Medicaid Administrator. Medicaid: Lessons for National Health Insurance, Rockville, Md., Aspen, 1975.

35. Periodic Medical Review: Assessing the Quality and Appropriateness of Care in Skilled-Nursing Facilities

KATHLEEN CONNELLY, PHILIP K. COHEN, and
DIANA CHAPMAN WALSH

Reprinted, by permission, from the *New England Journal of Medicine* (Vol. 296, pp. 878–879, 1977).

Mandated by Congress in 1969,[1] Periodic Medical Review (PMR) is a state-run program of external peer review of the care rendered Medicaid-supported patients in skilled-nursing facilities (SNF). In Massachusetts the Department of Public Health administers PMR on behalf of the Department of Public Welfare, which is the State Medicaid agency.

Based upon observations of patients in the facility and analysis of patients' records, the reviews are performed by three teams, each including two registered nurses, a physician and a social worker. The objectives are to appraise the quality of the care rendered and to assess whether patients are appropriately placed* so that remedial action can be taken when warranted.

PMR rates care of patients excellent, good, fair or poor in three categories, medical care, nursing care, and social services, and extrapolates from these findings an overall rating in each category for the facility. The percentage of patients in a facility inappropriately placed in skilled-nursing beds is also reported. Teams review 20 patients per day; because nursing care is considered central, the two nurses on each team divide the case load, and each reviews only 10 cases a day. Team members assess quality only in their own professional disciplines, but the team meets as a group to identify misplaced patients on the theory that factors from all three disciplines should condition that judgment.

PMR FINDINGS

In 1975 PMR reviewed 7700 patients in 215 Massachusetts nursing homes operating skilled-nursing beds occupied by Medicaid-supported patients. On the whole, care was rated fair or better (Table 1). Most patients (82 per cent) were reported appropriately placed. The distribution of misplaced patients among facilities was as follows: (Table 2) in 34 facilities (16 per cent of those reviewed), no patients were misplaced; 34 others had more than 30 per cent of their SNF patients inappropriately placed.

The 1975 ratings were analyzed to determine whether they correlated with other distinguishing characteristics of the facilities. A significant relation (chi-square

---

*Long-term care facilities in Massachusetts are classified at three levels according to the type or intensity of care provided: skilled-nursing facilities; intermediate-care facilities; and rest homes.

= 6.121, with 1 degree of freedom, for 214 facilities, $P \leqslant 0.01$) was found in a comparison of the ratings of medical care with the type of ownership: nonprofit nursing homes were more likely to be rated good or excellent (70 per cent of 27 homes) than proprietary homes (45 per cent of 185 homes). Standardizing variables, such as size of facility, staffing patterns, costs, reimbursement and other sources of income, were not applied, and the finding contradicts Levey's analysis of 1969 Massachusetts data, which revealed no statistically significant relation between type of ownership and quality of care.[2] Other variables examined (size of facility, location by health-planning region and proportion of misplaced patients) failed to correlate significantly with the quality ratings.

Comparisons among the quality ratings in the three categories revealed that they were in substantial agreement: 67.6 per cent of the medical and nursing ratings (chi-square = 27.508, with 1 degree of freedom, for 213 facilities, $P \leqslant 0.001$), 70.3 per cent of the nursing and social-service ratings (chi-square = 35.1, with 1 degree of freedom, for 212 facilities, $P \leqslant 0.001$) and 62.4 per cent of the medical and social-service ratings (chi-square = 11.768, with 1 degree of freedom, for 210 facilities, $P \leqslant 0.001$) were in agreement on quality of care to individual patients.

Table 1 PMR Quality-of-Care Ratings for 215 SNF's, Massachusetts, 1975

Rating	Medical Care		Nursing Care		Social Services	
	no.	%	no.	%	no.	%
Excellent	12	5.8	9	4.2	9	4.2
Good	91	42.3	111	51.6	91	42.3
Fair	102	47.4	85	39.5	103	47.9
Poor	8	3.7	10	4.7	9	4.2
Totals	213*	99.2	215	100	212	98.6

*Ratings were incomplete for 2 facilities in medical care and for 3 in social services.

Table 2 PMR of Appropriateness of Patient Placement in 212 SNF's, Massachusetts, 1975*

Patients Misplaced†	Facilities	
	No.	%
0	34	16.0
< 1	4	1.9
1-10	51	24.1
11-20	60	28.3
21-30	29	13.7
31-40	20	9.4
41-50	4	1.9
51-60	8	3.8
61-65	2	0.9
Totals‡	212	100

*7700 patients were reviewed, and 18.2% were determined to be inappropriately placed.
†% of total patients in the facility inappropriately placed.
‡215 facilities were reviewed, but information on patient placement was incomplete for 3 facilities.

FOLLOW-UP ACTION ON FINDINGS

Information gathered by PMR is referred for action to the Department's long-term-care program and to the Department of Public Welfare. The Department's surveyors visit facilities with low PMR ratings to determine whether regulations governing federal certification or state licensure are being violated and whether sanctions are indicated. A previous column[3] outlined the sanctioning process. Nurses from the welfare department also visit facilities rated poor, to ascertain whether the inadequacy of care warrants transfer of Medicaid patients, and to provide consultation to the facility on how to make improvements.

PMR's recommendations for transfer of patients to a lower level of care are made to the welfare department, which then requests the attending physician to re-evaluate the patient's placement. The physician must concur before any patient is transferred. The Department of Public Welfare does not routinely compile statistics on the number of transfers resulting from PMR reports, but incomplete data attest that transfers accomplished almost invariably occur within a multilevel facility rather than from one facility to another.

In theory, if follow-up action is effective, facilities rated poor one year should show improvement the next. The 1976 reviews have been completed for 13 of the 18 facilities rated poor in medical or nursing care in 1975. Of these facilities, seven received improved ratings in both medical and nursing care; only one was again rated poor in both categories. The degree to which PMR contributed to these improvements is unknown.

STRENGTHS AND WEAKNESSES OF PMR

The program's principal strength lies in its emphasis on the individual patient, which is unique among the State's regulatory activities. PMR nurses personally visit every Medicaid patient in each facility at the time of the annual inspection, prepared in advance with information from the patient's record about his or her condition. Over 90 per cent of SNF patients financed by Medicaid each year are reviewed; the remainder are short-stay patients who enter and leave the facility between PMR inspections.

The review's emphasis on the individual patient is accompanied by particular attention to functional status. PMR requires the facility to report each patient's functional capacity, on the basis of observations similar to those making up the Katz Activities of Daily Living (ADL)scale.[4] Most SNF patients are elderly, either convalescing from acute illness or operation or suffering chronic and debilitating illnesses associated with old age: heart disease, stroke, chronic brain syndrome and generalized arteriosclerosis.[5] More than half (58 per cent) of patients in Massachusetts SNF's are over 80 years old; only 5 per cent are under 60.[6] These characteristics make functional status an important index of the outcome of care—frequently a matter of slowing the patient's declining ability to function independently. To an extent, therefore, PMR is able to evaluate outcome by examining the patient's condition in the light of approaches to care aimed at maintaining or improving functional capacity: in the medical review, whether treatment plans are current and complete, particularly in orders for medications, diets, activities and special restorative care; and in the nursing review, whether rehabilitative nursing is adequate, including schedules for ambulation, proper positioning and skin care, and training in bowel and bladder control. This focus on outcome, as distinct from the input criteria predominating in licensure regulations, is a second strength of the PMR program.

A third is its relatively low cost. In fiscal 1975, nursing-home care for some 30,000 Medicaid patients in skilled-nursing and intermediate-care facilities cost the Commonwealth $183.5 million (35 per cent of the total Medicaid budget).[7] PMR costs about $26 for each of the approximately 8000 patients reviewed each year, or slightly more per patient than the average cost of one day in a skilled-nursing bed.

On the debit side, the program may be weakened by its possible lack of objectivity in the assessments of medical care and social services. The nursing review uses a 100-point scale to quantify 60 factors in five broad categories and arrive at an overall rating of the care that each patient receives. The medical and social-service ratings derive from the reviewer's professional judgment, without explicit criteria. However, the correlations found, in the 1975 review, between the quantified nursing ratings and the more subjective ratings of medical care and social service may suggest that the PMR ratings are at least internally consistent across categories of care.

A second deficiency is the program's very narrow perspective on the question of whether the patient is appropriately placed.

Nursing-home patients would be better served by PMR if the program could identify those with the greatest potential for rehabilitation and perhaps for eventual return home. But lacking information on the patient's previous family and community situation, the reviewers usually ask only whether the patient could be adequately cared for at the intermediate rather than the skilled level.

In short, as a mechanism for the State to monitor the quality of care available to Medicaid patients, PMR represents an important refinement. Additional sharpening remains to be done, particularly to increase the objectivity of the process and its effectiveness in balancing and integrating different professional perspectives to yield an overall picture of the facility's performance.

As a means of encouraging more rational placement of patients, however, PMR's potential remains largely unrealized. Transferring patients is administratively complex for the State, requiring the assent of attending physician and family. Distinctions between levels of care needed tend to blur, and PMR provides a single-snapshot view of a patient whose condition may change from day to day. Furthermore, a transfer to a different facility may itself cause the patient's condition to deteriorate. But where transfers are internal and less disruptive—in multilevel facilities, which account for about 73 per cent of the State's SNF beds—they have no direct effect on Medicaid costs because multilevel facilities receive a uniform rate of reimbursement for Medicaid patients placed at the skilled and intermediate levels of care. Thus, the financial incentives for transferring inappropriately placed patients are too remote to outweigh the difficulties.

REFERENCES

1. Social Security Act, Section 1902(a)(26).

2. Levey, S., Stotsley, B.A., Kinlock, D.R., et al: Nursing homes in Massachusetts: industry in transition. Am. J. Public Health 65:66–71, 1975.

3. Walsh D.C., Feeley, R.: Graduated sanctions to enforce nursing-home standards. N. Engl. J. Med. 295:222–224, 1976.

4. Katz, S., Chinn, A.B., Cordrey, L.J., et al: Multidisciplinary studies of illness in aged persons. II. A new classification of functional status in activities of daily living. J. Chronic Dis. 9:55–62, 1959.

5. Department of Health, Education and Welfare, Public Health Service, Office of Nursing Home·Affairs: Long-Term Care Facility Improvement Study Introductory Report (July 1975) (DHEW Publication No. [OS] 76-50021). Washington, D.C., Government Printing Office, 1975.

6. Massachusetts Department of Public Health: Health Data Annual. Vol. 1, No. 1. Boston, Department of Public Health, 1974, table 69.

7. Massachusetts Department of Public Welfare: Statistical Supplement to the Annual Report, Fiscal Year 1975. Boston, Department of Public Health, 1975, p. 21.

36. The Physician Ambulatory Care Evaluation Project: Computer-Assisted Peer Review of Ambulatory Services

JAMES Q. CANNON

Reprinted with permission from Conference Report: Patient/Provider Profile, pp. 130–179, June 7-10, 1977.

INTRODUCTION AND SUMMARY

The Physician Ambulatory Care Evaluation (PACE) program is a physician-directed professional review effort which utilizes claims data and an advanced automated system for building patient ambulatory case histories and screening them as to compliance with clinical guidelines. Both quality and utilization issues are addressed (with emphasis on the former). Where patterns of variation from peer expectations are observed, intervention is directed toward improving patient care. The approach involves educational contacts with providers rather than immediate punitive action. Interdiction of payment is only employed when other methods fail. Where aberrations arise that are not within the province of the provider to resolve, the matters are referred to the agency which can deal with them.

The PACE program is in full operation in Utah, performing review under contract with the Utah Medicaid program. Claims for physician services, lab and hospital outpatient charges, and prescription drugs, are added to the PACE patient history file and are subject to review. The program is conducted by the Utah Professional Review Organization (UPRO), a private nonprofit corporation, with data processing services currently subcontracted to Optimum Systems Incorporated (OSI). UPRO is closely tied to and predates Utah PSRO and is an offspring of the Utah State Medical Association.

The functions performed by UPRO and its subcontractor are currently supported out of state funds and operational MMIS funding, since the PACE data support system was developed under funding from the Medical Services Administration to be an MMIS module. While currently a contracted service between the State and UPRO, it is expected that, at some point, at least the professional review component of PACE will become a PSRO function.

A relatively clear division of responsibilities was worked out when the state of Utah contracted with UPRO to conduct a program which would satisfy state utilization review obligations for the types of services described above. The state is responsible for all MMIS functions including coding not done by the provider, data validation, entry, duplicate checks, fraud detection, pricing, and other aspects of administrative review. Furthermore, all communications with Medicaid clients or with social service

317

case workers and all payment sanctions are handled by the State. UPRO is responsible for all clinical determinations and associated contact with the provider. The PACE program operates under the same confidentiality requirements as the Medicaid agency, utilizes the same reference files, and is subject to state monitoring. Though the data support system for PACE is currently run by a private subcontractor, the system is fully compliant with the general MMIS systems requirements. Because UPRO adds information to the patient and provider history set in the form of exception messages indicating guideline failures and reviewer judgments, PACE patient and provider profiles are not routinely made available to state Medicaid officials; however, all files are open to authorized audit.

CRITERIA

One of the essential features of PACE as a means to peer review is the systematic and objective application of screening criteria to ambulatory medical care data and the reporting of instances where those criteria are not met. The concept behind PACE is that these guidelines be adopted based on the consensus of peers representing the leadership of each specialty and that screening be automated to the extent possible.

The system was designed to accept a wide variety of statements regarding expectations as to medical care in given situations. Such statements are not limited simply to the classical form, defining appropriate and inappropriate care for specified diseases or problems; rather, guidelines can also be written for medical procedures, drugs, types of patients, provider attributes such as specialty, and combinations of the above. Time limitations and episode definitions are also possible. A few examples illustrating the forms and types of guidelines now in use are shown in Figure 1. Table 1

Figure 1 Examples of Criteria Now In Use In PACE.

The following are subject to review:

1. Adult patient with pneumonia without follow-up chest x-ray during episode.
2. MAO inhibitors prescribed by nonpsychiatrists.
3. More than two EKG's per year for diagnosis other than heart disease, arteriosclerosis, or chest pain.
4. Lomotil® for children under two years.
5. Anticoagulant therapy lacking prothrombin time each month.

---

breaks the entire set of guidelines currently in use down by subject and type.

It is important to note that these guidelines are only used for screening. It is understood with regard to most of the matters addressed that some patients and situations will require other approaches. Generally, they are intended as a means to identify and examine *patterns* of current practice and patient care. Physician review of those patterns is necessary to determine whether they are inappropriate or not. Consequently, the guideline set is constantly being modified, with new guidelines being added as they are developed or refined, and with impracticable or outdated ones being dropped from the system after being tested.

AUTOMATED SCREENING

Weekly, the MMIS generates a PACE file containing data for all claims in the current run from clinics, pharmacies, hospital outpatient departments, independent labs and the majority of physician claims. (Anesthesiology, assistant at surgery, and professional component claims are excluded since the information they contain repeats other claims data.) Inpatient hos-

Table 1 UPRO PACE Screening Guidelines, by Subject and Type in use April 1, 1977

Type	Subject					
	Diagnosis (I)	Procedure* (II)	Drug (III)	Patient (IV)	Provider (V)	Total
A. Required service or therapy	55	6	3	0	2	66
B. Contraindicated service or therapy	30	12	53	2	1	98
C. Prerequisite history needed to justify service, therapy	0	10	1	0	0	11
D. Utilization limit for service or therapy	19	29	20	0	8	76
E. Untoward symptoms during therapy	0	0	2	0	0	2
TOTAL	104	57	79	2	11	253

*Includes all injections

Notes:

1. Study guidelines (which generate a patient treatment profile but register no exception) make up 3% of the guidelines.
2. Age or sex-specific guidelines comprise 16%.

pital claims data are also transmitted but are not currently utilized in PACE history. The file is transmitted to UPRO's data processing subcontractor via computer tape.

Figure 2 outlines the data processing sequence that ensues. The data are subjected to final editing to insure a match with patient and provider reference file information sent periodically and are then added to history. History data are organized and linked by patient and, secondarily, by provider.

When history files have been updated, screening begins. The first step in this screening process involves scanning the new claims data received for that week to determine which, if any, screening guidelines should be applied to a given patient's care. The application of a guideline is triggered by the presence of a data element on a new claim which matches the subject of the screening guideline. Each guideline contains a definition of the amount of patient history to be searched in either or both chronological directions from

the triggering data element. Also indicated is whether some additional patient care history is required before screening occurs. When a delay is specified, a record of the case is stored and screening is completed at a later time.

Screening involves examining patient history to determine if the care rendered exceeds the limits expressed in the guideline. Instances of care varying from the guidelines are recorded in the data base as exceptions and are listed in a set of reports to UPRO.

The PACE module was designed so as to be able to operate in a prepayment mode by means of "pend" guidelines, where an intervention prior to payment was felt to be necessary. Exceptions to such guidelines under such an operating mode would stop payment for that service until and unless a return disposition message were sent to the State endorsing the service for payment. It should be noted, however, that such screening in the Utah system resulted in a week's delay in payment to all physicians in

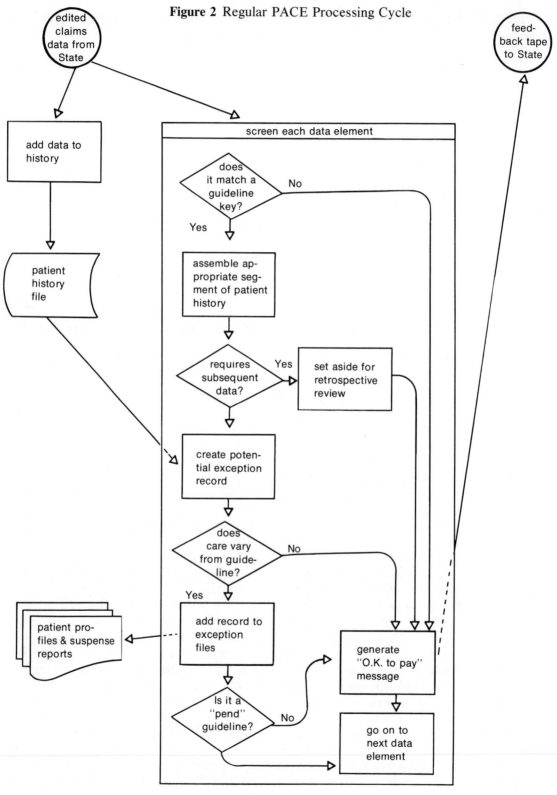

Figure 2 Regular PACE Processing Cycle

order to suspend payment for a handful. The benefits of the latter simply did not equal the disadvantages of the former. Consequently, the PACE-MMIS interface has been modified so that payment occurs as soon as claims clear MMIS. Any payment sanctions arising from professional review are currently imposed in the form of adjustments against future billings.

OUTPUTS OF THE PACE DATA SUPPORT SYSTEM

The MMIS/PACE module generates numerous outputs which are used by UPRO and OSI. Only three types are mentioned below. These are the most significant in the review process.

1. Patient Treatment Profile

The patient treatment profile is the primary tool in professional review under PACE. This report displays all services received by a patient during the past year or so that have been billed to Medicaid. Exceptional instances of care are indicated and a place is provided for a physician reviewer to record his evaluation of the appropriateness of each exception.

An example of a patient treatment profile is illustrated in Figure 3. The circled letters will be referenced in the text. As may be observed, the format is designed for readability by the physician reviewer. Identifying information on the patient is displayed in the upper right corner of each page (A). The contents of the history file for that patient are arranged chronologically according to date of service (B). The specialty and identification number of each provider of service are listed at the left (C). The body of the profile records the description (D) as well as the code (E) for each service and for the diagnoses for which those services were performed. Up to four diagnoses may appear per claim. An "E" in the "Dx Ref" column (F) indicates that the service related

to more than one of the diagnoses listed. Prescription drugs are similarly identified, and the dispensing date, the identification of the prescribing physician, where available, and the number of units dispensed (G) are shown. Though not shown in the figure, the actual computer-produced format displays the amount billed, the amount paid, and the claim and line numbers for each item on the right hand side of the profile.

All exceptions, regardless of when they occurred, are noted by means of a reference number in the "Flag #" column (H). Each new instance of exceptional care identified in the screening process is also starred. At the bottom of the page (J), each exception flag is footnoted with a description of the guideline not met. The fields to the right (K) indicate evaluations made of previous exceptions and prompt the reviewer to record one of seven possible review judgments for new exceptions. A review date and an identifying code for the reviewer are displayed for exceptions already evaluated.

A detailed examination of one aspect of this profile will help illustrate the process:

In early 1976, pharmacy claims data were transmitted to the PACE system indicating that a prescription had been filled on January 10, for 100 units of the drug propranolol. The prescribing physician was #11XX7, an internist.

The screening process identified three guidelines keyed to the drug class code for propranolol, which indicated that the following were subject to review:

1. Concurrent use of propranolol and aminophylline.
2. Propranolol prescribed in the presence of a history of congestive heart failure.
3. Concurrent use of propranolol and digoxin, except for patients with arrhythmia.

In addition, any concurrent use of sulfonylureas or phenformin with propranolol

Figure 3 UPRO PACE Patient Treatment Profile

PATIENT NAME: LEE xxxxxx
SSN: 519-00-0000
SEX: M   AGE: 59

(C) Prov Spec	Prov ID	(B) Date of Service	(H) Flag #	(F) DX Ref / (D) Description	(E) Diag	(G) Units	Proc/ Drug	(A) Amount Billed	Amount Paid
MED	11xx7	11/06/75		A .... Congestive Heart Failure	427.9				
				B .... Hrt Rhythm Disorder Nec	416.9				
				A Office Visit-Lmtd Srvc, Estab Pt			90050	12.00	9.00
MED	11xx3	11/12/75		<> Diazepam-5 MG Tabs		100	004000501	10.00	10.00
MED	11xx7	12/04/75	1*	A .... Congestive Heart Failure	427.9				
				A .... Office Visit-Lmtd Srvc, Estab Pt			90050	12.00	9.00
				E ECG W/Interpret/Prt, 12 Lead			93000	15.00	12.00
MED	11xx3	01/10/76		<> Diazepam-5MG Tabs		100	004000501	10.00	10.00
MED	11xx7	01/22/76		<> Propranolol-10 MG Tabs		100	046046191	8.00	6.00
PHAR	30xx7			<> Digoxin-0.25 MG Tabs		100	081024955	3.00	3.00
MED	11xx7	01/23/76		A .... Chr Ischemic Hrt Dis Nec	412.9				
				B .... Chest Wall Pain	789.2				
				E .... Office Visit-Lmtd Srvc, Estab Pt			90050	12.00	9.00
				E EGG W/Interpret/Rpt, 12 Lead			93000	20.00	16.00
MED	11xx3	01/27/76		<> Indomethacin-25MG Tabs		30	006002582	4.00	4.00
MED	11xx7	02/23/76		<> Diazepam-5MG Tabs		100	004000501	10.00	10.00
				<> Digoxin-0.25 Tabs		100	081024975	2.00	2.00
		04/06/76	2*	A .... Congestive Heart Failure	427.9				
				A Office Visit-Lmtd Srvc, Estab Pt			90050	12.00	9.00
				A ECG W/Interpret/Rpt, 12 Lead			93000	20.00	16.00

(J) Flag #

Guideline not met

Med Appro	Revw Incon	Non Prov	Educ	Warning	No Pay	Revw Unnec	Review Date	Reviewer
( )	( )	( )	( )	( )	( )	( )	03/26/7	24

(K)

1*Flag use of propranolol W/HX of congestiv Failure-past 90D
2*Flag more than 2 EKG's per 6 mos. for heart disease
(DXL #029)

was also reportable but for study purposes only.

Screening for compliance with the first and second guidelines occurred immediately upon receipt of the above mentioned pharmacy claim. The third guideline required an additional thirty-day period of history of following the dispensing date of the prescription.

The portion of the profile detailed in Figure 4 displays recent history information available for this patient at the time the pharmacy claim for propranolol was added to the PACE data base. A search of prior thirty-day period uncovered no use of aminophylline. However, the diagnosis of congestive heart failure had been recorded within ninety days prior to January 10, and thus an exception to guideline flagging propranolol with congestive heart failure was noted as exception #1 for this patient. Thirty days later, a subsequent search was made for compliance with the digoxin guideline. Though digoxin was prescribed on January 22 no exception was recorded

because the patient had been diagnosed as having heart rhythm disorders. The exception description section at the bottom of the page reveals that reviewer 24, in evaluating the profile on March 26, questioned the use of propranolol in this case and recommended an educational inquiry to provider #11XX7 regarding the use of propranolol. This decision was based not only on the provider's care of this patient but the fact that two other Medicaid patients had been similarly treated.

2. Review Requests

A review request is an automated search of history data for elements matching user-specified parameters. When a match is found, the entire patient treatment profile is assembled and printed. The search continues until the entire data base for the time period specified has been scanned or until the specified number of profiles have been produced. This function is most commonly used to retrieve a single patient's profile. In

Figure 4 Detail From Patient Treatment Profile

PATIENT NAME: LEE/xxxxxx
SSN: 000-00-0000
SEX: M   AGE: 59

Prov Spec	Prov ID	Date of Service	Flag #	DX REF	Description	Units	Diag	Proc/ Drug
MED	11xx7		1*	A.....Congestive Heart Failure			427.9	
		12/04/75		A	Office Visit-Lmtd Srvc, Estab Pt			90050
				A	ECG W/Interpret/Rpt, 12 Lead			93000
				<>	Diazepam	100		004000501
		01/10/76		<>	Propranolol	100		046046191
		01/22/76		<>	Digoxin	100		081024955

	Med Appro	Review Incon	Non Prov	Educ	Warn-ing	No Pay	Review Unnec-	Review Date	Re-viewer
				x				03/2/6/76	24

1*Flag use of propranolol w/hx of congestiv failur-past 90D-

addition to simply specifying a patient identification number, request parameters may involve any one or combination of the following:

a. patient age, sex
b. provider ID, specialty
c. diagnosis code range
d. procedure code range
e. drug code range

This function allows special investigations of the data base regarding matters not addressed by the screening guidelines.

3.   Summary Reports

Several reports can be produced which summarize, according to the need specified, the contents of the PACE exception file, the line-item file, and the review cases file. These are important aids in identifying and assessing patterns of care, in developing general comparative data, and in measuring project impact. These are designed to supplement, rather than duplicate MMIS S/UR reports.

STAFF SCREENING ACTIVITIES

The PACE system has been designed to eliminate the need for a large staff. The computer performs many of the clerical and screening functions which are handled manually in traditional claims review processes. The reason for this approach is not only to keep staffing needs down but to minimize the subjectivity of screening prior to peer evaluation.

The fact that the data processing system is sophisticated, however, imposes some significant demands on staff. Few, if any, physicians associated with the program can be expected to take sufficient time away from their practice to learn the intricacies of the system. Therefore, staff must be able to understand both the concerns of the professionals and the capabilities of the machine and provide a linkage between the two.

Staff screening involves the determination of the cases which are ready for physician review and is structured to make the professional review component as efficient as possible by selecting only those cases where there is some likelihood that inquiry or intervention will be in order. UPRO's philosophy is that isolated variations from guidelines, unless clearly inappropriate, should be discounted. This philosophy recognizes that the professional responsibility of the provider should be honored when his intent is unclear and details of the case are unavailable. Since most guidelines are designed to assist in the identification of inappropriate provider practice patterns, exceptions to such guidelines are generally not presented for physician review until a provider's care of multiple (usually three) patients is exceptional for the guideline. Thus, a review case often consists of several patients treated by a single physician. However, a case may be a single patient where the guideline is directed toward identifying:

1. Inappropriate patient utilization of drugs or services.
2. Situations where clear-cut risk to the patient exists that may be unknown to the providing physician.
3. Other cases where patient care varies substantially from the expected without any evidence of the reason or need.
4. Further instances of an exceptional provider practice pattern which should not be endorsed.

Twice monthly, staff screen the exception listings to identify new cases for physician review and request the relevant patient profiles for those identified. They also screen for continuing exceptional care patterns relating to patients or providers previously reviewed.

Back-up materials relating to other aspects of that provider's practice and earlier actions taken regarding either the provider or the patient are added by staff to the new profile(s) pertaining to the case. As needed, staff performs other background work to verify data, to highlight issues, to prompt reviewer consideration of certain factors, etc.

It should be emphasized that some exceptions registered by the computer are never presented for physician review. Some are isolated variations from a guideline for which only patterns are felt to be significant. Others require additional manual screening beyond what the computer logic can handle and are found to comply with the intent behind the guideline.

PROFESSIONAL REVIEW

An essential element of professional review process is individualizing the considerations to assure that extenuating factors which could appropriately modify the application of guidelines are taken into account. The nature of the data utilized in PACE requires a fairly extensive set of interpretations and inferences in reaching an evaluation as to appropriateness. The credibility of educational efforts depends on those judgments being made by peers who presumably understand the realities of medical practice first-hand.

Since most of the care reported to PACE has been rendered by primary care physicians, the bulk of the review is performed by physicians appointed from the primary care areas (family practice, internal medicine, pediatrics, and obstetrics/gynecology). Exceptions to guidelines written by other specialties are reviewed, when possible, by consultants from those specialties. However, because a substantial length of time is required in some instances to assemble enough work for a given specialty consultant to warrant his time, primary care reviewers are often involved in the preliminary appraisal of pattern data. However, no decisive action is taken on the basis of their review until the appropriate consultant has concurred.

Because of the importance of prescription drug information to the PACE review process, pharmacological consultation is an important component of professional review. Pharmacy consultants work closely with physician reviewers and provide important information as well as a link to the dispensing pharmacists.

A reviewer evaluates both the appropriateness of the individual aberration from guidelines and recommends an approach for dealing with the case. With regard to the first, six coded evaluation options are available which indicate the following:

1. The care failing the guideline is in fact medically appropriate.
2. There is insufficient data to conclude firmly that care is inappropriate but neither is justification for the care apparent.
3. The care does vary from peer expectations but the problem does not seem to arise from provider judgment.
4. The care is inappropriate and some educational intervention is in order.
5. The inappropriate pattern continues without justification and some further, more pointed intervention should occur.
6. Despite educational efforts, no response is apparent. The provider is to be informed that UPRO will not endorse for payment future inappropriate care of this type.

With respect to disposition approaches, the options are as follows:

1. Reconsider the patient later
2. Reconsider the practice pattern later
3. Close the case
4. Refer to a consultant
5. Refer to the Ambulatory Care Review Committee
6. Refer to the state
7. Contact the provider
8. Other

The provider is contacted by one of the reviewers when at least two reviewers have evaluated the exceptional case and agree that contact is in order. The issue at hand may be a matter of a variant practice pattern, apparently inappropriate patient activity, or simply a quirk in patient care arising from inadequate communication among the parties involved. Letters are the most common form of contact and are most readily documented, but phone and face-to-face contacts are also employed successfully. UPRO does not contact patients directly; the State is advised where some inquiry or information to patients is needed.

The tone of an initial communication is one of inquiry. Specifically acknowledged is the fact that information available to PACE is incomplete and subject to occasional misinterpretation. The provider is invited to discuss his approach with his peers and to make suggestions regarding review criteria. When behavior determined by peers to be unacceptable continues, the physician is put on notice that future claims of a specified type will no longer be approved. At this point, claims denials may occur. The decision for denial of payments rests with the State but is normally consistent with advice by UPRO.

In addition to individual contact with providing physicians, general circulation to the professional community of educational materials also occurs, usually under the auspices of the Academy for Continuing Medical Education, a subdivision of the Utah State Medical Association. These educational efforts take the form of articles, manuscripts, selected references, and other programs. Topics for such materials are those matters where the practice of a large number of physicians varies from best current information found in the literature.

Pharmacy consultants also participate in the feedback process by contacting the dispensing pharmacist in exceptional cases both in order to gather information and to encourage the pharmacist to monitor the drug profile involved. Normally, they do not contact the physician(s) shown as prescribing the therapy. This is felt to be the province of the physician reviewer.

A significant intervention opportunity involves reporting to the State those problem cases which require investigation or action outside the scope of PACE responsibilities and those changes needed in Medicaid program policy. For each special problem case encountered, UPRO describes the nature of its concern and provides the necessary identifying information so that the State can retrieve its own data on the case.

Frequently, these cases suggest the need for committing the responsibility for managing the patient's care to a single physician and pharmacy. Other cases require case worker involvement or special assistance, as is apparent in child abuse. For policy issues, UPRO normally serves as representative of the state medical association and indicates, for example, areas where the benefits package should be expanded or restricted or where new instructions are needed.

The intent of these PACE review activities is, as mentioned, to improve physician performance and patient care and to assure quality and sound utilization. Though the data deal only with care received by Medicaid recipients, the communications are intended to be generic so as to avoid catalyzing a double standard of practice or a reduction in the availability of medical care to Medicaid patients.

A managing committee made up of reviewers representing the primary care specialties is chaired by the PACE Medical Director. This group sets policy for ambulatory care review, acts on recommendations to make exceptional practices by certain providers subject to potential non-endorsement, determines all patients and patient care situations to be referred to the state, approves new types of letters to be sent, and a variety of other tasks. The Committee meets twice a month for a total of about three hours.

OTHER USES OF PACE

In addition to the regular PACE operations described in the previous section there are two other activities of UPRO/Utah PSRO for which the existence of the PACE data base is significant.

The first of these is the long term care review demonstration project being conducted by Utah PSRO. This demonstration is presently operating in 20 Salt Lake County nursing homes and it involves a combination of concurrent review and professional intervention techniques adapted from the experiences of our hospital review program and PACE. The project is currently limited to Medicaid patients in the participating facilities. One feature of the demonstration is an examination of the application of the PACE technology to this new care site.

The PACE data base already includes comprehensive drug information on Medicaid nursing home patients and a method is being developed to add diagnosis/problem information to the data base from our manually produced patient abstracts. This aggregation of information will permit the operation of a PACE-type screening system to nursing home patient data. In addition, comparisons will be made of drugs purchased versus those recorded in patient records as actually being dispensed. Some discoveries of interest have already been made in this latter area.

One of the measurement issues for the long term care demonstration relates to the extent that PACE data can be substituted for manual data collection and the efficiencies that might produce.

Concerning the PACE-long term care interface we are also exploring the possibility of adding Medicare crossover claims to the routine PACE data base. This addition has ramifications beyond the review of long term care demonstration. Discussions with state personnel are on-going.

Funding for these long term care review activities has been obtained from the Bureau of Quality Assurance, DHEW.

The second activity designed to test new uses for PACE would involve a linkage between current PACE data and information which can be gathered as part of our inpatient hospital review program (OSCHUR). Several issues have been identified where an aggregation of data from inpatient and ambulatory records will permit a more informed evaluation than either standing alone.

For the foreseeable future, the matching of information from the two data bases would be performed manually. During the next year, we expect to explore the range of clinical issues for which the expanded information resource may be productive and to understand the depth of data required for professional reviewers to make judgments. Whether this interface should ultimately be automated remains to be determined although some potential benefits are apparent.

RESULTS

UPRO is now processing an average of 64,000 Medicaid claims per month through the PACE system, of which 3/4 are pharmacy claims. Individual aspects of care fail PACE screening guidelines at a rate of 16.2 per 100 physician-patient encounters.

Physician and pharmacy review consultants are spending approximately 65 hours per month reviewing the exceptional cases produced. Slightly more than a third of this time is spent in committee review activity. Additional committee time is spent in the development and refinement of screening guidelines. Interest on the part of reviewers continues to be very high.

The number of contacts with individual providers has increased substantially during the current period as Table 2 indicates. Not only are UPRO review consultants writing to their peers individually when an exceptional practice is noted, but also they are corresponding to advise physicians of exceptional care arising from client behavior or involving several providers. In addition, communications with pharmacies have begun to encourage them to maintain drug profiles on their patients and to contact prescribing physicians where undesirable quantities or combination of drugs are noted. As would be expected, responses from providers to these contacts have been mixed, but on balance constructive.

Besides individual contact, generalized educational materials arising out of PACE and developed under the auspices of the UPRO Ambulatory Care Review Committee have been disseminated to the professional community on six occasions since October 1, 1976:

Subject	Recipients
Inadequate documentation that a psychiatric evaluation has been performed	All psychiatrists in Utah
Indications for pediatric use of tetracycline	All physicians in Utah
Gamma globulin use	All physicians in Utah
Misuse of hospital emergency services	All hospitals in Utah
Potential abuse of common psychotropic drugs	All physicians in Utah
Indications for tonsillectomy and adenoidectomy	All otolaryngologists in Utah

Table 2 Contacts with Individual Providers Regarding PACE Findings

	Current Contract (Oct. 1, 1976–Apr. 30, 1977)	Entire Project (May 1, 1975–Apr. 30, 1977)
Total Documented Contacts	359	532
Letters	315	423
Providers	245	283
Subjects	47	54

Since early 1976, UPRO has been referring matters to the state Medicaid Agency which require consideration, investigation, or other action by that Agency. Table 3 indicates the number of referrals for each type of situation referred.

A brief analysis was recently done to assess the PACE screening guidelines. The results are interesting in what they reveal about the way the PACE program operates and about the implications for review programs in general.

Exceptions reviewed during April, 1977 and provider contacts made during the first five months of 1977 were broken down by the category of the associated guideline using the scheme employed in Table 1. A comparison was then drawn between the relative shares of total guidelines, total exceptions, and total subjects for each type of guideline. Figure 5 displays those where

Table 3 PACE Referrals to State Office of Medical Services

TYPE	NUMBER	
	prior to Oct. 1, 1976	Oct. 1, 1976 –Apr. 30, 1977
Instances of nonendorsed care, where previous educational efforts to modify exceptional practice patterns have failed	19	187
Apparent duplicate billing not detected by MMIS	21	40
Exceptional client utilization	34	37
Children experiencing repeated injuries	20	94
Other	7	7
TOTAL	101	365

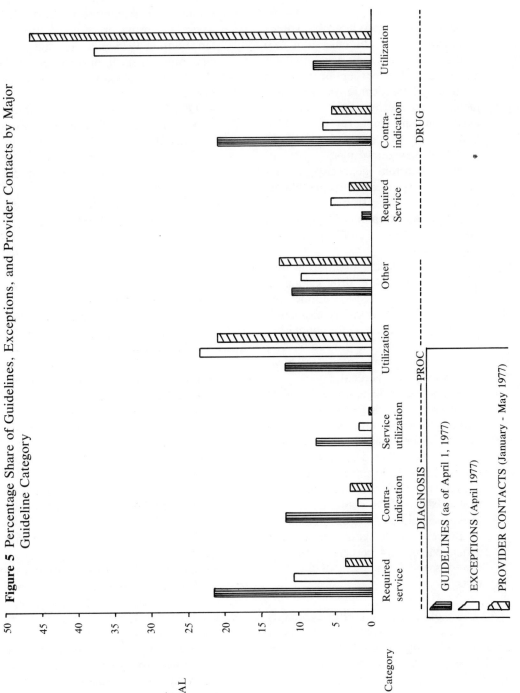

Figure 5 Percentage Share of Guidelines, Exceptions, and Provider Contacts by Major Guideline Category

significant variation among the shares is noted.

1. Though utilization-related guidelines represent only 30 percent (76 of 253) of the guidelines, they accounted for almost 2/3 of all exceptions and an even larger percentage of the contacts. The majority of the utilization exceptions and contacts (1020 of 1710 and 108 of 152) related to the 20 guidelines keyed to drugs.
2. Contraindications generally are described in 39 percent of the guidelines. However, exceptions to such guidelines make up only 15 percent of the total exceptions and 20 percent of the contacts.
3. Guidelines requiring monitoring during drug therapy (i.e. drug guidelines of Type A) generated 4 1/2 times the number of exceptions as expected, based on the share of the guidelines they represent (1.2 percent). The share of educational contacts, however, was only 3 percent.
4. In contrast, guidelines warning against the use of certain drugs because of potentially adverse effects or interactions failed less than one-third as often as expected (6.6 percent of the exceptions vs. 20.9 percent of the guidelines) and produced an even smaller share of the contacts.
5. Diagnosis-related guidelines comprise 41 percent of the guideline set but produced only 14 percent of the exceptions and 6.5 percent of the contacts.

A variety of efforts by UPRO as well as Health Care Management Systems, Inc., are now underway to assess the impact of the PACE program. The beginning results of UPRO's analysis are below.

1. A study was made of changes in exception rates for a provider regarding a single guideline for equivalent time periods prior to and following his receipt of a letter from UPRO on that subject. 116 situations were studied where the provider received the letter(s) during 1976 or earlier and sufficient subsequent information is available to compute post-letter exception rates.
   a. Of 108 written to *once* on a subject
      • 84.1 percent (92) show no exceptions at all or a clear decrease in their exception rate since the letter
      • no change is yet evident for 5.1 percent[6]
      • an increased number of exceptions has been observed for 9.3 percent[10]
   b. Of the 8 written to *more than once* on the same subject
      • 4 had already shown a decrease after the first letter
      • 7 evidenced a decreased exception rate after the second letter
      • for all who receive three letters, a marked decline was observed.
2. A guideline-by-guideline analysis is now underway. The only results available thus far are below:
   Tetracycline exceptions (i.e. prescribing tetracycline to children under 8 years of age) per 100 tetracycline claims:

May-June 1976	average 4.58
July-Dec. 1976	average 3.71
Jan. 1977	2.86

   Thus, a 37.6 percent decrease in 8 months
3. An analysis of utilization patterns regarding the most frequent injections covered under Utah Medicaid policy is reported in Table 4. It will be noted that injections of all types declined one-third in the year between June 1975 and June 1976 and almost as much between December 1975 and 1976.
4. Of the first 76 pediatric injury referrals to Protective Services, at least one-third have been validated and have led

Table 4 Injections per 100 office visits

| Most Common Injections | 1975 | | | | 1976 | | | |
| | 1st Half | | 2nd Half | | 1st Half | | 2nd Half | |
	Rate	Number	Rate	Number	Rate	Number	Rate	Number
90750 Unspecified Therapeutic	3.09	1408	1.69	887	1.54	926	1.28	643
90760 Steroids	1.20	546	.80	417	.82	493	.64	320
90762 ACTH	.26	119	.13	70	.12	73	.14	68
90776 Gamma Globulin	.80	365	.79	416	.92	554	.32	162
90778 Penicillin	15.19	6931	8.80	4609	10.00	6005	6.59	3323
90780 Other Antibiotic	1.84	841	1.65	863	1.52	911	1.06	533
TOTAL	22.38	10210	13.86	7262	14.92	8962	10.03	5049
Number of Office Visits	45,640*		52,391		60,126		50,420	
Change from 1st half 1975	–0–		–38.1%		–33.3%		–55.2%	
Change from 2nd half 1976	n/a		–0–		+ 7.6%		–27.6%	

*See attached note

to intervention beyond investigation. This validation rate is at least twice what UPRO had expected. As a result, UPRO has jointly agreed with Protective Services staff to modify the guidelines to capture injury patterns at an earlier point in their emergence. This will lead to more referrals, probably resulting in a lower validation rate, but a higher number of actual interventions.

Note to Table 4, Injections per 100 office visits:

An attempt has been made to explain the low office count in relation to injections for the first half of 1975 out of a concern that the injection rate might be overstated. No satisfactory explanations were found.

One would expect the relationship between office visit counts for the first and second halves of 1975 to be similar to that for 1976, which would require the actual count of office visits for early 1975 to be above 60,000. However, the reported ratio of visits to total line-items for early 1975 is consistent with that for other periods.

The hypothesis that the implementation of MMIS substantially increased the likelihood that a given claim would find its way to UPRO, explains the low reported counts for line-items and office visits; however, since there is no reason to suspect that the pre-MMIS system reported a greater proportion of one type of service to PACE than others, an under-reporting of claims data would not have distorted the actual injection rate significantly.

While it is true that data coding and entry switched from OSI to the State in July 1975, no changes to coding or entry procedures have been identified that were of sufficient magnitude to have caused the anomaly.

Thus, in the absence of an explanation to the contrary, one must assume the rate of injections for early 1975 to be reliable even though the number of office visits reported seems small.

COST

UPRO's contract with the State for PACE operations costs approximately

$6.50 per Medicaid client annually. The only additional costs associated with PACE are those required for State monitoring and supervision, for MMIS-PACE interface tape production, and for evaluation. Physician review, which is the objective of the service UPRO provides, is only 32 cents per enrollee annually but cannot occur without the support structure the other $6 plus provides. As a percentage of total Medicaid expenditures for the claim types reviewed, the PACE contract amounted to 5.3 percent of the $7,000,000 spent in 1976.

CONCLUSIONS

The UPRO PACE program represents a unique approach in the field of utilization review. A State government has contracted with a private professional review organization for a review program directed by the physician leadership of the State. The contractor assumes all responsibility for evaluation of ambulatory medical care and for communicating and interacting with the physician community regarding its findings and recommendations.

The review is clinically oriented. The focus is on the examination of episodes in the care of individual patients to identify unusual practices. The approach is based on a philosophy that the critical opportunities for achieving positive benefits for patients and the citizenry in general arise from quality-of-care issues, not from utilization issues *per se*. For the most part, the latter will solve themselves if the questions of appropriateness are answered successfully.

The program not only involves a method of exception detection, using clinical guidelines rather than statistical norms to measure variation, but also includes a procedure for evaluating those exceptional situations, which takes full advantage of physician expertise. In addition, a variety of courses of action are available to reviewers in their effort to improve ambulatory care which respect the professional responsibility of their peers and which provide incentives for voluntary response before they are faced with payment sanctions.

PACE represents a bridge in medical care review between administrative approaches and internal quality assurance programs. It operates on the assumption that others will deal with program policy issues (eligibility and benefits). Further, though it has some capability to detect and report potential fraud, it incorporates no investigative element. Because claims data provide only the outlines of medical care, PACE leaves to internal quality assurance programs the responsibility for matters such as whether lab results are followed up. Nevertheless, the definition of what PACE doesn't do should not result in an inference that it has limited power. PACE in Utah has provided more information about ambulatory care delivery than has ever been available. It has enabled the USMA's Academy for Continuing Medical Education to function in ambulatory care, it has given the state Medicaid agency more to deal with in the way of significant program and patient utilization issues than it has been able to handle; it has provided the Protective Services office with a large volume of information regarding suspected child abuse cases to investigate; and it has resulted in a level and kind of dialogue on ambulatory care issues within the medical community that has no precedent.

The impressions of physicians and staff associated with the program and the objective data which have been gathered to date regarding improvements in care associated with PACE interventions support the conclusion that the effect of PACE is significant and in the right direction.

The enthusiasm of physicians and other consultants knowledgeable about the program is high. The leadership of the medical profession as well as of the state Medicaid Agency continue to be supportive and committed. The rank and file physicians see the program as responsible and well-executed, despite occasional disagreement with the impositions of peer review.

Perhaps the most important conclusion to date is that each step in the development and implementation of the PACE approach has proven its potential and flexibility as a review tool. Many options are as yet untried. This ability to respond to the needs of reviewers represents an important aspect of its appeal to the profession. The program is designed to foster an individualized response to aberrations in medical care delivery and avoids the temptation to overreact to the visible but extreme case by the use of objective screening guidelines and the emphasis on patterns of care. Being able to respond differentially to a wide variety of issues and circumstances, the program transcends the need to be prematurely punitive or regulatory.

To date, PACE has not been implemented in a large-volume setting or with other data bases than Medicaid. Further, though it shares a common data base with S/UR, the linkage with that system or others is yet but an opportunity for future exploration. These areas will teach us more about the PACE approach and will bring about further evolution.

Finally, it must be emphasized again that the key to the success thus far of the PACE program lies in the fact that it is physician-directed. UPRO's experience is both that medical professionals will review their peers responsibly if given the tools to do so and that providers do respond to constructive encouragement to change. The societal assignment of the responsibility for medical review should clearly acknowledge review as an essential element of the profession of medicine.

Both the PACE module and the related approach to ambulatory peer review are in the public domain and may represent the best composite of medical, administrative, and systems thinking done to date. PACE is an important resource, the use of which must be expanded, explored and applied elsewhere.

37. Physician Involvement in a Successful Peer Review Program

A.R. KIRKLEY and JUDITH D. ANDERSON

Reprinted with permission from *Texas Medicine*, Vol. 74, pp. 72–76 (January 1978).

Nearly two years ago, the Texas Medical Foundation (TMF) implemented utilization review under the Texas Admissions and Review Program (TARP) in 18 hospitals. TMF had proposed its TARP plan to the Texas Department of Human Resources (TDHR) (then the Texas State Department of Public Welfare), and Department of Health, Education, and Welfare (HEW). Soon after, the foundation's plan was approved for implementation under a waiver from HEW as a superior state program. This review of Medicaid patients was funded by the TDHR.

To date, 172 hospitals have elected to sign agreements with the foundation to conduct Medicaid review. These agreements represent 73,000 annual Texas Medicaid admissions. Approximately 62% of all Medicaid review performed in Texas is now conducted under the auspices of the Texas Medical Foundation.

It is important that physicians understand the accomplishments of the TMF-administered Texas Admissions and Review Program. In the past, appropriateness of medical services for claims payment was overseen primarily by government agencies, government-appointed intermediaries, and/or health insuring agents. In Texas, employees of the health insuring agent screened the medical services provided to Medicaid patients against financial claims data. Screening for medical necessity of services was only a secondary and usually a retrospective activity.

Any claim that did not meet financial or dollar thresholds was rejected, and a long, involved process of medical necessity determination began. This process included costly and time-consuming correspondence with the hospitals. The system's requirements to obtain medical records and copies of charts for review caused lengthy delays, and many times the result was denial of payment or retroactive denial of reimbursement to hospitals.

TMF-TARP eliminates these denials by offering a unique program that includes a sound, uniform approach to review that will assure quality patient care in a cost-effective manner. It also protects the certified hospital from third-party requests for medical records. In accomplishing these aims, TMF seeks to place the major portion of decision making and responsibility of review in the hands of physicians in the local hospital setting.

But before the actual review process could be implemented, a task crucial to the process had to be undertaken by physicians through TMF, that of developing the

1. These graphs indicate the increase in the number of Medicaid admissions (left) and Texas hospitals (right) reviewed under the auspices of the   *Texas Medical Foundation from January 1976 through October 1977.*

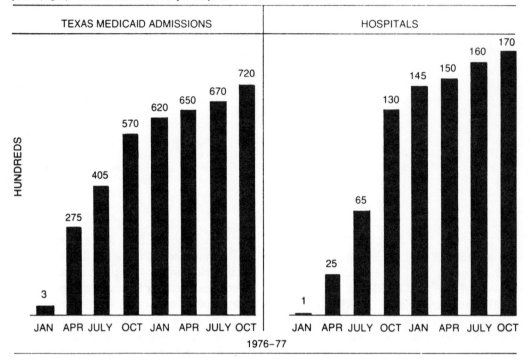

criteria on which the review would be based.

CRITERIA

The backbone of TARP is criteria. In workshops sponsored by TMF, representatives from Texas medical specialty societies participated in development of the criteria. Beginning with historical services data, workshop participants developed criteria based on medical care patterns of practicing physicians. Because TMF utilized the physician's experience and knowledge, its criteria more accurately reflect true medical care and service patterns provided to Texas Medicaid patients. TARP criteria only serve as guidelines for determining medical necessity; the ultimate authority remains with physicians themselves.

In addition to the input of physician workshop representatives, physicians at the hospital level also may participate in the development of criteria through their utilization review committee. When physician consultants meet to expand and revise the criteria, they consider suggestions and recommendations submitted by the hospital's utilization review committee.

While the Texas Medical Foundation was developing criteria, TDHR gathered information for the length-of-stay criteria based on its own computer-generated length of stay. The length-of-stay criteria were added after TMF had developed other facets of the program. Many physicians would like to see TDHR's length-of-stay criteria changed to reflect what they consider to be actual practice patterns. TMF's Texas Admissions and Review Program provides the necessary data and review documentation needed to revise TDHR's length-of-stay criteria. Through TMF's daily concurrent review, length of stay for many diagnoses has been reduced, and physicians generally agree that the reductions have not diminished the quality of care.

However, length-of-stay criteria modifications can work both ways. With the information being gathered and analyzed by TMF, the length-of-stay criteria for some conditions requiring longer hospitalization will be modified based on the newly collected medical data.

REVIEW PROCESS

TARP requires the interaction of three groups of people within the hospital: the utilization review committee, physician advisors, and medical care analysts.

The utilization review committee at each hospital was the primary responsibility for review under TARP. Committee membership is composed of physicians from the hospital's medical staff.

The utilization review committee also appoints physician advisors to carry out the primary physician responsibility for review at the local level. This presents a unique opportunity for practicing physicians to make medical necessity determinations on the spot. Consequently, there are no delays, since the review is performed while the patient is in the hospital, and there are no third-party medical determinations.

Although the major decisions concerning patient review lie with the physician advisor, the daily screening of patients' charts against physician-developed criteria is performed by trained nonphysician professionals, many of whom are registered nurses or registered record administrators. Medical care analysts perform daily review activities, and refer to physician advisors only those cases that do not meet the criteria for medical necessity. The medical care analysts relieve physicians of much administrative and paper work. Medical care analysts use physician-developed criteria to screen patient care, and when a need for necessity determination not covered by criteria arises, the analyst submits the case to the physician advisor for review.

In such cases, the physician advisor may consult with the attending physician to determine whether the treatment or service is necessary. If they agree, the physician advisor approves the service. If they disagree, the physician advisor and the attending physician take the case to a representative of the hospital's utilization review committee who is the final authority for approvals or denials of medical necessity. If the attending physician still disagrees with the decision, an appeal may be taken to the full utilization review committee whose decision, although it will *not* affect the determination, will be used for future policy decisions. If the attending physician is not satisfied with the utilization review committee's decision, further appeal may be made through TMF's appeal and denial process.

Physician advisors are important to the success of utilization review. In order for the Texas Admissions and Review Program to properly screen medical services against criteria, physician advisors must work within the guidelines of the program or they will jeopardize physician participation in the review process.

DISCHARGE PLANNING

One area of utilization review that has received only limited attention is discharge planning. It is important to physicians that their patients be prepared for hospital discharge. This preparation may include education in self care for the patient returning home or assistance for the patient entering an intermediate or skilled nursing care facility.

The foundation has conducted a special study of discharge indicators and discharge plans based on TARP patient abstract data. Although discharge planning is done for most patients, few hospitals have a formal discharge planning program.

To improve effectiveness in this area, TMF is emphasizing discharge planning when training medical care analysts. Future studies will be conducted to determine the effects of discharge planning on patients' length of stay.

DATA

TMF has gathered and established a sound, error-free data base of medical care; therefore, physicians now have access to analyzed medical data that will be useful in health care planning, improving health care, and furthering medical research.

The foundation gathers quality data from patient abstracts that are completed by its medical care analysts. The patient abstract itself contains nearly 100 elements of medical care data. Medical care analysts' error rate on patient abstracts is only 0.41 per abstract, and even this low error rate is eliminated in the Texas Medical Foundation's central office through correction.

Armed with quality data, physicians can improve and expand their participation and effect on present and future government programs. TMF data shows that physician involvement in TARP is a significant factor in the successful review of quality patient care. The physician advisor spends an average of 1½ minutes per patient stay and is involved in two out of every three cases. Twelve percent of the cases are reviewed for changes in length-of-stay, 47% for review of over utilization, and 7% for under utilization according to criteria.

Using these data, physicians also can show when review demands have exceeded cost effectiveness or when program decisions are being made from poor data. These data are far more useful to physicians than the financial claims data compiled by government agencies since they may be used to refute contentions that further intervention into the patient-physician relationship is justified.

But more importantly, with such data, physicians can begin to have an impact on health care planning for their communities based on needs of their patients.

TMF's medical care data also will be useful for insurance benefit planning and projections. Using this information, real patient needs are more apt to be covered in the benefit structure. Physicians often are accused of causing cost increases in health care. Many times, however, it is the benefit structure's use of financial data that allows a higher cost level of care than is medically necessary.

COSTS

The concept of utilization review is to improve quality of care in a cost-effective manner. Because TMF is under contractual agreement with TDHR, all review costs are covered by the government agency that requires the review. Therefore, when a hospital contracts with the foundation to assist in review, TMF reimburses physician advisors for their time and pays for medical care analysts, training, salaries, and review supplies. In addition, certified hospitals realize other cost advantages which include: (1) TMF assures compliance with government regulations, which assures hospital service reimbursement; (2) TMF guarantees payment for the first 24 hours of the patient's stay; in other words, it guarantees the admission without prepayment screening; and, (3) TMF assures the hospital that there will be no retroactive denials of Medicaid claims.

TMF's approach to daily concurrent review, that of combining quality of care review with utilization review of services, is a new process, but it has already proven to be both successful and cost effective. Recently, TMF secured access to sufficient data to conduct a number of studies concerning TARP's progress. A summary of these studies showed that TMF-TARP is cost effective and should become even more cost effective as volume of review increases and refinement occurs.

Daily concurrent review costs were compared with concurrent review costs of non-TMF hospitals and to original length-of-stay data now used in Texas. Daily concurrent review has reduced length of stay and use of ancillary services. The comparisons between the original criteria length of stay and present data show a reduction of approximately $46 in the cost of a Medicaid patient's hospital stay.

Another study shows that TMF-TARP's earlier projected costs of review per patient stay also have decreased. In 1974, cost for review of a hospitalized patient was estimated at $32 per stay. By 1976, that cost was projected to increase to approximately $40 per patient stay. TMF's recent figures show that the cost of review per patient stay declined 30% below the projected inflationary figure of $40 to $28. Based on these data, it appears that the review cost per patient stay will decline below the $25 level as the volume of reviews increases.

The cost effectiveness of TMF's program is beneficial not only to hospitals and physicians, but also to the taxpayers who support such programs as Medicaid. However, the greatest benefit is to the patient—*more* people receive *better* care with the funds now available, and physicians once again are able to assume a proper role in patient care.

SECTION FOUR

LESSONS RELATIVE TO FEATS, FRAUDS AND THE FUTURE

Medicaid can be viewed as an incremental movement toward a comprehensive national program of health care coverage for everyone in the nation. There can be no doubt that the Medicaid programs provided the wherewithal for poor people to receive a large amount of health care. There can be no doubt that the health care services rendered contributed to the improvement of the health status of those receiving Medicaid services. There can be no doubt that the health care providers, particularly some ailing institutions, received a shot in the arm from the financial input. There also can be no doubt that most of America probably thinks that the Medicaid program was and is a disaster. This holds true for the general public as well as the health care professionals.

Positively, Medicaid has championed the concept of the right to health care for all. Health care is no longer considered a privilege but is, or should be available to all. In addition, the fact that Medicaid has survived despite all the scandals, the investigations, the inadequacies, the inequalities and the bureaucratic bungling is a testament to its high intentions. Certainly, Medicaid is a response to a felt need of the nation and its legislators. Furthermore, Medicaid pro-

vided a testing ground for approaches to universal health care.

Negatively, Medicaid engendered public hostility and maintained the "welfare stigma." As many have noted, "A program for the poor is a poor program." Of course, this overriding mentality resulted in random eligibility requirements, state-to-state inequalities, uneven levels of care and severe governmental cutbacks.

A major outcome of the Medicaid program is the fact that health care and its related social and political problems have been exposed to the light in a volume never before noted. Wilbur J. Cohen, former Secretary of HEW and the creator of much of the national health legislation since the mid 1930s, put it succinctly,* "Medicaid has taught us things about the health care delivery system that we could not have learned in any other way. And in that sense, it's been a howling success."

Fraud and abuse in the Medicaid program has received a great deal of attention in the mass media and has probably contributed to the bad public image of the program.

---

*Emily Friedman. Medicaid: Uncertain Harvest. *Hospitals*. 51: 21, 77, November, 1, 1977.

Various guesstimates for fraud in the Medicaid program center about 5 to 10 percent. If overutilization and services to ineligibles are included, that figure jumps to 15 to 25 percent. Medicaid administrators have indicated that a tolerable waste level would be 1 to 2 percent. Outright fraud is a criminal offense and this is relatively limited. Critics often say, "Why commit fraud when you can make as much money with overutilization?"

What contributes to fraud and abuse in the Medicaid program? The following rationales have been cited frequently:

- Inappropriate reimbursement formulas tend to encourage providers to engage in practices to achieve their usual fees for services.
- Insufficient data on norms, standards and criteria are available to measure "abuse" when arguments can be made for the excessive services.
- Obstacles abound that tend to prohibit the vigorous enforcement of antifraud laws.
- Legitimate concerns for the rights of providers tend to encourage the governmental administrators to avoid taking a hard stand.

Of course, these may not be considered reasonable and there are probably many other rationales to explain some of the fraud and abuse. In addition, it should be noted that recipient abuse is also present. A 1977 report from the Inspector General for New York State reported that 370,000 Medicaid identification cards were returned as undeliverable by the post office. This indicated that a large number of people were not living at the given address, had given false addresses or in some other way applied for a Medicaid card fraudulently.

Passage of Public Law 95–142, the Medicare-Medicaid Anti-Fraud and Abuse Amendments Act of 1977, aimed to strengthen the capability of the government to detect, prosecute, and punish fraudulent activities under the two programs.

What about the future and the role of the Medicaid program? When the legislation was drafted, its developers felt that a national health insurance program would be in place in five years. Almost 15 years later, this nation still does not have a national health insurance plan. A number of experts maintain that a national health plan will take place in incremental stages and President Carter has indicated his projection also echoing that opinion.

If the national health coverage is to proceed in staged increments, Medicaid should provide health planners with huge bushelfuls of lessons. Among the major lessons for the future are those that respond to the projected costs of health care services prior to passage of legislation, the determination of adequate staff for administration of a program and the selection of the appropriate level of government for management and the control mechanisms required to insure high quality without fraud and abuse.

It is likely that Medicaid will be best remembered for the fraud and not for its accomplishments or for its experiences that could be applied to future health care services. As Shakespeare noted,* "The evil that men do lives after them. The good is oft interred with their bones."

Starting out with the feats, Davis reviews the achievements and problems of Medicaid. Considerable success was noted in providing adequate medical care to those in public assistance programs and in reducing the financial burden for those with limited financial resources. Utilization of health care services by the poor were nearly equal with the nonpoor and the health status also showed improvement. Linked to the achievements is the question of cost. Davis posits that Medicaid costs are high for the following reasons:

---

*William Shakespeare. *Julius Caesar* Act III Scene II.

- People receiving Medicaid services increased from 9 million in 1967 to more than 23 million in 1976.
- Medical care costs in the United States are generally high regardless of coverage by Medicaid.
- Medicaid has assumed the responsibility for meeting the health care costs of many elderly and disabled persons confined to nursing homes.

Four basic problem areas are detailed: rising costs; gaps in coverage of the poor and needy; limits on benefits; and limited participation in the program by private providers and institutions. Davis proposed several alternatives for reforms related to the four problem areas as follows:

- Maintain the present program with state governments continuing their authority to expand or restrict programs.
- Grant the states broader authority to use Medicaid funds for health services to the poor.
- Provide for tighter cost control through federal actions.
- Federalize the Medicaid program with uniform coverage of all poor persons and comprehensive coverage.
- Integrate the financing of health care for the poor into the funding of health services for all Americans through national health insurance.
- Reassess the existing financing-service delivery mix and use financing mechanisms to promote the development of health service delivery.

Ten reasons why physicians dropped out of the Texas Medicaid program are listed in the next article. A Committee of the Texas Department of Human Resources investigated the issue and concluded, ". . . physicians have been alienated and it is going to be extremely difficult to get physicians back into the Medicaid programs."

D'Onofrio and Mullen present information about consumer difficulties with pre-

paid health plans (PHPs) in California. State law encouraged the development of PHPs to enroll and provide health care for Medicaid eligibles. By 1975 more than 50 PHPs were operational. Consumer complaints involved high pressure marketing and enrollment drives, a lack of services, poor quality services and outright fraud by door-to-door salesmen. The authors compiled a list of danger signals to alert health care experts, legislators and consumers to potential pitfalls in PHP or like proposals:

- Poorly developed regulations and monitoring systems.
- Rapid program expansion without detailed prior planning.
- Inadequate screening prior to approval of PHPs.
- Lack of assistance from the state to the PHPs.
- Marketing on a per capita basis without a cooling off period for new PHP enrollees.
- No direct public accountability by PHPs.
- Lack of a range of sanctions and disciplines for PHPs that violate the regulations.

From the consumer's vantage, the need is stressed to form coalitions to fight the multiple vested interests. In concluding the authors note, "There is much to learn, then, from California's PHP experience, which should serve as an early warning system to identify possible points of breakdown in the effective development and expansion of HMOs (Health Maintenance Organizations) throughout the nation."

Almost immediately fraud and abuse within the Medicaid program took over the center stage in evaluations of the impact of the program. In testimony before the House of Representatives Subcommittee on Health and the Environment, Secretary of Health, Education, and Welfare Joseph A. Califano, Jr. commented on improper and wasteful payments in the Medicaid program. His testimony forms the content of this article.

Califano quickly pointed out the following reasons for wasteful payments:

- Payments linked to provider fraud and abuse.
- Payments for ineligible persons cost $1.2 billion in 1977.
- Claim processing errors cost $200 million in 1977.
- Payments that might possibly have been collected from third party payers totaled $600 million in 1977.

The Secretary described efforts to cut down on the waste including Project Integrity and the Medicaid Eligibility Quality Control (MEQC) program. Project Integrity includes the following initiatives:

- Ferreting out clear cut cases of fraud for criminal charges and others for civil and administrative charges.
- Developing data for the Medicaid claims processing system to spot weaknesses which permit fraud and to remedy them.

In relation to the claims system, Califano told the congressmen that limits have been established for 22 common medical procedures and 26 drugs and drug groups. Sanctions for violations include a warning letter and voluntary recovery, suspension of payments and suspension or termination of provider participation.

The MEQC program was adopted from private industry quality control techniques. In essence a statistical sampling approach is used to discover welfare agency slip-ups and track payments to ineligible people. Finally Califano told the Subcommittee that the federal government is planning to provide considerable assistance to the states to prevent waste and abuse.

Former U.S. Senator Frank E. Moss reports on his own personal experiences as well as members of his investigative staff as they traveled through the Medicaid mills. Moss opened a storefront pretending to be professional practitioners and almost immediately the phone began ringing. About 12 clinical laboratories offered kickbacks ranging from 25 to 55 percent if the doctors would send their Medicaid lab work to them. Next, the investigators, including Moss, posed as patients and visited Medicaid mills. They received unnecessary visits, each lasting 3 to 5 minutes, and were sent next door to get their prescriptions filled. When posing as businessmen, the sleuths were told by Medicaid mill owners, "how to maximize our patient revenues." Another owner gave this cynical assessment, "Medicaid isn't medicine, it's business. Curing patients is good medicine but bad business." Moss estimated Medicaid fraud at about 10 percent—$1.7 billion.

In response to the fraud and abuse in the Medicaid program, the U.S. Congress passed and the President signed into law the Medicare-Medicaid Anti-Fraud and Abuse Amendments (Public Law 95–142) on October 25, 1977. In this article, Suzanne Stone analyzes the major provisions of the law by Sections. These Sections deal with claims payments, fraud penalties, suspension of practitioners, disclosure of provider ownership, subpoena power for the Comptroller General, federal access to Medicaid records and uniform reporting systems.

It is altogether fitting that the last article in this book is by Wilbur J. Cohen reflecting on his 44 years working in the area of social policy. He comments that it is not possible to transfer foreign experience directly to the American environment. After noting the contributions of Medicaid and Medicare to the economics and politics of health care, Cohen states that, "We are dealing with a living and imperfect institution, which we can make better by applying our minds and our energies." Furthermore, the author cautions that it is wise to expect the unexpected when changes occur. Based on his experience Cohen concludes, "I believe the United States will never have a completed national health policy or program." He feels that program and policy will always be in process, always changing with new experiences. However, Cohen does think that the nation will achieve a comprehensive national health program for everyone, but that such a program will not be enacted overnight by a single stroke of the pen.

38. Achievements and Problems of Medicaid

KAREN DAVIS

Reprinted from *Public Health Reports*, Vol. 91, No. 4 (July-August 1976).

The Medicaid program, initiated in 1966 under the Johnson Administration, was one of many programs designed to help the poor and disadvantaged enjoy the fruits of a growing and prosperous economy. Among all of the Great Society programs, those devoted to financing medical care—Medicaid for the poor and Medicare for the elderly—received the largest and most rapidly growing share of budgetary resources. For fiscal year 1976, governmental expenditures under the Federal-State Medicaid program were an estimated $14 billion, providing medical care services for an estimated 23 million low-income persons.[1]

Dissatisfaction with the unanticipated high cost of Medicaid has plagued the program from its inception. Within a few years after its implementation, many State governments moved quickly to cut its cost. Some State governments sought to limit the drain on their budgets by tightening eligibility requirements, reducing the scope of benefits, and cutting back reimbursement levels to providers of medical care services (2–4). Beginning in the fall of 1974, unemployment rose rapidly and income and sales tax revenues declined. State governments experienced a fiscal squeeze, and once again severe pressures were put on them to make cuts in their Medicaid programs.

These actions, in turn, have contributed to the inability of the program to live up to the high expectations of low-income persons hoping to receive high-quality medical care and of providers hoping to receive suitable compensation for delivering it. Thus, Medicaid has cost more than was anticipated, while at the same time it has fallen short of providing all the benefits that were expected from the program.

In an atmosphere of frustrated expectations and seemingly unrestrainable high costs, it is perhaps not surprising that the Medicaid program has been subjected to numerous charges and accusations. Each affected group has pointed to others as the villains responsible for "the mess of Medicaid." A lot of myths and excessive rhetoric surround the program, hindering a dispassionate, objective appraisal of its effectiveness. Some claims regarding the inequities, inefficiencies, and spiraling costs of the program are true, but they are often exaggerated or taken out of context; others are blatantly false or misleading. Genuine reform of Medicaid is sorely needed, and a reassessment of an overall strategy for health care for the poor is in order. But these actions can best be undertaken in an atmosphere devoid of charges and counter-charges.

Concern with the cost as well as disappointment that the program has not fulfilled our high expectations, however, should not obscure the genuine accomplishments of Medicaid. Substantial progress has been made over the last 10 years toward its goals of insuring that needy persons receive adequate access to high-quality medical care and of relieving poor patients and their relatives and friends from the financial burden of medical expenditures. Any reform or replacement of the Medicaid program should be built on its achievements and accomplishments, so that the progress of the past will continue into the future.

WHY DOES MEDICAID COST SO MUCH?

Perhaps the best known fact about the Medicaid program is that the cost of the program has grown rapidly throughout its history—far outpacing original cost estimates. Combined Federal, State, and local expenditures increased from $3.5 billion in 1968 to an estimated $14 billion in fiscal

year 1976 (see table). This sixfold increase in Medicaid expenditures has been a major source of dissatisfaction with the program.

The fear, however, is unfounded that welfare costs and medical care costs for the poor are threatening to bankrupt State and local governments as well as to take over the Federal budget. Medicaid payments in recent years have not risen much faster than governmental expenditures generally. Medicaid accounts for roughly 2 percent of the Federal budget and 2 percent of State and local government expenditures, and this share of total expenditures has not changed markedly for several years. Thus, the cost of Medicaid is growing rapidly, but no more so than everything that governments pay for. Medicaid represents a fairly small, although politically vulnerable, part of overall government budgets.

Surprisingly, little is yet known about the reasons for the unanticipated high cost of Medicaid and its continued growth over time. Was the original cost estimate (of $1.5 billion combined Federal-State expenditures) totally unrealistic? Did providers of medical services take unfair advantage of

Medicaid payments adjusted for increases in recipients and prices, fiscal years 1968–76

Fiscal year[1]	Medical payments (in billions)	Medicaid recipients (in millions)	Payments per Medicaid recipient	Medical care price index[2]	Payments in constant dollars per recipient
1968	3.45	11.5	$300	100.0	$300
1969	4.35	12.1	361	106.9	338
1970	5.09	14.5	351	113.7	309
1971	6.35	[3]18.0	353	121.0	292
1972	7.35	17.7	414	124.9	331
1973	8.71	18.5	472	129.8	364
1974	9.74	21.1	461	141.8	325
1975	12.09	22.5	538	156.2	344
1976	14.06	23.2	606	170.8	355

[1]For 1968–70, table includes payments and recipients under the Kerr-Mills program.
[2]Medical care price index of Bureau of Labor Statistics with adjustment to make 1968 equal to 100; estimated for fiscal year 1976.
[3]Includes some recipients of aid under nonfederally matched assistance programs.
SOURCE: Data on the Medicaid Program: Eligibility, Services, Expenditures, Fiscal Years 1966–76. Reported in U.S. House of Representatives, Committee on Interstate and Foreign Commerce, Subcommittee on Health and the Environment. Medical Services Administration, Social and Rehabilitation Service, Department of Health, Education, and Welfare. U.S. Government Printing Office, Washington, D.C., January 1976.

the program to increase their incomes to exorbitant levels? Did beneficiaries of the program use medical care services excessively? Was the program incompetently administered? Or did the program serve far more persons than had been originally anticipated?

Accounts in the media have focused attention on the charges and counter-charges of different groups affected by Medicaid. Physicians earning $300,000 a year have been blamed by some as responsible for high costs. Exorbitant nursing home profits and kickbacks to State officials have been cited by others. Medicaid patients have come in for their fair share of attack—they have been accused of taking joyrides in ambulances, obtaining prosthetic shoes for normal feet, and having extensive gold dental work done. Arrangements between laboratories and physicians for fraudulent billing or overbilling for laboratory services have been uncovered.

These abuses and inefficiencies are inevitable in a program as large as Medicaid, and corrective actions should be taken to uncover and eliminate them. But fraud and abuses account for only a small fraction of total Medicaid costs. To achieve effective control of them, we must look to the genuine causes of the increased costs.

Since Medicaid is a Federal-State program and most decisions are left to State governments, some sources of the growth in costs are undoubtedly more significant in some States than others. On the whole, however, three factors are almost totally responsible: (a) the increase in the number of Medicaid recipients covered under the Aid to Families with Dependent Children program, (b) the rise in medical care prices, and (c) the high cost of nursing home care for an impoverished aged and disabled population.

Annual Medicaid payments per recipient in constant 1968 medical dollars (expenditures divided by the consumer price index for medical care services) averaged $344 per person in fiscal year 1975, compared with $338 in 1969 (see table). That is, from 1969 to 1975, all of the growth of Medicaid costs could be traced to the rise in medical care prices and the provision of services to more and more people. On the average, Medicaid recipients were receiving approximately the same real services in 1975 as in the early years of the program.

When looked at in relation to what is spent on medical care for the average U.S. citizen, Medicaid recipients do not appear to be getting more care or averaging higher medical bills than anyone else. In fiscal year 1973 the average expenditure for personal health care services by all Americans was $384 per person—compared with $320 for Medicaid welfare recipients and $749 for medically needy and institutionalized Medicaid recipients.[5,6] The average payment for services received by a child Medicaid recipient was slightly less than the average payment for a child in the U.S. population. Similarly, for adults 19 to 64 years, the average Medicaid payment of $349 compared reasonably with the average $386 spent by all Americans in that age group. Even among the aged, Medicaid expenditures for those receiving welfare payments were about the same as the direct costs for the elderly who were not covered by Medicaid; each elderly person on welfare received medical services costing on the average $436, a figure that corresponds roughly to the amount the average elderly person paid for medical care in addition to what Medicare paid. Only for the elderly who were in nursing homes or who were medically needy, were the costs considerably higher—averaging $1,742 per person.

In summary, Medicaid costs are high not because people get too much care or because the Government pays exorbitant rates for it, but because (a) 23 million people receive Medicaid services each year, up from 9 million in 1967, (b) medical care costs in the United States are generally high, whether the patient is covered by Medicaid or not, and (c) Medicaid has assumed the responsibility for meeting the health care costs of many elderly and disabled persons confined to nursing homes. To place any significant restraints on future Medicaid costs, these underlying causes must be addressed.

PROGRESS TOWARD MEDICAID GOALS, 1964–74

From its initiation, the Medicaid program has had two major objectives: insuring that covered persons receive adequate medical care and reducing the financial burden of medical expenditures for those with severely limited financial resources. Before the introduction of Medicaid, most poor persons had little or no private insurance, and many went without needed care. Some appealed to charity—either from the physician, public hospitals, or friends and relatives. Others attempted to pay all or part of their medical costs despite great hardship to the family. Medicaid attempted to alleviate this situation—if not for all poor persons, at least for those on welfare and the medically needy.

Although it is difficult to separate the effect of Medicaid from other health programs for the poor or from other changing conditions that affect the poor, recent evidence suggests that the program has had considerable success in meeting its original objectives. In fiscal year 1964, persons with high incomes saw physicians about 20 percent more frequently than did the poor.[7] By calendar year 1974 (according to unpublished data from the 1974 Health Interview Survey), the long history of lower utilization by the poor had been reversed, and the poor overtook persons with higher income in the use of physicians' services. Persons with low incomes saw physicians 13 percent more frequently in 1974 than did persons with high incomes. Poor children increased their use of physician services from 3.3 visits in 1964 to 3.7 visits in 1974. Children from higher income families reduced

their use of physician services over this period, thus reducing the differential in use of such services on the basis of income. While in 1964 children from higher income families had 66 percent more physician visits than children from low-income families, by 1974 they had only 15 percent more visits (reference 7 and the unpublished 1974 Health Interview Survey data).

Major gains were made by the poor between 1964 and 1974, particularly in the percentage who had seen a physician in the previous 2 years. In 1964, 28 percent of the poor had not seen a physician over the 2-year period; by 1973, 17 percent of the poor had failed to visit a physician for 2 years or more. Progress in this dimension was particularly evident for poor children, a third of whom had not seen a physician for 2 years or more in 1964. By 1973, this figure had been reduced to one-fifth of all poor children. Despite this gain, however, poor children were still 57 percent more likely not to have seen a physician in the 2 prior years than nonpoor children.[8]

Improvements in the prenatal care of low-income women were also noticeable between 1964 and 1974. The percentage of low-income women seeing a physician early in pregnancy increased from 58 percent in 1963 to 71 percent in 1970. However, in 1970 high-income women were still 20 percent more likely to have seen a physician early in pregnancy than low-income women.[9]

Although there are many conceptual and data difficulties in showing the effects of this greater medical care utilization on the health of the poor, there was considerable improvement over the 10 years in those dimensions of health status that are typically worse for the poor than for others and that are sensitive to improvements in medical care.[8] Infant mortality declined 33 percent from 1965 to 1974, and there were somewhat more rapid reductions in the postneonatal rates, rates which have historically been much higher for infants of low-income families. Declines of 50 percent or more were recorded for infant deaths from gastrointestinal diseases, influenza and pneumonia, and immaturity. The death rates for young children declined 14 percent from 1965 to 1973, particularly those for malignant neoplasms (26 percent decline) and those for influenza and pneumonia (48 percent decline). Age-adjusted death rates for the entire population declined by 10 percent between 1964 and 1974; deaths from diseases of the heart declined 16 percent, cerebrovascular diseases 18 percent, diabetes mellitus 7 percent, and arteriosclerosis 37 percent. Although a great many factors undoubtedly contributed to these gains, it is at least plausible that increased attention to medical care played a part in achieving this improvement in health. For better evidence we will have to await followup studies in which death certificate information is linked with other sources of data on income.

These trends in the patterns of medical care utilization and health status are encouraging, but five major qualifications should be made about the progress of the last decade:

1. Most important—differences in the use of physician services are not adjusted for the health needs of the poor, which continue to exceed those of other groups.[10, 11]

2. The increase in the use of services has not been shared by all of the poor; those who fall between the gaps and are unserved by either private insurance or public programs lag well behind other poor persons in the use of physician services.[11]

3. Trends for increased use of services by the poor have not been accompanied by a movement of the poor into "mainstream medicine" of comparable quality, style, and convenience to that received by the nonpoor.[11]

4. Averages for the poor as a whole conceal significant disparities for particularly disadvantaged groups such as the rural poor or minorities.[12]

5. Medicaid appears to have had only limited success in reducing the financial burden of medical expenditures for all poor persons.[13]

INEQUITABLE DISTRIBUTION OF MEDICAID BENEFITS

Perhaps the greatest deficiency in the Medicaid program is that it does not treat people in equal circumstances equally. The inequitable distribution of Medicaid benefits is caused in part by the joint Federal-State nature of the program and its tie to the welfare system. Other inequities arise because Medicaid is a financing program and therefore is less effective in overcoming the nonfinancial barriers to medical care that certain disadvantaged groups face.

Eligibility for Medicaid is linked to welfare eligibility, and thus the program shares the complexity of the welfare system. States must cover all families with dependent children that are receiving public assistance (AFDC). States may also cover all the aged, blind, and disabled recipients of supplemental security income (SSI), or they may restrict Medicaid coverage to those SSI recipients who would have met the more restrictive State Medicaid eligibility requirements of January 1, 1972, that were in force before the implementation of SSI. All but 14 States have elected to cover all SSI recipients.

In addition to covering recipients of cash assistance, States may also provide Medicaid coverage to the medically needy, defined as persons who would be eligible for cash assistance if their incomes were somewhat lower. Twenty-eight States and four jurisdictions (the District of Columbia, Gaum, Puerto Rico, and the Virgin Islands) extend such coverage to the medically needy.

Twenty-five States and two jurisdictions restrict eligibility for AFDC to families with only a mother present. Twenty-three States and three jurisdictions also extend AFDC and Medicaid coverage to families with unemployed fathers who are not receiving unemployment compensation. A limited number of additional States cover the children of families with an unemployed father, but not the parents. Thirteen States and three jurisdictions cover all children in families with incomes below the AFDC eligibility level—regardless of the employment status of the parents or the family's composition.

To be eligible for welfare, families must have incomes falling below a need standard established by each State. Need standards established by the States range from $2,208 for a four-person family in North Carolina (as of July 1974) to $5,472 in Wisconsin (slightly above the poverty level of $5,038 for a nonfarm family of four in 1974). Each State also may set limits on assets (homes, automobiles, savings, and so forth) in determining eligibility.

States covering the medically needy also establish tests for income, assets, and family composition similar to those for public assistance recipients. The income levels for a medically needy family of four as of December 1974 ranged from $2,200 in Tennessee to $5,600 in parts of Wisconsin. Families with incomes above these levels may also be eligible if their incomes fall below this level after incurred medical expenses are deducted (the so-called "spend-down" provision).

As a result of this complex set of restrictions, the following low-income persons are not eligible for Medicaid assistance:

1. Widows under age 65 or other nonelderly single persons
2. Most two-parent families—which account for 70 percent of rural poor family members and almost half of poor family members in metropolitan areas
3. Families with a father working at a marginal, low-paying job
4. Families with an unemployed father in the 26 States that do not extend welfare payments to this group and families with an unemployed father receiving unemployment compensation in other States
5. Medically needy families in the 21 States that do not voluntarily provide this coverage
6. Women pregnant with their first child in the 27 States that do not provide welfare aid or eligibility for the "unborn child"
7. Children of non-AFDC poor families in the 36 States that do not take advantage of the optional Medicaid category called "all needy children under 21"

Given all the holes through which a needy family can fall in trying to obtain assistance to meet their medical care costs, it is not surprising that a large number of poor people are not covered by Medicaid.

The magnitude of these gaps in coverage is not well known. There are few estimates of the proportion of Medicaid recipients with incomes above or below the poverty level; there is little information on the number of Medicaid eligibles at any given time. In fiscal year 1975, an estimated 22.5 million persons received Medicaid services—a figure that is similar in magnitude to the population below the poverty level, estimated as 24 million persons in that year. Some Medicaid recipients, however, have incomes above the poverty level, because of income standards being set above that level and because of the spend-down provision. The Council of Economic Advisers estimates that 30 percent of all Medicaid recipients have incomes above the poverty level (14). This proportion suggests that 15.8 million poor people were covered by Medicaid in 1975, or two-thirds of the poor. Thus, approximately 8 million poor people were excluded from Medicaid coverage. This estimate may be somewhat conservative, however, since the data on Medicaid coverage are for persons covered at any time during the year, while those for the population below the poverty level are based on the number covered at a given time. Counts of Medicaid recipients over the period of a year therefore overstate the number covered at any given time. If the movements in and out of Medicaid are adjusted over time, the results suggest that perhaps 40 to 50 percent of the poor population is not covered by Medicaid at any given time.

For some States, coverage of the poor is particularly restricted. In 1970, only 1 poor child in 10 was covered by Medicaid in the States of Alabama, Arkansas, Louisiana, Mississippi, South Carolina, and Texas. According to an estimate by the Medical Services Administration, Department of Health, Education, and Welfare, less than one-third of the poor in 17 States—Alabama, Alaska, Arkansas, Florida, Idaho, Indiana, Louisiana, Mississippi, Montana, New Mexico, North Dakota, South Carolina, South Dakota, Tennessee, Texas, Virginia, and Wyoming—received Medicaid assistance (1).

Medicaid represents almost exclusively a financing approach to health care for the poor. It pays for services that the covered recipients are expected to seek out and obtain. It was hoped that this approach would enable the poor to use private mainstream health facilities rather than being segregated in public hospitals or clinics. For some groups, however, removal of the financial barrier to medical care services is not sufficient to facilitate a use of medical services that is commensurate with their health needs. Instead, other nonfinancial barriers to care—such as transportation, long distances involved in obtaining care, discrimination on the part of existing health facilities and personnel, disregard for the patient's circumstances and the patient's dignity, limited patient education and limited information concerning the desirability and efficacy of medical treatment, and the persistence of past attitudes and past patterns of medical care use—frequently prevent the appropriate use of medical services, even when these services are provided free of charge.

Such nonfinancial considerations are particularly strong for residents of rural areas and for minorities in both urban and rural areas. Deterred from seeking medical care by nonfinancial barriers, these groups are more likely to receive less than their proportionate share of Medicaid benefits and to continue to use medical services that are less adequate for their health needs than other covered Medicaid recipients.

Poor people in rural areas are further disadvantaged because of the restrictions on eligibility for Medicaid. Only 40 percent of the poor in nonmetropolitan areas are elderly or members of one-parent families—the groups most likely to qualify for Medicaid. In metropolitan areas, 55 percent of the poor fall into the typical aged or one-parent welfare-eligible category.

In calendar year 1969 Medicaid payments per white recipient were 75 percent higher than payments per black recipient (12). Although part of this difference reflected the greater concentration of blacks in the States with limited Medicaid programs, even within broad geographic regions, blacks lagged substantially behind whites in the receipt of benefits. For example, in the Northeast, whites received on the average $362 in Medicaid payments while blacks received only $205. Differences among races, however, were most extreme in rural areas, where whites received more than double the benefits received by blacks. Disparities in Medicaid benefits on the basis of race were smallest for children and largest for the elderly. For nonaged adults, payments for whites were more than 33 percent higher than payments for blacks.

The lower benefits per black recipient were somewhat offset, however, by the tendency of poor blacks to qualify for Medicaid to a greater extent than poor whites. Since 65 percent of the poor blacks were either aged or members of one-parent families, compared with 43 percent of the poor whites, the poor blacks, particularly in the urban northern States, were somewhat more likely to be eligible for Medicaid.

Seven of 10 poor blacks received Medicaid services in 1969 compared with slightly more than half of poor whites. The average Medicaid payments per poor person, therefore, were 36 percent higher than the average payments per black person.

For those eligible for Medicaid, the disparity in benefits was particularly marked for nursing home care. The average nursing home payments per white person covered by Medicaid were almost five times as high as the average nursing home payments made on behalf of the blacks covered by the program. Most of this difference is related to the higher proportion of white Medicaid recipients placed in nursing homes. For persons admitted to nursing homes, average payments for whites were $2,375 in 1969, compared with an average expenditure of $1,857 for blacks. The rate for black patients in nursing homes was lower than the rate for whites partly because blacks die younger. Therefore fewer black Medicaid recipients were elderly and in need of nursing home care. But there also appears to have been substantial discrimination, both overt and institutional, in nursing homes in 1969. Some nursing homes refused to accept black patients. More commonly, however, blacks failed to get into nursing homes because of institutional discrimination arising from segregated housing patterns and physicians' referral of patients to only a limited portion of all nursing homes.

Payments for general hospital service did not differ greatly by the race of the Medicaid recipient. About 17 percent of the white Medicaid recipients were hospitalized, compared with 14 percent of the blacks. However, the average payments per person hospitalized were slightly higher for blacks. The reason may be that blacks were more likely to be treated in city-county public hospitals, where costs were higher and stays longer.

Payments for private physician services were 40 percent higher for white than for black Medicaid recipients. Sixty percent of the white Medicaid recipients saw a private physician during the year, compared with 52 percent of the blacks. The average payment for physician services was also higher for whites, either because they visited physicians whose fees were higher or because they went more frequently.

These higher payments to private physicians for white Medicaid recipients were offset, in part, by the greater use of hospital outpatient departments as a source of medical care for blacks. Thirty-eight percent of the black Medicaid recipients received care from hospital outpatient departments, compared with 26 percent of the whites. The average cost of care for those going to hospital outpatient departments appears to have been much the same, regardless of the race of the recipient.

Some caution should be exercised in extrapolating these data on Medicaid payments by race to current conditions. The data are based on the experience of 24 States reporting Medicaid data by race in calendar year 1969. Since that time, national statistics on medical care utilization indicate that blacks have made some gains in the use of physician services relative to whites, although they still lag behind whites in the number of physician visits per person. In 1969, many States in the South with high concentrations of poor blacks did not have Medicaid programs. Benefits for blacks, therefore, may have become more extensive in recent periods.

Data from the Georgia Medicaid program, however, reveal that differentials by race have not evaporated over time (15). In fiscal year 1974, white Medicaid recipients in Georgia averaged payments of $587 per person, compared with $271 for black recipients—more than twice as much for whites as for blacks. Poor blacks were somewhat more likely to be covered than poor whites. Georgia Medicaid covered 54 percent of the poor blacks and 43 percent of the poor whites.

Racial differences by type of medical service were much the same in Georgia as for Medicaid as a whole. A higher fraction of whites than blacks were hospitalized in 1974, but blacks tended to have somewhat more expensive hospital stays than whites. White Medicaid recipients in Georgia were almost six times as likely to receive nursing home services as were black recipients. Slightly more white recipients received private physician services, and the payments per person receiving physician services were 28 percent higher for whites than for blacks. Blacks in Georgia tended to receive more dental care than whites in 1974, but this benefit has since been discontinued by the State. Blacks in Georgia made relatively greater use of hospital outpatient facilities in 1974 than did white Medicaid recipients.

Rural residents, whether white or black, also face special barriers to receiving medical care services. Frequently, Medicaid does not cover rural families, since in typical poor rural families both parents are present, and hence the families do not qualify for AFDC in most States. Limited availability of medical personnel and transportation barriers also deter some of the rural poor from seeking needed medical services. Rural blacks may be even more affected by racial discrimination than urban blacks, since they have fewer alternative sources of care.

Again, the Medicaid program has not collected extensive data to document the distribution of benefits. Data for 1969 for 28 States reveal that Medicaid payments per poor person were 70 percent higher in metropolitan than in nonmetropolitan areas. Most of this difference reflects the greater coverage of the urban poor by the Medicaid program. Sixty-three of every 100 poor metropolitan residents were covered by Medicaid in 1969, compared with 38 of every 100 poor persons in nonmetropolitan areas. Thus, the metropolitan areas in the 28 States had 1.5 times as many poor people as the nonmetropolitan areas but 2.4 times as many Medicaid recipients.

DIRECTIONS FOR CHANGE IN MEDICAID

The Medicaid program has had a major impact on the health care of the poor in the past decade. Its many achievements have gone unheralded and largely unappreciated—obscured by an allconsuming concern with its unanticipated high cost. But there is little doubt that Medicaid has fallen short of our original high expectations. It continues to be afflicted by a host of problems. Reform is clearly needed.

Four problem areas should be addressed by a far-reaching reform of the program: the sources of rising costs, the gaps in coverage of the poor and needy, the limits on benefits and the limited participation in the program by mainstream medicine (private health facilities, physicians, and other health professionals), and the inequitable distribution of benefits by State, urban-rural residence, and race.

In seeking solutions to the seemingly unrestrainable increase in health care costs for the poor, we should look to underlying causes. Over the first 10 years of the program, three factors played a central role in rising costs. The first was the increased eligibility under AFDC (which was brought about by an increase in poor one-parent families), the increasing tendency on the part of the poor to register for the benefits for which they were eligible, and the high unemployment. The second factor was the generally rapid increase in medical care prices. The third was the high cost of caring for aged, disabled, and seriously ill persons who could not care for themselves or meet their own medical expenses.

Lesser factors that have added to Medicaid costs—and which have received the largest amount of press and public attention—include fradulent practices (such as billing for services that have not been rendered, or that have been provided by ineligible providers, kickbacks to physicians for referrals to laboratories or other providers, and the sale by patients of prescriptions or supplies obtained through the program); abuse of the program (such as by excessive hospitalization, excessive surgery, lengthy hospital stays, excessive laboratory services, injections in physicians offices, excessive prescriptions for drugs, physicians' mass visits to nursing homes, the padding of physicians' incomes through proliferation of services and repeat visits); and poor administrative mechanisms for checking and periodically reviewing eligibility and identifying abuses. Although the magnitude of the dollars involved in these abuses has never been demonstrated to be substantial, actions should be taken to eradicate the more costly or harmful aspects of fraud, abuse, and administrative inefficiency.

The second area of needed reform relates to the exclusion from the Medicaid program of many poor persons. The categorical restrictions on eligibility, the varying tests for income and assets, and State administrative actions to curtail costs by restricting eligibility have served to exclude many poor persons from the program. Estimates indicate that at any given time from one-third to as many as one-half of the population below the poverty level does not receive Medicaid benefits. These poor persons continue to lag well behind the rest of the poor in access to decent health care.

Even for the poor covered by Medicaid, restrictions on the level of services and the low rates of reimbursement for physicians and for other providers impede access to adequate care. It is clear that Medicaid has not achieved its objective of bringing the poor into mainstream medicine and providing them with treatment by the same types of physicians, community hospitals, and other health facilities as other Americans. Instead, State Medicaid programs have discouraged many physicians from partici-

pating by low rates of reimbursement for services, extensive red tape, delays in payment, the need for prior authorization of services, and numerous restrictions on covered services. A third needed reform is the institution of adequate methods of providing the poor with high quality care, care that is comparable to that received by all Americans.

Finally, serious inequities in the distribution of Medicaid benefits on the basis of State of residence or urban-rural residence within the State and on the basis of race need to be redressed through greater uniformity of benefits and coverage and through supplemental programs to encourage the establishment of health care delivery in disadvantaged communities.

A number of alternative directions can be taken to achieve some or all of these reforms. These include:

- Maintaining the present Medicaid program, with State governments continuing to exercise their current authority to expand or restrict eligibility, benefits, patient charges, and provider reimbursement
- Giving the State governments even broader authority to use Medicaid funds for health services for the poor—as President Ford's block grant proposal would do
- Providing for tighter cost control through Federal actions—as the proposed Talmadge Medicare and Medicaid Administrative and Reimbursement Reform Act would do
- Providing for federalization of the Medicaid program with uniform coverage of all the poor and comprehensive benefits—as in the proposed Long-Ribicoff Catastrophic Health Insurance and Medical Assistance Reform Act
- Integrating the financing of health care for the poor into the financing of health

services for all Americans through national health insurance

- Reassessing the current financing-service delivery mix of health care programs and using financing mechanisms to promote the development of health services delivery

Debate on these alternative future directions for the health care of the poor should be a key focus in the period ahead. Recognizing the strengths and weaknesses of our current programs, we can build new ones on the past and continue our progress toward the goal of decent health care for all Americans.

REFERENCES

1. Medicaid, 1977–1981: Major program issues. Medical Services Administration, Social and Rehabilitation Service, Department of Health, Education, and Welfare, Washington, D.C., July 1975.

2. Holahan, J.: Financing health care for the poor: The Medicaid experience. Lexington Books (D.C. Heath and Company), Lexington, Mass., 1975.

3. Klarman, H.E.: Major public initiatives in health care. Public Interest No. 34: 106–123, winter 1974.

4. Stevens, R., and Stevens, R.: Welfare medicine in America: A case study of Medicaid. Free Press, New York, 1974.

5. Mueller, M.S., and Gibson, R.M.: Age differences in health care spending, FY 1974. Soc Security Bull 38: 3–16, June 1975.

6. Numbers of recipients and amounts of payments under Medicaid, fiscal year 1973. DHEW Publication (SRS) 76–03153. National Center for Social Statistics, Social and Rehabilitation Service, Department of Health, Education, and Welfare, Washington, D.C., November 1975.

7. Volume of physician visits, by place of visit and type of services, United States, July 1963–June 1964. PHS Publication No. 1000, Series 10, No. 18. U.S. Government Printing Office, Washington, D.C., June 1965.

8. Health, United States 1975. DHEW (HRA) Publication No. 76–1232. U.S. Government Printing Office, Washington, D.C., 1976.

9. Andersen, R., Greeley, R. McL., Kravatts, J., and Anderson, O.W.: Health service use: National trends and variations 1953–1971. DHEW (HSM) Publication 73–3004. National Center for Health Services Research and Development, Health Services and Mental Health Administration, Rockville, Md., October 1972.

10. Aday, L., and Andersen, R.: Development of indices and access to medical care. University of Michigan Health Administration Press, Ann Arbor, 1975.

11. Davis K., and Reynolds, R.: The impact of Medicare and Medicaid on access to medical care. *In* The role of insurance in the health service sector, edited by R. Rosett. National Bureau of Economic Research, New York City, 1976.

12. Davis, K.: National health insurance: Benefits, costs, and consequences. Brookings Institution, Washington, D.C., 1975.

13. Anderson, R., et al.: Expenditures for personal health services: National trends and variations, 1953–1970. DHEW (HRA) Publication No. 74-3105. Bureau of Health Services Research and Evaluation, Rockville, Md., October 1973.

14. Council of Economic Advisers: Economic report of the President. U.S. Government Printing Office, Washington, D.C., January 1974.

15. Georgia Department of Human Resources: Medicaid report 2082, fiscal year 1974. Atlanta, Ga.

39. Why Texas Physicians are Dropping Out of the Medicaid Program

TEXAS MEDICINE

Reprinted with permission from *Texas Medicine*, Vol. 73 (September 1977), pp. 91–93.

What makes Texas physicians drop out of the Medicaid program?

A reimbursement rate that is too low, excessive paperwork, and delay in getting payment are just some of the reasons doctors answered in response to a letter sent to 1,200 physicians by the Texas Medical Association. The letters were mailed June 8, 1977, and as of June 29, 1977, responses were received from 77 physicians.

The letter was sent at the request of the Committee on Physician Participation in the Texas Medicaid Program of the Texas Department of Human Resources (formerly the Texas Department of Public Welfare).

The committee analyzed the responses, after the physicians were asked to provide their views on physician participation in the Medicaid program.

FEE REIMBURSEMENT

The primary reason that physicians gave for declining participation is fee reimbursement.

The secondary reason was "paperwork hassle." Other reasons included Medicaid not paying claims, the lack of responsibility of recipients in keeping appointments and following medical treatment plans, and the 90 day filing deadline.

Physicians responding indicated that the rate of reimbursement was ridiculously low. All of the physicians responding gave the reimbursement rate and the "paperwork hassle" as reasons for dropping out of the program.

Other reasons included problems with the intermediary in not replying to inquiries, arbitrariness, restrictive guidelines, and presumption of government and intermediary administrators that physicians are basically dishonest. Physicians responded that another factor is the publicity given to investigations rather than to the amount of time dollars actually contributed to the program by the physicians.

The lack of responsibility by Medicaid recipients in keeping appointments and in following the medical treatment plan prescribed often results in physicians spending more time with Medicaid recipients than with other patients, but receiving less pay for doing so, the physicians reported.

COMMITTEE GOALS

In performing the survey and other studies the Committee on Physician Participation in the Texas Medicaid Program is looking to answer two questions: "What are the reasons that more physicians are not participating in the Medicaid program?'' and "What changes should be made in the Medicaid program that would encourage more physicians to accept Medicaid patients?''

The committee has reviewed the report developed by the Task Force for the Evaluation of Medicaid in Texas and discussed the developments with the Department of Health Resources regional administrators and directors of medical assistance units.

In reviewing the report of the Task Force for the Evaluation of Medicaid in Texas, the committee found that Medicaid recipients are encountering extreme difficulties in finding physicians who will accept Medicaid. There are areas in the state where Medicaid recipients must travel considerable distances to find a physician who will accept Medicaid, the committee concluded.

In Houston, San Antonio, Dallas, and other metropolitan areas, it is not uncommon for Medicaid recipients to have to travel across town to the city/county hospital outpatient clinic to obtain service because they are unable to find physicians who will accept Medicaid, the committee reported.

COMMITTEE RECOMMENDATIONS

The committee findings indicate that physicians have been alienated and it is going to be extremely difficult to get physicians back into the Medicaid programs.

The committee recommended that immediate consideration be given to several areas to deal with problems in the Medicaid program.

The committee recommended that alternative methods of reimbursement of physicians be reviewed. The committee also recommended that the Department of Health Resources and the National Health Insurance Company review programs to improve paperwork and payment procedures.

Another recommendation is that resource persons be assigned to answer Medicaid questions. The committee recommended that the Medicaid program be presented to physicians by a physician on a regularly scheduled basis.

Improved recipient education on Medicaid usage and benefits was another committee recommendation.

The committee also recommended that the requirement for physicians to see nursing home patients every 60 days be reviewed. The committee recommended discontinuing publishing the list of Medicaid providers.

The committee recommended that a positive publicity campaign be conducted explaining the services provided by physicians to Medicaid recipients.

WHY TEXAS PHYSICIANS ARE DROPPING OUT OF THE MEDICAID PROGRAM

1. reimbursement rate too low
2. excessive paperwork and delay in getting payment
3. dissatisfaction with limit of two office visits per month without lengthy justification
4. Medicaid would not pay claims
5. lack of responsibility of recipient in keeping appointments and following medical treatment plans
6. 90 day filing deadline
7. adverse effect on cash flow
8. resent government publishing list of physicians making certain amounts from Medicaid or Medicare
9. procedure codes are being arbitrarily changed by carrier and payment reduced
10. dictatorial attitude of government employees about program

40. Consumer Problems with Prepaid Health Plans in California: Implications for Serving Medicaid Recipients Through Health Maintenance Organizations

CAROL N. D'ONOFRIO and
PATRICIA DOLAN MULLEN

Reprinted from *Public Health Reports*, Vol. 92, No. 2 (March-April 1977).

Escalating costs, uneven access to physicians, and lack of quality control in Medicaid programs have led policymakers to seek options to the fee-for-service system. In 1971, California led the nation in implementing a promising alternative—a statewide prepaid health program for Medicaid beneficiaries. This action was widely heralded as a solution to the problems of cost containment, guaranteed access, and quality assurance in the provision of health care to the poor.

Under California's program, prepaid health plans (PHPs)—modeled after prototype prepaid group practice organizations—contracted to provide comprehensive health care to Medicaid recipients in return for a predetermined per capita payment by the State for each eligible enrollee. Based on the results of studies of established prepaid group practices (1–4a), it was assumed that this arrangement would provide more benefits than available through fee-for-service coverage. More-

over, built-in provider incentives to keep members healthy presumably would result in a greater emphasis on prevention and improved quality of care, which, in turn, would reduce costs—saving millions of dollars in public funds (5).

California's program, however, has fallen so far short of its promise that many consider it scandalous. Because this situation has received little attention in the public health and medical care literature, our aim here is to alert public health professionals to the many possible pitfalls in applying the health maintenance organization (HMO) concept to programs for the poor. This alert is particularly important now that at least 14 other States are contracting with prepaid health plans to provide health care to Medicaid recipients (6), and more States are likely to begin such programs soon.

It is ironic that California's most recent experiment with prepaid health care has resulted in such a tempest, since the earlier successful experiences of its "first generation" PHPs—the Ross-Loos Medical Group, the Kaiser Foundation Health Plan, the San Joaquin Foundation for Medical Care, and others—contributed significantly to the development and passage of Federal HMO legislation. Although California's present stormy developments do not con-

The study was supported in part by grant CMERF-ROP-74E-76-145G from the Public Health Service's Regional Medical Programs to the School of Public Health at Berkeley for the development of that institution's role in improving the quality of health care.

cern all HMO-type organizations in the State, they do reveal a complex series of difficulties in providing quality health care to the poor through the HMO mechanism. At issue are not only operational dilemmas as to how publicly supported health care can be effectively planned, organized, financed, delivered, regulated, monitored, and evaluated, but also larger public policy questions fraught with political, economic, and legal ramifications of great import to those whose health is at stake.

Our central emphasis is on consumer problems with PHPs for several interrelated reasons. First, the poor have borne the greatest burden of California's experiment, and their statements of what went wrong are the most poignant of all. Second, consumer reports of difficulties with prepaid health plans, particularly as expressed through disenrollments, were the initial impetus for arousing more widespread concern which eventually led to the disclosure of underlying legislative, organizational, and administrative defects in the program. Third, at least until recently, the majority of consumer complaints were never followed up by the State (4b). Although two prior reviews of California's PHP experience (7, 8) take a consumer perspective, neither of these was published in a public health journal nor did the authors have access to certain data considered in this report.

Most important, as health educators, we saw the need to search out and analyze consumer problems in greater detail, since the achievement of PHP program goals depends to a large extent upon consumer behavior. Thus, in deciding whether to join a PHP, and if so, for how long to continue membership, consumers as a group will determine the extent to which enrollment targets are met, as well as the economic viability of the various participating plans. Similarly, consumer expectations for, perceptions of, and actual experiences with accessibility and quality of care will affect their satisfaction with the plan, their adaptation to a new system, and what they say about the plan to others. Because these factors affect both the size and stability of the PHP enrollment base, they bear heavily upon the actual quality of care which can be provided and ultimately upon the extent to which broader health goals can be achieved through the PHP mechanism.

In the following discussion, we consider the impact of California's PHP experience on consumers in three sections: (a) a brief overview of the program's history, (b) limited, but highly suggestive data emphasizing a special form of consumer complaint—disenrollment, and (c) program weaknesses revealed by our analysis and the thinking of others concerned with health care for the poor.

PROGRAM OVERVIEW

California's active restructuring of its Medicaid system began with the Medi-Cal Reform Act of 1971 (9). Although prior State legislation to implement Title XIX of the Social Security Act (Medicaid) specified that care for public assistance eligibles "to the extent feasible, be provided through prepaid health care or contracts with carriers" (10), only a few pilot contracts were developed under this authorization (11). To further encourage this pattern of care, the 1971 legislation authorized minimal constraints on full-scale State contracting with prepaid health plans. At the same time, it placed stringent restrictions on use of fee-for-service benefits, requiring prior authorization for more than two physician office visits and two prescription drugs monthly and for nonemergency hospitalization. Copayment charges on office visits and prescriptions were also imposed on about half of the beneficiaries—a cost-saving strategy conducted as an experiment under a special waiver from the Department of Health, Education, and Welfare (12–14).

Called the "carrot and the stick approach" by the State department of health, the law made PHPs relatively more attractive to Medicaid beneficiaries because of freedom from copayments, avoidance of delays caused by prior authorization procedures, and the provision of extra benefits such as transportation. At the same time, physicians were further deterred from accepting Medicaid patients under fee-for-service arrangements by the additional "red tape."

Those portions of the legislation that encourage development of new health services delivery organizations are germane to understanding many of the ensuing problems. The underlying philosophy was that without government interference, private enterprise would produce a cost-effective system with quality controlled through free competition in the marketplace (7a, 15). As in private enterprise, risks were also to be borne by the contracting PHPs. Accordingly, no provision was made for marketing assistance similar to that given to developing HMOs through the "dual option requirement" in the Federal HMO Act of 1973. No planning or startup monies were offered by the State. Additionally, no limits were placed on the number of plans that could be granted contracts in a given area. Nothing prevented PHPs from being composed entirely of Medicaid enrollees; but despite the vicissitudes of eligibility, continuity of membership for specified periods of time was not guaranteed.

Contracts were to cost less than the same services delivered under the fee-for-service system and were to be let on a nonbid basis, but qualifications for applicants were purposefully left vague. Although most PHPs chose to organize as nonprofit corporations because this offered them the least limitation from government regulation, under California law such organizations are permitted to subcontract with for-profit groups, the directorships of which may be overlapping. A final important point is that the law did not require contractors to provide services, only that they arrange for them. This feature, of course, is consistent with one classic model for organizing prepaid health care (16a).

The legislature authorized the State department of health to establish requirements governing PHP contracts, but the department followed the lead of the administration in taking a laissez-faire stance toward PHPs, both in the establishment of regulations and in their enforcement. Moreover, to encourage a rapid transition to the cost-saving PHP system, the State executed contracts as quickly as possible—with only cursory screening of applications and without adequate pilot experience.

According to the department of health, from the effective date of the first PHP contract on May 1, 1972, the program grew by the end of the year to include 21 plans with a combined enrollment of 147,569 persons. Only five of these organizations existed before that year. By the end of 1974, just 3 years after the 1971 act, the State was paying 54 contractors $84.6 million per year for the health care of 252,000 Medicaid recipients, roughly 10 percent of the eligible population (4c). The speed with which this development took place, as illustrated in figure 1, precluded the careful phased development built into the Federal HMO program, which generated only half as many operational HMOs in a similar timespan (6).

As new prepaid health plans sprang up in California, consumer complaints began to mount, flowing from aggrieved persons to the State health department through neighborhood groups, consumer organizations, concerned welfare workers, public health nurses, legal-aid societies, local health departments, medical associations, and comprehensive health planning councils. These complaints resulted in unfavorable newspaper publicity, decreases in PHP enrollments, increases in disenrollments, the development of consumer advocacy organizations, and a rallying of public support against these plans, as for example, through disenrollment campaigns. Reports prepared by the California Legislature (17, 18), the State auditor-general (19, 20), responsible Federal agencies (21), and various other of-

Figure 1 Average number of approved prepaid health plans per quarter, 1972–76

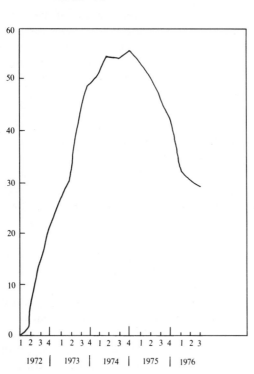

ficial and private organizations (4d, 22–24), pointed to the existence of serious problems.

Some statutory protection was obtained through the Waxman-Duffy Prepaid Health Plan Act, enacted in 1973 (25). This legislation set forth standards governing marketing, established a ceiling on the proportion of Medicaid enrollees, and required public hearings before renewal of existing contracts or entry into new ones—potentially an important source of influence for consumers. Such measures, however, did not bring the situation under control because they were not effectively implemented. For instance, the determinations of whether or not to renew a PHP contract were not necessarily based upon the hearing records (26, 27).

Consumer frustrations mounted, legal actions were filed (28, 29), county grand juries became involved, and the U.S. Senate in-

vestigated and held hearings on California's PHP difficulties in March 1975 (4).

Electrifying phrases cut through these various events: fraud, misrepresentation, profiteering, exploitation, moral bankruptcy, high-level mismanagement, negligence, incompetence, irresponsibility, deliberate coverup, failure, and abuse. The central issue, however, was sharply focused by Dr. Lester Breslow in testimony before the Senate Permanent Subcommittee on Investigations (4e):

> Excessive profits, sales misrepresentation, maladministration in government—such things, while deplorable, are not unique to PHPs. What is really bad about the development of these organizations in California is that the government has handed over the health care of tens of thousands of poor, and mainly unsophisticated, people to organizations that cannot provide and do not provide good quality care . . . often in situations where permanent damage to health, even death, may occur . . . The fact that people for whose health care government has declared itself responsible are not getting good care—that is the main issue.

Many of the entities with which the State contracted were little more than management shells that had been quickly thrown together by entrepreneurs who saw attractive profitmaking possibilities in the margin between capitation payments and expenses for services rendered. Some of the contractors were basically holding companies purchasing all their laboratory, pharmacy, physician, hospital, and other services from affiliates owned by the directors and their associates (17a). The absence of an adequate rate-setting mechanism, combined with loose contracting controls enabled some of the contractors to skim substantial profits from the monthly State payments in the form of excessively high administrative overhead (18) and, it is alleged, low enrollee utilization rates (4f).

Contrary to the intent of the State legislature in implementing Title XIX (10) and despite the potential of prepaid group practice to integrate the poor into one-class medicine (16b), a dual-track pattern emerged early on. Thus, many PHPs enrolled Medicaid recipients almost exclusively (7b).

Three years after the passage of the Medi-Cal Reform Act of 1971 there existed two types of HMOs in California: PHPs and non-PHPs. The majority are PHPs; of the 77 HMOs operational as of October 1, 1974, 58 or 75 percent were Medi-Cal contractors . . . The overwhelming majority of the PHPs have enrollee populations in which the Medi-Cal beneficiaries are disproportionately represented.

A department of health survey of 46 PHPs in early 1975 found that among those responding (all but 8 percent), the memberships of 74 percent consisted of three-quarters or more Medicaid recipients. Of this 74 percent, 57 percent had Medicaid members only (30). The legislature's effort to alter this situation through the Waxman-Duffy Act has largely failed.

California embarked on a fresh chapter in its PHP experience in 1975 when the present Governor assumed office and placed a moratorium on PHP contracting. A broad-based advisory team was formed, and after several months the new PHP director for the State testified that the team's investigation "confirmed much of what was suggested in other reports" (4g). The new deputy secretary of the Health and Welfare Agency and, at that time, acting director of health, also acknowledged significant PHP problems in his testimony before the Senate Subcommittee on Investigations (4g):

We . . . recognize our obligation to set the record straight that the California model—without necessary regulatory development and quality assurance

mechanisms—in general, does not provide a satisfactory level of quality to patients and encourages an unwholesome and complex network of big business relationships. . .

In June 1975, new and stricter standards were promulgated by the department of health. Other promising actions included the enactment of legislation that involved the California commissioner of corporations in the financial audit of PHPs commencing July 1, 1976 (31).

A vigorous PHP program director who was appointed later—the sixth in 5 years and the second in the new administration—began to weed out the marginal plans, and during his tenure the number of contractors was substantially reduced (fig. 1). But, in April 1976, this administrator was dismissed abruptly (32–34).

Once again consumers and their advocates were disappointed by what they perceived as a backing off from tough regulation by the department of health. Repercussions quickly developed. The State Assembly Subcommittee on Health Care Investigations conducted hearings in July 1976 and subsequently issued a blistering report calling for the termination of another Los Angeles PHP and a "systematic housecleaning" among State contract managers (35). Further State assembly hearings were scheduled for September. In the meantime, the U.S. Senate Permanent Subcommittee on Investigations again began to probe California's PHPs. Concurrently, the program is being investigated by the U.S. General Accounting Office and the DHEW Audit Agency. Federal concern for Medicaid beneficiaries in prepaid health plans was additionally evidenced in the new HMO amendments signed into law in November 1976. One of these amendments limits Medicaid matching payments to prepaid health plans which are federally certified HMOs. Since at the time of this writing only one of California's first and second generation PHPs meets this requirement, the impact of this legislation on the State's Medicaid program is yet to be determined.

In view of the preceding events, it is certainly not clear that the "good has driven out the bad," as once envisioned by the State administration under its free market-oriented philosophy espoused in 1971. Political ambitions on all sides continue to affect action, and the countervailing forces to meaningful reform are strong (33). The serious danger has not been dispelled that inferior plans might succeed financially and become firmly entrenched, making "extremely difficult future efforts to deal with them in the public interest" (4h). A second grave danger exists in that negative experiences with some PHPs may jeopardize unfairly the reputations of responsible plans, as well as the entire concept of providing health care to the poor through the prepaid mode. To the extent that this occurs, it may be more appropriate to say that "bad health care tends to drive out the good" (4h). One should keep in mind these perils and the existence of multiple problems in the fee-for-service sector when reading our following detailed examination of problems experienced by Medicaid enrollees in California PHPs.

CONSUMER PROBLEMS WITH PHPs

Assessment of the impact of California's PHP experiment on Medicaid enrollees is both a moral responsibility and a pragmatic imperative. Evaluation therefore is exigent not only to effect program improvements and to determine future program directions but also to judge the extent to which the program has fulfilled the public mandate to provide quality health care to the poor. Within the broad scope of evaluation needed, we have focused on sources of consumer dissatisfaction leading to disenrollments as indicative of underlying problems that need resolution if consumer decision making is to support the development of PHPs as a viable alternative for implementing Medicaid legislation.

Sources of Data

To develop a more comprehensive view than previously available of the difficulties experienced by Medicaid consumers in conjunction with the expansion of PHPs in California, we extensively examined certain public records, many of which have been relatively inaccessible. Documents reviewed included all available enrollment and disenrollment data from the State department of health, disenrollment forms collected by consumer groups in Los Angeles during the first 2 years of the program, and affidavits from lawsuits against individual plans. The information thus obtained was supplemented through personal interviews with consumers and those working on their behalf, as well as by newspaper articles, testimony presented before investigative bodies, and the findings of other evaluations and reports (7, 8).

Symptomatic of larger difficulties, State PHP records are inadequate and incomplete. These limitations are reflected in this paper and will certainly affect other evaluation attempts. A broader significance of these limitations however, is that the lack of adequate data has obviously affected the State's ability to identify problem areas for responsible monitoring of plans, as well as to manage the program as a whole. In fact, the State's data base is so disappointing that one wonders what combination of mismanagement, personnel turnover, naivete, and deliberate attempts to thwart scrutiny have produced the present system.

Thus, for example, although the monthly reports giving frequencies and rates of enrollment and disenrollment by plan are intact, tabulations of the reasons for voluntary disenrollment exist for only 13 months, 6 of which are from 1976. Much of the available information has not been tabulated for more than 1 month at a time; preparation of statistics to examine trends over time is complicated by periodic changes in the statistics collected, coding systems, and reporting formats. These problems, in turn, have created other data gaps, such as the lack of departmental analyses of program activity relevant to essential administration and policy decisions.

Although we found State health department personnel cooperative in opening their files for the present study, the department previously has been reluctant to make available PHP information that legally is a matter of public record. This reluctance has also contributed to holes in documentation, as illustrated most notably by the experience of the Los Angeles County Health Rights Organization in attempting to obtain PHP utilization data. A successful lawsuit (36) filed under the California Freedom of Information Act was required before the State acknowledged LACRO's right to gain access to monthly utilization reports. Shortly thereafter, the department halted compilation of these records, leaving raw utilization data on the computer where it was effectively inaccessible not only to the plaintiffs, but to the State itself—and we might add, to subsequent investigators.

In light of these problems, an important supplement to State PHP data has been our review of 769 disenrollment forms through which 2,099 persons sought to terminate membership in 28 Los Angeles PHPs. These forms were collected during 1972–73 by two consumer advocacy groups because people reported difficulty in disenrolling through the plans themselves (4i). Although lack of access to all disenrollment records listing the reasons for voluntary withdrawal from a plan precluded a representative sampling, other reports (4) clearly indicate that the difficulties revealed in these documents did not merely reflect a "reporting" bias, but rather a problem of epidemic proportions. Moreover, the documents available draw from an important Medicaid population, for Los Angeles has been a major PHP center. According to department of health records, more than half of the PHPs operating in the State at any given time have been located in the Los Angeles area, and between two-thirds and three-quarters of all Medicaid PHP members have been enrolled there.

Further data were obtained from affidavits representing some 132 consumers bringing civil suit against 1 Los Angeles PHP (28) and 8 additional affidavits involving 23 persons who initiated successful litigation against another plan in the San Francisco Bay area (29). Not all lawsuits against California PHPs have been examined, nor is the total number even known, but the civil actions considered here are especially important in that the plaintiffs are seeking not only personal damages but also injunctive relief—that is, basic changes in the organizational situation which led to their complaints.

The more complete data—disenrollment and enrollment reports—provide a backdrop against which to discuss the Los Angeles disenrollment forms and affidavits. Despite their obvious limitations, the latter sources serve to point out and emphasize the paramount issues in providing publicly supported prepaid health care from a consumer perspective.

The data available do not assure the identification of all problems which Medicaid beneficiaries have experienced with PHPs. Neither do they permit an accurate estimate of the frequency with which the problems revealed have occurred. What does surface therefore should be regarded as the "tip of the iceberg." As such, the following discussion should forewarn public health professionals to explore further the hazards involved before steering the Medicaid ship deeper into prepaid waters.

Enrollment and Disenrollment Trends

Figure 2 charts the actual and potential number of Medicaid enrollees in California prepaid health plans from the first nonpilot contract approval in 1972 through June 1976. As is immediately apparent, enrollments have fallen far short of the Medicaid memberships authorized by the State department of health and the targets that these

Figure 2 Actual and potential Medicaid enrollments in California prepaid health plans, January 1973–June 1976

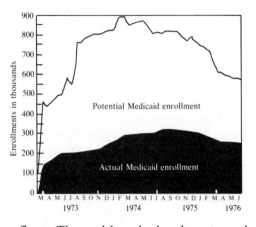

Figure 3 Prepaid health plans disenrollments, January 1973–June 1976

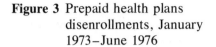
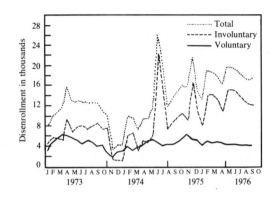

reflect. Thus, although the department's goal was to enroll half of California's 2 million Medicaid beneficiaries in PHPs during 1973, by the end of 1974 only 10 percent of this population had enrolled (4c)—a figure which has remained fairly constant since. While the authorized Medicaid membership capacity has decreased with recent reductions in the number of operating plans, enrollment potential is still more than double the number of actual Medicaid subscribers. Therefore, despite the State's attempts to effect major changes in the health care delivery system, California's poor have not enrolled in PHPs to the extent anticipated. This situation generally reflects the experiences of prepaid group practices elsewhere (37a).

Notwithstanding, the actual PHP membership curve suggests gradual and stable growth. This is deceptive, however, because rapid turnover and fluctuation in membership have been hallmarks of California's "second generation" PHPs. Monthly Medicaid enrollment figures mask this situation in that gains in new subscribers offset losses from disenrollments to produce the illusion of membership stability.

As figure 3 demonstrates, disenrollments have varied erratically, with monthly disenrollment statistics greatly affected by marked variations in involuntary disenrollments—primarily due to members' loss of Medicaid eligibility (8a), but also more recently to the reduction in plan contracts. Voluntary disenrollments, too, have been a steady drain on PHP membership; these result from subscribers moving from a plan's service areas or subscriber dissatisfaction.

The impact of enrollment and disenrollment on Medicaid membership in PHPs is exemplified by data for April through August 1973, when new enrollments averaged approximately 8 percent of the total membership per month and disenrollments averaged 5.5 percent. The voluntary disenrollment rate alone was 2.3 percent monthly, ranging from 0 to 21 percent for individual plans. Projected annually, this means that 66 percent of the total PHP Medicaid membership disenrolled per year and that nearly 28 percent of all Medicaid subscribers did so voluntarily.

By 1975, involuntary disenrollments were averaging 4.2 percent monthly. In addition, an average of 1.8 percent of the Medicaid PHP subscribers were still disenrolling voluntarily each month—a trend that persisted through the first 6 months of 1976. Individual plans also continued to vary in voluntary disenrollment rates, ranging from 0 to 8.1 percent during 1975 and from 0 to 6.2 percent in the first half of the following year.

The effects of these patterns on PHPs— and· on the Medicaid recipients for whose health they are responsible—have varied, depending not only on each plan's particular enrollment and disenrollment experience, but also on the proportion of the plan's total membership which Medicaid consumers represent. For the substantial number of plans relying mainly or solely on Medicaid enrollees, however, the failure to attract the expected number of subscribers has inevitably affected the range and quality of services. A prepaid membership base of 20,000–50,000 enrollees has been estimated as the minimum essential for economic survival and the delivery of comprehensive health care (8b, 16c, 38a), but the average Medicaid enrollment in California PHPs did not exceed 5,000 members until early 1975, and in March of that year only two plans had registered more than 11,000 beneficiaries (39).

Coupled with problems of size, membership turnover has resulted in tremendous marketing pressures, not only to achieve plan growth but to replace enrollees who became ineligible, moved, or withdrew PHP membership as a result of dissatisfaction. These factors, as well as the lack of an adequate enrollment "mix" to spread the risk of coverage, have also exacerbated the difficulties of providing quality care to new and continuing subscribers. Herein lie the major sources of consumer complaints against California PHPs as revealed in disenrollment forms and the other documents that we reviewed.

Consumer Complaints Against PHPs

In contrast to complaints against fee-for-service providers, which in California typically concern billing for services not rendered, consumer complaints against PHPs can be categorized into two broad groups:

marketing and enrollment practices and lack of services to meet member needs (4j). As previously noted, however, the lack of sufficient data makes it difficult to estimate the proportion of PHP Medicaid members registering such complaints and the frequency of specific alleged abuses.

Although State health department personnel began investigating complaints from Medicaid consumers shortly after the first PHP contracts were written, this activity was the subject of considerable intradepartmental conflict. As a result, systematic records of complaints were not kept and (4j):

. . . program staff responsible for contract supervision most often resorted to disenrolling a complaining beneficiary to solve the enrollee's problem rather than impose sanctions against the plan.

The disenrollment forms collected by the two Los Angeles consumer groups during 1972–73 therefore assume a special significance and provide the primary source of data on the dissatisfactions of Medicaid recipients with PHPs during this period.

Content analysis of these latter documents clearly reveals that PHP marketing and the accessibility and acceptability of services are the major problems. Not all reasons for consumer dissatisfaction may have been listed, however, since only one was required for a member to disenroll. The use of a single form to disenroll more than one subscriber and variations in the way documents were completed further complicate tabulations of frequencies, while changes in PHP membership, contracts, and plan service areas result in a denominator much too slippery to estimate the extent to which complaints stated on disenrollment forms represent the Medicaid population then enrolled in PHPs.

The earliest information on the relative frequency of consumer problems with prepaid health plans is provided by an analysis of 860 complaints on file with the State department of health as of September 1973.

Working from "typically handwritten telephone messages taken by PHP management staff during the past seven months" which . . . "gave no evidence of follow-up action or indication of referrals having been made," the then newly appointed chief of the investigations section found that 46 percent of these complaints were for poor service, 33 percent concerned marketing misrepresentation, and 17 percent involved transportation difficulties. Less common problems were failing to pay non-PHP providers for health care given enrollees in emergencies or outside the plan service area, as well as selective disenrollments of members who were seriously ill (4j).

Because the particulars of alleged abuses are numerous, we cite only a few of the most frequently reported reasons for grievances. Although these suggest related problems, only individual case histories can capture the frustration, bewilderment, and personal tragedy underlying consumer complaints against PHPs.

Marketing and Enrollment Practices

Repeated consumer protests strongly suggest that Medicaid recipients have been pressured into joining PHPs through a variety of deceptive enrollment practices, many of which were employed in door-to-door solicitations in poverty areas. One common report is that enrollers hired by PHPs misrepresented themselves by wearing physicians' or nurses' white coats, as well as by claiming to be welfare workers, employees of the State, or other government employees. The authority thus fraudulently established apparently was used to build credibility in marketing the plan, as well as to threaten sanctions for failure to join.

Although specifically prohibited by the Knox-Mills Acts of California (16d, 40), misleading advertising and misrepresentative statements about services covered allegedly also were used to recruit new PHP members. In some cases, ideal HMO benefits apparently were promised regardless of the plan's ability to deliver, but in other instances, not even a model HMO could fulfill the promises which plaintiffs claim were made. Alternatively, some PHP recruiters allegedly failed to make clear that a choice of health care plans was possible, advised people that they would lose their Medicaid benefits unless they joined the PHP in question, or provided so little information that consumers were enrolled unwittingly or without full understanding of the changes which PHP membership would effect in their health care coverage.

Typical is the statement of a woman who reported that a man claiming to be from the State came to her door and asked to see the family's Medicaid cards. In her words:

He copied our names and numbers from the cards. He filled out a paper and told me to sign it, saying that from now on we will have better care than we had before. He did not give me any printed material, nor did he explain anything about the plan to me. He did not say that we would not receive our regular Medi-Cal cards the following month.

Until she took her father-in-law to their family physician, this woman did not know that his services were no longer covered. When two of her children needed medical care, she did not go to the PHP clinic because it was too far and because she had heard that its services were not good. Instead, she took them to the family physician and paid for the visits and prescriptions herself. Not all PHP enrollees had sufficient money to exercise this option.

Further complaints held that peer pressure in several forms was exerted to obtain PHP enrollments. For example, an elderly Chinese man stated that he joined a plan after being convinced that most others in his senior citizens' group already had done so (29). Misstating that one person could enroll others, PHP representatives also allegedly urged new members to enroll their relatives and friends. In other instances, the enrollment of members through deliberate forgery was reported.

Problems in Obtaining Services

Although the intent of Medicaid legislation is to remove barriers to health care for the poor, another large category of consumer complaints concerns problems in obtaining PHP services. For those who sought promised care under the strain of illness or injury, the discovery that medical attention was not readily available often compounded personal pain and stress, sometimes in life-threatening situations. For others, the difficulties in obtaining even routine care created a crisis.

Distance and transportation problems represent obvious obstacles to obtaining health care, especially for the poor, and thus numerous consumer grievances related to transportation hardships. These hardships allegedly were compounded by providers' failure to keep scheduled office hours and appointments and by the enrollment of PHP members beyond the prescribed service area. Geographic limitations of PHP services, even when legal, have presented problems for consumers in other ways. For example, since plans are required to provide emergency care at only one of their locations, emergency services have been effectively inaccessible for all but the most extreme conditions to members living far away.

Consumers have criticized the availability of PHP emergency services on other counts also—that enrollees are sometimes required to get a physician's approval before they can use emergency facilities; that physicians are on call only for emergencies rather than being at the clinic on a 24-hour basis as required by PHP contract; that emergency treatment was denied because the appropriate specialist was not available; and that some plans do not even maintain an emergency facility or telephone contact with emergency providers.

Inordinate waiting time is another commonly reported hindrance. An extreme example is that of a 3-year-old with a severely and obviously painful fractured arm who waited with her mother in a PHP clinic from 10 am until 6 pm for an orthopedic specialist to arrive. At 6 pm the pair was sent home to await word about where to go for treatment. Unable to wait any longer by 9 pm, the enrollee took her child to an orthopedic hospital where she received attention immediately. Nevertheless, since the visit was not authorized by the PHP, the mother had to pay for it out of her own pocket (7b).

Poor Quality of Care

The documents reviewed for this study indicate that for the poor, quality is judged first by the availability of services. The more usual definition of quality, however, concerns the evaluation of care actually delivered. The blending of these two dimensions is apparent in specific consumer grievances regarding inferior PHP services. Thus, charges that the clinic atmosphere was unfriendly, that the physician would not prescribe the treatment the patient desired, or that no follow up service was provided tend to be associated in individual experience with difficulties of access, such as long waiting times or the unavailability of a specialist.

These consumer indicators of health care quality differ markedly from those used in professional evaluations which, nevertheless, have found PHPs seriously lacking in the quality of care provided (4k, 22). If we assume that consumer assessments of quality are related to expectations for health care, our data suggest that extravagant promises made in PHP marketing may well contribute to later disappointments with PHP services. Similarly, previous patterns of health care tend to shape notions of what adequate care should be.

Medicaid recipients accustomed to frequent prescriptions, laboratory tests, and hospitalizations under the fee-for-service system may be likely to complain when PHPs do not provide such services in the same volume, regardless of whether or not they are medically appropriate. Past inequities in services received by the poor as compared to those economically more advantaged may also condition Medicaid members of PHPs to expect "second-class treatment," thereby sensitizing them to perceive even the smallest deviations from usual practice as indicative of inferior care. This was illustrated by one enrollee's complaint that rather than taking a thermometer from a sterile container, a health plan nurse gave her one from a table, which she "of course, refused."

The results of several studies also indicate that the extent to which health workers, and particularly physicians, demonstrate interest in patients and try to communicate effectively with them about their medical problems is extremely important in consumer assessments of the quality of care (41). At the same time, there is evidence that the systematic organization of prepaid group practice tends to be associated with a less personalized form of physician care than is provided in fee-for-service medicine (1, 42). Consumers disappointed with the quality of the physician-patient relationship therefore may perceive problems in PHP services regardless of their technical adequacy. This situation does not preclude the possibility of overlap in the problems identified by differing consumer and provider criteria. Few providers, for example, would quibble with the complaint of a PHP member that she could not communicate with her physician who spoke only the language of the small Asian country where he was born and trained.

Voluntary Disenrollment as an Expression of Dissatisfaction

Many Medicaid recipients who joined prepaid health plans, whether or not under conditions of informed consent, and subsequently discovered that services were unavailable or of inferior quality quite naturally tried to disenroll and return to the fee-for-service system. In some instances where the PHP had no grievance procedures, or grievance procedures were unknown to the enrollee, or such procedures failed to resolve the problem, consumers may have seen disenrollment as their only recourse. In other cases, Medicaid beneficiaries who had been free to "shop around" under the fee-for-service system may have attempted to disenroll from the PHP before trying to resolve complaints through other channels. Hypothesized relationships among these complex factors are diagramed in figure 4.

Although the specific events preceding attempts of Medicaid recipients to terminate PHP membership obviously vary, the problems encountered in disenrollment were so severe that these form yet another major group of consumer complaints, including some which led to lawsuits (29). Dissatisfied PHP members frequently reported that they were not informed of their right to a fair hearing to resolve grievances, and indeed some plans apparently did not even have procedures for handling grievances. In addition, enrollees allegedly were not advised of their right to disenroll under certain circumstances at any time if dissatisfied; rather, they were told that they had to stay in the plan for at least 1 year.

Persons who insisted on exercising their right to disenroll reported numerous difficulties, including harassment in being questioned about reasons for wishing to do so; disenrollment forms which were hard to understand; hostile PHP personnel who gave consumers the run-around about being able to disenroll only at inconvenient locations during certain limited hours; and long waits to complete the necessary paperwork.

After necessary forms were completed despite these obstacles, plans allegedly failed to forward them to the State for several months, thereby continuing to receive

Figure 4 The dynamics of voluntary disenrollment from prepaid health plans (PHPs)

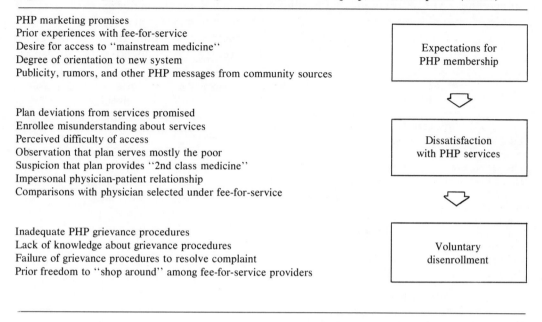

PHP marketing promises
Prior experiences with fee-for-service
Desire for access to "mainstream medicine"
Degree of orientation to new system
Publicity, rumors, and other PHP messages from community sources

Expectations for
PHP membership

Plan deviations from services promised
Enrollee misunderstanding about services
Perceived difficulty of access
Observation that plan serves mostly the poor
Suspicion that plan provides "2nd class medicine"
Impersonal physician-patient relationship
Comparisons with physician selected under fee-for-service

Dissatisfaction
with PHP services

Inadequate PHP grievance procedures
Lack of knowledge about grievance procedures
Failure of grievance procedures to resolve complaint
Prior freedom to "shop around" among fee-for-service providers

Voluntary
disenrollment

capitation payments without providing services (33). In some cases, this was because disenrolling members were so disillusioned that they chose not to return to the PHP for care while waiting to get their Medicaid cards back, but in other instances plans reportedly failed to inform clients that the PHP was still responsible for their health care until the new card arrived or refused to provide needed care to disenrolling members, particularly if the services required were expensive. In any event, the outcome was that consumers failed to receive the medical coverage to which they were entitled during the frequently extended disenrollment period.

Under persistent pressure, the State health department in 1973 set up a PHP Information Center in Los Angeles to handle the heavy number of complaints, to curb marketing abuses through enrollment verification, and to facilitate the disenrollments of dissatisfied subscribers. A subsequent decline in voluntary disenrollments (fig. 3) suggests that these actions had a positive effect.

Later data on reasons for State health department approval and disapproval of PHP disenrollment forms provide additional information of interest. The first available department report, covering December 1974, indicates that the most common approval code for that period was "enrolled over one year" followed by "return to prior treatment program" and "moved from service area." On the other hand, the beneficiary's desire to return to fee-for-service accounted for approximately 33 percent of the disapproved disenrollments, while the next most frequently used disapproval codes were insufficient explanation to determine or support the reason for disenrolling and a desire for a medical service that as one of the standard Medicaid benefits should have been provided by the plan. Similar data available for 8 months in 1975 are summarized in the table.

As apparent from the table, the codes used provide only limited information about sources of consumer dissatisfaction with PHPs. Neither of the codes accounting for the highest proportion of disapproved and

Reasons for State health department disapproval or approval of 20,187 disenrollment forms submitted by 51 California prepaid health plans during 8 months in 1975

Reason	Number of forms	Percent of total forms approved or disapproved[1]	Number of plans for which reason was coded	Number of plans for which reason was most common
Disapproval codes				
Insufficient explanation to determine or support reason	388	26	39	13
Desire to return to fee-for-service	323	22	40	8
Desire to change plan	158	11	21	5
Generally dissatisfied with plan	351	24	37	10
Not in plan 1 year and claims to have been	63	4	15	—
Wants a medical service that can be obtained from plan	64	4	20	1
Invalid lack of transportation claim	34	2	17	1
Other	94	6	25	—
Approval codes				
Enrolled more than 1 year	5,762	31	47	26
Dissatisfied with medical services (after 1 year)	1,639	9	46	—
Plan not explained completely or misunderstood plan representative	1,185	6	45	—
Requires Medi-Cal services not provided by plan	145	1	37	—
Return to prior treatment	2,652	14	49	5
Breakdown in physician-patient relationship	181	1	39	—
Transportation problems	2,102	11	45	2
Moved from service area	1,840	10	50	5
Other	1,424	8	47	2
Blanket approvals	1,782	10	23	7

[1]Percentages do not total 100 because of rounding.

approved disenrollments indicates *why* subscribers wished to withdraw from plan membership, and several other codes are equally devoid of explanation which would be helpful in preventing or resolving problems. Nevertheless, it can be assumed that approximately 90 percent of the voluntary disenrollment documents submitted, whether approved or not, were filed as the result of dissatisfaction by PHP members. Some requests for withdrawal can be attributed to specific complaints against a plan, while others may represent an unfavorable comparison of the PHP with the more familiar fee-for-service option. General exceptions include disenrollments approved because members moved from the PHP service area or required Medicaid services not provided by the plan.

During the time period considered in the table, an average of 93 percent of the disenrollment documents received by the State were approved, with approval rates ranging among plans from 69 to 100 percent. The actual number of documents approved per plan ranged from 1 to 3,953, with many documents typically disenrolling more than one Medicaid recipient. Because of the larger number of PHPs in the Los Angeles area, most disenrollment requests originated there, but the percentage approved did not differ significantly either by region or by the number of disenrollment forms which plans submitted.

Enrollment for more than 1 year was the most common reason for approval of disenrollments during each of the 8 months and for all regions, but this was not true for all plans as indicated by the two right-hand columns in the table. Similarly, not all approval and disapproval codes were applied to all plans, and differences in the rank order of reasons for disenrollment were noted. Certain regional differences also emerged. Thus, while transportation problems were the second-ranked reason for approved disenrollments in the Los Angeles area, this was the fifth most common code in San Diego, and eighth in northern California. In contrast, marketing problems accounted for 10 percent of approved disenrollments in the northern region, but 5 percent or less in other areas. Regional variations were also observed in reasons for disapproving disenrollments, for example, general dissatisfaction with the plan accounted for 27 percent of the disenrollments denied in the Los Angeles area, but only 17 percent of the disapprovals in both the San Diego and northern California regions.

DISCUSSION AND IMPLICATIONS

The preceding summary of consumer complaints and related allegations against prepaid health plans provides an important public perspective on what went wrong with California's program. If such problems are to be avoided in the future, this perspective cannot be ignored because it reveals the existence of PHP problems as perceived by those whose behavior ultimately will affect the achievement of PHP program goals. Thus, prompt resolution of consumer grievances is necessary not only to overcome dissatisfaction with the program, but also to stem the growth of public rumor and distrust which can jeopardize the viability of particular plans, as well as the prepaid health care concept in general.

Moreover, our analysis indicates that consumer complaints often reflect real problems in the program. Other reports and evaluations taken together acknowledge and corroborate the existence of each type of abuse which forms the basis for consumer protest and PHP disenrollment. Early attention to members' grievances therefore can serve to identify underlying program weaknesses so that these can be corrected before they become compounded into larger difficulties.

The best approach to these problems is, of course, to prevent their occurrence in the first place. Therefore, as new State PHP programs are initiated, public health professionals should scrutinize enabling legislation, accompanying administrative regulations, and procedures for implementing them in order to identify inadequacies that could result in program abuse. Above all, mechanisms must be developed to assure that PHPs have the resources necessary to provide acceptable health care coverage for the people they are contractually obligated to serve.

Many analyses indicate that predominant emphasis on the economic advantages to be realized both by the State and by PHP providers, rather than concern with quality of care for consumers, contributed heavily to the problems with which California's program has been associated. The following are particular danger signals:

- Laissez-faire or poorly developed regulations and monitoring mechanisms for assuring reasonable access of members to PHP services, acceptable quality of care, and effective PHP management—including safeguards against profiteering.
- Rapid program expansion without detailed prior planning and the develop-

ment of adequate supportive and regulatory mechanisms at the State level.

- Approval of PHP contracts without adequate prior screening for evidence of operational and delivery capability, including sufficient capital to assure service capacity development before enrollment of members.
- Lack of State assistance to PHPs, both financial and technical, during planning, organizational, and early implementation stages.
- Marketing on a per capita commission basis, no mechanisms for assuring consumer rights to an informed choice based on a fair representation of the plan and discussion of the consequences of membership, and no "cooling off" period for new enrollees to reconsider their decision to join.
- No commitment by individual PHPs or the State through a dual-choice requirement to attracting at least 50 percent of the membership from non-Medicaid groups.
- No preparation of the public for acceptance of the PHP concept, including establishment of criteria for judging plans.
- Lack of State guarantee of Medicaid eligibility for at least 1 year to prevent high involuntary turnover rates.
- No provision for orientation of PHP members to insure understanding of the plans' utilization procedures.
- Absence of clearly defined and operational procedures within the PHPs and in the State Medicaid office for reviewing and responding to grievances of members and for assuring members' right to speedy disenrollment if a problem cannot be resolved.
- Lack of mechanisms to assure direct public accountability by PHPs, as well as by the State, to PHP enrollees and to taxpayers, including disclosure of utilization rates, quality of care reviews, identification of financial interests in other organizations, and additional relevant data.
- Lack of a range of sanctions and procedures, in addition to contract cancellation, for disciplining PHPs with confirmed violations.

Even if such deficiencies are discovered, correcting them will not be easy. The stakes are high, the vested interests are strong, and the pressures are enormous. Therefore, in addition to working through administrative channels in the State health department, persons discovering PHP problems may well have to seek other strategies, including conferences with legislators and the mobilization of professional and community groups who together can counterbalance the forces of those attracted by the profit motive.

The importance of forming coalitions to fight the multiple vested interests in PHPs is pointed out succinctly by Singh (43): "When the tiger is in the garden, need the cobra fear the mongoose?" Tigers for the PHP garden can be found not only among public health workers and consumer organizations, but also in district attorneys' offices, social welfare associations, organized medicine, and the press corps, as well as among well-motivated PHP providers whose reputations can be tarnished by the unethical practices of other PHPs. Alerting these people to the issues, keeping them informed of program developments, and suggesting possibilities for cooperative efforts to effect needed change constitute a challenge that health educators especially have a responsibility to meet—but doing so promises to test both our commitment to the public and our courage in taking risks.

Health education is also significant in preventing PHP problems and in strengthening PHP programs, as indicated in detailed discussions by other authors (36, 44). Unfortunately, however, those who see PHPs primarily as cost-saving ventures or get-rich-quick schemes are likely to resist comprehensive and multifaceted educational efforts with the open communication, consumer involvement, informed decision-making, and public accountability toward which these are aimed. At the same time, there may be enthusiastic support for health education as an euphemism for manipulative tactics to increase PHP enrollments and to restrict the use of services without consideration of either population needs or the appropriateness of current utilization patterns. The employment of untrained or naive "health educators" to serve as blind instruments of the program is one way in which such perversion could be accomplished. Therefore, although PHPs may include health education as a funded benefit, it is critical to ask "benefit for whom?"

There is much to learn, then, from California's PHP experience, which should serve as an early warning system to identify possible points of breakdown in the effective development and expansion of HMOs throughout the nation. Although we have considered only a few of the problems associated with one State's program, we hope that this paper demonstrates that translating the promise of the HMO concept into the reality of improved health care for the poor is no simple task. Nevertheless, the opportunity is here and if we fail to seize it, others will exploit it for their self-interests.

REFERENCES

1. Donabedian, A.: An evaluation of prepaid group practice. Inquiry 6: 3–27, September 1969.

2. Greenlick, R.: The impact of prepaid group practice on American medical care: A critical evaluation. Ann Am Acad Polit Soc Sci 399: 100–113, January 1972.

3. Roemer, M.I., and Shonick, W.: HMO performance: The recent evidence. Milbank Mem Fund Q 51: 271–317, summer 1973.

4. U.S. Senate, Committee on Government Operations, Permanent Subcommittee on Investigations: Hearings on prepaid health plans, Mar. 13–14, 1975. 94th Cong. U.S. Government Printing Office, Washington, D.C., 1975; (a) pp. 53–56, (b) pp. 6, 39–45, 132, (c) p. 6, (d) pp. 59–61, (e) p. 59, (f) p. 101, (g) p. 111, (h) p. 62, (i) p. 7, (j) pp. 131–132, (k) pp. 59–62, 101–102, 144–145, 205–206, 211–212, 230–231, 311–318.

5. Fairbanks, R.: New gold rush—prepaid Medi-Cal franchises sought. Los Angeles Times, Dec. 10, 1972.

6. Seubold, F.H.: HMOs—The view from the program. Public Health Rep 90: 99–103, March-April 1975.

7. Schneider, A.G., and Stern, J.B.: Health maintenance organizations and the poor: Problems and prospect. Northwestern University Law Review, vol. 70. March-April 1975; (a) p. 126, (b) p. 134.

8. Greenfield, M., and Childs, A.W.: Prepaid health plans: California's experiment in changing the medical care system. University of California, Institute of Governmental Studies, Berkeley, Public Affairs Report, vol. 17, April 1976; (a) p. 5, (b) p. 2.

9. California Statutes, Ch. 577, 1971.

10. State of California. Welfare and institutions code, Div. 9, Pt. 3 Sec. 14000, 1965.

11. Gartside, F.E., Hopkins, C.E., and Roemer, M.I.: Medicaid services in California under different organizational modes: Medi-Cal project final report. University of California. School of Public Health, Los Angeles, December 1973.

12. Brian, E.W., and Gibbens, S.F.: California's Medi-Cal copayment experiment. Med Care 12:1, supplement, December 1974.

13. Roemer, M.I., Hopkins, C.E., Carr, L., and Gartside, F.: Copayments for ambulatory care: Penny-wise and pound-foolish. Med Care 13: 457–466, June 1975.

14. Hopkins, C.E., et al.: Cost-sharing and prior authorization effects on Medicaid services in California: Part 2: The providers' reactions. Medi Care, 13: 643–647, August 1975.

15. Brian, E.: California's emerging prepaid health plans. California Department of Health, Sacramento, 1972, pp. 6, 7.

16. Greenberg, I.G., and Rodburg, M.L.: The role of prepaid group practice in relieving the medical care crisis. Harvard Law Review 84: 887–1001, February 1971; (a) pp. 913–915, (b) pp. 934–935, (c) p. 949, (d) p. 977.

17. California. Legislative Analyst: A review of the regulation of prepaid health plans by the State Department of Health. California State Legislature, Sacramento, No. 15, 1973; (a) p. 8.

18. California Senate. Committee on Health and Welfare, Subcommittee on Medical Education and Health

Needs: Group health plans in California: Who regulates? (staff report) California State Legislature, Sacramento, 1974.

19. California, Office of the Auditor-General, Joint Legislative Audit Committee: Department of health prepaid health plans. Sacramento, Apr. 22, 1974.

20. California, Department of Finance, Audits Division: A review of the Medi-Cal program. Sacramento, Dec. 30, 1974.

21. U.S. Senate, Committee on Finance: Better controls needed for health maintenance organizations under Medicaid in California. Report by the Comptroller General of the United States, Sept. 19, 1974. U.S. Government Printing Office, Washington, D.C., 1974.

22. General Research Corporation: Evaluation of California prepaid health plans (PHPs), by D. Louis and J. McCord, under DHEW Contact No. HEW-OS-73-194. Santa Barbara, Calif., September 1974.

23. Comprehensive Health Planning Council of Los Angeles County: Prepaid health plans: The concept and the operation. Los Angeles, undated.

24. California, State Department of Health: Response to the legislative analyst's recommendations regarding the State department of health's regulation of prepaid health plans. Prepared for the Assembly Health Committee. Sacramento, undated.

25. California Statutes, 1972, ch. 1366.

26. Ortiz, et al. v. Lackner, et al., Sacramento Superior Court Case No. 254-434 (1975).

27. Ricketts v. Lackner, et al., Sacramento Superior Court Case No. 257-191 (1976).

28. Miller v. DePaulo Health Plan, Los Angeles Superior Court Case No. C-122-674, (1975), pending civil law suit.

29. Ortiz v. American Health Care Plan, San Francisco Superior Court Case No. 680-697 (1974).

30. California, State Department of Health, Division of Alternative Health Systems: Patient-health education practices in California's prepaid group health plans. Sacramento, July 1, 1975.

31. Knox-Keene Health Care Service Plan Act of 1975: California Statutes, 1975, ch. 941.

32. Fairbanks, R.: Brown aide fired over health reform. Los Angeles Times, Apr. 14, 1976.

33. Horrock, N.M.: New health plan controversy on coast centers on the dismissal of reformer. New York Times, June 14, 1976, p. 37.

34. Mullen, L.R., and Schneider, A.G.: HMOs and the poor: Another look at the California experience. Health Law Project Libr Bull 323, July 1976.

35. California Assembly, Special Subcommittee on Health Care Investigations: Report to Governor Brown. California Legislature, Sacramento, Aug. 2, 1976.

36. Los Angeles County Health Rights Organization, et al. v. Mayer et al., Sacramento Superior Court Case No. 252-035 (1974).

37. Galiher, C.B., and Costa, M.A.: Consumer acceptance of HMOs. Public Health Rep 90: 106-112, March-April 1975; (a) p. 111.

38. Myers, B.A.: Health maintenance organizations: Objectives and issues. HSMHA Health Rep 86: 585-591. July 1971; (a) p. 588.

39. Childs, A.W., and Greenfield, M.: California's experiment in changing the medical care system. Paper presented to the National Conference on Social Welfare, San Francisco, May 12, 1975.

40. Knox-Mills Health Plan Act: California Government Code 12530-39, West. supp. 1969.

41. Rivkin, M.O., and Bush, P.J.: The satisfaction continuum in health care: Consumer and provider preferences. In Consumer incentives for health care, edited by Selma J. Mushkin. Prodist. New York, 1974, pp. 304-326.

42. DeFriese, G.H.: On paying the fiddler to change the tune: Further evidence from Ontario regarding the impact of universal health insurance on the organization and patterns of medical practice. Milbank Mem Fund Q 53: 117-148, spring 1975.

43. Singh, M.: Maxims. Trans-India Educational Press, Hyderabad, 1973.

44. MacColl, C.S.: Health education in the HMO setting. In Selected papers on consumerism in the HMO movement. DHEW Publication No. HSM 73-13012. U.S. Government Printing Office, Washington, D.C., 1973.

41. Improper and Wasteful Payments in the Medicaid Program

JOSEPH A. CALIFANO, JR.

Statement before the Subcommittee on Health and the Environment, Committee on Interstate and Foreign Commerce, House of Representatives, November 1, 1977.

Since their inception over a decade ago, the Medicare and Medicaid programs have paid for health care to countless poor, elderly and disabled people in this country.

These programs will spend over $47 billion in federal and state dollars in the current fiscal year to promote health and alleviate suffering. Without them, the quality of health in America would be far worse.

For that reason it is vitally important that America's taxpayers continue to have faith in the viability of this system. We simply cannot afford to countenance waste and leakage from inefficiency, ineligibility, or fraud and abuse in these programs. We must make every effort to determine where such waste and leakage is occurring. And we must marshall all available resources to end, or sharply reduce, fraud, abuse and error.

In the Medicaid program alone, we have discovered a number of major areas where significant leakage has occurred:

- *First,* we estimate that many hundreds of millions of dollars will be lost in the current fiscal year through Medicaid provider fraud and abuse;
- *Second,* during fiscal 1977, at least $1.2 billion in Medicaid funds were paid for services to individuals who were ineligible for the program.
- *Third,* claims processing errors, such as duplicate payments, overpayments, payments for uncovered services, payments to ineligible providers and the like have led to an estimated loss of at least $200 million dollars during fiscal 1977.
- *Finally,* through our review of potential third party liability, we have estimated that the Federal government failed in fiscal 1977 to collect over $600 million dollars from third party payors, such as worker's compensation funds or private insurance companies, which should be covering certain health care costs before Medicaid dollars are used. I should note that of this $600 million, we estimate $300 million should have been collected by states from the Medicare program.

Although there may be a little overlap in these figures, the sum total would appear to indicate substantial and intolerable leakage of taxpayer dollars in the Medicaid program—more than $2 billion in fiscal 1977, depending on our estimates for fraud and abuse.

It is thus vital that we take aggressive action now to curtail this serious drain of taxpayer dollars.

In just the ineligibility, overpayment and third party areas alone, *we estimate we can save $500 million in federal and state leakage of Medicaid funds in fiscal 1979, and a total of more than $2 billion by fiscal 1981, or $12 saved for every $1 it will cost to put controls into effect for these problems.*

Through more aggressive identification and pursuit of fraud and abuse—under our recently launched Project Integrity, as well as with the new tools available to us from enactment of H.R. 3—we can also begin to cut down on funds wasted due to that problem.

Let me describe some of our efforts and initiatives for you in greater detail.

PROJECT INTEGRITY

Project Integrity was commenced by the Department last April, as a joint project of the Office of the Inspector General and the Health Care Financing Administration. It has three principal goals:

- To ferret out cases of clear cut fraud by Medicaid doctors or pharmacists and to refer such cases for criminal prosecution, where necessary;
- To identify cases of Medicaid abuse in which the doctor or pharmacist might stop short of outright criminal culpability, but might deserve civil or administrative sanctions for improper practices; and
- To develop the data for a careful overall examination of how the Medicaid claims processing system works so that weaknesses which permit such fraud and abuse to occur can be identified and remedied.

Project Integrity uses computer technology to search for fraud and abuse by quickly screening an enormous inventory of state Medicaid billing records. As you can imagine, we need a tremendous amount of cooperation from the states in this project, and their cooperation has generally been as enthusiastic as it is vital to the program's success.

I want to stress that this is the first time the federal government has organized a nationwide attack on Medicaid fraud and abuse, using consistent national ground rules for the selection of cases, and bringing together, in the same time frame, available federal and state forces to work as a team.

Over 350 state personnel have been assigned to Project Integrity around the country. These resources augment the very limited resources we have available within HEW—162 personnel in HCFA and the Inspector General's audit agency and Office of Inspections. Both state and federal manpower need to be increased, but the states have generally acted in exemplary cooperation with the Department in this effort.

I think it might be helpful to give you an overview of the way Project Integrity functions. I should note at the outset that we focused on doctors and pharmacists in the Medicaid program *not* because we thought doctors and pharmacists had different performance records than other types of providers, but because records for doctors and pharmacists were already computerized by the states, and we had already developed a method of analyzing the computer data at hand.

First, we sought to determine reasonable levels of medical service and drug prescriptions for individual patients for a number of different procedures and drugs. Parameters for these levels were established in close consultation among medical and pharmaceutical experts both within and outside the government.

For example, we determined that more than 40 office visits, 20 home visits, 25 injections, or one tonsillectomy for the same patient in one year might be *prima facie* evidence to warrant further inquiry. We were able to identify 22 common medical procedures and 26 drugs and drug groups, for which limits could reasonably be established.

Second, once these parameters were established, it became a relatively simple matter to ask a computer to screen *all* state Medicaid billing records to identify individual physicians or pharmacists whose billings were in excess of parameters. Their names, number of patients treated, total reimbursement from Medicaid and other statistical data were printed out as a result of the computer screen.

Once these printouts were available, further analysis of the data enabled us to identify and select the most obvious cases for further investigation. The first time around the 25 pharmacists and 25 physicians whose records were most indicative of possible fraud or abuse were selected in each state. We proceeded in each state—rather than on the apparently worst cases across the nation—in order to get as many states involved as possible. And we selected 50 apparent cases per state—rather than all promising cases in a particular jurisdiction—because of limited manpower.

Third, after preliminary screening and selection of 50 cases per state, the records in these cases were then subjected to a validation process. The claims-invoices were pulled out and the cases examined. The purpose of this validation was to determine that the data in the original computer printouts were correct. We also wanted to determine whether there were any obvious reasons why the statistically aberrant data might in fact be acceptable in a particular case.

Fourth, once this process was completed, cases were turned over to a three-person team in each regional office, whose responsibility was to oversee further investigations. These teams are led by the Inspector General's Office of Investigations and contain key personnel from HCFA's field force of Program Integrity specialists and from the Audit Agency. These teams are available to work with the states or to conduct investigations when states are unable to do so. They are supplemented in some instances by the FBI and the Drug Enforcement Administration. As a result of investigations, cases may be dropped, they may lead to administrative or civil actions, or they may be earmarked as potential criminal cases deserving still more intensive investigations. After further intensive investigation the most serious cases may be referred for prosecution or more stringent administrative or civil action may be sought.

Under Project Integrity, we have thus far screened a total of 250 million paid billings representing 275,000 providers in the 49 Medicaid states (Arizona does not participate in the program), the District of Columbia and Puerto Rico.

From that group, over 47,000 providers were printed out who exceeded the parameters we established.

Of those, we have thus far selected 2,434 cases which appeared to involve the most blatant forms of abuse.

Of these 2,434 validated cases, nearly 1,950 have been turned over to the states for review and participation in the investigation when possible.

Of those turned over to the states, over 500 are now being actively investigated in order to determine whether the providers' own records indicate the presence of fraud or abuse.

In some states, providers identified by the computer were already under investigation, and their cases have been merged with Project Integrity. In a few other states, grand jury proceedings have begun. But most cases are at this time in the stage of initial examination, with decisions still to be made on whether administrative, civil or criminal actions are appropriate.

Unfortunately, the impression has been created that we expect every Project Integrity case to merit criminal prosecution. That is definitely not so. It is difficult to predict how many cases will be referred for criminal investigation or how many will lead to prosecution, but we estimate that perhaps 5 or 10 percent will reach this stage, with the largest number requiring administrative sanctions.

In order to protect the rights of suspects and so that prosecutions or other administrative actions can be based on sound development of the facts, we are proceeding carefully, in conjunction with the states, during this investigative phase of the initial 2,434 cases. As these cases move through the pipeline—and investigative resources become available—we will continue to examine the list of other providers who appear to violate our parameters of sound practice.

The long term results from Project Integrity are likely to range far beyond the indictment of or assessment of penalties against doctors or pharmacists.

For in an important sense Project Integrity is merely an experimental first step toward widespread and systematic changes in the way we process and pay for claims in *both* Medicare and Medicaid.

For example, we plan to analyze the relationships between apparent physician and pharmacist abusers who appear in our first printouts and nursing home and hospital charges.

Further, we expect to use this data bank for analyzing the levels of services provided to recipients by physicians and pharmacists, on a state-by-state basis, to develop comparisons for further study.

In addition, learning from our experience with physicians and pharmacists, we plan to conduct a number of inquiries into the activities of other providers. We now have audit agency teams developing computer screening programs to analyze billing practices in the following areas:

- outpatient clinics;
- durable medical equipment;
- clinical laboratories;
- dentists;
- medical transportation; and
- non-medical providers such as chiropractors and podiatrists.

We expect the results of our current and future efforts under this project to accrue to the benefit of both the Medicaid and Medicare programs.

In addition, Project Integrity is only one anti-fraud and abuse effort in the Medicaid program. Some 2,000 state employees are directly involved in the investigation of fraud. In the year ending June 30, there were 63 convictions for fraud as a result of their work.

A contract has been made with the state of New York for a two-year Demonstration Study of hospital costs, with emphasis on disclosing fraud and abuse problems, techniques of uncovering these problems, and the most appropriate investigative and prosecutorial techniques. This project will be directed by Mr. Charles J. Hynes, New York Deputy Attorney General, who has had an outstanding success in his role as Special State Prosecutor for Nursing Homes.

We will also continue to give major attention to studies in the nursing home area, building in part on the lessons learned by Mr. Hynes.

With the enactment of H.R. 3, we expect these efforts to multiply and become more effective, as more states develop effective anti-fraud units. We hope to issue interim regulations and certify the first of these new state units by early 1978.

H.R. 3 also mandates a comprehensive study of Home Health Agencies, with a report to the Congress within one year. We welcome this assignment and have already begun an early field study with the Florida Department of Health and Rehabilitative Services.

We will be releasing guidelines in the near future for states to use in imposing administrative sanctions, where state law permits, against providers who have abused the program. These guidelines will help ensure proper handling of such providers as they are identified through state fraud and abuse control efforts. Examples of abuse include:

- billing for unnecessary services,
- consistent over-charging, and
- upgrading services on billing forms to claim higher reimbursement.

Appropriate sanctions or corrective actions include:

- A warning letter and voluntary recovery,
- Suspension of payments in whole or in part, or
- Suspension or termination of provider participation.

Following release of these guidelines, we will be making contact with each state to determine their impact on existing state procedures. Training sessions with appropriate state officials will also be conducted to assure proper and consistent application by states.

I suspect we have much to learn about how to apply appropriate administrative sanctions, and to that end I am asking the Administrator of HCFA and the Inspector General to conduct early conferences with state personnel to discuss these matters and seek to formulate more adequate remedies for the future.

For example, we are now developing model state legislation which may be necessary to permit states to act quickly to terminate participation of those providers who abuse or defraud the program. In Illinois, the state Supreme Court recently ruled that the state did not have authority to suspend a clinical laboratory which had pled guilty to defrauding the program. Over a hundred similar administrative suspensions were placed in jeopardy by this ruling.

In summary, we are pleased with the outlook for success for our various programs to expose and sharply reduce fraud and abuse and waste in the Medicaid Program. These are among our most complex problems, and we must put to use the most advanced management techniques to solve

them, working in full partnership with the states.

MEDICAID ELIGIBILITY QUALITY CONTROL

Fraud and abuse is not the only source of wasteful spending we have identified under Medicaid. We now estimate that one out of every eleven dollars spent by Medicaid at any given time is for an ineligible person. This has led to approximately 1.2 billion dollars of excess Medicaid expenditures by federal and state governments during fiscal year 1977.

Our ability to identify the magnitude of error and project the waste results from our Medicaid Eligibility Quality Control program (MEQC).

The MEQC program has been adopted from private industry quality control techniques. It is designed so that both the state and federal government can monitor the proportion of Medicaid payments to ineligible recipients.

Before I describe this program in detail, I should make clear what we mean by "Ineligible Recipients." There are currently 21.6 million Medicaid recipients. Eligibility for Medicaid is determined primarily on the basis of financial need for individuals in three basic categories:

- 10.8 million individuals who are in the AFDC program;
- 5.6 million SSI recipients; and
- 5.2 million individuals who may not qualify for AFDC or SSI, but who are eligible for Medicaid because they meet the state income requirements or because their health care expenses cause them to "spend down" to that income level.*

---

*If, for example, the state Medicaid level is $3,000 and the individual's income is $3,200, he or she would become eligible for Medicaid in some states *after* spending $200 on medical care.

When individuals are no longer eligible for Medicaid because they do not fall in one of the three categories outlined above, claims paid for them are not proper.

It is important to note, however, that such payments may be made to individuals who have just left or are about to be added to the Medicaid rolls and are thus only marginally ineligible. During development of the Administration's National Health Insurance Plan, we will, of course, be looking carefully at some of the larger questions regarding the appropriate scope and type of coverage for all low income individuals. I should also point out that, as part of the MEQC program, we are reviewing the number of persons who are denied Medicaid or who are terminated from the Medicaid rolls to protect against error in those areas as well.

The MEQC program does not actually draw its sample from the entire universe of Medicaid recipients. Rather, the sample is drawn from a population comprised of 3.2 million of the SSI Medicaid recipients and all 5.2 million of the third category of recipients I referred to above—those Medicaid recipients who are not categorically eligible for AFDC or SSI.

This is done so as not to overlap with eligibility reviews already underway for the AFDC and part of the SSI segments of the Medicaid population.

The population from which the sample is drawn accounts for 39 percent of the recipients and 55 percent of the total dollars spent under Medicaid.

The states themselves are required to review a statistical sample of 18,000 claims out of this population every six months under MEQC. Then, the federal government conducts an in-depth review of 3,500 of those claims to ensure that states have developed accurate and valid results.

From this review, we are able, within limits, to determine a statistically valid percentage of erroneous payments both in each state and in the nation as a whole. We then apply that percentage to the total dollar amount paid out to the particular categories of Medicaid recipients sampled, and we can determine relatively closely the total amount paid in error for that group.

Last April, we released the first six month MEQC survey, covering the period October, 1975, to March, 1976.

Today, I am releasing our latest data, covering the six month period between April, 1976, and September, 1976. Our analysis of the MEQC data collected for the latter period indicates that 8.6 percent of the payments made on behalf of Medicaid recipients were paid erroneously, compared to 9 percent in the earlier survey. The total annualized dollar amount of these errors is projected to be $882 million for the fiscal year 1977, compared to an annualized amount of $715 million for fiscal 1976, based on the earlier survey.

MEQC also enables us to determine the basic source of the errors, so that we can begin to take steps to reduce them.

Thirty-seven percent of the errors appeared to be client errors—clients erroneously filing claims, concealing income, not providing enough data, etc.—while the majority of errors, 63 percent were agency errors. The percentage of agency errors is higher in the most recent data than in the previous sample, when the figures were 42 percent client and 58 percent agency errors. The current high level and apparent growth in agency errors is disturbing, and we must redouble our efforts to eliminate these mistakes. Better training programs for eligibility workers, claims form and procedure simplification, and other technical assistance are clearly required.

When the error rate for the segment of the Medicaid population sampled by MEQC is combined with the estimated ineligibility rate for the AFDC and SSI populations, an overall payment error rate of 7 percent can be estimated. That rate resulted in nearly $1 billion in erroneous payments for ineligible recipients in fiscal year 1976 and in approximately $1.2 billion in such erroneous payments for the total Medicaid program for fiscal 1977.

In addition to ineligibility payment errors, the Medicaid program also experiences leakage in other significant areas.

For example, we have also identified approximately $600 million a year which is not being collected by Medicaid from third party reimbursers, such as workers' compensation funds, private insurance companies, and Medicare.

In another area, approximately 200 million dollars is being lost through claims processing errors such as: duplicate payments, overpayments, payments for uncovered services, payments to ineligible providers, and payments for services for which recipients are not eligible.

NEXT STEPS

There are a number of ways we can begin to plug up the holes and put an end to this leakage.

- We are expanding the MEQC program so that we can get even more accurate data for ourselves and for the states. We hope to expand the sample, and to apply it to the total Medicaid program, rather than just the smaller segment of the Medicaid population currently sampled.
- We are evaluating our manpower requirements in this area so we have a realistic assessment of the kinds of personnel needs we must fulfill if the program is to operate effectively at this stage in its development.
- We are exploring the possibility of new fiscal incentive for states, to encourage them to improve their control over eligibility errors, and claims processing and review procedures.
- We are planning to provide considerable additional technical assistance to

the states, in order to help them with error detection, claims form simplification, improved training of eligibility workers, and wider automation of antiquated systems. In this regard, we are reviewing efforts to get states to use the computerized Medicaid Management Information System (MMIS), and related computerized subsystems.
- With regard to collecting third party payments, we are encouraging states to adopt improved recovery systems. Last year, for example, the state of Michigan used a computer and a small third-party liability staff to recover over $3 million in Medicaid funds. Next year, with 24 people concentrating on third-party liability recoveries, Michigan expects to save $20 million.

We hope to be able to use these and other improved techniques and procedures to reduce erroneous payments for ineligibles by 1 percentage point each year over the next three fiscal years.

From an overall Medicaid rate of 7 percent this year, we hope to reduce errors to 6 percent in fiscal 1979, to 5 percent in fiscal 1980, and to 4 percent in fiscal 1981.

If we can do so, we will save $200 million in fiscal 1979, $300 million in fiscal 1980, and $800 million by fiscal 1981 in the ineligible claim area alone.

If you add in the potential savings of improved third party payments and claims processing, we can realize a total of over $2 billion in savings in the next three fiscal years under these improved procedures, or twelve times more than we will spend to implement them.

We are entering a new area of management capability in HEW. We want the Department to serve as a striking example that social programs can be managed in a fair, humane, *and* fiscally responsible fashion. Our efforts in controlling the fraud, abuse and waste in the Medicaid program will go a long way toward realizing that goal.

42. Through the Medicaid Mills

FRANK E. MOSS

Reprinted with permission from Legal Aspects of Medical Practice/*The Journal of Legal Medicine*, Vol. 5, No. 5, pp. 6–11 (May 1977).

"Medicaid isn't medicine, it's business. Curing patients is good medicine but bad business." This cynical assessment was given me by a Medicaid mill owner during the course of an investigation in which I posed as a patient.

Why had I, a U.S. senator, turned sleuth?

As chairman of the Subcommittee on Long-Term Care of the Senate Committee on Aging for some 14 years, I conducted since 1969 some 49 hearings related to Medicare and Medicaid abuse.

One result of this work was our 12-volume report on nursing home problems. One such report was an indepth study of the flow of drugs through nursing homes, which, we concluded, is essentially without controls. We were also able to provide a detailed discussion of what we termed "widespread kickbacks" between nursing home operators and pharmacists.

In September 1975, we started the first phase of our intensified investigation of possible fraud and abuse among clinical laboratories and related fraud perpetrated by owners of "Medicaid mills," which are small shared health facilities that checker the ghettos of major cities, catering to the walk-in trade.

Working with the Better Government Association, we rented a storefront in Chicago, pretending to be a group of practitioners opening for business. A sign in the window and a telephone number announced: "Professional Inquiries Invited." It wasn't long before our telephone started ringing off the hook. Representatives of 12 laboratories appeared at our storefront and offered our investigators kickbacks ranging from 25 to 55 per cent if we would agree to send all our laboratory business to their particular laboratory.

Armed with information that 12 laboratories gave kickbacks and knowing the general amount that was offered, investigators sifted through paid billings in the Illinois Comptroller's Office and constructed a profile on each laboratory. We knew precisely which physicians used each of the 12 laboratories. We then selected for interview 50 physicians from this list.

Our investigators found that the physicians were primarily foreign medical graduates working for Medicaid mills. When confronted with our information, most readily admitted receiving kickbacks from the laboratories as well as from other providers.

However, in at least half of the interviews, the foreign-trained physicians were not the recipients of the kickbacks. We learned that the illegal rebates were being paid to the businessmen who owned the

Medicaid mills. We were amazed to learn that many of these physicians were working essentially on commission. They were allowed to keep only 20 to 40 per cent of the monies they generated from seeing Medicaid patients. Clearly, their incentive was to "optimize patients"—that is, to see as many patients as possible and to order as many tests as possible. In our financial analyses, we found that some Medicaid mills receive over a million dollars from Medicaid each year. Of this amount, more than 60 per cent was going to various businessmen who owned or rented the Medicaid premises.

Our committee staff called attention to these matters in the report, adding a number of startling conclusions. For example, the report concluded that one dollar out of every five paid for clinical laboratory services is fraudulent. It concluded that a small number of laboratories control the bulk of Medicaid business.

In New York, 17 labs control 70 per cent of the Medicaid business. In New Jersey, 12 labs control nearly 60 per cent of Medicaid payments. In Illinois, 12 labs control over 65 per cent of the Medicaid business.

The report concludes that, at least in the states that came under investigation, kickbacks are widespread among labs specializing in Medicaid business. In fact, it appears to be necessary to give a kickback to secure the business of physicians or clinics who specialize in the treatment of welfare patients.

The average kickback to physicians or medical center owners in Illinois was 30 per cent of the monthly total the lab received for performing tests for Medicaid patients. Kickbacks took several forms, including cash, furnishing supplies, business machines, care or other gratuities as well as paying part of a physician's payroll expenses. Most commonly, it involved the supposed rental of a small space in a medical clinic.

Our report concludes it is apparent that the law passed by the Congress in 1972, prohibiting kickbacks and mandating a $10,000 fine and a year in jail upon conviction, is not being enforced.

When I was confronted with an early draft of this report, I was shocked by the conclusions the staff reached in their investigation with Chicago's Better Government Association. I decided to go to Chicago and see things for myself.

Accompanied by Senator Pete V. Domenici of New Mexico:

- I saw the proliferation of so-called Medical Clinics spreading like mushrooms all over Chicago.
- I saw their glaring signs beckoning Medicaid patients to utilize health care services.
- I visited a postage stamp sized clinical laboratory that billed Medicaid for almost $200,000 last year. There was little in the way of equipment and no lab technicians in evidence. While the owner assured us as to the quality of the work performed, I heard from the owner himself that he chose to send his wife's blood test to another laboratory.
- I visited the sparkling new Laboratory of Illinois Masonic Hospital and saw its sophisticated new machines, but I learned the hospital could not obtain much Medicaid lab business because of its refusal to offer kickbacks.
- I interviewed a physician who received over $100,000 from Medicaid last year. I asked him to check against his records nine lab invoices that had been presented to Medicaid for payment by D.J. Clinical Laboratory of Chicago. The doctor told us he had not ordered 55 per cent of the $259 total on those invoices of lab tests for which D.J. had billed the Illinois Medicaid program. This same physician told us that he received a rebate of $1,000 per month from the laboratory in exchange for

sending all this Medicaid business. The kickback was disguised as rent for a 6 × 8 foot room in the physician's office. The doctor's rent for the entire suite was $300 a month; yet he received $1,000 per month for the "rental" of a 6 × 8 room!

- Finally, I interviewed a businessman who owns two medical clinics employing foreign-trained doctors who received about $300,000 in Medicaid business last year. This man admitted sending all of his lab business to one company in Chicago. He told us he received a rebate of 50 per cent of the amount Medicaid paid for laboratory tests physicians in his clinics ordered for welfare patients.

I cite these facts in support of the contention that fraud and abuse is rampant in the Medicaid program. In my view, this is because of the bifurcated nature of the Medicaid program. Both the states and the federal government are looking to each other to prevent fraud and abuse. Legally, the states are responsible, at least this is my reading of Title 19.

In order to document this problem further, I decided to take an in-depth look at the operation of the Medicaid program in the state of New York. In addition to the normal investigative techniques, it was decided to have investigators pose as Medicaid patients entering shared health facilities for treatment. Our staff also posed as businessmen who answered ads in the *New York Times* in which every Sunday Medicaid mills are offered for sale. Our findings are contained in the report entitled, "Fraud and Abuse Among Practitioners Participating in the Medicaid Program." We learned much from this experience.

The provider abuse and surveillance activities in the city and state of New York are in a shambles. Despite the fact that federal funds have been made available at the rate of 90 per cent for development and 75 per cent of the operating costs of automated data systems, the management systems at the state and county level have not been modified since the start of the Medicaid program 10 years ago. New York City, despite an impressive computer capability, does not have such rudimentary fraud detection aides as provider, vendor, and recipient profiles. All of its files beyond the past three months are stored in cardboard boxes in a warehouse in Ryerson Street in Brooklyn. Efforts to prosecute cases have been hampered by the inability to retrieve the original providers' invoices from these cardboard boxes, which are often broken open and scattered about. One city employee on the scene told us that "if we can recover 50 per cent of the invoices we want, we're lucky."

As an example of what happened when perfectly healthy Senate investigators entered Medicaid mills posing as derelicts, I offer the following:

- Private Roberts entered Gouveneur Medical Center in the Lower East Side of Manhattan, New York City, complaining of burning and discharge in his urinary tract. He was given a general physical and a tuberculosis test, told he had a heart murmur and given an electrocardiogram. A second shopper, Investigator William Halamandaris, entered the same clinic several minutes later complaining of a possible head cold. His "head cold" was diagnosed as "sinusitis." He was given a general physical, an ECG, a TB test, told he had a severe heart murmur and that he probably had rheumatic fever as a child. In addition, the doctor ordered a series of x-rays of the patient's sinuses and chest, and referred him to the heart specialist—*all in the space of three minutes.*

  A third shopper, Patricia G. Oriol, chief clerk of the Senate Committee on Aging, entered this same clinic a month later complaining of a possible cold. She, too, was told she had a severe heart murmur and high blood pressure and told to return for further tests.

All three shoppers were given a large amount of medication and specifically instructed to have the prescriptions filled "at the pharmacy next door." (It is a violation of New York state law to recommend a specific pharmacy.)

- At the Riis-Wald Medical Center on the Lower East Side, Private McDew was given a general physical, referred to the chiropractor and the podiatrist. The podiatrist informed Private McDew that he had hammer toe and flat feet (for which the podiatrist placed "arches"—actually small pieces of sponge in his tennis shoes). He was also told his feet sweat. Subsequently, the same shopper met the same podiatrist (again on referral as a result of a "ping-pong") in a second clinic in Uptown Harlem. The podiatrist, after putting face and name together, checked his notebook and informed our investigator: "Remember what you had before? Well, you've got it again." He placed another set of "arch supports"—this time in the investigator's oxfords. In addition to arch supports, Private McDew received skull and chest x-rays (more than 10) and was ordered to return "next week" for additional tests. When Private Roberts entered Riis-Wald clinic, he received a general physical and was referred to the chiropractor who ordered a full set of x-rays. He was also referred to the podiatrist but had to refuse treatment because his toes had been painted the previous day by another podiatrist.
- At the East Harlem Medical Center, Private McDew asked to see a podiatrist. He was sent, instead, to the general practitioner and owner. The doctor listened to his chest and referred

him to the chiropractor. He saw the podiatrist only after he had seen all other practitioners in the facility. Despite the nature of his complaint, "The bottom of my feet hurt," blood and urine samples were taken and his chest and feet were x-rayed. The podiatrist prescribed ankle braces, which Private McDew was told to obtain "down the street" from a particular supplier. He was specifically referred to the East 116th Street Pharmacy to fill three pharmaceutical prescriptions, which included two antibiotics. Private Roberts entered this same clinic complaining of tiredness and received a general physical. He was referred to the podiatrist and given a future appointment to see the psychiatrist. Blood and urine samples were taken. His feet and chest were x-rayed and he was given two prescriptions, which he was told to fill at the adjoining pharmacy.

I, too, posed as a Medicaid patient and sought treatment at the East Harlem Medical Center and two other "mills" in New York. From that experience, I formed some impressions as to what it is like to be a Medicaid patient. At our recent hearings, I gave these impressions:

If you are a Medicaid patient, you can expect to be treated in a clinic located in a dilapidated part of the city.

The outside of these clinics, or Medicaid mills, are garish. Most offer a brick facade. They may be brightly painted, with awnings, banners, and pennants attracting the eye. The front window lists an impressive array of services—everything from a psychiatrist to a podiatrist.

Inside, the mill will be cramped and sparsely furnished. It will be dirty. Cleanliness is not prized in Medicaid mills; it costs too much money. The floors look like they haven't been swept in a month and the restrooms are abominable.

As you enter a mill you will be greeted by a receptionist or someone who looks like a nurse. This is important because you never know for sure. This "receptionist" will ask for your Medicaid card. She will Xerox it a number of times. You may be asked whom you want to see or what is your medical problem. Or you may not.

Now you wait for an hour, sometimes two. While you wait the receptionist or someone else may suggest that you should see Dr. So-and-so, the chiropractor, or Dr. XYZ, the podiatrist.

When you do get to see a practitioner, your visit will be brief—usually from three to five minutes—and the examining room will be tiny.

You will be given a general examination no matter how specific your complaint. If blood pressure is taken or a stethoscope is used, the odds are it will be done through your clothing. It is likely that you will not be touched. Medicaid doctors do not like touching their patients.

At some point, the doctor will take blood. The taking of blood confirms that treatment has been rendered to the patient. But, perhaps just as important, samples presented to clinical laboratories will generate a return of $15 each from the laboratory.

In addition, you are going to be asked for a urine sample; you will be given a number of x-rays and perhaps a shot or two. You can count on receiving several prescriptions. In most cases you will be directed to a particular pharmacy to have your prescriptions filled.

If you're not sick, you won't be told you're not sick. If you are sick, the odds are you won't be helped. Patients who are cured may stop running through the mill, generating reimbursements for the owners.

From our experience posing as businessmen who were trying to buy into the Medicaid mill business, we gathered totally incredible information. Mill owners told us "how to maximize our patient revenues," how to cheat and not get caught, and that protection against the enforcement of existing standards could be purchased by payoffs to appropriate city health officials.

Accompanied by a physician, we sometimes got down to dickering on the price we would pay. One owner wanted to make us a package deal and throw in some of his "Medicare mills" in Miami. Still other owners spoke of the involvement of organized crime in the business. They spoke of using arson as a means of disposing of an unprofitable mill—collecting the fire insurance. They spoke of some union officials who allegedly are running a protection racket charging a "finder's fee" for allowing a mill to be located in a particular area.

All of these facts were turned over to the U.S. Attorneys in the Southern District of New York and Northern District of Illinois, with whom we were working closely. The investigations continue.

From my firsthand personal experience, I am outraged. I am angry that money the Congress has appropriated for care of the aged, blind, and disabled is going to line the pockets of a few businessmen and real estate operators who own shared health facilities in the ghettos of our large cities. I am angry that more than 10 years after the enactment of the Medicaid program we find the resurrection of that abhorrent dual track of medical care that provides one standard of care for the rich or comfortable and another for the poor. I am angry that so much of the taxpayers' hard-earned dollars are lost to fraud and abuse. Our citizens work too hard for their money to be able to stomach the fraud and abuse that by now must be evident to anyone who subjects the Medicaid program to even the slightest scrutiny.

If I were to estimate how much fraud there is in Medicaid, I would guess about 10 per cent, or $1.7-billion. This is just an educated guess—many people who have worked in this field tell me its more like 20 per cent. However, I suggest the size of the theft is not the worst problem. There is abundant evidence that Medicaid is not working. Our inability to manage this program casts a cloud over our ability to manage a 10 times larger national health insurance.

By way of solutions, I endorse the fraud and abuse bill that the Congress is considering. This will help in the short run. Last year I sponsored a bill creating an Office of Inspector General in HEW, which the Congress accepted. I also suggest creating a new division of Health and Welfare Fraud within the Department of Justice to prosecute fraud in government health care programs. The rationale for this idea is that we learned that thousands of dollars were being lost to the Federal Treasury every day because of the running of the statute of limitations. Numerous lawbreakers escaped punishment as Medicare and Medicaid cases languished on the desks of our U.S. Attorneys.

By way of long-run solutions, I think the Congress must take a hard look at the way we finance government health care programs and fashion appropriate solutions. The abuses call for prompt and effective remedies.

43. H.R. 3. The Medicare-Medicaid Anti-Fraud and Abuse Amendments

SUZANNE STONE

HR-3. The Medicare-Medicaid Anti-Fraud and Abuse Amendments. Major impact: on all Medicare and Medicaid providers, including pharmacists. Passed by the House on September 23, 1977. Passed by the Senate (as S-143) on September 30. Both bills referred to Conference. Conference report agreed to on October 13. Signed into law as HR-3 (Public Law 95-142) on October 25. President Carter's observation on signing the legislation: "This bill will go a long way to eliminating fraud in the administration of the health care programs of this country."

Passed by Congress under the scrutiny of a body politic energized with a Watergate watcher's sensitivity to public and private sector dishonesty, HR-3 puts strong teeth into federal programs designed to prevent fraud and abuse in the Medicare and Medicaid programs.

No provider of Medicare or Medicaid—including pharmacists—is left unaffected by the legislation, and *American Pharmacy* asked APhA staff member Suzanne Stone to prepare the following analysis of the law's major provisions.

Section 2 (Prohibition of Assignment of Claims; Medicaid Claims Payment Procedures). The provision of HR-3 which will be most welcome to pharmacists is Section 2. It requires state Medicaid programs to eliminate the long delays many pharmacists have experienced in obtaining payment of their claims.

Specifically, state Medicaid programs will be required to pay 90 percent of all "clean" (defined as not needing further substantiation) claims within 30 days of filing, and 99 percent of such claims within 90 days. This provision applies to claims submitted by pharmacists, and stipulates that a state would not be found in noncompliance with this requirement if HEW found the state was acting "in good faith" to achieve this.

Section 4 (Penalties for defrauding Medicare and Medicaid) strengthens existing penalty provisions. Most fraudulent acts are now classified as felonies and are subject, upon conviction, to a fine of not more than $25,000, imprisonment for not more than five years, or both. *Any person* who solicits or receives any remuneration (including kickbacks, bribes, or rebates)—(1) in return for referring an individual to a person for the furnishing, or arranging for the furnishing of items or services; or (2) in return for the purchasing, leasing, or ordering, or arranging for, or recommending the

393

purchasing, leasing, or ordering of goods, facilities, or services—is subject to the penalty provisions.

Similarly subject are people who offer or pay any remuneration (including kickbacks, bribes, or rebates) to someone to induce him to take part in similar activities which would be subject to the penalty provisions.

The legislation specifically excludes the practice of discounting or other reductions in price from those financial transactions considered illegal, but only if such discounts are properly disclosed and reflected in the cost for which reimbursement could be claimed.

Also defined as a felony under the new law is requiring contributions (gifts, money, and donations) as a condition of entry or continued stay at a hospital or long-term care facility for patients whose care is financed in whole or in part by Medicaid.

Section 7 (Suspension of Practitioners) provides for an additional penalty—suspension from the program—whenever the HEW secretary determines that a practitioner has been convicted of a criminal offense related to that practitioner's involvement in Medicare or Medicaid. The secretary can suspend the practitioner from participation in the program for as long as he wishes.

Section 3 (Disclosure of Provider Ownership and Financial Information) requires, as a condition of participation, certification or recertification in either Medicare, Medicaid, or the Maternal and Child Health program, or Title XX of the Social Security Act, that participating "entities" disclose specified ownership data to HEW or the appropriate state agency.

"Entities"—which are defined to include providers of services—must supply full and complete information as to the identity of each person who:

1. has a direct or indirect ownership interest of five percent or more in the entity;

2. owns (in whole or in part) a five percent interest in any mortgage secured by the entity;
3. is an officer or director of the entity, if it is organized as a corporation;
4. is a partner in the entity, if it is organized as a partnership.

Where disclosing entities which provide services under Medicare or Medicaid own five percent or more of a subcontractor, or where a subcontractor has more than $25,000 in annual business transactions with a reporting entity, similar ownership information must be disclosed about the subcontractor.

A related provision requires disclosure of information on specific business transactions. For example, if a pharmacist owns both a long-term care facility and a pharmacy which supplies drug products to that facility, full and complete information about business transactions between these two facilities for the prior five years must be disclosed if requested by the secretary of HEW or an appropriate state agency.

Section 8 (Disclosure by Providers of Owners and Certain Other Individuals Convicted of Certain Offenses) requires that all *institutional* providers of service be required, as a condition of participation, certification, or recertification in Medicare, Medicaid, or Title XX, to disclose in the application for ownership or certification the names of people who have a five percent ownership interest. Disclosure is also required of those who are owners, officers, directors, agents, or managing employees and who have previously been convicted of fraud against the Medicare, Medicaid, or Title XX program.

Section 6 (Issuance of Subpoena by Comptroller General) authorizes the U.S. Comptroller General to sign and to issue subpoenas to obtain necessary information for, and to facilitate review of, all Social Security Act programs. The Comptroller

General is further authorized, upon resistance or refusal of an individual to obey a subpoena, to request a court order requiring compliance with the subpoena.

Under Section 15 of the law, any provider of services participating in Medicare is required to notify the HEW secretary promptly of its employment of an individual who, at any time during the preceding year, was employed in a managerial, accounting, auditing, or similar capacity by a Medicare fiscal intermediary or carrier that serves the provider.

Section 9 (Federal Access to Medicaid Records) allows the federal government access to the records of people or institutions providing services under Medicaid, just as such access is presently provided to state agencies.

Certain administrative changes are effected by the passage of these Amendments:

Section 17 (Funding of State Medicaid Fraud Control Units) provides for special funding of programs within a state to establish an office to prosecute cases of suspected fraud and abuse in Medicaid provisions. The law also authorizes the HEW secretary to arrange for demonstration projects designed to develop improved programs for detection, investigation, and prosecution of fraud and abuse.

Section 19 (Uniform Reporting Systems for Health Service Facilities and Organizations) requires HEW to establish for each type of health service facility or organization a uniform system for the reporting information.

There are a total of 28 sections in the new law. Copies of the law may be obtained by sending a self-addressed mailing label along with a request for a copy of P.L. 95–142 to the Document Room, The House of Representatives, Washington, D.C. 20515.

44. Experience Teaches That NHI Will Be Gradual: What I Have Learned

WILBUR J. COHEN

Reprinted with permission from *Hospital Progress*, March 1978. Copyright 1978 by The Catholic Hospital Association.

I began working in the area of social policy some 44 years ago in 1934 when, as a young man, I became the research assistant of Edwin E. Witte, then executive director of President Franklin D. Roosevelt's Cabinet Committee on Economic Security. One of my first assignments was to study the social security, unemployment insurance, and health insurance programs of foreign countries. Since that time, I have continued to follow the experiences of other nations in social security and health insurance with interest and fascination, visiting a dozen countries and studying their programs at first hand.

From these studies I have learned that it is not possible to transfer foreign experience directly to the American environment. Our political and economic institutions differ from those elsewhere. Our social policies and attitudes regarding work, leisure, family, and government are also different. Thus, even if the lessons to be derived from foreign experience in the health and welfare areas are crystal clear, the American voter is not necessarily knowledgeable about or impressed by them.

The American situation is one in which experience is the teacher—new policies and programs emerge and evolve through the trial and error of experience. The American voter, taxpayer, and citizen is less philosophical and ideological than he or she is pragmatic and realistic. The typical American, however, also tends to be idealistic, although this idealism is tempered by realism. The vast improvements in the status of the poor, women, social and religious minorities, and other disadvantaged groups in recent years testify to these general observations.

From these lessons in analyzing both foreign and American experience and temperament, I have become convinced we must develop a national health policy and program in the United States on an incremental basis—adopting a step-by-step, gradual approach, rather than attempting quick and total immersion.

Because of my close association with the formulation of both Medicare and Medicaid during the period from 1943 to 1965, I am often asked what I think about their success or failure. Certainly, faults, errors, and problems exist in these fragmented programs, just as they do in other services and institutions—the family, marriage, business, church, government, mail service, and tax system. But Medicare and Medicaid have provided payment for services to the aged, children, and minorities—payment that very likely would not otherwise have existed. In addition, both programs have taught the nation a great deal about the complex problems involved in the health care delivery system that we could not have learned in any other way. And they have taught us more about the economics and politics of health care than we ever knew before. In these respects, they have been a tremendous success. No longer are we dealing with a general theory or a vague concept of health care financing. We are dealing with a living and imperfect institution, which we can make better by applying our minds and energies.

A tremendous achievement of Medicare and Medicaid has been the breakdown of segregation in many hospitals, clinics, nursing homes, and doctors' offices. The South offered a minimum of opposition when the programs were put into operation in 1965–1966, and the "white" and "colored" signs over water fountains and rest rooms came down overnight. As a result of Medicare, today minority individuals in every state in the union receive medical care without loss of their dignity and respect. Medicare and Medicaid came at the right moment in history to help make this possible. These accomplishments taught me that an ethical ideal can be achieved through institutional change and that it is always wise when changes occur to expect the unexpected. I have also learned this from 43 years of following legislative developments in Congress.

Will the United States ever have a comprehensive national health program for everyone in the nation? I think we will. I doubt, however, whether such a program will be enacted overnight by a single stroke of the pen. I believe we will take further steps toward it within the next few years. They will be important steps—some big, some little—but not perfect or complete. Finding the accommodation between legislative objectives and administrative reality will be a long and continuing process.

A number of questions must be discussed and resolved as we go about planning a program. In my judgment health insurance involves so many sensitive and complex political, emotional, and financial issues that it should be in the hands of a board, not in the hands of a single administrator, no matter how competent. Arrangements must be such that physicians and hospitals can perform their services efficiently and cooperatively. Benefits should be phased in gradually. And a comprehensive public information and health education program should be part of the total effort in order to further key issues and to prevent excessive demands on the medical care system. Others will have proposals to be considered as we take the initial steps toward national health insurance. Future generations will also bring suggestions for improving the system.

I believe the United States will never have a completed national health policy or program. Neither policy nor program will be static; both will always be in process, changing and becoming as we constantly profit from our experience, because—in the American ethos, as I have learned—experience is the great teacher.

INDEX